ONCE UPON A TIME

Born, raised and educated in Edinburgh, Ian Bell is a past holder of the George Orwell Prize for Political Journalism and the award-winning author of *Dreams of Exile*, a biography of Robert Louis Stevenson. Formerly the Scottish editor of *The Observer*, he is a columnist with *The Herald* and the *Sunday Herald*.

Once Upon a Time
The Lives of Bob Dylan

IAN BELL

MAINSTREAM
PUBLISHING

EDINBURGH AND LONDON

First published in Great Britain in 2012 by

MAINSTREAM PUBLISHING COMPANY

(EDINBURGH) LTD

7 Albany Street

Edinburgh EH1 3UG

ISBN 9781780575735

Printed in Great Britain by
Clays Ltd, St Ives plc

1 3 5 7 9 10 8 6 4 2

For Sean

Contents

A Series of Dreams

SOMEONE HAS JUST USED THE NAME JUDAS. IT IS A SHOUT, NOTHING more, in the protective darkness of a provincial English concert hall a long – long – time ago.

The cry, two vowels stretched, is intended as a kind of remonstrance, a denunciation from the congregation. Instead, it confuses style with substance, sincerity with art, past with present, and worse besides. At a push it might count, if someone is being generous, as the impassioned defence of integrity, real or imagined. It would not be mistaken for wit.

As insults go it is oddly old-fashioned, Sunday school prim, strangely neurotic. Even in a nominally Christian country the idea that a popular entertainer could resemble the betrayer of the Saviour-of-all-Mankind is beyond stupid. Such seems to be the entertainer's opinion.

It happens, though, and then it's famous: *Ju-das!* Christ-killer. Yet in this case, for a novelty, the apostate has somehow managed to murder his own sanctified self. Without even trying. At a pop concert. Things are about to become legendary.

This cry, this bubble of emotion, is pique expended on trivia. The heckler, like all the people applauding his indignation, has just paid good money to be outraged. Yet there are no surprises here: the blasphemy in question – let's render that one unto little Caesar – has been well advertised. The miscreant has toured the world affronting his audiences. It's been in the papers and Britain is his last stop. But two things are really taking place.

First, the accused has never claimed allegiance to the thing betrayed. He is not – and he insists on this point – an adherent of the near-comical cult that has formed like a cyst around his name. Not interested.

Second, he has a history of his own. Among other things, he was born a Jew. Where else but in provincial England, as the century passes its middle age, could someone libel a Jew as Judas?

9

The accused, no doubt narcotised – many would like to believe it – certainly assailed, currently existing within the still centre of the cold flame of his own artistic firestorm, has a precise line of response to such attacks. It is almost a matter of rhetorical principle.

He says: 'I don't believe you.'

He adds: 'You're a liar.'

Then, turning to his musicians, all but inaudibly: *'Play it fucking loud.'*

One way or another, art is in the room. One thing ends, another begins. From that, and then, to this.

*

The noise that follows, 'bootlegged' for decades, dishonoured by abysmal reproduction on cheap stereos, mythologised and misrepresented, denied and embraced and denied, is like the sound of a crashing wave. There is fury, too, in the music and the words, as though the singer is disputing gravity itself while it hauls him down, inch by inch, among those sullen listeners *who are just like the character in his song*. And they don't even know it. How about that?

In another mood, on a different night, he would have seen the humour, but now he's tired, exhausted. After fewer than five years as a recording artist he has evolved from an ingratiating impersonator, the grubby sprite echoing a sick man, the prodigy stealing the histories and songs of others, into something without obvious precedent. He has been both lauded and misconstrued (and that *is* funny), congratulated and conscripted. Many want to believe he is *sui generis* yet 'universal', fashionably subversive but, for them at least, always reliable. And, above all, *a leader*.

Of what? They act as if they own him, especially when he sings about freedom. They say he is wholly new. Yet somehow he seems to know all about an old tradition that binds things together, the perverse tradition that obliges him to seem to break, and break decisively, with all that is purportedly traditional.

Even that isn't really what's going on. This performer, this night, is still more evidence that everything comes from somewhere. Originality, says the cliché, is the ability to see afresh, and hear afresh, things that are familiar. In truth, the music that has baffled a jeering section of his English audience could be traced like veins beneath the skin all the way to a heartland. Sometimes he says as much. Sometimes he claims that it all adds up. Periodically throughout his career he will talk mysteriously of the underlying 'mathematical' logic of his music. Here, in these monstrous, blazing songs, is a progression – not necessarily progress – founded on first principles.

The skinny young man with the wild hair, sharp suit and glowing eyes did not invent rock and roll, or R&B, or the blues, or the structures of popular song. The auditory hallucinations promised by an electric guitar's pick-ups have been explored many times before, by better players. The division of labour within small bands of musicians, 'rhythm' and 'lead', is a practice born of economic necessity, not revolutionary intent. On the face of it, there is nothing – barring a voice that sometimes causes eyebrows to rise – that's new about this noise.

Besides, only a handful of years before these events the smart record-industry money was declaring the 'pop group' passé, the boom ended, a flash in the pan. That might have been one reason why this ferociously ambitious performer became a singer of 'folk' music to begin with. As the '50s became the '60s it had seemed as though the fires of rock and roll were going out one by one. Pastiche and inanity, harmless music controlled by cynical old men, had become the residue. The word was *phoney*. Hence the reverent fidelity, currently fashionable, to folk's older gods. Even for him, in the beginning, old songs had been the new wave, 'the underground'.

Now a lot of people are aggrieved, even furious, because the performer has seemed to abandon – how best to put this? – the musical settings appropriate to properly serious and 'literate' songs of the folk type. Specifically, they hold that a hollow-bodied guitar derived from the Spanish original sounding into a free-standing microphone is good, honest, authentic and true. An instrument with a solid body and embedded transducers is the howling symbol of venality, vacuousness, mere cash and tawdry thrills. It's offensive. It sounds like a betrayal. They say he has bartered away that precious integrity. The tab runs to 30 pieces of silver (and then some). Hence the tantrum in the dark.

But offensive is good for someone, and scandal is better: at this moment that might as well be the only law in pop's little world. No record sales will be harmed in the making of a famous concert. Perhaps this is one reason why a section of the crowd have paid to be disgusted: the bedlamite's horror has admirers too. Some people, very shallow people, actually like this *new stuff*.

On this English night, in any case, the performer cuts an ambiguous figure. He doesn't much enjoy being insulted, but he will defy anyone for the right to make music as he chooses. He doesn't have to suffer the abuse, yet he persists. He has been backed into a corner, yet he does not retreat. Bob Dylan is mulish, but no one's fool.

There's more. These days, as though by nameless instinct, he seems to sense a need to split and scatter his audience, to provoke and challenge them, if he is to make any headway. Just as he has taken the familiar elements of American popular music and rearranged them into strange kaleidoscopic configurations, so he expects his listeners to reorder their preconceptions. Or boo him. As he sometimes tells his band: if people have paid hard cash for their tickets, they can boo all they like.[1] That's their privilege. They get it or they don't. It is that sort of decade.

The date in question is 17 May 1966; the place is Manchester, a monochrome industrial city in the north-west of England. Dylan and five musicians have been around the world in eight months with only a very few short breaks. It has been hard, heavy going. The scandal – some truly think in those terms – has been unfolding bit by bit since the folk and blues festival at Newport, Rhode Island, in July of the previous year. Three ferocious songs performed with a high-class pick-up band at that event have set off derisive echoes (and some handy publicity) at every other stop on the latest tour. Audiences have been placated, even lulled, with 'acoustic' numbers in the first act of the little touring melodrama, and have applauded accordingly. The least of them have betrayed the poverty of their borrowed opinions by taking it for granted that the choice of instruments alone guarantees folk music. But if they have missed the point it is because they had no pressing interest in finding the point. They know what they like.

In fact, if lyrics alone are the issue, these solo performances, with their phantasmal harmonica passages endlessly sustained, are scarier than anything you might hear from a Fender Telecaster. 'Visions of Johanna', 'It's All Over Now, Baby Blue', 'Desolation Row' and the rest are thick with dissociated imagery, dark with foreboding or ecstatically vivid, but bereft of 'messages'. Sceptics say they are bereft of any meaning. They say these songs are just a juvenile's ill-digested idea of

---

1   Commenting on first reactions to his 'new sound' at a press conference in San Francisco in December of 1965, Dylan had said: 'They certainly booed, I'll tell you that. You could hear it all over the place. I don't know who they were . . . they've done it just about all over . . . I mean, they must be pretty rich to go some place and boo. I mean, I couldn't afford it if I was in their shoes.'

poetry beneath a patina of 'significance'. Try reading the verses, they say. They say that a lot. Then they set to work on the performer's so-called singing voice.

Yet these songs, like the old folk blues, arise from psychic deeps. They share that ancient sense of supernatural mystery and fundamental truth while breaking apart the familiar linkages between image, metaphor and meaning. They are old/modern, weird/familiar. No one, fan or not, says they are anything other than strange. This is no accident. These are no more the folk songs of audience expectations than Dylan is a Peace Corps volunteer.

Still, thanks only to his choice of guitars, the singer, a few days shy of his 25th birthday, gets away with the opening half of the Manchester show. At this juncture the customers keep their bafflement to themselves. Many are even prepared to tread gingerly on the path being marked out: the 'Mr Tambourine Man' tune remains an infinitely seductive thing, after all. What's it 'about'? That's the funny part. Those who don't mind the voice can never quite say why, or to what, they respond. A few have *theories*, though, and even in Manchester the crowd will accept novelty if it doesn't sound heinously 'commercial', or just too bloody loud. They are not yet ready to notice the deconstruction and reconstruction of the entire art of songwriting.

In Manchester, the first set goes well. An intermission follows. Afterwards, as though in response to a supernatural dog whistle or a malign secret chord, all hell erupts. The annals, wherever they are kept, acquire a new chapter.

When recordings from the night are released to the wider public a generation later, one legend will be extinguished and another encouraged. The former is a slight matter: the bootleggers got it wrong, as many had long since known or guessed. Illicit copies of the tapes were ascribed for years to London's Royal Albert Hall – all spoke of 'the Albert Hall concert' – not Manchester and its century-old Free Trade Hall, with its ghosts of Mr Charles Dickens and *his* theatricals. But there were no regal Beatles in the audience to encourage Dylan against the groundlings on 17 May up in the North-west. Hence the second legend. When, in 1998, Columbia issues *The Bootleg Series Volume 4: Live 1966*, the packaging on the handsome box asserts that 'Dylan blazed a trail of confrontational' – red ink for that word – 'performances that changed rock and roll' – more red ink coming – 'forever'. Partly true.

The sleeve notes themselves observe that though 'some cheered' others barracked the band or 'simply walked out'. In the usual story, opinions were less evenly divided: they hated it. So how did that work? Why is anyone still talking about Bob Dylan in the twenty-first century when the received account tells of a majority reaction so baleful, so murderous, in Britain and around the world, that it should by rights have destroyed his career? If so many people detested the second half of the 1966 shows so much, surely no one would remember the artist or the concerts, far less care. When you fail to keep the customer satisfied you go out of business. Someone must have enjoyed those performances enough to grant the Manchester concert and the artist an abiding legend and a singular reputation. Or was it his bad luck that only fools were buying tickets that year?

The 1998 release had the effect of setting a myth in stone. This, it said, was the unparalleled moment. Here was the transformative gesture, the confrontation, that defined Dylan's pre-eminence in his generation, and in his art. This artefact above all others needed to be heard and understood with the urgency that attended its making. But the surviving contraband evidence differs. It says that the previous night's performance at the unglamorous Gaumont in Sheffield was just as remarkable – arguably the superior concert, in fact – and that the show given at the Liverpool Odeon on the 14th was also better than pretty good. Manchester was just another stop on a long tour, its set list – in 1966 an oddly rigid thing by Dylan's later standards – no different from all the other set lists. What marked out the date, the place and the recording was only partly to do with music. This was the *Judas* album, and the moment.

Another thing. What did separate the supposedly acceptable acoustic set from the ensuing electric heresy? Mere noise? By the standards of what was usual in 1966 Dylan opened with a performance a thousand degrees of separation from his old folk-minstrel civil-rights persona. Those spooky, angular songs, that harmonica like the sound of an animal refusing to die, that voice with its precisely mangled timing, every word bent and twisted, and each number going on forever – they went for all that without a murmur? So the recorded evidence seems to suggest.

The word 'counter-culture' wasn't yet in use in 1966,[2] but most of the legend of Manchester arose from its vainglorious assumptions about

---

2   Theodore Roszak's *The Making of a Counter Culture: Reflections on the Technocratic Society and its Youthful Opposition* (1969) put the term into general use. *Merriam-Webster* dates its first appearance to 1968.

art. All true art had to be – didn't it? – novel, 'challenging', dissident, 'out there' and always, above all, misunderstood. The whole point was that the straights would never get the point. Thus (apparently) would the world be transformed. So Dylan's difficulties with audiences and electromagnetic induction that year were taken to be symbolic, whether he liked it or not, of a bigger quarrel. Given the choice, he might have preferred enraptured applause.

Clearly, outrage made a bigger spectacle of itself in Manchester than appreciation. Yet the fact is that Dylan won through in the end, his rising star undimmed, his sales of vinyl increasing. The song that followed his exchange with the accusing voice in the darkness, performed in the teeth of the storm, had already provided him with his first top-five single almost a year – so who was really shocked? – before the fracas at the Free Trade Hall.

The concert recordings show, nevertheless, that many in the crowd were truly, thoroughly pissed off, despite being forewarned, by those drums, keyboards and guitars. If they knew anything at all, they knew that Bob Dylan was the most unusual talent in the music business and knew, as all the critics agreed, that he was to be taken seriously. Yet in Manchester and in many other places a large part of the hip, educated demographic went nuts, and not in a good way, when he and his band plugged in.

Perhaps the crowds were merely dedicated audiophiles who deprecated abysmal sound systems. Perhaps the loudest noise most of them had ever heard robbed them of their wits. Or perhaps they wanted the fight.

There are still some old leftish folkies who mourn the Dylan they lost, missing in inaction, in the pop-culture wars. For a few brief years he really mattered, and mattered deeply, to them. It wasn't just the changing-the-world stuff, or the decision to exchange a pristine, truth-telling gift for mere wordplay, Top 40 hits and fancy boots. It went deeper. Their Dylan was antithetical. In the first wave of his creativity he dissented from all the fraudulent capitalist games of the music industry and the denatured society it represented and sedated. This was an article of faith. His art was pluralist, of 'we' and for 'us'. Protest songs had been written because, as it happened, there were a lot of things to protest against. That had been his story, too, for a while.

Some of those same people would soon be wondering how Dylan could keep his mouth tight shut while Vietnam descended into a bloodbath, or while a president of the United States conspired against his country's constitution. As the years passed the singer would make a virtue of his indifference, of being (in the proper sense) disinterested. His social conscience would re-emerge intermittently, but as often as not he would appear to believe that formal politics was, is, beside the point. His aversion to the political press gang ran deep.

In 1966, the committed and the disappointed – generally one and the same – were asking aloud what Woody Guthrie would have made of the spectacle unfolding at his protégé's behest. Rock and roll? The automaton Presley, with his wilfully dumb movies and dumber tunes, was what remained of rock and roll's fading memory. Pop groups? Beatlemania – prepubescent hysteria and trite little words you could scarcely hear – was the best bid from that quarter in 1966.[3] Small wonder the born-old crowd wanted a fight.

And perhaps Dylan wanted them to want it. At this distance in time it seems likely that he was thinning his audience deliberately in order to win a new sort of listener for a new sort of music, the never-defined thing clumsy journalists were about to call 'rock'. He wanted a career on his own terms. He wanted rid, you suspect, of the sort of people who would yelp 'Judas!' and they, those six-string Stalinists, were happy to oblige. At the Odeon in Glasgow on 19 May, and at the ABC 'Theatre' in Edinburgh (both venues were movie houses) on the 20th, Dylan was to be subjected to slow handclapping and walkouts, in part the alleged result of a solemn decision by Scottish Communists to punish the singer for his manifest betrayals.[4] *Let's teach the sell-out a lesson*, concluded alert Marxist thinkers, *by paying him money*. The tale is all too plausible. When this writer first came to Dylan, some three years after the Manchester event, there were still plenty of older, none-the-wiser types insisting that it had been downhill all the way since *The Freewheelin' Bob Dylan*. That was his second album, recorded when he was just 21.

There is an odd fact, too, that gets overlooked when the legend of '66 is invoked. The barracking was anything but universal. In some places, by all accounts, the show went over well, with no fuss and a

---

3   *Rubber Soul* had just appeared, in the previous December. Brian Wilson's *Pet Sounds* was released on the day before the Manchester concert.

4   CP Lee, *Like the Night* (1998) and *Like the Night (Revisited)* (2004). In either edition Lee gives a fine, forensic account of 1966 and 'the road to Manchester'. Anyone who was ever on nodding terms with the old Scottish Communist Party will hear the ring of truth.

lot of applause. There was no booing. So some people thought the latest Dylan was abominable and some, a few dozen miles away, thought he was just terrific? That doesn't make much sense. Years later, nevertheless, it would give rise to the belief among astute commentators that some of the dissent was indeed – to some extent – organised, 'political', the calculated revenge of a British folk scene under stern Communist influence. The influence was a demonstrable fact; the sheer comedy of it all a matter of taste. So here they were chastising an individual as a matter of *political principle*, and all because he had apparently lost his taste for politics. Then he had picked up the wrong sort of musical instrument: *blasphemer*. Amidst it all the useful idiots, the people who just liked 'the old stuff' best, had joined the chorus. How bourgeois can you get, exactly?[5]

Having travelled the world for the sake of these indignities, Dylan had acquired a broader view. On the 17th it was as though the Mancunian crowd were being made to answer for the insults from all points of the compass that he had suffered since Newport. The sort of people liable to walk out or treat him to a slow handclap were the sort of people he didn't desire or need – who in their right mind could? – and would never persuade.

Nor would they alter his course. Those around him in 1966, the musicians in particular, have vouched for the fact that Dylan showed not a single sign of self-doubt about the course he had adopted. He knew what he was doing. Or rather, he knew why he was doing whatever it was he was doing. Had they thought twice, some among the disgusted folk-left would have recognised a version of a theatrical technique then in vogue: *Verfremdungseffekt*, alienation.

This doesn't mean that 'Like a Rolling Stone', the actually perfect riposte to the semi-biblical curse, was anything other than vicious as a whip that night. It doesn't mean that Dylan wasn't angry: the song, as he said once of its composition, is a song about revenge. If his reaction was merely theatrical, on the other hand, the act was

---

5   In the December/January 2010/11 edition of *Socialism Today* the former (meaning disenchanted) West Lancashire Labour Party activist Frank Riley drew on CP Lee's work for a long article entitled 'We Live in a Political World: Bob Dylan and the Communist Party'. Riley concluded: 'there is little doubt that some . . . members were cheerleaders in the extraordinary events of the 1965–66 tour, based on a twisted Stalinist interpretation of "proletarian culture" dashed with an unhealthy dose of nationalism.'

immaculate. But no one, for or against, had heard anything like this music before. On this night, they get it or they don't.

*

'Like a Rolling Stone': four brutal verses explaining to someone, a Miss Lonely, what her life has been and will become. Down the years various women in the public eye will be nominated as the song's victim, but that's a parlour game. The internal rhymes that agitate each stanza, false endings dramatically and metrically, are more interesting than the list of suspects attached to a song that has come into existence as 20 (or thereabouts) 'pages of vomit'. Thanks to his chosen medium, Dylan has managed the trick that eludes much of twentieth-century American poetry, combining common speech, fast and loose, with the ribbed structures of verse. Out of an incident, an idea or a mood, he has created a cinematic drama, complete with a cast of enigmatic characters sprung from some perverse *Pilgrim's Progress*, in 36 lines (less chorus). He has demonstrated that a pop song can be any length it needs to be. (This one is a breath beyond six minutes, or forever.[6]) He has made a morality play from a once-upon-a-time fairy tale, like Fellini's *La Dolce Vita* done for real, and forced it to a conclusion that is part tragedy and part farce. He has shown what is possible (at least for him) in a juvenile medium. This song is his breakthrough.

You can tell as much by a simple test: everything else in pop music has been the clear outcome, more or less predictable (in hindsight at least), of prior events. Styles have developed almost organically, one thing growing into the next, through influence, imitation and shameless theft. This one, whatever its deeper roots, whatever the debts it owes, was impossible to predict. It was actually unthinkable.

Furthermore, 'Like a Rolling Stone' satisfies one of art's usual demands: it renders the particular universal. That would be the chorus, the question. You might remember: *'How does it feel?'* The song's victim is being forced to ask this of herself, as few ever do, for the first time. The genius of the thing, what with humanity's persistent condition, lies in the fact that 'it' can be almost anything: success, degradation, applause, pain, pride, loss, betrayal, obscurity, the final surrender of the self. The irony, a fine one, is that Dylan will feel the backwash for decades to come as exultant audiences – never a lonely miss among

---

6   Though chopped in two – there is nothing radical about the music industry – for Top 40 radio.

them – shout the question back at him. Will it still mean anything by then, to either party? By the summer of 2012 his own website will claim – though who really knows? – that the 70-year-old has performed 'Like a Rolling Stone' in concert on 1,953 occasions. The song goes on and on. And how does that feel?

Countless songs have told stories. 'Frankie and Albert', from the dreamtime of the blues, tells its story over and over. Woody Guthrie told of Tom Joad and Pretty Boy Floyd and numberless others. The ballads of the British islands evolved as common stories edging into myth. Miss Otis will never cease to regret her passion's story. One way or another, there is a tale for every tune: humanity craves narrative, even when there is nothing more at stake than the old, predictable story of romantic love, the immense legacy, unmatched in art, of some Provençal troubadours. *Once upon a time* . . .

All of that flows beneath and through 'Like a Rolling Stone'. The difference is that a myriad of the old lyrics can be caught and held. One way or another, they still abide by the courtly conventions. This song shifts and blurs even as Miss Lonely's fate is being told to her face. There's one reason: in its best-known version, the one plucked from the air, manifested like a spasm of the subconscious in a New York recording studio amid a rainstorm in the summer of 1965, the song, this bitter and vengeful song, is joyous.

Those who got it responded to that before they began to delve, if they ever did, into the things going on in the lyric. It had the mark of pop's fugitive greatness within it, the ineffable sense that one recording only is *right*, unimprovable, definitive, a life force. But that's not what the words intend: they mean harm.

The paradox is in Dylan's performance. He is enjoying Miss Lonely's ruin, glorying in every second of his own spitting anger. He is destroying her utterly and taking pleasure in his ability to do so. Do we draw conclusions from that? The Manchester performance of 'Like a Rolling Stone' is a man lashing out at the world: the statement is general. The studio original is venomously specific. Even if we neither know nor care who she is, Dylan sings with the adrenalised contempt of one who can see a certain face crumpling before his eyes. And he loves it. Hatred and anger give this song, above all pop songs, its majestic energy. So where does that leave us?

At no point in 'Like a Rolling Stone' does Dylan (or the imagined speaker; let's remember a possibility) begin to doubt his right to judge a person, to put her down and take her apart. 'He' grants himself every moral privilege. There is no possibility that he could be unjust or wrong. Yet imagine this hyper-cool, groundbreaking piece of song-poetry 'rock and roll' in another setting and the performer could be any seventeenth-century Puritan branding and casting out a fallen woman.

Who says he is entitled to loathe anyone in this fashion? He says. Who says he's the only truth-teller among liars? He does. That thread, the moralising rhetoric, the sense of entitlement, will run through Dylan's entire career. It is one reason why he will be compared so often in the 1960s to the callous, unparalleled, irresistible, fuzzy-haired French poet Arthur Rimbaud. You could call it lacerating honesty – why not? – but you could also call it mere self-righteousness. One who is without sin (apparently) is casting, to confuse a metaphor, the first rolling stone. And he will retain the habit: listen only to some of those religious songs of praise for the selected saviour written at the wrong end of the 1970s and you hear the hanging judge of 'Like a Rolling Stone'. It seems he missed the class on mercy and forgiveness.

So vicious is the song you forget even to ask: what has she done to deserve this? Failed to gather moss, forgotten to form lasting attachments, fallen in with the bad-faith crowd? And this has earned her a verbal beating as bad as the ones Dylan used to hand out to those masters of war?

In Manchester, 'Like a Rolling Stone' acquires an entirely different set of resonances simply because it pitches Dylan, standing alone, against a sea of hostility.[7] This 'put-down' song, this extended act of vengeance, renders him heroic. Those people were judging *him*. They justified his anger. To keep things simple: they asked for it.

Who does that?

*

Still, a question: why should anyone really care about this famous Manchester 'confrontation'? It's a tiny rhetorical war. No one's dead. Pop songs and singers come and go: like mayflies, that's their purpose.

---

7   Fans of banal explanations should be aware that apostasy is available. In 2002, narrating his own, dull *Bob Dylan – World Tour 1966: The Home Movies* ('Here's Buckingham Palace!'), the drummer challenged the legend. Mickey Jones suggested that Dylan never said, 'Play (it) fucking loud.' Nor, claimed this witness, did the cry issue from any of the other musicians. Jones thought the credit went to a nameless roadie. Probably.

Why the sense – and on this there is general agreement – that this singer matters, or could matter, and that these songs are something out of the ordinary, for better or worse? Seriously: who in any crowd gets quite so angry, even in damp Lancashire, even in a self-involved decade, over a bad night out? And how does that individual's indignation become part of the founding myth of what we are pleased, these days, to call an art form?

Anyone can make a guess and call it a theory. Let's say that in 1966 there is something uncanny about Dylan, something to do with his instincts and his speeding intellect. He seems connected to people and things and places he could not possibly know. He appears to believe that the public face of his society does not begin to represent its older, deeper, mysterious nature. His talent is a root system, his personality a lightning rod. He can flip between the personal and the universal in a phrase. His wit could flay you alive. Jean-Jacques Rousseau on a good day could not have contrived this savage boy, or a gift as seeming certain as a compass needle. He has arrived out of nothing and nowhere, so it seems, with a fully formed idea that what he does is art. Where did the belief come from?

Others have written and performed songs of political dissent. Others have encouraged the idea that poetry – or the strategies and metaphorical density of poetry – might be possible in popular music. Plenty of people have felt the need to write of love and loss, hate and death. There is nothing new, either, in stylistic eclecticism over the piece: it's the American way. The idea that an artist can embody and represent his national community is also, like the necessary creative revolution, old hat. Why Dylan? Good question.

To this day there is something dreamlike about his long career. He likes (or needs) to be elusive, but that fact doesn't explain much. Wounded former friends, dropped like litter down the years, tend not to offer glowing character references. They say – and they have been saying it since the early 1960s – that he does not give a damn. That doesn't seem relevant either. If artists were to be disqualified from the cultural steeplechase on the grounds of obnoxious behaviour, few would make the starting line. That's probably why nature's groupies advance the faintly preposterous idea that a true creator is obliged – the Rimbaud thing again – to be a cold-hearted son of a bitch. Geniuses: what can you do?

You do not arrive at a body of work like Dylan's inadvertently. Others have sustained long careers, have piled up the honours, racked up the platinum and gold discs, and commanded the loyalty of paying customers decade after decade. Dylan is a different case. Most of those who achieve professional longevity do a few things supremely well, year after year. They carve out a space and stick to it. He has staked innumerable claims, worked the seams and moved – or drifted – on. Sometimes he has emerged empty-handed from the labour, but equally he has escaped with treasures too often for anyone to confuse his successes with luck.

What's so special about Bob Dylan? You could offer the minimum, Pulitzer or Grammy award style: a greatly gifted songwriter who through a long and distinguished career has influenced . . . etcetera. You could invent a citation for one of those honorary degrees, and remember to paraphrase a title or two: voice of a generation . . . and every generation . . . touched us all . . . winds blowing, times a-changing . . . Etcetera and etcetera.

All the strands of American popular music save one (jazz[8]) come together in Dylan. Most of the concerns of American literature, stretching back to Whitman and Twain (and arguably before), form a confluence in his work. American history, the kind that moves through the back roads and battlefields and city streets, is in the fabric of his songs. He has knocked out stick-in-the-skull tunes – never mistake this for a small matter – to match old Tin Pan Alley's finest. He has taken a by-product of the entertainment business, the pop song, and turned it into a literary form. He is – should the dry dust ever settle over definitions – the central poet of the long, fading American century and the pre-eminent songwriter of his period.

Yet there is, too, a European cast to the mind under that big, ironic twenty-first-century show-time Stetson, and a British folk consciousness, and a French Symbolist awareness, and old European Jewry's sense of continuity and discontinuity, virtue and sin. This makes him utterly American, in the old sense, and anything but parochial.

When he was very young, back in his first days in New York's Greenwich Village, everyone, even his devoted girlfriend, called him 'a sponge'. They said he seemed to absorb influences and ideas as though from the air. Others said, in so many words, that he was a plagiarist, a master thief. Both characterisations have persisted down the years. Challenged once to explain his 'influences', he answered that you only have to open your eyes and ears to be influenced. But

---

8   'If Dogs Run Free' (*New Morning*, 1970) does *not* count.

his embrace is vast, continental. More to the point, he has never ceased to reach. And Dylan has meantime done the writerly work that tends to be remembered, the unending job of exploring, without maps, what it means to be alive on the planet.

He is a moral artist and a rowdy artist, a spiritual writer and a sexual writer, a political creature without politics, a believing sceptic and a sceptical believer, an improviser and a craftsman. He gives a lot of concerts, too, which pleases a lot of people. Dylan is a public artist who keeps himself to himself, the self-effaced screen on which his society, America and the world, projects its presumed realities. Then he sings, and ignores all this stuff.

*

Manchester is a determining moment. Henceforth, it will shape Dylan's career. Henceforth, everything he says and does will be pored over amid arcane calculations designed to identify a sum greater than all the parts. Fame – notoriety, genius, celebrity, unrequited global affection – will ensure that each instant in his life, private or public, is analysed for the meanings it might yield. In any human sense, this is bizarre. Casual statements will be treated like pronouncements. Stolen recordings – the 'electric' set at the Free Trade Hall among the first – will pass among the faithful like relics. Bad performances will gain as much attention – for what could they portend? – as great performances. The circumstances of his birth, childhood and youth, his studies, habits, loves and beliefs, will be written about (yes, I know) at encyclopedic length. Before long, for some, nothing trivial will remain. Each new album of songs will be treated as a cultural event and a guide to his interior life. This too is stupid, but entirely of its times.

It will leave him aghast, as often as not. Hopelessly, helplessly, he will say over and again that all he ever meant to do was write songs and perform. The disavowals, too, will be analysed. A great many of his admirers will see nothing even slightly funny in that. His name will become a magnet for comment on anything – spiritual, political, literary, philosophical, historical, sociological – that happens to preoccupy his fans. Soon enough, books will begin to appear. Saints and presidents and historic villains will never earn his shelf space. In time, the phenomenon of his fame, the fascination it exercises, the obsessions it allows, will also attract a book or two. Ironic, that.

*

With the 1966 performances he stages a hit-and-run version of the modernist rite of passage, alienating an old audience for the sake of the new. The act may be instinctive, born of anger and impossible stresses, public and private, but it is not reckless. Drugged or not, Dylan knows what he is about.[9] And he knows full well what certain of his hitherto most devoted fans, those who have become so very angry, are about.

At the Odeon in Liverpool, three nights before the Manchester show, there had been that wry, nose-wrinkling distaste after another accusing shout from the crowd. 'There's a fellah up there looking for *the saviour*,' Dylan had drawled. 'The saviour's backstage. We have a *picture* of him.' 'Ballad of a Thin Man', a song about explanations (and other things), had followed. Enough was enough.

This, the gesture of repudiation and all, is what must be. Everything is urgent. Manchester will become his Armory Show, his *Rite of Spring*, his 'Heartbreak Hotel': the comparisons are not even slightly fanciful. In 1966 he is moving so fast his personality resembles a torrent of misrelated images caught and frozen by a spectral camera's motor drive. Which one is him? Yet again, the several selves named Bob Dylan are collapsing inwards, one upon the other. And it is, all of it, wearing him out, shaking him to pieces.

*

Manchester almost finishes him. It comes near the end of a trip that will have packed forty-three stops into four months and a day before Dylan drags himself back to the starting point, the kick-off, at the Westchester County Center in White Plains, New York, on 16 June. By then, he will have been *around the world and back again*. For a time, for its star, this will have seemed like the only never-ending tour. Then he's gone: he's not there. Over the following seven years he will perform on a public stage on precisely five occasions.

When he and The Band agree to face audiences again for a fast 40-date American tour and a ton of money early in 1974, the changes wrought will be plain. The kid who started out with a guitar and a

---

9   The difference between his speech and his singing is startling on the 1966 recordings. Whatever the chemicals at work, he displayed remarkable powers of intermittent recovery, with perfect timing. He certainly managed to deliver some well-practised lines. The pieces of film restored for the 'Martin Scorsese' documentary *No Direction Home* are not wholly conclusive, however. Heroin, 'confirmed' decades later, remains the candidate.

harmonica in Greenwich Village was a joker, a droll, chattering and laughing, starry-eyed, with the crowd. In '74, he doesn't waste time on pleasantries, even on words. A face has begun to turn to unyielding leather.

Dylan's hide was cured between February and June 1966. That process is part of this story. America, Canada, Hawaii, Australia, Sweden, Denmark, Ireland, England, Scotland and France, all in 132 days, all to learn, the hard way, how adulation can become possessive contempt, how art must fight for its survival. It stood Dylan in good stead when he returned to large-scale touring in the 1990s, perhaps, but in Manchester things crystallised. It was, by any stretch, a hell of a ride. Or simply a season in hell. The San Franciscan poet Kenneth Rexroth had written:

> The last time I saw Dylan, his self-destruction had not just passed the limits of rationality. It had assumed the terrifying inertia of inanimate matter. Being with him was like being swept away by a torrent of falling stones.[10]

The avalanche metaphor is nice. A little uncanny, too, since Rexroth was writing in 1957, and writing about the *other*, Welsh Dylan. In 1966, the singer who shared the name had also passed the limits of rationality. He too had been swept away. If he had nothing else in common with a semi-namesake he had this: the art of poetry imposed a price, and paid a price.

Was he a poet? It is long past time to settle that argument. You can begin, perhaps, with a simple question. If Bob Dylan isn't a poet, what is he, exactly?

*

Three years and less of fame: a blur, a delirium, something unstoppable. He had not banked on that. They sold his soul while his back was turned. They handed him the keys to the kingdom. They gave him everything he thought he wanted and demanded everything he had, and then a little more, in return. That was a surprise. Now he trembles before his own shadow.

So: Play it fucking loud.

---

10 'Disengagement: The Art of the Beat Generation', first published in *New World Writing* No. 11, 1957.

I'm Not There, I'm Gone

A picture – you buy it once, and it bothers you for forty years; but with a song, you sing it out, and it soaks in people's ears and they all jump up and down and sing it with you, and then when you quit singing it, it's gone, and you get a job singing it again. On top of that, you can sing out what you think . . .

Woody Guthrie, Bound for Glory

LATE IN NOVEMBER OF 1961, IN COLUMBIA'S STUDIOS IN NEW YORK City, a raggedy 20-year-old college dropout with a taste for inventing fantastic tales about himself is trying to make a long-playing record. For this, he is the envy of friends and rivals alike. Down in Greenwich Village, where the weightier issues of the folk movement are decided, some people are wondering aloud why the great John Hammond is granting an unequalled opportunity to a coffee-house beginner who can 'barely play', the one who calls himself – a joke, surely? – *Dylan*. Certain executives of the mighty Columbia Records are wondering over the same thing. A *five-year* contract?

Approaching 51, the tall, close cropped and patrician Hammond has seen it all, so they say, and done most of it. He has empathy, taste and the gift, sometimes, of prescience. This is the moneyed New Yorker, great-grandson of a Vanderbilt, who first saw Bessie Smith sing back in the 1920s, who later presided over the last recordings the Empress made, and who, in 1936, prodded Benny Goodman into recruiting a black vibraphonist named Lionel Hampton to the ranks of a white band. As though for a needless encore the executive has just persuaded Columbia to reissue the ethereal works of Robert Johnson, long-lost 'King of the Delta Blues Singers'. Everyone from Count Basie to Billie Holiday, Big Bill Broonzy to Aretha Franklin, owes something – in certain cases everything – to John H. Hammond II.[1]

---

1   See Dunstan Prial's *The Producer: John Hammond and the Soul of American Music* (cont.)

His eminence is founded in part on the vast knowledge acquired during a long career, but in another part on an enduring passion. Where black music is concerned, Hammond gets it, has always got it. He has also done as much to oppose racism in the industry and beyond as any other Ivy League-educated white man. Hammond knows the blues. Yet here he is producing an act turned down by every label in town with even the slightest interest in folk or blues, and Hammond is doing so on the strength – so it appears – of a single press review. And the kid is terrible.

Raw talent is one thing. It is a producer's job to find, cut and polish the diamond within the dull stone. So where's the gem? Robert Shelton's catalytic *New York Times* review – another occasion for envious muttering in the Village – has spotted 'a bright new face' on the stage of the Gerde's Folk City 'cabaret' on West 4th Street. The journalist has described 'a cross between a choir boy and a beatnik' beneath 'a Huck Finn black corduroy cap', a slight individual who is 'vague' – or lying through his teeth – 'about his antecedents'. Shelton has also admitted that 'Mr Dylan's voice is anything but pretty'.

'Consciously,' and predictably, the singer is 'trying to recapture the rude beauty of a Southern field hand musing in melody on his porch.' Busily musing, the youngster's 'scarcely understandable growl' and 'highly personalised approach toward folk song' stray close, sometimes, to 'mannered excess'. There is, nevertheless, 'the mark of originality and inspiration', whatever those might be currently, upon him. The heading on the *Times* piece mentions 'a distinctive stylist'. An ill-lit single-column half-tone shows 'Dylan' with his puppy fat still evident. It isn't much to go on.

In the studio on 7th Avenue, in fact, there is less than that. This Dylan resists even the elementary disciplines of the recording process. As Hammond will one day recall, the youngster pops every 'p' and hisses every 's'. He wanders off the microphone. Time is money; timing is music. Does he want to make a record? This one can't even be

---

(1 cont.) (2006). Hammond, says the author, 'sensed from an early age that there was a reason this music was as deeply passionate as it was. It was uniquely American music, written by and played by people who had known the harsher realities of life, firsthand. In particular, it was music by and for people whose skin colour kept them perpetually at the bottom rung of American society. Listening to this music helped awaken Hammond to the vast class differences that separated him from the servants in the basement.'

bothered to take an interest in retakes. Worst of all, Dylan refuses to accept basic instruction from people – and that would be everyone – who know better than him. The Columbia executives who damn this signing as 'Hammond's folly' might have called it right.

So what is it, exactly, that John Hammond hears?

*

In fact, he has already heard Dylan play, just a little, first at an apartment rehearsal, then in the studio while producing the third album by a rising singer named Carolyn Hester on the day after the appearance of Shelton's review on 29 September. The youngster contributed some harmonica to the session thanks to Hester's urging, the advice of the Village veteran Liam Clancy and the enthusiasm of John Jr, the producer's teenage son. As legend will relate, a cursory audition, plus the news that the young man tries to write his own songs, prompted Hammond to offer both the session job and, verbally, the contract 'on the spot'.

Years later, in his long-delayed biography of Dylan,[2] Shelton will offer his own memory of a Friday night at Folk City just after the *Times* review has hit the streets and drawn a big, inquisitive crowd to the club.

> Later in the evening, Dylan steered me to a quiet corner and said: 'I don't want you to tell anybody about this, but I saw John Hammond Sr this afternoon and he offered me a five-year contract with Columbia! But, please, man, keep it quiet because it won't be definite until Monday. I met him at Carolyn's session today. I shook his hand with my right hand and gave him your review with my left hand. He offered to sign me without even hearing me sing! But don't tell anyone, not one single soul! It could get messed up by someone at the top of Columbia, but I think it is really going to happen. Five years on Columbia! How do you like that?'

Something of the sort must have taken place. On the other hand, biographers and autobiographers tend to forget that the verbatim conversation plucked magically from memory is about as trustworthy as a standard recording contract. Or a Dylan tale. It juices up a narrative, no doubt, but it flirts with fiction. Did Shelton truly recall every legendary word, just like that? Didn't he once say, 'What do you mean, *without even hearing you sing?*'

---

2   *No Direction Home: The Life and Music of Bob Dylan* (1986), p. 113.

Accounts of Dylan's big break will be at odds ever after. Hammond, for one, will always be impatient with the idea that he could have offered a deal without, in fact, listening to the kid. Later he will *seem* to recall that a studio audition of some description took place. Looking back – though this doesn't really count for much – Dylan will mention no such event. Hammond will also dispute the suggestion that he was influenced by Shelton's review: in his recollection the decision to sign the beginner was made before the *Times* review had appeared. Yet the producer, his memory 'fuzzy', will one day remember that the boy's guitar playing was 'rudimentary' – the harmonica too was 'barely passable' – but claim to have believed, simultaneously, that 'Bob was a poet, somebody who could communicate with his generation'.[3] In the late autumn of 1961, at the moment the famous contract manifests itself, neither description fits the bill. Dylan, who will never be a virtuoso in the usual sense, is a musician capable enough to hold down club jobs. But *a poet*? Not yet.

*

This, though, is how it will be: episodes in this career will become luminous, burnished, told and retold. Dylan himself will wind up as a folk tale. Each event in his life will become a kind of fable, each fable with its own concordance, its innumerable footnotes. Soon enough they will be looking for miracles and stigmata. Soon enough – too soon – each and every one of this young man's utterances will be studied. Before long they will be going through his garbage, literally and metaphorically. Comment on his deeds will become a minor industry.

Too few will find the business weird, or stop to wonder just what it is about modern times that can produce this phenomenon. In the end the career of an invented character will itself resemble nothing so much as an elaborate piece of fiction. Even the parts that are true. Even the true parts about the person who fabricated the character who tells the tales. Immaculate hindsight will dictate every word.

In 1961, he wants to be a singer. Soon he will want to write a lot of songs. That won't be good enough. Like Hammond, the devout – the word isn't too far from the mark – will talk about poetry instead, but struggle to name the last time they gave a damn about an American poet. In an age of cult and celebrity 'Bob Dylan' will not be allowed

---

3   Shelton, *No Direction Home* (1986), pp. 114–15.

mere art. Numberless articles and books will interpret the meaning of a life even as it is being lived, and spin one life into many lives. That he has performed exactly the same grisly operation on the remains of one Robert Allen Zimmerman, a Middle American youth from a nowhere town, will not go unnoticed. The real miracle, in any case, will lie in the fact that he manages to get any work done at all, and that some of the work lives up to its billing.

In November of 1961, in Studio A, a devoted girlfriend at his side, all of this lies ahead as the 20-year-old rattles through a bunch of songs in a matter of hours. He can't begin to guess – no one can – where this will lead. But recordings bend time even as time passes. They allow the illusion that we can catch the light of a star being born. There is no one left now who can hear the album called *Bob Dylan* as it was first heard. Whatever Hammond hears on this first afternoon, however, it isn't yet any sort of poet.

*

Perhaps the producer has truly acted on instinct, or – more likely – on the recommendations of those he trusts: talent scouts and A&R people take such risks. Besides, *'Five years on Columbia!'* is not precisely the deal, a fact that will soon begin to haunt the singer. Dylan – who has signed without apparent hesitation, and with no regard for the fine print swimming beneath his myopic eyes – has won nothing more than is granted by Columbia to any new act. 'Five years' means the guarantee of one album only, with *an option* on another four.

It remains the case, meanwhile, that Dylan in this moment is a near-unknown quantity. Or rather, he is a known and hitherto mistrusted quantity. His Village club following is loyal, but small. His friends are supportive, but partisan. There is a buzz around him, certainly, but the noise has not carried far. Village sceptics, aghast at the bestowal of Hammond's blessing and Shelton's approval, swarm.

The journalist, always wedded to those magical verbatim testimonies, is at least a reliable witness to 'jealousy, contempt and ridicule'. Later he will note that 'very few musicians were pleased' by his *Times* review. In fact, a couple say he needs a hearing aid. Fred Hellerman, writer and guitarist with the pioneering and persecuted Weavers, stops Shelton on the street to ask, 'How can you say that he is such a great this-and-that? He can't sing, and he can barely play, and he doesn't know much about music at all.' From which we can deduce this much: the boy Dylan is tough. When the folk police are laying down the law, he has to be.

After the best part of a year in New York it is not obvious, however, that he is going anywhere, far less somewhere. Hammond thinks he has 'something', but lots of folk singers and would-be folk singers have that. Some of them have knowledge too, and vast technical expertise, and useful experience of the world, and clear ideas. Most of them at least manage to be less alarming. Dylan is the beneficiary of a mere hunch.

There is another puzzle: just why does he want to be a folk singer anyway?

*

Forty-three years after he stepped up to a microphone in Columbia's studios, Dylan told his own tales in *Chronicles*, his first volume of memoirs. The book was praised lavishly and derided comprehensively when it appeared in 2004, sometimes in the same review. An engrossing piece of writing, it was agreed. But – always but – there he goes again. *What is it with Dylan and facts?* (What is it with the facts and Bob Dylan?) In pointing out the author's many lapses, errors, omissions and abuses of the documented record, some commentators managed to sound as though they were correcting overdue homework. Clearly, they knew more about him than he ever knew about himself. Most lacked the simple wisdom brought to the business of recollection by Suze Rotolo, that old girlfriend from the earliest days in New York, when she came to publish her own memoir, *A Freewheelin' Time*, in 2008. Her book, Rotolo wrote, 'may not be factual, but it is true'.[4] For Dylan, those were 43 years long gone: this wasn't yesterday.

His memory offered up the following. First, Hammond had heard only a pair of the compositions – a mere handful existed in 1961, in any case – that Dylan could call his own. Second, folk was still being dismissed in those days as second rate, the province of small labels. Big-time outfits dealt only with the palatable music of the select few. Someone like the younger Dylan would never have been allowed near those Olympian heights had Hammond not been a remarkable character, one who had not a minute to squander. And neither, as we are allowed to understand, had Bobby Dylan.

---

4   On 24 February 2011, when the foregoing was being written, Suze Rotolo, 'the girl on the cover', was reaching the end of a long illness, aged 67. Whatever her relationship with Dylan came to mean to Ms Rotolo, she will remain one of the great muses in recent literature. The cause of death was lung cancer.

It amounts to a brief yet revealing passage near the memoir's beginning. Funny, too, as much for what it doesn't say as for what it does. Either Dylan is suffering a bout of patented all-purpose false memory, allowing us to understand that one extraordinary individual had detected a second of the type, or – you never know – he is just telling the truth as he understands it.

Second-rate folk stuff was fit only for small labels? Those small operations – Elektra, Folkways, Tradition, Vanguard et al. – had all turned him down.[5] He would never have been allowed near Columbia except under circumstances far out of the ordinary? So what were those, exactly? Just that a man of taste heard him play harp and perform a couple of imitative tunes?

Dylan conspires in the legend he otherwise says he despises, or at least indulges, for he has the gift, in the old American folk art of the taller-than-average tale. Did Hammond have a claim to fame? Of course, but apparently it was not yet confirmed. Wasn't this just another routine record-industry signing, a big company plugging a gap in its roster in the face of a new fad and taking a chance, as even big record companies must, on an untested talent? Or was fate showing her designing hand?

After all, in this remembered account Hammond didn't waste his valuable time on juvenile performers. Patently, the neophyte Dylan was older and wiser than his years. What's more, he was hewn, Hammond apparently declared, straight from the long folk-blues tradition. With his usual accuity and prophetic insight, the producer explained to the untried youngster – or so this story goes – that he had a sure belief in what lay ahead

Perhaps he did. But what was the conviction based on, exactly? The surviving recorded evidence from the period, home-made and professional, offers only flickering glimpses of Dylan's near future. What seemed like insight could as easily have been old-fashioned guesswork. You can only wonder, yet again, about the actual words John Hammond

---

5   In a 1978 interview Moses Asch, founder of Folkways, said: 'That isn't true. Bob Dylan immediately went to Columbia Records. Pete Seeger and John Hammond brought him to Columbia; he never came to me. I never rejected him for rejection's sake.' No one else has suggested that Seeger had a role in Dylan signing for Columbia, however.

On the other hand, Jac Holzman of Elektra supposedly abandoned a sojourn in California after hearing Dylan's first album, realising that his label had missed out.

used for this ordination rite. The miraculous recognition of lineage is pure folk myth. Did the executive really dub Dylan the natural heir to a vast tradition, rather than merely flatter his sophomore artist? Was it clairvoyance that caused Hammond to confuse Dylan's glimmering early talent with, say, the gifts of a Robert Johnson?

Either Dylan's memory has succumbed to his ego, or it's all true. That ego is meanwhile in the authorial driver's seat: this is his version of events. But Hammond did indeed sign him, and apparently without much hesitation. Didn't the producer – as the author of *Chronicles* hints – have a clear eye for a born talent? You are invited to believe it.

In any case, he also gave the youngster that contract, though at no great cash cost.[6] It is the one part of the tale that is beyond dispute. Hammond and Columbia, biggest of them all, signed Dylan. Why? Just because folk music had come into vogue? That might have been part of it. The recording industry of the period had no understanding of, or use for, creative autonomy. The rule admitted few exceptions. If the young people were keen on the folk stuff, you rounded up a few players, put them in the care of a reliable producer and left it to him to turn hokey peasant melodies, real or faked, into something that might shift units. 'Authentic' was fine, but only if it sold. Outside the Village, and sometimes within, the boy Dylan was a hard sell.

In the mid-1970s, in fact, John Hammond would allege that Columbia at first refused even to authorise the contract. In this version 'Bob Dylan' almost didn't happen. As the producer recalled: 'Hammond's folly. The vice-president of Columbia Records said [it] just right off – the most horrible thing he'd ever heard in his life. Hammond's folly . . . I signed him anyway.[7] This first brush with higher powers was scarcely encouraging, however.

On the other hand, Suze Rotolo – who was there, after all – gives an account of the first Columbia sessions that is unaffected and almost persuasive. Having taken a moment to dismiss the old tale, put about

---

6   In Hammond's semi-serious recollection, the entire recording costs for Dylan's first album came to 'something like' $402. For years it was alleged that the sessions ended 'when they ran out of tape'. Clinton Heylin (*Dylan: Behind Closed Doors – The Recording Sessions 1960–1994*) instead cites Columbia's files to establish that there were in fact two three-hour sessions.

7   As recalled by John McDonough of National Public Radio, 'John Hammond: The Ear of an Oracle', NPR website, December 2010.

by Shelton, that Dylan had used her lipstick case as a guitar slide (she didn't wear lipstick), Rotolo writes:

> During the sessions, John Hammond did not interfere with Bob's process but watched and listened, letting Bob do as he wished. Columbia planned to rush his album into stores within two months, believing Dylan to be the next big thing. I watched Bob as he sang and saw his focus, his loyalty to the work at hand, the art he was making. Bob was intense, both sure and not sure of what he was doing. Afterward he'd ask: What do you think, what do you think?[8]

The next big thing could 'do as he wished'? He was 'sure and not sure'? Columbia came nowhere near to hitting the two-month release target – almost four months would pass – and the idea that Hammond would simply sit back while the beginner popped all those 'p's is hard to credit. It's more likely that he was too stylish and too smart to play the martinet. This producer often *appeared* to be doing next to nothing in the studio, sometimes lounging with a magazine or a newspaper while the artist brought forth his art. But Rotolo conveys an essential idea: beginner or not, this was Dylan's record, and the choices made were his choices.

So: *What do you think, what do you think?*

*

His first album, *Bob Dylan*, was recorded in a matter of hours and flopped horribly, totally. Most accounts put the dismal sales figure for the first year at fewer than 5,000; Mitch Miller, then Columbia's head of A&R, estimated the tally at half that number. At the time, the few who knew whereof they spoke said the disc, though worthy enough, failed even to represent the artist's repertoire, far less his emerging gifts. Those who knew his club work said it wasn't a Dylan they recognised. The rest of the world didn't care.

Half a century later, the twenty-first century listener can say one thing: John Hammond knew his job. All the software there is could not approach the clarity and compelling immediacy of this otherwise abortive record. If Dylan messed up, if he misrepresented himself by trying too hard and choosing too carefully, Big John almost saved the day. His reminiscences to the contrary, the producer who never appeared

---

8   *A Freewheelin' Time*, p. 159.

to do anything persuaded the kid to respect the microphone and extracted performances worth preserving. For all his subsequent adventures in recording studios Dylan would find it hard, some would say impossible, to rediscover the simple virtues of this gauche debut. I'd say it took him more than 30 years.[9]

The artefact we have now is in one sense primitive; the songs are mostly folk-scene staples, or have become so. Yet on this record, here and there, between the many missteps of a youngster straining at the leash, the ballads and blues are invested with a commitment that can make you forget most of the facts attending their performance. The album was made in a hurry – Dylan was impatient, even by the standards of 1961 – yet the production catches lightning in a bottle just as it has begun to flash. There are no studio effects, no fancy tricks: just voice, guitar, harmonica. Simplicity approaches purity: that's what catches the ear today. Even as an example of Hammond's cut-to-the-chase studio technique, long lost to a digitised world, the album still *sounds* very fine. All that this singer needs, you these days conclude, is better songs.

It wasn't that he had failed to prepare. According to Carla Rotolo, his girlfriend's older sister, 'He spent most of his time listening to my records, days and nights. He studied the Folkways *Anthology of American Folk Music*, the singing of Ewan MacColl and A.L. Lloyd, Rabbit Brown's guitar, Guthrie, of course, and blues . . . His record was in the planning stages. We were all concerned about what songs Dylan was going to do. I remember clearly talking about it.'[10] Perhaps there was a little too much talk.

Dylan still sounds, in places, like the real thing: he is anything but that. This beginner has to tell frankly ridiculous tales about himself – of life on the road, life with the carnival, life on the streets, of parents dead and gone – to make an otherwise ordinary existence even halfway interesting. This is no mere showbiz stratagem: he lies outrageously,

---

9   Until the albums *Good As I Been to You* and *World Gone Wrong* in 1992 and 1993 respectively. These sets, his 28th and 29th studio collections, were technically 'primitive' and contained only traditional material. They seemed like perverse gestures at the time, or still more evidence that Dylan had run dry. If so, the old songs effected the old cure, inaugurating yet another burst of invention.

   How primitive? For *World Gone Wrong*, it is alleged, Dylan knocked off 14 songs in a matter of days, old style, and never once changed his guitar strings.

10 Clinton Heylin, *Bob Dylan: Behind the Shades Revisited*, p. 81.

lies when there is no need, habitually, even compulsively. There is a misaligned facet to this character, an internal contradiction.

His voice, though, is fabulous, in both senses. If you knew no better, and if you forgot to look at the weirdly reversed picture on the album's cover – he hasn't been shaving long, or well – you might be fooled into thinking that an old-timer had descended from the West Virginia hills. You might even – and wouldn't he just love it? – mistake him for black. The truth, now and henceforth a slippery notion, is that he's just another college dropout with a guitar, that most of what he knows about life he has gleaned from old songs and that his album's two 'original' cuts are wholly derivative.

That's not actually a crime. In 1961 Greenwich Village swarms with people pretending to be other people. Such is the New York way. It had been the way in the Village, *quartier* of lost souls, scam artists, fantasists, lunatics and geniuses-in-embryo, for decades. If the junior Dylan is a performance, fake name and all, the act is exquisite. He has the absolute conviction of the sincere fraud.

When he pulls it off, when he sings something like 'See That My Grave Is Kept Clean' – for a 20-year-old knows all there is to know of death – he isn't Blind Lemon Jefferson, or even close, but he is wholly present within the cold universe of the song. He inhabits the thing like an actor consumed by a role. Or rather, he somehow persuades you to imagine that he is, supernaturally, the true author of another man's song. Where others treat the blues with the reverence accorded to museum pieces, Dylan looks for the emotional pulse first and last. It will define his approach to song, writing and performance, ever after. Here, then, is a hint of Hammond's 'something'.

How does the youngster do that? You don't train, as such, for the art Dylan has chosen. You can learn the notes, copy the guitar patterns, steal and study the old recordings – he can't stop himself – that are the folk scene's currency. But in the Village there are numerous earnest young white men from comfortable homes who would dearly like to be mistaken for cowboys or mountain folk or hobo jungle refugees. They all want to be the real thing – as they imagine it – and they all sing as though attempting a second language. Dylan's impersonations are near effortless. The conclusion is therefore irresistible: the personae of the songs are the people he wants to be. He's performing, but not kidding. To fake authenticity in this manner you must somehow believe the fantasy. So what's wrong with who, as a matter of fact, he is?

Even his record's pair of semi-original songs, though they give no inkling of wonders to come, are valid, by their lights, and revealing. Here no guesswork is needed. If the boy could be anyone in the world late in 1961, he would be Woody Guthrie, the great authentic – if you believe every word – pioneer of democratic song. So Dylan offers 'Talkin' New York', a piece of mimicry in the sardonic, guttural, dust-in-the-pipes Guthrie style. As a loving homage to his hero, meanwhile, he performs 'Song to Woody', pastiche as fealty, a hymn to that freedom highway. It's not great, but good enough to last, as these things go. Hindsight will make sure of it.

In fact, should you wish to identify the first, fragmentary, publicly available recorded evidence of real emerging talent, here it is. Not in the melody, not by any stretch (it was one of Woody's 'own'), nor even in the sentiments. But there is a hard sliver of self-knowledge lodged in this attempted impersonation. Dylan places himself squarely inside the Guthrie myth, 'Walkin' a road other men have gone down'. He meditates routinely on a sick and hungry world, does honour to Woody's comrades, the outsider troubadours Cisco Houston, Sonny Terry and Lead Belly, but concludes: 'The very last thing that I'd want to do / Is to say I've been hittin' some hard travelin' too.' This time the apprentice is modest. This time, for a breath, he admits he has never done his ramblin' the hard way. Someone was liable to call him on that.

*

Shelton, doubling up as 'Stacey Williams', contributes liner notes to the first album, and makes one unequivocal assertion: the 20-year-old, the one who 'doesn't know much about music at all', is in fact 'one of the most compelling white blues singers ever recorded'. This happens to be true. The mystery lies in why – and how – it could possibly be true.

Seventeen songs are recorded; five are cut in single takes; four of those – rat-a-tat, effortlessly – are done consecutively as the sessions draw to a close.[11] So what? That was how it was done in 1961. Woody and Cisco had once recorded 'forty to fifty songs' for Folkways, straight to glass acetates, in the space of twenty-four hours.[12] But this is different. This is not, as anyone who has heard the numerous home-recorded bootlegs from the period will know, Dylan's tried-and-tested repertoire. It's not even close. He has performed fewer than half of

11 Heylin, *Behind Closed Doors* (1995), pp. 7–8.

12 Jim Capaldi, 'Conversations With Mr Folkways: Moe Asch', *Folk Scene* magazine, May–June 1978.

these songs publicly, if ever. Either this is a demonstration of speed-learning, of facility and creative thirst, or of a certain confusion. Or both.

Whose songs, in any case? Here, at the very beginning, Dylan dives headlong into the swamp of controversy over folk tradition, artistic ownership, originality, love and theft. He is careless, or ignorant, or ruthless, or some mixture of all three. He purloins his friend Dave Van Ronk's arrangement of the venerable 'House of the Rising Sun' despite being asked, specifically, to leave it alone. He claims to 'arrange' 'Man of Constant Sorrow', 'Gospel Plow' and the antique Scottish standard 'Bonnie Lass o' Fyvie'/'Pretty Peggy-O'. On an old (and lousy) CD copy of the album, indeed, 'In My Time of Dyin', sometimes known as 'Jesus Make Up My Dying Bed', is attributed to one 'Bob Dylan', a coincidence that must have come as news to fans of the endlessly eclectic Josh White, more so to the shade of Blind Willie Johnson, that ineffable Texan genius of the slide guitar. Such lapses will recur uncomfortably often as the years come and go.

The more important point is that while Dylan will henceforth be marked with the 'folk' brand, his real successes in this recording debut are with the blues. It feels natural and yet it *cannot*, surely, be natural. Still more extraordinary is the fact that he has reached this position of authority at lightning speed. Whatever the fibs, in November of 1961 he is still only 20 years old. Scarcely two years back he was presenting himself as just another hick juvenile rock and roll piano player, one with a lot more enthusiasm than skill. Graduating from a small-town high school in the summer of 1959, he was swearing undying allegiance to Little Richard, not – who? – to Bukka White.

In blues, he has attitude, empathy, instinct and attack. If this is fake – for what other explanation is possible?   it is vastly more remarkable, somehow, than the real thing. Charley Patton could bellow forth from Sunflower County in the Delta, astound every listener, die on the plantation in his 40s, and still make perfect sense. His was a black man's music, defined by America's racial agonies and its endless, imperfect apologies. A white Jewish near-juvenile striking a pose? You can steal the blues or live the blues. This youngster, though he plays fast and loose with authenticity, sounds alive *in* the music.

For all that, Dylan is dismissing his own efforts even as Hammond's tape ceases to roll. Hardly has his excitement over that contract subsided than the youth is swallowing his disappointment, as though in one gulp, and trying to behave as though the record does not exist. He is honest, almost brutally so, with himself. In one instant he is a rank studio amateur who has stumbled across one of those once-in-a-lifetime chances; the next he's certain this precious debut is nowhere near good enough. This isn't what he seeks. So he bids goodbye to the record and, somehow, to the person who made the record. He doesn't look back.

*

That's just as well. The album will not lead to fame and fortune. It will not, of itself, justify Hammond's faith. It will not attract much attention beyond the tiny Village world. Above all, it won't sell. The young singer, fearful he may have missed his chance – for he understands the import of the famous contract soon enough – won't settle for that. His ambition is vast, amplifying whatever small talent he may seem to possess in 1961 and '62. In later life Dylan will affect diffidence towards fame, and talk as though things just happened, and seem to say that global celebrity and wealth were prices he had to pay for the pursuit of his calling. You can believe it if you like. The boy Dylan wanted very badly to be a star, whatever it took, whatever it meant. He wanted to be someone, something, other. The life into which he had been born had failed to convince, or to make sense. Years later, in 1978, he would tell a *Playboy* interviewer: 'I was born in, grew up in, a place so foreign that you had to be there to picture it.' Reality was the fake.

*

Robert Shelton's review did not strain against the grandly grey journalistic conventions of the *New York Times*. What made the piece unusual was the praise it lavished on a performer who was just the opening act (to the Greenbriar Boys) at Gerde's. Actually prosaic, the rave – worth a pretty penny to any singer, far less a beginner – reads now like a communiqué from one side of the cultural fence to the other. It is couched in the high-end media language of the day, slightly patronising despite itself, determined to be fair to the young folk and their enthusiasms, but inhibited by the usual assumptions about youth and cultural hierarchies. Were *distinctive folk-song stylists* to be taken seriously by serious people?

Yet Shelton[13] was a pioneer, of sorts, and his paper was doing its

---

13 Robert Shelton – originally Shapiro – was born in Chicago in 1926 and died, criminally neglected, in Brighton, on the English coast, in 1995.

level best to show it sensed something interesting, perhaps important, afoot in the Village and the college towns. The liberal hacks at the *Times* certainly understood recent political history as well as anyone. Shelton knew it better than most.

He had once been a staff news reporter for the *New York Times*. He had also been subpoenaed in 1955 by the Senate's Internal Security Subcommittee and ordered to testify before a grand jury over 'possible ties' – his or any he might have heard of – to the Communist Party USA. Beforehand, Shelton and 33 colleagues had been warned by a *Times* house lawyer that if they were impertinent enough to exploit their constitutional rights and plead the Fifth Amendment their employment would be terminated instantly. In 1955, New York's bastion of liberalism was not in a heroic mood.

Shelton had simply refused to answer questions. He had also refused to inform on Matilda Landsman, a Linotype (typesetting machine) operator, CPUSA member, and trade union activist. Shelton had then been convicted for contempt and sentenced to six months' imprisonment. That sentence having failed 'on a technicality', the grand jury refiled the charges. Once again, the writer was convicted and sentenced. Once again, he beat the rap. The court exchanges would rumble on into the mid-1960s, when the state dropped the case, but their immediate effect in the mid-'50s had been simple. Shelton had ceased to be a newsman. Shuffled into the Siberia of 'arts and entertainment', he had become the person – with a good enough reason to take an interest in politics and folk music – liable to review dumb-luck youngsters with 'something to say'. Robert Shelton's stake in protest song was personal.

Folk itself, once teetering on the banks of the pop mainstream, had fallen under suspicion amid the witch-hunts and blacklists of the 1950s. One by one its leading lights, democracy's victims, had been forbidden the national stage. That fact gave a context, and a certain edge, to reports of the folk fad and its appeal to youth. This American music was also (sometimes) subversive music, red music. The *scene* was bohemian and politically dissentient. Literate, too. Some of its performers and proponents even termed it a movement. Old-time songs were the coming thing.

Rock and roll, say the snapshot histories, had lost its way. There is something in that. An age that takes the form for granted, as though it has always been around, forgets that it was never expected to last. Just as Dylan was beginning to find his feet in the Village, four Liverpudlians were being told that 'guitar groups are on the way out'.[14] Rock and roll had been a mere aberration, a brief teen craze, said the received wisdom among the relieved middle-aged men of the record industry. Elvis Presley had been neutralised by military service; Buddy Holly was dead; and the charts were full of clean-cut kids in attractive knitwear, regular Rock-a-day Johnnies who were, with a few exceptions, offensively inoffensive. Any half-alive young person with half a brain wasted no time on that stuff. On the college campuses, in particular, folk was making urgent claims. It wasn't dumb, it wasn't phoney, it summoned satire and serious themes alike, it treated language as something more than cliché and filler, and it seemed apt, perfect indeed, for the era of the Bomb, the boycott and the march.

Tastes change. Plenty of people now speak well, if selectively, of the pre-Beatles pop music of the late 1950s and early 1960s. Folk, in contrast, has seemed to require any number of revivals over the years. Each new wave has undermined attempts to define and contain the form. Though purists of all stripes persist, 'folk' today as often as not describes mere ambience, certain motifs, a choice of instruments and arrangements. And this, even this, only after another long spell in which the music was mocked, not unfairly, for self-regarding earnestness.

That was one irony among several in Dylan's arrival as a recording artist. Even as he was setting out to light up the landscape, folk was succumbing to its pieties. Few real *folk* could be found in the Village clubs that were already becoming tourist haunts. Few of the tastes of real working people could have survived the strictures of New York's disputatious pedants. A tendency among the arbiters to confuse tradition with musical conservatism, and conservatism with a party line, was evident even before Dylan laid down his first track. That was what made him sound so fresh, 'untutored' and new, at least to some. But the folk scene's proscriptive streak was never well concealed. Dylan, who loved and loves the music, would catch on quick.

It remains an oppositional music, nevertheless, in whatever form it takes. The critique may be implicit and the call to oppose no more than a hint. But 'folk' says several things. First, it cannot be manufactured to order. Second, even in dilute form, it contains the memory of origins, of roots. Third, it is not overwhelmed by pop's lyrical conventions, those romantic tropes as rigid as anything heard

---

14   In the aftermath of a notorious audition for Decca Records on New Year's Day 1962.

in a Victorian drawing room. Finally, folk's sense of the past, sometimes called 'tradition', offers escape from the assumptions of the present, the political assumptions not least.

Should you be growing to adulthood in the belief that the popular music on offer is fakery amounting to a lie, therefore, and should you further notice that your elders are both hidebound *and* attempting to blow up the world, folk might seem a reasonable choice. If you are ambitious, stifled, restless in your given identity, eager for experience and gifted in ways you cannot quite name, this high road to music might seem like the only choice. For a while, at least.

*

By the time *Bob Dylan* was released in March of 1962, the featured artist was trying to forget its existence. By that March, for one thing, he was long gone, musically, and could just about have put together a respectable collection of original (more or less) compositions. He had understood a possibility. Now he was writing furiously, if haphazardly, and learning on the job. Already he was learning one part of the art: he had to dare to fail in order to succeed. In 1962, he would turn out a great many songs at speed, but a great many of those would be near worthless. Somehow, nevertheless, quantity became the key to quality. Everything was an experiment.

In *Chronicles* Dylan's memory runs dry when the subject of artistic beginnings comes up. Or rather, he resorts to a disclaimer that could be read as ambiguous, reporting that he is unable to say when the idea of songwriting first came to him. Most other people would surely remember, or at least persuade themselves, after a few decades, that they possessed a hazy recollection of just when a life's work began. Not this artist. He grants, nevertheless, that a writer needs to discover his own manner, that curiosity over where art might lead is at the heart of the impulse. Then he explains, usefully, that none of this is easy.

Easy or not, *Bob Dylan* had been gathering dust on the racks for scarcely three weeks before a curtain parted to allow the featured artist a glimpse of what might lie beyond. Others have tried and failed to claim rights in the song that materialised. The tune (an old spiritual[15])

---

15 In his booklet notes accompanying *The Bootleg Series Volumes 1–3 (Rare & Unreleased) 1961–1991* (1991) the late John Bauldie credits Pete Seeger with identifying the melody as an adaptation of the spiritual 'No More Auction Block'/'Many Thousands (cont.)

probably struck its first listeners as somehow-almost-familiar. The melody itself, performed by Dylan at a steadfast walking pace, amounted to a musical reassurance. Loved and loathed, mocked and lauded, 'Blowin' in the Wind' changed everything, less for what it was – and what was it, exactly? – than for the liberation it represented.

Written, supposedly, in ten minutes, and first performed before a tiny crowd at Gerde's in a half-finished version on 16 April, it allowed Dylan to see that lyrics did not exist merely to be handed down like heirlooms. You could truly 'do things your way', wherever that led. The song answered no questions save one: what does it mean to create?

Songwriting ceased to be a matter of easy or hard and became inevitable. The boy pretending to be 'Bob Dylan' meanwhile became, irreversibly, Bob Dylan. He got what he thought he wanted. But what he thought he really wanted has never been clear, and was never obvious.

Much later, a persistent *Rolling Stone* journalist with a taste for the oracular and a fancy quotation for every occasion let slip the belief that 'A genius can't be a genius on instinct alone'. Dylan, for once agitated by the challenge, gave a straight answer. 'Well, I disagree,' he said.[16] 'I believe that instinct is what makes a genius a genius.'

So: from where does an instinct spring?

(15 cont.) Gone'. The singer himself has – just for a change – conceded every connection freely, perhaps because the borrowing is, for most listening purposes, well enough disguised.

16   Interview with Jonathan Cott, November 1978.

Beyond the Horizon

'My childhood is so far away . . . it's like I don't even remember being a child. I think it was someone else who was a child. Did you ever think like that? I'm not sure that what happened to me yesterday was true.'

Interview with *Rolling Stone*, 1978

BOB DYLAN WAS BORN – AND ROBERT ALLEN ZIMMERMAN WAS BORN, and Shabtai Zisel ben Avraham also was born – when half the world was at war and the other half was edging towards its Bogart-in-*Casablanca* moment. This was in May of 1941, the 24th,[1] in Duluth, Minnesota, a shipping port in the path of the winds that traverse the vastness of Lake Superior, where sometimes in winter the ice sheet is thrust twenty miles from the shore for three unending months of the year.

The town has two seasons, Dylan has said: damp and cold. Once mocked as 'Zenith City', Duluth slips towards the water's edge from a worn volcanic rim of hills. 'The train yards go on forever too,' the native son has observed. 'It's old-age industrial, that's what it is.' Or it was. 'It was as if Duluth sat,' recalled one visitor, 'on an edge of infinite blueness.'[2]

Six years after the child's arrival at St Mary's Hospital, Abram and Beatrice 'Beatty' Zimmerman would migrate 70-some miles northwards with their firstborn to Hibbing, a mining town whose best days were about to become a bleached memory and whose disappearing mineral wealth was memorialised in the rusty deeps of the biggest man-made hole – or so the depleted community would boast – on the planet. Hibbing, properly South Hibbing, was a long way from anyone and everything.

---

1 Strangely, the front of the booklet supplied with the 1991 compendium *The Bootleg Series Volumes 1–3 (Rare & Unreleased)* displays what purports to be Dylan's passport, issued in 1974, due to expire in 1979. Thus: hair brown, eyes blue, height – it says here – five eleven. And a date of birth: 11 May 1941.

2 William Least Heat-Moon, *Blue Highways: A Journey into America* (1983).

From anyone who counted as anyone, that is, and from everything that someone might someday want. But Abe, like anyone, needed work.

Hibbing – 'We're Ore and More' – was a small town then and has grown smaller since.[3] The city limits are spread wide, but by 2009 the population had fallen to 16,237, down 4.9 per cent on the 2000 census. A century ago, just after the open pits of the Mesabi Range had been consolidated into one big operation and given birth to US Steel, the new township contained perhaps 20,000 souls. Getting things out of the ground still preoccupies their descendants. Recent city statistics record that near 20 per cent of local men are engaged in mining, quarrying, and the extraction of oil and gas. Another 10 per cent are in construction. Women work, as often as not, in health care or education.

They are white, overwhelmingly (97 per cent), these progeny of German, Norwegian, Irish, Swedish, Finnish, Serb, Croatian and Italian settlers. Churchgoers, too: half these days say they are Roman Catholics; one in five are affiliated to the Evangelical Lutheran Church in America. With household incomes only two-thirds of the Minnesota median, not many are rich – 11.7 per cent live below the poverty line – but they don't suffer much from crime, as averages go. Often enough they are staunch still for the Democratic-Farmer-Labor interest. In 2008 each and every county in the Iron Range came out for Barack Obama.

Minneapolis, the only real city within touching distance, is 170 miles or so from this hard land; Chicago is 464 miles distant. In winter, the weather is fierce, often touching 40° below, and given to dumping 100 inches of snow annually on the hinterlands of Lake Superior. Meanwhile, that giant hole, the Hull-Rust-Mahoning Open Pit Mine, counts nowadays as a tourist attraction. Locally, the statistics are boasted. Three and a half miles long, two miles wide, 535 feet deep, the void – a National Historic Landmark since 1966 – is evidence of a billion tons of iron earth taken and gone.

Old North Hibbing, such as remained in Dylan's childhood, was a ghost town, sucked dry and abandoned for the sake of the ore, the creaking ruins a spooky allegory of progress. Between 1919 and 1921, 200 buildings – houses, stores, even hotels, some cut in half for the purpose – were evulsed from this first settlement to make way for the Oliver Mining Company and dragged down the First Avenue Highway

---

3   Founded in 1893 by a German named Frank – the key, obviously – who for reasons obscure decided to call himself Hibbing. His town is twinned with Walsrode in Lower Saxony.

like so many surreal carnival floats. The parade continued, inching along, for decades thereafter. In *Chronicles* the singer remembers poking around, a curious child, amid what was left behind.

A strange land. In his 1980 book *American Dreams: Lost and Found*, Studs Terkel, memorialist and oral historian, transcribed an interview with an 81-year-old Minnesotan, Andy Johnson, who understood the strangeness. Brought from Finland, 'the Old Country', as a child in 1906, Mr Johnson recalled logging and homesteading and mining on the Iron Range.

> Your American Dream? You got a terrible-looking hole down in the ground where we used to live once. It's filled with water, and the wealth is taken out of the land. I don't know what it's good for. On the other hand, people live in nice houses, they're painted well. There's jobs for those that have jobs, and there are a lot of people on welfare in this country.
>
> I see a wonderful future for humanity, or the end of it.

Judging by photographs, bits of film and reminiscences, North Hibbing's surviving sister community would have passed for any version of the old, ubiquitous Main Street USA in the days before Wal-Mart crushed the heartland in its embrace. In the winter snows it could have been Bedford Falls, waiting for Jimmy Stewart to dream again.

In fact, the author of *Chronicles* paints a pretty picture, possibly in imitation of one of Norman Rockwell's discards, of Dickensian scenes never dared by Dickens, of streets full of sleighs, angel decked Christmas trees, carol singers and wreaths on storefronts. Hibbing becomes a place frozen in time and snow. Remembering the town in winter, the writer could as well have been composing the notes for a festive Bob Dylan album (had anyone suspected that possibility in 2004). In his nostalgia – or in his joke at nostalgia's expense – he writes of believing that his greeting-card Christmas was a universal experience. All that's missing is 'Happy Christmas to all, and to all a good-night'. The point being: Dylan knows this perfectly well.

Where are the Jewish people in this tableau? As a matter of fact, if it was Christmas Eve the Zimmermans were probably attending midnight mass at the local Roman Catholic church. As Bob's mother would explain in a 1985 interview, Christian neighbours would always be invited over for potato pancakes on Hanukkah; come the Christian holiday, the gesture would be reciprocated. It was all part of fitting in – two of Beatty's brothers had married non-Jews, after all – and of being, whenever possible, if permitted, a part of the community. Hibbing's Jews, business people dependent on goodwill, families with children whose schoolmates were invariably Gentile, understood what was required.

Dylan's father and uncles, selling their electrical appliances from their store, were part of that. His mother's family, the Stones, selling clothing to mining folk, were part of that. Yet even when the boy was growing Hibbing was notable, if notable, only because it seemed less remote than forgotten. Somehow it felt as though it didn't connect with anywhere, or anything.

That wasn't actually true: at the peak of its output the North Country was producing and shipping 80 per cent of America's iron. Raised though he was on the republic's fringe, Dylan grew up in an industrial landscape, even if nature was always close at hand. There were contrasts all around: mundane and remarkable, wild and tamed, a small town in a big landscape. His Hibbing was an ordinary place in an extraordinary physical circumstance, seemingly lost in a complicated terrain. That would have left its mark, you suspect, on anyone's imagination. Yet where did 'Bob Dylan' originate? Nowhere to speak of.

People there were like people everywhere, nevertheless. In Dylan's childhood most Americans still got their milk delivered. They wore few man-made fibres. The mail came twice a day. Everyone – 85 million of them – went to the movies every week. People smoked cigarettes without shame or fear and men drank beer from returnable bottles. They didn't go to malls. They made do with one bathroom to a family, if they even had indoor plumbing. Everyone listened to the radio – on 44 million sets – but only the cities had their own stations; the rest of the country took pot luck with far-distant 50,000-watt 'clear-channel' transmitters that played all sorts of things, if the weather allowed. To fly in those days was rare, and four-lane highways were few. There was no welfare worth the name and in every town save the biggest telephone calls were still placed through an operator. Long distance was expensive.

Standing proud in a ruined world, America then seemed more or less content, or more or less complacent. By the war's end its money had bought a weapon, the biggest weapon of all, called simply 'the Bomb'. That instrument was meant to keep Americans safe, but already it was making them a little afraid. They had seen the newsreels. The years of Dylan's infancy, the years of bloody conflict, had reminded people that the world beyond their borders was a dangerous place. What would happen if, more likely when, their enemies acquired the Bomb that ate cities? Already allies of recent memory were hoisting enemy colours. The America of immigrants, the America of refuge, minding its own business in its own backyard, no longer seemed inviolable. The people had won one war, they felt, only to begin to prepare, in their hearts and minds, for another.

Harry S. Truman, a Democrat, was still in the White House in those days, but his era was fading by the time young Bobby began to come to terms with Hibbing life: 'To err,' ran the joke, 'is Truman.' Racism, sexism and most of the other *isms* bar Communism were endemic then. Old Europe's radical creed dismayed some, angered others and drove a few to vindictive lunacy. Not for the first time or the last, the idea of America was in dispute.

Eight million hunting licences were handed out at the war's close to men who had become accustomed to guns. Divorce rates were meanwhile going down, birth rates were going up and most women married, said the statisticians, at the age of 21.5. Three in every four mothers stayed at home. Male life expectancy was 65.6 and a loaf of bread cost 14 cents. Fully half the workforce was unionised.

Who remembers? And who is reminded, in an America seemingly locked in the familiar cycles of patriotic war and national defence, that the past truly is another country? Dylan has been investigating that cliché for the last 20 years, perhaps longer. Approaching old age he inveighs against the iniquities and the blindness of these 'Modern Times' – mortal sin or digitised recording technology, according to his mood – but two things need to be understood.

First, the world in which he was raised is in every sense a long way distant. That really was another, vastly different America: the people who lived there didn't even *think* the way people think now. Second, Dylan has endured the revolutionary's fate. Once the voice of the modern, of now and tomorrow, he has become the echo of all the ghost voices, raised from the grooves and plucked from the airwaves, of a lost past. It colours his outlook somewhat.

Meanwhile, in Hibbing's public library there stands a disconcerting papier-mâché statue of a long-gone native son, frozen in place and time, to bear silent witness. Each May brings the town's 'Dylan Days', and those are a lot of fun, they say. Each May, Bob Dylan's own Hibbing days slip a little further into the ethereal past.

*

The boy who invented and named the person was dislocated at birth. First, geographically: the North Country, a cartographer's insult to

Canada, was defined by the compass, as though the Iron Range drew the needle inexorably to a long stretch of nothing. Grown up and long departed, the singer would fantasise sometimes that all the iron ore in the cold ground, the latent magnetic force, could do strange and mystical things to people's heads.

Second, this 'Dylan' was set aside by his genetic markers: his Jewish family, its forebears found in Lithuania, Latvia and Ukraine, were part of a tiny minority amid Hibbing's Scandinavian-Finnish-German-Irish majority.[4] In 1937, 285 Jews resided in the town; by 1948 the figure was only 268.[5] They dominated a modest business district around Howard Street and First Avenue, but their community was a small and discrete entity. Beatty's family on her mother's side, the Edelsteins, owned several movie houses – one named the Lybba, in 1947, after Beatty's grandmother – while other Jewish people were busy in insurance, groceries, a department store or pharmacies. Abe's two brothers, Maurice and Paul, ran Micka Electric, and were expanding that business to encompass all the new labour-saving appliances bewitching a victorious America flush with money to spend.

For all that, the community could not support a full-time rabbi, or so it is said, and its small-time entrepreneurs were not conspicuously devout. They 'shaved their beards', as Dylan has recalled, 'and, I think, worked on Saturday'. In reality, those Jewish men failed to observe the Sabbath in the conventional sense simply because they had no other practical choice. Their businesses would not have survived Saturday closures. But their heritage, like their synagogue, like Dylan's upbringing, was Orthodox.

So what does that make him? Or rather, what kinds of identity and allegiance were made in Hibbing, in that small, remote community? *Chronicles* is silent on the question: its author has never had much patience for such enquiries. Over the piece, Dylan has been as spiritually promiscuous as any questing rock star, accepting Jesus at one moment, drawing close to the Hasidic Chabad-Lubavitch movement at another, but capable of declaring Old and New Testaments to be equally 'valid'. He has also seemed happy, as often as not, to detach himself from fixed religious loyalties and local patriotism. He cuts himself loose,

---

4   The Zimmerman name first appeared in medieval Prussia, commonly among Ashkenazi Jews, with its roots in Middle High German. It once meant 'carpenter'.

5   According to Andrew Muchin, 'Dylan's Jewish Pilgrimage', JewishJournal.com (March 2005), quoting *The American Jewish Yearbook*.

time and again. Is that, perversely, Hibbing's mark? That was his story, once upon a time.

No one is left now to judge. Hibbing's Jews, but for a handful, are gone, just as they are gone from every corner of the Iron Range. It is as though the tide of migration that once swept them in has carried them away. The synagogue known to Bobby Zimmerman and his parents was abandoned a generation ago. He severed all the ties save memory's tether, but the once tenacious community into which he was born has faded entirely. That wasn't Bobby Zimmerman's doing; he didn't cause the old world to disappear. Still, in the twenty-first century nothing important remains of his past except halts on a local Bob Dylan 'heritage' trail.

In Britain in 1965 a reporter from the *Jewish Chronicle* put the question bluntly: 'Are you Jewish?' Dylan answered: 'No, I'm not, but some of my best friends are.' In 1978, a *Playboy* interviewer asked him if he had thought much about being Jewish while he was growing up. He replied: 'No, I didn't. I've never felt Jewish. I don't really consider myself Jewish or non-Jewish. I don't have much of a Jewish background.' In another encounter with the press, he was asked directly if he had been 'aware of any anti-Semitism' as a child.

> No. Nothing really mattered to me except learning another song or a new chord or finding a new place to play, you know? Years later, when I'd recorded a few albums, *then* I started seeing in places 'Bob Dylan's a Jew,' stuff like that. I said, 'Jesus, I never knew that.' But they kept harping on it; it seemed like it was important for people to say that – like they'd say 'the one-legged street singer' or something. So after a period of time, I thought, 'Well, gee, maybe I'll look into that.'[6]

In Dylan's childhood, despite vicissitudes, the Zimmermans earned their share of American dreams – Pop in his store, Mom in her kitchen – and suffered no overt bigotry, or so it used to be said. Beatty herself insisted, on one occasion at least, that the family encountered no problems with their Gentile neighbours. Robert Shelton nevertheless quoted 'a teacher at Hibbing High' who vouched that 'the Finns hated the Bohemians and the Bohemians hated the Finns. Nearly everyone hated the Jews.' It has also been alleged that Abe Zimmerman, a keen golfer, was barred from the local 'restricted' Mesaba Country

---

6   Interview with Kurt Loder, *Rolling Stone*, June 1984.

Club. In Minnesota, back then, that wasn't even half the story.

When Dylan was a child the state had a tainted reputation. In 1946, the writer Carey McWilliams, later editor of *The Nation*, described Minneapolis as 'the capital of anti-Semitism in the United States'. In 1948, a survey commissioned by the city's mayor, the future presidential candidate Hubert Humphrey, found that 63 per cent of local firms employed no Jews, blacks or Japanese-Americans. In the late 1930s, when Abe and Beatty were embarking on married life, job ads in Minnesota had still carried the qualification 'Gentile preferred'. In 1938, one Elmer Benson had faced a viciously anti-Semitic assault in his doomed attempt to succeed Floyd B. Olson as the state's Farmer-Labor governor: the party, said his enemies, was 'run by Jews'. In the Depression, William Dudley Pelley's fascist Silver Shirts, the 'Silver Legion of America' in their leggings, stormtrooper caps and bizarre glittering blouses, could muster 6,000 members in the state, according to an extensive investigation conducted by the *Minneapolis Journal*.

So did someone say, 'Jesus, I never knew that'? He managed sarcasm and denial simultaneously. He knew all about being a Jew in small-town Middle America, yet refused to accept that it mattered. Anyone inclined to ponder Dylan's persistent ambivalence towards Judaism and his Minnesota roots might want to bear the strategy in mind. Certainly Tony Glover, the musician and journalist who was a close friend in Minneapolis at the start of the 1960s, would later suggest that Bobby Zimmerman's change of name to Dylan was 'a racial thing', a response to the possibility of anti-Semitism.[7]

After the war, anecdotally, discrimination became 'discreet' in Minnesota as reforms were enforced. You sense, nevertheless, that the rarity of Jews gave rise to circumspection, even in little Hibbing. They kept to themselves, as ever, and attended to their own affairs: that made sense. Judaism, whatever it has meant or truly means to Dylan, was in those days a cultural force in the big cities of the new American land, but no Jew ever forgot the old story of pogrom and flight. Dylan's paternal grandfather had seen it unfold at first hand. Zigman (Zisel) Zimmerman had arrived at Ellis Island in 1907 from Odessa, in Ukraine, after the infamous Kishinev pogrom in which hundreds, perhaps thousands, of Jews were hunted out and murdered.

Nor had the promised land ever been free of the poison: from the Civil War onwards anti-Semitism was a reliable card for American

---

7   In a contribution to Scorsese's *No Direction Home*.

demagogues to play. The census of 1860 had identified 31.4 million Americans, with four million slaves among them, but by most estimates Jews were numbered in a few tens of thousands before that time. Mass migration, transforming America and Europe alike, began with the arrival of some 200,000 German Jews on the eve of the struggle between the states. Between 1882 and 1914, when Dylan's forebears made their way to the heartland, four million of their coreligionists crossed the Atlantic. Bigotry was by then ingrained, in some places almost respectable.

When Abe and Beatty were preparing to marry, one Father Charles Coughlin, 'the Radio Priest', was pumping out anti-Semitic propaganda from Chicago to an audience of millions. Coughlin and his allies denounced Franklin Roosevelt for conspiring with Wall Street's 'Jew bankers' while the German American Bund, swastikas on its banners, was parading in New York City. Equally, it was not just in Minnesota that Jews found it hard to join certain clubs, enter certain professions or even holiday at certain resorts. By the war's end, as though to complete the lesson, hideous news was on its way, yet again, from Europe. Safe enough, the child Robert, known from the first as Bobby, was nevertheless birthed, ready or not, into that category called 'different' in the North Country. Forty nationalities had converged on the Iron Range mines at the beginning of the century, but Jews were, for some, still Jews.

That reality foreshadowed the third thing. Dylan has sometimes struggled to explain, perhaps most tellingly in *No Direction Home*, the 2005 TV documentary overseen by Martin Scorsese, that Hibbing was never a place in which he felt comfortably rooted. He loved his mother, they say, and in 1968 he wept over his father's death, but somehow *home* was always elsewhere. No doubt he was talking to the film's title when he tried to describe his uneasy relationship with his origins. On the other hand, the bare facts of his life and long, itinerant career seem to confirm the claim. 'I was born very far from where I was supposed to be,' he told the camera, 'so I'm going home.'

Over the years Dylan has sometimes sounded almost wistful about a distant, snowbound – forever snowbound – home town where the aurora scratched the horizon, a billion trees whispered and life depended on wresting iron from the earth, but always he seems to pull himself back to wherever else he happens to be. In October of 2009 he sat down with the author and broadcaster Bill Flanagan for the benefit of the North American Street Newspaper Association to talk about a Christmas album, of all things. Nostalgia, homesickness and the young man who struck out for New York City were mentioned. Dylan wouldn't have it. He said: 'I didn't bring the past with me when I came to New York. Nothing back there would play any part in where I was going.' *So I'm going home.*

In America, that land of transients, there are millions who would probably make similar statements. Heading off to the big city is a rite of passage; travel has a meaning so plainly symbolic it is hardly worth discussing. The journey towards new beginnings is fundamentally American. So what does it mean, then, if you never cease to travel on? Old western movies liked that motif, but so did Homer. Hibbing, as Dylan has painted it, was one of those near-featureless towns surrounded by a lot of empty ('You probably couldn't even find it on a map') seemingly created just to drive off the young and ambitious. In him, nevertheless, the reaction was near metaphysical, the feeling indelible.

In April of 1963 he produced verses entitled 'My Life in a Stolen Moment' by way of programme notes for his concert at New York's Town Hall. This time he didn't deny Hibbing, or his parents, yet nor did he offer the truth and nothing but. Equally, the absence of any affection for his home of a dozen years was plain enough.

> Hibbing's got the biggest open pit ore mine in the world
> Hibbing's got schools, churches, grocery stores an' a jail
> It's got high school football games an' a movie house
> Hibbing's got souped-up cars runnin' full blast
>   on a Friday night
> Hibbing's got corner bars with polka bands
> You can stand at one end of Hibbing's main drag
>   an' see clear past the city limits on the other end
> Hibbing's a good ol' town
> I ran away from it when I was 10, 12, 13, 15, 15½, 17 an' 18
> I been caught an' brought back all but once
> I wrote my first song to my mother an' titled it 'To Mother'
> I wrote that in 5th grade an' the teacher gave me a B+
> I started smoking at 11 years old an' only stopped once
>   to catch my breath

These days, reportedly, Dylan owns many of the fine houses Americans persist in calling 'homes'. He even has a place in Scotland, a mansion near the small Highland town of Nethy Bridge.[8] But *a* home? He says

---

8   Aultmore House, a handsome, ten-bedroom Edwardian mansion set amid (cont.)

not and you are inclined to believe him. The fact that all of this fits neatly with a well-worn native mythology – of *Shane*, Huck Finn who has to 'light out for the Territory ahead of the rest', Blind Blake singing 'Packing up my duffle, gonna leave this town' – is no coincidence. Still, Dylan has earned those credentials many times over. The American frontier has long gone, 'the road' has become fiction, but his restlessness is incurable. So the story goes. Whatever he likes to claim about the life of a working musician, he has been touring relentlessly, as these things are measured, for almost a quarter of a century. He does not, or cannot, linger. 'The great affair,' as Robert Louis Stevenson once foresaw, 'is to move.' The story also goes that Dylan has felt this way for as long as he can remember.

Still, consider this. The introduction to Peter Guralnick's fine book *Lost Highway: Journeys and Arrivals of American Musicians* (1979) is subtitled 'Trying to Get Home'. Its first few pages amply confirm Dylan's matter-of-fact claim that travelling is just what a real musician *does*. But Guralnick – who never once mentions Bob Dylan – is doubly illuminating. Here, for example:

> For someone like Ernest Tubb, the road has become almost an escape, providing him with a welcome refuge from all the nagging problems that assault him at home . . . As one of his long-time associates says, 'I think Ernest will die right in the back of that damn bus.'

Or here:

> Similarly for Bobby Bland, the road has become a refuge, it has insulated him against all the distractions of 'the street', given him an aura and a retinue that serve to mask his fears and insecurities, indeed his helplessness in the face of tasks that seem commonplace to those who live in the square world of nine to five.[9]

(8 cont.) 25 acres of woodland within the Cairngorms National Park. It was purchased by Dylan and his brother David towards the end of 2006 for, reportedly, £2.2 million. The selling agents boasted of formal terraces, lawns, two gazebos and a grotto, no less. The house was built at the turn of the twentieth century by a Scottish entrepreneur grown rich from the ownership of pre-revolutionary Russia's first department store. Locals say it now contains recording facilities.

9 Tubb died in Nashville in 1984, aged 70. Before emphysema and other (cont.)

In the other world, in Dylan's world, there is no way home, nor any real desire to get to such a place, irrespective of the poetic truth he offered to Scorsese's film-makers. Yet he is not, or not quite, consumed by his legend: that above all is resisted. He has returned to Minnesota often enough over the years (a farm there is one of those numerous 'homes'). He can and does live anywhere he pleases. An existential sense of dislocation, deep as it might be, is one thing. But he will not be typecast, even by his own words. So he grows irritated when people, journalists or fans, keep talking about his 'Never-Ending Tour'.[10] It has become another Dylan cliché passed off as a mystery, a conceit too alluring to be tested. For his own part he told Jon Pareles of the *New York Times* in 1997:

A lot of people don't like the road, but it's as natural to me as breathing. I do it because I'm driven to do it, and I either hate it or love it. I'm mortified to be on the stage, but then again, it's the only place where I'm happy. It's the only place you can be who you want to be. You can't be who you want to be in daily life. I don't care who you are, you're going to be disappointed in daily life. But the cure-all for all that is to get on the stage, and that's why performers do it. But in saying that, I don't want to put on the mask of celebrity. I'd rather just do my work and see it as a trade.

Nevertheless, Guralnick's invocations of Tubb, Bland and others besides might explain some things, or at least leave you wondering about roads not taken. Is Dylan still searching for home as he travels, as he buys 'home' after 'home', the better to shelter his wealth?[11] Or has he understood that for the likes of him there never was, and never will be, a final destination, personally or artistically, and that

---

(9 cont.) problems forced him off the road in 1982, he was still doing his customary 200 shows a year, latterly hauling an oxygen tank around on the 'damn bus'. Bobby 'Blue' Bland was last sighted – in the summer of 2011 – performing, aged 81, at Bert's Jazz Marketplace in Detroit.

10 In his sleeve notes to *World Gone Wrong* (1993) he says firmly that the Never-Ending Tour ended in 1991. Then he proceeds to reel off successive, separate tours, each with a different name, and all of them, he says, 'with their own character and design'. It is demonstrable, too, that Dylan's alleged 'obsession' with the road does not interfere with the holiday seasons.

11 The biographer Howard Sounes cites a 1998 law suit brought by Victor Maymudes, a former retainer, in which 17 'properties' in the United States alone were declared.

for as much as it matters the road will be his refuge too, until the end? What does that say about him? What does that say about the place where he was raised? This is as American, mythic and actual, as it gets.

*

Just as the newest Zimmerman was busy being born in 1941, lusty and cute, a 28-year-old singer of populist sentiment and democratic intent was securing a month's paid work in Oregon, and grateful for it, with the Bonneville Power Administration. Woodrow 'Woody' Guthrie had cut a few records and done some radio, but the jobs had dried up. With a bunch of blond children to feed he had seized the chance to become an Everyman-narrator for a documentary film on the dams and electricity schemes that were harnessing the Columbia River. The picture never got properly made, and his role was soon curtailed by jittery producers, but in his 30 days' employment Guthrie experienced an upwelling torrent of his own.

Twenty-six songs in a month, or so the legend would run, all manner of songs, arch and artful, 'artistic' yet accessible, but taken together they formed a montage with a clarity and instinctive sympathy no camera could match. Political, of course, perhaps (the Feds and worried film-makers guessed) *red* – even if Guthrie was never clear about such details – but intrinsically American. While Soviet propaganda boasted of a revolution to tame nature itself, sweat-salted democrats were raising their own monuments to progress, and inching towards their own kind of brave new world.

Or so Guthrie told it. Each day he would travel the wild river's banks, watching, seeing, talking, scribbling. Always scribbling. He was catching the voices and giving voice. And each night back in Portland he would refine the words. He was a man entranced.

Two decades later, a boy besotted with Guthrie, flattering his hero into myth by dint of imitation, would feel his own dam burst and let the songs come out. He would absorb Guthrie, right down to the bare stolen bones of those Okie speech patterns, but then he would digest the legacy. He would swallow it whole. The 'Bob Dylan' who hitched a ride to New York in the unspeakably cold January of 1961, and thereafter took the bus to New Jersey's Greystone Park Hospital just to play Woody's songs to Woody – because he knew '200 of them' – soon surpassed the old man without appearing to try. But then, the others, the rest of them, did not appear even to try.

Huntington's chorea, an inherited degenerative disease,[12] had turned Guthrie's body into a shambles by the time Dylan knew him. Despite medication, the jerks, spasms and tremors were near uncontrollable, the formerly sure dry voice often almost indecipherable. The dying man's biographer[13] would later assert that a 'real rapport' developed between Guthrie and Dylan. Visits from 'the boy' were eagerly awaited, it was said, and the baton passed: 'That boy's got a voice . . . He can really sing it.' Others have declared categorically, sometimes with asperity, that by this stage in his terrible illness Guthrie was often barely capable of recognising his oldest friends, or of making himself understood, far less of bestowing his blessing on another guitar-playing acolyte. Howard Sounes, in his portrait of Dylan, quotes Pete Seeger and Harold Leventhal, Woody's manager, to that effect: they detected no special bond. Variations have been added to the theme. In a widely circulated yet unattributed account – one that nevertheless surfaces in Guthrie's Wikipedia entry – Woody seemed at first to take a shine to Dylan but later, on his 'bad days', berated the youth. In the end, it is claimed, he had no idea who the young interloper might be.

So which was it: a deep and instant affinity, intrinsic to the Dylan legend, or no big deal? Given the nature of Huntington's disease, the probable answer lies somewhere between the two. In notes based on researches in the Woody Guthrie Archives, Thomas H. Conner makes frequent mention of the singer's irrational 'rages', those first symptoms of his affliction.[14] Guthrie's violent behaviour, long misdiagnosed as alcoholism or schizophrenia, had caused his second wife, Marjorie, to fear for the safety of her children back in 1952. Berating Dylan, or anyone else, was the least of it.

As Woody's body began to shut down he sometimes fell into 'a sort of trance, and no one could reach him'.[15] The extent of his awareness

12 An 'autosomal dominant neurodegenerative disease'. The cause is a genetic defect. Together with the increasing lack of physical control – 'chorea' – the symptoms of the disease can range from irritability to hallucinations and psychosis. Huntington's operates by an iron law: if either of your parents is affected, you have a 50 per cent chance of acquiring the disease gene. There is no cure. Guthrie's mother was a victim.

13 Joe Klein, *Woody Guthrie: A Life* (1980).

14 'Tracking Woody's HD: From Instinct to Institution' (2000), which can be found at woodyguthrie.org/archives/trackingwoodysHD.htm.

15 Klein, Ch. 12.

of his surroundings was far from clear. He had a lot of young visitors, meanwhile, and they all sang Woody Guthrie songs: when able, the sick man demanded no less. It isn't obvious that one devoted boy was picked out for praise or abuse. He no doubt received his share of each.

Dylan, though, has never wavered in his devotion to his hero. Twenty-first-century interviewers still comment on the fact. You might also say, equally, that he has never wavered in his loyalty to his youthful self. The kid who found something in Woody's songs – the history-in-tradition, the mythologised loner, the truth-to-power truculence, the humour, the idea of authenticity – found his own voice and identity in an act of loving impersonation. So the older Dylan sticks by that boy. He also abides by the bargain struck: true to the music still, as he conceives it, and true to the idea of America that is embedded in Guthrie's ballads. Things would have been simpler if Dylan had remained a Little Richard fan.

Woody was a fake in his own way, of course, a master phoney, and incurably feckless with it. For one thing, he was not raised poor. Before things went sour in the 1920s his father, Charley, was a prosperous and politically ambitious property speculator – a staunch anti-Communist too, ironically enough – with 30 rental properties to his name, and the first automobile in Okemah, Oklahoma. Woody explained all of this well enough in his 'autobiography', *Bound for Glory*, but somehow managed to sound as though little of it had anything to do with him. For his part, he preferred to play the cornpone singing philosopher, a conventional enough pose in his chosen field in the late 1930s. That he would soon become deeply serious in his ragged anger and in his compassion is beyond question. But 'Woody Guthrie' was a deliberate creation just as much as 'Bob Dylan' ever was.[16]

Granted, Woody rode the rails and stood by the workers. He knew their lives and understood their hopes and fears: the songs are his vindication. Guthrie had seen some hard times of his own, and experienced at least one 'Great Dust Storm'. But he was never an authentic part of the 'great migration of Okies and Arkies in second-hand trucks piled high with possessions and heading west',[17] never a proletarian dirt farmer driven by the wind. Unlike such refugees, he *chose* to make for California in 1936 – deserting a young wife and

16 See Ed Cray's *Ramblin' Man: The Life and Times of Woody Guthrie* (2004).

17 Klein, Ch. 2.

family in the process – because, well, Woody felt like it. Barely a year after quitting Texas, he was a radio star in LA, exploiting the craze for novelty 'cowboy' singers and laying on the Okie accent for all he was worth.

For much of his time Woody Guthrie was an accomplished writer and performer, a professional entertainer with a conscience. But when Dylan was being born Guthrie was creating the music *for which* Dylan was being born. Not that anyone suspected such a thing.

*

America had joined the effort to eradicate the Axis powers before he could walk. Guthrie and others of the formerly pacifistic, non-intervention, union-organising left had changed their tunes, or at least their lyrics, with Hitler's invasion of the Soviet Union. By the evening of Sunday, 7 December 1941, with Pearl Harbor a blazing ruin and the US Pacific Fleet shattered, they were finding new songs for what Woody called 'the new situation'. 'This Machine Kills Fascists' said the famous warning pasted on his guitar. Suddenly, the loner's line was national policy. And Bob Dylan's first president, the first of many, was Franklin Delano Roosevelt.

Before the child was much older 12.1 million Americans were in uniform. News of war was ubiquitous, but the conflict itself was a distant thing in Minnesota, though it kept the mines busy. At its end in 1945, as Europe crawled from the rubble, as cauterised Japan contemplated its scars and the Soviet Union counted 24 million dead, Americans had some good reasons to be content. There were 140 million of them then and their wages had roughly doubled since 1939.[18] With consumer goods in short supply in the war years, they had salted their earnings away, $30 billion worth. Now they were ready to spend. The great prosperity, the unparalleled age, beckoned. It would endure, economists reckon, until 1973. This was the American Century and here, never bashful, was 'the American Way of Life'.

These days, the singer can count to a round dozen if he ever stops to wonder about the men in the White House who followed FDR. In *Chronicles* Dylan talks of being a child at the end of the 1940s, and of hearing Truman speak in Duluth. He recalls that Minnesota folk were not inclined towards Republicanism in those days. Instead, they embraced the remnant American Left of the Farmer Labor Party, social

18 William L. O'Neill, *American High* (1986).

democracy, socialism and Communism. Yet by the close of polling in the general election of 1960 Minnesota was too close to call in the struggle between Democrats and Republicans. In the end, the state granted John F. Kennedy only 50.6 per cent of the vote.

In the present era Dylan is a citizen of a wider country in which, for perhaps half the population, a 'liberal' is the next worst thing to a red, in which the state rescue of a corrupt banking system is labelled 'socialist', and in which the white God's enemies plot and swarm. The fear of a vast conspiracy against America, a terror supposedly confirmed by the 9/11 atrocities, seems ubiquitous in the world's most powerful country. True, a black man has occupied the Oval Office, finally, but the world of Dylan's childhood, of FDR, Guthrie, radicals and 'Social Democrats', is a forgotten dream. Forty per cent of the singer's fellow Americans identify themselves consistently in opinion polls as firmly, morally, socially and politically 'conservative'. Things have changed.

Which is to say, again, that Dylan's native land is long gone. He came into an America utterly alien and entirely lost to most twenty-first-century Americans. His attitudes, his responses, his tradition are each as fragile now as ancient movie stock. The old-time musical stuff over which he exults – and which he preserves – was once the stuff of his life. He, too, is a kind of conservative.

If anything, in fact, his responses to the age are reactionary in most senses of the word. The old progressive crowd from Greenwich Village and their heirs, the people who still from time to time mourn Dylan's willed absence from the ideological front line, don't grasp the half of it. On most matters, he's with the God-happy 40 per cent.

Which side are you on, boy? That was one of Woody's favourites. An answer, pieced together, would not thrill the standard *soi-disant* liberal of today. Dylan doesn't care for modern times, even if – especially if – there are no others available. It is no coincidence at all that the second chapter of *Chronicles* is entitled 'The Lost Land'.

*

His parents were married fully six years before his birth, in a country still attempting to crawl from the wreckage of the Great Depression. Clearly, the two facts were connected. Guthrie's Okies were still being blown westwards from the Dust Bowl to California when Abe and Beatty were joined in Hibbing, her home town, before moving to Duluth, Abe's birthplace, to start married life in his mother's busy household. Dylan's father had begun his working life as a messenger boy for Standard Oil, rising steadily. By the time of the son's birth Abe was a manager with the company, 'senior', by some accounts, or just the man in charge of the stock department in other versions. It was no road to riches. Instead, the Zimmermans seemed to have a degree of security, and that was neither a small nor a bad thing.

When genius appears the temptation always is to attempt to find the child in the parent, or to account for the fact that lineage seems to explain nothing. What was there of Bobby in Abe? The father was a steady man, it seems, a hard worker (from the age of seven onwards), briefly a (company) union personage, not too tall, sometimes affecting a cigar, deliberate in speech, and in all appearances a methodical soul. He was also something of a moralist: not doctrinaire, but devout enough and dead certain about what he knew of right and wrong. When his pretty firstborn was lauded by family and friends as precocious and bound for glory, Abe – in Shelton's account – didn't buy it. His greatest discernible gift to his son was that he did not manage to impede Bobby by much.

The infant liked to perform; Abe did not. It seems he had played some violin in his own childhood, in a little family ensemble, but there is no evidence that he encouraged or discouraged his boy. Instead, he and Beatty did all the right things, as things were measured in 1940s America, but without flamboyance. Hibbing, its streets still full of the sounds of elderly immigrant voices, had never been in their plans; nor did they rush – a sense of caution, of common sense, hangs over the pair – to build a family until circumstances and Abe's career allowed. They had waited six years to have their first home and their first child, and close to a further five for their second boy, David Benjamin Zimmerman. Then events, their sequence unclear, combined to test them.

David was born in February of 1946. Abe lost his Standard Oil job just before or (more likely) shortly after the birth. In that year, in any case, a vicious epidemic struck the country and left Dylan's father a different, diminished man. Polio, the terrifying poliomyelitis, tended to lay waste children and adolescents, crippling, paralysing or killing them. It struck without warning, often with no symptoms at all. If the virus got into the blood and the central nervous system, however, the carnage wrought on motor neurons was absolute. In 1946, the scourge claimed Abe. It changed his life, and Dylan's life, and yet, nine years before the introduction of Jonas Salk's vaccine, the elder Zimmerman was among the lucky ones. So too, if you stop to think about it, were his children. There would be 25,000 reported cases of polio in the US that year; by

1952, the figure reached 58,000, a national emergency in that older, other America. As a doctor who was near at hand in 1946 remembered:

> The first summer when I was home in Minnesota was that gosh-awful polio epidemic they had there . . . Maybe two or three hours after a lot of these kids would come in with a stiff neck or a fever, they'd be dead . . . At the height of the epidemic, the people in Minneapolis were so frightened that there was nobody in the restaurants. There was practically no traffic, the stores were empty. It just was considered a feat of bravado almost to go out and mingle in public. A lot of people just took up and moved away, went to another city . . .[19]

Bobby was oblivious to all of this, as far as we know, but what we know isn't much. In 1978, already older than Abe had been amid the crisis, Dylan told a journalist from the French newspaper *L'Express*: 'My father was a very active man, but he was stricken very early' – Abe was then 35 – 'by an attack of polio. The illness put an end to all his dreams, I believe. He could hardly walk.' Dylan would also say that his father 'suffered much pain his whole life. I never understood this until much later, but it must have been hard for him.'[20]

In *Chronicles*, nevertheless, a slightly strange claim – among several – is made. There Dylan writes that the ravages of polio had prevented his father from joining up during the war. The disease was not rare in the first half of the twentieth century, but 1946 suffered what was, as *Time* magazine noted, America's 'worst polio year in three decades'. Outbreaks in the war years were far less severe. Philip Roth's novel *Nemesis* (2010) involves an imagined, metaphorical epidemic taking place in Newark, New Jersey, in 1944, but Roth chose that year precisely because there was no epidemic. Perhaps Dylan's childhood memories failed him, or perhaps he was applying his imagination to a problem: namely, his father's failure to enlist when his uncles had served in the forces and survived the ordeal. Shelton interviewed the elder Zimmerman and was specific about 1946 as the grim year when Abe was left to 'crawl up the front steps like an ape'. He had been 30 for just a couple of months when Pearl Harbor was bombed. What prevented this 'very active man' from joining up?

In 1946 he emerged from hospital relatively quickly, outwardly

---

19   Richard Aldrich MD in the 1998 television documentary *A Paralyzing Fear*.
20   Interview with Cameron Crowe, *Biograph* booklet (1985).

almost unscathed, but after six months spent recuperating at home, and condemned to carry a slight limp – no one thought he could 'hardly walk' – his chances of reclaiming his job with Standard Oil, or finding another, were slim. For his family's sake, he had no choice: Hibbing it was.

*

Micka Electrics opened for business in the summer of 1947. Maurice and Paul took brother Abe on as 'secretary-treasurer' – bookkeeper, in effect – in a town whose future seemed suddenly precarious. Hindsight could construct a tiny metaphor for the American century at its apogee from little Hibbing, immigrant melting pot, in that moment. The country was victorious, the country was rich, but suddenly, unthinkably, the ore seemed to be running out. Who could have suspected such a thing? The Mesabi Range – in Ojibwa the word means 'giant' – is, or was, a strip of iron ore deposits 110 miles long, between one and three miles wide, and in places 500 feet deep. Nevertheless, in a handful of decades it had been consumed. Wealth, even American wealth, was not infinite, and Hibbing had been left vulnerable by pit owners who had spent years 'minimising' their tax obligations. Miners were restive; strikes would follow; more than once, the town faced straitened times.

> Come gather 'round friends
> And I'll tell you a tale
> Of when the red iron pits ran plenty
> But the cardboard filled windows
> And old men on the benches
> Tell you now that the whole town is empty

'North Country Blues', recorded in 1963 for Dylan's third album, *The Times They Are a-Changin'*, was one token of an unbroken connection with Hibbing, that town 'very far from where I was supposed to be'. Barry Feinstein's monochrome cover portrait of the singer with rough-cut hair and well-worn work shirt even makes him resemble some downtrodden miner (not that he would ever have accepted that fate), or a sharecropper fugitive from the pages of *Let Us Now Praise Famous Men*.[21] Nevertheless, for this piece Dylan adopts the persona of a miner's

---

21 Text by James Agee, photographs by Walker Evans (1941).

wife widowed with three children. A folk convention or a disguise? He had been none too forthcoming – meaning downright evasive or hilariously dishonest – about his Minnesota roots in his rise to cult stardom during 1963. He paid no attention, then or later, to the indigenous folk music of the northern Midwest. Yet in this song a cliché is jolted into life: 'North Country Blues' is layered with home truths.

The widow tells of mines shutting down ('your ore ain't worth digging') and of a husband, John Thomas, dead and gone. That was Hibbing's story, at least until the unlovely taconite process seemed to save the industry.[22] But the last verse concludes: 'My children will go / As soon as they grow / Well there ain't nothing here now to hold them.' That was Dylan's story.

*

First there was the dreamtime of childhood. It fell, as it falls for most, into two phases: paradisal innocence, then the experience, gathering pace, of restlessness and inevitable revolt. Dylan took it further than most. His Hibbing years seem now, in his songs and scattered statements, like a parable of all that was and might have been in America: love, loss, time out of mind, a world gone wrong. Reality might have been another matter, of course: even Dylan now tells the *story* of his early years.

The Zimmermans lived first with Beatty's mother, Florence Stone, on 3rd Avenue East. Bob's mother went back to work as a clerk at Feldman's Department Store; his father began his duties at the appliance store on 5th Avenue. Soon enough, Bobby would be hanging around, sweeping up or accompanying his uncles on wiring jobs and the like. After a year or so, Abe moved his family to a solid three-bedroomed house at 2425 7th Avenue, a short walk from the high school, from the downtown district, from numerous relatives, and from anything and everything, the great endless outdoors included, that Hibbing might have to offer.

In the composite portrait the child is shy, a little sensitive, but wants for nothing. As he would later observe, no one in his home town was conspicuously better off or worse off than anyone else; the real mining

---

22 Once considered waste rock, taconite is a low-grade iron ore. As the supply of high-grade natural iron ore diminished, the industry began to reconsider its view of taconite. The rock is blasted apart, scooped up by giant diggers and dump trucks, crushed, separated by magnets, rolled in clay and baked into pellets. None of this is pretty.

wealth, like the ore itself, was shipped out. Still, Bobby had plenty of friends. In Duluth he had attended kindergarten; in Hibbing he grasped the point of the Alice Grade School[23] – it lasted *all day* – and wore the occasional insults of those who teased him because of his odd, complicated name. It seems, too, that he acquired the retentive, sponge-like capacity of near-infinite memory: he opened his eyes and his ears.

What he saw and heard can seem impossibly quaint now, or utterly bizarre. In *Chronicles*, Dylan would recall schoolchildren trained to dive beneath their desks when the sirens sounded. This was supposed to save them, and children all across America, from the Russians and their bombs. Those same Russian hordes – the Russians his uncles had encountered as allies – were even then poised to come parachuting down on little Hibbing. Few doubted it. Yet in another part of a child's world the sight and sound of the railroads, crossing the country roads, halting traffic at intersections, was a guarantor of security. When the trains were running the world was complete, and incapable of change. This mixture, confidence and dread intertwined, was entirely of its time.

Duck and Cover, said Bert the Turtle, a friendly cartoon, in the 1951 civil-defence movie designed to provide America and its children with the illusion that a nuclear war could be endured. *You Can Survive*, said the official government pamphlet, cultivating ignorance and optimism in equal measure. Kids of Dylan's age were encouraged to wear ID tags, the better to identify the corpses – though the fact was not advertised – should the government be mistaken in its confidence. The Soviets had set off their first atomic bomb in Kazakhstan in August of 1949, adding a footnote to one war and commencing another. Even in the North Country, where miners daily blasted rock as old as the planet, the political aftershocks would be felt for decades. No American child was left innocent. Meanwhile the ore trains, hauled by the big Yellowstone locomotives of the Duluth, Missabe & Iron Range Railroad, Hibbing's lifeline and reason to exist, went rumbling off into a child's memory.

He did OK. He played in the woods and on the spoil-heaps-become-hillsides. He listened to those unending ore trains as they snaked through the landscape. He tried the Boy Scouts, but it didn't last. At ten or eleven – said Shelton, curating Beatty's proud memories – he even tried writing poetry, for Mother's Day. Somehow that idea endured. In due course 'Bob Dylan' became a voice, a form of words.

*

---

23 These days the site is a parking lot: they paved paradise.

A nice, white, ordinary Jewish boy was raised by decent, caring parents. There wasn't much more to it than that. His faith was a little out of the ordinary in a town that was a little out of the way in an early 1950s America whose reality long ago blended with movie myth and nostalgia. But that, too, was OK, more or less. You could arrange the pieces. In 1952, the Zimmermans, early adopters, acquired a TV set to receive news – the signal came and went – from a new age. In 1953, Ethel and Julius Rosenberg, a Jewish couple, were executed for selling the secrets of the Bomb to the Soviet enemy. In 1954, a US senator named Joseph McCarthy was censured finally for un-American activities against those he had deemed un-American and a new Bomb, the hydrogen one, turned a blameless Pacific atoll into vitrified slag. In 1955, a western drama named *Gunsmoke* was the electrifying sensation among all the new cowboy shows on all the new TV sets while the black people of Montgomery, Alabama, were boycotting city buses just for the right to sit where they chose.

In 1955, at the J&M Recording studio in New Orleans, a frustrated 22-year-old former jump blues performer named Richard Penniman began to mess around on the piano, trying his luck again with one of his old stage numbers, a risqué little ditty called 'Tutti Frutti'.

In 1955, in Nashville, a 20-year-old piano player from Louisiana named Lewis, a handsome devil who had been kicked out of Bible school for adding boogie-woogie to God's Word, was looking for luck and finding none. The record company guys said he should switch to guitar.

In 1955, one Charles Hardin Holley, Buddy to his friends, had the great good luck to be picked as the opening act for a show in his home town of Lubbock, Texas, with an attentive agent in the crowd and a record deal about to happen.

In 1955, on 15 October, the 19-year-old Buddy Holly was followed on stage by another minor, a 20-year-old sometimes known as the Memphis Flash, sometimes as the Hillbilly Cat, whose act tended to enrage teenage boys and most grown-ups. Over in Odessa, Texas, still another 19-year-old, Roy Orbison, was prepared to drive 355 miles to Dallas just to see and hear what Holly was seeing and hearing. Hibbing, Minnesota, though, had seen nothing yet.

A lifetime later, in that world gone wrong, 'Bob Dylan' and Bobby Zimmerman were reunited briefly. Together they said: 'When I first heard Elvis' voice I just knew I wasn't going to work for anybody; and nobody was going to be my boss . . . Hearing him for the first time was like busting out of jail.'[24] Rock and roll could make anything seem simple. In the mind of the young Zimmerman, nevertheless, consciousness of a two-fold problem was forming, day by day, year by year. Steadily it became a conviction. He was the wrong person in the wrong place.

---

24 *Us Weekly* magazine, August 1987.

Forever Young

The beginning was there in Minnesota. But that was the beginning before the beginning.

> Interview with Studs Terkel, WFMT (Chicago), 1963

IN MAY OF 1954, ON THE SABBATH BEFORE HIS 13TH BIRTHDAY, ABE and Beatty Zimmerman's eldest became a *bar mitzvah*, a son of the commandment. By joining in the ritual public reading of the Torah he marked the beginning, in the religious sense, of his adult life. He came of age. In Hibbing that year there were few enough youngsters of his faith who could say as much. His proud parents would summon 400 relatives and friends from Duluth and beyond to the resplendent Androy Hotel on East Howard Street to celebrate the happy event, but an aged Orthodox rabbi had to be imported all the way from New York to prepare the boy. As Dylan would tell *Spin* magazine in 1985:

> Suddenly a rabbi showed up under strange circumstances for only a year. He and his wife got off the bus in the middle of winter. He was an old man from Brooklyn who had a white beard and wore a black hat and black clothes. They put him upstairs above where I used to hang out.
>
> I used to go up there every day to learn this stuff, either after school or after dinner. After studying with him an hour or so, I'd come down and boogie . . .
>
> The rabbi taught me what I had to learn, and after he conducted this bar mitzvah, he just disappeared. The people didn't want him. He didn't look like anybody's idea of a rabbi. He was an embarrassment. All the Jews up there shaved their beards, and, I think, worked on Saturday. And I never saw him again. It's like he came and went like a ghost.[1]

---

1   Andrew Muchin at JewishJournal.com says Dylan was describing 'the Rev. Reuven Maier, probably a nonordained religious functionary. He lived on Howard Street above the then L&B Cafe.' Muchin adds that, contrary to the singer's tale, (cont.)

One way or another, a good deal of Hebrew had to be mastered and memorised. According to Robert Shelton's researches Bobby applied an alert ear to the job of phonetic mimicry. More than that, the youngster who was already spending time in his room writing poetry – or what his mother remembered as poetry – had to immerse himself, consciously or not, willingly or not, in religious language and imagery. The experience left its mark. Whether the Agudath Achim ('Society of Brothers') synagogue on 2nd Avenue West still counted as Orthodox in 1954 is a good question, but the mysterious cross-country rabbi certainly occupied that category.[2] There is evidence enough, meanwhile, that some amalgam of Jewish teaching and Abe's adamantine moral code would give Bob Dylan a certain cast, shall we say, of mind.

In 1966, effortlessly quotable, he would sing of how 'To live outside the law you must be honest'. It was probably a line, one of many, adapted from a movie.[3] No doubt it was a comment on criminal justice and personal morality, on society's rules and integrity. But in Judaism the bar mitzvah ceremony is also the moment at which the child-man becomes spiritually 'subject to the full force of the law'.

In 1954 he was a good kid, quiet and shy, slightly asthmatic, never in trouble, doing well at school – though developing curious aversions; to the study of history, for one example – but as keen as any all-American boy on bowling and movies and all those TV cowboy shows. He liked music, too. Or rather, he liked the idea of music.

In Shelton's version, presumably derived from family sources, there was, first, a piano and 'home dance records'. The former is identified as a Gulbransen spinet model – 'never recommended for serious students', according to a modern buyers' guide – that sat in the Zimmerman front room, disdained by Bobby after a single infuriating lesson from a female cousin. Various brass instruments followed, each horn attempted, insulted and discarded. As to the phonograph records, Shelton mentions Billy Daniels, a veteran cabaret act of the day, the purveyor of 'That Old Black Magic'.

(1 cont.) 'Maier stayed in Hibbing at least another two years, according to the 1956 Hibbing City Directory.'

2 The Agudath Achim synagogue disbanded during the 1980s. In May of 2011 the temple was on the market as a potential residential property, priced at $109,000.

3 In a 2007 *Harper's* article Jonathan Lethem, novelist and essayist, nominated a 1958 Eli Wallach gangster flick entitled *The Lineup*. Thus: 'When you live outside the law, you have to eliminate dishonesty.'

Looking back in 1984 on the luck or fate that first brought him to the attention of Columbia Records,[4] a label that had somehow managed to miss the entire point of rock and roll in the 1950s, Dylan said:

> You know, nostalgia to me isn't really rock and roll. Because when I was a youngster the music I heard was Frankie Laine, Rosemary Clooney, Dennis . . . what's his name? Dennis Day? And you know, Dorothy Collins . . . the Mills Brothers, all that stuff. When I hear stuff like that, it always strikes a different chord in me than all the rock and roll stuff.[5]

Such was pre-history for most white Americans of his generation. In their cliché the 1950s was the bifurcated decade, a world split like the atom (the one that promised a nuclear-powered home for the nuclear family and doom, simultaneously) by titanic forces. For the survivors, music is shorthand: first there was this, then *that*. They talk of the decade – through their movies, books, songs and other fictions – as though once upon a time there was only yesterday and tomorrow, with today no better than a fuzzy notion. Hindsight says they talk like teenagers, a breed they say they invented.

Most of Dylan's contemporaries, on either side of the Atlantic, would share that sensibility, and seem to emerge from the after-war years as though coming up for air. Post-imperial Britain had a special, shabby tedium of its own, but the argument was the same. For that generation pubescence and adolescence coincided with a supernatural change: the world itself was altered. One of them, John Lennon by name, would say: 'It was the only thing to get through to me after all the things that were happening when I was 15. Rock and roll was real. Everything else was unreal.'[6] The remembered history is this: before, after, and nothing ever being the same again. Even the language employed to describe the metamorphosis is full of transatlantic echoes. Thus Keith Richards, barely a couple of years younger than Dylan, in his 2010 autobiography, *Life*:

> The one that really turned me on, like an explosion one night, listening

---

4   Interview with Bert Kleinman and Artie Mogull, Westwood One Radio, 1984.

5   'The sort of pop songs John did listen to, when he listened to any, were by Johnnie Ray and Frankie Laine. "But I didn't take much notice of them."' Hunter Davies, *The Beatles* (1985), Ch. 2.

6   Lennon (born in 1940) in an interview with Jann Wenner. *Rolling Stone*, 1971.

to Radio Luxembourg on my little radio when I was supposed to be asleep, was 'Heartbreak Hotel'. That was the stunner. I'd never heard it before, or anything like it. I'd never heard of Elvis before. It was almost as if I'd been waiting for it to happen. When I woke up the next day I was a different guy.[7]

Memories are imperfect, however, and made for tricks. The existence of the little Gulbransen spinet piano in the Zimmerman front room, to which Bobby would soon find a reason to return, is not disputed. Shelton's account of a child torturing the brass section sounds plausible enough. The point at which Dylan elected to attempt the instrument that would not defy him creates a small argument, however, between biographers, witnesses and the recollections of an individual who has turned 'hazy' into anecdotal art. So Dylan's version has become Dylan's truth. Events and experiences are conflated. But memories of childhood are like that. Who remembers the *second* record they bought?

So Kurt Loder of *Rolling Stone* was assured in 1984 that Bobby Zimmerman first heard Hank Williams 'one or two years before he died. And that sort of introduced me to the guitar. And once I had the guitar, it was never a problem. Nothing else was ever a problem.'

Hank Williams, still the greatest single thing ever to come out of country music, died aged 29 of a heart attack – what with the booze, the morphine, and the rest[8] – on New Year's Day 1953, when Dylan was 11. So how much time elapsed between being 'introduced' to the guitar and actually attempting to derive a tune from the thing? And why would it really matter if a middle-aged (and older) man has failed to assign verifiable dates to each and every event in his childhood? In one of his earlier interviews, nevertheless, Dylan claimed he was first inspired to attempt the art of songwriting itself after hearing Williams. But he didn't say when.

The tale changes with each retelling. Sometimes it is as though Dylan is simply picking the version that feels right at a given moment. By the time he faced the cameras for the sake of Martin Scorsese's 2005 documentary, he was claiming to have 'found' his first guitar at

---

7   Richards, Ch. 2.

8   'I'll Never Get Out of This World Alive', sang Hank, reasonably enough. Still, eleven number-one records in five years (1948–53) give one measure of his importance. Dylan's guiding presence on 2011's *The Lost Notebooks of Hank Williams*, a collection of new settings for old, previously overlooked lyrics, is another.

the age of ten, 'in the house my father bought'. For good measure, he offered 'mystic overtones', explaining that 'one day' he had opened the lid of an old-style mahogany gramophone and found a 78-rpm disc resting on the turntable. Dylan said it contained a gospel track (one written in the 1920s) entitled 'Drifting Too Far From the Shore'. It might have been the Monroe Brothers (a 1936 version) or Roy Acuff (1939), but it was surely fate, at least in his telling. Years later, Dylan would even find a use for the song's title. 'The sound of the record made me feel like I was somebody else, that, you know, that I was maybe not even born to the right parents or something . . .'

Why would a mere tune, with Jesus to the fore, make you doubt your own parentage? The question is not idle. Even during his brief spell as a college student Dylan was a noted – the polite word – fabulist. In his early days in Greenwich Village he told whoppers relentlessly, sometimes for 'professional' reasons, sometimes, it seems, just because he could. Sometimes, often enough, he seemed to feel a strange compulsion to conceal the truth, however innocent. The tall tales don't matter much, in themselves. But some myths are sacred, even to the myth-maker. When you have lived your entire adult life under an assumed name a back story becomes imperative, if only to explain yourself to yourself. On the other hand, psychologists have devoted a good deal of attention to those they call *confabulators*. Dylan has been asked time and again about his first encounters with music and with the guitar. The records that first moved Bobby Zimmerman to music – was it really Johnnie Ray[9] and Hank Williams? – and caused him to attempt the instrument are part-answers to a fundamental question: where did Bob Dylan come from? In 1978, he told still another interviewer:[10]

> I didn't create Bob Dylan. Bob Dylan has always been here . . . always was. When I was a child there was Bob Dylan. And before I was born there was Bob Dylan.

For that to be true, even poetically, 'he' had to exist before the flood,

---

9   Dylan's persistent resort to the 'Nabob of Sob' verges on the Proustian. Ray and the splendidly named Four Lads made number one on the *Billboard* chart late in 1951 with the hysterical (in almost every sense) 'Cry'. Dylan has described its impact on his ten-year-old self repeatedly.

10   Jonathan Cott, *Rolling Stone*.

attuned to the music and already playing, already prepared, fully formed, before anyone else even knew the flood was coming. So who was this remarkable boy? In the early 1950s the answer was incomplete. But the idea that rock and roll could ever have taken Bobby Zimmerman by surprise, and turned his world upside down without warning, is judged too prosaic. *Bob Dylan has always been here . . .* So the initiation into the art of the guitar is summarised, the moments compressed:

> First I bought a Nick Manoloff book.[11] I don't think I could get past the first one. And I had a Silvertone guitar from Sears. In those days, they cost thirty or forty dollars, and you only had to pay five dollars down to get it. So I had my first electric guitar.[12]

As hindsight tells it, this was an epiphany. Bobby Zimmerman didn't need – or want – anything else. If there was anti-Semitism in Hibbing, he didn't notice. If he began to seem a little aloof around the house, or to falter in his schoolwork, he didn't care. In his early teenage years he was a model student, often cited on the Hibbing High honor rolls. After rock and roll, such distinctions were few, and the boy's relationship with his father became fraught, no doubt as a consequence. *As long as I had a guitar, I was happy.* Many thousands of his peers were about to succumb to a mere craze, a season's delirium. Dylan's addiction, runs this fragment of legend, was of a different order from the start. He was incurable.

*

---

11 *Manoloff's Basic Spanish Guitar Manual* (says Shelton). If so, Dylan is in good company. In a 2004 interview to mark his induction to the Academy of Achievement, B.B. King said he learned how to tune a guitar after ordering Manoloff's guides from the Sears Roebuck catalogue. Chuck Berry meanwhile told the *New York Times* in 2003 that he first mastered a borrowed four-string tenor guitar thanks to a Manoloff chord book.

From the 1930s onwards the mysterious Manoloff, apparently a lap steel specialist, produced numerous guides to anything with strings, and marketed his own line in bars and branded picks. Arguably, an entire generation of American guitarists learned to play by his fondly remembered Method.

Manoloff also took 'arranger' credit on numerous standards used in various movie soundtracks. One notable success, if you enjoy a coincidence, was a 1936 rendering, with a lap steel tuning, of the Russian folk song 'Dark Eyes'.

12 Kurt Loder, *Rolling Stone*, 1984.

One historian has summed up the Eisenhower years of Dylan's youth as 'in general ones of comfortable lethargy'. It is a precis of the standard description, but like most of history's verdicts it depends on the facts selected and the perspective claimed. The soporific conservatism seeping from the White House certainly seemed to suit a mostly prosperous country. The president himself called it 'the politics of tranquillity'. On the other hand, those who grew up in the period always claim to remember a neurotic and hidebound era – 'the Fatuous Fifties' – in which imagination was not much prized, big business owned the government, and uniformity was a virtue.

Some fretted over the torpor even as it took hold. Adlai Stevenson, the great lost hope of 1950s liberalism, once enquired: 'With the supermarket as our temple and the singing commercial as our litany, are we likely to fire the world with an irresistible vision of America's exalted purpose and inspiring way of life?' In Europe, the US was caricatured, much as now, as rich but crass, hugely powerful but utterly parochial. Distant foreign intellectuals mocked the things in which Americans took pride when the Yanks were not agitated, like Stevenson, by the cash nexus and commercialism. One only had to look. As it turned out the surface of things was deceptive, and even that surface was in equal measure disturbed and disturbing to those who were paying attention.

When Eisenhower was the unlikely president of Columbia University in the late 1940s and early '50s, a joke did the academic rounds. Don't send the general too much paperwork, they said, or his lips will get tired. Nevertheless, it was a wily Democrat, Truman, who dropped the Bomb. It was Truman who led the United States into a 'United Nations' war as the new decade began after Communist North Korea tipped a strategic domino and invaded the south of the peninsula. It was Truman, too, who presided over the first splutterings of anti-Communist paranoia in the early years of the so-called Second Red Scare, the mania that was to see thousands of Americans, most of them merely incautious of speech or liberal in opinion, harassed and persecuted on suspicion – an endless, self-sustaining, near-totalitarian suspicion – of disloyalty and subversion. More than a few of the victims were allied to the Left and its folk songs.

TV and the 'singing commercial' told one story in Dylan's childhood; political reality another; and life in little Hibbing, Minn., a third. In New York, Hollywood and elsewhere many victims of the witch-hunts and the blacklists were Jews: at the time it was alleged, convincingly enough, that the House Committee on Un-American Activities was a poorly veiled exercise in anti-Semitism. Yet when a junior senator from Wisconsin named Joseph McCarthy produced a list of 205 alleged 'card-carrying' Communists at work in the State Department, little Bobby Zimmerman was living in a dream landscape of snow, trees and hypnotic silence, lost in music, far from those incomprehensible troubles. Some of his peers in the big cities grew up in the shadow of McCarthyism; not him.

Were there ever Communist subversives peddling red revolution in Hibbing? Over the years the mine unions had contained their share of radicals: given the rapacity of the iron barons, that had been inevitable. Workers of Scandinavian and east European extraction, in particular, had adopted the aims of the Socialist Party, and later of the Communist Party. In the 1920s these stubborn men had fought off attempts by Minnesota's burgeoning wing of the Ku Klux Klan to prevent 'foreigners', Catholics above all, from unionising. During the Depression Hibbing's union hall had been a redoubt for left-leaning 'Rangers'. Gus Hall, born Arvo Kustaa Halberg of Communist parents in a nearby hamlet, would later become the Stalinist general secretary of the CPUSA and, on four occasions, its supremely optimistic presidential candidate.

For all that, most of the Mesabi miners did not win a contract with US Steel until 1943, after almost half a century of struggle. Theirs was a collectivist political culture, but hardly 'subversive'. In *Chronicles*, Dylan would attempt to describe the North Country's detachment from the world's affairs and throw in – inadvertently, no doubt – a little political comment. After claiming that fallout shelters were rare in his region of Minnesota, he would deny the existence of anti-Communist paranoia on the Iron Range. According to Dylan, there was no fear of the red menace and a certain scepticism that such a menace even existed. Instead, Communists symbolised invaders from outer space. The mine owners were a bigger threat, and a greater enemy.

It's a neat inversion: deeply serious film scholars will always maintain that movie aliens were symbolic of the red menace. But Dylan also allows, after some comedy on the bomb shelter's potential as a status symbol and the Iron Range's disdain for *that* sort of thing, that his Minnesota shared the fears of the age. He had ducked and covered in school with the rest. In the North Country folk had worried as much about a nuclear holocaust as anyone. The people, in his account, simply had no truck with salesmen peddling anxiety. That applied to red scares, too.

Abe Zimmerman was no miner, and nor was he inclined towards radical politics. For one thing, he was responsible on behalf of the electrical store for repossessing the goods of miners' families who had fallen behind with their payments. Hibbing was meanwhile about as far as it was possible to get from the centre of national events. In truth, any notion that the facts of political life were being prepared for the future attention of this infant, or for any child of Hibbing, was preposterous by definition. This was Dylan's America, nevertheless. It was where he came from.

*

In the spring of 1954, in still another world entirely, Woody Guthrie was broke, sick, drunk, chaotic and finished as a performer. In Greenwich Village, a lot of actors and folk singers couldn't find jobs because of the blacklist. It was, like a lot of things, no longer Woody's problem. That summer he was still trying to ride the boxcars, but company was hard to come by. There were no more hoboes and few people thought of him as much of a hero. The diagnosis was in: Huntington's, the implacable disease that had caused his mother to end her days in an insane asylum, was to be his fate.

Guthrie had been given $500 and a contract to write a book – a coincidence, but an appealing one – in the year of Bob Dylan's birth. Once the vast manuscript was trimmed somewhat, *Bound for Glory* made a legend of Woody. His *chronicles* didn't always fit the facts, exactly, and sometimes didn't approach the truth at all, but who among the New York left-folk crowd was about to contradict the authentic Okie voice of liberty?

On the book's publication in 1943 the *New Yorker* – required reading in every hobo jungle – had deemed Woody 'a national possession, like Yellowstone or Yosemite'. Back in Oklahoma, in contrast, one of his cousins decided to sue the memoirist for libel. Certain facts, it was alleged, were at odds with the author's truths. Guthrie became a Manhattan celebrity regardless until he was persuaded by the government, and by his comrade Cisco Houston, that the need to fight fascism might require more than a few USO tours. Woody and Cisco had therefore joined the merchant marine for a spell until Guthrie's reputation as a red fellow traveller – though he was never a Communist Party member – saw him drafted into the army at the war's end.

Afterwards, he had enjoyed a few fruitful years living out on Coney Island and raising another brood of children. That was the last of Woody's luck. By the end of the 1940s, though no one then knew why, his behaviour, never predictable, had spun out of control. Diagnoses had ranged from alcoholism to schizophrenia (later, the romantically ignorant would even blame advanced syphilis). Then an arm had been disabled in a campfire accident. By 1954, with a third wife in tow, he was back in New York. But Bob Dylan's future inspiration could no longer play his fascist-killing guitar.

*

Soon afterwards, Bobby Zimmerman began to hear things. Through no fault of Micka Electric, the family's prized TV, like every TV in town, was an erratic appliance. Sets in Hibbing picked up signals haphazardly, for a few hours each evening, and often managed only a snowy picture: just what the North Country needed to see. In the big cities a few rich, crazy souls were paying $1,000 a time by 1954 for the first of the new, if tiny, colour sets, but on the Iron Range decent monochrome reception was for long afterwards a question of luck and weather. Radio was another matter.

The craze for TV was sweeping all before it. Between 1949 and 1959 the number of American households with sets would rise from 940,000 to 44 million. Yet, as one historian puts it, 'The more it prospered the more bland and conventional television became.' Barely born, it was 'becoming a great industry but a failed art',[13] one dominated by the reactionary instincts and dedicated crassness – as Dylan would discover in his turn – of advertising sponsors. Few viewers seemed to care. Soon enough what was seen on TV began to pass for normal. People began to ape television's prescriptions and proscriptions, to 'aspire', in the language of a later world, to its idea of glittering suburban-zombie perfection. The box in the corner preached: sometimes insidiously, sometimes overtly. If 1950s America thereafter acquired a reputation as a stupefied and conformist decade, one worth rebelling against, the smiling folk on the television screen could take a bow. Radio, though it had lost its supremacy, was an alternate reality. It wasn't always phoney.

Dylan would remember that. By no coincidence at all, his very own *Theme Time Radio Hour* was to be the delight of his late years, and a

---

13   O'Neill, *American High*, Ch. 3.

delight for everyone with ears who heard it.[14] What you heard there was Dylan's idea of a remembered dream, like a dial being spun through an infinity of channels to alight on music famous and obscure, songs linked – if you got the joke – by whimsical, near-arbitrary 'themes' and by a single receptive consciousness. A 1990 Van Morrison song, 'In the Days Before Rock and Roll', takes the selfsame conceit for its lyric: radio, transmission, magic and inspiration coming through the ether to succour the beleaguered. In simple truth, without radio there would have been no rock and roll. It would have remained a regional curiosity, a kind of folk music.

In the 1950s you had to search. Presumably, you had to have some idea of what you were looking for when you coaxed the dial to catch distant stations, even when the broad sweep of the Mississippi River flatlands carried signals almost unimpeded, as though on a tidal race, from the south. It was one thing to hear Johnnie Ray and his 'strange incantation', or find yourself transfixed by Hank Williams – if he hadn't already been fired because of his suicidal boozing[15] – at the Grand Ole Opry. The weekly shows from the venerable Nashville institution had been reaching most of the country on a 50,000-watt AM clear-channel transmitter, as near immune from interference at night as radio could be, since before Dylan was born. During his early teens the Opry was available almost everywhere in America thanks to NBC. But the dangerous exotica that was black music?

> Late at night, I used to listen to Muddy Waters, John Lee Hooker, Jimmy Reed and Howlin' Wolf blastin' in from Shreveport. It was a radio show that lasted all night. I used to stay up till two, three o'clock in the morning. Listened to all those songs, then tried to figure them out. I started playing myself.

A nice story, told in 1984.[16] It suggests that the blues, the good stuff

---

14 One hundred shows featuring any sort of music you could name were broadcast from the entirely fictitious 'Abernathy Building' – situated wherever Dylan happened to be – between May 2006, and April 2009. The 'themes' were supported by invented calls and emails. The host also indulged his fondness for some of the worst jokes ever told.

15 As he was in 1952, just before his death, inconvenient though the fact is for the standard Dylan narrative.

16 To Kurt Loder, of *Rolling Stone*.

from the Chess or Vee-Jay labels, inspired the youngster to play. It has also led at least one over-eager biographer[17] to assert that 'Bob had stumbled upon the basic forms of American popular music, before Chuck Berry, Little Richard, or Elvis Presley. The hillbilly songs and heartbreak lyrics of Hank Williams made him think. The libidinous riffs of Jimmy Reed and Howlin' Wolf inspired him to play.' Just like that.

Robert Shelton has Dylan making his first attempts at the guitar – it 'almost sounded like music' – at 'about 14'. No sooner than the summer of 1955, then. Clinton Heylin demonstrates that a vastly more plausible year was 1957.[18] Yet from another biographer we have the nonsensical myth entire: a Dylan who 'stumbled upon' the Platonic forms of American song before Presley, before he had even heard of Presley, or that jailbreak. And it is Dylan – speaking at the age of 43 – who would have us believe it. In this fantasy he could never have just been a kid out in the sticks, like a million others, swept up by the tidal wave of rock and roll, like a million others. Memory is not alone in playing tricks.

Dylan told Shelton this: '"Henrietta" was the first rock 'n' roll record I heard.' Though the claim was repeated – in the *Biograph* booklet and elsewhere – that doesn't seem very likely. Not because there was no chance of a teenager catching a number by San Antonio's Jimmy Dee and the Offbeats that sounds *just a bit* like Little Richard. The Texan appeared on Dick Clark's *American Bandstand* and the raucous 'Henrietta' made 47 on the *Billboard* Top 50. It got some exposure.

But that didn't happen until early in 1958. Bobby Zimmerman was 16 by then, the ideal age for rock and roll perhaps. 'Henrietta' – 'Do your love so fine / Henrietta / The way you love me mine / You're always on the move / Handing out such a line' – could certainly have taken a young man's fancy. Yet is it actually possible that any American teenager, anywhere in the country, could have got to 1958 without hearing just a couple of other specimens of rock and roll first?

In Dylan's own version – in the version directed by Martin Scorsese, at any rate – the music on the radio caused him to become 'bored being there', meaning Hibbing. Revealingly, he has also said that when he first heard rock and roll he 'thought it was pretty similar to the

---

17 Sounes, *Down the Highway*, Ch. 1.

18 *Bob Dylan: Behind the Shades Revisited* (2003).

country music I'd been listening to'. If nothing else, he shared that sense of connections and relationships with Presley.

Whatever Bob Dylan has come to think of 'Bob Dylan', of myths, fictions and inventions, he still cultivates more than a few blooms in that garden himself, as though still trying to justify the fantasies of a kid from the back of beyond. It's touching, in a way, a testimony to how much the music, to being at the heart of the music, and to finding himself at its heart, has mattered. The need runs deep: that part is true. He always wants to believe that Bob Dylan *always was*.

The irony would be, of course, that he certainly did listen to blues 'blastin' in from Shreveport', sooner or later, after he had learned that the musical sensations grabbing at his heart had a history, and a story. First, though, he had to be like every other teenager in the country, set aflame by an underground movement that was just about to show its colours. The bare, obvious fact is that Bobby Zimmerman was living in Hibbing, Minnesota, at the heart of nothing much at all, when the rock and roll story broke. Why else would he soon develop such a consuming urge to get out and on?

In 1968 and early 1969 a young writer named Toby Thompson attempted a version of the (then) New Journalism with a ramshackle investigation of Dylan's home-town background. When not talking about himself, the writer spoke to, among others, B.J. Rolfzen, Dylan's 11th grade English teacher. Thompson's well-lubricated paraphrase went as follows:

> Robert. Robert was a quiet boy, aloof. Used to sit in the front row of B.J.'s class, to the left of the desk. Never said a word, just listened. Got good grades, B plusses . . . Took life seriously. Spent a lot of time by himself, must have been thinking and writing – though B.J. never saw anything young Robert produced. Liked motorcycles, had a slew of them. And to have owned a motorcycle in the middle fifties, one would've *had* to be considered . . . well, could never have labeled Robert wild or *hoody* . . . he was always such a sharp dresser . . . but perhaps, *eccentric*.[19]

And so on. In point of fact, 'B.J.' – Boniface – Rolfzen provided young Zimmerman with what sounds like a decent grounding in literature, both American and English, at the vast, ornate high school built with

---

19 *Positively Main Street: Bob Dylan's Minnesota* (1971, rev. ed. 2008).

mining company money.[20] The 2004 Experience Music Project exhibition *Bob Dylan's American Journey, 1956–66* included, among other things, a section of the student's 1958 essay on Steinbeck's *Grapes of Wrath*. One Hibbing girlfriend, the most famous of them, would remember that 'Bob was always reading something' by Steinbeck, and acquiring 'his strong feelings for the Depression Okies'. Echo Helstrom also seemed to recall the works of Dylan Thomas and other poets in her beau's possession.

You can – and people do – make too much of this sort of thing.[21] The only surprise would have been if someone as ferociously literate as the songwriter in question had not had his dose of Steinbeck, a writer whose reputation had begun to flat-line in the late 1950s just as his novels were becoming set texts. How many bright-enough teenagers didn't read *The Grapes of Wrath* and absorb its message? B.J. considered Dylan to have had an unusual interest in literature, and clearly did his best to encourage that interest. But a study of high-school reading lists doesn't actually tell us much.

Dylan's closest friend in Hibbing was a working-class boy named John Bucklen, a year Zimmerman's junior in school but his equal, it appears, in instinctive curiosity where music was concerned. Somehow these youngsters knew that 'out there' was something more. Towards the end of the decade, during their last couple of years at Hibbing High, sometimes with others in tow, the two would hitch to the Twin Cities, Minneapolis and St Paul, in search of music. Bobby also had family in Duluth and Superior on whom he could call. Thanks to a friend from summer camp, he even knew *black people*. It is almost needless to add that these expeditions followed Highway 61, US Route 61, the artery than runs – or ran – for 1,400 miles from New Orleans to the Canadian border.

Who knew that the lifeblood of the blues ran through America on this near-endless highway? No one had thought to turn it into an album title; 66 and kicks made better metrical sense. Zimmerman and Bucklen had some vague inkling, no doubt, of what their journeys

---

20 In part-compensation for uprooting the community from North Hibbing.

21 See 'Hibbing High School and "The Mystery of Democracy"' by Greil Marcus, an account of the writer's visit to the shrine – my word, not his – published in *Highway 61 Revisited: Bob Dylan's Road from Minnesota to the World*, ed. Colleen J. Sheehy and Thomas Swiss (2009). The 'multi-disciplinary anthology' was the result of a 2007 conference at the University of Minnesota concerning a former occasional student.

promised. In those days, from their perspective, 61 was a beginning, the start of something. Everything lay ahead and beyond. But the idea that Bobby had already ingested all the essential musical knowledge he would need is fanciful.

In a 1990s interview with a Dylan fanzine, Bucklen would recall that by 'maybe the summer of '59' they were listening to late-night radio, to KTHS from Little Rock, Arkansas, to 'Brother Gatemouth, Stan's Rockin' Record Shop review' and to a show named *No Name Jive*. This was the real thing, the hard core, from Chuck Berry to Ray Charles to Lightnin' Hopkins. The youths 'ordered a lot of records from Stan's Rockin' Record Shop'. They also discovered a DJ in Virginia, Minnesota, named Jim Dandy, a voice in the wilderness, an individual who played R&B for an hour or so each night. John and Bobby tracked this black man down – 'the only black guy within 50 miles' – and he gave them a priceless education. If Dylan's own *Theme Time* show was to have a presiding patron saint, you suspect, it was this lone guru, talking of the blues.

But that came later. Which came first? Not 'Henrietta', certainly. Bill Haley, the unlikeliest rocker ever born, had covered Ike Turner's 'Rocket 88' in the summer of 1951, but that was a little early for the Dylan myth, and for most people. The former western swing stylist with the retreating cowlick and the mad grin had tried again in '54 with 'Shake, Rattle and Roll', and topped the R&B chart. That scarcely mattered. 'Rock Around the Clock', a B-side re-released in May of 1955 to accompany the movie *Blackboard Jungle*, is the likeliest candidate for primary platter in the emergence of the Bob Dylan who has 'always been here'. It's not something anyone would boast about – Haley, *30 years old*, soon stood revealed to appalled teenagers as the palest of imitations – but it fits. That summer, the dismal track, a novelty number in all but name, was everyone's candidate, in every corner of the world. It is difficult to believe that Bobby Zimmerman, just turned 14, was immune.

Chuck Berry's 'Maybellene' made top five on the *Billboard* Best Sellers in Stores chart in September of that year. Little Richard put out 'Tutti Frutti' in October. RCA Victor, having bought up the billion-dollar mother lode for $40,000, began to re-release Presley's Sun recordings shortly thereafter. 'Heartbreak Hotel' – and the deluge – followed in January of 1956.

Shelton, who interviewed Dylan's parents at the Zimmerman family home in the spring of 1968, just before Abe's death, was shown around the basement recreation room at 2425 7th Avenue East.[22] 'Piles of mouldering 78s and 45s stood in a corner, a cross section of the 1950s' – and of an adolescent life – said the journalist. There lay 'Heartbreak Hotel' and 'Blue Suede Shoes'. There too survived 'Tutti Frutti', Holly's 'Slippin' and Slidin'', Gene Vincent, Johnny Ace, Bobby Vee, Haley, the Clovers and, like a guilty secret, Pat Boone, tireless white copyist of black music. There stood the honky-tonkin' Webb Pierce, 'a flood of Hank Williams's lonesome blues' and *Hank Snow Sings Jimmie Rodgers*.

Dylan was still naming that album of songs in 1997, and remembering that he was 'drawn to their power'. The statement is slightly odd. *Hank Snow Salutes Jimmie Rodgers*, containing 'My Blue-Eyed Jane', a song Dylan would later cover for a tribute record, had certainly appeared in 1953. *Hank Snow Sings Jimmie Rodgers Songs* didn't come out until 1960, when 'Bob Dylan' was already an irregular visitor to Hibbing. Either he had absorbed Snow and Rodgers at a very early age, or he was catching up.

Dylan himself probably could not name the what or when of rock and roll. Nevertheless, it seems that in late '55 or early '56 he developed a sudden respect for the Gulbransen spinet piano in the Zimmerman front room. He may even have realised that the 'compact' instrument doesn't offer much room for a player's knees, and is sometimes better played standing up. And played, if you lack something in the way of skill, loud.

*

In Hibbing, black music entered a white world from afar. Elsewhere in America, things were less simple: the 'races' whose commingling was transforming popular culture were otherwise kept apart, sometimes by unstated prohibitions, sometimes by law and sometimes by sheer brute violence. One unmistakable fact of the rock and roll revolution, the fact that made Presley seem unspeakably transgressive and Little Richard downright dangerous, was its context: skin colour, and attitudes towards skin colour, mattered. 'Race' meant strife and trouble; for black people the word and all its connotations meant misery and pride simultaneously. When Dylan was a child 17 states in the Union enforced racial segregation in schools. Many whites, even in the supposedly

---

22 The wood-framed, two-storey 'Mediterranean Modern'-style house was reportedly sold on eBay in 2001 for $94,600. The purchaser used the name Srueff. Understandably enough, the 'current occupants' ask not to be disturbed.

civilised states, thought it a wise and responsible policy, especially if people were conveniently 'separate but equal'.

In 1954, however, the Supreme Court of the United States decided, after a long struggle among the justices, to do its job and protect the constitution. In the case of *Brown v. Board of Education of Topeka* the court interpreted the 14th amendment to mean that 'equal' treatment was irrelevant: segregation was harmful in and of itself to black youngsters, and unconstitutional. The idea that racism could have a 'scientific' basis was dismissed.

In Topeka, Kansas, this did the trick. In the American South, however, racists persisted in their attempts to defend segregation for a decade and more. They didn't stop with children. On 1 December 1955, a black seamstress named Rosa Parks refused to give up her seat to a white man on a crowded bus in Montgomery, Alabama. For this spontaneous act of rebellion – spontaneous but deliberate – Mrs Parks was arrested for a breach of the segregation laws.

It was no isolated incident, nor was it the worst. In August of that year, in Mississippi, an 'adult-looking' 14-year-old from Chicago named Emmett Till made the mistake of flirting – to her alarm, it was alleged – with a white woman. A few nights later Carolyn Bryant's husband, Roy, and his half-brother took the youth to a barn where they beat him bloody, gouged out one of his eyes and shot him in the head. Emmett's body, barbed wire wrapped around its neck, was recovered from the Tallahatchie River after three days.

Scarcely half a dozen years after the fact a young songwriter, barely a beginner, would 'borrow'[23] a tune from a friend and compose a ballad about the murder, a farcical trial and the killers' acquittals. It was intended to remind his fellow man 'That this kind of thing still lives today in that ghost-robed Ku Klux Klan'. In truth, it wasn't much of a song, even as a prentice piece, and Bob Dylan disowned it soon enough. But the civil-rights movement, born in its modern form when Mrs Parks took her stand and Emmett Till died, was another unnoticed backdrop to Bobby Zimmerman's childhood and youth. The music he came to love, and the music the young Bob Dylan would make, was torn from a disfigured national psyche. Or as Barry Shank has said,

---

23   'Stole' is the accurate word, as Dylan would confess in a 1962 radio interview, having lifted a melody from his Greenwich Village colleague and friend, the African American folk singer Len Chandler. The result was 'The Death of Emmett Till'. According to *Chronicles*, Chandler did not appear to object. We have Dylan's word on it.

Dylan's earliest musical tastes, desires, and ambitions were profoundly intertwined with the history of race relations in the United States; he learned about race through his study of popular music.[24]

*

Knowledge was born from a collective memory, too. Some things were hard to forget, and some persistent, ugly facts of American life did not fit the usual caricatures. One convenient caricature said that racism was 'a Southern thing'. Too many people knew better.

For example: in June of 1920, when Abe Zimmerman was an eight-year-old in Duluth, the circus came to town. One night, two local teenagers, 19-year-old Irene Tusken and James Sullivan, 18, decided to spend time behind the big top watching black workers dismantling tents and loading wagons. Something happened – no one is sure quite what – but young Sullivan would later claim that he and the girl had been assaulted and held at gunpoint. Then, so the story went, she had been raped by a group, five or perhaps six strong, of the black men.

A subsequent examination by Irene's own doctor showed no physical evidence of such a crime, but it didn't matter. Six of the black workers were arrested. Incensed by press reports and rumours that the girl had died, a mob then broke into the city jail – the police did not resist – seized three of the men, beat them senseless, and lynched them.

There is a postcard of the event's aftermath, 3½ inches by 5½ inches, showing an unabashed white crowd posed around three black corpses, each stripped to the waist. The victims are depicted hanging together from a pole on the corner of 1st Street and 2nd Avenue East,[25] a site almost as far as it was possible to get from the 'notorious South'. The inscription on the card – though the date is erroneous – reads: 'Three Negroes lynched at Duluth, Minn. for rape. Oct, 1919 by mps.'

In the years after the First World War such postcards were commonplace in America. James Allen, who has spent 25 years

24 'That Wild Mercury Sound: Bob Dylan and the Illusion of American Culture', published in the journal *boundary 2* (Spring 2002).

25 Abe's family had lived on West 1st Street during his infancy, but had moved to Lake Avenue North before the murders.

collecting and documenting the evidence, remarks acidly on the website withoutsanctuary.org[26] that the cards were once 'common as dirt, souvenirs skin-thin and fresh-tattooed proud, the trade cards of those assisting at ritual racial killings and other acts of a mad citizenry'. Allen states that the surviving postcards represent 'an original photo population of many thousands'.

In 1919 lynchings and 'riotings' had occurred in at least 25 cities across America. Were such things possible in Duluth, far in the north, with all its newly arrived Europeans versed in oppression and oblivious to the legacies of the war between the states? The Minnesota Historical Society observes that a city 'on the rise' in 1920 contained 100,000 souls, but only 495 of those – according to that year's census – were black. They did the usual work – 'as porters, waiters, janitors and factory workers' – and were treated in the usual fashion. As the society's account of the 15 June lynchings observes: 'Certain restaurants did not serve blacks. A downtown movie theater forced blacks to sit in the balcony. Blacks working for US Steel were paid less and excluded from living in Morgan Park, an idyllic "model city". . . Many settled in nearby Gary, a poor neighborhood with substandard housing.'[27]

After the event, many citizens were outraged by the lynchings, but others were unperturbed. In Superior, Wisconsin, just across the bay from Duluth, the acting Chief of Police declared, 'We are going to run all idle negroes out of Superior and they're going to stay out.' The historical society cannot say if the threat was carried out. It is known, however, that 'all of the blacks employed by a carnival in Superior were fired and told to leave the city'. The belief that racism was a Southern disease died when the Duluth mob – anywhere between 1,000 and 10,000 of the city's upstanding citizens – laid hands on Elias Clayton, Elmer Jackson and Isaac McGhie.[28]

What did Abe know of the killings? If he knew, what did he remember? If he remembered, what did he say in later years? The Duluth lynchings were within the living memory of some of the older local folk, white and black, who would soon hear of a native son

---

26 The site is remarkable, but – if you need to be warned – just as appalling as you might expect. Allen's book *Without Sanctuary: Lynching Photography in America* was published in 2000.

27 Minnesota Historical Society, Duluth Lynchings Online Resource.

28 Three seven-foot bronzes depicting the dead men, erected in 2003, now watch over a memorial set on a plaza in Duluth.

become the chosen voice of civil rights. But there's another point. James Allen had not begun his researches in 1965. At that date the city of Dylan's birth had not recovered its memory; the Minnesota Historical Society had not set to work. Yet in 1965 there was this:

> They're selling postcards of the hanging
> They're painting the passports brown
> The beauty parlor is filled with sailors
> The circus is in town
> Here comes the blind commissioner
> They've got him in a trance
> One hand is tied to the tight-rope walker
> The other is in his pants
> And the riot squad they're restless
> They need somewhere to go
> As Lady and I look out tonight
> From Desolation Row

*

America's Jews knew all about bigotry. By the 1950s, in any case, the truth of the European Holocaust had ended every lesson. The idea that Bobby Zimmerman could be growing up almost oblivious to that, too, and to Judaism, even after his bar mitzvah, was never remotely plausible. When you understand how he spent his adolescent summers the disavowals become ludicrous, intriguing and odd.

For many years, nevertheless, Dylan would deny both his faith and reality. No one obliged him to do so. Somehow he didn't seem to *notice* any bigotry in Hibbing, or *feel* Jewish, or grasp the purpose of the town's Agudath Achim synagogue, the former Lutheran church where he had stood with his prayer book to recite from the Torah. Somehow he *forgot* that his father had been president of the Hibbing B'nai B'rith lodge, and his mother president of the local Hadassah group.[29] That makes no sense at all, of course. He wasn't driven from his faith or his family. He made a choice. Something about that choice, about his faith and his father, seems to nag at him still, even in his 70s. Even now, none of it represents 'home'. Even now, Dylan presents himself – Rimbaud once

---

29 Respectively, a prominent organisation long dedicated to community work, Jewish rights and opposition to anti-Semitism, and 'The Women's Zionist Organization of America'.

did the same – as an orphaned soul. What has to be decided is whether he was truly abandoned, emotionally, or whether he chose to abandon his family. If the answer is the latter, the question is why.

*

Summer camp is an American institution, taken for granted, central to all the juvenile rites of passage beloved of movie-makers. When Beatty decided that her boy should enjoy the privilege, Bobby, by all accounts, was less than keen. But Camp Herzl at Webster, Wisconsin, offered more than the usual character-building adventures in the woods. From 1953 onwards Dylan would spend fully four summers there.

Founded in 1946 by a couple from St Paul, Minnesota, named Harry and Rose Rosenthal, Herzl was – and still is – dedicated to Zionism. Inspired by Theodor Herzl, the father of the movement, the camp was aimed at youngsters:

> from dozens of small communities where Jewish children had few role models and no readily available cultural institutions. At Herzl Camp, they learned what it meant to be Jewish, to practice cultural and religious traditions, to live a Jewish life with others of the same faith.

As the camp's own history relates:

> In its first brochure, Herzl Camp's aim was 'to bring a child closer to Jewish life and the Jewish people . . . to prepare the child to absorb the content and values of modern Palestine . . . to enlist the child's interest and help in building of the Jewish national homeland'.[30]

Campers were selected, moreover, 'on the basis of merit, personality, Jewish background, *possibilities for leadership* [my italics] and general interests'. If Bobby Zimmerman was ever vague about his identity before his first visit to Herzl in the summer of 1953, the uncertainty was soon dispelled. As the camp's current literature states, here were 'Our concepts of ruach[31], involvement, acceptance and learning about ourselves, Israel and Judaism in a fun environment . . .'

---

30 Camp Herzl website.

31 Ruach Elohim, a Hebrew name for God. In the *Tanakh* the *ruach* means 'wind, breath, mind, and spirit'. It also involves the idea that life possesses reason, will and conscience.

In 1954, the camp was expanding fast under a new director, Rabbi Zvi Dershowitz, with between 250 and 300 youngsters enrolled for the summer. Clearly, middle-class Jewish parents with ambitions – and in Beatty's case a desire to see her boy meet nice Jewish girls – thought the place ideal for their children, and something more than a mere seasonal recreation.

> There were boat trips and camping trips, as well as a kibbutz building adventure, where campers would be awakened in the middle of the night to do the work that was done in Palestine to establish Jewish communities as quickly as possible. Campers would arrive at a site, some by truck, some on foot, some by boat, and would make campsites, cooking sites, resting accommodations, all in a spirit of cooperation, singing the songs of Israel.[32]

There was swimming and tennis, too, and canoeing, and cookouts. In most respects it was the standard, invigorating, hale-and-hearty summer-camp experience. From the start, nevertheless, Herzl's primary purpose was to endow its youthful participants with a thoroughly Zionist education. These campers were enjoined to 'speak Hebrew in the dining hall, call buildings by Hebrew names and dress in white for the Sabbath'.[33] If you believe a word, all of this had somehow slipped Bob Dylan's mind by the time anyone thought to ask him about his Jewishness. Decades would pass before the mask slipped – with a visit to Israel in 1971, and with a song ('Neighborhood Bully') on 1983's *Infidels* album – but even then he would refuse to deal straightforwardly with his history. It seemed never to fit, least of all with born-again Christianity. Or rather, much of the time, he would not allow it to fit within the scheme of his chosen narrative. In point of fact, he would attend the camp each August until 1958.

Today, by all accounts, Herzl is still going strong, and still true to its original mission as 'a welcoming, independent camp where young people become self-reliant, create lasting Jewish friendships, and develop commitment and love for Judaism and Israel. Herzl Camp

---

32 Camp Herzl website.

33 Dave Engel, *Just Like Bob Zimmerman's Blues: Dylan in Minnesota* (1997). This is an invaluable account by a Wisconsin journalist and historian – certainly invaluable for the writing of these pages – of Dylan's earliest years. Absurdly, the book has long been out of print, but remains available – at a price – online.

creates a vibrant Jewish community of future leaders.' Judging by the wilful evasions of one 'future leader', the place might never have existed.

Yet Bobby Zimmerman made friends there, and even encountered some kindred spirits. In August of 1954, during his second stay, he was giving his attention to the piano in the recreation room, the Ulam[34], when a 12-year-old from St Paul named Larry Kegan asked him how he knew the (supposedly) blues-inflected tune. Reportedly, Bobby mentioned something about a radio station and the conversation turned to music. A bond was forged that endured for the rest of Larry's difficult life.

Howard Rutman, also from St Paul, was another of the Herzl gang whose musical tastes came close to meeting the young Zimmerman's exacting standards. The three formed a trio, of sorts, and on Christmas Eve in 1956 were to take a crack at one of those music-shop make-your-own-record facilities that fascinated so many teenagers of the period. A few minutes of horsing around would later be granted the status of an artefact – *the earliest known recording*, indeed – but these efforts were never especially serious. All that matters is that Bobby was still just a rough-and-ready piano player, and that he stuck by these friends – Louis Kemp, a scion of a Duluth fisheries business, was another – ever afterwards, as best he could. People he knew before the craziness were luckier than a host of others down the years. Kegan, Rutman and Kemp, and a handful more besides, became witnesses to the fact that Dylan never did leave Minnesota behind entirely.

At Herzl there were girls, too, in the time-honoured way: crushes, curiosity, infatuations, efforts to impress. Nice Jewish girls, of course, as nice as Beatty might have hoped: a Harriet Zisson, a Judy Rubin who lingered, intermittently, in Bobby's affections for several years, and perhaps others. After several returns to the camp, and a bit more practice, he could impress them and anyone else with his 'rock and roll' piano playing. In 1957, he even attempted to amaze the whole camp with his literary gifts.

'Little Buddy', he called it. Eleven verses of doggerel dedicated to a dog – 'Then he left the fluffy head / But the little dog was dead' – the 'poem' was submitted to the camp's *Herzl Herald* and saved for decades after the paper's editor realised just how famous the boy-scribbler had

---

34 Historically, the antechamber to the Temple in Jerusalem. Herzl's educators missed no opportunities.

become. In 2009, the handwritten and signed manuscript turned up in an auction of Dylan memorabilia. Proceeds were intended for the summer camp's $8-million fund-raising effort, with the writer's blessing. (Which is to say, 'Do what you want with it.') The 'experts' at Christie's auction house thought the treasure might fetch all of $15,000.

A spokesman told the Associated Press: 'It's a very early example of [Dylan's] brilliance. It comes from the mind of a teenager [with] some very interesting thoughts . . . percolating in his brain.' Artdaily. org chipped in with the view that 'The poem reveals the prodigious talent of the prolific singer-songwriter who is regarded as one of the most influential figures in the 20th century . . . Foreshadowing Dylan's gift for storytelling, "Little Buddy" is a dark and mournful poem, about the murder of a boy's dog . . .'

Fascinating stuff. Not half as fascinating, though, as the near-instant response on the indefatigable Expecting Rain website from Dylan watchers who know their man, in this regard at least, as well as he knows himself. The truth was this: as though rehearsing the bad habits of a lifetime, Bobby had simply copied out a Hank Snow song – not for the first time or the last[35] – down to the last inept rhyme and grisly sentiment, and passed it off as his own. It was certainly a very early example of something. *That* was revealing.

To be strictly fair, Beatty Zimmerman later vouched that her pride and joy was a voracious reader, then and later. He spent a great deal of time in the library, she told Shelton. At home he was forever writing and drawing. Even his comic-book choices leaned, mom said firmly, towards those 'that had some meaning, like *Illustrated Classics*'.

It was just as well. This was amidst the 'great comic-book scare', when parents across America (and Britain) convinced themselves that lurid tales of horror and superheroes might be morally toxic. A self-promoting but respected psychiatrist, one Fredric Wertham, had published the bestselling *Seduction of the Innocent* in 1954 to 'prove' the point. Superman was 'a fascist' (obviously) and Wonder Woman a blatantly sexual (ditto) lesbian with a bondage habit. 'I think Hitler was a beginner compared to the comic-book industry,' declared

---

35 In 1993, the Dylan fan magazine *Isis* published verses in the singer's hand as 'a poem' dated to 1952–5. This was also a Hank Snow song, 'The Drunkard's Song', itself probably plagiarised from a work by Jimmie Rodgers, 'A Drunkard's Child'. Perhaps it was just the young Zimmerman's aide-memoire. But 'influence' is a strange process. Habit-forming, too.

Wertham, dead to irony, as public bonfires of the ten-cent tales were staged, a congressional inquiry was launched, hundreds of artists and writers were fired and sage editorials were written in the polite press on the connection between cheap fiction and juvenile delinquency.

At a time when comic-book sales were running at 100 million a week in 625 separate titles in America alone, Wertham argued against an outright ban. Deadly serious, he recommended that this insidious juvenile pulp should be forbidden to minors lacking parental consent. Instead, like Hollywood before it, the industry got its very own censor, the Comics Code Authority, to pore over daft plots and outlandish imagery. Production duly collapsed.[36]

Beatty got off lightly, then, with her high-minded son. If she was talking about comic books, however, it seems she was confusing *Illustrated Classics* with *Classics Illustrated*, a series that ran from 1941 to 1962 and did exactly as its title claimed by abridging – gutting would be the better word – the plots of great Western literature. *Robinson Crusoe*, *Oliver Twist*, *The Three Musketeers*, even (improbably) *Les Misérables*: all were rendered into four-colour storyboards at 15 cents a time, each worthy title calculated to reassure parents that their children were being inoculated against excitement. *Classics Illustrated* was intended as culture-made-easy, and as an alternative to the lurid stuff. Wertham condemned a couple of the titles regardless.

Dylan might have learned something about storytelling 'with some meaning' from all this, but America was in a strange mood. The strangest part was that few seemed to notice. Even children were marked as incipient threats to the social order; even juvenile fantasies were fit for censorship and control. Theories purporting to explain the rise of the 1960s counter-culture overlook the shared memory of a time when adults tried to take away *comic books*. In the early 1950s it was as though a country living under the shadow of the Bomb had become addicted to panic and fear. And not even a patriotic Superman was allowed to save them. Something had to give.

*

There were plenty of other reasons for unease amidst the 'comfortable

---

36 See David Hajdu's *The Ten-Cent Plague: The Great Comic-Book Scare and How It Changed America* (2008). Hajdu is also the author of the very fine *Positively 4th Street: The Lives and Times of Joan Baez, Bob Dylan, Mimi Baez Fariña and Richard Fariña* (2001, 2nd ed. 2011), a certain cure for hero worship.

lethargy' of 1950s America. It could prove surprisingly difficult, for one thing, to get poetry published if your verse did not conform to the seemingly folksy patterns of a Robert Frost. On 25 March 1957, for example, US Customs seized 520 copies of some weird, obscene stuff that had been printed in England for San Francisco's City Lights bookshop. The author called it 'Howl'.

Twenty-nine-year-old Allen Ginsberg from Paterson, New Jersey, drunk, arms and eyes wide, had climbed to his feet to give the first reading of the work at the city's Six Gallery on 7 October 1955. A sensation, the birth of a movement, the intervention of the customs men, and an obscenity trial had ensued. A long, wide-angled poem in line of descent from William Carlos Williams, Walt Whitman, William Blake and Christopher Smart, 'Howl' also became, soon enough, the presumed locus for Bob Dylan's first notions of poetry. When he opened his eyes to it, he was influenced. But the same could have been said of a lot of young people.

Ginsberg was never short of theories to explain the poet's art. Those who retained a belief in metrical discipline would dismiss most of them as bunk, as mere self-justification, but that was no deterrent to a writer who relished controversy. William Carlos Williams had previously attempted to construct an argument for a 'variable foot' derived from his belief that colloquial American language contained its own rhythms, rhythms owing little or nothing to Europe. The Paterson baby doctor had thus arrived at a twice-broken poetic line, the 'stepped triadic'. After 'Howl', Ginsberg would come up with the successor notion of the 'breath unit' and would explain, always game, that the lines in his poems were long because he took big breaths when speaking or declaiming. Each unit had a 'fixed base'. His verses were free, therefore, of weary formalism and its inherent deceits. Real poetry, his poetry, was as human, colloquial and honest as breathing, even if it didn't seem to 'work on the page'. Attempting to explain himself, Ginsberg would invoke the 'bop refrain' of the jazz he knew best.

If he had a central, consuming political idea, meanwhile, it was this: America was destroying its own, and driving its 'best minds' to madness, their last and only refuge. The poet's own mother had wound up in the 'foetid halls' of the institution that would house Woody Guthrie. Ginsberg detected something corrosive and deadening in the culture, a loss of affect, a denial, above all, of life, energy and the old, visionary America. So he took it all on: militarism, capitalism, imperialism, consumerism, all of the *isms* of the age:

Moloch! Solitude! Filth! Ugliness! Ashcans and unobtainable dollars!
Children screaming under stairways! Boys sobbing in armies!
Old men weeping in the parks!

Though the poet duly regained his First Amendment right to free speech
– and won the court's certification of his poem's 'redeeming artistic
value' – 'Howl' was an authentic (and wholly satisfying) *succès de
scandale*, with its transgressive sex (sodomy was illegal in every state),
its unabashed drug references and its 'crack of doom on the hydrogen
jukebox'. This was 'Tutti Frutti' in a parallel universe: the record, that
bowdlerised gay howl, was released within mere days of Ginsberg
astonishing the gallery crowd. All of a sudden, the supposedly placid
1950s had a new sort of writing and a new sort of pop music to edify
or appal the citizenry, and to energise the young.

They called the writers Beats. As in *beatific, beatnik, upbeat, deadbeat*,
heart and metrical *beat, beaten* and ground down by existence. The
New York Times magazine had made the title official, as shorthand for
'a generation', as early as the winter of 1952, thanks to an article by
John Clellon Holmes, a 26-year-old 'sometime member' of the sometime
movement.[37]

> The origins of the word 'beat' are obscure, but the meaning is only too
> clear to most Americans. More than mere weariness, it implies the feeling
> of having been used, of being raw. It involves a sort of nakedness of
> mind, and, ultimately, of soul; a feeling of being reduced to the bedrock
> of consciousness. In short, it means being undramatically pushed up
> against the wall of oneself. A man is beat whenever he goes for broke
> and wagers the sum of his resources on a single number; and the young
> generation has done that continually from early youth.

Beat's practitioners preferred bop jazz to rock and roll, as often as not,
but Beat writing and rock and roll had much the same intent, conscious
or not: free the spirit, refuse the phoney conformity of the age, and
live.

Dylan would respond to that. Soon enough, he would attempt to
write poetry-for-the-page in something like that manner – some would

---

37 Also author of the 1952 'Beat' novel *Go*. Published, if not written, five years before
his close friend Kerouac's *On the Road*, it revolves predictably, not to say interminably,
around life with Jack and Neal and Allen . . .

even call him the last of the Beats – and would run across Ginsberg himself in due course. The new writing would touch his writing, too. Somehow, nevertheless, he had an ability to outgrow his inspirations, and do so at frightening speed. His art would never be built on instinct and native genius alone.

In *Chronicles*, for example, Dylan would write that no sooner had he arrived in New York than his interest in the visionary promise of Kerouac's *On the Road*, and all it had once signified, began to dissipate. He still loved and admired the prose of a book that had been like holy writ to him, but suddenly Dean Moriarty's version of the Beat adventure seemed purposeless, a victim's tale. In fact, Kerouac's character seemed liable to inspire nothing more than stupidity. Dylan saw through it all.

*

In his mid-teens he applied himself to the piano, less to master the instrument – he remained essentially a black-key player – than to force from it a semblance of the noise coming from the radio and the records. He began to work on his hair, and his attitude. He began to reimagine himself. As month by month 1956 came to resemble the *annus mirabilis* of legend, Bobby Zimmerman began to think about bands. Irrespective of the experience and skills of those who were actually making real recordings in real recording studios, the new music was planting an idea, one that would be rediscovered by punks 20 years on: anyone could do this stuff. What was Presley? Not – didn't everyone say so? – a real musician. And what did that matter?

When they went to work, the historians would observe that rock and roll had been brewing for years, certainly since the war's end and prosperity's arrival. Even poor, sobbing Johnnie Ray would be judged a forerunner of sorts, though no one said as much at the time. At the time they said rock and roll was primitive, crude, dangerously arousing and – above all – *negro*. Confusingly, they further said that 'jungle music' was just a fad, a hula hoop of a style. Alarmed, the elders nevertheless had the sense to grasp that this was music coming up from under, as though through fissures in society's crust. It had not flowed like warm molasses from all those millions of family TV sets. Even when cleaned up, some of the lyrics were plainly *filth*. Even when placed under close moral arrest, the movements and sounds involved were demonstrably, blatantly sexual. Worst of all, the audience were that new American breed, teenagers, each one of them, patently, a potential juvenile delinquent.

Then as now, America affected an ignorance of class. Somehow even to acknowledge the existence of such a thing would have been to deny democracy's purpose. Talk of class was by definition subversive. But one other thing was obvious about rock and roll: it came from the poor. In time, the sociologists and musicologists could nominate influences and confluences: the black migration from the South to the cities; the radio signals that defied segregation; the migrating folk music of mountain whites; the way the blues mutated through electricity; the way gospel found its secular outlets; the ways in which country music discovered an urge to swing and in which hillbilly music became rockabilly; the way jazz permeated all American music and allowed boogie-woogie to become more than the sum of its parts; the way in which a need to dance found the backbeat; above all, the way in which the poor connected, one with the other, black with white, again and again.

In time, a knack for colour-blind affinity, honest respect and cross-cultural kicks would be named as Presley's instinctive, eclectic genius. But rock and roll was the music, as the twenty-first century would have it, of an underclass looking for a good time. What was there for a teenager to dislike? What was there for adult, official, racist 1950s America to embrace?

Somehow, those disturbing teenagers didn't need to be told. Rock and roll was a kind of telepathy, inspiring strange and impossible thoughts. As a high-school yearbook entry, joking or serious, would attest in 1959, Abe and Beatty's eldest was anything but immune. What did he want most from life? He put it in words. Ambition: 'To join Little Richard'.[38]

*

You can just about picture him. He wears a jacket very like the one the dead movie star used to wear. He smokes his cigarettes with an attempt at that heavy-lidded gravitas, but nervous energy consumes him. Sometimes he puts people on, sometimes he couldn't be more serious. Most of them don't know if he's kidding about that electric guitar with the gold sunburst finish, or if he really means what he says with his wild talk about the music business. In Hibbing? Hibbing where the cold

---

38 When the 'legendary' statement is invoked, the rest of the yearbook entry is generally overlooked. It reads: 'Latin Club 2; Social Studies Club 4.' In the former enterprise Bobby Zimmerman and his fellow students of the dead language would 'promote the study of Roman life and customs'. *Poeta nascitur, non fit.*

could freeze you to the spot and the winter wind could send you into a trance? Besides, he doesn't know anything about any sort of business. He just hears something in the music, so he says, and something through the music. But who doesn't? He has an answer to that question. In his head, only a very few people get what he's talking about, especially when he's talking about records, and what lies within the records. Sometimes he talks and talks, but he can't put that part into words. Why not? Perhaps he felt this way before there was any music.

Something else is strange: he wants to know who the person is who could think such things.

*

Dylan once claimed that in Hibbing there was no right side of the tracks and no wrong side. It wasn't strictly true. There may have been no great or conspicuous wealth among the locals, but there were certainly those who had a good deal less than others. The Zimmermans were middle class (in the European sense) and comfortable, but Echo Star Helstrom, a white-blonde girl of Finnish extraction whose family lived in woodlands on the outskirts of town, was 'poor folk'.

Her claim to be the 'Girl From the North Country' has been disputed. Then again, every likely candidate's claim to a place in a Dylan love song has been disputed. In Hibbing, Echo has the plaque, and the pictorial endorsement of a Howard Street establishment named Zimmy's ('The Art of Food and Drink'). It's one strange way to memorialise a brief teenage love affair. Nevertheless, Helstrom certainly seems to have been the most enduring of Dylan's Hibbing girlfriends. On the other hand, his behaviour towards her seems to have been only too typical. She wore his ring; he done her wrong. Music brought them together, the bejeaned girl in the leather jacket and the boy on the Harley 45, but it couldn't – someone should have written a song – keep them together. Not that such a thing was ever likely.

If you believe the nudge and wink of a late Dylan tale, as related for the benefit of the *No Direction Home* film, Echo Helstrom was not his first flame, however. Before he got around to serenading the girl from the North Country, another had 'brought out the poet in me'. Poetry can take a joke, after all.

> The first girl that ever took a liking to me, her name was Gloria Story. *Gloria Story.* That was her real name.

And that was his story. He and Echo first met properly, it seems, in 1957. In Helstrom's version he was glimpsed standing on a corner alone, playing his guitar to himself in the snow as she made her way to the L&B Café with a friend. Continuity faltered a little, for in the next scene Bobby arrived with his high-school buddy John Bucklen, with whom he played (and taped) music now and then, and with whom he shared most tastes. The boys and the girls fell to talking. Echo won his heart over sodas – this movie never ends – because she knew plenty about rock and roll. How could Bobby resist a buxom blonde who raved about 'Maybellene'?

Certain writers have tried to make something of the fact that the young Dylan formed bonds with those such as Echo and John Bucklen, and others besides, who came from tough backgrounds. It is worth stating, too, that though raised in an all-white town, in an era of casual and institutionalised racism, he never hesitated to seek out and befriend black people. To Dylan, as to Presley, they were just people; in fact more, because of their music, than *just* people. It might sound absurd to suggest otherwise of the author of all those songs, but young Zimmerman gave not a damn about class and race at a time, and in a country, in which 'sensitivity' to such 'questions' was uppermost in a lot of minds. In order to protest it was necessary first to empathise.

You could speculate further: he was an outsider too, in a town in which Jews were almost as rare as black citizens. More importantly, he felt like an outsider, and embraced the feeling. Echo would relate that while the Zimmermans were a social and economic notch above the Helstroms, Bobby never had much money. Abe was strict – relations were deteriorating fast – and she bought the hot dogs. Until, that is, her beloved confessed he had lost his virginity to one of her friends, and until she grew tired of his road trips and all the antics involved. Bucklen recalled several tearful phone calls.

All more or less true, no doubt. But tight-fisted Abe purchased his son a Harley. In Hibbing, reportedly, it is still said that Bobby Zimmerman charged sheet music and records from Crippa's Music Store to his father's account. At one point the teenager seems also to have acquired a car (though its make and colours vary, according to the source of the tale). He went to the movies when he felt like it. He acquired an electric guitar from Sears, albeit a cheap one, with 'pocket money', though Shelton claims he had no allowance. He was never badly dressed, and never short of cigarettes. The idea that Abe Zimmerman was less than generous in a material sense seems implausible, on that evidence. It doesn't seem likely, either, that his son earned enough down at the store to pay for flashy jackets and smokes, far less guitars. For a while Abe had obliged Bobby to put in a few hours at Micka Electric, but the only interesting thing about the fact is that it could still cause a superstar in his 60s to sound like a resentful adolescent.

> The first job I ever had was sweeping up the store. I was supposed to learn the discipline of hard work or something, and the *merits* of employment.

What becomes obvious, through all the anecdotes, all the Dylan half-truths and misremembered facts, is that he began to live inside his own head at a very early age. Something drew him and something spooked him. He was alienated from his parents – he alienated himself? – for no reason that is obvious or clear. He was drawn to music with an intensity that spoke of need. He was faking an identity almost from the moment he knew who he was *supposed* to be, and rejecting a Jewish heritage wholesale into the bargain. He told lies, a lot of lies, to shore up a personality he had constructed and he got out of Hibbing just as quickly as he could. One of his prime deceits, very early in his career, involved the improbable number of times he claimed to have run away from home long before he actually left.

Clearly, he wanted it to be true. The strange part is that somehow you don't blame him. When you ask, 'Where on earth did Bob Dylan spring from, with those gifts and that desire?' a long-gone teenager seems to answer that it sure as hell wasn't Hibbing, Minnesota. He didn't want to be there. Later, for a while, he would hate to admit that he had ever been there. Dylan's teenage years are the tale of a boy who was waiting impatiently for the movie to begin.

There is something slightly wrong with the script, nevertheless. Dylan became estranged from his parents: it happens. He ran a little wild, and faltered at school: it happens. He was at odds with his father: that happens too. He came to deny his faith and his origins: that certainly happens. Then he quit town as soon as he could: many did in those days, as the mines around Hibbing became exhausted and the local economy struggled.

But the plot goes awry. Dylan changes his name legally, and pretends his parents are dead. He denies that he was ever 'really' Jewish despite his Zionist camp experiences, and in time turns to thunderous, born-again Christianity. Meanwhile he persists in rejecting any possibility of an emotional connection with the town in which he was raised, or with his own ancestry. He tells tales, year after year, that don't add up. Finally, he winds up sounding, even as a grandfather, like a man with serious, unanswered resentments.

You can only speculate. Shelton has Abe still somewhat raw in 1968 over the presence of 'those friends' and, indeed, 'that girl' in his son's life. Supposedly, Abe and Beatty told their eldest that Echo 'wasn't good enough for him'. But in Dylan's own extraordinary account his father also told him once that it was possible to become so 'defiled' his parents would abandon him. He said this, moreover, while receiving a Grammy 'lifetime achievement' award from Jack Nicholson in 1991, with his mother in the audience.

> Well, my daddy, he didn't leave me much, you know. He was a very simple man, but what he did tell me was this. He did say, 'Son,' he said [Dylan paused, as though lost in thought, while some in the audience laughed hesitantly], he say, 'You know it's possible to become so defiled in this world that your own father and mother will abandon you, and if that happens God will always believe in your ability to mend your ways.'

A few years later, a contributor to Expecting Rain, the Dylan fan website, explained that the award recipient had been quoting almost verbatim from Rabbi Samson Raphael Hirsch, a leading intellectual light in the development of nineteenth-century German Orthodox Judaism. In a commentary on a psalm, the rabbi had written: 'Even if I were so depraved that my own mother and father would abandon me to my own devices, God would still gather me up and believe in my ability to mend my ways.' So was Dylan quoting Abe quoting a long-dead scholar? Or was he just putting words in the old man's mouth to explain these modern times of ours? He had some memory, in any event, of Abe's attitude towards 'defilement'.

Echo Helstrom was poor, blonde and anything but Jewish. David Zimmerman certainly told Shelton that two out of three was bad enough as far as his parents were concerned. Did everything flow from those facts? By the time Dylan got to Minnesota in 1959 he was telling new friends how much he detested his father. Presumably that meant he detested some of the things for which his father stood. On the other hand, Echo had already ceased to be the only girl on his mind. Besides, plenty of people felt the urge or the need to quit Hibbing.

Lesser careers have been shaped by bigger events, whatever the truth. On every level, estrangement fits the symbolic bill almost too perfectly. But still, the interviewer who even now asks Dylan about Hibbing, or why he changed his name, or how he feels about Jewishness, is liable to receive some mumbled, evasive and contradictory answers. Even the occasional pleasantries can be confounding. The picture isn't over.

I ask Dylan if he minds people visiting Hibbing or Duluth or Minneapolis searching for the root of his talent. 'Not at all,' he surprisingly says. 'That town where I grew up hasn't really changed that much, so whatever was in the air before is probably still there. I go through once in a while coming down from Canada. I'll stop there and wander around.'[39]

*

For a while in those teenage years there were actual movies, too, the other American art, and a better brand of fantasy and fiction for his distraction, education and inspiration. Hollywood responded to the new age of the teenager, and Dylan, on cue, saw 'something' of himself in James Dean and *Rebel Without a Cause*, late in 1955.

A friend calculated that Bobby saw the picture at least four times, and bought the red jacket, and lived the frustrated, 'complicated' suburban life to whatever degree an incoherent flick allowed. But then, so did a great many others. Even adolescent rebellion became an entertainment-industry product the instant it could be identified, dramatised and sold back to the young. When James Dean (or 'Jim Stark') destroyed his Porsche 550 Spyder and himself on Route 466 in California in September of 1955, just before the picture's release, it was a perfect marketing moment. Dean's performance in *Rebel* did its job, too. What better way to appeal to the inarticulate young than through an inarticulate – or misunderstood – hero? Throw in some 'generational conflict' and you have a movie with a certain calculated appeal. The Dean character said it was OK to be in rebellious turmoil for reasons that needn't or couldn't be explained to your elders. There would be a lot of fancy talk in the decade ahead inspired by that non-proposition.

It would take Bobby Zimmerman, recast for the part, less than a

---

39 Interview with Douglas Brinkley, *Rolling Stone*, 2009.

decade to realise, as Dean never had the chance to realise, that it doesn't pay to be any generation's spokesman. That sort of thing could get you killed. Worse, you could be misunderstood.

*

First he had to learn things the hard way. There were those friends from the Herzl summer camp, Larry Kegan and Howard Rutman. Together, the three called themselves the Jokers, and it was apt. Then there were the Shadow Blasters,[40] a band as brief as a breath: more friends, more enthusiasm than skill, with Bobby still battering the keyboard. On this occasion, the group even got a crack at a school concert, and the Zimmerman kid got a crack at Hibbing High's treasured Steinway Grand. The anecdote would be told over and over: of the bequiffed Dylan pounding and wailing, standing up to hammer the piano, of kids astonished (or in stitches). What's noteworthy is that the self-appointed star of this little band, otherwise known as a shy youth, was utterly undaunted by a less than rapturous reception. He had crossed the performer's first hurdle, and done it, for better or worse, his way. This would be the spring of 1957.

Then came a garage band before the term meant anything, with a sound that didn't (by all accounts) mean much either, who called themselves the Golden Chords. Like an omen, Little Richard had just quit rock and roll for God when Bobby, LeRoy Hoikkala (drums) and Monte Edwardson (guitar) were given a second chance to impress at an afternoon school show.

This was the beginning of February of 1958 and one Golden Chord – all the legends agree – intended to be heard. For once, everyone was amplified, but Bobby somehow found a few extra microphones for his piano and his voice. The Steinway got the treatment worse than before: in one authoritative version he tried to stamp a pedal to death while howling out 'Rock and Roll Is Here to Stay'. It wasn't. Equally, whatever Dylan was doing – and whatever some biographers claim – it wasn't the Danny and the Juniors number. That would not be released for another month. Still, the principal, playing his teen-movie part to perfection, did order the power to be cut and the racket halted. No one thought of taking an axe to the cables, but the sentiment was there.

Usefully, the trio didn't know what they were doing, and therefore didn't know how to be deterred. A month after the high-school outrage,

---

40 According to Dave Engel.

'Hibbing's Own Golden Chords' actually got a paying job as the intermission diversion during a 'Rock & Roll Hop for Teenagers' at the National Guard Armory. Next up was a 'Winter Carnival Talent Contest' in which the Chords placed second to a tap dancer. A TV spot in Duluth – *Polka Hour*! – followed. It was not the Chords' finest moment, by all accounts, but it was more or less their last.

Bobby's comrades, a little tired of his purist approach and eager for an audience that didn't actually hate them – a motif is born – decided, as they might have said, to split. Decades later Dylan was still grumbling over the way his teenage bands were each 'stolen' and suborned by the malign power of someone's money, or lost to him thanks to the pull exercised, so he says, by some local bigshot or other from the nefarious mercantile class. Few other accounts suggest that LeRoy and Monte required much persuasion to desert the hardcore Zimmerman for the crowd-pleasing Rockets.

Bobby tried again, fitfully, with a cousin, but the moment was passing. Half a century and more after the fact, when rock and roll has its halls of fame, its movies, its mountains of memorabilia, and its place of honour in the cultural history books, you can easily forget how brief that moment was. The first wave of rock and roll, the truly revolutionary gesture, came and went, apogee to perigee, in no time at all. You could make a case for saying that everything since, everything in white music at any rate, has been mere aftermath.

In October of '57, in Australia, Little Richard mistook Sputnik's launch for a great ball of fire signalling the apocalypse. He threw an $8,000 ring into Sydney Harbour, renounced – if that's the word – his homosexuality, signed up as a Seventh-Day Adventist and quit the Devil's music.

Just before Christmas in '57 Elvis Presley received his draft notice. John Lennon would later decree this to be the moment at which rock and roll ended, but already, less than two years after 'Heartbreak Hotel', Elvis was being sucked into the routine of crass movies and careless ballads that would manacle his talent for almost a decade. In March of 1958 he was inducted into the army and given his basic training in amphetamines, their deployment and destructive power. RCA maintained a release schedule from a formidable stockpile for the following two years, but none of it was prime Presley.

In May of '58, meanwhile, Jerry Lee Lewis made the mistake of touring Britain in the company of a third wife – he was a ripe old 22 – named Myra Gale Brown. That she was his first cousin once removed was of less importance than the fact that Myra was only 13 years of age. It didn't help when Lewis and his management told the British press that – honest to God – the child was certainly all of 15. The tour was cancelled; Lewis was blacklisted on American radio; and his fees, when he could get the work, went from $10,000 a show to $250.

In February of '59 Buddy Holly was stuck, miserably, on a 'Winter Dance Party' tour through the American Midwest. On 31 January, a 17-year-old named Bobby Zimmerman caught the show.

> Yeah, sure. I saw Buddy Holly two or three nights before he died. I saw him in Duluth at the armory. He played there with Link Wray. I don't remember the Big Bopper. Maybe he'd gone off by the time I came in. But I saw Ritchie Valens. And Buddy Holly, yeah. He was great. He was incredible. I mean, I'll never forget the image of seeing Buddy Holly up on the bandstand. And he died – it must have been a week after that. It was unbelievable.[41]

In 1998, they gave Bob Dylan three Grammy awards for the album of the year, *Time Out of Mind*. For once, he was compelled to attempt to explain something about himself, and about music. He said:

> And I just want to say that when I was 16 or 17 years old, I went to see Buddy Holly play at Duluth National Guard Armory and I was three feet away from him . . . and he *looked* at me. And I just have some sort of feeling that he was   I don't know how or why   but I know he was with us all the time we were making this record in some kind of way.

The loss of Holly's small chartered aircraft near Mason City, Iowa, in the early hours of 3 February 1959 marked the day, as keening Don McLean lamented, 'the music died'. Soon enough, Chuck Berry would be jailed, amid astonishingly racist proceedings, for having sex with a 14-year-old Apache waitress he had happened to sack from his thoroughly integrated St Louis club. Soon enough, a taxi carrying the multiply talented Eddie Cochran, a 21-year-old from a little Minnesota town, would wrap itself around an English lamp post. The omens agreed: it was over. No one in the music business was in any doubt about that.

There was still Pat Boone, if that helped, busily turning black music into something pallid and lucrative. There was Ricky Nelson, still almost

---

41   Interview with Kurt Loder, *Rolling Stone*, 1984.

bearable. There was Chubby Checker, still raising a smile. There was Marty Robbins and Paul Anka, Johnny Mathis and Brenda Lee. Presley's big release in 1960, *in absentia*, was 'It's Now or Never', a track that did only slightly better in the *Cash Box* year-end rankings than the guy singing of an 'Itsy Bitsy Teenie Weenie Yellow Polka Dot Bikini'. That was about right. But a teenager's ambition – 'To join Little Richard' – suddenly seemed beside the point. Irrespective of the question, pop music wasn't the answer.

That can be disputed, of course. Michael Gray, for one, attempts to explain (in his *The Bob Dylan Encyclopedia* and in *Song and Dance Man III*) that the idea of rock and roll's death is another part of the rock and roll myth. Gray makes a persuasive case for believing that there was no 'day the music died', that the early 1960s were not a musical wasteland, and that, by implication, there was no self-evident need for young Zimmerman to become 'Bob Dylan', or to trade his Supro Ozark electric for a Martin 00-17 acoustic in 1959.

There's some truth in that. The collated 1960 *Cash Box* Top 50 has plenty of dispiriting stuff, but it also embraces the Everly Brothers, Roy Orbison, Sam Cooke, Jackie Wilson, Duane Eddy, and the Ventures. You could get by on those. Besides, there was a *lot* going on in black music as the 1960s began, whether involving Ray Charles, James Brown or a couple of labels newly launched in Detroit named Tamla and Motown. Dylan, formerly so assiduous in his researches, seems to have missed all of this. Or rather, he was no longer much interested. He was entering another world. So much, it seems, for Little Richard.

What was missing in 1959 and 1960 was the shock of the new. Young Zimmerman had absorbed rock and roll, much as he would absorb and for a while discard his next great obsession. The meaning of Little Richard in his adolescence had everything to do with timing. But, just as he felt a compelling need to be clear of Hibbing, so Dylan clearly felt a need, whether he yet knew it, to pursue his instincts, whatever they turned out to mean. He would go back in time in order to go forward in art. Standing still was no sort of choice. In this instance, it is safe to take him at his word, and trust his memory.

By the early months of 1961 he was in Greenwich Village, standing in the kitchen of the Café Wha? and listening idly to Ricky Nelson on the radio. As *Chronicles* tells it, Dylan had once been a big fan. He still liked Nelson's music well enough, but realised, in this minor epiphany, that its limitations had been exposed, that its time had gone. It could never hope to achieve meaning. In the kitchen of the Wha? the young folk singer passed a judgement permitting no appeal: pop was a lot cause.

Thus spoke the Dylan who was never known to make a foolish move, who dumped one kind of music for another in answer to the imperatives of a career as well as a creative need. At this moment he had not begun to think seriously about songwriting, or even about where folk music might take him, if it took him anywhere. He had glimpsed the future, and it did not lie with pop. Bear in mind, meanwhile, that in 1997 Dylan told *Der Spiegel*, 'I think rock and roll never was of any great importance to my work.'

In the strict sense, that's perfectly true. Rock and roll, the real and original thing, would play a vanishingly small part in any of the records 'Bob Dylan' would make. 'Like a Rolling Stone', *Blonde on Blonde* or the 1966 concerts involved nothing that Presley, Chuck Berry or Jerry Lee would have recognised. When finally Dylan plugged into an amplifier an entirely different sort of sound emerged.

By '59 he was, according to Shelton, 'dabbling' in the art of the non-amplified guitar, and in 'the strength of strings'. He may have already heard a few things; descriptions of his initiation into this new music are as vague and confused as the earlier tales of rock and roll. Odetta has been mentioned, as often as not by Dylan himself, along with the forever mysterious gift, out of the blue, of a Lead Belly collection. Dates are vague. The fact is that at this point he knew very little about folk music, but instinct, whether for art, mere fame or escape, had begun to do its work. The only emotion never mentioned, by Dylan or those who knew him, is self-doubt.

*

In 1959, America was wondering whether it could bring itself to elect a Roman Catholic to the presidency: the presumed natural order then was still white, Anglo-Saxon and Protestant. Those who spoke for that constituency's God questioned whether a candidate could be loyal to his country and to the Church of Rome. The prejudice was as old as the republic.

America was pondering, further, on whether this grinning 42-year-old was 'too young' for a job that hitherto had been the preserve of sonorous father figures, war heroes and assorted portly crooks. Youth was not yet so esteemed in the Western world as to render its value self-evident. Jack Kennedy, the senator from Massachusetts, also struck some as too premeditated in his demeanour, too perfectly designed – 'a masterpiece of contrived casualness', said a columnist for the *New York Times*[42] – to be a trustworthy candidate. The risk of his actually winning seemed slight, however. In 1959, Kennedy remained an outside bet for the Democratic nomination. The smart money also said that the over-eager hopeful – hindsight should pause – was *a poor public speaker*. As the decade ended, America didn't fully know its own mind. America didn't know that, either.

*

> The air is so pure there. And the brooks and rivers are still running. The forests are thick, and the landscape is brutal. And the sky is still blue up there. It is still pretty untarnished. It's still off the beaten path. But I hardly ever go back.[43]

So said a 68-year-old man in 2009, close to 50 years after he quit the old, untarnished world. Dylan has often talked this way, as though a restless farewell was never truly made. Again and again he has described the way in which a Minnesota upbringing acted on his imagination, in the days before TV ruled existence, in the days before rock and roll. In the same interview, conducted far from America, he connected two words: 'It was a more innocent way of life. Imagination is what you had and maybe all you had.'

You need not doubt his sincerity to wonder about the teenager alienated from home, faith and family, driven by an urge to succeed, determined to be anywhere *but* Minnesota. There's nothing new in the story. If you take him at his word, however, the reason for going wasn't the place, not as such. Perhaps he simply needed to leave in order to understand what it was he had left: that impulse is as old as literature. Perhaps, too, he needed to grow up before he could understand. Perhaps the trouble with his father ran deeper than anyone knew or yet knows. One simple truth, however, is that he was no different from his peers. Most of Hibbing's young people left because there was no reason to stay.

Interviewed by Nat Hentoff for *Playboy*'s March 1966 edition, Dylan would state the plain facts (even while still pretending that he had 'run away from home six times between the ages of 10 and 18'). He said:

---

42   James Reston, quoted in Robert Dallek's *John F. Kennedy: An Unfinished Life 1917–1963* (2003), Ch. 7.

43   Interview with Douglas Brinkley, *Rolling Stone*.

Hibbing, Minnesota, was just not the right place for me to stay and live. There really was nothing there. The only thing you could do there was be a miner, and even that kind of thing was getting less and less. The people that lived there – they're nice people; I've been all over the world since I left there, and they still stand out as being the least hung-up. The mines were just dying, that's all; but that's not their fault. Everybody about my age left there. It was no great romantic thing. It didn't take any great amount of thinking or individual genius, and there certainly wasn't any pride in it. I didn't run away from it; I just turned my back on it. It couldn't give me anything. It was very void-like. So leaving wasn't hard at all; it would have been much harder to stay. I didn't want to die there. As I think about it now, though, it wouldn't be such a bad place to go back to and die in. There's no place I feel closer to now, or get the feeling that I'm part of, except maybe New York; but I'm not a New Yorker. I'm North Dakota-Minnesota-Midwestern. I'm that color. I speak that way. I'm from someplace called Iron Range. My brains and feeling have come from there.

So here was another version of the honest truth. It was more plausible than some of the stories Dylan would offer up. Imagination – 'maybe all you had' – is the fount of creativity, and of invention, and of sheer, compulsive fabrication. 'Art is the lie that tells the truth,' said Picasso, taking a crack at honesty. All of this youth's imagined needs were to be answered soon enough.

That's another fragment of legend, nevertheless, as though Bobby Zimmerman became 'Bob Dylan' just by snapping his fingers, as though he was reincarnated in one supernatural moment. It's not *exactly* true, but close enough.

Don't Think Twice

dogs wag their tails good-bye to you & robin hood watches you from a
stained glass window . . . the opera singers will sing of YOUR forest &
YOUR cities & you shall stand alone but not make ceremony . . .

Tarantula

PROSPERITY WAS NEVER UBIQUITOUS IN 1950S AMERICA: THAT TOO
was a myth. Average earnings rose steadily, but the period saw a pair
of recessions, with unemployment rising beyond 7 per cent. During
the middle part of the decade economic growth stagnated while Japan,
western Europe and the godless Soviet empire seemed to forge ahead.
As the 1960 presidential election approached only 22 per cent of
foreigners were prepared to tell opinion pollsters that American prestige
had increased.

At home there was scary talk, spurious as it turned out, of a 'missile
gap' that somehow had left the United States vulnerable to a sneak
Soviet attack. Handsome John Kennedy and the generals told the lie
relentlessly, over and over, until it became a useful truth. The fear of
annihilation seeped into the bright new suburbs like a chill fog from
the Cold War front line.

Wealth was meanwhile too often apparent rather than real: by the
decade's end the 'poverty rate for all Americans was 22.4%, or 39.5
million individuals'.[1] No one could call this a triumph. Need was most
conspicuous, equally, in certain regions, and among certain ethnic
groups. Complacency was not, as it turned out, a universal habit of
mind.

The detonation in '56 that went by the name Presley was no symptom
of lethargy. Nor could drunken Joe McCarthy, hunting red subversives
in every corner of society, be dismissed for a lack of obsessive zeal. In
those days the movies of furious James Dean, beloved by the teenage

---

1   National Poverty Center, University of Michigan.

Dylan, were mesmerising the young. Allen Ginsberg's 'Howl' was calling all America to account in 1956 just as Elvis was breaking out; Jack Kerouac's *On the Road*, that manual for dazed pilgrims, was to appear in the following year. As rock and roll seemed to come and quickly go, the folk revival was demanding a hearing, red-baiters permitting. If life in the heartland felt conformist and lethally dull to alert young Americans, that was because they knew things were happening elsewhere. The trick was to get to wherever those things happened to be.

That was becoming easier. Eisenhower, elected in 1953, was neither an ambitious nor an energetic president. He attempted little, they said, and achieved less. Ike had seemed to stand aside even while McCarthy was running amok. They said – and he hated the slur – that this leader 'reigned but didn't rule'. The alternative truth was that Eisenhower defined himself as the honest man in the middle, struggling to hold the ring, happier to talk about God and prayer than ideology. Perhaps as a result he would remain, though the fact is too often forgotten, a popular leader without seeming ever to do much.

Passive or not, complacent or not, one of the detached president's legislative acts changed America permanently. You could put it this way: the National Interstate and Defense Highways Act of 1956 was probably as important in shaping Bob Dylan's career as any movie star, poet or musical influence.

The new highways cut memory and imagination in two, separating the old, remembered country from its modern successor. The roads drew deep dividing lines on the landscape even as they connected the cities. Slowly but surely, the blacktop altered forever the *feel* of America. What people could see of the country beyond the flaring tail fins of that year's model was suddenly reduced and receding. Perceptions changed; life changed.

The experience was hardly unique to one teenager from the back of the great beyond, but the legislation committing Washington to a $25 billion[2] road-building programme all but silenced the railroad engine's lonesome cry, placed the automobile finally at the heart of American life, destroyed much that was once uniquely regional, accelerated migration (especially black migration) and helped to bury the old world beneath suburb, mall, motel, strip conurbation and sprawl. Communities were exiled to back roads that led nowhere; rural

---

2   It took 35 years, and in the end cost $114 billion.

music retreated. Memory too seemed to disappear beneath the concrete and tar. A single act of government consigned the past to another country. In time the fact would cause Dylan to inhabit and preserve an America of the mind, authentic but no longer real. It also turned folk music into a living museum.

Suddenly in the late 1950s the United States was on the move as never before, and yet simultaneously the frontier – or the once-boundless idea of the frontier – was closed, finally and for good. The popularity of those cornball TV westerns was probably a kind of collective subconscious reaction to the fact. In the space of a decade, in any case, the number of automobiles on the road doubled, to 80 million. Even the names of the models were an attempt to preserve the myth of liberation: the Dodge Sierra, the Buick Roadmaster, the DeSoto Adventurer, the Oldsmobile Holiday, the Thunderbird. People embraced the dream precisely because it was a dream. Car-loving Americans could go wherever they wanted to go, but where, what, was left? Kerouac's *On the Road* was born out of the question. Looking for America amid the witch-hunts and the Cold War paranoia, Sal Paradise and Dean Moriarty travelled like pinballs – New York to New Orleans, to Mexico City, to Denver, to San Francisco, then back to Chicago and New York – going nowhere at all at speed. On speed. Benzedrine provided the illusion of a destination.

Yes! You and I, Sal, we'd dig the whole world with a car like this because, man, the road must eventually lead to the whole world. Ain't nowhere else it can go – right?[3]

The Beats esteemed feeling above reason, says the critical snapshot.[4] In the case of 'Moriarty' (Neal Cassady) it led to death from exposure on some railroad tracks in 1968. For 'Paradise' (Kerouac), the end of the line was reached a year later, just as the Woodstock 'Aquarian Exposition' was encouraging a new fantasy of endless possibilities, when the booze exacted its final price. His novel's idealised freedom – 'Where we going, man?' 'I don't know but we gotta go.' – turned out to be as problematic and puzzling as Guthrie's hobo legend. This romance was a response, of sorts, to the moral paralysis of the

---

3   *On the Road,* Part Three, Ch. 9.

4   *On the Road,* said Kerouac, was 'really a story about two Catholic buddies roaming the country in search of God. And we found him.'

Eisenhower years, but not much of an answer. The only real travelling done by the Beats was psychological and emotional, deep inside the head. The last echoes of the pioneer tradition, the idea that essential liberty was contained in a man's right to up sticks and move on, were disappearing even as the interstates and freeways were being built. The car and the blacktop brought a new sort of myth into being. The internal combustion engine became a fetish object, not least for impatient teenagers. Dylan would make a legend of at least one rambling road trip, but that too was a gesture. Pre-history, real freedom and the founding belief in an endless continent were left in the dust. America was energised; America shrank. All anyone could really do was revisit old Highway 61 and dream of drifting down those 1,400 miles, all the way from Duluth to New Orleans. It was that or Disneyland, the entertainment sensation of 1955.

Dylan took the bait, in any case; many did: life as a road movie, escape as autonomy. As a teenager he itched just to *go*. Or rather, to be gone. As a dusty old man he cannot, or will not, cure the habit of mind, or the habit of ceaseless travel. Nevertheless, the sensational appearance of Kerouac's novel was a clue offered to anyone who could see only the waxen conformist surface of '50s American life. Beneath the 'comfortable lethargy' energies were accumulating. Tops were about to blow, as Dean or Brando probably said. And Dylan was one of the forces, so it turned out, of America's nature.

Via the gift of hindsight's perfect vision, he explained it – and probably idealised it – as well as anyone in an interview staged to accompany the *Biograph* box set in 1985. Even before arriving at the University of Minnesota in 1959, even before taking his first real steps into the 'underground' music of folk, he

> had already decided that society, as it was, was pretty phony and I didn't want to be part of that . . . Also, there was a lot of unrest in the country. You could feel it, a lot of frustration, sort of like a calm before a hurricane, things were shaking up.

Dylan went on:

> America was still very 'straight', 'post-war', and sort of into a gray-flannel suit thing. McCarthy, commies, puritanical, very claustrophobic and what ever was happening of any real value was happening away from that and sort of hidden from view and it would be years before the media

would be able to recognize it and choke-hold it and reduce it to silliness.

It was impossible, in any case, to maintain one's ideal lethargy while facing the threat, apparently imminent, of nuclear annihilation. That sort of thing affects a person. This was the era of pointless survival drills in classrooms and public places, of bomb shelters in backyards and barely metaphorical science-fiction movies waiting to become ghastly 3D reality. Complacent is hardly the word for a period in which the likely casualties from a nuclear exchange were discussed, publicly and often, in terms of multiples of millions and 'mutual assured destruction' (MAD, of course) was a black joke awaiting its punchline. The movie-makers and the science-fiction pulp writers made it all seem almost inevitable. In that regard the young Dylan was an average American raised in the shadow of the mushroom cloud, waiting for a hard rain to fall. 'Our reality,' he has said, 'was fear that at any moment this black cloud would explode and everybody would be dead.'[5]

The United States had engaged in two major wars within recent memory and believed a third was more than likely. Most said that in some sense, off in the shadows, it had already begun, cold but growing warmer. The word often used, with no irony, was biblical: Armageddon. Albert Einstein joked gravely that World War III would be fought with nuclear weapons, but number IV would be fought with sticks and stones. America's grinning soldier-president seemed to want nothing more than a quiet life, meanwhile, but even he feared the emergence of something he would call the 'military-industrial complex'. It was a polite way to describe the alliance of money, killing machines, chauvinism, economic dogma and politics whose evangelists were colonising discourse. By the mid-1950s the US government had 40,000 military contractors on its payroll. A stubborn streak of isolationism still ran through American affairs, but the outside world was disquieting for all. This was a strange sort of lassitude. Nightmares infested the grey-flannelled republic's slumbers.

Not for the first time or the last, a country liable to believe itself chosen by God had turned to religion. Thanks to Billy Graham and other salvationists, a full-scale Christian revival was under way. Moreover, a country with a constitution built around the separation of church and state had allowed its body politic to succumb to religious

---

5   *No Direction Home* (film).

fevers. 'Under God' had been inserted into the Pledge of Allegiance in 1954, to popular acclaim, and Eisenhower himself had submitted to a belated baptism in February 1953, mere weeks after his first inauguration. It had become routine for politicians and their favoured preachers to identify America's democracy with its faith, and to set those in logical, fundamental opposition to 'godless Communism'. Cold War doctrine was underpinned by religious doctrine.

It is impossible, in that context, to overstate the extent of the young Dylan's isolation as a Jew – whether he 'noticed' or not – in the Hibbing of the mid-1950s. Christianity was dominant; Christianity was normal. Christian prayers in school attracted no real controversy: their opponents were patently eccentric or subversive. The statement that America was the country selected by a Christian God was taken as a statement of the obvious. Any attempt to understand the later, born-again Dylan depends on an understanding of this America. It *believed*. And belief, in a country built by immigrants from every corner of the world, was both democratic and exclusive. America's faith explained 'American exceptionalism', its sense of itself and its attitude towards the world. Fundamentalist belief did not alleviate all of the nation's nightmares, however.

One was actual, not theoretical or imagined, and it had nothing to do with foreign powers. It was the legacy of the war between the states, whose memory penetrated every corner of American culture. Already in the 1950s there were those who imagined that euphemisms were sedatives, so they called it a 'question'. It might have been a question of liberty, or of justice. Instead, they called it 'the negro question'.

As a historical fact, probably the largest in American life, it allows a bald statement: born on the fringe of the country he may have been, but Bob Dylan was raised in a racist society. Growing up, he had few contacts with black people, but assumptions about race were common, even in the far north, even among those who considered themselves liberal. The Ku Klux Klan, the KKK, had once been well supported in Minnesota. Hopeful descriptions of the 1950s tend to invoke the civil-rights struggle (and assume it to have been won) but ubiquitous racism, racism defended with tooth, claw, club, gun, law and common opinion, was a tenacious fact of life. Harry Truman, the Democrat heir to Roosevelt, had failed utterly to prevent Southern senators from talking reform legislation to death with congressional filibusters. Basic rights, simple rights – even the right to buy a home – were denied routinely to black Americans. Many of them had to fight – non-violently, it is still amazing to recall – even to vote. Segregation, their apartheid, stained vast tracts of the republic. The grim story continued when Eisenhower occupied the White House, and for years afterwards.

In *Chronicles*, and with the benefit of inescapable hindsight, Dylan would dismiss the 1950s as a culture heading for a fall. It didn't necessarily seem that way at the time. Equally, his ability to treat a subsequent decade of upheaval as of no great consequence said more about Bob Dylan than it said about his times. He might have taken to folk songs as to a religion, and might have believed they involved truths more profound than anything in society at large, but art did not vanquish every fact.

Calendars are arbitrary, in any case. The 1950s became the 1960s, but the decades were not antithetical. Nor were they ever capable of being characterised as equal and opposite states of mind. Nothing changed overnight. The counter-culture, whatever it signified, was slow in coming. The persecution of Lenny Bruce, for one example, began as the '60s began and ended only with the comedian's death in 1966. In 1961 J. Edgar Hoover, busy turning the FBI into an American Stasi, asserted publicly, sinister and hilarious, that 'beatniks' were one of the three *greatest threats* to the country. That year Jack Kerouac was getting drunk with former military men who told him, 'Why do you want to run around with those radicals, Kerouac? You're an American, not like your fucking Jewish friends.'[6] The anti-Communist witch-hunts had abated, and a young 'liberal' president was in the White House, but the early '60s were not the best of times for a Jewish boy to be launching a career as a radical folk singer. No one had yet asserted that the times were changing.

Dylan began to shape his own future as one decade ended and yet, like a lot of other people, he did so after listening hard to songs made by those who were long gone. Such was the modern world: at every turn, in nostalgia or in fear, in cowboy dramas or political conservatism, it stole backward glances. Preoccupied with a past that was already lost, America was learning to worry about the future.

The pattern would be echoed in Dylan's life and career: first the embrace of the new, then the retreat into older traditions. The cycle repeats and repeats. First Hank Williams and Jimmie Rodgers, then rock and roll; next ancient folk ballads, then 'Like a Rolling Stone'; next the inventory of a basement full of antique noises and a country idyll, then religious fads and a glib superstar's decadence and decay;

---

6   Gerald Nicosia, *Memory Babe: A Critical Biography of Jack Kerouac* (1983), Ch. 12.

next a return to the oldest blues of all, like an immersion in a deep, cold stream, as the preface to another – final? – summation.

You could as easily characterise the process, plain enough in the songs, as an oscillation between complexity and apparent simplicity, between 'Stuck Inside of Mobile' and 'I Dreamed I Saw St Augustine', between 'Tonight I'll Be Staying Here With You' and 'Idiot Wind'. It has nothing whatever to do with sophistication, or a lack of sophistication. Simple needn't be stupid and complexity is not, however tangled up, necessarily clever. But when a teenager put rock and roll behind him for the sake of some very old and entrancing stuff (that happened also to be the new stuff) he was establishing his own precedent. Put it this way: Bob Dylan is an avant-garde conservative.

*

In June of 1959 Robert Allen Zimmerman was done with Hibbing High School, and had played his last teenage show – no damage reported – in its vast, grandiose auditorium. His grades were good enough for the University of Minnesota, but his enthusiasm was slight. With all the hubris of youth he had already decided that formal education did not meet his requirements. He took himself off to college, it appears, because it was expected, and because Abe – more tolerant than the boy ever seemed to realise – would probably have raised hell over the idea that 'poetry', or some such nonsense, could ever be the equivalent of an honest job. Young Zimmerman had no better ideas.

College was a bigger deal then than now. In those days, fewer than half of the American population graduated from high school. Of those, fewer than 10 per cent went on to gain a college degree. If Abe and Beatty laboured the idea that education was a passport to freedom as *they* understood it, they had a point. It was no small thing to throw all that away. Besides, as ever, Abe was footing the bills. He didn't seem to be getting much for his hard-earned money, respect least of all.

Give the kid a break, nevertheless: colleges then, as now, were full of people doing the right and sensible things. The things that interested this juvenile were not taught, or could not be taught in a lecture hall. So what was he supposed to do? It is not fanciful in the slightest to say that music spoke to the youth, that the songs produced psychic-emotional emanations to which he responded, and hinted at a wisdom that demanded his assent. It was powerful stuff. It wasn't phoney.

Truth (and lies) were to be Bob Dylan's preoccupation. But it surely took a lot of honest courage for a near-child simply to shrug aside adult advice, parental expectations and common sense. In his father's version, a deal was struck: Bobby could have 'free rein' to be a folk singer, for a while, but only to get the strange passion out of his system. Abe told Shelton:

> He wanted to be a folk singer, an entertainer. We couldn't see it, but we felt he was entitled to the chance. It's his life, after all, and we didn't want to stand in the way. So we made an agreement that he could have one year to do as he pleased, and if at the end of that year we were not satisfied with his progress, he'd go back to school . . .[7]

We couldn't see it: who could have blamed two well-intentioned parents for that? Neither background nor experience had made Bobby Zimmerman a likely candidate for a career in the entertainment business, far less as a 'folk' – and what was that, exactly? – singer. Juvenile amateur-hour rock and roll had failed to produce an extensive CV; no one was hailing the boy as a natural. You have to wonder, too, what these parents made of the music that bewitched their son. The pop stuff was at least explicable, if unappealing: people made hit records, and therefore money. But folk? It was no part of their tradition. Those odd, obscure songs had not been handed down through their generations. Nevertheless, the progress Abe and Beatty had in mind bore no resemblance to the path glimpsed by their stubborn son. There was no future in poetry? Then there need be no past, either, for a poet busy being born.

*

First came a couple of curious episodes, all the more curious   what with the fictions their protagonist was already beginning to weave – because they *probably* happened. It seems Bobby Zimmerman had already been struck by Lead Belly's music as by a bolt from the clear blue, but in the summer of 1959 he was far from sure that folk music represented his future. He knew little enough about it, for one thing. Becoming someone famous, another *kind* of person entirely, unencumbered by the identity blind chance had allotted in a speck of a township on the Iron Range, with a family he struggled to locate in his mental universe, was another matter. That might as well have been ordained.

He was musically eclectic, to say the least. His tastes were still

---

7   *No Direction Home*, Ch. 1.

forming. Nothing as fancy as an artistic choice had yet presented itself. So why not play piano, in the key of C for preference, for a touring one-hit pop wonder? Bobby Vee – formerly Velline; who didn't change their name? – wasn't Little Richard, exactly. But Bobby Zimmerman wasn't 'Elston Gunn' for too long either. In all the long and frankly tedious debates over the choice of the name Dylan, certain small mercies are forgotten. *Elston Gunn*?

It goes like this. High school concluded – he 'left the very next day' – young Robert was spending time with relatives in Fargo, North Dakota, and working as a busboy in a local café, the Red Apple. One day in a record store he got himself introduced to the guitar player Bill Velline, elder brother to Bobby, and ventured the preposterous claim that he was a hot-shot piano player who had been paying his dues – hadn't Bill heard? – playing for Conway Twitty.

Bill Velline and his brother, Fargo boys who had just recorded 'Suzie Baby', their first minor hit, had not been in the business long (Bobby was almost two years Dylan's junior). They had got their own break thanks only to the death of Buddy Holly earlier that year, when an opening had appeared – unavoidably, permanently – on a local concert bill. They bought Dylan's nonsense. According to Vee, who told his story more than several times, this Elston Gunn even played one or two small shows before becoming surplus to requirements. For the want of a piano – the band couldn't/wouldn't buy/didn't give a damn – one possible career was lost.

Vee also alleged that 'Elston' chose to spell his last name with a third 'n': *Gunnn*. He was 'a neat guy'. The brothers bought him a matching shirt, paid him '15 bucks a night', and tried to work around the fact that the ace pianist lacked even a little Wurlitzer to call his own. It was all, said Bobby Vee later, 'ill-fated'. 'The story is that I fired him, but that certainly wasn't the case,' the singer would say. Instead, the band chose not to hire him.[8] There was a difference, though the fact was of scant comfort to Elston *Gunnn*.[9]

The twist to the believe-it-or-not tale, according to John Bucklen, was that on his return to Hibbing Dylan did not merely boast of having played with Vee, but claimed to *be* the teen idol. He had been 'recording', he said, under the pseudonym. In Scorsese's *No Direction*

---

8   *Goldmine* magazine, 1999.

9   *Peter Gunn* was a hit TV private-eye drama. Henry Mancini's 'Peter Gunn Theme' was its legacy, thanks mostly to the movie *The Blues Brothers*.

Home it was suggested, furthermore, that some people even believed him.

Attention-seeking adolescents have done worse. The appetite for fame induces all sorts of foolishness. But three small details surrounding this footnote stand out. First, even by 1959 Dylan had yet to represent himself as a guitarist. Second, he was none too fussy about musical vehicles, even when they involved something as anodyne and Holly-lite as 'Suzie Baby'. So try this for counter-factual speculation: what would have become of folk, protest, singer-songwriters and 'rock' if the Vellines had found a few dollars for a cheap piano?

Finally, there's the compulsion to prefer fantasy to truth. It was already so well established you can only wonder if Dylan didn't half-believe the 'Bobby Vee' farrago. He could have been having fun at the expense of the gullible – another habit that would last a lifetime – but if so it was an odd, complicated sort of joke. How would he have explained himself when the real Bobby Vee played Duluth?

It all counts as Dylan trivia, of course, and there are volumes of that stuff. But there is also a serious point. In 1959, clearly, young Robert's grip on reality was none too reliable. Four years later, authentic fame would detach him from commonly understood reality for the rest of his days. Yet if this singer's art is 'about' anything it is about penetrating the nature of the real, of shared human existence. He can only do that, it seems, because he has never been mired in ordinary life often or for long. He stands on the outside. The strange little tale of Elston Gunn(n) and Bobby Vee suggests that perhaps he always did, and that his lies were more than a career strategy. Bluntly, Dylan was strange from the start.

The second curious episode from that summer, more a matter of biographical speculation than documented fact, might have a bearing. Call it the Red Wing Tale, or the Jailbird Story. Some years later, as though to embroider the narrative of his 1963 song 'Walls of Red Wing',[10] Dylan would supposedly tell the New York journalist Al Aronowitz (not the ideal witness) that he had done time at the Red Wing Reformatory, a granite-walled 'correctional facility' to the south of Minneapolis. Soon enough, and for years afterwards, people would come forward claiming to have been locked up with Dylan, or – better still – to know someone who had shared his fate, and heard him play

---

10 Scots recognise the melody of this 'Dylan composition' instantly: it's that old Hogmanay (New Year) staple, 'The Road and the Miles to Dundee'.

his lonesome guitar in the dark night hours. They didn't explain how his song could be wrong about every physical detail of the real Red Wing institution, however.

Then there were those who said that, no, this spell of lost time – not found again – was spent at a discreet, low-security 'boarding school' establishment in the vicinity of Pennsylvania. Reportedly, a psychiatrist (never named) even vouched for Dylan's presence. In neither case has documentary evidence for a spell inside been produced, nor has anyone managed to fill a gap in either marvellous tale: *what was he supposed to have done to deserve this?* Affronted his folks once too often? Dodged school too frequently? There is certainly no word, documented or anecdotal, of a criminal offence. It's all worse than flimsy, even for an era liable to believe that juvenile delinquency was a pandemic. Dylan's relationship with his father became strained, no doubt, but the idea that Beatty Zimmerman would have countenanced having her son locked up tests credulity. It smacks of a desire to find tales to suit the legend.

Beatty told Shelton that Dylan spent that summer in Denver and Central City, Colorado. Dylan would later claim to have been fired from a joint in Central City named the Gilded Garter, and later seem to prove to the satisfaction of his acolytes that he knew the place. But whether this was in 1959 or in the summer of 1960, when he had a slightly better grasp of 'folky songs', is hard to establish. Beatty and Dylan's contemporaries differed. Alerted by Monte Edwardson, the former Golden Chord, he also spent a few weeks in one or other summer exploring what there was of musical life in Denver. It seems he ran into Jesse Fuller, the late-blooming one-man band, who apparently showed the youngster how to play a harmonica in a holder, and also met a young talent named Judy Collins. But then – so the story goes – Dylan was chased out of Central City after stealing money from the boss of the Garter and acquiring some records on permanent loan, without the owner's consent, in Denver. He would certainly make a habit of that, but it is equally possible he was making no headway with the management at the city's Exodus club. He said that this establishment, the only place of its kind in Denver and relatively prestigious in folk circles, wouldn't give him a job. What did they know? Besides, college awaited. That was the mundane truth.

As is often the case with the young Dylan of lies and legend, you can take your pick: Denver one year, or Denver the next. Just as his own tales seem to evolve according to his mood, so admirers and detractors select an episode in the *Bildungsroman* – reform school, boarding school or dive – according to taste. Forever missing from the picture is the simple story of a teenager who had seen little of the world and done nothing out of the ordinary. These were omissions he meant to rectify with all possible speed: that was the real point of every tale.

*

In the summer of 1959, when Bobby Zimmerman enrolled at the University of Minnesota, lodged between the Twin Cities of Minneapolis and St Paul, his country was deep in a Cold War with an alien power while other aliens, the movie sort, seemed to be coming out of the sky with every matinee. The white portion of his rich country was mired in a struggle between hatred and decency over its dispossessed black portion. The rich portion of the white portion was meanwhile locked in the usual internecine combat for ascendancy in government while some of the country's youth wondered what any of it – Bomb, racism, high politics and anti-Communist paranoia – had to do with them.

And then the white Jewish boy from the North Country sang the blues. How come?

> I had another band with my cousin from Duluth. I played, you know, rock & roll, rhythm and blues. And then that died out pretty much, in my last year of high school.
>
> And after that, I remember I heard a record – I think maybe it was the Kingston Trio or Odetta or someone like that – and I sorta got into folk music. Rock & roll was pretty much finished. And I traded my stuff for a Martin that they don't sell anymore, an 0018, maybe, and it was brown. The first acoustic guitar I ever had. A great guitar. And then, either in Minneapolis or St. Paul, I heard Woody Guthrie. And when I heard Woody Guthrie, that was it, it was all over.[11]

In 1958, the Kingston Trio would have been difficult to avoid. Their single 'Tom Dooley', choirboy folk as most folk had never before heard it, was released in August and had sold a million copies before the year was out. The Trio's influence on Dylan, if any, would not last long. Odetta, Odetta Holmes, was another matter. A black woman with opera training and theatrical experience, she had been singing

---

11 Interview with *Rolling Stone*, June 1984.

folk songs since the beginning of the decade. *Odetta Sings Ballads and Blues*, released in 1956, had been her first album in her own right, and it had contained several traditional songs that would form the basis of Dylan's first repertoire. As he told *Playboy* in 1978, Odetta represented 'something vital and personal. I learned all the songs on that record.' She was his first important folk influence. Then again, she was a big influence on a lot of people.

*

He had taken to calling himself Bob Dylan. Which theory on that mauled topic would suit? The Welsh poet, some Midwest football star, a character in a TV cowboy show, a familiar home-town name and address, 'a town in Oklahoma', the old lie about some 'uncle' named *Dillion*? In December of 2004, publicising *Chronicles*, he told interviewer Ed Bradley on the CBS show *60 Minutes* that the name Dylan was 'destiny'.

> Some people . . . You're born, you know, the wrong names, wrong parents.
> I mean, that happens. You call yourself what you want to call yourself.
> This is the land of the free.

So: the self-hating Jew theory, then, the one that fits so neatly with the memories of college friends who claim he avoided his coreligionists? The one that coheres with all the denials of any 'consciousness' of anti-Semitism, the apparent willed amnesia despite all the summers spent at Camp Herzl, and all the scripture the bar mitzvah boy had committed to memory, and – let's not miss the wholly obvious – all the words in all of those songs? Was he 'making a grand gesture, denying that he was his father's son'?[12] That would make sense, given the accounts of friends remembering tension and mutual incomprehension between Bobby and Abe. But Dylan's attitudes towards his origins, and towards 'Bob Dylan', are so tangled they deserve to be called a psychological condition. It's complicated because he made it complicated. It's complicated when there seems to be no reason for complications. All the limp meditations on a pop star's 'reinventions' overlook the old, fundamental human issue of identity. Who is this person?

In his 1997 biography of Mark Twain, that other great all-American

---

12 Heylin, *Bob Dylan: Behind the Shades Revisited*, Ch. 2.

contraption of a personality, Andrew Hoffman argued that Samuel Langhorne Clemens came in time to hate the real/unreal character he had created with such care. Hoffman proposed an explanation for the revered one-man double act:

> Traditional interpretation of the man dictated that Clemens had such a large personality that he needed a separate persona in which to carry it. That premise seemed to me fundamentally false. Anyone who has ever performed, whether on the stage or at a dinner party, knows that maintaining a false persona places a huge strain on one's ego. The larger the ego, in fact, the more difficult it becomes to sustain the invention. To live as someone else, to fully inhabit an invented self, the root self must have nearly no ego, or at least one so handicapped by insecurities that it might as well not exist.[13]

It's a theory. A useful one, too, if your subject has 'ever performed' on the stage. It might help to explain why Dylan has seemed to move so easily between identities, and why he is always described as essentially a shy man, lacking in ego. There is evidence enough, too, of an individual 'handicapped by insecurities'. You need only add that Mark Twain's difficult upbringing also left him with few strong roots.

Equally, though, you could settle for mundane answers. Back then, Dylan did not know 'who he was': that's a commonplace of adolescence. Nevertheless, he understood, somehow, that any star of stage, screen or radio had to assume a persona that was better than real. Later, for the sake of his privacy – and because he was ever drawn to life's mysteries – he came to enjoy mystique for its own sake, and used it like a weapon. But here's the thing: an artist who venerates truth, abstruse or otherwise, who began by scorning 'phonies', who has devoted his creative life's blood to emotional honesty, has never been honest, in the plain sense, about himself. In order to answer one old question – where did Bob Dylan spring from? – you must attempt to answer another.

How does it come about that a man in his 60s can still be talking about being born with 'the wrong names, wrong parents'? What happened within the head of a child to convince him of this truth almost at the first moment of self-awareness? And why was this idea, this fantasy, so powerful as to make it stick through life? These rhetorical questions have a point. Bob Dylan doesn't wear a mask. The mask is

---

13 *Inventing Mark Twain: The Lives of Samuel Langhorne Clemens*, Prologue.

the person now, and the person – *masked and anonymous* – sometimes calls himself Jack Frost, too, just to keep things interesting.

Fame eradicates personality: that's the cliché. Become a public spectacle, a continuing performance, and you lose yourself, the person you once were. A Presley or a John Lennon has rendered testimony sufficient, post-mortem, for that thesis. But the point is this: Dylan was a self-alienated individual – denying his family, his religion, his home town – long before anyone cared whether or not he had an ounce of talent. There is a difference between a teenage fantasy – 'to join Little Richard' – and the act of will, Rimbaud style, that aims to turn an assertion into a fact, and another cliché: 'I is another.' In the end, however, there is no 'I'.

The curious sense that there is no such person as Bob Dylan, that he is unknown even to Bob Dylan, began when a college kid declared that his name – and who didn't laugh? – was *Dylan*. He laid waste a life for the sake of a fiction: that's beyond strange. A person makes the art, but the art has no personality. So authorship is challenged: another thesis awaits. So the art attracts endless allegations of 'borrowing', plagiarism and theft. So the work arises from the lives of others. The great irony is that Dylan has become as impersonal and as anonymous, in his writing and his performances, as any nit-picking folk purist could wish. And he has done this time and again, shedding identities – not mere roles – like sloughed skins.

It therefore made perfect, twisted, ironic and 'postmodern' sense when Todd Haynes released a movie in 2007 entitled *I'm Not There* and cast six actors – known and unknown, male and female, white and black – to depict 'Bob Dylan', or a 'Woody Guthrie' in the imagination of an invented 'Bob Dylan', or even 'Arthur Rimbaud' striking a Dylan pose. In that movie, some of the actors play people pretending to play people who might be playing someone who might be Dylan in a film invented for the film. Narrative is plastic: who cares? All the allusions, visual, musical and metaphorical, are fun to spot. But you are left, just for irony's sake, with a question: why? What's the purpose of this game?

Dylan himself experimented with such themes in his 1978 film *Renaldo and Clara*. In that long, never coherent subversion of Marcel Carné's *Les Enfants du Paradis*, Dylan played the hero but Ronnie Hawkins, The Band's old mentor, played 'Bob Dylan' (while sounding the spit of Ronnie Hawkins). Sara Dylan played Clara, but the singer Ronee Blakley was given a credit as 'Mrs Dylan'. Hats and masks were worn. Dylan appeared in white-face. David Blue talked a lot about the old days. Fiction and 'documentary' were interspersed. The music was pretty good and a flower became important.

It must have seemed valid, clever and *Dylanesque* at the time, like a lot of good ideas about to go wrong. Given the amount of his time, money and effort invested in the project, Dylan's sincerity – on screen almost painful to behold – is not in doubt. But his attempt to deal with the question of identity, his identity in particular, winds up seeming like another elaborate evasion. In the inevitable *Rolling Stone* interview,[14] it led to a faintly hilarious exchange. Here the journalist makes his play:

> 'So Bob Dylan,' I surmise, 'may or may not be in the film.'
> 'Exactly.'
> 'But Bob Dylan made the film.'
> 'Bob Dylan didn't make it. *I* made it.'

So what, you might be tempted to ask, is the big deal? And what is the point in insisting that 'I' made this movie if you have neither the desire nor the intention to say who that person might be? It would make perfect sense for Dylan or anyone else to observe that the numerous upheavals in his life, not to mention the erosive effects of celebrity and fame, have left him with a fluid sense of identity. 'Bob Dylan' must often wonder who the hell he really is. Hence *Masked and Anonymous* (2003): that would be another movie designed to labour the point, or to confront the audience with its own metaphysical comedy quandary. Dylan doubts himself; we should all doubt the reality of self. The fundamental point, though, is that he has been this way *from the start*.

Someone writes the songs and sings them. He has a physical presence, a carcass you can label, a career you can describe. It might be, though, that this long epistemological argument began as something mundane. Maybe Bobby Zimmerman just decided, back in 1958 or 1959, that you don't get to be a star if you're Bobby Zimmerman, from little Hibbing – where the hell? – in Minnesota.

Echo Helstrom would certainly pin the moment to the spring of 1958, and ventriloquise a youth saying, 'I know what my name's gonna be now,' and specifying (though her story altered over the years) the spelling. Supposedly he even had the poet's book under his

---

14 With Jonathan Cott, January 1978.

arm when he broke the news. It sounds just a little too perfect. On the other hand, John Bucklen would also maintain that the Welsh writer's name had been appropriated, right down to the spelling, by Christmas 1959.

Dead Dylan Thomas was a big enough deal in 1950s America, less for his overwrought assonance than for the manner of his extinction: suicidal boozing in Greenwich Village was the last word, not least for him, in bohemian style. Mere pneumonia was less glamorous, of course, but Thomas, dead in November of 1953, set an example for any number of rock stars with literary pretensions. Farcically, his end was also taken as symbolic, as a kind of rebuke to a hidebound era. Live fast, die young, but – as no one remembered to say – be careful not to leave a pallid, chubby corpse behind.

In a 1978 *Playboy* interview, the question was asked, yet again: 'By the time you arrived in New York, you'd changed your name from Robert Zimmerman to Bob Dylan. Was it because of Dylan Thomas?' Answer:

> No, I haven't read that much of Dylan Thomas. It's a common thing to change your name. It isn't that incredible. Many people do it. People change their town, change their country. New appearance, new mannerisms. Some people have many names. I wouldn't pick a name unless I thought I was that person. Sometimes you are held back by your name . . .
>
> But getting back to Dylan Thomas, it wasn't that I was inspired by reading some of his poetry and going 'Aha!' and changing my name to Dylan. If I thought he was that great, I would have sung his poems and could just as easily have changed my name to Thomas.

Thomas tends to appeal to teenagers of all ages, perhaps because he invests each line with a certain portentous self-regard. The young John Lennon was a fan, no doubt for that reason. The Welshman never *sounds* less than profound. Attempts to detect his influence on the other Dylan's writing falter at first sight, however, and at first hearing. This youngster, so easily and willingly influenced, didn't think Thomas was 'that great'. There is nothing in his subsequent writing to suggest he ever believed otherwise.

Then again, why not a poet's famous brand? As stories go, it remains as good as any. The real point about *Dylan* is obvious: the name could hardly be less Jewish. (The origins are certainly Welsh, possibly referring to the sea, or to a god of the sea, or to tides.) Hibbing had been settled early by an individual named Dillon, and there was a local road bearing the name. That might also have stuck, consciously or not, in the mind. But there was never the slightest chance of Bobby Zimmerman becoming Bob Merman.

It would not actually be necessary to hate your identity to realise in the late 1950s and early 1960s that very few entertainers, comedians aside, went by their given Jewish names. Even if they had, Zimmerman didn't exactly roll off the tongue. Tony Curtis was born Bernie Schwartz: why did he change his name, do we think? Woody Allen is not Woody Allen. Lenny Bruce was born Leonard Schneider. Paul Simon, only five months Dylan's junior, would claim in 2003 that Columbia's decision in 1964 to present 'Tom & Jerry' as Simon & Garfunkel was the first example of a pop act being allowed – in this case encouraged – to declare their ethnic identity. Ethel Merman (of all people) really was a Zimmerman too, and once made a showbiz joke about the wattage required to put *that* family name in lights.

Bob Dylan is a pretty good handle, in any case, as a teenager attuned to music and movies no doubt realised. At least its bearer did not suffer the pop-world indignity of having an identity picked for him. It might simply have been the case that Dylan rebelled against the idea of being defined in any fashion, whether by name or religion.

Besides, a change of name was scarcely a novel gesture for the descendants of immigrants. Dylan's maternal grandfather had called himself Ben Stone, but *his* father's name was Solemovitz. Was 'Stone' any less of a repudiation than 'Dylan'? Or was it no sort of repudiation at all? In a would-be star a touch of glamour and the avoidance of bigotry equal pragmatism and ambition.

More important are the conjunctions. They go something like this. Still in his teens, Dylan had rejected and denied his parents, his name, his home town and the faith of his fathers. By an act of will he had metamorphosed, utterly plausible, into the legatee of black tradition and a folk culture rooted squarely in a shared American Christian memory. He had destroyed one identity and created, or borrowed, another. He had done this, with no sense of irony, in reaction to a society he held to be 'phoney'. To describe the act of self-immolation as reinvention is beyond glib. This was not some cute career move, and 'impersonating' Woody Guthrie wasn't even the half of it. This was never just a question of picking a stage name and liking the

Gentile sound of 'Bob Dylan'. Bobby Zimmerman and Shabtai Zisel ben Avraham were eradicated for Bob Dylan's sake.

But. By the time he and the world got to 2004 and *Chronicles*, the name-above-the-title was once again having fun with people who puzzle over his hide-and-seek identity. Yet another story was stitched together. A good one, too.

It turns out that he had intended to call himself Robert Allen the minute he left home, because – in one half of his identity at least – that was the person he believed himself to be. He also thought the name had the sound of a Scottish king about it. Later he would come across an article in *Downbeat* magazine involving – so he remembered – a California sax player named David Allyn. Dylan suspected that the individual's original name had been Allen, but the alternative spelling had been judged more appealing. Bobby Zimmerman had been taken, it is alleged, with the same notion: Robert Allen would become Robert Allyn.

Just like that. It probably wouldn't spoil things too much to observe that David Allyn was a jazz *singer* who started out in the 1940s, and who changed his name, it seems, from DeLella. He even made an album in 1975 entitled *Don't Look Back*. But Dylan is rolling: here, after all those years, comes a poet.

Finally it is admitted, casually, that he had indeed come across the poetry of Dylan Thomas. Then there is the memory of struggling to decide between Allyn and Dylan. Then, supposedly, came the decision to prefer the initial consonant over the vowel. He was none too sure about 'Robert Dylan', but plainly he was certain – if you choose to believe a word of it – that it was worth taking pains over the decision.

Meanwhile, there were far too many people named Bobby around. Bob Allyn would have evoked someone who sold used cars for a living. So in the Twin Cities, when he was asked, a young man answered 'Bob Dylan' without a single pause for thought. All that hesitating over a name and suddenly there's no hesitation? As for Bobby Zimmerman, he'll give you the plain, verifiable facts. *That* Bobby, it turns out, was an early president of the San Bernadino Hell's Angels, run down and killed in a moment of general idiocy by one his own pack. That Bobby is no more. Another one bites the dust. *True story.*

There are no recorded examples of Dylan cackling. Yet he knows, still, that people want to know, like it or not, about the source of this pointless, enveloping cloud of self-created mystery. Even the acknowledgement of Robert Allen as 'my identity' is a contribution to the endless game. In law he became Bob Dylan – or Robert Dylan, according to publishing contracts and an old passport – in 1962. Yet still he intrigues against the simple fact that he bumped off Robert Allen Zimmerman at the first opportunity and still can't or won't say why. The striking part about the great identity switch is in a single remark. It was what 'I was going to do as soon as I left home'. The instant a door closed behind him he was another person.

Sober commentators have meanwhile noted, more than once, that in fact Dylan's choice was nothing out of the ordinary, historically speaking. The old American tradition of 'blackface minstrelsy' is adduced. White performers have been impersonating black people and stealing their culture, often enough to gruesome effect, for a long time. What really happens when a white Jewish boy decides to sing the blues? In an essay published in 2002, Barry Shank observed:

This . . . personal transformation, whereby a young white male attempts to remake himself through performing black music, is the classic trope of the great American tradition of blackface minstrelsy. From at least as early as the 1830s, when TD Rice observed a dancing slave and created the international sensation 'Jump Jim Crow', American popular music has formed a crucial cultural ground, where the meanings of blackness and whiteness have been reproduced, renegotiated and renewed.[15]

For Americans this old story has profound and complicated implications. Even in Britain, the blues boom of the early 1960s produced, in some listeners, a certain queasy wonderment. If it was strange to see and hear white Americans passing artistically for black, how odd was it – worrying, too – when Eric Clapton from Surrey or Keith Richards from Kent claimed an identity with the musicians of Chicago and the Delta, and got stinking rich (unlike their role models) in the process?

In Dylan's case it isn't quite the whole story. Contrary to one of his own songs, he was no mere minstrel boy, an Al Jolson, even metaphorically, for the age. Nor, despite his love for the music, did he invest himself entirely in the blues. The early 'Bob Dylan' would also borrow music from the Irish, Scottish and English traditions, among other things. Above all, a complicated cross-cultural history fails to

---

15 'That Wild Mercury Sound: Bob Dylan and the Illusion of American Culture', *boundary 2* (Spring 2002).

explain his sheer need. If adopting the blues meant putting on blackface then it is fair to say that's exactly what he did. Why? Why was this common-enough transformation tied to a compulsion to erase an identity?

But here's the funny part: it worked. He was vindicated a thousand times over. The mystery lies in the impulse, and in the cost. 'Bob Dylan' is a lonely place to be, I think. These days he jokes sometimes about having struck that old, bad and inevitable deal at the crossroads. He told Ed Bradley: 'It goes back to that destiny thing. I mean, I made a bargain with it, you know, long time ago. And I'm holding up my end . . . to get where I am now.'

The devil, as he always was, is in the detail.

*

Dylan was a dropout even before he arrived at university. Though enrolled to pursue 'liberal arts' – with music as his major – he seems to have had not the slightest intention of once clouding his ambitions with study. His parents had entertained high if naive hopes that their hand-raised genius would soon get the fanciful stuff out of his system. They should have known better: he didn't attend a single class. In 2005, Dylan said, blandly, 'I just didn't feel like it.' Instead, his plans long formed in secret dreams, the boy was drawn to what passed for bohemia in the Twin Cities as a pigeon is drawn to home. He was an early adopter, as these things went, of what was soon to be known as 'alternative'.

> I was a musical expeditionary. I had no past to speak of, nothing to go back to and nobody to lean on.[16]

If literature is the topic, however, it is worth bearing in mind that this American poet had no higher education worth the name. Schools of this and schools of that, critical theory and metacritical *whatever*, had neither traction nor influence on him as a writer. He would become formidably well read – this poet knows his poets, and knows some of them inside out – but not because of received wisdom. Essentially he was an autodidact from the start, educating himself by listening, reading and trying to write. Dylan created this Dylan, and gained his own perspective. It meant that those who sought to define or dismiss his gifts as a poet would have to work harder on their terms and assumptions.

---

16 *No Direction Home* (film).

It could have been otherwise. Among the benefits offered by the University of Minnesota in the autumn of 1959 were classes taught by the poet John Berryman. Most say he was a brilliant teacher; some that he was mad; a consensus further holds that against his capacity for wholesale self-harm and inexhaustible vanity no one – no one sober, at any rate – could have borne a candle. Berryman was nuts, and a genius. Dylan never knew. Thanks to his conviction that school had nothing to offer, and to his indolence, the juvenile missed out on illumination. So their boats passed, one drunkenly, in the night. Odd echoes persist, nevertheless. In his 2003 book *Dylan's Visions of Sin*, Christopher Ricks makes a passing mention of the coincidence, but in terms of American poetry it feels more like synchronicity.

In Berryman's *77 Dream Songs* (1964) parallels to many of Dylan's syntactical tricks and perverse diction in the songs of the mid-1960s can be found. The older poet's abrupt switches in tone, from high vernacular comedy to low Shakespearean posturing, are often reminiscent of *Tarantula*. Berryman – whose birth name was not Berryman, who revered the blues, who found and lost God often enough – used alter egos to speak in his stead, and turned his cracked-sonnet sequences into a minstrel show, whites in blackface and all, involving 'Henry' – 'Mr Bones' – a stock character called 'Friend' and a presence named 'Ruin'. It was as though he understood the complications of 'blackface minstrelsy' intimately. For a while in the 1960s Berryman was the biggest thing in American poetry. Thanks to fads among tenured hacks his reputation's tide has ebbed since.

Citationists find a resemblance, nevertheless, between 'Ballad of a Thin Man' and Berryman. There's Mr Jones and Mr Bones. There's a slight correspondence, too, between Dylan's 'There ought to be a law / Against you comin' around' and Berryman's fourth dream song ('There ought to be a law against Henry'). In the song there are, of course, 'the professors', and the invocation of Minnesota's own F. Scott Fitzgerald. There is, above all, Dylan's dismissal of those with pencils in their hands, who try so hard and don't understand.

The relevance is probably slight. The important thing is that the Berryman of *The Dream Songs* was a wild master of voice, sacred and profane, in every register, one whose intellectual intonation, whose poetic identity, was peculiarly all-American. Like Whitman, like William Carlos Williams, like Ginsberg – though there was precious little else held in common – Berryman discovered America in its language. Dylan missed him at college, but caught up, I think, when it mattered. One critic summarised the habitual Berryman mode – it wasn't praise – in terms that could sound familiar.

> The unmistakable, catchy, melancholic manner of the *Dream Songs* – the gags and ampersands, the jumble of baby-talk, minstrel-talk, slang, high eloquence and quotation, the cubist pretzels of syntax, the dimestore, frail mask of 'Henry' – has been adored, imitated, even made into a cult; it has become the 'Berrymanishness' of Berryman.[17]

'Dylanesque' might stand as a worse fate. It is worth wondering, though, whether a later investigation of a poet he had missed entirely in college, along with every other class, might not have acted on Dylan's writing with at least the force of Beat rhetoric. As noted, those *77 Dream Songs* appeared in 1964, just as the protest singer was allowing himself to be called a poet.

In 1969, Berryman was on a reading tour. By then his unquenchable alcoholism, sundry manias and a fixation with a father's suicide were in a three-horse race towards the finish. That would come, as though on a too-often postponed whim, on a January day in 1972, when the poet jumped for the first and last time from the Washington Avenue Bridge in Minneapolis. In 1969, he visited himself upon academic hosts in Seattle. Berryman, they say, tended to shout. On this evening he shouted that

> He would never forgive that 'young upstart' Bob Dylan for stealing *his* friend, Dylan's, name. Oh, Bob Dylan was certainly a real-enough poet. All he had to do now was learn how to sing.[18]

*

In 1940, in 'a fleabag hotel on the corner of Sixth Avenue and Forty-third Street' in New York,[19] Woody Guthrie had written 'This Land Is Your Land'. He had become sick and tired of hearing Irving Berlin's 'God Bless America' and had jotted down six verses with the title, and

17 Robert Pinsky, *New York Times* book review (1977).

18 Paul L. Mariani, *Dream Song: The Life of John Berryman* (1990), p. 445. In the survey *Twentieth Century Literature* (1976) Charles Molesworth reported: 'Adrienne Rich [the feminist poet] has suggested that only two men in this age know what the American language is, in all its fullness and impurity, and they are Bob Dylan and John Berryman.'

19 Klein, *Woody Guthrie*, Ch. 5.

refrain, 'God Blessed America for Me'. On the manuscript, dated 23 February – when the European war was a long way off and much of the American left was still failing to grasp a 'new situation' – 'Woody G' had added, 'All you can write is what you see.' But then, according to his biographer, 'he completely forgot about the song and didn't do anything with it for another five years.'[20]

In the meantime, Guthrie had gone off to Washington and a studio at the Department of the Interior to record his songs and his anecdotes over the course of three long days for the folklorist Alan Lomax, then assistant-in-charge of the Archive of Folksong at the Library of Congress. The results were not to be released for a quarter of a century, but the sessions, his first serious recordings, counted as Woody's 'discovery'. Here was a son of the soil, a natural talent, an authentic type, and a template for 'folk'.

Lomax's father, John, by then in his 70s, had been a legendary folklorist, a pioneering collector who had enlisted his student son's help on recording trips in the South on the library's behalf in the early 1930s.[21] The experience had politicised Alan (though not his parent) as he came face to face with the realities of existence for America's poor, especially its poor blacks, and the black prisoners in its Southern jails above all. In 1933, on the infamous prison farm at Angola

---

20 *ibid.* It was four years, in point of fact, before Guthrie recorded the song, along with seventy-five others in a single day. 'This Land' has acquired and lost numerous verses over the years. In Guthrie's original draft, verse four talks of 'a big high wall there that tried to stop me / A sign was painted said: Private Property / But on the back side it didn't say nothing.' This was considered too political, it seems, when the 'original' 1944 version was recorded. Equally, two further 'variant' verses were omitted when the song was published in 1945. One of these ran, 'Nobody living can ever stop me, / As I go walking that freedom highway; / Nobody living can ever make me turn back / This land was made for you and me.' When Dylan performed the song at the Carnegie Chapter Hall in New York in April of 1961 that vexatious verse stayed in.

21 As Klein explains – *Woody Guthrie,* Ch. 5 – both Lomaxes were held in some suspicion by academic folklorists, Alan because of his politics, Lomax Sr because of his methods. Though John Lomax's 1910 anthology *Cowboy Songs and Other Frontier Ballads* had preserved the likes of 'Jesse James', 'Sweet Betsy from Pike' and, most famously, 'Home on the Range', the collector's habit of compiling 'favourite' versions was controversial. On the other hand, he gave full credit to that forgotten breed, the black cowboy, for supplying some of the most famous songs in the book.

(officially the Louisiana State Penitentiary), father and son had encountered and recorded a 12-string guitar player by the name of Huddie Ledbetter, known to most as Lead Belly.

Subsequently, Lomax Sr had hired the singer as a driver and attempted, briefly, to manage his career before a quarrel over money and control, ironically enough, ended the relationship. Lead Belly – when you survive a gunshot wound to the stomach, you get to keep the name – called the father 'Big Boss' and the son 'Little Boss'. Admirers of either Lomax struggle to explain that detail. Lead Belly subsequently sued for release from his management contract, but then struggled to find much success on his own. After another spell in prison in 1939, however, he began to achieve prominence on the folk scene, falling in with Guthrie, Pete Seeger, Sonny Terry and Brownie McGhee.

Woody had meanwhile allied himself with the Almanac Singers, an agit-prop Greenwich Village folk troupe specialising in topical material, often union songs, in the service of the Popular Front, that loose alliance of shades of left-wing and left-liberal opinion. Guthrie had met Seeger just after jotting down 'This Land Is Your Land' and had been introduced, subsequently, to Millard Lampell, Lee Hays and an apartment they called Almanac House. To begin with it had been a casual, bohemian affair, but the point was both musical and political. The folk revival, as it came to be known, was ideological from the start.

The Almanacs – sometimes joined by the likes of Josh White, Burl Ives or Cisco Houston – had dressed casually and sang vehemently of socialism, racism, militarism and the rights of the working man. They even had the temerity, as it was thought, to ridicule Roosevelt, not least for introducing a military draft bill when America was at peace. Their first album, *Songs for John Doe*, released in the spring of 1941, had taken it for granted that the European war was 'phoney', another big-business plot. Despite all that had been learned in the Spanish Civil War, the group had followed the Communist Party in demanding non-intervention. Their confusion, even as they proffered political answers, ran deep. War saved them from absurdity by making them folk heroes.

But what were those, exactly? Dylan's later travails when his songwriting changed and the charges of betrayal began to be levelled have been misrepresented. 'Purists', it is said routinely, turned against him, but the word is misapplied. It confuses musicological issues with political arguments. By one truly purist account the Almanac group themselves were never folk musicians: Guthrie wrote his own songs;

he, Seeger and others 'borrowed' and adapted freely. They saw nothing wrong with that. Yet, as all the dictionaries explain, folk music is music 'handed down in the popular tradition of the people', or 'traditional and typically anonymous music that is an expression of the life of the people in a community'. Many folklorists have stated the case baldly: 'a true folk song has no known author'. The Almanacs were often enough named authors; they got paid, sometimes. Patently, they were professional entertainers. Yet they helped themselves to songs or melody lines and excused the habit as 'traditional'.

At their peak, the Almanacs were hardly unknown; most of them wrote a little or a lot; Woody wrote hundreds of songs. They were 'folk' only because of their claimed connection with 'the people'. That was political. Yet music made to *speak for* the people failed pure folk's demand for anonymity. The real grouse against Dylan when fame arrived sprang from politics: he deserted the cause and supped with the capitalist devil. Which is not to say that the Almanacs or the Weavers refused the chance to make hit records: they too were pop stars, of sorts. It's not to say, either, that the true folk purists, insisting on tradition, community and songs with unknown authors, did not define *that* as political. The folk revival was a series of arguments, most of them incoherent. Dylan would slash through every Gordian knot.

*

John Bucklen recalled that Bobby was given an album of Lead Belly 78s in 1959, as a high-school graduation gift. Typically, the source of this Mephistophelian bounty – 'One of his relatives,' said Bucklen; 'Gifts from strangers,' said Shelton; 'One of Bob's uncles,' said Howard Sounes – has not been identified. Supposedly the records simply lay on the dining-room table after the big party (a party Bobby had attended under the usual teenage protests). So which individual from Hibbing or Duluth, Zimmerman or Stone or family friend, would have accounted Huddie Ledbetter ideal for a teenager who had been busying himself with rock and roll nonsense?

The 'King of the 12-String Guitar' – and a lot more besides – had died in 1949. He was not a hit-maker, exactly, not on his own behalf. Nor do we know the titles of the songs that split the air for Bobby. Perhaps the gift was a down payment. Clinton Heylin transcribes a fanzine's interview with Bucklen thus:

Just after he'd left high school but before he left for Minnesota he called me on the telephone, as he'd done so many times before, and he said, 'I've discovered something great! You've just got to come over here!' . . . One of his relatives had given him some rare Lead Belly records, old 78s, and he was flabbergasted by them . . . He thought it was [all] great. I thought, this isn't great – it's okay.[22]

Earlier, Shelton had jotted down *almost* the same story:

Bucklen: 'Bob almost shouted over the phone: "I've discovered something great! You've got to come over here!" [They listened, and Bob was flabbergasted.] "This is the thing, this is the thing," he repeated. Leadbelly [*sic*] was too simple for me in 1959. There was another example of Bob's being ahead of us all.'[23]

This is the thing. A gift from nowhere, from thin air, from person or persons unknown: and this explains Bob Dylan, the folk blues, the singer-songwriter, the Nobel nominations and a 50-year career? Then again, why not?

He heard something somewhere: so much is plain. He was, in that old, underused sense of the word, inspired. Yet in that he was in no sense unique: all over America, all over the world, youngsters were experiencing the same urge as coffee houses and clubs sprang up, each one filled instantly by guitar players, most of them forgettable, all of them possessed by the desire for a music that 'meant something'. What did they mean by that?

In 1959, when Dylan was enrolled at the University of Minnesota, Keith Richards was a student at a minor art school in south London, beginning to learn the blues on 'a borrowed f-hole archtop Höfner', finding a way to make this music flow 'straight from the heart to the fingers'. The future Rolling Stone was no unique phenomenon either. He stands as witness, even yet, to the fact that a generation shocked into life by rock and roll had already begun to find maps to the riverine source of the music.

Yet again, nevertheless, the tale goes that Bobby Zimmerman – looking younger than his years, chubbier and heavier than he would ever be again – was forewarned against the hurricane. He didn't,

22 *Bob Dylan: Behind the Shades Revisited*, Ch. 2.
23 *No Direction Home*, Ch. 1.

couldn't, just pick up the blues and a rudimentary sense of the folk tradition from a small-city college bohemian crowd. That would have been too simple.

*

At first, like a proper freshman, he roomed at an outpost of the Sigma Alpha Mu fraternity network, a Jewish house. That didn't last long. There was a dispute, supposedly, over unpaid dues, though all concerned seemed to realise from the start that this ostentatiously eccentric youth was no frat boy. He quit the Sammies without a backward glance. The thought of studying, irrespective of any arrangement made with his parents, was also exorcised soon enough. Some say Bobby applied himself for a short while – Dylan says otherwise – but soon devoted himself to the guitar and the freewheelin' life. One account has him 'writing night and day' after giving up his studies, though the results were 'pretty infantile'. Still, if the young Zimmerman had been granted licence by Abe, he used it.

Beyond the campus precincts lay Dinkytown, a name that could have been coined to describe the district's limitations as a bohemian ground zero. Dylan didn't know that. Huddled around the junction of 14th Avenue Southeast and 4th Street Southeast in downtown Minneapolis, Dinkytown contained bookshops, a drugstore, a cinema and a coffee house, the Ten O'Clock Scholar, newly opened. There was music, art, new styles and new ideas. There were new and impressive people to meet. Dylan had scant experience of that sort of thing, but he was eager. Dinkytown wasn't the Left Bank, exactly, but in comparison to Hibbing it offered the next best thing to cocktail hour at La Coupole.

> Where I was at, people just passed through, really, carrying horns, guitars, suitcases, whatever, just like the stories you hear, free love, wine, poetry, nobody had any money anyway. There were a lot of poets and painters, drifters, scholarly types, experts at one thing or another who had dropped out of the regular nine-to-five life, there were lots of house parties most of the time. They were usually in lofts or warehouses or something or sometimes in the park, in the alley, wherever there was space. It was always crowded, no place to stand or breathe. There were always a lot of poems recited . . . It was sort of like that and it kind of woke me up . . .[24]

---

24 Interview with Cameron Crowe, *Biograph* booklet (1985).

Rock and roll was not well regarded in this milieu. Rock and roll was not well regarded period. Whatever it had meant, it was over. Even back in Hibbing Dylan and Bucklen had begun to have their doubts about Elvis – so Bucklen would say – when the fuss became intense. But a college crowd given to reciting poetry had a particular disdain for the cheap, manipulated, industrial product offered by Presley and his kind. As the record industry's payola scandal was demonstrating, even the idea of a pop hit was probably phoney. Those busy giving Dinkytown its ambience had no interest in the music of adolescents, a music that no one had yet begun to associate with art, and a fad that seemed, in any case, to have passed. Students requiring 'substance' turned instead to jazz or, increasingly, to folk and blues. Rock and roll was trivia, with 'nothing to say'.

For obvious reasons, a lot is made of Dylan turning to folk music, but in one sense he had no choice. Fitting in on the Dinkytown scene, a small world if ever there was one, demanded no less. He may have arrived prepared, in some manner, but Dylan truly 'woke up' soon enough. Equally, you suspect that much of his early rhetoric concerning music and music-industry phonies echoed the received wisdom of the Minneapolis crowd. Nevertheless, in 'My Life in a Stolen Moment', the poem committed to print in 1963, this moment in his life went through the Dylan fantasy filter:

Later I sat in college at the University of Minnesota
    on a phoney scholarship that I never had
I sat in science class an' flunked out for refusin' to watch
    a rabbit die
I got expelled from English class for using four-letter words
    in a paper describing the English teacher
I also failed out of communication class for callin' up
    every day and sayin' I couldn't come
I did OK in Spanish though but I knew it beforehand
I's kept around for kicks at a fraternity house
They let me live there an' I did until they wanted me to join
I moved in with two girls from South Dakota
    in a two-room apartment for two nights
I crossed the bridge to 14th Street an' moved in above
    a bookstore that also sold bad hamburgers
    basketball sweatshirts an' bulldog statues
I fell hard for an actress girl who kneed me in the guts

an' I ended up on the East Side a the Mississippi River
with about ten friends in a condemned house underneath
the Washington Avenue Bridge just south a Seven Corners
That's pretty well my college life

There was a girl or two, certainly. As ever, attempts have been made to link one or another with this or that Dylan song. What they seem to have had in common, as a minimum requirement, were tastes in music that matched his. Some of the women have reminisced serially over the gauche proto-Dylan who could rouse protective instincts. One girl, Bonnie Beecher, to whom he was especially close, has remembered buying Dylan his first harmonica holder before he had quite mastered the instrument. In every aspect, he was a work in progress.

The Ten O'Clock Scholar – 'a diller, a dollar, a ten o'clock scholar' – was one of the newly opened coffee houses, much like all the rest, springing up across America. In the memories of those who shared a youth long gone it offered cheap sandwiches, decent coffee, chessboards and music to a clientele of students, dropouts and assorted 'bohemians'. The Cabaret Voltaire it was not, but Dylan began to haunt the place soon after his arrival in the city. He began to acquire a reputation, too.

In all the interviews and memoirs attributed down the years to Dylan's Minneapolis contemporaries a note of affection is often hard to detect. In truth, only a few seem to have liked him much. Those who did find time for him also found Dylan disconcerting, even puzzling. His subsequent career – for who can argue with that? – lends respect to hindsight. Still there is a kind of wariness. The recurring theme is a lingering astonishment, mixed now and then, just below the surface, with a residual resentment, as though they still cannot believe that *he*, of all people, could have made it. Many have been big enough to confess that they never saw it coming. In those days, Dylan wasn't the best folk musician in Minneapolis. In the beginning, he wasn't the best musician in the Scholar, even on a slow night. But his tenacity was formidable. As often as not – and the word would reappear when he reached Greenwich Village – this 'Dylan' was a pest.

A poseur, too, in a juvenile way. That's well remembered: everything about the teenager seemed to be an act. While his contemporaries performed with imaginary guitars in front of forgiving bedroom mirrors, he was striking attitudes in public. He had a lot of nerve, and a vast amount of self-belief mined from somewhere deep inside. Perhaps he meant to prove something to his parents. Perhaps he truly did feel driven to follow the music. Perhaps he was just living out his fantasies. What is certain is that he needed to be noticed. He was determined to succeed when all around thought he was a joke. He refused to be rejected.

One regular at the Scholar, older than Dylan by a few years, as most were, catches the persistent 'sceptical' note. In an online memoir[25] Stan Gotlieb, subsequently a writer based in Oaxaca, Mexico, recalls that in 1959 'a rather pushy college sophomore named Bobby Zimmermann [*sic*] began dropping in. Most of us reacted negatively to him, probably as a balance to his own inflated estimates of his ability as a guitarist and as a poet.'

In the Scholar, it seems 'there was universal agreement that [Dylan] was definitely second rate'. Gotlieb also remembers that 'we sometimes hooted at him when he performed'. Dylan was worth only $2 a gig, if he was lucky, when others could command all of $5. Thus, when this no-hoper 'decided he was ready for the big time in the Big Apple, I, like almost everyone he knew, told him to forget it; that he didn't have the talent . . .' These days Gotlieb at least admits that this 'was one of a long line of outrageous mistakes I have made in my life'.

The competition included John Koerner, 'Spider John', an erstwhile US Marine who told Shelton that he didn't remember Dylan talking about 'making it'. 'We were more interested in immediate things,' recalled this guitar player, 'in making up songs.' Koerner, certainly numbered among those reckoned superior talents, struggled to connect the later Dylan with the kid he had known at the Scholar.

It is believed, in any case, that the new arrival got his first chance in January of 1960 in a St Paul establishment called the Purple Onion Pizza Parlor. He began to play with Koerner in the Scholar in the following month. Spider John would later say that Dylan 'was writing some songs'. These were 'those folky spirituals that were popular'. Once again, a fondness for Odetta was mentioned. The young man had 'a pretty voice, much different from what it became'.

The kid took to carrying a notebook around. One witness also saw 'a book of French Symbolist poetry' on the person of the non-student. Dylan lingered in the memory as eager, competitive, annoying and probably deluded. When you piece the accounts of his brief spell in Dinkytown together there is rarely a sense of a youth who kept people close to him. Nor is it clear that he or those around him had much idea of what this 'folk' music was supposed to be. Things had not

25 'An Inappropriate Life', realoaxaca.com.

yet come into focus. In their reminiscences they talk of Odetta, of Josh White and of Guthrie. But you sometimes wonder: what did they think it meant, any of it? Just something that wasn't dumb pop?

Listen, if you can, to folk music as it was understood in mainstream America in the 1950s. Many of the people who are now esteemed for their pioneering efforts look and perform, say the recordings, as though for a church social. Authentic folk musicians meanwhile sprang from another era – from another world – and from times and places long gone. The choices available, in short, were sanitised cabaret folk, the ghostly voices captured in Harry Smith's *Anthology of American Folk Music*, or musicians recently 'discovered' in the lost lands beyond the cities. The fascination with folk is understandable, in one sense. The desire for something radical and real in a phoney world of consumerism and hypocrisy was rational. Worries over the lusts of mass culture preoccupied the era. But in Dinkytown the price, it appears, was a wholesale rejection of rock and roll, the music that had been obsessing Dylan only months before.

One of his contemporaries, Harvey Abrams, was interviewed by Shelton in 1966. He remembered Bob *Dillon* – 'all of his music billings here were spelled Bob Dillon' but also said that his old friend was 'the purest of the pure' where folk was concerned, forever intent on pursuing the original record or the original song. 'If anyone had played him a Beatles or a Rolling Stones record,' said Abrams, 'he would probably have broken it.'

Before Dylan arrived at college a few chart hits had been scored with folk-type songs. Even self-declared purists had accommodated themselves to the people's choices, and to popular arrangements. But listen to Lead Belly perform 'Goodnight, Irene' and then listen to the Weavers' 1950 number-one hit. The latter troupe are due a great deal of credit for their courage in the face of the blacklists. Their abuse of the music, on the other hand, has long gone unpunished: it was 'folk' only because these earnest white people said it was. A twenty-first-century listener meanwhile wonders why they should have been performing a black writer's music to begin with. If Elvis could be charged with theft, what was this? Even the most radical of the folk crowd had a habit of patronising black culture. Only if it was rendered white would it sell. Who went along with that? Everyone.

And who was 'authentic', exactly? By which criterion was it decided that rural folk were somehow culturally pure because – let's not beat

143

around the undergrowth – they didn't know shit? The habit of treating America's peasantry as a collection of lost tribes required a good deal of self-deceit. You had to believe that these people had never seen a movie, never picked up a magazine, never served in the armed forces, never guessed at the bright lights and the big city, that they existed in a kind of redneck Brigadoon. This was, of course, impossible, as a handful of the wiser pioneers of the folk revival understood almost from the beginning.

Smith's vastly influential *Anthology* might have sounded like music from the beginning of time, but in reality the most ancient thing collected was dated to 1926, only three and a bit decades before Greenwich Village was discovered by *Time* and *Newsweek*, and barely twenty years before New York experienced its first 'folk boom'. The 78 rpms hustled by Smith, who had a hazy notion of copyright, were in any case products of modernity. Extensive lineages might have been involved in certain lyrics and melodies, but Smith's six long-players, first released by Folkways in 1952, were evidence only of a *previous* recording boom. He said as much himself: the purpose of the *Anthology* was to mark the moment when 'electronic recording made possible accurate music reproduction' before the Great Depression blew 'commercial folk music' away. If Richard 'Rabbit' Brown or Bascom Lamar Lunsford echoed in Village ears like near-alien voices, that had more to do with a failure of America's collective memory than with proletarian purity. Those sounds had been pop songs in their time.

The young Dylan's reputed purism is interesting, therefore. Harvey Abrams said he would track down a song all the way to an original Library of Congress recording, as though following a trail of counterfeits. Yet his knowledge of folk before his arrival in Minneapolis was necessarily slight, as he has admitted often enough. Rock and roll records had been hard enough to acquire in Hibbing; folk music was rare indeed. Did he become a purist almost overnight because that was the modish thing to be in the Scholar? Then again, he wasn't *exactly* a purist. Finding the source was supremely important; arguing over what was and was not legitimate and allowable held no interest for him.

What's odd, though, is that he was almost instantly hardcore, with no obvious preamble. What's odder still is that he had arrived at college announcing himself as a folk singer. Clearly, his trip to Denver had not, after all, been fruitless. Nevertheless, the conclusion must be that having set his course – and having abandoned his classes within a matter of weeks – he studied music intensively. He had to *know*.

*

He is generally remembered as quiet, 'shy', yet always eager to perform. Some of those who at first enjoyed his singing and playing got tired of it soon enough. No party was spared 'Dylan'. He was dressing the part too, in a version of the outfits by which the world would soon know him: 'Levi's, loafers or boots, and a blue denim shirt; in the winter, an old tweed sports jacket and a thick scarf. Always some kind of eccentric hat or cap.' He had also taken to saying – 'long before it was fashionable' – that school had no relevance to life. Given what he didn't know about life, this counted as a bold assertion. Such is the picture, the after-image, he presents, somehow shy and insufferable, ill-tutored yet confident. He had hitch-hiked to Denver and come back talking like an Okie. He had stolen records from people who trusted him. This too was an education. So Jon Pankake and Paul Nelson, editors of the small but influential *Little Sandy Review*, soon enough discovered that some precious English produced albums by a Guthrie copyist named Jack Elliott had disappeared from their collection. In legend, threats and menaces (and a flourished bowling pin) were required to secure the records' return.

Dylan meanwhile read Ginsberg and Kerouac and a lot else besides in short order, not because reading came naturally – quite the opposite, or so it has been claimed – but because again he needed to know. When a friend, Dave Whitaker, loaned him a copy of *Bound for Glory* in September of 1960 or thereabouts, an awestruck Dylan began instantly to behave as though the discovery was his alone, and Guthrie his personal possession. Then he began to possess Woody's music, song by song. He had found one of the things he was looking for.

By this point, depending on whether you believe his mother or his biographical stalkers, and date the visit to 1959 or to 1960, he had hitched to Colorado, played in a strip joint in Central City named the Gilded Garter, enjoyed a liaison with one of the performers and in effect been run out of town for thieving. Back on the road a few years later, Dylan was certainly able, according to those present, to display a knowledge of Central City. On the other hand, who on earth would give a job sight unseen, even in a dive, to a teenage black-key piano player from 750 miles away? Supposedly, the nameless stripper got him the gig, presumably in the absence of anyone local who could manage a tune. In an interview late in the 1970s, Dylan would claim to have offered delights such as 'Muleskinner Blues' between the main disrobed events. The old blue yodel in a strip joint? He would certainly be playing the song thereafter, and still performing it in Montreal by the summer of 1962. But this is one of those stories: the facts, if any, might as well be fiction.

In Minneapolis, come the autumn, we catch the sound of the real 'Dylan' of the period. Though Guthrie has already hit him hard, Spider John Koerner's memory is accurate: this is a prototype, a voice still testing the possibilities of a new style. Bootlegs aside, it can be heard on the 'soundtrack' album to Scorsese's *No Direction Home* delivering 'Rambler, Gambler'. In truth, the tape shows that Dylan still isn't much good.

*

One trope of twentieth-century Western life, in the United States as elsewhere, was the nagging thought that modern existence was unreal, fake, inauthentic. The Romantic movement in England had promoted the notion even as ordinary folk were being pitched into the entirely real horrors of the Industrial Revolution. Equally, the Romantic ideal was born, screaming, as a reaction to that revolution. A century or so on, T.S. Eliot was fretting over the spectacle of London, 'unreal city'. A couple of generations later, a self-described counter-culture found one of its manifestations in hippies escaping to communes, oblivious to their antecedents in millenarian sects, Zionist nation-building or Stalinist collectivism. It was all of a piece: the modern world, getting and spending, was a fake, an unnatural condition. Dylan was still using the word – always one of his favourites – in that *Biograph* interview: phoney.

This counted as a historical oddity: no sooner had America achieved unparalleled prosperity, no sooner had it risen to become the richest, most powerful nation the planet had seen, than it began to question its good fortune. People who had come through the Depression and the Hitler war were raising children who could do nothing better, it sometimes seemed, than bitch about their lot. The home-grown *isms* of post-war plenty had no obvious connection with the old ideologies. Smart young folk complained of *materialism*, or *commercialism*, or *consumerism*. They mocked the new suburban paradise. Books were published with knowing, cynical titles, books like *The Lonely Crowd*, *The Power Elite*, *The Organization Man* and *The Affluent Society*. They argued, sociologists or singers, satirical novelists or shrinks, that there was something hollow at America's heart.

And how could plain, honest, God-fearing people approve of that? They had tried to do the right things. They had fought for their country and worked hard. They *liked* their suburbs and their supermarkets, their appliances and their TV dinners. An antagonism was growing between the generations. By the 1960 election 90 per cent of households contained a TV set; 13 per cent had two. The box whispered soft encouragement, shouted its affirmations, poured forth news of the latest consumer wonders and amended reality for the sake of decency. Surely the ratings proved that this was what the people wanted? When the people repeated the Pledge of Allegiance, in a ritual that struck other democracies as odd indeed, they meant every word.

Congress had inserted 'Under God' into that oath after the Korean War. The legislature had ordered that 'In God We Trust' be inscribed on the coinage. A movement to establish a state religion was halted only by a higher power, the sacred constitution. In this, at least, the lawmakers understood the people: the country had returned – had flocked back, indeed – to faith during Dylan's childhood and youth. The idea that the United States was a nation wedded to religious belief from the moment of its founding is a myth of modern times. The tide ebbs and flows. God made his comeback in the 1950s.

In 1940, church membership had stood at 64.5 million; by 1960 the figure was 114.5 million. A better way to describe the numbers is to say that just before the war half of all Americans felt no need to join a church. By the time Dylan was 19, and preparing to launch himself on New York, where quizzical tunes on the consequences of blind belief awaited, only 37 per cent of the population resisted organised religion. Their numbers were falling steadily, too, in part because a general sense of vague faith had coalesced for social and political reasons, in part because of simple-seeming logic.

America was blessed; the evidence was all around. America was the exception among nations; one glance at the world proved it. Blessed, then, by Whom, and for what purpose? The answer to that question, taken to be the obvious conclusion, provides tinder for the fire in American politics to this day. Dylan, born Jewish, seeming agnostic – though not a line in any song says any such thing – would one day be drawn towards the heat in his turn.

In his childhood and youth the Protestant ethic was the definition of virtue. So how was materialism to be reconciled with Christ's endorsement of poverty? You get a clear sense of the times if you consider Norman Vincent Peale, a Protestant minister who in 1952 published *The Power of Positive Thinking*. As a historian would put it: 'The message of the Bible, according to Peale, was that God wanted you to get ahead.'[26] Sometimes it could seem that whatever America wanted or thought it wanted was fine by the Almighty. Even wars could be fought – as someone would shortly sing – 'with God on our side'. Nevertheless, Peale's book sold, like his other unashamedly optimistic perversions of the Christian message, in their millions. Jesus was no Commie. Bobby Zimmerman invented Bob Dylan not in a country infested with subversive attitudes, but in a nation awash with faith. He attuned himself to that, too, though it took a while for anyone to notice. God was there, in all sorts of disguises, from the start. It was, as it remains, an American thing.

*

I just got up one morning and left. I'd spent so much time thinking about it I couldn't think about it anymore. Snow or no snow, it was time for me to go. I made a lot of friends and I guess some enemies too, but I had to overlook it all. I'd learned as much as I could and used up all my options. It all got real old real fast. When I arrived in Minneapolis it had seemed like a big city or a big town. When I left it was like some rural outpost that you see once from a passing train. I stood on the highway during a blizzard snowstorm believing in the mercy of the world and headed east.[27]

Dylan quit Minneapolis, as he artfully suggests, because there was no reason to linger. He weaves a folk tale from the decision – suitcase, guitar, falling snow and a big world waiting – but the story is more or less true. The city that had seemed so big at first glance quickly shrank. This, surely, is how he was: greedy for experience, consuming knowledge and relationships with a voracity that spoke of a deep, gnawing need. Dinkytown was a dead end.

If folk music was the thing, in any case, there was only one place to be. It must certainly have made 'finding Woody Guthrie' seem like something better than a foolish idea. *Bound for Glory*, the great discovery, had no doubt given Dylan the belief that ramblin' off to New York was exactly the sort of thing his hero would have done, *had* indeed done, in his fashion.

---

26 O'Neill, *American High*, p. 212.

27 Interview with Cameron Crowe, *Biograph* booklet (1985).

DON'T THINK TWICE

Whether Woody would have picked the depths of a hard winter for his travelling season is open to question. In every possible way, the idea was crazy, and yet the decision had a sense of inevitability about it. You can believe the youngster had been thinking about it for what seemed a long time. Fame wasn't going to come looking for 'Bob Dylan' in Dinkytown.

Besides, there was a whole new audience waiting for the person he had decided to become. That job was the work of a lifetime.

I Was Young When I Left Home

There now is your insular city of the Manhattoes, belted round by wharves as Indian isles by coral reefs – commerce surrounds it with her surf. Right and left, the streets take you waterward. Its extreme down-town is the battery, where the noble mole is washed by waves, which a few hours previous were out of sight of land. Look at the crowds of water-gazers there.

Melville, Moby Dick

IN LOWER MANHATTAN, JUST BEFORE THE ISLAND'S 'EXTREME DOWN town', still defying the tyrannical grid of New York's street plan, sits the enclave of Greenwich Village. West of Broadway, north of Houston Street, south of 14th, and east of impossible for those who will never afford celebrity rental prices in gentrified bohemia, the Village is these days a 'historic district' watched over by a city commission charged with the preservation of architectural memory. The priority in any new works undertaken – for irony never sleeps – is to 'preserve the main facade'. Greenwich Village is not dead, exactly, but vital signs are sparse.

Self-evidently, this wasn't always the case. When modern arrivals pay top dollar for their nineteenth-century Revival-style apartments they pay for the illusion of cultural osmosis, for 'heritage', and for the chance to remark that Tom Paine wandered thereabouts, that Henry James Slept Here, that Mark Twain has just left the building. You name them, for Villagers can, or once could: James Fenimore Cooper, Herman Melville, Edgar Allan Poe, Walt Whitman, Edith Wharton. Locals who know of it can also summon the legend of Madame Katherine Blanchard's rooming house, the 'House of Genius' once situated on Washington Square South,[1] an establishment that at one time or

---

1. Luc Sante, *Low Life* (1991), Ch. 16. Even by the 1920s, Sante writes, the Village had become 'a theme park of bohemia'. 'Art is grand and literature is wonderful,' said Madame Blanchard. 'But what a pity it is that it takes so many barrels of liquor to produce them.'

another bedded down the talents of Theodore Dreiser, O. Henry, Eugene O'Neill, Willa Cather, John Reed and John Dos Passos. These days memories are short-to-vanishing, but in the old Village, on certain evenings, Stephen Crane fought the law (who won); Isadora Duncan danced; William Faulkner drank; and Edna St. Vincent Millay opened a playhouse.

Greenwich Village, specifically the precinct known now as the West Village, has been at the heart of America's culture and radical politics since the 1840s. In the first half of the twentieth century, when rooms were cheap – the prerequisite for an artistic ferment in any age – the trick was to remember who wasn't around. In the 1920s the cast included merely Marianne Moore, Hart Crane, e.e. cummings and Thomas Wolfe. As the writer Martin Green has observed, 'The Village lived in perpetual secession from the rest of the country.'[2]

One Gertrude Drick, known as Woe ('Is Me'), with Marcel Duchamp and four of their artsy chums in tow, had already cracked that joke in January of 1917 when the gang climbed a disused staircase to the top of the Washington Square arch.[3] Equipped with food, wine, Chinese lanterns and hot-water bottles, the expedition released red balloons and fired cap pistols into the freezing night air to celebrate the founding of the 'Independent Republic of Greenwich Village'.

In 1844 Poe had completed 'The Raven', so it was said, while starving in an attic on West 3rd Street, then known as Amity Street. In the 1850s Whitman had commanded his own table at Pfaff's vaulted beer cellar on Broadway, just above Bleecker, and there held court with Ada Clare, 'Queen of Bohemia'. In the 1890s, oblivious to his pending fate as Britain's Poet Laureate, John Masefield had been a teenage sailor down on his luck and scrubbing floors in a salubrious joint called the Working Girls' Home on the corner of Greenwich Avenue and Christopher Street. In 1912 the heiress Mabel Dodge had cultivated artists, writers and reds in a weekly salon at 23 5th Avenue while the Armory Show was plotted. By 1919 Hart Crane was subletting at 45 Grove Street; the next year he was living on Van Nest Place (nowadays Charles Street), all the while boozing himself into insensibility nightly

---

2   *New York 1913* (1988).

3   Gertrude, a poet of uncertain temperament, carried black-bordered calling cards featuring the single word WOE. Hers was the second attempt at secession. In 1913 the socialist (later fascist) journalist and activist Ellis O. Jones had made a similar declaration in Central Park. Few people showed up; it rained; arrests were made.

and writing the verses that would become *White Buildings* (1926). Crane's poetry was held by the smart critics to be startling, admirable and utterly incomprehensible: emblematic Village art.

In 1912 John Reed had joined the editorial collective of *The Masses* in their Greenwich Avenue headquarters. Like good socialists, the journalist and his comrades would hold votes on the poems and articles they were prepared to accept, if not pay for. A few years later Reed would write *Ten Days That Shook the World* while hiding out from government agents in the top-floor room of Polly Holliday's Greenwich Village Inn on West 4th Street, but in 1912 the comical tensions between art and ideology among the *Masses* crowd prefigured certain Dylan-shaped controversies. As an anonymous Village wit remarked of the 'Ashcan' illustrations favoured by Jack Reed and his friends:

They draw nude women for the *Masses*
Thick, fat, ungainly lasses –
How does that help the working classes?[4]

Bohemia, like 'bohemian', was the nineteenth century's best guess at a counter-culture. Politics, conventional morality and the death-grip of establishment art played their usual parts. Equally, the ancient impulse just to live for the day, and for the hell of it, brought bohemia's New York outpost into being. In every era disaffected youths, difficult artists and cussed dissidents were drawn from every corner of America. The Village was a refuge for anyone on the run from philistinism, family or themselves. In the shelter of this patch of Manhattan they could shed old lives like old clothes.

In another sense bohemia's lure was simple: it offered what couldn't be had elsewhere, whether that was new art, adventurous bookshops, relaxed morals, a touch of the exotic, or hard-drinking raconteurs with firm opinions. Amid the red-baiting, the Christian revivalism, and the soporific reassurance of Ike-the-father, these amenities were worth something in the middle years of the twentieth century. South of 14th was the place to be even for those, like Dylan, who had only the haziest idea of the nature of the place itself.[5] Robert Shelton reckoned that

---

4   Quoted in Robert A. Rosenstone's *Romantic Revolutionary: A Biography of John Reed* (1975), Ch. 7.

5   'Don't ever, if you can possibly help it, go below 14th Street. The Village literati are scum.' H.L. Mencken, advice to a young writer, *c.*1920.

in the late '50s the folk singers inherited an audience that had come in search of crazy Beat writers.[6] By the time the youth from Minnesota turned up, distinctions were already being made between curious visitors and the self-selecting citizens of the semi-autonomous urban republic. Their toehold on the island was much as it had been in John Reed's time.

> Low rents were one of the attractions, but no more so than the feel of an authentic village, protected by its meandering pattern of roads and lanes from the implacable rush of Manhattan. Here were quiet, twisting streets like Gay, Minetta and Christopher, tiny cul-de-sacs like Milligan Place and Patchin Place, charming mews on MacDougal Alley and the inviting oasis of Washington Square, all surrounded by swarming Italian and Irish ghettos, with raucous bars, homey restaurants and cheap grocery stores where credit was easily available.[7]

Things have changed. The theatrical life of the Village may be off-off Broadway still, but few of the celebrity-people who favour this section of lower Manhattan need dream now of fame or success, far less of revolution. All the artists have gone, so they say, to Brooklyn and beyond. A museum of a kind remains to mark their passing, one patronised by tourists, occupied by the daughters of former Republican presidents and haunted by misinformed enthusiasts still hoping to catch the echo of Kerouac and Ginsberg, of the hootenanny, and of a certain harmonica player.

*

As the story goes, Dylan arrives in New York City either in the fearsomely cold ('coldest winter in 17 years') December of 1960 or, more likely, in the last week of the dismally freezing January of 1961.[8] It is hellish, in any event. For 17 straight days the mercury is stuck below zero. 'Snow Coats City; Commuters Face New Tie-up Today; Fall Up to 9 Inches Feared; Icy Roads Slow Cars,' says the *Times*. Meteorologists

---

6 'At the time, the crowds of tourists were enormous, and one of the things they were coming for was to hear Beat poets say the f-word. So folksingers would alternate sets with poets, and gradually the folksingers began to predominate.' Tom Paxton, liner notes to *I Can't Help But Wonder Where I'm Bound* (1999).

7 Rosenstone, *Romantic Revolutionary,* Ch. 7.

8 The 24th of the month, a Tuesday, is generally nominated.

calculate that the bleak season is in fact the coldest in fully 28 years while the city authorities prepare to ban all non-essential vehicles from Manhattan's beleaguered streets. The newspaper is otherwise taken up with January 20th's inaugural ceremonials for America's 35th president, the youngest yet, one who has, in the vigorous modern style, kept his historic speech nice and brief.

All of that's coincidence, of course. Dylan *presumably* does not time his arrival in New York to catch the beginning of an era. Nor is John Fitzgerald Kennedy, just 43, quite the saint of hopes and democratic dreams whose slaying will somehow give a point to every protest song. JFK's tendency to hot war will do that instead. Still, for the purposes of context the conjunction is perfect: they begin together, in fast changing times, this pair. One day the music and the grainy pictures will blend. 'Let the word go forth . . . that the torch has been passed to a new generation of Americans,' exhorts Kennedy this snowy January. Up to a point, Mr President, as a representative of that new generation will soon enough seem to reply.

On arrival, Dylan is not yet 20 years of age. The unshakeable legend will say he has travelled halfway across the country just to find and meet Woody Guthrie. There is no reason to doubt it. But there is also little doubt that a youngster with precious little experience of the world and no readily discernible talent – no talent, that is, discernibly different from a thousand others – has also set out to find a life that will fit the identity he has begun to fashion. Even in his slow dying Guthrie is a symbol for all the music, and therefore the way of being, around which this 'Bob Dylan' has begun to form.

That said, the kid doesn't lack for courage: he is throwing himself, heedless, into the great unknown. He is lucky to be so naive. But he is also, as everyone will recall, ravenously ambitious. In all his early adventures there is never the slightest sense that Dylan has turned up in the Village just to try his teenage luck, to see how things might work out. He isn't hoping against hope: his conviction – or his need – is absolute. Nowhere among the many anecdotes is it said that he once contemplated returning to Minnesota with his tail between his legs. He stuck to his tale, too. Dylan would probably have wound up in New York had Woody never existed. Still:

> Woody Guthrie. He had a particular sound. And besides that he said something to go along with this sound. That was highly unusual to my ears . . .

I couldn't believe that I'd never heard of this man. I could listen to his songs and *actually* learn how to live . . .[9]

Woody's songs were about everything at the same time. They were about rich and poor, black and white, the highs and lows of life, the contradictions between what they were teaching in school and what was really happening. He was saying everything in his songs that I felt but didn't know how to [say].[10]

Such is the story even 44 years after the fact. Hearing Guthrie in Minneapolis or St Paul, Dylan has been struck to his core, says that story, as though by a revelation. *Bound for Glory* has affected him more deeply than any of Kerouac's *On the Road* riffs. Woody has changed his life, given it a purpose and a point. He has travelled east 'to visit Woody Guthrie' with just 'a suitcase and a guitar', with 'ten bucks in my pocket'. Of all the Dylan tales, this remains one of the best remembered. It is supposed to tell us something, no doubt, about art, inheritance and elective affinities. But unless you are also a naive teenager with an emotional reach greater than your grasp, it doesn't make much sense. All things considered, a pilgrimage in the depths of a fearsome winter, with no guarantee whatever that the traveller will be allowed anywhere near his hero, is a dumb move. Equally, in brutal truth, Guthrie is the least-likely role model.

Becoming Woody does not promise fame: by 1961, sickness has turned him into a spectre, a legendary ghost. Despite constant medication all the premonitory 'little twitches and shakes' have become 'gross, unpredictable lurches of his arms and legs and torso'.[11] It is a slow, cruel and ghastly business. In February, Guthrie's friends will gather at the One Sheridan Square basement theatre in the Village to sing, play and make their farewells. Handsome Cisco Houston, weeks from his own death from stomach cancer and about to record a final album, *I Ain't Got No Home*, will kiss the trembling forehead of his comrade for the first and last time. To men of Cisco's vintage, such gestures are available only *in extremis.* For these heroes, it's over.

Does Dylan therefore mean to take their place? If so, it's not what a later generation will call a career move. Woody is in no sense a star,

---

9   *No Direction Home* (film).

10   Interview with Robert Hilburn, *Los Angeles Times*, April 2004.

11   Klein, *Woody Guthrie*, Ch. 12.

or even particularly well known: his real fame will arrive after his death. On the other hand, Guthrie is as far removed from the experiences of a Camp Herzl-schooled youth as it is possible to be. Deracination is a word that has been put to ugly purposes, but often it seems to fit this 'son of Woody'. Again, this is no accident. Whatever the motives, this is his choice.

Inspired or not, the young Dylan isn't much good: former Dinkytown acquaintances agree on that. As a player and singer he is, at best, 'ordinary', and certainly near indistinguishable from all the many others struggling to sound like the real thing. Some will say he has improved greatly since that trip to Colorado, but a lot depends on the yardstick employed. The Village is more exacting than Minneapolis. To succeed in New York 'Dylan' will have to offer something better than decent. For now, he doesn't know much at all about folk music beyond the fact that it is a bit outré and agreeably bohemian, inherently oppositional and a dropout's handy excuse. He's learning fast, taking every opportunity that comes his way, but compared to some of the people he is about to encounter he knows nothing.

Since he isn't stupid, however, he certainly knows that *Bound for Glory*, first published almost 20 years before his arrival in New York, is less a handbook on how to live in the 1960s than a piece of social history. He probably also realises that Woody's memoir isn't necessarily believable in every particular. A lot of it is heroic fiction, the ballad of everyman versus the boss class. None of that will matter later, in the often-told Dylan tale. Nor will it bother many in 2004 that his *Chronicles* contains more than a few trace elements of *Glory*'s nearly naive prose in its alchemical mix. Guthrie, his career and his active life at an end, meanwhile doesn't know this youngster from the son of Abram. Still, the fable will say, the spark of genius – that 'something to go along with this sound' – will cross the generations, as though willed by fate.

*

It's a good story, improved by the fact that it all happened more or less as Dylan has described. He was *besotted* with Guthrie, and visited the sick man devotedly, and was nourished, somehow, just by being in the hero's presence. The ambition 'to join Little Richard' had been eradicated in the space of months by the need to find Woody. The great discovery was this: folk music was the antithesis of phoney; old songs could map the way to a new life. And life, as Guthrie seemed to show, was a gallery of possibilities. You could choose, be altered, become another person. New York was the *tabula rasa*, the blank page. For this Minnesotan, doubly negative and positive when he remembered, or thought he remembered, it was 'some place which not too many people had gone, and nobody who did go never came back'.[12]

Despite it all, the feeling persists that Dylan would have made his way to New York and the Village no matter what. This was more than a pilgrimage or a juvenile's romantic notion. Sick Woody Guthrie had provided the impulse, but not the motive, for Dylan's journey and for his metamorphosis. A career as a performer mattered, always mattered, as much as affirmation.

His consuming love for folk music was the biggest fact in his existence in 1961, but what he loved was its mysterious past, its enduring collective wisdom and strange mythic power. Scuffling around the dingy clubs and sad cafés of Lower Manhattan in those first weeks, amid a left-field music-business boom already approaching its end, among a hidebound seen-it-all crowd with a tendency to doctrinal cant, was another matter entirely. To begin with, the youngster was marked down as just another Woody Guthrie impersonator, passing the basket via the 'kitty girls' who cajoled customers into sparing change for hopeful performers.

It is safe enough to assume, though, that in one part of his mind he was also a little ambivalent about aspects of his new-found vocation. Even in Minneapolis, his lack of interest in all those *profound* arguments over tradition and authenticity had been noted. He was obsessed with originals, with the sources of the music, but cultural factionalism was never his style. He wanted the thing itself, not a debate over the thing. One of his talents, even then, was an ability to get to the point, and to avoid being pinned down. It could make him seem bumptious and self-involved. It could, and did, arouse suspicion.

In the end, the folkies were right, of course. He was interested in the music mostly because of where it might lead. That some of them deserved no better, laying down their laws or turning native song into effete nonsense, rowing Michael's boat ashore or discoursing on the relative merits of old Cecil Sharp's 22 discovered variants of 'House Carpenter', has too often been left unsaid. He 'used' them? That was the charge. So what was it they had in mind for him?

---

12 Interview with Cameron Cowe, *Biograph* booklet (1985).

I WAS YOUNG WHEN I LEFT HOME

At the end of 1961 Hunter S. Thompson would write an article for *Rogue* magazine – they declined to publish[13] – that captured something of the atmosphere of the Village and the folk scene's odd mixture of hip, fake and weirdly, implacably sincere. The Greenbriar Boys, Thompson's subjects/victims, would play their supporting roles in Dylan's story in due course.

> New York City. The Scene is Greenwich Village, a long dimly lit bar called Folk City, just east of Washington Square Park. The customers are the usual mixture, students in sneakers and button-down shirts, overdressed tourists in for the weekend, 'nine to five types' with dark suits and chic dates, and a scattering of sullen looking 'beatnics' [*sic*]. A normal Saturday night in the Village, two parts boredom, one part local color, and one part anticipation . . .

Even at 10.30 the place on the corner of West 4th Street and Mercer Street was so dead, wrote Thompson, 'even a change of scenery would have been exciting'.[14]

> So I was just about ready to move on when things began happening. What appeared on the tiny bandstand at that moment was one of the strangest sights I've ever witnessed in the Village. Three men in farmer's garb, grinning, tuning their instruments, while a suave MC introduced them as 'the Greenbriar Boys straight from the Grand Ole Opry'. God, I thought. What a hideous joke!
>
> It was strange then, but moments later it was downright eerie. These three grinning men, this weird, country-looking trio, stood square in the heartland of the 'avant garde' and burst into a nasal, twanging rendition of, 'We need a whole lot more of Jesus, and a lot less rock-n-roll.'

Thompson recorded that he was 'dumbfounded' when the crowd cheered and the Greenbriars answered with an Earl Scruggs arrangement of 'Home Sweet Home'. The writer mentioned smiling tourists and a 'bohemian element'. These were 'decked out in sunglasses, long striped

---

13 The piece, 'New York Bluegrass', was later collected in Thompson's *The Proud Highway: Saga of a Desperate Southern Gentleman, 1955–1967 (The Fear and Loathing Letters, Volume 1)*, ed. Douglas Brinkley (1997).

14 Formerly a restaurant, Gerde's had only recently opened for business – in January of 1960 – as a folk venue. The original building was demolished in the 1970s.

shirts and Levis'. A 'howling version' of 'Good Ole Mountain Dew' brought a (relatively) thunderous ovation.

> Here in New York they call it 'Bluegrass Music' but the link – if any – to the Bluegrass region of Kentucky is vague indeed. Anybody from the South will recognise the same old hoot-n-hollar, country jamboree product that put Roy Acuff in the 90-percent bracket. A little slicker, perhaps; a more sophisticated choice of songs; but in essence, nothing more or less than 'good old-fashioned' hillbilly music. The performance was neither a joke nor a spoof. Not a conscious one, anyway – although there may be some irony in the fact that a large segment of the Greenwich Village population is made up of people who have 'liberated themselves' from rural towns of the South and Midwest, where hillbilly music is as common as meat and potatoes.

The journalist discovered, predictably enough, that the Greenbriar Boys hailed from Queens and New Jersey, and not 'straight from the Grand Ole Opry'. Thompson called them 'fraudulent farmers', but allowed 'a distinctly un-hillbilly flavour' in their banter, even 'a distinct odour of Lenny Bruce in the room'. All things considered, Thompson concluded, 'the avant garde is digging hillbilly'.

> Here I was, at a 'night spot' in one of the world's most cultured cities, paying close to a dollar for each beer, surrounded by apparently intelligent people who seemed enthralled by each thump and twang of the banjo string – and we were all watching a performance that I could almost certainly see in any roadhouse in rural Kentucky on any given Saturday night.

Not too many years later the same writer would conclude that Bob Dylan was one of the most important men alive. Thompson wasn't kidding. Improbably, he would introduce a bunch of Hell's Angels to *The Freewheelin' Bob Dylan*, dedicate *Fear and Loathing in Las Vegas* to the singer in thanks for 'Mr Tambourine Man' and – according to his literary executor, Douglas Brinkley – regard any Dylan concert bootleg as 'the greatest thing of all time'. When the writer's ashes were blasted from a cannon at his Colorado farm after his suicide in 2005, 'Tambourine Man' was playing. Most of the millions of critical words expended on the singer could meanwhile be reduced to a single inimitable Thompson remark: 'Dylan is a goddamn phenomenon, pure gold, and as mean as a snake.'

That phenomenon was not commonly available at the end of 1961. Thompson – perhaps prompted by Shelton's 29 September review of Dylan and the Greenbriars in the *Times* – was sharp enough to see that *something* was going on in the Village, and knowledgeable enough to identify its models and inspirations. But why was Hip Central, NYC, suddenly besotted with the old-time music of rural, conservative America? Why 'hillbilly', of all things? As Thompson wrote, this was 'neither a joke nor a spoof'. So what was it? Something new was coming out of something old. The journalist was smart enough to spot it, but in December of 1961 an explanation was beyond him.

*

That was understandable. There were weird paradoxes at work. Folk was unquestionably the latest thing for Thompson's avant-garde and those 'beatnics', but already it was showing the symptoms of ossification. On the one hand, this movement had a lot to say about change, liberation and phoney materialism. It was, in someone's parlance, hip. Simultaneously, it was the only music ever to have been defined by a committee. In 1954 the International Folk Music Council[15] had ruled that folk was, inter alia,

> the product of a musical tradition that has been evolved through the process of oral transmission. The factors that shape the tradition are: 1) continuity which links the present with the past; 2) variation which springs from the creative impulse of the individual or the group; and 3) selection by the community which determines the form or forms in which the music survives.

As though to cover its bets, the council had also granted a dispensation to 'music which has originated with an individual composer and subsequently has been absorbed into the unwritten living tradition of a community'. This was one way of saying that no one quite knew what folk was, but they knew what it was not. It was, roughly, communally produced, orally transmitted, associated with specific regions or nations, the product, invariably, of native or working people and somehow impervious to ruthless capitalist systems of production.

---

15   Founded in 1947 at a meeting in London of delegates from 28 countries, presided over by Ralph Vaughan Williams. It is nowadays known as the International Council for Traditional Music.

It was also an ideal candidate for varieties of Marxist theory: any mention of 'the people' generally did the trick. As Barry Shank has written, understating the case, 'A folk singer is an odd sort of performer.' Amidst the warm solidarity of the sing-a-long, a Pete Seeger has 'immersed himself in the anonymous passing on of tradition that is the romantic view of the folklore process'. In this idealised communion folk singers 'erase self in the authentic performance of community'.[16] And no one gets paid.

An apostate could therefore err thrice over. Deviation from a correct interpretation of 'tradition' was heinous. Failing to be appropriately 'absorbed into the unwritten living tradition' before aspiring to recognition as an individual composer was odiously bourgeois. Selling out to commerce and copyright while failing to heed your obligation to 'the people' was the worst sin of all. Three strikes were not required: one would do.

Some people believed this stuff; some still do. Mercifully, most of the folk who made the music, on the plantations or in the mountain shacks, in union halls or in recording studios, city or country, were not numbered among the sophists. Yet as Dylan would remember almost a quarter of a century later, 'The first bunch of songs I wrote, I never would say I wrote them. It was just something you didn't do.'[17] The folk movement's problem, as scholars would have it, lay in the tension between 'autonomy and authenticity' (and in knowing what was meant by authenticity). Dylan would come to embody that tension.

*

As far as his parents knew, he was still involved in nothing more than a year's sabbatical, still getting music out of his system, still bound by a promise to return to college if things didn't work out. As far as friends and acquaintances in Minneapolis knew, he was embarked on a mad adventure. These are not minor details: *no one* believed in him. America's campuses swarmed with young men dragging guitars around. Most of those who could play were playing much the same songs as Dylan. His slight edge, if that, was an extravagant wealth of knowledge where Woody Guthrie's work was concerned. Driving towards New York in that fierce winter, after the

---

16   'That Wild Mercury Sound: Bob Dylan and the Illusion of American Culture', *boundary 2* (Spring 2002).

17   Interview with Cameron Crowe, *Biograph* booklet (1985).

loneliest of Christmases and a couple of diversions that had done nothing to raise his spirits, he had no reason for optimism. Guthrie was a talisman, but the talisman was also an excuse. All Dylan had was self-belief founded on a kind of guesswork. Only guesses begin to explain what persuaded him to believe he stood a chance. This one, for example: his alienation from Hibbing, his sense that it could never be the place for him, had evolved into a faith. That faith survived everything simply because there was no alternative. Music or bust: 'It was a way of life. And it was an identity which the three-button-suit postwar generation of America really wasn't offering to kids of my age: an identity.'[18]

*

Folk music is where it all starts and in many ways ends. If you don't have that foundation, or if you're not knowledgeable about it and you don't know how to control that, and you don't feel historically tied to it, then what you're doing is not going to be as strong as it could be.[19]

These days, Dylan commands universal respect as a master of the American folk tradition. Less clear is the means by which he achieved that eminence. A random example: in 2008 one music blogger will return to the 1993 album *World Gone Wrong*, Dylan's 29th in the studio, by confessing: 'What has always been amazing to me is that Dylan was familiar with so many and different types of traditional songs. These songs would literally define him as a person and musician just as well as most of his own compositions.'[20] Others have made similar observations. Even when his music seems as far from folk as it is possible to get, Dylan's verses contain what the critic Robert Christgau once called 'the non sequiturs, sudden changes of heart, and received or obscure blank spots in these buried songs'.

This was not a case of spontaneous artistic combustion: Dylan applied himself. More important is the fact that his outlandish originality as a songwriter, his revolutionary talent for the form, was deeply rooted. In his tyrannical 1919 essay 'Tradition and the Individual Talent', T.S. Eliot had asserted:

---

18 Interview with Mikal Gilmore, *Rolling Stone*, December 2001.

19 *ibid.*

20 David Bowling, 'The Discographer', at blogcritics.org, October 2008.

No poet, no artist of any art, has his complete meaning alone. His significance, his appreciation, is the appreciation of his relation to the dead poets and artists. You cannot value him alone; you must set him, for contrast and comparison, among the dead.[21]

The word from the captain's tower had it, furthermore, that 'what happens when a new work of art is created is something that happens simultaneously to all the works of art which preceded it'. Tradition is a two-way street. What we understand by the folk blues today we understand in part because of Dylan, and that understanding is in turn based on his first 'relation to the dead poets and artists'. Eliot also said that when 'the really new' turns up it alters what has gone before. The poet has to live in 'the present moment of the past'. Such was Dylan's instinct. If he thereafter revolutionised songwriting, it was thanks to dozens of old ghosts.

In 1961, all of this has yet to be learned. In the twenty-first century there is a romantic myth involving a Dylan who sprang up fully formed, an instinctive folk singer. Anything but. What will mark him out in his first months in the Village will be the speed with which he makes the myth seem plausible. Mimicry, theft, admiration yielding to sincere imitation, obsession, the immersion in the past: all of these will play their parts in transforming Bobby Zimmerman from Duluth, Minn., who has never done a day's manual labour in his life, or seen hard times, or marched out on strike, or ridden on a freight car's stinking boards, or prayed to a Christian God, or lived beneath Jim Crow laws, into the supposed embodiment of *folk*. One simple fact, still remarkable, is that he becomes 'Bob Dylan' at frantic speed. Another truth is that the part suits him.

In the bitter January of 1961 he sings Woody Guthrie songs all the way from Chicago to New York, annoying the hell out of his companions. Two students, Fred Underhill and David Berger, have invited 'Dylan' along to share the driving for the long, non-stop haul from city to city in, he will recall, a 1957 Impala.[22] His 'monotonic' singing is, so Berger will later remember, 'a pain the ass. As we got into New Jersey, I finally told him, "Shut the fuck up."'[23] In Manhattan,

---

21 Collected in *The Sacred Wood* (1920).

22 Fans of American cars say there was no such vehicle. Dylan must have meant the '58 model, the first of its kind. Obviously.

23 Interview with Berger published in Dylan fanzine *The Telegraph*, autumn edition, 1992.

the first of many non-fans drops his co-drivers amid the deep snow. Even the North Country boy finds the cold 'brutal'. Freezing, Underhill and Dylan catch the subway, supposedly, straight to the Village.

The first sighting is *probably* in the Cafe Wha?, a hole-in-the-wall establishment at the corner of MacDougal Street and Minetta Lane, between Bleecker and West 3rd Street. If this is journey's end, it leaves everything to the imagination. Why this club? The author of *Chronicles* says he was advised to go there, but doesn't say by whom. On a bone-chilling Tuesday afternoon the place is half-empty, but anyone who cares to offer unpaid entertainment to bored customers is invited to take a chance. When you have nothing, there's nothing to lose.

*

Dylan doesn't mention companions in his memoir. He says he spent the 24-hour ride from Chicago (perhaps via Madison, Wisconsin) nodding off in the back of the car (perhaps having already agreed to shut the fuck up). New York City, even at first sight, didn't intimidate him at all. Even then, right at the start, he knew he could rise above any obstacle. He was not in search of mere wealth or affection. In this telling, in fact, the youthful hero was already sure of his insights and his gifts. He knew himself to be tough and he required no one's approval. He was single-minded, inflexible, in thrall to an idea. He had no interest in doing the sensible thing. If he knew not a single person in a cold, forbidding city, meanwhile, that problem would be rectified soon enough.

It's another peculiar, elliptical and arresting little self-portrait. That Dylan was rash is easy to state: his decision to take off for New York was proof enough. But what of his inflexible certainty, his absolute self-belief? He wasn't yet 20 years old, and just starting out. His beliefs were about to undergo any number of changes. Yet he was also going to take the folk scene by storm, and he knew it? Bravado aside, there's that note again, the brazen sound of the self-created myth, the fantasy taken on faith. Bob Dylan was 'Bob Dylan' from the first instant. He was there from the beginning. So he says.

At this point, there's a movie dissolve. Suddenly we are sitting in Manny Roth's Café Wha? basket house, and Dylan is on stage, playing harmonica for a singer and writer of some talent called Fred Neil. This was the person he had been told to seek. On the other hand, as Shelton will attest, Roth was in the habit of 'offering jobs to young musicians who drifted in'. In another version it was hootenanny night – Guthrie had once used the old hillbilly nonsense word to describe rent parties – and an opportunity for anyone who fancied his chances to take the stage and pass the basket. But if this was a Tuesday night rather than the afternoon, as is sometimes supposed, with snow feet deep on the streets, witnesses to Dylan's New York debut must have been few indeed. He and Underhill took the opportunity, nevertheless, to ask if anyone had a floor they could sleep on. Again, it seems, they were in luck.

What happened when? Anyone who says they know for sure where Dylan was and what he was doing during his first days in the Village has mystical powers or a touching faith in narrative coherence. At this point the story is composed, at best, of incidents capable of being arranged in any number of permutations. Dylan might fib, but no one else who was present, or who claims to have been present, has ever managed to get the chronology straight: contradictions multiply. To begin with, it appears, the new arrival depended on the kindness of strangers, not least for his sleeping arrangements. As for the rest, no one is entirely sure. Dylan himself cannot, or doesn't care to, remember clearly.

In 1966 he would sell Shelton a tale of time spent hustling around Times Square for clients both male and female in the company of 'a friend' ('he's a junkie now') during those winter weeks. According to Dylan, he went nowhere near the Village during his first two months in New York. Instead, he and the friend were making up to $250 a night hanging around in bars, looking for clients: 'And we would do anything you wanted, as long as it paid.'

Though he entitled this section of his book '11 p.m. Cowboy', Shelton, the reliable Boswell, did not mock the story. Nor did he point out that James Leo Herlihy's novel *Midnight Cowboy* had just been published when Dylan was concocting a tall tale placing himself at the Times Square scene. As with his many other fabrications, you begin to wonder: did he really think he could get away with this? Did it amuse him to wonder about the things people would fall for? Dylan seems to have been gripped, somehow, by his own confabulations. The anecdote's only contact with plausibility came with the hero's belated arrival in the Village: 'I didn't have anyplace [sic] to stay, but it was easy for me. People took me in.' And they did.

*

The Village was not a tidy place. The singer Tom Paxton would remember that in this golden age many quaint doorways and entrance halls stank, for reasons you probably didn't want to imagine. Gentrification had yet to arrive and the precinct wasn't pretty, but the Village had any number of clubs, cafés and bars, and that was what counted. Few of the folk establishments were even in the neighbourhood of glamorous, but their proliferation in the late 1950s and early '60s was fundamental to the musicians of Dylan's generation. The money was lousy, generally, but the opportunities to play, listen, learn – and to steal ideas – were unmatched. This was an era of live music, sometimes licensed, and the Village was a bustling, hustling conservatoire. To that extent, Dylan's instincts were faultless: no other city in America, and certainly not in Minnesota, could offer a musical crash course, or a freewheeling bohemian life, to rival his new-discovered world on an isle full of noises. Soon enough people would say, in wonder, that he 'sprang from nowhere'. It was true in one, limited sense. But it was also true that Dylan received a folk-music education money couldn't buy.

Before long – in far-off 1963, indeed – he would be bathing his first forays into the clubs in nostalgia's vivid glow. Supplying sleeve 'notes' for Peter, Paul and Mary's *In the Wind* album, Dylan wrote:

Snow was piled up the stairs an onto the street that first
winter when I laid around New York City
it was a different street then –
it was a different village –
Nobody had nothin –
There was nothin t get –
Instead a bein drawn for money you were drawn for other people

In one version, Dylan's very first performance at the Wha? was *possibly* – Shelton says 'in early 1961' – as a harmonica accompanist to Fred Neil and *perhaps* the extraordinary Karen Dalton. Certainly a surviving photograph of the three, shot by Fred McDarrah of the *Village Voice*, looks about right for the period – the new arrival in cap and waistcoat, Neil hitting his 'big dreadnought guitar', Dalton like a Cherokee beatnik princess – but whether this was truly the first public noise made by Dylan in the Village is open to question, and probably beyond proof. Some have dated the picture – by what means it is hard to say – to February, and suggest it shows the trio at the Bitter End. If so, that club had only just opened its doors to the paying public. Shelton also wrote that his subject 'first performed in the Village at the Commons coffeehouse', a basement place on the west side of MacDougal, also later known as the Fat Black Pussycat.[24] *Chronicles*, as ever, sheds little in the way of light.

In the beginning, in any case, Neil was a guide and inspiration to any number of young hopefuls. Odetta would later testify: 'There are two voices I heard in my life that no microphone can possibly capture. Paul Robeson is one, and the other is Fred.' A former Brill Building songwriting pro, Neil would go on to supply the 1969 movie version of *Midnight Cowboy* with its remembered song, and Harry Nilsson with the matching hit, 'Everybody's Talkin'', when Dylan's 'Lay Lady Lay' was submitted 'too late'. In those early days Neil embraced the folk scene's prevailing attitude, almost its ideology. As John Sebastian, the folk and rock veteran (and someone who was actually born and raised in the Village), would say, 'He's a good friend of Lenny Bruce's, and of these jazz musicians, and they equated commercialism with some kind of selling out. With some kind of a denigration of what they did. And so this kind of selling out was something that Fred was very afraid of.'[25] Needless to say, most of those haunting the Village didn't have the option.

Neil would quit the music business soon enough, to all intents and purposes, to live off his 'Everybody's Talkin'' royalties and reinvent himself as a protector of dolphins down in Coconut Grove, Florida. His influence was and remains substantial, nevertheless, perhaps precisely because – the music industry is perverse – his name is now so little known.

You could say as much, and more, about Karen Dalton. In her time she represented the dark and bright sides of the Village simultaneously. A rare talent, arguably unique, she had a voice that was impossible to forget and an attitude towards living that was impossible to survive. Glibly, they called her – and Dylan was one – folk's answer to Billie Holiday, but the description did no service to either woman. Alive, Dalton made only two albums, neither perfect but each crackling with the static of a singular, hazy voice. She could not or would not handle

---

24 Formerly a theatre, latterly a Mexican restaurant named Panchito's whose owner in June 2011 described the original Commons/Pussycat as a 'cesspool'. Eighty-four-year-old Bob Engelhardt, owner of the building since 1963, told the *Wall Street Journal*: 'When you wanted to get drugs, get into fights and get with underage girls the Pussycat was where you went.'

25 In Richie Unterberger's *Urban Spacemen and Wayfaring Strangers* (2000).

the consequences of her talent. She disliked the recording process and, moreover, disdained her own songs. She was more receptive to drugs and drink, heedless, it seems, of her ravaged beauty. Dalton died in 1993, aged only 55, apparently of AIDS. In *Chronicles* Dylan remembered her fondly. White blues singers who sound the way Dalton sounded are hard to forget.

Shelton, paid to haunt the clubs and coffee houses, remembered a circuit to which 'an army of folk musicians . . . struggling for recognition' laid siege. The competition was fierce. Joan Baez and a few others had already begun to demonstrate that careers and hit records could be made uptown from old songs accompanied by a certain attitude. By 1961 the irrepressible former merchant seaman Dave Van Ronk – five years older than Dylan, a performer since 1956 and a recording artist since 1959 – was beginning to resemble a club veteran. Among younger musicians the likes of Len Chandler, Tom Paxton and Noel Paul Stookey – later the Paul in Peter, Paul and Mary – were already around, already working (just) and already ahead of the game. If anything, Dylan was a late arrival to this scene. In early 1961, folk was no longer a secret. Once again, the mainstream audience was starting to take an interest. 'On weekends, you couldn't move on the sidewalk, and all the coffeehouses would be crammed,' as Paxton remembered.[26] Bohemian or not, the Village was already a stop on the tourist trail.

In the beginning, Van Ronk was as important to Dylan as anyone in New York. A couch was always available at his 15th Street apartment when the youngster wasn't off in New Jersey on his Guthrie quest, or otherwise distracted. Van Ronk's wife, Terri, even attempted to find club work for Dylan, but it was an uphill struggle. If folk was then defined as the harmless noise of the Kingston Trio, or the painfully pure tones of Joan Baez, or the aching sincerity of Pete Seeger, Dylan was close to beyond the pale. That voice was hard to take; that big guitar was sometimes barely in tune. In legend, he looked a little *too* much like a hobo for the club owners' tastes. He was punk – and you can hear it on the early recordings – to the folk revival's easy listening.

It was a peculiar moment in urban American life. Folk was emerging both from the shadows of the red scare and from a long period of record-company disdain. Why, though, the sudden big-city enthusiasm for an old-time musical religion? Some of the answers are complicated, some self-contradictory. On the one hand, it is said, mainstream pop was an arid wasteland (as ever), unspeakably bland and entirely bogus. Yet the Village was full of people, like Dylan, who had been consumed by rock and roll only a few years before. The latest folk revival had already begun to find its voice with the Weavers' reunion concert at Carnegie Hall on Christmas Eve 1955, just as Presley was about to hit. Paxton would certainly attest that the album of the concert – 'Rock Island Line', 'Lay Me My Money Down', 'Wimoweh', 'When the Saints Go Marching In' – was where everything began for the younger generation of singers. Folk might have been a response to corporate values, conformism and the rest therefore, but not to the music that had gripped young America: the lines were drawn before rock and roll consumed the planet.

Equally, the idea that the revival was political in its origins, a mark of the Left's renewed confidence and the beginning of the counter-culture, is tricky to demonstrate unless you subscribe to the JFK myth. Being a red, or being called a red, was no more comfortable at the start of the 1960s than it had been a decade earlier. Mainstream America had internalised its anti-Communism, as Kennedy knew perfectly well. Joe McCarthy had been a close friend of the president's father, after all, and godfather to one of JFK's nieces: the shining new generation had old and grubby connections. America's power elite had not gone soft on radicals.

The likes of Seeger might have stayed true and fought through the bad times. The Village might have remained as politically liberal as ever. None of that explains the new, growing audience for old minority music. They wanted authenticity, all of a sudden, in the age of the organisation man, in the plastic age? Perhaps. But you could as well explain the folk revival as a form of nostalgia for an older, better, less complicated America. The phenomenon recurs periodically in the country's history. It can be seen in the unending cycle of religious revivals, even in the periodic moral panics. It can manifest itself as easily in right-wing politics as in the politics of the left. But then, when it came to music any number of Village radicals were also deep-dyed conservatives. The folk movement contained tensions enough in the early 1960s – old purist academic school versus Young Turk individualist school above all – and envy was never in short supply. Still, what had seemed a ludicrous ambition for the young Zimmerman in Hibbing or Minneapolis did not seem wholly absurd to the callow Dylan in the Village. *If* he could survive.

It was, almost literally, a hand to mouth existence. What came back when the basket had been passed around a listless audience could mean the difference between eating and going hungry. Living arrangements were improvised, at best. Friendships and loyalties could also be makeshift and perfunctory. But the folk who played the new folk music were ripe for Dylan, as he was for them, despite the rough edges. The confused anecdotes of his Village days all point in one direction: his timing was immaculate, almost supernatural.

*

The year 1961 begins with another Elvis hit, 'Are You Lonesome Tonight?'. Harper Lee's *To Kill a Mocking Bird* is entering its 23rd week on the *New York Times* bestseller list. *Floating Bear,* a poetry 'newsletter' contrived by Diane di Prima and LeRoi Jones, is meanwhile arriving in the mailboxes of the Village cognoscenti. Robert F. Wagner, breaking with Tammany Hall, is about to win his third term as mayor of New York, this time on the 'Democrat-Liberal-Brotherhood' ticket. His Honor has been attacking discrimination, and ensuring that black people get their share of city jobs. His liberalism doesn't extend to gay bars, however: those are harassed constantly by the Catholic mayor's cops. Gay men are entrapped routinely; even serving them drinks could lose a bar its licence. No one is singing radical folk songs about that issue: there are no such songs.

In a parallel universe rockin' Elston Gunn is on piano for the Bobby Vee smash 'Take Good Care of My Baby'. Anyone who knows better than the Greenbriar Boys can meanwhile catch Miles Davis at the Village Vanguard, or a 19-year-old Barbra Streisand singing 'I Want to Be Bad' at Bon Soir on West 8th Street. In this January, in 'folk', Michael is still rowing his damnable boat thanks to the Highwaymen, those harmonising frat brothers from Wesleyan University in the badlands of Connecticut. Country music is meanwhile proving yet again that Hank Williams died in vain by elevating Jimmy Dean and the tale of 'Big Bad John' to the top of the charts.

In this year a young Jean Redpath will arrive in the Village from Scotland to sing at Gerde's and give a Fifeshire lesson in tradition. She and Dylan will briefly become more than friends. In this year Tom Paxton, a US Army typist, will spend his leave time from the New Jersey front line and become the first truly Greenwich-made folk artist with a writer's gifts. A year on, Paxton's self-financed first album, *I'm the Man That Built the Bridges*, will seem more substantial than a self-aggrandising thing entitled *Bob Dylan*.

In May of 1961 the chairman of the Federal Communications Commission, Newton Minow, will give a speech denouncing TV as a 'vast wasteland'. It's worse than offensive, Minow will say: it's horrifically, corrosively *boring*. In this year traffic in Manhattan will move at six miles per hour, half the pace achieved by horses in 1911. In this year the Italian families who have called Greenwich Village their own for three generations will begin to summon the cops as wild 'hootenanny' noise disturbs their hard-earned sleep. On the first Sunday in April, 500 of the noise-makers will gather at Washington Square to sing and play. The cops won't care about peace, harmony and whatever: heads will be cracked, arrests made and 'the Washington Square Folk Riot' rendered into another Village legend.

*

Dwight Eisenhower's era ended on 17 January 1961. Three days before leaving office, the soldier-president addressed his people. He gave them warning, in terms as plain as any heard from the Oval Office. Then as now some wondered why he had waited eight years to find his voice, but at the end Ike did not equivocate. An obsession with defence spending risked turning America into a garrison state, he argued. The appropriation of power by a self-selecting elite – a conspiracy in all but name – had given rise to a 'military-industrial complex'. Eisenhower urged Americans not to 'live only for today, plundering for our own ease and convenience the precious resources of tomorrow'.

The idea that this president represented a kind of cultural entropy, a death-by-prosperity or a conservative coma, is another fragment of the Dylan story. Didn't the folk singer, as much as anyone, help to destroy that suffocating complacency and inaugurate the mind-altered 1960s? Many modern historians would argue, instead, that Eisenhower got a raw deal, and a bad press. For one thing, he left office with a 59 per cent Gallup approval rating.[27] For another, he had spent most of his eight years in office struggling against those who were determined to turn America into an armed camp. Cold War or not, Eisenhower – who also ended segregation in the armed forces after Truman had tried and failed – kept a lid, most of the time, on defence spending. It was his successor, the sainted JFK, the bright shining hope of the new decade, who pandered to the 'complex'.

In 1957, America was spending $38.4 billion on national defence;

27 O'Neill, *American High*, Ch. 10.

by 1961, it was $43.2 billion, with much of the increase due to inflation. A year after taking office, Kennedy raised the defence budget by 27 per cent, launched 'an unrestrained nuclear arms race', and approved the pointless and vastly profligate Apollo project to put an American on the moon. It was JFK's brightest and best, above all his defence secretary, Robert McNamara, who came up with the demented logic of 'mutual assured destruction'. If required, these suave liberals would bring down a hard rain.

In the January snows of 1961, Kennedy took office with a famous warning of his own. 'Let every nation know,' he said, 'whether it wishes us well or ill, that we will pay any price, bear any burden, meet any hardship, support any friend, oppose any foe to assure the survival and success of liberty.' Days later, the first full-scale test of the Minuteman intercontinental ballistic missile was carried out successfully.

Most people working in Greenwich Village could not have put a tune to that noise. Another American affliction was easier to describe, if just as hard to comprehend. Once again, Kennedy's engagement with 'the question' was slow in coming. As a senator, he had been less than conspicuous in the struggle against racism – in the era of red-baiting, he had been all but a cheerleader for McCarthy – but there were those who stood ready to force his hand. Their heroism is ill remembered. John Kennedy's attitude is meanwhile well documented if you care to see beyond the Camelot myth. As one of his biographers puts it:

Jack's interest in civil rights was more political than moral. The only blacks he knew were chauffeurs, valets, or domestics, with whom he had minimal contact. He was not insensitive to the human and legal abuses of segregation, but as [special counsel and speechwriter Ted] Sorensen wrote later, in the fifties he was 'shaped primarily by political expedience instead of basic human principles.' He could not empathize, and only faintly sympathize, with the pains felt by African Americans.[28]

During 'the great civil rights debates of 1957–60' the new man in the White House had been 'largely motivated by self-serving political considerations'. That was, of course, the Kennedy code, the standard operating procedure for the tribe. But in May of 1961 John F. would begin to run out of places to hide.

28   Dallek, *John F. Kennedy: An Unfinished Life*, Ch. 6.

Dylan was back in Minneapolis in that month, showing off his new skills, some of them impressive, to old friends, singing Woody's songs – 'Pastures of Plenty', 'This Land Is Your Land' – and others besides into Tony Glover's tape machine in Bonnie Beecher's apartment. In New York, he had begun to pick up some real gigs, finally. He had also, fatefully, begun to master a harmonica technique that would serve. As bootlegs of the tape reveal, 'Dylan' was coming into focus, albeit hesitantly. There was an irony in that fact to which, through no fault of his, he was at first oblivious.

In the American South, in the region that gave birth to the blues and hence, in convoluted lineage, to the art of Bob Dylan, a reminder was being offered that May of all the reasons why the music existed. Even in the Kennedy Camelot, those couldn't be ignored. That May, while the young Dylan was showing off in Minneapolis with 'James Alley Blues' and 'Man of Constant Sorrow', white people were firebombing a Greyhound bus full of innocent citizens in rural Alabama.

In 1960 the US Supreme Court had declared segregated facilities for interstate passengers illegal. In Alabama and elsewhere, the ruling was ignored. Some 400 non-violent volunteers – three-quarters of them under 30, half of them black, a quarter among them women – had therefore decided to oblige their government and their new president to enforce the law. The gesture was dangerous.

The bus travelling the Alabama back-country was first bombarded with rocks and bricks. Then its tyres were slashed and its windows shattered with axes. After the bomb was thrown in, and after smoke and flames had begun to fill the Greyhound[29], the mob barricaded the door. 'Fry the goddamn niggers,' shouted one philosopher. Even when state troopers arrived to aid the occupants in their escape, the passengers were attacked with baseball bats. Shortly afterwards, legal travellers both black and white on a Trailways bus were assaulted brutally after some dared to enter 'whites-only' waiting rooms and restaurants at bus terminals in Birmingham and Anniston, Alabama. Then *the victims* were arrested, charged and convicted of 'breach of the peace'.

These were the Freedom Riders: college students, civil-rights workers, young men and women of religion from all over the country. In October of 1960 some of them would found the Student Nonviolent Coordinating

---

29 A company founded in Hibbing, Minnesota, it so happens, in 1914 by Carl Wickman, a North Country Swede who guessed there was money to be made from transporting thirsty iron miners to the bars Hibbing lacked.

Committee. Only in 1965 would the Supreme Court overturn their Alabama convictions. In 1961, they were asking questions of America, and of John Kennedy. Soon enough, Dylan would be asking the same questions, and adopting the same cause. Black music, 'the real thing', was entangled in profound moral issues. The singer who had barely an original chord change to his name would rise to this occasion within the space of months. His transformation would be extraordinary. Before Dylan turned his back on the political hope of folk music he had first to give people that hope. When they bombed the bus, he was still ten days away from his twentieth birthday.

*

People took him in. The elusive, enclosed, unknowable Dylan of later years was nowhere evident in those days. Not in public places, at any rate, and not for those prepared to indulge his taste for fantastic yarns. He made friends easily enough in the first months. Kevin Krown, an acquaintance from Colorado and Illinois, introduced him to a talented player and singer named Mark Spoelstra in a café when coffee was all that the hungry aspirants could afford. Spoelstra was already finding work, of sorts. Soon he and Dylan were playing together at the Wha? Guthrie and blues, of course.

Then there was Fred Neil, messed up but amiable, willing to pay small change to backing musicians, or the New World Singers, ready to allow Dylan a few minutes on stage, make some meaningless introductions on his behalf and believe whatever stories he was telling about carnivals and life in New Mexico. Always there was Van Ronk, patient mentor, scholarly Trotskyist, no-nonsense teacher and provider of hospitality. At Folk City, meanwhile, Dylan often got to meet the nearly famous visiting acts. Then Woody's wife Marjorie introduced him to Eve and Mac McKenzie, friends of the Guthrie family who became, for a while, surrogate parents. Thanks to this couple Dylan met a dancer named Avril, possessor of an East 4th Street studio apartment, who seems to have been both deeply smitten and capable of forgetting the guitar player easily enough when the tears had dried. Other girls have been mentioned. So it went on: one thing led inevitably to another in folk's tiny community.

Visiting Guthrie in New Jersey, Dylan was introduced to a character newly returned from Britain who called himself Ramblin' Jack Elliott. The former Elliot Adnopoz had reputedly run away from his native Brooklyn (where the buffalo didn't roam) to join the rodeo while still an adolescent. Along the way he had been inspired to learn the guitar, or actually taught to play the instrument – the facts were subject to revision – by a real live singing cowboy. Ten years older than Dylan, Elliott had been a disciple of Woody since 1950. He had travelled with his hero and had even lived for a while in the Guthrie family home, the better to master the art of being an authentic egalitarian troubadour. He too had been inspired by *Bound for Glory*. He too had become a Guthrie facsimile, unabashedly absorbing the slightest details of Woody's voice and mannerisms until the original was reputedly heard to observe, 'Jack sounds more like me than I do.' Elliott had also been born a Jew. The parallels with Dylan were better than comical.

It didn't end there. The two became firm friends and Ramblin' Jack became Dylan's Guthrie surrogate. Soon it was Elliott's turn to be aped and followed everywhere. Soon the impersonator's impersonator had moved into a room a few doors away from his scale-model Woody in the shabby Hotel Earle (these days the Washington Square Hotel) at Waverly Place and McDougal. Jack was untroubled, it seems, by the absurdity of it all. Dylan was so eager for knowledge he didn't pause to be embarrassed. He was deaf to mockery, too. You can only wonder, queasily, how this fanboy would have behaved had Guthrie been fit and well. In the end, it didn't matter: Dylan was doing what he wanted to do. None of that book-learning; no more parental sighs and gripes; no more Hibbing, lost to the great world. Liam Clancy said:

> Do you know what Dylan was when he came to the Village? He was a teenager, and the only thing I can compare him with was blotting paper. *He soaked everything up.* He had this immense curiosity; he was totally blank, and was ready to suck up everything that came within his range.[30]

Those were wild times and innocent times. The Village bohemia was fulfilling its traditional function as an entertainment and an education. The little republic was full of tales in the making. In due course even the mundane episodes of a youngster's freewheelin' days would become near mythological, argued over and interpreted like symbolic panels in some illuminated manuscript. Hindsight rendered them magical. In early 1961, in hard reality, Dylan was just about getting by.

*

---

30 Interview with Patrick Humphries. First published in *The Telegraph* issue 18 (1984). Reprinted abridged in John Bauldie (ed.), *Wanted Man: In Search of Bob Dylan* (1992).

He had begun a serious attempt to write his own songs. There is evidence, slight enough, of certain previous efforts. The researcher and author Clinton Heylin, conspicuously, appears to have tracked down every last rumoured and half-heard, alluded to or fondly imagined effort. Wonderful stuff, no doubt, wherever it might be. The spring of the year 1961 brought the first actual evidence that Dylan was composing material – or at least writing lyrics – intended seriously for public performance, and for incorporation in his club repertoire. This was daring, or naive, or impertinent. It certainly wasn't standard practice in the Village, where mastery of the old, received songs generally counted for as much as 'originality'. Dylan, still in thrall to Guthrie, seemed to treat the development as natural, if not inevitable. He was not content simply to be a 'stylist' eager for the praise of the *New York Times*.

In 1961, Allen Ginsberg would publish lines dedicated to the memory of a mother who had perished in 1956 after time spent in the same 'asylum' that contained the often misdiagnosed, sometimes violent, Guthrie. 'Kaddish' began:

> Strange now to think of you, gone without corsets & eyes, while I walk on
> the sunny pavement of Greenwich Village.

In 1961, the bipolar alcoholic genius Robert Lowell would emerge from a locked ward at New York's Columbia-Presbyterian Hospital to publish several versions of Baudelaire, one of which, a rendering of 'La cloche fêlée', had the lines

> . . . sitting out the winter night, I hear
> my boyish falsetto crack and disappear
> to the sound of the bells jangling through the fog.

Less than a decade later, Lowell would give a surprisingly evasive assessment of Dylan. 'Bob Dylan is alloy,' the poet would say, 'he is true folk and fake folk, and he has the Caruso voice. He has the lines, but I doubt if he has written whole poems. He leans on the crutch of his guitar.'[31] This was some years after Dylan had claimed the previously unsuspected ability to hold his breath for three times as long as the

---

31 Ian Hamilton, 'A Conversation with Robert Lowell', *The Review* 25 (Summer 1971). The piece was reprinted in *Robert Lowell: Interviews and Memoirs*, edited by Jeffrey Meyers (1988).

legendary Enrico Caruso – if he *wanted to* – and 'hit all the notes' as a bonus. Lowell, you must suspect, wasn't aware of the joke. So he allowed lines but not – of course – whole poems, and a crutch rather than a poet's instrument. One critical tone was set.

How do you write? In all the endless discussions of Dylan, that primary, adolescent question is never addressed. 'Genius', the non-word, does service for an excuse instead: he did it because he could. There are other examples of extraordinary artistic development, fast as lightning, striking out of nowhere, but they don't help much. Hence the lazy habit of measuring the precocious Dylan against a Keats or a Rimbaud. It is worth asking, nevertheless, how a teenager whose formal education had been average, at best, got from 'Song to Woody', a piece 'written in the 1960th winter', 'in five minutes', with inimitable artlessness – 'I just thought about Woody, I wondered about him, thought harder and wondered harder'[32] – to 'A Hard Rain's a-Gonna Fall' in a little over a year. Neither melody has any claim to originality: just the reverse. But the Dylan who began as a rewriter of endlessly rewritten folk clichés found a lyric power in – and you can count them – a matter of months and a handful of seasons.

Reviewing *Chronicles* for the *Wall Street Journal* in 2004, Nat Hentoff – who would come to know Dylan as well as any journalist in the first half of the 1960s – probably spoke for most of those who had taken an interest in the new arrival on the folk scene.

> I first heard Bob Dylan in 1961 at Gerde's Folk City on West Fourth Street in Greenwich Village. He was 19 and wore a leather cap, blue jeans and well-worn desert boots. I was not impressed with his voice, and certainly not with his rather rudimentary guitar playing, but the lyrics to his original songs were intriguing.

'Song to Woody' tends to be nominated as his first 'real' or 'significant' composition. In 1961, though he scribbled constantly, there would be little enough in the way of competition for that title. Like some nineteenth-century art student learning life drawing by sketching the frozen forms of plaster busts, Dylan was acquiring proficiency by imitation, and by repetition. He was learning how to construct a myth, too. 'Song to Woody' was another of those songs, in fact the first of them, supposedly written in moments. Dylan believes in inspiration,

---

32 Interview with Gil Turner, *Sing Out!*, 1962.

remember, and wants us to believe that his songwriting operates like a sort of Zen poetry: long contemplation, then the flashing strokes of art. He clings, too, to the Kerouacian notion of spontaneity, almost of automatic writing. None of this can or should be explained to anyone, of course, and certainly not – the word that became a curse – *analysed*. Then again, as a wealth of evidence proves, Dylan is, and always was, a careful editor and reviser of his own verses. As with Kerouac, his spontaneity sometimes requires assistance. From the start, he worked hard at words.

His first success is an odd one, nevertheless. 'Song to Woody' is effectively a Woody Guthrie number about Woody Guthrie. It rests on a melody lifted from Guthrie – '1913 Massacre', a song commemorating the Italian Hall disaster when 73 people, copper miners and their families, died at a Michigan Christmas party – that Woody himself had adapted from older Irish or English songs to support a lyric derived, down to its 'echoes', from eyewitness accounts of a tragedy caused by the mine-owners' thugs.[33]

Whether Dylan understood much of this at the age of 19 is open to doubt. What he did grasp, untutored, was persona, role, the need to inhabit a song and a part, both as a performer and as the character he called Dylan. In 'Song to Woody' he borrows Guthrie's style, somewhat, but the person being invented and impersonated, real but not real, is this new character. That Dylan is the one a thousand miles from home, walking the roads, seeing America and its people. Young Bobby Zimmerman had done no such thing, of course. People have made much of the psychology implicit in the act of impersonation. Instead, you could say he was surrendering himself to a performance that would last a lifetime. The song itself, this pleasant-enough little thing remembered only because of its author, hardly matters.

A question, therefore: did imitation, perhaps even in Robert Lowell's poetic sense, cause originality? The enquiry will be relevant to the art of Bob Dylan for a long time to come. In 1961 imitation was, in one

---

33 Guthrie's melody relates to a group of songs – 'One Morning in May', 'The Nightingale', 'Green Bushes' – from the early nineteenth century, possibly by way of the standard 'Sweet Betsy from Pike'. That melody in turn, in the workings of tradition, has its roots in Britain in the 1820s. As Pete Seeger attested, Woody wrote his song on the Michigan massacre after reading *We Are Many*, the autobiography of the union organiser Ella Reeve Bloor, 'Mother Bloor', who witnessed what happened on Christmas Eve 1913.

sense, just what people on the Village folk scene did: fealty to 'tradition' encouraged the habit. Woody himself had never wasted too much time thinking up original melodies. But the example of 'A Hard Rain', one of the oldest tunes in any canon, well worn in the Scottish borderlands long before America was founded, would point to a talent capable of making the old seem startlingly new.

Everything comes from somewhere. 'Lord Randal' (or Rendal, or Ronald, or Donald) was a song long before it was revived in Walter Scott's 1802 *Minstrelsy of the Scottish Border*, or collected by Francis James Child in the 1880s. It lived all over Europe for centuries in one form or another before it became Dylan's news from the world's end. Scott – who managed a few ballad 'imitations' on his own account – decided it was 'not impossible, that the ballad may have originally regarded the death of Thomas Randolph, or Randal, earl of Murray, nephew to Robert Bruce, and governor of Scotland. This great warrior died at Musselburgh, 1332, at the moment when his services were most necessary to his country, already threatened by an English army. For this sole reason, perhaps, our historians obstinately impute his death to poison.'

Dylan decided he had other things to say about poisons at the start of the 1960s, and that six centuries long gone were no impediment. Scottish tradition, like all the traditions of the anglophone world, also spoke to him.

> O where ha you been, Lord Randal, my son?
> And where ha you been, my handsome young man?
> 'I ha been at the wild wood; mother, mak my bed soon,
> For I'm wearied wi hunting, and fain wad lie doon'

*

His first meeting with Woody Guthrie – if meeting is the word – was at the home of the Gleasons, Bob and Sidsel, in East Orange, New Jersey, less than a week after Dylan's arrival in New York. Each Sunday the couple, fans become friends, provided Guthrie with a respite from the 'booby hatch'. Which is to say they held open house for any cronies, acolytes and curious visitors who happened to drop by. The young folk singers among them would sit at Woody's feet and sing his songs. As Joe Klein records, 'he only liked to hear *his* songs'. When he could, Guthrie would cajole, correct and encourage his students. When they sang, so it is said, they tended to mistake the effects of Woody's illness for a vocal style, and copied those slurred efforts. It made Marjorie Guthrie more than a little uncomfortable. Of all the apprentices, though, Dylan is remembered, in the usual story, as the favourite.

There are other versions. In one, the first encounter with Guthrie takes place at the hospital. According to a story related in Lawrence J. Epstein's 'Dylan Watch' on the Best American Poetry website, four people – Dylan, Kevin Krown, a Mark Eastman and a forgotten other – travelled together to Greystone on that first weekend in New York.[34] They found Woody looking 'like a prisoner from Auschwitz', hard to understand but 'happy and excited to have company'. For reasons unexplained (as ever), he 'really bonded with Dylan'. All present 'felt that something significant was happening'. Guthrie asked a hospital attendant to fetch his guitar. Somehow he managed a few of the chords for 'This Land Is Your Land'. And then – of course – 'Bob and he sang the song together.'

Call it a variant tale. There are plenty of those, just as there are many people prepared to insist that Guthrie took to Dylan instantly at the Gleason house, and then asked after him when he was absent and extolled his virtues to anyone who would listen. Those witnesses are matched by people – Pete Seeger for one, Guthrie's manager and staunch friend Harold Leventhal for another – who insisted that Woody was too sick, and too far gone from the world, to manage any of that. It isn't just Dylan who shapes myths, or mishandles history. Sometimes memory falters. Sometimes the story is told for the sake of things as they should have been. Sometimes it helps to make 'Bob Dylan' real. Sometimes everything is just a story.

*

He's wearing sheepskin and denim and suede. Either that or a big, black oversized overcoat that brushes the ground. Beneath there will be the usual thick flannel shirt, the jeans or khaki trousers, and the motorcycle boots. It probably still isn't enough to keep him warm; he probably doesn't care. He has on that funny little corduroy hat – the 'Huck Finn' cap, the fisherman's hat – that he picked up somewhere along the line. Indoors he can't sit still: the fingers drum, the boot heels tap, the knees jiggle. Erect he bounces, dashes, hustles and bustles through the days and the nights. He doesn't understand repose. He even believes he sings too fast. The smoking habit he picked up early

---

34 Epstein got the story from Eastman, who died in 2008. Epstein admits that he 'cannot verify the facts'.

is as bad as ever: when he isn't holding a guitar, one cigarette follows another. He eats what he can – his mother would worry – and when he can. He lives on tips, spare change and whatever arrives from home. Yet he's still a little chubby, and he still has the waif's grin he knows how to use. He listens intently to all the music and to his elders – they are all his elders – and doesn't give much away. Most of the time he says very little and most of what he says is a lie or a disarming joke; when he drinks the lies take on cartoon lives of their own. Did anyone really believe that stuff about the freight cars and growing up in New Mexico? None of it really matters. The Village is his world, the music is his life. He has no business dreaming of success and no ability to think about anything else. It's not something he needs or wants to explain. He's been to the Guthrie family home in Queens. He's taken the 90-minute bus ride, pilgrim-devout, from the 42nd Street terminal all the way to the old, gloomy Greystone Park psychiatric hospital at Parsippany in cold northern New Jersey. He's been in Woody's presence, and sung Guthrie songs for Woody. He has the great man's card in his pocket. *He knows Woody.* Now the tiny stage at Gerde's – 'Open Every Night', 'Never A Cover Charge', 'Air Conditioned' – is free for a brief while. He can give his songs another shot.

Was that how it was?

There used to be a club called Gerde's Folk City. One night, Dave Van Ronk and I – apparently, we had already done our three songs apiece – [were] sitting there drinking beer, and this scruffy kid in a black corduroy cap – what they called a Huck Finn cap – and a harmonica rack and, I think, a Gibson guitar, got up and sang three Woody Guthrie songs. And both Dave and I, who were not easy, said, 'Yeah, not bad. Ooh, this guy's all right.'

So, in next to no time, Bob Dylan was the most talked about, argued about artist in the Village. I mean, they were accusing him of being a Woody Guthrie clone, which was nonsense. He didn't sound like Woody Guthrie. Jack Elliott, in his early days, sounded much more like Woody than Bob ever did. But Bob had a tremendous repertoire of Woody Guthrie songs. He knew Woody Guthrie songs no one else knew. And perhaps Woody didn't write 'em. Perhaps Bob did. But who knows?[35]

*

---

35 Tom Paxton, video interview with Ken Paulson, *Speaking Freely*, November 2000, available at the website of the First Amendment Center.

What is known is that after two and a half months in New York Dylan lands a fortnight's real work as a support act for John Lee Hooker at Gerde's Folk City. This is notable progress. Hooker, too, is getting his share of the folk boom (boom) after all those years scratching a living with electric boogie. He is another of those black musicians willing enough – and why not? – to play along with white liberal preconceptions. He and Dylan hit it off. Of the handful of songs the youngster is allowed as an opening act, one is probably the piece 'Written by Bob Dylan in Mills Bar on Bleecker Street in New York City on the 14th day of February, for Woody Guthrie'. The inscription on the manuscript left with the McKenzies speaks of post-adolescent pride, as do the Gerde's handbills – a named performer! – he sends off to Minneapolis to impress sceptics and friends. Hooker is described on the flyer as a country blues singer; Dylan is just a name. He meanwhile earns $90 a week, or $15 a show, or $3 a song. It isn't much, even in 1961. But the chance to meet, talk to, drink with and share a stage with Hooker is the greater compensation.

Then in May he returns to Minneapolis, perhaps to show those friends and sceptics what he has made of himself in a few months, a pop gun becoming a big shot, and perhaps to make the break with unhappy Avril as clean as it ever can be. One strand of biography and reminiscence has plenty to say about Dylan and women, his charisma and his confidence, the need for a girlfriend and the simultaneous infidelities. At this point, there is a less complicated story: he's not yet out of his teens. In other accounts he is also supposed to be shy. These things will become complicated later. For now, the notable fact about his early songs, real or rumoured, is that they do not yet encompass emotional intimacy. The Guthrie template, as Dylan conceives it, does not allow for that kind of lyric, and the apprentice lyricist does not feel the need. The 'singer-songwriter' will come later.

In fact, the indifferent home recording made in Bonnie Beecher's Minneapolis apartment in May could have the listener believing that this singer doesn't write at all: it's Woody still, in song after song, save for cautious excursions into the blues and one piece of novelty fluff, 'Bonnie, Why'd You Cut My Hair?', at the tape's end. The performances do not amount to much – he sounds hesitant, even nervous – but they are better than anything Dylan could have managed before his departure for New York. Listeners are impressed. People might actually pay money for this.

Back in New York, he also finds himself back with the McKenzies.

Avril has declined to wait around, patiently or otherwise, and gone to California. Disconsolate to some degree, no doubt, and unable to persuade the girl to think twice, Dylan begins to work seriously on his lyric writing. It's no pushover. Contrary to any tales later put about, genius does not manifest itself on command. 'Becoming Woody Guthrie', if that's still the ambition, is not as easy as it looks or sounds. Becoming something and someone more than Woody, a talent to pin to the name he has chosen for himself, is more difficult still. Dylan begins to get through a lot of paper, but none of these efforts make it into his repertoire or his records. Fortunately or not, the McKenzies preserve many of his discards.[36]

Dylan is undaunted, publicly at least, just as he is undeterred by the oratorical firefights among Village factions, each hung up on definitions of what is fit and proper behaviour for a true folk singer. He sings the traditional songs – often he sings nothing but – yet sings them in a style that is beyond individualistic. That's what everyone notices, the reason he becomes, as Paxton will remember, 'the most talked about, argued about artist in the Village'. For some, this Dylan's style is anathema, the antithesis of the people's music. Apparently the people are to remain forever anonymous. He senses the error, and perhaps the insult, inherent in that notion. Besides, whoever heard of an anonymous star?

*

There's a problem with some of this, however. Part of the Dylan legend depends on the image of the young maverick genius ranged against a stubbornly conservative folk establishment. The way the story is told these cultural commissars – 'a clique', as he would call them – ran the Village like a one-party state. Some accounts can make it sound as though humourless veterans patrolled the clubs nightly handing out cease-and-desist orders to anyone whose intonation wasn't up to scratch. Hence, supposedly, all the outrage when Dylan erased his political persona – overnight, in this symbolic

---

36 In December of 2010 Dylan's single-sheet block-capital pencil-written manuscript of the lyrics to 'The Times They Are a-Changin'', inherited by the couple from Kevin Krown, was sold by their son Peter at Sotheby's in New York for $422,500. Peter McKenzie had sold other Dylan jottings previously. On this occasion the successful bidder – of all the songs in all the auctions in all the world – was a hedge-fund manager.

drama – and began to work with amplified bands. He has not discouraged the idea.

> Folk Music was a strict and rigid establishment. If you sang Southern Mountain Blues, you didn't sing Southern Mountain Ballads and you didn't sing City Blues. If you sang Texas cowboy songs, you didn't play English ballads. It was really pathetic. You just didn't. If you sang folk songs from the thirties, you didn't do bluegrass tunes or Appalachian ballads. It was very strict. Everybody had their particular thing that they did. I didn't much ever pay attention to that. If I liked a song, I would just learn it and sing it the only way I could play it . . . But it didn't go down well with tight thinking people. You know, I'd hear things like 'I was in the Lincoln Brigade' and 'the kid is really bastardizing up that song.' The other singers never seemed to mind, though.[37]

This isn't true. Or rather, it *can't* be true. If the 'strict and rigid establishment' had possessed that sort of grip, Dylan would never have got a job. If he was hired, it was because the club owners were serving an audience – Hunter S. Thompson described them – far broader than the 'clique'. Tourists, so called, easily outnumbered the purists. The average customer on an average Village night didn't know the difference between a southern blues and a mountain ballad, and didn't care. That sort of person formed Dylan's small crowd: he *sounded* like a folk singer, but performed like someone who knew a pop song when he heard one. It's why he stood out. Around the clubs, nevertheless, there was something in the folk-type line for everyone.

Equally, though, the lone wolf Bobby who 'didn't ever pay attention' to anyone's strictures is another hero from the singer's imagination. To begin with, he also had his 'particular thing', his specialism. He was, so they said, the Woody Guthrie impersonator, seeking his own niche in a crowded market. To those who wanted to mock, he was less than that. In the beginning, for a brief while, he was a shadow to Ramblin' Jack Elliott's shadow.

But hold on: even *that* isn't quite true. Numerous Village veterans have certainly stepped forward over the years to testify to the sight and sound of Dylan as the never-forgotten 'son of Woody', the disciple, the copyist, the 'Guthrie jukebox', echo of an echo, trailing after Jack

---

37 Interview with Cameron Crowe, *Biograph* booklet (1985). The erratic capitalisations are as printed.

Elliott like an eager pup. Perhaps so. The discrepant fact remains that he sounded nothing like Guthrie.

There is not a track on his first album, not a song among the early bootlegs – even the tapes that are full of Woody's songs – that would cause you to mistake the young Dylan for his hero. For peculiar reasons of their own very few people, with honourable exceptions such as Paxton and Van Ronk, chose to remember the fact. Affected mannerisms were one thing. The tendency to fake an Okie accent was probably comical enough to stick in most minds. But while Ramblin' Jack was truly the Village equivalent of a tribute act, Dylan mostly sounded like Bob Dylan, even then.[38] Besides, which of the clique's pedants would have objected to a reverent rendition of a Dust Bowl ballad? That's not what the kid was doing. Too many people who didn't understand what he was doing simply invoked Guthrie as the handiest explanation. The myth would persist.

*

No one ever paused to wonder about the number of Americans who could have found Vietnam on a map in 1961. Representatives of their country had been dispensing advice to approved combatants on that Cold War front 'officially' since November of 1955 while the French, humiliated and defeated, prepared to quit the country. In 1959 two US 'advisers' had become the first Americans to die in this Vietnam in democracy's name. In May of '61, undaunted, John Kennedy would dispatch 400 of his finest special-forces troops to hand out more advice and oversee the training of a corrupt regime's army. JFK would have a lot to ponder in his first year in office: the aftermath of April's CIA-sponsored Bay of Pigs debacle in Cuba, the sinister and symbolic wall erected in Berlin in August and the endless travails of 'neutral' Laos. In 1961 he did not mean to pitch his combat troops into a long, bloody ground war. He guessed that the consequences, political and military, would be 'adverse'. Where Communism was concerned, nevertheless, lines had to be drawn, mostly – JFK knew his westerns

---

38 Elliott's albums of the period tell the story. There's *Ramblin' Jack Elliott Sings Songs by Woody Guthrie and Jimmie Rodgers*; *Jack Elliott Sings the Songs of Woody Guthrie* (both 1960); *Songs to Grow On by Woody Guthrie, Sung by Jack Elliott* (1961). The sentiment is no doubt admirable, but redundant. A track like Elliott's version of 'Talking Miner'/'Talkin Centralia' from *Jack Elliott at the Second Fret* (1962) leaves the listener with a single question. What's the point?

– in the sand. As the new president would tell the *New York Times*: 'Now we have a problem making our power credible and Vietnam looks like the place.'

Most other places would have served just as well. New York's freezing winter could equally have served as token of the chill that had consumed world affairs while Dylan's generation were edging towards maturity. The anti-Communist witch-hunts had been a sideshow to the real contest between democracy in the American manner and totalitarianism in the Soviet style. No one knew where it would lead. In the case of Vietnam, no one, least of all the advocates of military engagement, had begun to guess. Such was the background noise, nevertheless, in 1961, the distant rumbling beneath folk melodies in the Village and TV's gurgling *laff box*. In Vienna that summer the USSR's Nikita Khrushchev would tell Kennedy, 'If the US wants war, that's its problem.' It was Kennedy, nevertheless, who increased American troop numbers in Vietnam from 500 to 16,000 during his brief term, and inaugurated the nightmare.

Dylan was entering a milieu in which politics was urgent, the fears (and a few hopes) all too real. JFK was the sort of peacemaker who would not shirk from war: the charge of weakness was judged a worse fate. But the kind of war that seemed most likely in 1961 gave all the songs, old and new, a cold edge. Rational people thought it entirely possible that the world would end soon enough. 'Topical' was one poor word for folk music's response. The fact lends perspective to one aspect of a career. Launching himself onto the scene that year, the young Bob Dylan could scarcely have been anything other than a 'protest' singer. He had the wit to grasp the fact.

*

The girl in the picture was Suze Rotolo, Susan Elizabeth Rotolo. The picture was made on Jones Street near West 4th Street by Columbia's Don Hunstein in February of 1963; she had come into the world two decades before as a 'red-diaper baby', the thoroughly politicised child of the Communist working class, born in Brooklyn but raised beyond the bridge in Sunnyside, Queens. Suze was a native New Yorker. You can tell as much, if imagination allows, just from the *Freewheelin'* cover shot. Bohemia was home from home for her. She was Dylan's lover for three years, but she was also his teacher when it mattered. He took lessons from her in literature, art, theatre and politics that he probably would not have accepted from anyone else. Both were perilously young when they met – she 17 to his 20 – and Suze was on the side of the angels.

Her sister Carla, then working as an assistant to Alan Lomax, made the introductions on a hot day towards the end of July 1961, at a Riverside Church concert on Morningside Heights. Dylan was appearing along with Van Ronk, Tom Paxton, the Greenbriar Boys and Ramblin' Jack Elliot in an all-day event staged to launch a radio station dedicated to folk music. In *Chronicles*, Dylan remembered the girl as eroticism personified, a vision beyond his experience, with a smile that could illuminate a city thoroughfare. He compared her – stinting nothing after all the lost decades – to a Rodin statue made flesh. When he encountered Suze for the first time, says our poet, banana leaves swirled through the air. In New York City, too. Rotolo just liked the way he played his harmonica.

So: bananas? You cannot read *Chronicles* for long without realising that there is more to contend with than the issue of the author's reliability. Why banana leaves, of all things? Dylan wants you to wonder. Note then that the Buddhist *Vimalakirti Sutra* 'uses the image of the banana plant, its frail leaves in the wind, its watery trunk, as a metaphor for the human body and its impermanence', at least according to the Hermitary website ('reflections on hermits and solitude'). It sounds impossibly abstruse, but it fits. Why else use such an image? Reference is also made on the site, via the *Harvard Journal of Asiatic Studies* (v. 16, 1953), to the twelfth-century Japanese poet Saiygo. He wrote:

> When the wind blows at random
> go the leaves of the banana;
> Thus is it laid waste;
> Can anyone rely on this world?

One relationship was destined to go nowhere, in other words. It was doomed from the start. Decades on, it is safe for the author to say so: no harm done. *Chronicles* is full of these sly little ciphers, messages and hints. Only Dylan knows why.

Suze had seen him around, and had seen him perform at Gerde's, mostly with Mark Spoelstra or as an accompanist (harp players being something of a rarity, oddly enough) to others. She had 'noticed him more then but didn't think much about it'. No banana leaves were sighted.

I thought he was oddly old-time looking, charming in a scraggly way.

His jeans were as rumpled as his shirt and even in the hot weather he had on the black corduroy cap he always wore. He made me think of Harpo Marx, impish and approachable, but there was something about him that broadcast an intensity that was not to be taken lightly.[39]

She was organising for the Congress of Racial Equality (CORE) while designing posters and flyers for Gerde's in her free time; he was still trying to work out what his own ideas, if any, were worth. They flirted that day. In her book Rotolo summed up Dylan and their relationship, formed in an instant: 'He was funny, engaging, intense, and he was persistent.' Moreover, 'he was not linear'. They began to meet at Gerde's or one of the other clubs. She commenced his education – Picasso's *Guernica* at the Museum of Modern Art was not a bad start – and they talked, 'very earnest', about poetry, philosophy, art and politics.

That Dylan remained 'evasive and secretive' was troubling to a teenage girl in the grip of a strong attraction. 'His paranoia was palpable,' she wrote four and more decades later. The young Rotolo set that aside, for a while: lots of people in the Village told tall tales. Come the autumn, after Shelton's *Times* review and the Columbia deal had helped to put a little money in Dylan's pocket, they moved in together. Home was a tiny top-floor apartment above a furniture shop in a four-storey building at 161 West 4th Street. It would become Rotolo's private theatre.

Still you wonder. *A Freewheelin' Time* was written with the benefit of decades of hindsight. Who truly remembers a teenage self, the events as they happened or the emotions at stake? Judgement had been passed on Dylan many times by many people in the years separating the girl on West 4th Street from the woman facing death from lung cancer. There were no more first impressions available. But Rotolo, living with the memory of old wounds, makes assertions that would sound downright peculiar to anyone unfamiliar with Dylan's reputation. For example, even in 1961 her new boyfriend, this youth, acted 'as if he expected someone to show up and blow his cover and expose him'.

Who was expected? Exposed as what? Why was a cover story quite so important? As Rotolo records, no one in the Village much cared about the tall tales he told. Performers compose all sorts of fantastic narratives to embellish the ordinary for the interview or the standard bio. Confronted with facts, most would just laugh off the fictions. But for

---

39   *A Freewheelin' Time*, p. 91.

Dylan, with that 'palpable' paranoia – at 20? – the need for secrecy was urgent. 'Self-mythologising' doesn't cover it. He was in hiding. On stage.

*

Nevertheless, 'Dylan' was still under construction. Robert Zimmerman did not adopt the name legally until 1962, but the fact that he did so at all speaks of a determination to discard an entire prior existence, not to mention a family. Some performers get by with a mere stage name without destroying their histories. This one became Bob Dylan even when he had no clear idea of who that character might be. When forced to look back, the older man talks as though there has been a clear continuity between his several selves, as though he always understood the things he understands now, but in the first years of the 1960s the persona was little better than a sketch.

Obliged to provide a back story, the boy would spin yarns and tall tales, weaving traces of fact into the fictions. Sometimes, for no obviously apparent reason, he would lie outright. He killed off, disowned or erased his parents several times. Five pages into his memoir he describes giving an early interview to Billy James, Columbia's head of publicity, in which 'Bob Dylan', 'kicked out' from home, has just arrived from Illinois by freight train. The author concedes that this was – no kidding – 'pure hokum', but doesn't bother to explain himself, even 43 years after the fact. Either he simply doesn't think it matters, or the confession is itself a sleight of hand.

The person remembered by friends in Minneapolis meanwhile bore no resemblance to the person who appeared in the east. There he talked gruff of riding the rails, of working on a carnival ('when I was about 13'),[40] of Muddy Waters' Chicago bar and travels in Texas, New Mexico and North Dakota. The prodigy got his age right, usually, but even the circumstances of his arrival in New York were to be amended within a few years. He was good at telling stories, perhaps because he wanted them to be true, perhaps because he couldn't help himself. And perhaps because these fabrications were the story.

He had gall. People who knew what they were talking about, and who made a habit of telling the truth, were less likely to make a romance out of itinerant poverty. Cisco Houston was one. In February 1961, less than two months before his death, Woody Guthrie's old

---

40 Also from the interview with James. The game was played at around the time *Bob Dylan* was being recorded.

companion, once forced out on the road as a teenager by the Depression, sat down for an interview with Lee Hays, bass singer with the Weavers. Houston talked of being stranded, flat broke, in West Texas towns when he was no older than Dylan. He remembered the railroad bulls who persecuted hobos remorselessly, and the two men he saw killed on the tracks, crushed by freight wagons. 'It's no fun on the road,' Cisco said. 'There is *no* romance or glory doing it on freight trains. Buy a car instead.'[41]

'Reinvention' is one of the clichés of popular music, or rather, of things written about popular music. The talent picked up on the notion long ago. Every singer with pretensions and a career in need of a jolt can present a costume change, a new producer or a fresh set of session players as a grand gesture. Dylan is generally given credit for having pulled off more of these redrafts than most – 'electric', 'country', 'gospel', 'rock', 'Americana' and ever on – but these choices have had to do with artistic instinct. What's truly interesting is that the metamorphoses have rarely been in his immediate commercial interest. The creation of Bob Dylan himself – or should we say his emergence from Robert Allen Zimmerman? – is more puzzling. For one thing, the boy had the name before he had the need. He claimed the name before he had the talent to match. Above all, the name's adoption involved a deliberate act of self-destruction. It was not some showbiz career strategy. Who does that?

Neither the chosen name nor the manufactured identity would be mistaken for Jewish: was that it? Jews were less than prominent in Dylan's home town, and scarce enough in his home state. But testimony as to episodes of overt prejudice suffered by the boy has been hard to come by. Perhaps anti-Semitism – it wouldn't be the first time – preferred discretion, a whisper and a hint. You could as well believe that his parents' frosty attitude towards poor, blonde, Gentile Echo Helstrom had itself provoked an antipathy towards Jewishness. As in: if that was their attitude, they could keep it. The denial of his origins was a big deal, in any event. The wholesale denial of self, the subsuming of Robert Allen Zimmerman within Bob Dylan, was meanwhile to be a life's work. If you happen to believe that all of it was done somehow to insulate the real and original person, it becomes a work with few parallels.

---

41 'Lee Hays interview' in the 'Cisco's Words' section of the website Cisco Houston: The Web Home.

Suze Rotolo's memoir certainly testifies, and testifies repeatedly, to the young Dylan's profound reluctance to acknowledge his true identity. She discovered his real name only accidentally, on a night in the little West 4th Street apartment when he got home 'really drunk', dropped his wallet and spilled his draft card. Clearly, it was a detail he had meant to keep to himself. In other words, he had hidden the truth even from someone he loved and trusted more than any other. Years later, Suze said:

> The discovery of his birth name didn't have to be anything astounding or earth-shattering. I didn't mind his keeping secrets from others. I was accustomed to that, having grown up in the McCarthy era, when it was necessary to be wary of prying outsiders. But it was suddenly upsetting that he hadn't been open with me. I was hurt.[42]

More than that, Rotolo, having noted that Dylan was already 'paranoid' over his trivial secret, 'couldn't shake feelings of doubt about him' after the incident. Such was the price he would choose to pay, then and for years afterwards. Yet already, even on West 4th Street, 'Bob Dylan' had become a full-time job. If the job then came to seem a burden, if it earned him worlds of needless grief, he had no one to blame but himself. Privacy is one thing: this character was to have doubts about his need even to exist.

*

He was very young, she was younger: too many of the memoirs and tales seem to forget a simple fact. When Dylan first dared to play in the Village he was called a kid, often enough, simply because that's what he was. Ramblin' Jack had a decade on him; Van Ronk five years; Paxton four; Fred Neil five; Len Chandler six. Bob Gibson and Peter La Farge were another pair of veterans each with ten years of living – holding down jobs, travelling around, serving the country, going to war – to draw on. They had all been juveniles once, but Dylan was treated as a prodigy for an obvious reason. Even Phil Ochs, who didn't arrive in the Village until 1962, was a touch older than the singer to whom he would always defer. The fact that Dylan should begin so quickly to hold his own among this crowd contradicts the libel that he was some jumped-up juvenile who couldn't sing and could 'barely

---

42 *A Freewheelin' Time*, Ch. 10.

play'. Simple deduction says there was, for there generally is, a reason for the jealousy reported by Shelton. Dylan might not have been ready to make a record in the winter of 1961, but John Hammond was not mistaken: he had 'something'.

*

On the October day when the first recording contract was signed, as one party would later recall, the same John Hammond gave Dylan an advance copy of *King of the Delta Blues Singers*. The gift of 16 recovered Robert Johnson tracks was perfectly judged for a youngster addicted to old records and obscure sounds. It might also have been Hammond's sly way of guiding his protégé, as though to say, 'Here. You think you know something. You don't know about *this*.' Few did, in 1961.

Those who believe that Hammond did not contribute much to *Bob Dylan*, or to Dylan's development, forget the producer's musical hinterland. Those who believe, meanwhile, that the veneration of Robert Johnson in the 1960s by Dylan, Eric Clapton, Keith Richards and the rest has distorted the history of the blues outrageously do scant justice to John Hammond. His first response to Johnson, the guitarist who could sound like three men playing simultaneously, was unconditional; he knew he had heard something extraordinary.

Hammond had written about this discovery for *New Masses* (under a pseudonym) as far back as 1937, stating flatly – impertinently but not wrongly – that 'Johnson makes Leadbelly [*sic*] look like an accomplished poseur'. Just over a year later, Hammond had made efforts to find the wandering phenomenon for the first of his 'From Spirituals to Swing' concerts at Carnegie Hall. Though the impresario didn't know it, Robert Leroy Johnson had already died at the age of 27, probably of strychnine poisoning, in Greenwood, Mississippi. Twenty-four years later the producer knew exactly what he was doing, nevertheless, when he handed Dylan an acetate of *King of the Delta Blues Singers*.

The album assembled in 1961 thanks in part to Hammond would acquire a vast influence, among white audiences at least. It would also, it is true, give rise to all sorts of legends and half-truths about the blues and about Robert Johnson. On the most severe account, *King of the Delta Blues Singers*, issued on Columbia's Thesaurus of Classic Jazz series, was near pernicious, still another example of a white world rendering the black experience mysterious and alien. The tale found no room for a guitarist who, as a matter of fact, was happy enough

193

playing white pop tunes. The sleeve notes, written by the jazz producer and editor Frank Driggs, certainly did not hesitate to fill the gaps in Johnson's brief biographical record.[43] Driggs would later confess that there was plenty he didn't know about the guitarist, but ignorance had been no impediment.

> Robert Johnson appeared and disappeared, in much the same fashion as a sheet of newspaper twisting and twirling down a dark and windy midnight street. First, he was brought to a makeshift recording studio in a San Antonio hotel room. A year later, he was recording again, this time in the back of a Dallas office building. Then he was gone, dead before his twenty-first birthday, poisoned by a jealous girlfriend.

Johnson had expired, as noted, at the age of 27. His death certificate gave the cause as syphilis, but the story that he was poisoned – by whom is not known – appears to have been true. Was he transformed, though, from a ham-fisted guitarist into a genius in the space of months thanks to a midnight pact with the Devil made at the crossroads of Highway 61 and Highway 49? Dylan would use that piece of supernatural nonsense to his own advantage late in 2004, telling Ed Bradley of CBS that he too had 'made a bargain'. The amused look on his face said the noun was open to all kinds of interpretation.

In reality, Robert Johnson had practised hard, found a good teacher[44] and listened attentively to records and the radio. His mastery of the blues depended, too, on promiscuous 'borrowing' from his elders and peers, but in truth this Delta king was obscure in 1961 mostly because

---

43 See Barry Lee Pearson and Bill McCulloch's *Robert Johnson: Lost and Found* (2003). Elijah Wald's *Escaping the Delta: Robert Johnson and the Invention of the Blues* (2004) also lays to rest myths and ghosts alike.

44 Reputedly a farmhand named Ike Zinnerman, a figure of mystery, so Dylan writes in *Chronicles*, unknown to the history books. Some research suggests, however, that Ike was real enough and that his name was – true story – *Zimmerman*. Teacher and pupil are said to have practised in graveyards, for the sake of quiet rather than for the Devil's sake. The Satanic pact myth was meanwhile as old as Robert Johnson, and first attached, before the First World War, to *Tommy* Johnson, later best known for 'Canned Heat Blues'. This Johnson acquired his skills from Charley Patton, to whom – to keep things symmetrical – Dylan would dedicate the song 'High Water' on the 2001 album *Love and Theft*.

his records had failed to sell in the 1930s. In that respect, he was the opposite of unique.

The Depression had almost destroyed the recording industry. Sales in 1929 were somewhere between 100 million and 150 million; by 1933, they had fallen to 10 million, possibly to as low as 6 million. With black workers hit savagely hard as *average* unemployment in the US reached 31 per cent, the audience disappeared. Across America, jazz and blues musicians saw their careers destroyed: becoming "obscure' was easy. In the northern cities, six in ten black men could find no work; in the south, devastation was absolute. In a single April day in 1932 one-quarter of the farm acreage in Johnson's native Mississippi was auctioned off. The state then had a debt of $14 million and only $1,000 in its accounts. Nor did the Depression hit bottom, as is too often supposed, during the following winter. A few months after Johnson made his first recordings in November of 1936, the Roosevelt administration, always more orthodox than its rhetoric, decided to impose spending cuts. A deep, 13-month recession followed, pushing unemployment back to 20 per cent and ending whatever hopes Robert Johnson had entertained for a recording career.

By 1961, less mundane explanations were preferred. Johnson was turned into a stock character in the usual white narrative of black American art. The sleeve notes to Hammond's gift to Dylan also made the basic error, seemingly impossible to resist, of interpreting the lyrics to Johnson's songs as slices of autobiography. That habit would not die easily.

Dylan was entranced, nevertheless, by *King of the Delta Blues Singers*. It was, as he would write much later, like Woody all over again. Why had this profound secret been kept from him? Hammond said this guy was a match for anyone. Dylan heard an artist who seemed to have appeared fully formed from the brow of a god.

Johnson was like no one else. His songs, their couplets fluid, intertwined and apparently careering in all directions in their subject matter and tone, were like no other songs. Somehow they were complete and perfect in themselves. Yet in the space of a few verses these songs seemed to give off a consuming blaze.

Such would have been a fair description of Dylan's own writing a little way down the road. In 1961, Dave Van Ronk told him only that Johnson lacked originality, that he had borrowed a lot – and this was perfectly true – from the likes of Skip James. Dylan understood the point. He understood, but didn't bother to argue because it didn't matter, and because he didn't care. He understood something else entirely, something coming from deep within the music of Johnson that made his own creative sense respond like a vibrating echo chamber.

The youth became desperate to understand how this magic was accomplished. He began to copy Johnson's words onto scraps of paper for closer study, stripping the verses into their component parts, analysing their mechanisms, identifying the techniques of free association and allegory, working out how the bluesman could conceal so many large human truths within what sounded, at first hearing, like throwaway nonsense. Sixteen Johnson songs (from a legacy of only twenty-nine) were giving Dylan the education of a lifetime. In his memoirs, he would compile what amounted to an artistic autobiography from the tale of his first encounter with the Delta king. Large truths and apparent nonsense: remind you of anyone?

Everyone talks about Dylan and Woody Guthrie, as they should. Robert Johnson tends to be mentioned within the generic categories of 'blues' and 'influence'. You can't blame Dylan for that: he has been insisting on the primary importance of Johnson to his work for decades. In 1973, persuaded to publish *Writings and Drawings*, his first collection of lyrics and other pieces, he included a dedicatory poem

> . . . to the rough riders, ghost poets,
> low-down rounders, sweet lovers,
> desperate characters,
> sad-eyed drifters and rainbow angels – those high
> on life from all ends of
> the wild blue yonder.

And then:

> To the magnificent Woody Guthrie and
> Robert Johnson
> who sparked it off . . .

One of Johnson's traits as it related to Dylan is worth remembering. If the bluesman was mysterious, it was a matter of choice or necessity. As an itinerant musician, Johnson travelled the length of the country, from the Delta to Canada. Along the way, he would pick up friends and lovers. But he took extreme care – and no one is quite sure why – to ensure that the girl and the folks in one town knew nothing whatever about the folks and the girls in any other town. By one count, Robert Johnson went by at least eight different names, each one accompanied by a different story.[45] His early life was already obscure, his date of birth uncertain. Only two photographs are certain to exist, though a third – published in *Vanity Fair* magazine in 2008 – certainly *looks* plausible. The elusive Johnson's self-created myth makes the young Dylan's fantasies seem almost plausible too. Perhaps the affinity was deeper than even he realised.

*

Dylan had arrived in New York just as the 35th president's inaugural address was sounding in the country's ears. On 20 January 1961, John Fitzgerald Kennedy had invited his fellow Americans not to 'ask what your country can do for you. Ask what you can do for your country.' The thought of what America's interior darkness, the excrescence of something latent and brutal, might do to a president had not been guessed. Dylan's ascent would depend greatly, nevertheless, on the things that were happening, and about to happen, in his country. The songs would begin to appear at precisely the right moment.

By sheer coincidence, a 29-year-old *New York Times* hotshot writer named Gay Talese and the photographer Marvin Lichtner were to publish a portrait of the city in the year of Dylan's arrival. *New York: A Serendipiter's Journey* is an odd mixture of gee-whiz and would-be hip, but in striving to render the sights and sounds of the world-city in 1961, it gives the tang of another age. Some of it is weird and arresting enough for a Dylan song, too. Talese wrote:

New York is a city for eccentrics and a center for odd bits of information. New Yorkers blink twenty-eight times a minute, but forty when tense. Most popcorn chewers at Yankee Stadium stop chewing momentarily just before the pitch. Gum chewers on Macy's escalators stop chewing momentarily just before they get off – to concentrate on the last step. Coins, paper clips, ballpoint pens, and little girls' pocketbooks are found

---

45 See Ted Gioia's immaculate *Delta Blues: The Life and Times of the Mississippi Masters Who Revolutionised American Music* (2008).

by workmen when they clean the sea lions' pool at the Bronx Zoo.

Each day New Yorkers guzzle 460,000 gallons of beer, swallow 3,500,000 pounds of meat, and pull 21 miles of dental floss through their teeth. Every day in New York about 250 people die, 460 are born, and 150,000 walk through the city wearing eyes of glass or plastic.

A Park Avenue doorman has parts of three bullets in his head – there since World War I. Several young gypsy daughters, influenced by television and literacy, are running away from home because they do not want to grow up and become fortune-tellers. Each month one hundred pounds of hair is delivered to Louis Feder at 545 Fifth Avenue . . .

Forty-three years later,[46] Dylan for once explained his reasons for moving to New York without reference to the sanctified image of a young pilgrim kneeling at the bedside of Woody Guthrie. Los Angeles was never considered, he explained, 'because everything I knew came out of New York'. By that he meant baseball and radio shows, but also 'all the record companies'. In his head, even in 1961, with scarcely a public performance worth the name under his belt, he was already under contract and in the studio. 'It seemed,' he said in 2004, 'like New York was the capital of the world.' He was very clear about that.

Folk music was big there. Rock and roll, a four-year fancy, had been swallowed in the corporate maw; Elvis was in the army; and the payola scandal had confirmed the belief of the pure in heart that 'commercial' music was all about money. Folk – cheap to play, cheap to stage – was the principled alternative. Folk was serious, literate, intellectually credible, and it had a political point for anyone dissenting from the national smugness. It wasn't – that word repeated, thesis and antithesis – phoney.

Its aficionados could be a little self-righteous, perhaps. Dylan wasn't entirely wrong about overbearing cliques. Some had a tendency to lecture, and a habit of judging. Certain of them would even make out that money didn't matter. Prominent Village types also had an unfortunate knack for turning egalitarian song into an elitist affair. The little tin gods were jealous gods. Such people could be quick to forget that their cherished traditional songs had once been someone's cheap pop. They wanted to believe that the singers of blues and the makers of mountain music, the anonymous banjo players, cowboys, union organisers and hobos, had been more *authentic* in their poverty

---

46 *Los Angeles Times*, April 2004.

than the consumer society's TV-addicted, advertising-led majority. Authenticity was important. Folk music was a way of keeping in touch with the original, essential spirit of America, and of keeping it alive. It was all, in the pure sense, political.

Politics crossed oceans. The folk revival, and hence the blues revival, was born of certain ideological assumptions, and those were international. Over in little England, the pre-Stones Keith Richards encountered exactly the sort of contradictions that were soon to bedevil Dylan, and at much the same time. Just loving the blues wasn't enough.

> The purists thought of blues as part of jazz, so they felt betrayed when they saw electric guitars – a whole bohemian subculture was threatened by the leather mob. There was certainly a political undercurrent in all of this. Alan Lomax and Ewan MacColl – singers and famous folk song collectors who were patriarchs, or ideologues, of the folk boom – took a Marxist line that this music belonged to the people and must be protected from the corruption of capitalism. That's why 'commercial' was such a dirty word in those days. In fact the slanging matches in the music press resembled real political fisticuffs; phrases like 'tripe mongers', 'legalised murder', 'selling out'. There were ludicrous discussions about authenticity.[47]

Suze Rotolo, child of Communist parents, knew all about this species of sectarianism. One odd theory even holds that she was somehow being used at this time to keep her boyfriend on the ideological straight and narrow. Her older sister, Carla, was working as a secretary to Alan Lomax, the musicologist and reputed Communist – the charge was a banal smear – liable to be at the heart of any folk clique. Dylan spent a lot of time listening to Carla's extensive record collection. He was thereby claimed, supposedly, on behalf of the people's music and progressive song. The FBI's attempts to entrap Lomax were less ingenious. Still, as Suze remembered:

> Bob Dylan had to be the Next One, the Prophet. He fit the bill with the extraordinary songs he was writing, which expressed wisdom beyond his

---

47 *Life*, Ch. 3. Lomax had moved to England in the early 1950s in an effort to escape the McCarthyite frenzy. His influence on the British revival was much as Richards describes. In 1957, *Punch* magazine published a cartoon depicting a weary farmer, with the caption: 'I've got these Alan-Lomax-ain't-been-round-to-record-me blues.'

years. The old-left wanted to school him so he would understand well and continue on the road they had paved . . . Bob listened, absorbed, honored them, and then walked away . . . He didn't want to accept the torch they were trying to pass to him.

The scary thing was that many from the so-called New Left of the sixties felt equally betrayed by Dylan. The orthodoxy that had kept the left cemented to Stalinism should not have even remotely been carried forward into the movements of the sixties. But old philosophies and attitudes tend to linger on and have an influence even after the declaration of their demise.[48]

Yet what, artistically and politically, was the left's 'position', their working hypothesis? Essentially, that poverty and oppression, suitably idealised, were the guarantors of authenticity: without suffering, there was no truth. Their 'real' folk music depended on the misery of others. What became of sharecroppers' blues if black people gained their liberty and their economic rights? What would remain of the fine old mountain music if real hill folk got decent jobs and a few consumer durables? Some of their children might even hanker after TVs and cars and electric guitars. To put it no higher, certain of the presiding spirits in the Village, and all the bourgeois types who trailed in their wake, hadn't thought things through.

It didn't occur to them, for example, that the finest American folk music in recent memory had probably emerged from 706 Union Avenue, Memphis, Tennessee, and the studios of Sun Records. Nor did they pause to doubt their right to decide what was, and was not, acceptable as folk music. Even the fact that the cherished memory of the Popular Front was tainted utterly by Stalinist bad faith got overlooked. Dylan's brief, tortured relationship with the politicised folkies, from acclaim to ordure, would bring the whole argument into sharp relief. No definition of folk music has ever contained or embraced all the people from whom folk music emerges. A tricky detail.

Yet who is this Dylan today if not the purveyor of purest *Americana* – not that he cares for the word – the one who tells interviewers why folk music is fundamentally important, the senior citizen who is held up as the artist above all others who is truly connected to those old, ancient roots? These days he dedicates songs to Charley Patton, the Mississippi farmer born who-knows-when and dead circa 1934. The

---

48   *A Freewheelin' Time*, pp. 266–7.

twenty-first-century Dylan even objects to the latest recording technology, and to kids 'tuned out to real life' with their ears welded to MP3 players. He sounds as though he would take an axe to it all, if he could.

Back then, he was preoccupied with the creation of something new. He worked hard, soaking up music, and learned all he could from anyone who would teach him, taking what he wanted when the need arose. It was no easy task, either, to maintain the persona of the Bob Dylan who had, apparently, just blown in off the street, and who just happened to have a guitar to hand. Being Dylan was a serious business, as Suze Rotolo recalls in that slyly affectionate memoir:

> Much time was spent in front of the mirror trying on one wrinkled article of clothing after another, until it all came together to look as if Bob had just gotten up and thrown something on. Image meant everything. Folk music was taking hold of a generation and it was important to get it right, including the look – be authentic, be cool, and have something to say. That might seem naive in comparison with the commercial sophistication and cynicism of today, but back then it was daring, underground, and revolutionary. We believed we could change perceptions and politics and the social order of things.[49]

'Be authentic, be cool, and have something to say': Rotolo's precis all but sums up the primary-stage Dylan who signed John Hammond's contract on the last day of September 1961. He could not be properly authentic – hence those tall tales – but cool was a function of his charisma. And he had plenty to say. The fixed legend of the 'controversy' over his eventual adoption of the electric guitar – or rather his return to the instrument, fair warning having been given – overlooks the power of his writing in the second half of 1962 and in 1963. In that period he invested the topical song, so called, with invective, wit and a lyrical weight that no one else could match. Soon enough he would joke or complain about the 'protest singer' tag, but he occupied the moment with genuine commitment. So it seemed, at any rate.

*

Slowly, he was becoming someone. On stage and in his first, fumbling efforts to write, a character was beginning to form. It could have been

49   *ibid*, Ch. 1.

anyone except Robert Zimmerman. When he appeared in his first real concert at the Carnegie Chapter Hall – $2 a ticket, but no sell-out of any sort – in November of 1961, the programme notes were both copious and preposterous. Revealing, too, in hindsight.

> Bob Dylan was born in Duluth, Minnesota in 1941. He was raised in Gallup, N.M. and before he came to NY earlier this year, he lived in Iowa, S. Dakota, N. Dakota and Kansas. He started playing carnivals at the age of 14, accompanying himself on guitar and piano. He picked up the harmonica about 2 years ago.
>
> The University of Minnesota gave him a scholarship. He went there for some five months, attended some dozen lectures and left. He learned many blues songs from a Chicago street singer named Arvella Gray. He also met a singer, Mance Lipscomb, from the Brazos River country of Texas, through a grandson that sang rock and roll. He listened a lot to Lipscomb. He heard Woody Guthrie's album *Dust Bowl Ballads* in South Dakota. In fact, Bob Dylan has sung old jazz songs, sentimental cowboy songs, top 40 Hit Parade stuff. He was always interested in singers and didn't know the term 'folk music' until he came to New York.

Truth and lies. He wove them together with care – Duluth involved a birth certificate, after all – but not carefully enough. The fantasies of this weary veteran of the dusty road would be picked apart before long. Arvella Gray (James Dixon) was real enough, a blind bluesman – he liked to sing 'Corrine, Corrina' – who could probably have been found performing out on Chicago's Maxwell Street on the very day of Dylan's concert. Mance Lipscomb was better than real, and certainly Texan. Having been 'rediscovered' down on the farm, he had issued albums in both 1960 and 1961. 'Rocks and Gravel (Makes a Solid Road)', a song Dylan would attempt in 1962 – and impertinently copyright in 1963 – was featured on the second of these. Gray, 'the Singing Drifter', had no records of his own in circulation but had appeared – in 1961, by remarkable chance – on a Heritage label anthology of Maxwell Street musicians. Dylan was therefore claiming an acquaintanceship with men whose names were new even to blues aficionados: that was clever. Meanwhile, his imagined childhood self was still rolling and tumbling through those dusty old fairgrounds. Yet even in this torrent of nonsense, the prodigy managed to say one pertinent thing: 'I can offer songs to tell something of this America, no foreign songs – the songs of this land that aren't offered over TV and radio and very few records.'

The fantasies spring from somewhere: they have roots. It is far too easy to talk of Dylan in this period as a 'Woody Guthrie impersonator', or even (that old favourite among the rock writers) 'a myth-maker'. What does that mean, if it means anything? Dylan was hardly the only scam artist in the Village inventing weird tales, but he had a very precise idea of who he would *rather* have been. This 'Bob Dylan' wasn't just invented on the spur of the moment.

Equally, though it is clear he was telling people what he thought they wanted to hear, it's fascinating to wonder how he *knew*, from the start, what it was – who it was – they wanted in hip, progressive New York. It seems obvious, for example, that he picked on Blind Arvella Gray, who would not get to make his only album until 1972, precisely because the musician was profoundly obscure. That sort of thing would go down well with the cognoscenti. Somehow Dylan knew it. He had empathy.

His 'Dylan', this possessive character, was cast in line of descent from Huck Finn, John Ford, Steinbeck and Woody. He was, even in 1961, a recognised American type, a ghost from the back roads. And Bobby Zimmerman wished he had been that type. It was the only way he could make sense of himself.

*

Dylan had written 'poems' in childhood. His mother had a memory of a son spending part of his teen years writing. His first attempts to set verses to music didn't amount to much – Clinton Heylin counts twenty-seven songs for 1961, only three of which would be taped for his first album – but these were folk prentice pieces, not verse. In Montreal, a certain Leonard Cohen, senior to Dylan by six and some years, was already well travelled on that road. He had published his first book of poems, *Let Us Compare Mythologies*, in 1956, while still an undergraduate. When Dylan was arriving in New York, Cohen was in Montreal readying a second volume, *The Spice-Box of Earth*, for the press. Here was a sophistication and an intellectual verve that the young folk singer could not begin to match. Cohen's work, always very different from Dylan's, would in time provide one answer to the question of whether song lyrics could 'survive on the page' and therefore deserve to be recognised – by those equipped for the job, naturally – as poetry. But 1961 was a confusing year, in any case, for anyone still interested in the art of verse.

On the one hand, Allen Ginsberg would publish *Kaddish and Other Poems* in San Francisco. In near diametric opposition, Robert Lowell would release the austere free translations, or rereadings, he called *Imitations*. LeRoi Jones, Theodore Roethke, Denise Levertov, Richard Wilbur: each of these notable Americans would also publish in Dylan's first New York year, but confirm only the variety of American verse. It did not amount to guidance. There was, as usual, an argument going on. Besides, it isn't obvious that the youngster was reading any of this stuff. His education under the guidance of Suze Rotolo and others had not yet begun. He knew his Beat writers; in later years he would claim a thorough immersion in Poe and Whitman. What he read and when is less clear. By his own account, partially rebutted by others, he certainly wasn't reading dead Dylan Thomas. Some day, someone will ask the obvious question: if not, why not?

In those days, every teenager in the Western world with the slightest interest in verse took the Welshman as a starting point. *Bob* Dylan would deny borrowing the name, but by the end of his first year in New York he was acquiring the habit of denying anything that failed to suit whatever plans were in his head. He was becoming lost in those denials. The only consistent statement amounted to this: nothing was owed to anyone save to Woody, dead blues singers, and the thing he and Suze knew as 'the truth'.

If Dylan became, however briefly, a political singer, the credit probably falls to Rotolo. She certainly provided a lot of the information – on race, Cuba, the Left's heritage and politics generally – that would help to shape a topical songwriter. On one occasion he admitted that he 'checked the songs out with her'.[50] Suze certainly did not discourage the idea of protest. Many years later, she was still making large claims for Dylan's minor works in the civil-rights era. Of 'Hattie Carroll', 'Emmett Till', 'Medgar Evers' and the rest, she wrote: 'These songs are not just newspaper stories rewritten in rhyme; they speak to the human condition, and to human conditioning. That makes them timeless.'[51]

Soon enough, Dylan would dissent from that fond, slightly foolish endorsement. The lists of his most enduring songs do not often include the ballad written upon the death of poor Emmett Till. But as the writer David Hajdu,[52] among others, has noticed, the singer would

---

50   In conversation with Robert Shelton, *No Direction Home*, Ch. 4.

51   *A Freewheelin' Time*, p. 90.

52   See *Positively 4th Street: The Lives and Times of Joan Baez, Bob Dylan, Mimi Baez Fariña and Richard Fariña* (2001/2011) for the correlations between Dylan's personal life and his changes in artistic direction.

leave the girl behind at around the time he was leaving 'the movement' – politics, folk, solidarity and the rest – behind. This, it is concluded, was hardly a coincidence. The great betrayal, if betrayal it was, was personal, too.

*

Israel 'Izzy' Young, operator of the Folklore Center on MacDougal Street where Dylan would while away afternoons in the back room among records and 'extinct song folios of every type', took a gamble on that first concert at the Carnegie Chapter Hall. This was on the first Saturday in November, just a couple of weeks or so before Dylan and John Hammond were due to set to work in Columbia's studios. First, the singer was interviewed by Oscar Brand on WYN. Before the performance, Dylan gave a performance.

> Brand: Now let's return to our guest this evening. His name is Bob Dylan and on November 4th he will be at Carnegie Chapter Hall in a very exciting concert of songs that he's collected since his first days, when he was born in Minnesota, and then he went down to the south-west. He travelled around the country with carnivals and, as we heard earlier, he's collected many songs from many people. Bob, I know that that means when you travel that much that you hear a lot of songs. But doesn't it also mean that you forget a lot of songs that way?
>
> Dylan: Oh yeah. I learned, forgot quite a few I guess. An' once I forgot 'em I usually heard the name of them. I looked 'em up in some book and learned 'em again.
>
> Brand: Can you read music?
>
> Dylan: No, I can't. But this here song's a good example. I learned it from a farmer in South Dakota. An', er, he played the autoharp. His name was Wilbur, lived outside of Sioux Falls, when I was visiting people and him, heard him do it an'. . . I was looking through a book sometime, saw the same song and remembered the way he did it. So this is the song. ['The Girl I Left Behind' follows.]

Some say only 52 people were in the audience at the Chapter Hall, some that 53 attended: perhaps they counted the artist. In any event Young, the promoter for the evening, had not promoted conspicuously well. Fifty-some people at $2 a time had to be set against a booking fee of $60 for the little hall on West 57th Street. On the partial bootleg of the show that survives it doesn't quite sound as though Dylan was playing to a near-empty room, but since the venue was capable of seating 225 people, the occasion could probably be classed as intimate. The performer was game, nevertheless. He could charm a crowd – or even a small group – with the best of them.

> Kind of got lost coming up here tonight. Took a subway. Got off somewhere on 156th Street, started walking back. I got hung up in a Cadillac store an' . . . So I'm not here on time. Almost run over by a bus, so I took another subway. On to 34th street an' I walked up here . . . Come pretty prepared tonight. I got a list on my guitar. This is a new list. I used to have one on my guitar about a month ago, that was no good. Figured I'd get a *good* list. So I went around an' put the list on first. Then I went around to other guitar players an' I sort of looked at their list, copied down songs on mine . . . Some of these I don't know so good . . .

Of the 21 or 22 songs he performed only a handful would make it to the *Bob Dylan* sessions. He had the nerve to sing Guthrie's '1913 Massacre' early in the set, however, and finish up with 'Song to Woody', its bastard sibling, second to last. But this beginner put on a good show, for all that, given the paucity of his experience. Sometimes belief conquers all.

*

As that year ended, eggs were 30 cents to the dozen and gas 28 cents a gallon. *La Dolce Vita* was the seductive foreign language movie hit, but Dylan wasn't aiming to live that sweet life. *Breakfast at Tiffany's*, another big-grossing picture, involved a New York he didn't recognise. There had meanwhile been yet another nuclear test beneath the Nevada sands: people were supposed to feel reassured. That spring the Soviets had put a man in space; a month later an affronted America had retaliated by pitching Alan Shephard through the surly atmosphere for 15 minutes in a tin can named *Freedom 7*. Back on earth, the world was as divided as it had ever been. The USSR would soon be erecting a wall in Berlin to mark the fissure. That spring, all of Times Square had been cleared of its pedestrians and its cars, its hustlers and tourists, for a futile civil-defence air-raid drill. No one explained how the exercise was supposed to help if missiles came over the pole, but everyone was talking World War III. Dylan was scanning the newspapers, taking all of this in and hoping for a 'topical song' for his pains. Why not? That year Elvis had delivered one of the biggest-selling records ever made, but he had done it with a truly terrible thing called 'Surrender'. It was as though he too was disowning rock and roll once and for all, a king preferring abdication. You could almost see Presley's point. There was no future in that.

*

As the year ended Dylan had professional representation, a local reputation, the approval of a *New York Times* reviewer, a record deal, a loyal girlfriend, a big-name producer and a bunch of songs laid down, for better or worse, on Columbia's high-grade tape. He had even managed to write some songs of his own, too, after a fashion. Ready or not, he was Bob Dylan, finally. There was no one else left. He had no inkling of what the fact entailed.

Boy in Search of Something

Here I was in New York, city of prose and fantasy, of capitalist automatism, its streets a triumph of cubism, its moral philosophy that of the dollar. New York impressed me tremendously because, more than any other city in the world, it is the fullest expression of our modern age.

Trotsky, *My Life*

THE LEGEND SAYS THAT IN THE MIDDLE OF APRIL 1962 DYLAN TURNED up on a Monday night at Gerde's Folk City with two-thirds of a song he had jotted down in a nearby café. Forty-two years later he would tell the *Los Angeles Times* that 'Blowin' in the Wind' was written 'in ten minutes', and that he had merely 'put words to an old spiritual'.[1] Perhaps so. By the twenty-first century nonchalance had become a Dylan habit. Any piece of work the world deemed important was probably just some little thing he had put together, and no big deal. Yet even if his memory served him well, this song's alleged origins belied its consequences. Covered since by hundreds of performers in hundreds of mostly improbable ways, and still liable to intrude on Dylan's concert repertoire,[2] those three verses with their nine unanswered questions changed a 21-year-old's life. They also, it is entirely fair to say, transformed popular music, the art of the age. Enter the singer-songwriter.

After a fashion: others had of course written and performed their

---

1   Usually identified (not least by Dylan) as the 'slavery song' 'No More Auction Block'/'Many Thousands Gone', a spiritual said to have originated among runaway slaves in the 1830s. The musicologists may be right about the old melody, but a casual listener to Dylan's version of 'Auction Block', as recorded in October of 1962 and released finally on 1991's *The Bootleg Series Volumes 1–3*, would not rush to that conclusion. 'Blowin' in the Wind' at best lifts a few bars of its supposed original.

2   By July of 2012 he had played the song on 1,091 occasions in public places, according to his alarmingly specific website.

own songs long before Dylan tried his hand. Woody Guthrie would be only one conspicuous example, but he was, equally, one of very few. Columbia Records, still struggling to swallow its doubts over producer John Hammond's latest beyond-category discovery, had signed a performer, not a writer. As far as the music industry was concerned in 1962 the only relevant singer's art, the folk singer's art in particular, was interpretation. No one of real note wrote and sang. The only surprise in Dylan's first album had been the inclusion of even two 'self-penned' – the journalese is itself revealing – folk-type numbers.

Guthrie had been a rare exception to the folk rule. He got away with it, you might say, in part because he was profoundly gifted, but also because of his genius for representing himself as the horny-handed common man, folk personified. Even then, Woody's writing had tended always towards the public realm, to 'issues', topicality and a tradition shaped to suit current events. The other early stars of the folk revival – the Almanacs, Burl Ives, Odetta, the Weavers, Seeger and Harry Belafonte – were no different. Big names they might have been, but their music was in essence anonymous. The huge early success of Joan Baez was founded on a repertoire of Child ballads and traditional laments. The Weavers' reunion concert at Carnegie Hall at Christmas 1955 might have carried political weight in the aftermath of their blacklisting, and might have launched the 'second revival', but the music was strictly singalong, a communal affair. In 1960 Belafonte would be given a Grammy, richly deserved. The award was for 'Best Ethnic' – no decoding required – 'or Traditional Folk Recording'. The album honoured was called *Swing Dat Hammer*, a collection of work songs abetted by the harmonies of 'The Harry Belafonte Singers'. That, when Dylan shuffled forward, was folk.

The idea that a song could be in any sense autobiographical was highly unusual to anyone's ears, and a little strange. Devotees of tradition might even have called it vainglorious. Were they inclined towards stricter versions of socialism, they would have deemed it an example of bourgeois individualism, one step from show business and far removed from the people's music. No one attempted what Dylan had attempted. Lyrics of a personal sort were the business of the hacks, some of them touched by genius, of Tin Pan Alley.

True, the likes of Buddy Holly and Chuck Berry were expert, witty writer-performers who had enlarged the industrial conventions of rock and roll. But they were not in thrall, like Dylan, to a folk movement that claimed to venerate 'anon', that depended on the idea of communal composition by poor or safely dead unknowns, and moreover attached a political meaning to its sources. Nor, superficially at least, did the rock and rollers spend too much time exploring the tedious labyrinthine topic that was to bewitch the remainder of the century, 'the personal'.

They wrote to order, to find and fill gaps in the market, and because they were smart enough to see, long before most of their peers, that management types were making big money from publishing rights. They had no obvious interest in the interior life. Dylan's little anthem for the perpetually bewildered altered the terms of the argument once and for all.

This doesn't mean to say, of course, that he intended any such thing. He had been trying hard to turn himself into a writer. He was making good progress. But you can be fairly well assured that in April of 1962 Dylan, too, had no clear idea what a 'singer-songwriter' might be. So what did he think he had written? He has never addressed the question.

*

The tale of the song's creation has been told and retold. The late David Blue (once Stuart David Cohen) told it twice (at least), on one occasion – presumably at Dylan's bidding – for his chorus role in the film *Renaldo and Clara*. The version given to author and journalist Robbie Woliver[3] said that in the Fat Black Pussycat late one afternoon Dylan 'began to strum some chords and fool with some lines he had written for a new song'. Then Blue was asked to handle the guitar 'so he [Dylan] could figure out the rhymes with greater ease'. Those 'ten minutes' of composition thereafter elapsed several times over as the prodigy worked at the song. Or as Blue put it, 'We did this for an hour or so until he was satisfied.'

Gil Turner, editor and songwriter, was hosting at Gerde's when the pair arrived that evening – still more time having elapsed – at around 9.30 or 10 p.m., fighting their way 'through the crowd down the stairs to the basement where you waited and practiced until your turn to play was called'.

---

3   *Hoot! A 25-Year History of the Greenwich Village Music Scene* (1986, reissued 1994).

Bob was nervous and he was doing his Chaplin shuffle as he caught Gil's attention. 'I got a song you should hear, man,' Bob said, grinning from ear to ear. 'Sure thing, Bob,' Gil said. He moved closer to hear better. A crowd sort of circled the two of them. Bob sang it out with great passion. When he finished there was silence all around. Gil Turner was stunned. 'I've got to do that song myself,' he said. 'Now!' 'Sure, Gil, that's great. You want to do it tonight?' 'Yes,' said Turner, picking up his guitar, 'teach it to me now.'

Dylan showed Turner the chords 'and Gil roughly learned the words', but took a copy of the incomplete lyrics with him when he went back upstairs.

Gil mounted the stage and taped the words on to the mike stand. 'Ladies and gentlemen,' he said, 'I'd like to sing a new song by one of our great songwriters. It's hot off the pencil and here it goes.'

He sang the song, sometimes straining to read the words off the paper. When he was through, the entire audience stood on its feet and cheered. Bob was leaning against the bar near the back smiling and laughing.

In this apotheosised moment, amid all that stunned silence and awestruck acclaim, the idea of the singing poet is let loose. It springs from simple confusion, from the idea that anyone composing verses from a singular and personal perspective must surely be engaged in some sort of poetry. In another sense, though, it has to do with language and with the rhetoric Dylan employs in his still unfinished song. Even in its first, two-verse form the piece is 'metaphorical', ambiguous, open to interpretation and apparently from the heart: just like real poetry.

*

There were plenty of European precedents for poem-songs and poet-singers, but what did Dylan know of those? Some coincidences are intriguing. For one example, Jacques Prévert's *Paroles* (1946) had been translated in 1958 by Lawrence Ferlinghetti and published by the latter's City Lights Books.[4] In Europe, the volume would in time sell a million copies. Along the way, any number of its poems would be set to music and performed by the likes of Yves Montand, Édith Piaf and Juliette Gréco. Serge Gainsbourg did a tribute number, 'La

---

4   Pocket Poets Series No. 9. Reprinted in a bilingual edition 1990.

chanson de Prévert', in 1961. But this European habit also passed into English: Nat King Cole would attempt the French poet's words, as would Joan Baez. Johnny Mercer, one of the greatest of the mainstream American lyricists, had turned Prévert's 'Les feuilles mortes' into 'Autumn Leaves' as early as 1947. Only in America was a poet of song a novelty.

Circumstantially, there may have been more to it than that.[5] Writing in 1990, Ferlinghetti quoted a French critic of the 1940s who had described Prévert, spookily enough, as

> the voice of the wise street-urchin – precocious, mocking, bitter, dupe of nothing and no one. He is even compared to Daumier for the way he unmasks and deflates judges, generals, presidents, popes and academicians – all those he thinks keep us from joy.[6]

If your tastes run to quiz-show synchronicity and odd parallels, note that Ferlinghetti also mentioned 'one American poet' (unnamed) who said that Prévert (1900–77) had 'a tinpanalley [sic] ear for a cadence, and the cheapest mind this side of Hollywood, with the least integrity, and the most eagerness to fake and crib and puff himself up'. In France, the poet is meanwhile remembered for once remarking, '*Fort heureusement, chaque réussite est l'échec d'autre chose.*' Prévert *did not* say, 'There's no success like failure.' He did say (approximately), 'Fortunately, each success is the failure of something else.' More interesting are certain of his actual verses, available in all good, hip bookshops in the early 1960s. This one, for example, from 'Pater Noster':

> The masters with their priests their traitors and their troops
> With the seasons
> With the years
> With the pretty girls and with the old bastards
> With the straw of misery rotting in the steel
> of cannons.

---

5 One further connection is that Prévert was the screenwriter for Marcel Carné's *Les Enfants du Paradis*, a movie with a clear and distinct influence on Dylan's 'surrealist' 1978 adventure in film, *Renaldo and Clara*.

6 Gaëton Picon, quoted in 'Translator's Introduction', *Paroles* (City Lights, 1958, bilingual edition 1990).

Or this, from 'J'en ai vu plusieurs' ('I've Seen Some of Them'). The attitude towards punctuation and layout was nothing out of the ordinary at the time in America or in Europe, but it was echoed by Dylan each time he hit the typewriter.

> I saw one of them dragging his child by the hand
> and shouting . . .
> i saw one of them with a dog
> i saw one of them with a sword in a cane
> i saw one of them crying
> i saw one of them enter a church
> i saw another one come out . . .

It has meanwhile been claimed[7] that there is a very close resemblance – the reader can decide – between Prévert's poem 'Le temps des noyaux' (a title inaccurately rendered by Ferlinghetti – perhaps he was clairvoyant – as 'Hard Times') and Dylan's 'The Times They Are a-Changin''. This suggestion is better than plausible. The poem begins:

> Soyez prévenus vieillards
> soyez prévenus chefs de famille
> le temps où vous donniez vos fils à la patrie
> comme on donne du pain aux pigeons
> ce temps-là ne reviendra plus
> prenez-en votre parti
> c'est fini

> ('Be forewarned you old guys / be forewarned you heads of families /
> the times when you gave your sons to the country / as one gives bread
> to pigeons / that time won't come again / resign yourself to it / it's over')

---

7. Certain of these speculations were prompted by suggestions made in 2010 by Manfred Helfert to a blog – Humming a Diff'rent Tune – operated by Jürgen Kloss. Helfert runs the heroic (for various reasons) Bob Dylan Roots website. Like him, I had been wondering about Dylan and poets, Ginsberg, William Carlos Williams, and Ferlinghetti in particular. That led back to the Prévert translation, then to the discovery that Helfert was way ahead of me. Thanks are due to him. Kloss, with interesting things to say about Dylan, Brecht and much else, also runs the remarkable justanothertune.com.

In 1962, the French singer Hugues Aufray had been working as a support act for Peter, Paul and Mary at the Blue Angel club on East 52nd Street. As he would tell it,[8] he had one night found himself in a 'real dive' named Gerde's Folk City where a 'young guy with a harmonica' was performing. The two had met and formed a friendship, one that would endure – unusually for Dylan – for many years.[9] Aufray would next return to France and score his first real hits in the land of *yé-yé* pop with 'a whole bunch of American songs' he had collected, thereafter going on to translate and perform many Dylan songs. His 1965 album *Aufray chante Dylan* would have a big influence on the tastes of his compatriots. So: would a young French singer have failed to mention Prévert, the best-known French poet of the day, in 1962, when his new friend was deep in the study of verse? Would the well-read Suze Rotolo have known nothing about *Paroles*?

She had certainly been influencing Dylan's reading. Thanks to her, he had investigated, among others, François Villon, Rimbaud, Robert Graves, Byron, Yvegeny Yevtushenko and Bertolt Brecht. Yevtushenko, a dissident poet with an oddly charmed life, was on the cover of *Time* magazine on 13 April 1962, representing 'Russia's New Generation' Western journalists never failed to say that in his native land he was received 'like a pop star': some Russian exiles held less favourable opinions. Plays aside, Brecht had meanwhile been a guitar player in 1920s Berlin, a vastly popular Marxist writer and performer of ballads who 'borrowed' (or 'stole with genius') unhesitatingly. Soon enough he would be making a guest appearance in some Dylan liner notes. 'With the sounds of François Villon echoin' through my mad streets / as I stumble on lost cigars of Bertolt Brecht.' Legend adds that Villon was another thief.

Taking up the idea of Dylan as a poet, the besotted Village was out

---

8   RFI Musique interview, November 2009.

9   Aufray's dedication to Dylan was unwavering. They performed together, in fact, in Paris and Grenoble in 1984. In 1995 the Frenchman released *Aufray trans Dylan*, and in 2009 a collection of Dylan duets, *Newyorker*. Among several treats, the latter has the difficult-to-forget sound of Johnny Hallyday attempting 'Jeune pour toujours' ('Forever Young') and Jane Birkin performing 'Tout comme une vraie femme' ('Just Like a Woman'). Aufray's solo renditions of 'La réponse est dans le vent', 'Les temps changent' and 'L'homme orchestre' ('Mr Tambourine Man') are meanwhile better than most. Responses to 'Commes des pierres qui roulent' ('Like a Rolling Stone') might depend on your native tongue, however.

of date, or out of touch. Jack Kerouac had often read his poetry with a free-jazz accompaniment. Lawrence Ferlinghetti worked with the sax player Stan Getz. Kenneth Patchen had gone deeper into 'jazz poetry', the idea that the two arts could actually be combined, than anyone, particularly with his 1959 Folkways album *Kenneth Patchen Reads With Jazz in Canada*. In 1964 Amiri Baraka (formerly LeRoi Jones) would perform his 'Black Dada Nihilismus' with the New York Art Quartet.

In any case, the belief that there was a deep connection between blues and jazz and poetry went back at least as far as Langston Hughes and the Harlem Renaissance. Working as a busboy, the young Hughes would often sing his 'blues poems' in his head during their composition.[10] Then again, the notion that there was anything new about the relationship between music and poetry was out of date before Robert Burns (of whom Dylan is a big fan) began collecting and adapting songs in eighteenth-century Scotland. When Dylan appeared Ferlinghetti, for one, was quick to point out that Europe had been harbouring poet-singers for a very long time. That much was true; it should have been obvious. But there was no need – though it might have helped – for Dylan's admirers to know anything about medieval Italian 'sung poetry', or the troubadours of Occitania, or Ezra Pound's attempts to translate their lyrics. The anglophone tradition made the case unaided.

There was nothing new, nothing at all, in the claim that folk song deserved the status of poetry. Cf., as they say, *Lyrical Ballads, With a Few Other Poems*, and Wordsworth's prefatory defence of his art: 'The principal object, then, proposed in these Poems was to choose incidents and situations from common life, and to relate or describe them, throughout, as far as was possible in a selection of language really used by men . . .' Wordsworth was in turn a fan of Thomas Percy's *Reliques of Ancient English Poetry* (1765), with its 180 ballads, many filched from broadsides collected by Samuel Pepys. Wordsworth was thereby inspired to imitate these old songs; Walter Scott was moved to collect songs – and 'adapt' them – on his own behalf. And so on.

This is lecture-hall stuff, elementary to musicologists,

---

10 See *The Big Sea: An Autobiography* (1940). A comparison between the account of the poet's early years and Woody Guthrie's own *Bound for Glory* (1943) is interesting, not least for all the things the authors failed to reveal. Both would suffer the attentions of red-baiters. The familial relationship between their memoirs and the Dylan of *Chronicles* also becomes plain.

ethnomusicologists, literary scholars and the rest long before the second revival of (sometimes) traditional song in the '50s. One explanation for the reception given to Dylan would surely begin with the almost childish wonder he evoked. A real, living person was *really* writing these things in the here and now, singing in and to the modern world. Poetry: how about that?

*

The fact that Dylan's 'Blowin' in the Wind' would be published within weeks of its composition in the folk scene's newly founded *Broadside* magazine, and thereafter in *Sing Out!*, wouldn't hurt the case being made for the song and the singer. Dylan was working with words for their own sake. Some people thought the words were worth printing. Imagine.

The only thing missing from the story is the answer to a simple question: what moved him to write such a song? When the lyrics were published in *Sing Out!* in June Dylan accepted the invitation to add a few comments, taking care to ensure that he didn't explain anything much. He was 'only 21', after all, not 'older and smarter'. He was artfully gauche instead.

> There ain't too much I can say about this song except that the answer is blowing in the wind. It ain't in no book or movie or TV show or discussion group. Man, it's in the wind – and it's blowing in the wind. Too many of these hip people are telling me where the answer is but, oh, I won't believe that. I still say it's in the wind and just like a restless piece of paper it's got to come down some.

*

The first album, released finally in March of 1962, had not done its job. Which is to say that it had done nothing good for Dylan's self-esteem, or for his career. The earliest copies had worn a sticker on their sleeves announcing 'A New Star on Columbia Records', but the claim had been wishful PR thinking. Few in those days were accustomed to that voice. Those who knew the singing style, a small enough band, were meanwhile unimpressed by the choice of material, or merrily scornful of the performer's credentials. Dylan regretted the recordings as soon as they were made. That fact remains intriguing for what it says about his character and ambition. After all, he had told Shelton (according to Shelton) that the journalist's fanciful-insightful sleeve notes – packed full of half-truths and entire lies though they might be – were preferable to anything on the record. Such humility, if that's what it was, had no practical consequences. It didn't help. What was it about his first album that he disliked so much?

Returning to Minneapolis and Bonnie Beecher's apartment late in December of 1961 he had been taped by Tony Glover while turning in a wholly different sort of performance. Without John Hammond fretting over popped 'p's Dylan had torn through the likes of 'Dink's Song' and 'Baby, Please Don't Go' as though clearing his head.[11] Praised often enough, rightly enough, over the course of half a century, the 26 recordings nevertheless give no useful clues to Dylan's development as a writer. His own words are almost entirely absent. Instead, the tapes mark the speed of his evolution as a performer since the first, hesitant Minneapolis session all of seven months before. That was the context in which his first professional album could seem like a backwards step, and a missed opportunity. He had failed to recognise the multiple creative possibilities offered by the old music. He had missed a trick. His first record had been based on a misunderstanding of his own evolving persona. He knew there was more to Bob Dylan than *Bob Dylan*.

The passage of time has shown the first album to be a far better record than most thought on its release, but disappointment had caused the debut act to reconsider, to think hard and fast. What was it he wanted to achieve? The Guthrie impersonations were falling away, or at least becoming more obscure: those four strange songs about VD victims recorded by Glover were never likely to have mass appeal. 'House of the Rising Sun', aside from almost having cost him his friendship with Van Ronk, was wearing thin.

It may be, too, that Dylan was beginning to recognise a problem with old songs and folk music generally. They involved a kind of rote learning, a habit of going through the motions. It didn't matter how 'original' you were: someone would always compare your version to another version. Around the Village, in some quarters, a bizarre dogma still held sway: in order to represent the people's music, a performer couldn't actually be a distinct person. His personality had to be subservient to, and submerged within, the received song. Constraint was inherent in the idea of tradition. Dylan would have to arrive at his own solution.

---

11 Long known as the 'Minnesota Hotel Tape', though no hotel was involved, and probably the first – if not the first – of the Dylan bootlegs.

Besides, a flop was hardly likely to encourage those doubting Columbia executives to press on with the famous five-year contract. As his memoirs almost make clear, Dylan's break had owed everything to John Hammond's standing in the business. The company suits had been prepared to back the famous producer's hunch: his hunches were the reason he had been hired (or rather rehired) as 'director of talent acquisition'. But Dylan had been a personal choice. Another executive – any other executive – would have dismissed the youngster out of hand. If even the folk labels had failed to notice his gifts, or understand his appeal, why would a big, mainstream company waste its time?

And why Columbia, biggest of all companies? In 1962, the people in charge at 'Black Rock', the black-granite-clad 6th Avenue headquarters of CBS and its record label, thought the jolly New Christy Minstrels were *probably* folk. The closest they had come to Dylan's understanding of the term was with the Clancy Brothers and Tommy Makem (and they had been signed for a $100,000 advance). In 1962, the big news at Columbia would be the Tony Bennett album *I Left My Heart in San Francisco*. That year the company would sign Barbra Streisand, Andy Williams and Patti Page. It would put its might behind Robert Goulet's *Sincerely Yours*, Doris Day's *You'll Never Walk Alone* and *Hymns From the Heart* by Johnny Cash. If the company needed to show its class, it meanwhile had plenty of serious music to offer in 1962, from Stravinsky to Thelonious Monk's *Monk's Dream* and Jimmy Giuffre's *Free Fall*. It had no particular need for Hammond's folly.

Suddenly, with an abortive album to his name, Dylan had to improve, and quickly. As the long, slow and fraught gestation of *The Freewheelin' Bob Dylan* would show, he understood perfectly well that there was a lot at stake, Columbia and its contract options – even with a miserable 2 per cent royalty – above all. 'Blowin' in the Wind' materialised at exactly the right moment.

*

Implicitly, the song did claim the status, if not the stature, of poetry. Suddenly authorship and an individual sensibility mattered. As in literature, this individualism implied a specific relationship between artist, art and audience. It thereby extended the possible range of a songwriter's subjects beyond the usual affairs of the heart, even if most of the singer-songwriters (though not Dylan) were thereafter preoccupied, to the point of narcissism, with the confessional mode. The blunt way to put it is that 'Blowin' in the Wind' seemed (the important word) to be about things that 'mattered'. Simply because it was a product of an individual's art, the song contested music-industry assumptions.

How could the cry of a lone human confronting the cold universe ever be mere entertainment-business 'product'? That naive inquiry followed Dylan's nine questions and set the tone for an entire decade and beyond. Here, rather than in transient political protest, was the real counter-culture: art against the corporate machine, the poet's liberated voice (on the wind) to oppose bland conspirators doling out production-line entertainment. A lot of people were to build very decent careers from that pose. Some were even to put it about that they did not make music for the sake of anything as tawdry as money.

Dylan's new song strained for a universal effect. It would shortly be adopted by any sensitive adolescent capable of staying in tune, and by hordes of professionals keen to develop a serious side. But it 'spoke' to people, they said, and it asserted that popular music could be grown-up, serious, mature, literate, and all the other reassuring stuff. On the other hand, what sounded like poetry to some sounded jejune to others. The list of serious musicians who would dismiss it, led from the first by Dave Van Ronk, would be long. Pete Seeger certainly disdained the effort. This was presumptuous, you might think, from the man who (half) wrote 'Where Have All the Flowers Gone?' with a melody that had been original once upon a time, and with lyrics 'adapted' from a Cossack song Seeger had picked up while reading Mikhail Sholokhov's novel *And Quiet Flows the Don*.[12] As the fatuous ditty enquires, 'When will they ever learn?' Tom Paxton was another performer who (just) counted as Dylan's senior, and one who was also embarking on a career in the songwriter's craft: he never did esteem 'Blowin' in the Wind'. Such figures of local influence would be outvoted, in a landslide, by the wider public.

---

12 As described in Seeger's notes to *Where Have All the Flowers Gone: The Songs of Pete Seeger* (1998). The godfather of folk's habit of telling the world where Dylan picked up this or that melody thereby acquires a context, one might feel. By Seeger's account, Sholokhov and the Cossacks provided the bulk of the song. Joe Hickerson, of the Oberlin College Folksong Club (later director of the Archive of Folk Song at the Library of Congress), then added two verses. Seeger's central contribution – though the song is known as his to this day – was that 'I added the handwringer's personal complaint, "When will they ever learn?"'

Dylan himself said soon enough that he was never 'satisfied' with the piece, but it was not that kind of song: his opinion didn't matter. Nor did it matter to anyone but the singer that in the spring of 1962 he was *already* growing tired of the word 'protest'. In April, in a performance at Gerde's of which a recording survives, in an effort to explain 'Blowin' in the Wind' and himself, he said it plainly: 'I don't write protest songs.'

This must have puzzled most of those listening. It would certainly have puzzled most of those who bought Dylan's next two albums during the first gusts of fame's hurricane, who read all the things being written about him or who saw him perform. It was the sort of defiant statement that would become typical. Don't classify or compartmentalise me, Dylan was saying. Don't think you know what I'm about. So what sort of songs did he think he was writing and recording?

It happens to be a good question, one that gets to the heart of Dylan's later problems with the folk-political crowd who placed him front and centre in idealism's onward march, or saw fit to tell him where his duty lay. He was insisting, it seems, that any of his reactions to anything, politics not least, were strictly personal. He had nothing else to offer. He served no collective, even when opinions coincided. He might get as angry about racism or nuclear weapons as the next liberal, but his response was his own. It didn't belong to anyone, and neither did he, even (or especially) when the songs sounded like so many anthems for the common man. Bob Dylan spoke for himself: nothing would get in the way of that. Yet again, this was not, whatever anyone alleged, an obvious career move.

He could have made a good living out of topical songs. Instead, his 'desertion' from the cause would deprive the movement of its oxygen. That probably explained some of the resentment he would attract: his gesture deprived several notable folk people of the chance to ride comfortably on his coat-tails. Consciously or not, in any case, he was posing a serious (if familiar) artistic question. How is a stubborn individualist supposed to function within a collective endeavour? Does it aid his art – or his ego – even to make the attempt? As it turned out, Dylan didn't spend too much time on the question. Despite anything said subsequently, and despite the persistent efforts of headline writers, he was a protest singer for a very brief time.

Then as now there were those who said that 'Blowin' in the Wind' was vacuous in any version, not to say portentous, and pretentious, and utterly juvenile. In the Village, parodists took the piss. Those questions: what did they amount to beyond the hint that life's a puzzle, eh? And those images: man on life's hard road, more than one road indeed; and that Noachian white dove of peace (bearing a spooky resemblance to a confused albatross); and 'cannonballs' defying progressive legislation; and folks failing to attend to unpleasantness generally; and death getting more than its share. Dylan's peers, envious or not, went out of their way to disparage the song. When Peter, Paul and Mary's spun-sugar version appeared just over a year later it served only to confirm all the criticisms.

Yet the facts are inconvenient. That campfire rendition by the unctuous apostolic guys and the sanctified blonde sold close to a third of a million copies in a little over a week, and has sold many times more over the piece. Within a couple of years of its composition the song had been covered – not that this should count as posterity's criterion – by everyone from Bobby Darin to Sam Cooke, the Kingston Trio to Marianne Faithfull to Johnny Cash. Even Elvis would get around to 'Blowin' in the Wind' in the end.

Does this mean Dylan composed an upmarket version of one of those novelty songs that from time to time exercise an inexplicable grip on the public? Does it mean that the folk, the people, the audience for whom the folkies claimed to speak, were just stupid? Or does 'Blowin' in the Wind' possess a greater power than sophisticates have been prepared to allow?

An adequate answer is hard to come by, if only because this song, the foundation of a remarkable career, a new style of songwriting and the counter-cultural ethos, is simply too familiar. Children aside, who can actually hear it now in the way it was heard by Dylan's Greenwich Village audience, or by the Top 40 audience?

The song was certainly novel. The mass audience was not accustomed to 'philosophical' hits. Still, was it also *platitudinous*? That takes care of large parts of the Bible, where the language of the song is rooted. In any case, what is implied by those famous questions? Simply that the fundamental truths of existence are unknowable. Certain noted philosophers concur, but don't sing about it. Certain religious believers – Dylan would probably be one – say the same about their God. The very fact that those famous questions are rhetorical is, of course, a statement. You begin to see why Dylan became so averse so quickly to people demanding 'answers'. 'Blowin' in the Wind' makes it clear, in fact, that from the start he had no answers to give: the song says so.

It is a music-industry truism, nevertheless, that some songs become hits thanks to the serendipity of context and timing. One fact is that 'Blowin' in the Wind' is a song – 'an anthem', indeed – of the 1960s. It is of an era. Another fact is that the song would probably have had a slim chance of success at any other time.

*

Oddly enough, by some dating evidence Dylan had already written a better one. 'Let Me Die in My Footsteps' would not be released to the wider public for almost 30 years, but it remains a convincing demonstration of what protest song might have become had its practitioners learned to leave slogans alone. The song – apparently inspired by the sight of a large public bomb shelter under construction – is 'about' the nuclear threat, and could hardly have been more topical. It reeks, in places, of Guthrie, and in other parts surpasses Woody effortlessly. It is not sententious in the manner of 'Blowin' in the Wind'. Above all, it has a purely American spirit, a different kind of patriotism. No matter what, this singer isn't going to cower in a shelter; he'll die on his feet

Let me drink from the waters where the mountain streams flood
Let the smell of wildflowers flow free through my blood
Let me sleep in your meadows with the green grassy leaves
Let me walk down the highway with my brother in peace
Let me die in my footsteps
Before I go down under the ground

Unlike 'Blowin' in the Wind', 'Let Me Die in My Footsteps' is not ambiguous: few would have mistaken Dylan's meaning in an America deeply divided, as never before, over the definition of patriotism. At the song's end he invokes the country's founding purpose, the original dream. The freedom to perish in a holocaust for freedom's sake had been no part of the prospectus, nor had the plotting of the military-industrial complex. 'Blowin' in the Wind' was sufficiently wistful and vague – its critics were right about that – to appeal to a mass audience. 'Footsteps' was a real protest song. Its dissent from the bomb-happy chauvinism dominating the political establishment in 1962 was explicit: some people wouldn't care for that.

It hardly mattered: one song would blow all before it. The jejune tune would make Dylan moderately famous. His dissent, like his lyricism, his youth and the grisly pretence that he was just plain folks, would be part of the package. He would not merely be the writer of a hit tune, either: he would be *important*.

*

Eisenhower's big idea had been to contain Communism and the USSR. The idea of being contained – encircled, as Moscow saw it – had meanwhile been a profound Russian fear since long before the 1917 revolution. To some on the right, and to the likes of Kennedy, America was confronting a godless creed with designs on the entire globe. For some on the left, Americans included, the United States had acquired a distinctly imperial idea of what constituted its backyard. Each superpower was active, or so it seemed in 1962, in every corner of the world, and there was nothing much the world could do about it.

Dylan was never political: that much seems clear. His politics was that of the citizen. His early fans confused a belief in justice with a belief in political programmes, and mistook a dislike of illegitimate power for an identification with mass movements. When did Dylan ever vote, and for whom? In 1964, backing out of the political limelight, he would tell the journalist Nat Hentoff: 'Me, I don't want to write for people anymore – you know, be a spokesman. From now on, I want to write from inside me . . . I'm not part of no movement . . . I just can't make it with any organisation . . .' By 1965 he was telling a reporter: 'I don't believe in anything. I don't see anything to believe in.' As late as 2009 he was sounding like a bar-room philosopher who has just worked out that party politics is a scam. Dylan's faith in democracy was not conspicuous:

> Politics is entertainment. It's a sport. It's for the well-groomed and well-heeled. The impeccably dressed. Party animals. Politicians are interchangeable.[13]

As just about everyone has since observed, his escape from the political world coincided almost exactly, certainly conclusively, with the ending of his relationship with Suze Rotolo. That doesn't mean he had failed to reach his own conclusions, or that he and Suze were not, for a while, kindred political spirits. The fact remains that her influence was persuasive, and that he wrote exactly the sort of 'protest' songs liable

---

13 Promotional interview – on Dylan's own website – with Bill Flanagan.

to chime with her egalitarian, anti-racist, anti-war beliefs. She herself wrote: 'He once told me that he couldn't have written certain songs if he hadn't known me . . .'[14] On the other hand, Dylan would have received a political education in the Village with or without his muse. Politics was inescapable and left-wing veterans plentiful on any street corner.

In her memoir, all those years later, Rotolo was still praising the long-gone topical songs written when she and Dylan were together. Yet what do those actually amount to? There's nothing as lofty as ideology involved, and no concept more complicated – or more valuable – than the simple idea of dignity. Even in 1962 it would have been difficult, whatever anyone believed, to attach a manifesto to Dylan's songs. Their writer became important because he understood what 'universal' actually meant.

*

It is a mistake, though, to confuse 'importance' with quantifiable success, or influence with authentic celebrity-stardom. The twenty-first century holds it to be self-evident that Dylan exercised an 'incalculable' (or some such word) effect on his society. In point of fact, that's hard to demonstrate. In the early 1960s Dylan was a big noise in a small world. His music – folk, protest, the singer-songwriter idiom, whatever – attracted plenty of attention in the high-end media among college-educated types looking for significance in the new youth culture. The younger professors all liked his looks. They wanted something to talk *about*. His songs were meanwhile impressing his professional peers mightily, but that was not translated into popular success or sales. The buyers of Top 40 records were less easily swayed, says the evidence, by Dylan or by the folk-music movement generally. Those could seem a little cerebral, a little worthy, even a little dull. In the scheme of things they were minor phenomena. Theirs was not the loudest boom ever heard and you certainly couldn't dance to that folk thing. To this day people are sometimes astonished by how few records Dylan has sold in the course of five decades.

In 1962, the pop world he had left behind in Duluth was managing well enough without him. The mistake is to believe that this singer, and folk generally, had a revolutionary impact from the start. What it had instead was an excellent press. When Dylan was jotting down

---

14 *A Freewheelin' Time*, p. 290.

'Blowin' in the Wind' Little Eva was recording the million-selling 'The Loco-Motion' elsewhere in New York. In that same month Sam Cooke would put two remarkable songs – 'Having a Party' and 'Bring It On Home to Me' – on one disc. That month Elvis would release 'Can't Help Falling in Love' (a song to which Dylan would return). In 1962, Booker T and his 'Memphis Group' would release 'Green Onions', Gene Chandler would put out 'Duke of Earl' and Dion would record the mighty 'Wanderer'.

There might have been a political need for protest song that year. The advent of the singer-songwriter might have had many – if you must – profound cultural consequences. As ever the world might have stood in need of a lyrical genius. But in 1962 pop and the folk who bought it were doing just fine. Protest did not transform society or popular taste. History is distorted by anyone who writes about Dylan and forgets the fact.

*

Peter Yarrow, Noel Paul Stookey and Mary Travers had lost the important parts of their names in 1961, at Albert Grossman's behest. He had first meant to call them the Willows, for reasons best known to himself, but the talent had demurred. The manager had been plotting a group to rival the Kingston Trio for two years, pondering – and toying with – this singer and that before settling on the three who would work financially rewarding wonders with 'Blowin' in the Wind'. After constructing his perfect folk-type weapon, Albert had then put Peter, Paul and Mary through seven months of rehearsals. Their first album was released in the spring of 1962 and duly went to number one; in time, two million copies would be sold. Meanwhile, Grossman set about adding a songwriter to his collection. So it was that when 'Blowin' in the Wind' went tearing up the charts he was in a position to collect big, and do far better financially than any of those who did the actual writing, singing or playing. Grossman would have a large piece of two acts, of the record revenues, the publishing, the performances and all the many *sundries*. It took a kind of genius just to keep track of all the revenue streams flowing through a manager's meaty hands.

That summer, while his relationship with Suze Rotolo began to hit reefs and rocks, Dylan was engaged in the serious but oddly haphazard business of making his second album. All in all, *Bob Dylan* had demanded barely the equivalent of a day's work, its creative processes amounting to no more, supposedly, than an occasional approving remark from John Hammond and a refusal by the singer – an early piece of Dylan nonsense – to attempt retakes. In contrast, the spring's first drafts of *Freewheelin'* would be discarded entirely. The album would only begin to come into focus in July, approach full realisation in the winter and be brought to completion in the following spring.

There were external problems and distractions along the way, and plenty of them, but Dylan's real difficulties had to do with his own talent. That summer he was writing furiously, continuously, wherever he happened to find himself. The inevitable result was that he left his own songs behind almost in the instant they were written. There was always something new and better coming along. In 1962, according to Clinton Heylin's wholly persuasive account, Dylan would write 41 songs.[15] Some of those were trivial. Others had titles such as 'Let Me Die in My Footsteps', 'Blowin' in the Wind', 'Tomorrow Is a Long Time', 'A Hard Rain's a-Gonna Fall', and 'Don't Think Twice, It's All Right'. It was not a modest beginning.

On 2 August, meanwhile, Bobby Zimmerman of Hibbing, Minn., went off to the New York County Supreme Court on Centre Street and never came back. Bob Dylan – as a matter of legal record, 'Robert Dylan' – returned instead. Did this in some manner mark the approach of Grossman, and a contract about to be signed? Was the formal recognition granted to Bob Dylan a signal that all deals were in place? Was the singer anticipating success for *Freewheelin'* and preparing the last details of the persona that would henceforth hold title to the person? Or was he just getting it over with, once and for all, reconciling finally the name on the playbills, the one to which he answered, with the paperwork?

Dylan has been so obsessively evasive on this topic, and for so long, no one can say. He has turned everything into guesswork. The perverse irony is, of course, that the effort has been entirely self-defeating. People won't shut up about what he did and, more to the point, why he did it. In one version he acted on Grossman's advice. That may well be true, but it is hard to see why a legal change in his prospective client's name would matter to the manager. Many performers with stage names choose not to become welded in law to their alter egos. It made no difference to Grossman's contracts or

---

15 *Revolution in the Air – The Songs of Bob Dylan Volume 1: 1957–73* (2009) pp. 64–114.

percentages if Dylan was legally Dylan or not. It mattered to the son of Abe Zimmerman, however.

In 1962, in any event, he had turned 21. He was free to achieve an old ambition, whatever it signified. Robert Allen Zimmerman was eradicated. He ceased – and Dylan had a piece of paper to prove it – to exist. There are only a very few reasons why anyone would do such a thing.

A few days later Dylan returned again to Minnesota and taped a rough account of a lonely song of crooked highways and lost love, among several others, once again for Tony Glover, this time at Dave Whitaker's place. Dylan was in a strange position: he had every reason to feel unutterably bereft just at the moment when his life, from the outside looking in, was going well, better than he could have hoped. Things were beginning to happen.

*

In one sense, perhaps the most important, the decade itself had begun in February 1960, when four students, young men of instinctive genius, gave the world an idea by refusing to vacate their seats at a Woolworth's diner in Greensboro, North Carolina. They stayed until the store closed. On the following day, some 20 black men appeared at the 'whites only' joint and requested service. They got no joy. On the third day, 60 polite protesters arrived to face the heckling and a statement from Woolworth's corporate headquarters honouring 'local custom'. Three hundred people joined the protest.

The tactic, this insistent non-violence, spread instantly across the South. In Greensboro, a boycott was imposed on all the stores and diners that took black citizens' money but insulted their dignity. By April of 1963, just as *The Freewheelin' Bob Dylan* was being prepared for release with 'Blowin' in the Wind' as its opening track, Martin Luther King was launching a non-violent campaign to challenge segregation and racist hiring practices in Birmingham, Alabama, a city with no black policemen, firemen or elected representatives. On the 12th of that month, Dylan performed the song in his first major concert at Town Hall in New York.

In the spring of 1961, meanwhile, President John Kennedy had ordered the disastrous Bay of Pigs operation against the Cuban coast and the Castro regime. In October of 1962, thanks to U-2 spy photographs, JFK had discovered that there were Soviet ballistic missiles on the island. For the rest of the month the United States and the USSR had inched towards a confrontation for which definitive nuclear war seemed the only likely conclusion. Faced with extinction, the world had flinched. Memories were less fresh than raw when Dylan's album made its appearance. The first side opened with 'Blowin' in the Wind' and closed, prophetically it seemed, with 'A Hard Rain's a-Gonna Fall'.

Those were the times. Each day's newspaper supplied reasons for topical song and cause for protest. *Freewheelin'* was released in May of 1963; Peter, Paul and Mary's ineffably content account of 'Blowin' in the Wind' appeared in the middle of June and began to sell better than hotcakes ever did. The trio, this folk 'supergroup', were under the management control of Dylan's own supposed Svengali, Albert Grossman, so there was no coincidence in that. But it is hard to overlook the conjunction of dates that saw JFK give a famously defiant democrat's speech to a quarter of a million cheering West Berliners on the Cold War's front line on 26 June 1963, just as the dimwits' preferred version of Dylan's song began its climb up the *Billboard* chart.

In July, the Newport Festival closed with Dylan, Pete Seeger, Joan Baez, the Freedom Singers, Theodore Bikel and Peter, Paul and Mary delivering the new anthem. In August, each of the performers was present at the March on Washington, amid 250,000 others, when King told the world that he had a dream of an America delivered from racism. Dylan sang 'Only a Pawn in Their Game' and 'When the Ship Comes In' that day, leaving 'Blowin' in the Wind' to the hit-making trio. In September, a black church in Birmingham, Alabama, was bombed, and four children were murdered. In November, Kennedy was shot dead in Dallas, Texas. That was 'context'.

*

Dispassionately, 'Blowin' in the Wind' is not the peak of Dylan's stupendous 1962 output. It is not as fine an example of a singer-songwriter's stance as 'Let Me Die in My Footsteps'. It lacks the brooding, apocalyptic, imagistic force and metrical daring of 'A Hard Rain's a-Gonna Fall'. But 'Blowin' in the Wind' was the song, and the moment, around which things crystallised. It was proof that Dylan could reach above and beyond the folk crowd. It justified the persona he had created and vindicated his presumptuousness. With it, he demanded the artist's privilege: to be a public figure, but not public property; to speak to people, but always to speak for himself. No one had quite done things in this way before. As for a poet 'finding his voice', as all the one-note critics recommend, that job was done.

Still, no one in 1962 could know exactly which way the wind might blow next. The records say that Dylan first put three versions of 'Blowin' in the Wind' on tape at Columbia's New York studios on 9 July 1962, during the early phases of his work on *The Freewheelin' Bob Dylan*. Whatever his thoughts on the art and craft of the protest song, Dylan knew he had something. One Albert Grossman knew it too. June had not ended when he purchased the emerging talent from a gentleman named Roy Silver: one management contract, ten grand down. Sam Phillips had got four times as much for Elvis. By August, the deal with Dylan himself was sealed, just after Bobby Zimmerman disappeared.

What did he truly make of Grossman, this epitome of the hustler, this stereotypical predator of the music business? A couple of elliptical Dylan songs are assumed to tell all, but those name no names. The collapse of the relationship in 1970 was acrimonious enough: 'Albert' had, after all, awarded himself a wickedly good deal when he deigned to handle the young singer's affairs. That much became clearer still at the start of the 1980s, when the former manager had the gall to sue Dylan for back royalties. A barrage of counterclaims ensued, each founded on the allegation that Grossman had made millions by gaining and abusing his client's trust (to say nothing of his soul), and by taking an over-generous slice from every piece of revenue – fees, royalties, publishing, record deals, 'arrangements' with promoters: name it – that could be sliced. In another line of work Grossman's speciality would have been called skimming.

But his reputation preceded him. He was well known in the clubs as a silent, sinister eminence, but not well liked. Dylan knew this, and knew some of the reasons, and still he succumbed to – what? – to temptation? Or was it the honest truth that he had no head for business, and better things, as he believed, to think about? Did he figure that he needed a heavy to do the inevitable dirty work? In *Chronicles*, Dylan renders Grossman as a kind of Damon Runyon figure, but makes no clear judgements. Elsewhere he has conceded that Albert 'did some good things' for him when they were together. Meanwhile we have Robert Shelton's word that he 'advised Bob to consider Grossman's bid seriously', apparently because the manager had 'discovered Baez'.

Others – Van Ronk was one – have tried to say that Dylan's rapid ascent owed a great deal to Grossman's ruthlessness and drive: the manager's desire to get rich did the client no harm, in other words. Some devotees even persist in saying that he deserves most of the credit for the singer's stardom, that the otherwise reviled hustler was a great manager. Shelton, who plainly had a softish spot for Albert, saw 'a man not blessed with the infallibility he projected'. The journalist also told at least one story to Grossman's credit. Informed that 'some people' were indeed putting it about that Dylan 'would never have made it without him', the manager is said to have replied, 'That's ridiculous! He would have made it without anyone.' The fact remains that Dylan allied himself freely with a character who would indeed 'rob you with a fountain pen', and did so without a second thought.

A round month before the effective contract between the pair became formalised 'Blowin' in the Wind' was registered for copyright protection with M. Witmark & Sons. Grossman arranged the deal. He also arranged that he would get his cut from his singer *and* a cut – 50 per cent of the company's resulting income, it seems – from the publisher. He didn't bother to tell Dylan about the second part of the compact. Albert was prospecting for gold.

There were other seams waiting to be mined, and other ways to make art. In June of 1962 an engineer at EMI's Abbey Road studios in London had sent his assistant running to the staff canteen to fetch producer George Martin. An audition session had turned up something out of the ordinary. Unusually, two of the four Liverpudlians involved claimed to have written the thing they called 'Love Me Do' all by themselves.

*

Half a century on, the motives for protest song can seem self-evident. Racism, the nuclear threat, the advent of youth culture, the beginnings of a sexual revolution, prosperity for some and dispossession for others, the arts in ferment, ideologies in conflict, a bright shining hope in the White House: the confluence was formed, says the usual narrative, of volatile elements. A free citizenry might well have availed itself of the right to protest. But how many people noticed, or cared to notice, back in 1962?

That June, certain college and youth organisations long associated with the Old Left gathered in Michigan to form Students for a Democratic Society (SDS). After a lot of the usual sectarian wrangling, that first conference managed to adopt a manifesto from a draft written by Tom Hayden, he who would later marry Jane Fonda and enter mainstream California politics. The 'Port Huron Statement' began:

We are people of this generation, bred in at least modest comfort, housed now in universities, looking uncomfortably to the world we inherit.

When we were kids the United States was the wealthiest and strongest country in the world: the only one with the atom bomb, the least scarred by modern war, an initiator of the United Nations that we thought would distribute Western influence throughout the world. Freedom and equality for each individual, government of, by, and for the people – these American values we found good, principles by which we could live as men. Many of us began maturing in complacency.

As we grew, however, our comfort was penetrated by events too troubling to dismiss. First, the permeating and victimizing fact of human degradation, symbolized by the Southern struggle against racial bigotry, compelled most of us from silence to activism. Second, the enclosing fact of the Cold War, symbolized by the presence of the Bomb, brought awareness that we ourselves, and our friends, and millions of abstract 'others' we knew more directly because of our common peril, might die at any time. We might deliberately ignore, or avoid, or fail to feel all other human problems, but not these two, for these were too immediate and crushing in their impact, too challenging in the demand that we as individuals take the responsibility for encounter and resolution.

The Bob Dylan fan club was forming. While having plenty to say about the 'warfare state' and the political corruption inherent in 'Dixiecrat' dominance of the Congress, the SDS also declared that 'we have no sure formulas, no closed theories'. More than that, the newborn movement made a telling confession. The 'vast majority of our people', it admitted, 'regard the temporary equilibriums of our society and world as eternally-functional parts'. These eloquent young people were a minority of a minority, and they knew it. The same could have been said of a protesting folk singer.

In 1956, 42.5 per cent of Americans were reported in opinion surveys as believing that their chances of staying out of another war were 'getting better'.[16] By 1960, the figure had fallen to 18.9 per cent. The proportion of those who thought America's hopes of avoiding conflict were diminishing, on the other hand, had risen to 36.2 per cent. Nevertheless, by 1961 the polls said that 47.6 per cent wanted more

---

16   Philip E. Converse, Jean D. Dotson, Wendy J. Hoag and William H. McGee, *American Social Attitudes Data Sourcebook 1947–1978* (1980).

money spent on defence, with only 6.2 per cent favouring cuts. Kennedy's 'missile gap' ploy had worked.

The numbers would change as the SDS and a host of others made their protests during the '60s. By 1969, when Dylan's 'Masters of War' was embedded in the culture, only 13.8 per cent of Americans wanted still more defence spending. The fact remains that in 1962 patriotic conservatism, born of an ingrained pessimism and deep-rooted fear, was the order of the day. Greenwich Village was an enclave still.

*

Dylan was prospering; his relationship with Suze Rotolo was not. The fact would make both of these young people unhappy, and lead to some very fine songs. Their writer was alive to that ancient irony, no doubt. In her book, Rotolo still sounds bruised by the memory of a few brief years spent with Dylan. Even then, even as a hapless observer and incidental player in the developing drama, she felt as though her identity was being stolen. Already his charisma was a ring of fire.

The end might have been inevitable. Youth, ego, ambition, paranoia, infidelity, strange hours and stranger company: these did not comprise the formula for enduring bliss. Dylan's habit of evolving at a faster pace than anyone around him couldn't have helped much either. Suze, for her part, began to doubt her capacity for self-sacrifice early. She was intent on defending her independence. Dylan, it appears, could not cope easily with that.

The *Freewheelin'* photograph is one perfected image. By the time the shots for the cover were taken, however, other images of a relationship had begun to intrude. Rotolo had already begun to fear her eventual fate, 'on the screen, under glass, and written about in books, forever enshrined and entombed alongside the Legend of Dylan'.[17]

*

Upstairs, on the first floor, in the back, there was a little apartment that the Gaslight rented or owned or something, just kind of a storage room. And we set up a table in there. We had this penny-ante poker game that was continuous. And my room-mate at the time was a guy named Hugh

---

17   *A Freewheelin' Time*, p. 3.

Romney, who became, later, widely known as Wavy Gravy. And he was a poet, a Beat poet. And he had this portable typewriter, or what we would call now a laptop typewriter, that he had left in this room for general use.

So, one night, I came in early for work, and Bob was in there tap, tap, tapping, and had just finished this long poem. And he said, 'What do you think of this?'

So I looked at this thing, and I said, 'Well, this, you know, wild imagery, you know, what are you going to do with it?'

And he said, 'Well, I, I . . .'

I said, 'Are you gonna, you know, put music to it?'

He said, 'What? You think I should?'

I says, 'Yeah, I mean, 'cause otherwise it's just something to go in some literary quarterly or something, but this way, you know, you'll have a song out of it.'

So, the next night . . . Bob never worked at the Gaslight, but he was there a lot and would get up late at night and do a set. And he got up, and he sang this new song called 'It's a Hard Rain's a-Gonna Fall'.

And nowadays, when I hear him sing it, and it gets into, like, what seems like the 20th minute, I think, 'Did I make the right decision in advising this?' No, I'm just kidding. It's a great, a great song . . .[18]

*

Grossman had become Dylan's manager, officially at least, in August of 1962. To say that this economics graduate – Roosevelt University, Chicago – was not well loved in the Village is, it seems, to say the least. Even before anyone was making real money, Albert Bernard Grossman was attracting epithets from those who saw the enemy personified. Without much effort, he won the starring role as first villain in folk's abiding morality play, *Art Versus Filthy Lucre*. Grossman was denounced, sometimes even to his face, as a pudgy, cold-eyed, manipulative and malign combination of Colonel Tom Parker, Svengali, Dracula, 'rock and roll's Citizen Kane'[19] and any other species of predator that sprang to mind. In *Chronicles*, Dylan describes an early sighting of this music industry cliché looking for all the world like Sidney Greenstreet in *The Maltese Falcon*. Grossman was a big man,

---

18 Tom Paxton, video interview with Ken Paulson, *Speaking Freely*, November 2000, available at the website of the First Amendment Center.

19 Rory O'Conner, 'Albert Grossman's Ghost', *Musician Magazine*, June 1987.

unmissable and conventionally attired, as often as not commanding a corner table. A former Chicago nightclub owner, he seemed to growl rather than speak. He was, as Dylan vouches, no country bumpkin.

Every star in the making needs an Albert. It gives shape to the myth: artist as victim, manager as parasite, money as the cipher for creativity's travails. It might be worth remembering, though, that Grossman's devotion to folk music was almost as sincere as his devotion to a big slice of the gross. He was a fan *and* a leech. His style made him better suited to the mainstream pop world, where his deals and his demeanour would have raised very few eyebrows. Instead, 'the Bear' claimed his Mephistophelean role in a story many were desperate to believe, the tale as old as show business, of Bobby's Seduction. The part where someone held a gun to Dylan's head tends to be overlooked.

The manager favoured confrontation. As an approach, it had the merit of persuading his charge that there was nothing Albert would not do for Bobby while ensuring that any benefits accruing to Dylan would also accrue, in quantities capable of being counted, folded and banked, to Grossman. It wasn't pretty. Those who disliked the singer's new representative on earth were outnumbered, it appears, only by those who despised him. Dylan could seem to stay pure, turning a blind eye for most of seven mostly fat years, while Albert did the dirty work. There was hypocrisy on both sides: if anyone symbolised the ethical corruption of 'business' – and he didn't often waste time on symbolism – it was Grossman. Dylan must have noticed. The manager, on the other hand, liked to behave as if he cared only for the welfare and needs of 'his' artist. It was quickly apparent that he cared about a few other things besides, and took more than one pound of the talent's flesh. Both men conspired in the illusion: together against the world.

Grossman's first and enduring target was Columbia. His tactics were simple enough. Whatever the label did, it was never enough. As a first step, or as a negotiating ploy, the manager tried to extricate Dylan from his contract. The claim was that the singer had been under legal age at the time of signing. Where did that leave the management contract Albert had bought from Roy Silver in June of 1962 for a miserable $10,000? That agreement had also been reached when Dylan was only 20. Grossman had assembled a new deal at the end of August 1962 – taking 20 per cent of the singer's overall earnings but 25 per cent of the *gross* recording income – so why had he bought out Silver? It hardly mattered. Where money was concerned, as the manager understood, Dylan had not a single clue.

John Hammond was the opposite of naive. Infuriated by Grossman's ploy, he persuaded his errant protégé to 'reaffirm' the original agreement. This, in turn, angered the new manager. So the producer became an enemy. No one was to be allowed to come between the ringmaster and his performer. Hammond was too large a figure; Hammond commanded Dylan's respect. Legend or not – or because he was a legend – Hammond had to go.

*

Madhouse on Castle Street has not entered the literary canon. As a piece of TV drama it no longer exists, having been subjected to the mercies of BBC archivists in 1968 and dumped without a second thought. The corporation had no further use for an old monochrome recording of a play that received mixed reviews when it was first broadcast, even if the reels did contain early performances by an artist who was well enough known in '68, you might have thought, even among BBC executives.[20] In January of 1963 the *Times* reviewer thought the play 'freewheeling', and deemed the songs by a Mr Bob Dylan 'haunting'. Five years later, few remembered and no one cared.

In the winter of 1962–3, Britain was freezing to the bone. It was colder than it had been in more years than anyone could remember; in some places it was the coldest season, reportedly, since 1740. Dylan had flown into London just before Christmas after another attempt to finish *Freewheelin'*. On the day after the holiday, on the 26th, snow would begin to fall on the south of England and keep on falling. In January, the 'Big Freeze' would commence, with temperatures dropping below minus 16° centigrade. Britain would be paralysed; blizzards would follow and there would be no thaw until March. Yet again, Dylan had managed to arrive in one of the world's great cities in the teeth of the worst weather imaginable. For what reason?

It's another peculiar tale. Almost by chance, a BBC director named Philip Saville had seen Dylan perform in the Village in the autumn of 1962. As Saville remembered: 'I was talking to W.H. Auden who lived in, I think, West 4th Street in New York. He mentioned I should go to Tony Pastor's.'[21] The poet apparently remarked: 'Everybody goes

---

20 Audio recordings of the four Dylan performances were recovered, after a fashion, for a 2005 BBC documentary film, *Dylan in the Madhouse*, made to accompany a showing of Scorsese's *No Direction Home*.

21 Caspar Llewellyn Smith, 'Flash-back', *The Observer*, 18 September 2005.

there who is anybody. It's like going to the place up in Liverpool, that place that the Beatles were found.'[22] (Wystan was presciently hip. 'Love Me Do' would not be released until October.)

Saville later said he was taken aback by what he heard and saw. He recalled: 'When I heard Bob play, well, I thought this is too good to be true. If I can get the BBC to agree to it.' First, however, he had to secure Albert's agreement. Grossman, overlooking the fact that his client possessed not a shred of acting experience, but probably mindful of a 25 per cent cut coming his way, decided the opportunity would enable Dylan to 'enlarge his repertoire'. A fee of 500 guineas – then just under $1,500 – was agreed.

Dylan was first lodged, none too easily, at the Mayfair Hotel near Berkeley Square. He soon set about making his way around the local scene: Bunjies Coffee House, possibly the Establishment and Les Cousins, reputedly the Troubadour cellar on Old Brompton Road, indisputably a place then called the Pindar of Wakefield, a pub on Gray's Inn Road. Dylan was allowed to play a few songs there on 22 December, in the face of certain objections.

Pete Seeger's half-sister Peggy, who had moved to London from America in the late '50s, would long afterwards give one version of events. 'What might have puzzled Dylan was the non-nightclub atmosphere the folk clubs had,' she said. 'There were no lights, there were no microphones . . . There was no ritualised nightlife to it. It was a bunch of ordinary people coming to their pub.'[23]

It was nothing of the sort. This was the Singers' Club and it was ruled by Seeger's future husband, Ewan MacColl, the British revival's gatekeeper. His wife would tell the Dylan biographer Howard Sounes that, where the American visitor was concerned, 'Ewan and I were rather standoffish at that time and perhaps we were not welcoming enough.' The biographer nevertheless described the pair, entirely accurately, as 'hidebound traditionalists'. To which add: and then some.

MacColl had befriended the exiled Alan Lomax and derived from

---

22 Anything's possible. It's also true, however, that Tony Pastor's Club at 130 West 3rd Street was owned 'at mid-century' by the Mob figure Joseph Cataldo. This individual was linked to Jack Ruby after the murder of Lee Harvey Oswald. The Cataldos were also involved in the gangland wars provoked by Joe 'Crazy Joey' Gallo, who would one day have a Bob Dylan song written in his honour. It's almost too good to be untrue.

23 Llewellyn Smith, 'Flash-back'.

the American certain notions of what did and did not constitute authenticity in folk music. He was thereafter as purblind as only a dedicated Stalinist could be. MacColl had the sort of mind that could not only adopt the Communist Party of Great Britain's 1951 programme, 'The British Road to Socialism', without question – it had been approved by the infallible Stalin, after all – but even regard a pamphlet on 'the American threat to British culture' as an artistic blueprint. If Dylan thought he had encountered purists in the Village, he had seen nothing to compare to this commissar. In a career littered with fine songs – 'Dirty Old Town' and 'The First Time Ever I Saw Your Face' being the best known – MacColl had also written 'The Ballad of Stalin'. The piece was not satirical.

It wasn't relevant, apparently, that his sense of authenticity did not extend to his own name. Nor did the former Jimmy Miller from Lancashire worry too much over the art of 'adaptation'. There, however, the similarities with the American kid ended. This was a pity: Dylan was a fan. The fact did him no good when MacColl decided that the upstart – who also lacked deference, it seems – had transgressed against the rules of honest socialist folk song. Ignorance was no excuse: Dylan was an abomination. The CPGB's vanguard-in-person would return to the topic more than once. His opinion carried weight, too, with like-minded brethren on both sides of the Atlantic.

To describe the attitudes of MacColl and his kind is to risk sounding like a Monty Python sketch involving a less-amusing wing of the Judean People's Front. How did Dylan offend? He failed to observe the 'policy rules', for one thing. This wasn't a joke. MacColl and his followers had decided that the workers of the world should not be united in song. They had decreed, with absolute seriousness, that an English singer should perform only English music, an American only American material. Definitions of what was amateur, traditional, commercial, 'ethnic' and the like were also handed down. By these lights Dylan could not possibly be an authentic folk singer. He could sing 'Masters of War' and 'Hollis Brown' until he was deepest red in the face – and he did, that evening in the Pindar of Wakefield – but he would remain an agent of the class enemy.

This was ludicrous, of course. It helps to provide an answer, nevertheless, to the question, 'Whatever happened to the CPGB?' There are those in the British folk world still who despise Dylan and venerate MacColl without once asking about the nature of the man who remained true to his creed after the Hungarian uprising in 1956, one whose homophobia was never well concealed, and one whose understanding of gender politics was, it seems, primitive even by the standards of the early 1960s. And Dylan, they said, perpetrated the great betrayal? When he was blowing Newport away, MacColl was trying to impose 'self-criticism' – this also is not a joke – on British folk singers.

London was Dylan's first real taste of folk fanaticism, the weird conviction both that song could change the world and that only a certain type of song could be allowed. He could not have guessed it on entering a London pub, but his real crime in singing 'Masters of War' and 'Hollis Brown' was to employ British melodies. Patently, his cultural imperialism was blatant. Some allege, meanwhile, that this was where the barracking and booing of 1966 had its origins, in Britain at least. That seems, on the evidence, like the dismal truth.

Perhaps the real point about MacColl was twofold. First, he had tried and convicted Dylan long before the possibility of an electric guitar had even been mentioned. Second, the apparatchik had an influence within the American folk revival, particularly with Pete Seeger and Lomax. At Newport, this fact would have its effect.

In various utterances, MacColl would assert that Dylan was 'a youth of mediocre talent', that he had merely 'rehashed Ginsberg' and meanwhile 'muddied the pool where folk song is concerned'. In *Melody Maker* in September of 1965 he would declare: 'Dylan is to me the perfect symbol of the anti-artist in our society. He is against everything – the last resort of someone who doesn't really want to change the world . . .' In *Sing Out!* MacColl wrote: 'Our traditional songs and ballads are the creations of extraordinarily talented artists working inside traditions formulated over time . . . But what of Bobby Dylan? Only a non-critical audience, nourished on the watery pap of pop music, could have fallen for such tenth-rate drivel.'

Popular music, it is fair to say, was a great disappointment to the former Jimmy Miller. As many surviving recordings show, his own performance style was preposterously mannered. He sang in exactly the way the British working class do not. It was left to his daughter, Kirsty, to one day redeem the MacColl name. As a pop singer.

For his part, Dylan made the best of things. Saville would vouch that he 'loved' London: it's not self-evident. The TV play was made and broadcast, for better or worse, but it seems to have provided only the first evidence of an enduring fact: Dylan was no actor. The difficulty was merely technical, inasmuch as the drama's lengthy speeches were entirely beyond him. The director was obliged to hire another thespian to fill in the many blanks for his visiting American.

The real value of the trip was as a song-collecting expedition. Away from MacColl's louring presence, Dylan fell in with Martin Carthy, later one of the most important figures in modern British folk, a traditional singer and acoustic guitarist of enduring power who would one day have no problems with 'electric' music. After their first meeting in the King and Queen pub in Fitzrovia's Foley Street, Carthy, the elder by a mere three days, would introduce Dylan to the English repertoire, not least his own arrangement of 'Scarborough Fair'. In time that version was to make a few dollars for Simon & Garfunkel,[24] but it would also give Dylan all he needed to create 'Girl From the North Country'. Carthy's account of the ballad 'Lord Franklin' meanwhile became 'Bob Dylan's Dream', just as Dominic Behan's 'The Patriot Game' would shortly reappear as 'With God On Our Side'. To add insult to that imagined injury – can you steal stolen goods? – Ewan MacColl had recorded a couple of albums with the rumbustious Irishman.

Whether Dylan enjoyed London and its folk scene or not, his work was enlarged by the experience. The connections between the music of the British islands and that of America was an old story for most, but not, perhaps, for this beginner. He was still capable of being startled. He was meanwhile incapable of restraint when he heard a tune that caught his imagination. 'Adaptation' (or theft) was already central to his creative process. A tune in his head would put words in his head. Not for him the fastidiousness of Carthy. At the beginning of the 1970s he would be central to Steeleye Span's electric sound, yet in 2000 he could still tell an interviewer: 'I think it's actually immoral to claim songs you've reworked as being your own. It's public domain; it does belong to the people.'[25] Dylan's view was, as it remains, that everyone

---

24 In 2001, after years of complaints by Carthy, the remastered edition of *Parsley, Sage, Rosemary and Thyme* was still asserting 'All songs written by Paul Simon . . . except "Scarborough Fair/Canticle" written by Paul Simon and Art Garfunkel . . .' Nat Hentoff's notes for *Freewheelin'* meanwhile state that 'Girl From the North Country' was 'first conceived by Bob Dylan *about three years* [my italics] before he finally wrote it down in December 1962'. The performer of 'Lord Franklin' – 'whose name he recalls as Martin Carthy' – is at least given a nod.

25 In an interview with Tony Montague on the Rogue Folk Club website. A version of the piece also appeared in the Vancouver publication *The Georgia Straight* in 2000.

adapts, everyone – 'the people' not least – in some sense thieves from what has gone before. There are fine distinctions at stake. On the other hand, some of 'the people' have a quaint taste for being paid for their labours.

One odd result is this: Dylan is lauded as one of the most original artists of the age and accused, simultaneously, of relentless plagiarism. So what if both claims are true? And would music be better off if Bob Dylan had never borrowed?

*

Three of his first four albums would contain his name within their titles. There was nothing so unusual about that. This was an era before the acts began to get above themselves by imagining that long-playing pop discs deserved to be named like volumes of verse. Those Liverpudlians were *With the Beatles* or *Beatles for Sale* in early incarnations. The Rolling Stones were eponymous twice over, in Britain at least. But somehow *The Freewheelin' Bob Dylan* seemed apt from the start. The title was the youth in the picture, and the youth's persona – grave, funny, angry, poetic, compassionate and hip was in the performances as it had never been in *Bob Dylan*, and never would be again. *Another Side of Bob Dylan*, aside from being a dumb pun, was meanwhile a title neither chosen nor admired, so he said, by the performer who had to carry the can.

Of all Dylan's albums, *Freewheelin'* probably remains the most beloved. Its parts seem to fit together as though fated. It does not intimidate. It says decent things, serious things, droll things, and happens to contain two of the finest love songs ever written. A lot of people would never forgive Dylan for leaving the boy in the picture behind. Their grievance was not mere pique over the 'betrayal' of the politics of protest and social responsibility. In simple terms, they just liked the boy in the picture best. That was their youth, too, whatever age they happened to be. For many, he seemed to contain all the echoes of idealism and hope, of who they might have been and what they might have done. But Dylan would never be freewheelin' or free again.

The title turned out to be ironic, in any case. There was nothing freewheeling about the making of the album. Hesitations, second thoughts, stalled releases and abandoned experiments abounded. That was understandable. The first record had flopped badly. There were murmurs in the wings that Columbia's patience might not endure for much longer. *Freewheelin'* had to be right. One result, years down the line, has been the efforts of bootleggers to convince anyone who will listen that the collection you can purchase in the stores or download is not quite the real album. Most musicians would retort: no album ever is.

Recording began in April of 1962 and continued, off and on, for a year. In that time *Freewheelin'* was released and recalled. Songs were added and subtracted, controversies ensued, excitement rose in New York and beyond as Dylan played Carnegie Hall. Then he was off on that quixotic but useful trip to London: 'Girl From the North Country' was one unexpected result. Long before the album was let loose some of the songs Dylan was writing trance-like would convince Columbia that John Hammond had been innocent of folly after all. Hammond, on the other hand, would find himself removed from the project even as Dylan tried to capture quicksilver. Grossman had made it clear who was in charge. He knew better what was good for his boy than any producer, however legendary. Columbia – and this is one measure of a dawning understanding of the talent the company had acquired – could only agree. Albert intended to brook no rivals of any description; Hammond was dumped, fired from the job, and replaced for the final recording session in April 1963 by one Tom Wilson. Grossman, still making threatening noises over contracts, wanted Dylan's undivided attention.

The result of all this should have been a calamity. Instead, an indisputably great record emerged. *Bob Dylan* had contained only two of the singer's own compositions; of the thirteen tracks on *Freewheelin'* only one was 'trad' and one freely adapted from another man's song. Other borrowings were, shall we say, smuggled in. Yet in the period of the album's gestation Dylan wrote at least enough material to fill the record three times over. Some of the songs he discarded – 'Let Me Die in My Footsteps', 'Walls of Redwing', 'Worried Blues' – would have been seized on gratefully by any of his contemporaries. Dedicated fans argue over the choices made to this day: collections of outtakes are still among the most popular bootlegs. The real point is that Dylan had embarked on a five-year period of unmatched creativity. Everything he understood about himself and about the world would henceforth be swept along on the torrent. In consequence, his every word and deed would acquire an unspeakable 'importance'.

*

One example: even the version of the album that was recalled on the orders of Columbia's lawyers would in time become a minor phenomenon. Whether or not 'Talkin' John Birch Society Blues' provoked fears of a libel action before or after Dylan walked out on *The Ed Sullivan Show* in defiance of censorship in the second week of May 1963 is a long and tangled argument. In the end four tracks rather than just one were dropped from the recalled record – and why was that? – despite a few early copies having been pressed and dispatched. The songs themselves – 'John Birch Society', 'Let Me Die in My Footsteps', 'Rocks and Gravel' and 'Gamblin' Willie's Dead Hand' (otherwise 'Rambling, Gambling Willie') – are now freely available on *The Bootleg Series*. No big deal, then.

But should you happen to run across a fugitive version of *Freewheelin'* in its first incarnation, look for CS 8786 [S] with "360 Sound Stereo" in black (no arrows) on the label. Make sure the four errant tracks are listed. Then establish that either "XSM-58719-1A" or "XSM-58720-1A" is on the trail-off. Then collect your $35,000. That's at least as much as some will pay for this most valuable of Dylan artefacts. It is also one mad measure of his 'importance'

*

Another, better example: *Freewheelin'* effected a revolution, especially in folk. Before the album's release a singer was liable to be shown the door in many clubs if he or she sullied the ambience by attempting anything 'self-penned'. For some perfectly serious, dedicated and intelligent people the very idea was sacrilegious. It flew in the face of everything the folk revival had (supposedly) been about. You didn't preserve a tradition, according to this argument, by tampering with sources. Even Pete Seeger 'always got criticized by the purists for taking liberties with the folk songs, like Alan Lomax was, with patching them together'.[26] Seeger's habit, learned from Woody Guthrie, of affixing new political lyrics to old melodies was also looked on with disfavour. After *Freewheelin'*, everything began to change. Suddenly the singer who couldn't write was at a serious disadvantage.

Even in pop, where writer-performers were neither novel nor controversial, Dylan's album raised the bar to unsuspected heights. Famously, it captivated the Beatles. As George Harrison would

---

26 Irwin Silber, former *Sing Out!* editor, interview with Richie Unterberger, 2002, for the book *Turn! Turn! Turn!: The '60s Folk-Rock Revolution*.

remember, they found it 'incredibly original and wonderful'. 'We just played it, just wore it out,' said the Liverpudlian who would become closer to Dylan than any of the quartet.[27] Others in the Top 40 world lost their inhibitions – and sometimes made fortunes from publishing – when they took inspiration from Dylan and began to write their own material. Soon enough the practice was normal, as it has remained.

*

What did *Freewheelin'* offer that *Bob Dylan* had not? Better songs is one obvious answer. The second album also contained two things that the first had lacked: 'protest' and love songs. The character, the boy in the picture, acquired an identity. In luminous contrast to the juvenile dressing-up act on the cover of *Bob Dylan* this individual had wit, politics and personality. The comic songs were actually funny, the political stuff had real venom and the things that seemed personal were conveyed with an emotional depth that would never become commonplace. 'Better songs' does not begin to describe the advance Dylan had made. At a stroke – or so it seemed – he had expanded the possibilities of traditional music. And no one paused to worry, publicly at least, about 'authenticity'.

That was one way to pay tribute to his gifts. Dylan could make his own responses, his own outrage and anger, seem more authentic, and certainly more pertinent, than some reverently preserved ballad or union song. 'Oxford Town' is an exact case in point. Startlingly brief at well under two minutes, it was written after *Broadside* invited Village songwriters to come up with comments on the enrolment of James Meredith at the hitherto segregated University of Mississippi on 1 October. The case had been national news.

Meredith's idea had been to exercise the rights idealised in John Kennedy's inaugural address, and in the process force a reluctant JFK to confront bigotry. Twice the university had turned the applicant away. Then the National Association for the Advancement of Colored People had filed suit, pursuing the case all the way to the Supreme Court. That body had ruled in the applicant's favour, holding that Meredith was entitled to be admitted to 'Ole Miss'. Then Mississippi's governor, one Ross Barnett, the white supremacist son of a Confederate veteran, had devised a law forbidding anyone guilty of a state crime from attending a state school. Meredith had been convicted of 'false voter registration'

---

27 *Mojo* magazine, December 1993.

under rules designed to keep black Americans away from the ballot box. At that point Robert Kennedy, the Attorney General, had intervened.

Meredith's enrolment had taken place amid rioting on the Mississippi campus at Oxford. Bobby Kennedy had then dispatched 500 US Marshals and soldiers to restore order. Still more fighting had broken out; many people were injured; two were killed; and the governor was arraigned for contempt. Meredith, faced with continual abuse and harassment, would stick it out with remarkable courage and subsequently gain his degree in political science.

How to get all of that in a song? Dylan didn't even bother to try. Phil Ochs, always a dedicated protest singer, offered *Broadside* a ballad; Dylan gave them a brilliantly condensed set of images in fewer than 150 words, like frames pulled from a reel of film. He made no mention of Meredith by name: there was no need. 'He went down to Oxford Town / Guns and clubs followed him down', went the song, catching the essence of racist violence and proving that Dylan had understood something fundamental. A gift for phrases was one thing; the poetic line mattered. But in a song – and especially in a song intended to deliver a message – editing was the heart of the process. By happenstance and design, *Freewheelin'* itself went through several editorial stages before Dylan let it go.

Misconceptions still attach themselves to this 'historic' album, nevertheless. It was a big hit by the standards usual for a Village club act, and certainly a hit when set beside the vinyl wasted by Columbia on the singer's debut. But in conspicuous contrast to Peter, Paul and Mary's success with 'Blowin' in the Wind', *Freewheelin'* reached only 22 on the American chart. It became a number-one album in the United Kingdom, it's true, but not until 1964.

What the set did achieve was to alter perceptions of Dylan, above all in the upmarket media. Here was a true novelty: a voice of youth with something to say, quotable almost to a fault. Measured in terms of sales alone, however, his record did no better than to turn him into a cult among students and the like, and hence – to his profound disgust – into 'a spokesman'. Or as he was to describe it in *Chronicles*, into a lump of human flesh tossed to the media hounds. He had made himself too interesting for his own comfort.

*

One aspect of Dylan's life with a direct bearing on the making of *Freewheelin'* was the absence, for much of the time, of Suze Rotolo.

Fame had barely begun to eat into his well-defended ego before she decided that the attention, and the man, were becoming hard to live with. Suze was a teenager still, yet she found herself being tethered, it seemed permanently, to this 'Bob Dylan' who had attempted to conceal even his real name from the person he professed to love. Rotolo had doubts, and good reason to have doubts.

In the summer of 1962 she had also been given the chance to flee to Italy: she had taken that chance. The experience had worked wonders for Dylan the writer. For ramblin' Bobby, however, it was a lesson in loss, one of young love's condign punishments. By the second half of September all he had for consolation was the thought of an appearance at Carnegie Hall and the chance to show off still another new song.

'A Hard Rain's a-Gonna Fall' doesn't wear thin. Of all the 'protest' songs, it endures, bigger than any era. Tom Paxton was still struggling decades later to express his astonishment. The song's Scottish-European antecedents, fascinating though they might be, are essentially of no account. Suze's Poetry 101 course, on the other hand, appears to have had an effect more profound than even Dylan realised. In that regard, one thing needs to be said: if this song, rather than 'Blowin' in the Wind', marked the emergence of a real poet, nothing was owed to the Beats. It's not their language, not their manner. This piece seems almost to take the entire folk tradition – an impossible idea, of course – as a metaphor. The past is in the present. That's part of the point of its conventional/ borrowed opening line: nothing important separates Lord Randal, poisoned and dead, from anyone's blue-eyed son taken for war. Where has either been in the world? In places where nothing good can happen.

'Blowin' in the Wind' has soft edges: whatever transpires, there's the hope of that white dove finding rest in the sands, and the hope of answers to those questions. 'A Hard Rain' comes from a nightmare landscape, from a post-apocalyptic world. All the highways are crooked, the oceans are dead, wolves are gathering, trees drip blood, the waters are poisoned and the executioner is waiting. Dylan piles up the images relentlessly. That, too, is part of the effect: this is Whitman's chant. This is, equally, a world become medieval.

That the song was not written in direct response to the Cuban missile crisis – Clinton Heylin has settled that argument – is almost beside the point. The coincidence was close enough; the world could be understood through Dylan's words. 'A Hard Rain' is an end-of-the-world song, but it says, obviously enough, that the rain's 'a-gonna fall': here's prophecy, biblical in scale. If the crisis had not begun in Cuba, it would have begun somewhere else. In 1962, that was all but taken for granted. Dylan would explain some of this – as much as his syntax would allow – in the spring of 1963. Asked about 'atomic rain' he would say:

No, no, it wasn't atomic rain. Somebody else thought that too. It's not atomic rain, it's just a hard rain. It's not the fallout rain, it isn't that at all. I just mean some end that's just gotta happen which is very easy to see but everybody doesn't really think about [sic] is overlooking it. It's bound to happen. Although I'm not talking about that hard rain meaning atomic rain, it seems to me like the Bomb is a god in some sort of a way, more of a god and people will worship it actually. You have to be nice to it, you know. You have to be careful what you say about it. People work on it, they go six days a week and work on it, you have people designing it, you know, it's a whole new show.[28]

In this track, meanwhile, the audience, or some of it, begins to get the point and purpose of Dylan's voice. In 'A Hard Rain' it's flat, almost affectless, more so than usual. He doesn't need to emote like Jacques Brel to add anything to these words: they don't need 'performance' in the sense customary in 1962. This is the first real glimpse of what poetry will mean within the art of Bob Dylan. This is the first synthesis, poetry in song, as song, and song in poetry. The professors will struggle with that. *A great songwriter, but not a poet*: that makeshift judgement will stand for decades. It will overlook a problem: against which songs, exactly, is this greatness being measured. Who else is there?

*

Pete Seeger introduced Dylan to the Carnegie Hall stage for a hootenanny on 22 September. Five of his songs were heard that night, but only one of those would feature on *The Freewheelin' Bob Dylan*. Seeger had organised these affairs before, in 1958 and 1959, as *Sing Out!* benefits. This time the paterfamilias was 'introducing new talent', of which, on the night, there was an over-abundance.

The story goes, in the Seeger version,[29] that when the performers were told they could have only ten minutes each, Dylan raised his hand from the mob of musicians, asking, 'What am I supposed to do? One of my songs is ten minutes long.'

---

28 Interview with Studs Terkel, WFMT (Chicago), May 1963.
29 See Heylin's *Revolution in the Air*, p.96.

A nice tale. It involves, for one thing, believing that Seeger listened to this 'ten-minute' song – auditioned it, if you like – amid the chaos before the show and pronounced it a marvel. Perhaps he did. That still doesn't explain why Dylan in fact did four entire songs, including what is thought to be the first public performance of 'Ballad of Hollis Brown', before getting around to 'A Hard Rain's a-Gonna Fall'. That song meanwhile came in, according to the surviving bootleg, at under seven minutes, yet Dylan still did a twenty-five-minute set.

It's a trivial detail. The only important point on the evening in question was a song that caught its moment. But the tale also illustrates two things. First, the Dylan legend gets in the way of the truth, and the truth, if you can find it, is generally preferable. Second, the idea that Dylan is an inveterate 'myth-maker' is slightly unfair. He lied relentlessly, in public at least, but a lot of other people surrendered to fiction and false memories in his presence. The pressure on this young man was always to be what they wanted him to be. Seeger was as guilty as any, and more guilty than most: Bob Dylan met a need.

Come Gather 'Round People

Art is artillery.

Dylan to Douglas Brinkley, *Rolling Stone*, 2009

IN THE LATE AUTUMN OF 1963, THE ANNALS SAY, DYLAN WAS FINISHING up his third album.[1] The last track from the sessions, soon to form the collection's elegiac conclusion, was laid down on 31 October, as if as an afterthought. 'Restless Farewell' exhibited one of the singer's trademark tricks: at 22 he sounded ancient, weary to the bone. The song also borrowed liberally from the Woody Guthrie travellin' man myth, as though ol' Bob truly meant to chuck everything, burgeoning career and all, bid farewell, and 'be down the line'. For good measure, the born-jaded youth was rehearsing his defiance in the face of oppressive fame, 'the dirt of gossip' and 'the dust of rumors'. He had, of course, seen nothing yet. Still, making 'his stand', he rhymed 'as I am' with not giving a damn, and seemed to take his bow.

It was a lovely if, as all good folkies knew, melodically derivative little thing – based on an Irish song, 'The Parting Glass' – yet it showed Dylan edging yet again towards a new direction. The traditional personae were fading. Like the matching (though superior) 'One Too Many Mornings', the song was obviously personal, plainly autobiographical. Or rather, it sounded exactly like autobiography. In reality, this too was Woody's *Bound for Glory* dodge, the near-autobiographical half-truth, the illusion of confession. It worked like a charm. In 1963, a great many members of the paying public were still prepared to believe that Dylan was exactly what and who he said he was. Given that a great many also harboured dreams of becoming just like him, the imagined boy on the *Freewheelin'* cover, disbelief surrendered to its suspension without a fight. Impersonators were

---

1   Recovered and collated from the CBS archive and other sources in Clinton Heylin's *Dylan: Behind Closed Doors – The Recording Sessions 1960–1994*.

beginning to appear. Work clothes and 'Huck Finn' caps[2] were becoming uniforms for young men who haunted the Village, sneering at uniforms.

Dylan was meantime inaugurating a mode that would engulf pop music in the 1960s and 1970s. It endures to this day, a stylistic orthodoxy, taken for granted, assumed. Many people, oblivious to the contradictions, even call it 'folk' music. But here, in 1963, was the singer-songwriter, the walking first-person narrative, the personal supplanting the political. The journey to the humid interior of Self had commenced, even if Dylan was travelling by unmarked routes. It is probably beyond ironic that his of all egos – armoured, defended, disfigured – should be the moving force in all of this. His 'personal issues' were nevertheless becoming one source of his credibility.

Pop sociologists and social historians looking for the origins of the 'Me Generation' should always bear the singing poets of the 1960s in mind. Those who wonder about the American addiction to therapeutic chat should heed the soundtrack. Soon enough, everyone who could manage the style – and many who couldn't – had begun to explore the recesses of I and Me, those supremely important characters. Whether this was ever Dylan's intention is another matter entirely. His exercises in apparent autobiography are rarely what they seem.

His contemporaries were also beginning to discover, or rediscover, that writing credits could be valuable. Few managers or label owners had ever overlooked this detail – and few black performers had ever been acquainted of the fact – but suddenly it was realised that there was money in the copyrighted confessional. A respectable number of performers had already begun to cover Dylan's songs. Peter, Paul and Mary had laid their claim early, thanks to the offices of Albert Grossman. Others were quick enough to follow. In 1965, the Byrds, devoted adapters of the folk-singing Dylan, would have a bigger chart hit than the writer ever enjoyed with 'Mr Tambourine Man', a song probably composed – because it was certainly performed – just weeks after the release in January 1964 of *The Times They Are a-Changin'*.

---

2   Who came up with this bizarre description for the black corduroy cap? Shelton was first, presumably, in his September '61 *New York Times* review. For pedantry's sake, note only that in Edward W. Kemble's original illustrations for *Adventures of Huckleberry Finn* Huck is shown, in every instance, wearing a broad-brimmed, broken-crowned straw hat. Dylan's long and strange relationship with hats generally is another matter.

Pieces such as 'Don't Think Twice, It's All Right' and 'Girl From the North Country' had already demonstrated, in any case, that Dylan wasn't all about 'protest', satire and the reverent reanimation of dead bluesmen. Now, tentatively, he was on to something. Properly handled, it would demolish preconceptions of what a pop song could or should be. Did he know it? He knew his own instincts. Henceforth he would write what he needed to write. Others would follow, in their droves. Later, in another context entirely, someone would come up with that phrase 'the politics of the personal'. The poetics of the personal would have been more apt.

*

That wasn't the dominant tone of the third Dylan album, however. For the most part, the record created during the usual hit-and-run raids on Columbia's New York studios was full of what were then called 'messages'. 'Protests' rang out, too, in raging abundance, each marked by the sort of righteous moral certainty that would later give the singer the horrors. Here were documentary songs, songs dedicated to the commonweal, to a public purpose, to socially useful truth-telling in a world full of lies and injustice. Dylan was a natural. He may have found the mantle suffocating soon enough, but – lest history be obliterated entirely – he embraced the spokesman role without difficulty in the late autumn of 1963.

So much had been evident, in any case, in the spring of the year with the release of *The Freewheelin' Bob Dylan*. Veterans of the Greenwich scene had considered 'Blowin' in the Wind' glib, unresolved, juvenile or just plain dumb. Several were rude about it. It was, they thought, a beginner's *idea* of a folk-type song without the hard core of centuries of common experience. It lacked authenticity, later known as 'roots'. Also, it was damnably popular: for some that was reason enough to patronise the windy little ditty. No one else cared: a hit was a hit.

In point of fact, Dylan had solved an old problem of the radical, proselytising left. To wit: nice rhetoric, but how will it all work? Probably inadvertently – for he never claimed to be a political scientist – the youngster had evaded the nuisance of hard answers by not bothering to pretend to provide any. Like his generation, he was asking questions. His song was full of them. Since these were, in any case, eternal questions he caught the mood of confused times, and of confused youth. Yet barely had the song been written than he was denying its status as 'protest'. 'Blowin' in the Wind' was a song about the *search*

251

for meaning. Searches were good; they got a writer from couplet to couplet. They moved a song along. But actual meaning, if any, was the preserve of those who dared to claim to know.

When Dylan got down to cases he was more to the liking of folk's arbiters. 'Masters of War', that unaccountably popular dirge, was a key example. People who sometimes catch the news and see foreign policy being carried out from 30,000 feet still find value, apparently, in one of the dullest melodies Dylan ever stole.[3] There is also a healthy market still for statements of the entirely obvious. War, it turns out, is a bad thing. Those who wage it and profit from it are bad people. Just to prove a devotion to peace and non-violence, a right-thinking person would rather see those bad people dead, and watch over their graves just to be sure.[4] To the politicised types who were ready to take the prodigy in hand, this was more like it. This was 'profound'. Some still think so.

'Talkin' World War III Blues' did the same job, Woody style, but with laughs. 'Oxford Town', a brilliant snapshot of racial hatred and brutality, was the essence of the civil-rights struggle in a half-dozen breaths. Dylan had a ton of other stuff that didn't make the album, but the centrepiece of *Freewheelin'*, morally and artistically, the song that supposedly placed him at the head of a movement, like it or not, was 'A Hard Rain's a-Gonna Fall'. It caught Allen Ginsberg's ear. Supposedly it prompted Leonard Cohen to wonder if his poetry, too, could be turned into songs. This was protest and prophetic trance rolled into one. This was not a newspaper-headline song. This was as authentic as hell on earth, visionary and 'relevant'. In point of fact the song, closely examined, contained no protest to speak of. It was descriptive, a dispatch from a world to come, and closer to something William Blake might have written than to anyone's analysis of an international 'situation'. Yet, for all its marvels, 'A Hard Rain' bound Dylan to a role and a cliché: voice of a generation, singer with a message. He and the song were better than that, but it took a while for most of his audience to notice.

---

3   Lifted, without the slightest effort at concealment, from 'Nottamun Town', an English song possibly older than several hills. Specifically, Dylan had helped himself to Jean Ritchie's arrangement. The point would be that he didn't care who knew it. A copyright claim by the Appalachian 'Mother of Folk' was settled with, it is said, a $5,000 payment.

4   To be strictly fair, Dylan has claimed that this was the only song he ever wrote in which he wished anyone dead.

COME GATHER 'ROUND PEOPLE

Dylan had just turned 22 with the release of his second album, but even in 1963 he was no one's fool. The skill he brought to the craft depended on a simple insight: the proselytiser must never resemble a propagandist. Anyone who heard the album in the spirit intended could easily spot Dylan on the side of the sane. Suze Rotolo would attest that he held all the correct beliefs, and held them sincerely. But actual politics? An ideological position? Even an idea of how the world works beyond good and evil, right and wrong, truth and deceit? If the singer harboured any of those thoughts, he kept them to himself. The uses to which his songs would be put, then and since, were another matter.

Certainly in performance he would slip in jokes about red-baiters and crazed militarists. He would sermonise as required on the follies of war and racism. Audiences knew where he stood. A minor – less than that – example would be 'You've Been Hiding Too Long', a hit-and-run song if ever there was one, performed at Town Hall in April of 1963 and never heard again. A bootleg recording explains the swift and irrevocable decision to ditch the tune. Its anger is eloquent, certainly, towards the hypocrite-coward who sends people off to do battle and die. Dylan spits those words. But what function did emotion serve other than to reassure the right-thinking crowd that their hearts and minds were in the right places, even if those minds were not being put to any noticeably useful purpose? Long before the phrase came to be used and abused, 'You've Been Hiding Too Long' was politically correct in the worst way.

Get out in the open, stop standing afar
Let the whole world see what a hypocrite you are
I ain't joking and it ain't no gag
You bin hiding too long behind the American flag

One poor song doesn't justify an indictment. Even at this time Dylan was never merely, even on a bad day, an agit-prop singer. In fact, for those who needed slogans and doctrinal positions he could be infuriatingly vague. A few even wondered if he was somehow sending up the whole folk-song movement. Instead, he was keenly aware of the fact that he was in no position to offer solutions to anyone. A lot of his peers would be less circumspect. Dylan had faked many things, but he could not fake real knowledge. He didn't know much about anything: it was one good reason to decline the spokesman's job. He might also, just possibly, have had a few ideas of his own. At any rate, like Woody, he avoided formal political entanglements. If that was an accident, nothing in his subsequent career makes any sort of sense.

Hence the allegation, shortly to become widespread amongst former friends, colleagues and self-appointed comrades, that Dylan simply exploited a situation. Protest was just where the action was. He applied his facile gift, they said, merely to give the customer what the customer seemed to want. Protest was a career move. That those who made the charge could never come close to matching his eloquence seemed only to amplify their irritation. They seemed to say, in short, that he didn't deserve his talent. Disdain for anyone who happened to be well paid for their work was near universal in the Village. The record industry, like the entertainment business in general, was the father of lies and bad faith. Everyone said so – until the offers came in.

It did Dylan no good to explain forever after that his interest in politics, in platforms and parties and political operators, was less than slight. In time he would satirise those who needed to believe otherwise, even putting words – a comedy routine, indeed – into the head of a 20-year-old who had just signed for Columbia. Writing in *Chronicles*, Dylan would claim the perspective of a primitive, a rustic with a taste for populism and a fondness for Senator Barry Goldwater of Arizona, a figure who reminded the writer of the venerable Tom Mix. According to the older Dylan his younger self had never been comfortable with polemical babbling, or much interested in current affairs. The news, all of it bad, just made him nervous. He preferred yesterday's news.

Goldwater, as Dylan and the older American readers of *Chronicles* would know perfectly well – though only one of them was laughing up his sleeve – was easily the most conservative mainstream politician of the early 1960s, a man obsessed with Communists, trade unions and the pernicious effects of welfare. Goldwater supported Joe McCarthy from the start, opposed the Civil Rights Act, and caused a lot of people, even in his own party, to conclude that his finger would itch unstoppably over the nuclear trigger if he ever reached the White House. In other words, Barry Goldwater stood for everything opposed by the protest songs of the young Bob Dylan.[5]

---

5   The young Dylan also had fun at the senator's expense. 'I Shall Be Free No. 10' from 1964's *Another Side of Bob Dylan* proposed that Goldwater could test anyone's notions of tolerance:

Now, I'm liberal, but to a degree

In his prime the senator certainly seemed keen on a confrontation with the Soviet Union, and by any means necessary. Sometimes he talked like a bit player from *Dr. Strangelove*: a nuke in the men's room of the Kremlin would solve America's problems, he said. This sally tickled the senator; many voters who failed to see the joke, or the charm of the 'battlefield' nuclear devices advocated by Goldwater, were not amused. Their fears were palpable. Lyndon Johnson understood this and exploited it ruthlessly, not least with a notorious TV ad depicting a four-year-old girl in a sunlit meadow at the last instant before incineration. As a result, LBJ was able to hand a historic whipping to his Republican opponent in the presidential elections of 1964.

Late in 1961, just after Dylan had recorded his first album, Goldwater had even told a news conference that 'sometimes I think this country would be better off if we could just saw off the eastern seaboard and let it float out to sea'. Most people in the Village would probably have taken him up on the offer. The author of *Chronicles* and his 20-year-old self were both perfectly well aware of all this. Tom Mix was meanwhile the long-dead star of old-time western movies full of white hats and black hats: that may have been the joke.

Still, when the movement to halt America's Vietnam war approached its zenith a few years later Dylan was nowhere to be seen. When the counter-culture was being embraced by his peers Dylan was dismissive, holed up with his wife and kids, making 'surreal', somehow ancient music and drifting inexorably, it seemed, towards Nashville, of all places. In late 1963, when the time came to make a third attempt at a long-playing record, he was merely hinting, between messages, that there was probably more to human existence than Old Left or New Left. Sometimes, nevertheless, he slipped the chains he had forged for himself.

Why so uneasy? The common mistake is to say that he never really cared enough about people and their causes. A second error, almost equivalent, is to assert that he was forced to escape artistically from a suffocating – always 'suffocating' – folk consensus. You could find

---

I want ev'rybody to be free
But if you think that I'll let Barry Goldwater
Move in next door and marry my daughter
You must think I'm crazy!
I wouldn't let him do it for all the farms in Cuba.

evidence for either argument. In the former case, you could point to vast ambition, the lure of stardom and Grossman's influence. For the latter claim you could summon the voices of all those busy imposing obligations on the socially responsible artist.

The trouble is, no proof exists that Dylan ever felt under much pressure to write or record in any manner not of his choosing. From the second album onwards he was composing 'personal', non-political songs and being lauded for them. He was to make a few Marxist diehards deeply uneasy with *Another Side of Bob Dylan* in 1964, but even when their comments crept close to denunciation he gave no sign of being daunted. Besides, that sort of nonsense did not befall him in a serious way until Newport and the hurricane years, 1965 and 1966. By that time his songwriting had already left 'protest' far behind. It is perfectly clear, meanwhile, that his conscience remained in working order throughout. His ego expanded; his tongue was sometimes roughened; he made a lot of money. Is it suggested, though, that he overnight ceased to care about racial hatred? There is no shred of evidence.

A better guess would be that Dylan began to reach certain conclusions about the purposes of song, and about an individual's relationship to art. Some of the more zealous sorts attached to folk, the ones who talked in terms of a movement, seemed to believe the best songs were those designed by a committee, for a collective purpose. This gave reassurance to lesser talents such as Pete Seeger or Joan Baez – people with a lot to overcome – but it misunderstood Dylan utterly. Who was there equipped to tell him how to write? The important fact is that he chose the more difficult route. It would have been easier, too easy, to stick with protest and tradition. But that would have meant a lifetime spent stating the obvious. It would also have landed him with the activist's dilemma: agree with one thing and you have to agree with it all. Dylan wasn't made that way.

As to politics, he did have one gift. If he understood anything, he understood the art of lying. Again and again, those protest songs return to truth and lies. Dylan could spot deceit at a hundred paces, catch it in the tone of a voice, decipher it in slogans, body language and the speeches of self-advertising political types. He knew *phoney* by its sound and smell. That, as much as lyric power, was his weapon. He was an expert on lies, after all.

*

Towards the end of January 1963, Dylan is performing 'Masters of

War' at Gerde's. In March, listeners to Oscar Brand's radio show are being allowed to hear two more new songs, 'Girl From the North Country' and 'Only a Hobo'. In April, somewhat hastily as it transpires, Columbia begins to send out the promotional copies of *Freewheelin'* that will one day provide decent little nest eggs for lucky collectors. Yet by the end of the month Dylan is returning to the studio to make a final stab at completing an album capable of satisfying audiences, executives, record-company lawyers and the artist himself. First, however – on 12 April – there is a real, proper, big-time concert.

The surviving tape of the show is a lot of fun. This is the Dylan who so entrances his first audiences, the irreparably scruffy youth who can be funny and serious, the engaged would-be poet desperate not to be misunderstood, the endearingly 'Chaplinesque' – whatever that meant – young man who has 'something to say'. He certainly has the kind of easy charm that can persuade an audience to applaud even his screw-ups and his endless fumblings – thanks to his devotion to non-standard tunings – with his guitar. It should also be said that at this date, on this Friday night, this devoted crowd would run him out of New York town should he dare to claim that he sings no songs of protest.

'Blowin' in the Wind', 'A Hard Rain', 'With God On Our Side', 'Master of Wars', 'Hiding Too Long', 'John Birch Paranoid Blues', 'Hero Blues': the Dylan manner, in this 'first solo concert' – the Chapter Hall show having been erased from history – is to intersperse his topical songs with personal numbers. With the former, he is not leaving much room for ambiguity. Disillusionment has not yet bitten deeply.

'This is for all the, uh, boys who know girls who want them, uh, to go out and get themselves killed,' he announces before launching into 'Hero Blues'. 'I believe in the Ten Commandments,' he says before his penultimate number. 'The first one is "I am the Lord thy God." It's a great commandment if it's not said by the wrong people. So here's this is [*sic*] called "Masters of War".'

Whatever his private doubts, at Town Hall Dylan is embracing the public role of the folk propagandist without hesitation. If he refuses to be anyone's spokesman, he is nevertheless more than eager to speak out: that's the contradiction. It's hardly surprising that a lot of people are taking him at his word. Nevertheless, something more significant is going on, something fit to be recorded in those annals. For the first time, Bob Dylan is performing only Bob Dylan songs. The concert is a showcase, as they call it in the business, but he has the material now to do himself justice.

Harold Leventhal, Woody Guthrie's old friend and manager, has promoted the show in cahoots with Grossman. Town Hall, at 123 West 43rd Street, has been a favoured venue of jazz performers for years, with a capacity reckoned at around 1,200. Tonight, one unkempt individual has to attempt to fill the place on his own. Though Leventhal and Grossman will afterwards claim the concert has been a sell-out, Shelton – whose review for the *Times* will be yet another 'rave' – reckons that only 900 seats are filled. This is hardly a disgrace. On the other hand, it gives a measure of precisely how limited the Dylan 'phenomenon' still is on a spring evening on his home turf. Some in the audience will later claim that the show sticks in the memory as one of those defining moments, as the night when the marvellous youngster crosses the great divide and enters the afterworld of stardom. It might be better to say that this is the night when 900 people believe they see stardom coming. Many others have stayed away.

Shelton, ever loyal, will observe in the *Times* that Dylan is 'a folk musician who breaks all the rules of songwriting except those of having something to say and of saying it stunningly'. The *Times* headline writer, working with a palette of purest in-house grey, won't go quite so far, observing 'BOB DYLAN SINGS HIS COMPOSITIONS; Folk Musician, 21, Displays Originality at Town Hall'. Still, it's news fit to print.

*

The bootleg of the show is of excellent quality, as these things go. This no doubt reflects the fact that it was a Columbia recording, with a commercial release – as one part of an album, at any rate – in mind. Clearly, big plans had been laid: suddenly someone had acquired confidence in an artist whose first studio record had flopped and whose second had yet to reach the stores. No doubt the idea for a live album was inspired by the pop-chart success of *Joan Baez in Concert: Part 1*, released the previous autumn, nominated for a Grammy, and still selling in April. Columbia's executives must have been just a little disconcerted, therefore, when their young poet chose to end his performance with an actual poem.

'Last Thoughts on Woody Guthrie', delivered at breakneck speed, is two things. First, it's not at all bad, at least by the standards of certain pieces Dylan was passing off – 'Go Away You Bomb', would be one – as verse. Second, more importantly, it's a valediction, and that makes it odd. Woody was a very sick man in April of 1963, but a long way from dead. Nevertheless, here was Dylan making his farewells, cutting loose, marking an end to one period in his life and inaugurating another. This was a public declaration. Was he callous or merely clear-sighted?

The visits to Guthrie during Dylan's early New York days are central to the tale. No one forgets those. They do forget to ask another question, however: how often thereafter did he return to the sick man's bedside? Joe Klein, Woody's biographer, recalled that after 1964 young men following the Dylan pilgrimage trail became a problem for the Guthrie family. But Dylan himself? Between the early visits and a phone call made to Harold Leventhal offering – demanding – to be part of any memorial service or commemorative concert after Woody's death was announced in October 1967, there is a gap in the record.

Still, if Town Hall was a moment for last words, justice was done. Had the show happened a few decades later, rap and 'performance poetry' would probably have been mentioned. Dylan would certainly declare himself a big fan of the former, and have sane things to say, now and then, about the latter. 'Last Thoughts on Woody Guthrie' is a poem that requires performance, preferably by its author. All the claims soon to be made about Dylan's literary standing would turn on that consideration for proof or rebuttal: could anything of his ever 'work' without that voice? On 12 April 1963, nevertheless, he chose to dedicate the last spot of his first big night to Woody.

Your eyes can only look through two kinds of windows
Your nose can only smell two kinds of hallways
You can touch and twist
And turn two kinds of doorknobs
You can either go to the church of your choice
Or you can go to Brooklyn State Hospital
You'll find God in the church of your choice
You'll find Woody Guthrie in Brooklyn State Hospital
And though it's only my opinion
I may be right or wrong
You'll find them both
In the Grand Canyon
At sundown

Perhaps there were private visits after fame arrived: in those years Dylan could not move freely in public. Perhaps, given Guthrie's state of health, the pilgrimages ceased to matter. In his biography Klein would recall a report in *Sing Out!* in January of 1964 stating that Woody had 'deteriorated in the past year' and that visitors were being discouraged. 'By 1965,' Klein would write, '[Guthrie] had stopped speaking entirely and could only communicate by pointing a wildly flailing arm at "yes" and "no" cards . . .' Such was and is the horror of the disease. The lacuna in the otherwise extravagantly well-documented life of Bob Dylan is strange, nevertheless.

Chronicles fails, as ever, to shed any light on the matter. If Dylan stayed in touch with 'the true voice of the American spirit' after those first visits long lost to mythology, he isn't telling. Those last thoughts on a 'last idol' spoken in a torrent at Town Hall were written in homage, certainly, but they were also a declaration of independence.[6] It should be borne in mind: no one had asked him to inter the memory of a sick man, least of all on a public stage. He might have been moving on; Guthrie had no such choice.

*

In 1963, Dylan's world is changing almost by the day. In May, exactly a month after the Town Hall concert, he walks out on *The Ed Sullivan Show* – the *Sullivan* show, where Elvis had stood head, shoulders and hips above all others in '56 – after CBS corporate zombies forbid the performance of 'Talkin' John Birch Paranoid Blues'.

The legal herd have been spooked by the risk of a defamation suit from sensitive sorts on the lunatic right-wing fringe. Since CBS owns Columbia, Dylan's walkout is brave: it isn't obvious, in 1963, that the blacklists have been abandoned entirely. Whether the TV lawyers have talked to the record-company lawyers about his comedy song, or vice versa, is neither here nor there. The timing suggests that the record label's suits have panicked first, but the outcome is the same: the early copies of *Freewheelin'* are withdrawn. 'John Birch' then disappears, along with three other tracks. In dumping four entire songs Dylan uses a small crisis as an excuse to tinker again with his crucial album.

As ever, he has new songs to hand. As ever, he prefers the latest thing on his mind to anything that might have been around for longer than a breath. This, too, marks him out from his contemporaries. It also marks the beginning of a lifetime's habit. He doesn't care what

---

6   Devotion to the music did not cease. As late as December of 2009, Dylan was performing Guthrie's 'Do Re Me' with Ry Cooder and Van Dyke Parks during *The People Speak*, an all-star documentary – Matt Damon, Springsteen, Morgan Freeman – inspired by Howard Zinn's *A People's History of the United States* (1980).

anyone else thinks about a song. It doesn't matter if a piece of work earns extravagant praise from critics, fans or friends. If it fails to satisfy him, it's gone, erased, forgotten. He doesn't hoard his treasures. In these months it takes a special piece of work to meet the standards of his internal editor. There is always another, better song waiting to be written.

In the end 'John Birch', 'Let Me Die in My Footsteps', 'Rambling Gambling Willie' and 'Rocks and Gravel' fail to make the cut. Aficionados of the 'real' *Freewheelin'* will affect mourning for the choices made for years to come. In time, Dylan will give them many more reasons to mourn. In the spring of 1963, however, only one deletion – 'Footsteps' – counts as a significant loss. Of the four substitutes, 'Masters of War' is a poor bargain. 'Talkin' World War III Blues' is a near like-for-like exchange with 'John Birch', but funnier. 'Bob Dylan's Dream' will stand as a long-underrated piece of work. But one result of these editorial decisions, enforced or not, will remain startling: there is actually a point at which *The Freewheelin' Bob Dylan* is intended for release without 'Girl From the North Country'. Then a butterfly flaps its wings somewhere and everything falls back into place.

The slightly interesting fact is that the newer songs have been recorded before the *Ed Sullivan Show* incident. Long afterwards it will therefore be argued, in particular by Clinton Heylin, that Dylan was under pressure from Columbia over 'John Birch' well before the TV lawyers set to work. In 1963, the only really important point is that 'Girl From the North Country' comes to occupy the patch of vinyl at side one, track two. Reality resumes.

*

Suze Rotolo would one day remember that in the late spring of 1963 she was working at the Sheridan Square Playhouse on a 'bare bones' revival of a show called *Brecht on Brecht*. It was a six-handed, second-string production of a pastiche revue that had run for 200 performances at the Theatre de Lys on Christopher Street only the year before. That staging, in its turn, had exploited the record-breaking success of Brecht and Weill's *The Threepenny Opera*, albeit in Marc Blitzstein's compromised and 'tempered' version, over six years and 2,611 performances. Kurt Weill's wife, Lotte Lenya, had been the authentic star in both of these triumphs. She was not featured at Sheridan Square.

Bertolt Brecht, poet, playwright and singer-songwriter, was probably not well represented either. The huge success of *The Threepenny Opera*, that Weimar hit reconstructed from John Gay's *The Beggar's Opera*

– itself an eighteenth-century 'anti-opera' built on broadside-ballad pop – had been the exception to the Broadway rule. The Great White Way didn't care for Marxist dramaturges with fancy theories who thought they could overthrow society with their didactic plays. At the time of his death in 1956 Brecht was one of the most important playwrights in the world, revolutionary in several senses of the word, but America had never been impressed. *The Threepenny Opera* aside, he was a flop. Even with that exception allowed, even in a tuneful, bowdlerised version of the original 1928 show – for Marc Blitzstein's own Communism was long behind him – off-Broadway theatres and audiences of Village leftists were the core of Brecht's support.

No one should have been surprised. The refugee from the Nazis, blacklisted in Hollywood, had returned to Europe in 1947 on the day after his date with the House Un-American Activities Committee. In that comical interview he had denied Communist Party membership, made a few unintelligible jokes-in-translation, sported his usual drab overalls and drawn tirelessly – a certain contempt was detected – on one of his foul cigars. As a biographer has observed, Brecht 'did not aspire to American citizenship'.

The denial of party membership was entirely truthful, however, perplexing as that must have seemed to Washington red-baiters. At the hearing Brecht 'simply withdrew into his role of author who wanted to write and do what he thought right, and whose life's work was inconsistent with membership of the Communist Party'.[7] Some comrades would later denounce this statement of fact – certain parallels might amuse – as a betrayal, but they too missed the point. Brecht was certainly a Marxist, indisputably a plagiarist, probably a coward, demonstrably a liar, deficient in most of the usual human virtues and utterly self-seeking. 'Literary property is an item that should be classed with allotment gardens and such things,' he had said grandly after being caught red (deepest red) handed 'borrowing' another writer's translations of François Villon wholesale for the benefit of *The Threepenny Opera*. (Parallels might now be counted hilarious.) Brecht was also a genius. Without his larceny and his poetry the history of culture in the twentieth century would be missing a chapter. The artist's personality was neither here nor there. Dylan had never been exposed to this character, or to his songs. Of *Brecht on Brecht*, Suze remembered:

---

7   The quotations in both cases derive from Klaus Völker's *Brecht: A Biography* (1976), Ch. 28.

I told [Bob] to meet me at the theater earlier than usual so he could catch a few rehearsals. I really wanted him to see the play and one performance in particular: the actress Micki Grant singing 'Pirate Jenny' . . . It is a compelling song of revenge and as sung by Micki Grant, a black woman, it took on another dimension. This was the civil rights era, and listening to her sing the song was a powerful piece of living theater. I knew Bob should not miss it. He sat still and quiet. Didn't even jiggle his leg. Brecht would be part of him now, as would the performance of Micki Grant as Pirate Jenny.[8]

Not quite. Dylan did not embark on a Marxist analysis of actually existing reality, as Brecht would have hoped, on becoming transfixed by 'Pirate Jenny', but nor did he identify the song as a proto-anthem for the civil-rights movement. Instead, he responded to the artist who at 20 had been 'writing new poems, ballads and songs every day', who had been performing his 'Song of the Red Army Soldier' in Gabler's tavern in Augsburg at the age – exactly the age – when Dylan was getting his start at Gerde's Folk City, and who had made shock his stock in trade. In *Chronicles*, the memory of hearing 'Pirate Jenny' was translated into the eternal present tense. One phrase scurries across your path; another punches you on the chin. A ghost chorus is always present, telling of the omnipresent black ship that encloses the narrative and tightens the tension. Dylan judges this a malevolent song, one performed by a fiendish anti-heroine. When she's finished, there is nothing more for anyone to say. The audience is left breathless, stunned. In the confines of the little Sheridan Square theatre the effect is visceral and, for one listener at least, unforgettable.

In *The Threepenny Opera* Jenny is an abused serving maid in a cheap hotel dreaming in song, as the play's narrator informs us, 'of her revenge on Mack [Macheath, 'the Knife'] – and all other men'. Quite how she counts as fiendish – her desire to slaughter the bourgeoisie wholesale aside – is one for Dylan to explain. It is also worth remembering that 'the black ship', usually a 'black freighter', is Blitzstein's invention, an adaptation of the original thereafter adopted by most performers of the song in English. Brecht's original chorus said only that 'a ship with eight sails / And with fifty cannons / Will lie at the quay'. In Dylan's imagination, nevertheless, the ship would go on sailing.

Its first harbour is usually identified as 'When the Ship Comes In' and the album *The Times They Are a-Changin'*. The connection seems obvious.

---

8   *A Freewheelin' Time*, pp. 234–5.

But that song's jaunty hopes for justice are a little too millenarian and too biblical, too much of a civil-rights anthem, for Pirate Jenny's implacable dream. The vessel's fleeting reappearance amid a fleet 'with tattooed sails' in the 1964 song 'Gates of Eden' is also worth mentioning, but it functions there as a premonition: such wasn't Brecht's style.

Dylan responded, as he always responds, to a technical achievement in songwriting. He cared less for what the song signified politically than for the means with which 'Bert', the cynic's cynic, had pulled it off. Dylan and Suze were both right about one thing. 'Pirate Jenny' is, proudly, 'a nasty song', a 'song of revenge', an assault. Granted her dream, Jenny would offer no mercy: she would run up her flag and kill them all. Could an idea so brutal be offered as entertainment?

In terms of technique, Dylan would soon enough have a use, and a desire, for Bertolt Brecht's lesson. The sly German was tough, relentless; he used his art as a bladed weapon. He had a lot of nerve.

*

Just before his own record at last appears, Dylan flies to California for an appearance at the Monterey Folk Festival, the west coast's answer to Newport, on the weekend of 17–19 May. It is his first trip to the coast and it becomes what is known as fateful. Predictable would also serve. Whatever his feelings have been for Suze Rotolo, they do not preclude an entanglement that still seems, years later, somehow premeditated. Love is just a four-letter word. But so are pact, deal, work and game.

He has met Joan Baez previously, at Gerde's in 1961 when he was an unknown opening for John Lee Hooker and she was a regal young star expressing a desire, never fulfilled, to record 'Song to Woody'. As Baez will remember it:

> He was not overly impressive. He looked like an urban hillbilly, with hair short around the ears and curly on top. Bouncing from foot to foot as he played, he seemed dwarfed by the guitar. His jacket was a rusty leather and two sizes too small. His cheeks were still softened with an undignified amount of baby fat. But his mouth was a killer: soft, sensuous, childish, nervous, and reticent. He spat out the words to his own songs. They were original and refreshing, if blunt and jagged. He was absurd, new, and grubby beyond words.[9]

---

9   From Part 2, Ch. 3 of *And a Voice to Sing With* (1987), the second autobiography, no less, by Baez.

A second encounter has taken place at Boston's Club 47 in April of '63: something must have been said. After they perform 'With God On Our Side' together at the Monterey Fair Grounds, Dylan and Baez make the 20-odd-mile trip to her house in the warm hills of the Carmel Valley. An affair ensues. Years later, she will make a poor enough job of trying to explain the fatal attraction.

> He was rarely tender, and seldom reached out to anticipate another's needs, though occasionally he would exhibit a sudden concern for another outlaw, hitchhiker, or bum, and go out of his way to see them looked after. He was touching and infinitely fragile. His indescribably white hands moved constantly: putting a cigarette almost to his mouth, then tugging relentlessly at a tuft of hair at his neck, inadvertently dumping the cigarette ashes in dusty cavalcades down his jacket. He would stand thinking, his mouth working, his knees flexing one at a time, right, left, right, left. He seemed to function from the center of his own thoughts and images, and like a madman he was swallowed up by them.[10]

People have made a lot of it: how she helped him, how he didn't return the favour when it mattered; how one conceived a dazzling political mission for folk's anointed golden couple, how the other had other, better ideas. It seems to be agreed that Dylan and Baez were in love for a while, she more passionately – or foolishly – than him. In one of her memoirs there is even mention of the possibility of a child being discussed: they talked about names, it seems. Baez also alleges that Dylan made some sort of half-hearted marriage proposal. But the professional and the personal were tangled from the start: one enlarged ego made use of the other. He was a trophy for her, she for him. All in a good cause, of course.

Baez and her fans have inclined to the view that Dylan misused her, especially when a woman named Sara came along without warning, as though out of the blue. The fact that Suze Rotolo had already received the treatment Baez would receive – thanks in large part to Baez – muddies that narrative, somewhat. You can call it a legendary romance, or file it as one of the usual tales of celebrity, self-regard and fleeting desire. Dylan hasn't bothered to explain himself. The only enduring pity is that in roughly two years as an item he and

---

10 *ibid.*

his lover attempted duets together. They were, to put it no higher, stylistically inimical, and sounded horrible. They also held opposing ideas about the nature of the singer's job. Baez never did come to terms with that difficulty. She would always be foremost among those fretting over Dylan's retreat from the barricades, and would write a truly terrible reproachful song, 'To Bobby', in the early 1970s, as though to inflict her distress on posterity. In 1987, in her second ill-written and mispunctuated memoir, Baez was sticking with the programme:

> Bob Dylan's name would be so associated with the radical movements of the sixties that he, more than all the others who followed with guitars on their backs and rainbow words scribbled in their notepads, would go down forever in the history books as a leader of dissent and social change, whether he liked it or not, and I gather he doesn't much care one way or the other.

When the affair began she was unquestionably the bigger name, and possibly the biggest draw that folk had to offer. Though only six months older than Dylan she had already recorded three gold albums, starting in 1960, by the time they met. Her first appearance at Newport, and her name, was made as far back as 1959. She had been on the cover of *Time* magazine in November of '62, been taken up by Seeger and granted no small amount of credibility. Baez, with her immodest sincerity and her concert-perfect soprano-with-vibrato, was folk music's idea of a folk singer. By the twenty-first century, when she had ceased to take herself entirely seriously, she would tell one interviewer that even in her earliest days as a performer

> I was like a lion-tamer. In Club 47, where I sang, if somebody was reading a book and they turned a page, I would stop the song and maintain a stiff silence until they straightened out and realised why they were there, which was for the queen, of course.[11]

In the same interview it was claimed – though not by Baez herself – that Dylan 'introduced her to the peace movement which she took to instantly; it gave a focus for her dissent and brought fire to her otherwise flimsy folk songs'. That doesn't seem likely. No doubt they talked about issues of the day, but it was Baez, not Dylan (mercifully), who would sing 'We Shall Overcome' at the March on Washington only three

---

11 Interview with Emma Brockes, *The Guardian*, 24 January 2006.

months after his stay in the Carmel Valley. It was her hit concert album that had included the Malvina Reynolds anti-nuclear song 'What Have They Done to the Rain'.

It hardly mattered. 'Protest' would define them both; he briefly, she for the span of a career longer even than his. Yet by the time things had fallen apart in her relationship with Dylan, Baez was overshadowed utterly. The bright young hope was rendered passé very quickly. *The Freewheelin' Bob Dylan*, released while the pair were still in the first flush of their California romance, had something to do with that.

*

It was necessary to learn something about politics before learning to despise politics. In July of 1963 Dylan instead discovered at first hand what his possible contribution to decency's cause might be, and whether it might actually have some point. The answer to every such question was ambiguous.

His ignorance of the American South had hitherto been near absolute. He had never been there. Before the summer he had known only the ancient history of the blues and newspaper stories. He had acquired the usual rational opinions and heard all the arguments, not least from Suze, whose commitment to CORE was unshakeable, but he had never encountered American apartheid in its own backyard.

In that, Dylan was no different from many of the white liberals whose outrage towards Southern racism could sometimes verge on the patronising, certainly on the naïve. Either was still a lot better than nothing, in the circumstances. In April, Martin Luther King had been arrested during protests in Birmingham, Alabama. In May, Theophilus Eugene 'Bull' Connor, the city's 'Commissioner of Public Safety', with charge of the fire service and the cops, had turned hoses and snarling dogs on demonstrators. In June, in Jackson, Mississippi, the NAACP's field secretary, Medgar Evers, had been assassinated in the driveway of his home, shot in the back by a sniper who would escape justice for over 30 years.[12] Just a few hours earlier President Kennedy had gone on television to announce that finally he was ready, so he claimed, to enforce civil rights with legislation. Kennedy had said:

---

12 Forty-three-year-old Byron De La Beckwith, a member of the 'White Citizens' Council' and subsequently of the Klan, was first arrested in June of 1964. Two trials in that year failed to reach a verdict, but he was convicted finally in 1994. Beckwith died in prison in 2001.

ONCE UPON A TIME

One hundred years of delay have passed since President Lincoln freed the slaves, yet their heirs, their grandsons, are not fully free. They are not yet freed from the bonds of injustice. They are not yet freed from social and economic oppression. And this Nation, for all its hopes and all its boasts, will not be fully free until all its citizens are free.

Kennedy had not been the only one with something to say. Dylan's timing that July had been perfect, as so often, just like the new song he had written. There had been nothing amiss with his sincerity, either.

*

Voter-registration drives were being held all over the South in an effort to combat the bigots' old trick of denying black people access to the ballot box. One was to be held at Greenwood, Mississippi, on 6 July. After some prevarication from Grossman, Dylan was persuaded to lend his moral and musical support. It was a quick trip, made with the Village veteran Theodore Bikel and at his urging. The pair slept in a church loft and sat crouched out of sight in their car when they were driven the next morning to Silas McGee's farm. This wasn't play-acting. The killing of Evers had left everyone on edge. But Greenwood in Leflore County had been on edge – had been close to war – for a long time.

This was the heart of the Delta, and the heart of darkness. Other Southern states had their bigots, their discriminatory laws and their racist violence: Mississippi was the worst of all. Seventy per cent of its black people still lived in rural communities; 85 per cent existed below the poverty line; and only 7 per cent ever finished high school in a system that allowed pennies per head for their education. White Mississippians had a median income three times that of black citizens and the state was run, still, by an oligarchy of plantation owners whose methods and attitudes had not altered much, if at all, since the Civil War. In Greenwood, many black workers were still earning 30 cents an hour and returning huge profits for these Dixiecrat barons. For those who toiled in the fields there seemed only one hope.

The ratio of black people to white was higher in Mississippi than in any other state in the Union. In many rural counties, in fact, blacks were in a majority. The plantation owners and their white minions understood the threat perfectly well. They therefore rigged 'literacy tests' for prospective voters, either by relying on low educational attainments or by demanding a mastery of arcane test pieces stuffed with legal jargon. For good measure, the supremacists imposed poll taxes and 'whites only' primaries. They staged arrests, assaults and killings. They unleashed the KKK, above all, as a matter of course. The result was that by 1961 less than 7 per cent of Mississippi's black population was registered to vote.

The issue had split the SNCC, the Student Nonviolent Coordinating Committee. Roughly half of its activists wanted to continue with direct-action campaigns against segregated lunch counters, bus stations and the like; the rest believed that black hopes could be transformed by voter registration. The latter group also saw a chance to put pressure on a Kennedy administration that had shown no appetite for the battle. The White House had in fact called for protests to cease in favour of electoral organisation. So be it, said this wing of the SNCC. After some fierce debates, the smart decision was reached: the organisation would pursue both strategies.

Exactly a century after Lincoln's Emancipation Proclamation, things in the South seemed to be going from bad, if it was possible, to worse. In the winter before Dylan and his friends turned up local white supremacists had attempted to starve Greenwood's blacks into submission by cutting off federal food programmes to sharecroppers and labourers. In February of 1963 Klan 'night riders' had turned a machine gun on a car occupied by activists. In March, the SNCC's Greenwood office had been firebombed and destroyed. Homes had then been attacked; dogs and clubs had been used repeatedly against peaceful demonstrators; and the Kennedy administration had taken 'no noticeable action'.[13]

The world's media – and some folk singers – had paid attention, though, forcing Bobby Kennedy, the Attorney General, to cut a deal with the great state of Mississippi. It wasn't much to celebrate. Food supplies would resume and wrongfully jailed demonstrators would be freed by a magnanimous governor. In exchange, the Department of Justice would decline to act against local officials for interfering with the right to vote. It was enough to take press heat off the Kennedys. It did nothing whatever for Greenwood's black citizens.

---

13 This, as with much of the Greenwood narrative, is derived from crmvet.org, the website of the Civil Rights Movement Veterans. Its article on events in Leflore County in 1963 makes no mention, incidentally, of the efforts of any folk singer.

So much for context. If nothing else, it helps to explain why Dylan could be quite so brilliant as a protest singer. It is also a reminder, if a reminder is needed, that his topical songs were happening as events unfolded: they were as 'relevant' as music could be.

The new song he performed at Silas McGee's farm on a hot July day was entitled 'Only a Pawn in Their Game'. It dealt with the murder of Medgar Evers but, singularly, it did not blame his assassin. That might not have pleased too many SNCC activists, but the point of Dylan's song – a Marxist point, in all but name – was that the South's poor whites were victims too, the oligarchs' tools, their prejudices cultivated, their fears exploited. They too were left in their 'poverty shacks', treated like 'a dog on a chain'. They did the mindless killing while those in power, actually calling the shots, stayed free and clear. And the poor whites were no better off for it. If Dylan knew nothing about the realities of Southern life before his trip, he caught on quick.

The realities endured, nevertheless. Caught in the newsreel cameras – a partial clip would surface later in the documentary *Don't Look Back* – he was entitled to ask himself what good a protest song ever did. No white racists were ever converted, as best anyone knows, by 'Only a Pawn in Their Game'. Nothing Dylan said and nothing he sang was liable to change Mississippi for the better. If he didn't know as much about the loose connection between art and politics before the trip to Greenwood, he learned better at Silas McGee's farm. Beneath the headline 'Northern Folk Singers Help Out at Negro Festival in Mississippi', the *New York Times* reported:

Greenwood, Miss., July 6: Three Northern folk singers led by Pete Seeger brought a folk-song festival to the Deep South this evening.

They sang in the yard of a Negro farm home on the edge of a cotton patch three miles south of here. The song festival, or hootenanny, was sponsored by the Student Nonviolent Coordinating Committee, which has been conducting a voter registration drive among Negroes in Mississippi delta towns for more than a year.

The festival was attended by 250 to 300 persons. Most of them were Negroes. There were a score or more of young white people, plus several white newsmen and a television camera crew of four white men from New York.

Three cars with white men in them were parked in a lane across the highway from the scene of the sing [sic]. There was also a highway patrol car with two policemen sitting along the road. There were no incidents.

Joining Mr. Seeger in leading the songfest, in which most of the audience joined at one time or another, were Theodore Bikel and Bobby Dillon [sic], who, like Mr. Seeger, are white. There was also a Negro trio, the Freedom Singers, from Albany, Ga. All paid their own expenses for the trip and sang without a fee.

One of the more popular songs presented by a local singer was one dedicated to Medgar W. Evers, the Mississippi field secretary of the National Association for the Advancement of Colored People, who was slain last month in Jackson, Mississippi. A Greenwood man, Byron de La Beckwith, has been indicted in the shooting.

The refrain of the song was that the man who shot Mr. Evers didn't know what he was doing and should be forgiven: 'He's only a pawn in their game.'

The sing was to have begun at 10 a.m. but it was a blistering hot day, with a high of 97 degrees. So it was postponed until the sun had almost gone down, and it proceeded into the night.

Protest from well-meaning Northern performers could only ever be a gesture. If its purpose was political 'consciousness-raising' it had precious little effect on segregationists. They knew all the arguments. They had been hearing them for over 100 years: they knew and didn't care. In the *Don't Look Back* clip Dylan sings like someone who is uncomfortably aware of these facts.

Some of his fans wouldn't be too troubled by that. They would spend years explaining the real 'significance' of Silas McGee. As follows: a farm, name starts with M . . . Surely it's the pun that explains 'Maggie's Farm', they would all agree, and hence unlock the allusive electric song's supposed justifications for Dylan's withdrawal from folk and protest. The actual politics with which 'Maggie's Farm' is riddled would somehow be of no account. Maggie talks 'to all the servants / About man and God and law' while 'the National Guard stands around his door': this is Dylan's 'protest' against the folk scene? In fact, some of 'Maggie's Farm' makes better sense if you stop to imagine a Mississippi sharecropper and a plantation owner in a white America liable to demand that you 'sing while you slave'.

Well, he hands you a nickel
He hands you a dime
He asks you with a grin

If you're havin' a good time

Silas McGee was an SNCC organiser, not a metaphor. In August of 1964 he would be shot and critically wounded by KKK terrorists, but survive. Later in the year his family home would be torched. Dylan's *The Times They Are a-Changin'*, 'Only a Pawn in Their Game' and all, had already made the *Billboard* Top 20 by then.

As 1964 began, back in the real world, there were 10,000 white voters in Leflore County, Mississippi, and only 268 black people registered to exercise the franchise. At that moment black people made up 60 per cent of the county's population.

*

The tasteful version of 'Blowin' in the Wind' by Grossman's two-men-and-a-blonde trio was meanwhile continuing its ascent towards the top of the pop charts. That summer, as a consequence, a common enough question was beginning to prove difficult for its subject: who was this Bob Dylan? Was he truly the author of the effete anthem, or the uncompromising and unkempt performer with the rocks and gravel voice? Could he possibly be both? At the Newport Festival in July, just three weeks after his trip to Mississippi, one tentative answer was forthcoming: in the small world of folk music, he was now a very big deal indeed.

For one thing, he was granted the honour of contributing one of his poems to the festival programme. In reality, it was not the biggest privilege imaginable, given that Shelton (once again disguised as 'Stacey Williams') was acting as the publication's editor, handing out the commission and yet again operating as Dylan's unpaid PR man. The publicity, like the verse, was free, but the rambling 'For Dave Glover' wasn't necessarily what Shelton or the fans expected. That may be why the author published the 'poem' again in November, in *Broadside* 35. 'Dave' was Tony Glover, an individual from whom Dylan presumably expected understanding. There were some things he wanted to explain.

Once, back in Woody's day, it had been simple. There had been two sides, clear and obvious, or so Dylan maintained. He forgot, if he knew, that Guthrie and his comrades had disdained the 'capitalist' war against fascism before Russia and Pearl Harbor were attacked. But a folk singer's choices had been easy back then, thought the poet. Now

I don pretend to know what happened man, but somehow all sides lost
  their
  purpose an folks forgot about other folks–
I mean they must a all started goin against each other not for the good
  a their side but for the good a jes their own selves–
An them two simple sides that was so easy t tell apart bashed an
  boomed an exploded so hard an heavy that t'day all'ts left and
  made for us is the one big rockin rollin
COMPLICATED CIRCLE–

Late in the piece, after doing homage to the 'old songs' of traditional
folk, and after explaining tradition in terms of its apparent moral
simplicity, this confused and determined almost-poet had this to add:

Now's a complicated day–
An all I'm sayin' is 'at I gotta make my own statement bout this day–
I gotta write my own feelins down the same way they did it before
  me in that used t be day–
An I got nothin but homage an holy thinkin for the ol songs and
  stories–
But now there's me an you–
An I'm doin what I'm doin for me–
An I'm doin what I'm doin for you–

It still makes sense, by its lights. The world is not what it was: why
make songs in the way they once were made? If Newport wasn't ready
for that in 1963, the folk crowd could not say they hadn't been warned.
But Dylan's verse-piece makes one other thing abundantly clear:
'electric', amplification, bands of punk musicians and the choice of
guitars were never the crux of the matter, the meaning of what he did
next, or the reason why he did it. The songwriting changed first. It
was Dylan's self-inflicted problem if the songs on the album he would
make in the autumn of 1963 showed precious little evidence of the
transformation that was already taking place.

He emerged from Newport in the last weekend of July 1963 as the
boy-man of the hour. Peter, Paul and Mary repaid their debt to their
fellow Grossman artist; Baez sang 'Don't Think Twice' as though
sending a message to the distraught Suze; and Dylan and his new love
performed their 'With God On Our Side' duet yet again. One mission
was accomplished: he had made it. Folk singers massed behind *him*

for the big collective finish after his performance. It wasn't his fault, particularly, that the song they sang was 'We Shall Overcome', or that the fine sentiment expressed did nothing useful for the disenfranchised people of Greenwood, Mississippi.

Newport '63 was the zenith for Dylan as the singer of protest's community chorales. His reputation would be sealed when he accompanied Baez on tour – ending, whether he admitted it or not, his relationship with Rotolo – and magnified when he stormed New York's Carnegie Hall on 26 October. He would be there for Martin Luther King's March on Washington at the end of August, and sing in the shadow of the Lincoln Memorial. He would have his protest album and his pregnant song, 'The Times They Are a-Changin'', ready to go just as a president was being killed in Dallas. Newport, nevertheless, was when it all came together: if a crown had been handy, they would have given it to him.

What had he performed there on his own behalf? 'Talkin' World War III Blues', 'With God On Our Side', 'Only a Pawn in Their Game', 'Talkin' John Birch Paranoid Blues' and 'A Hard Rain's a-Gonna Fall'. The set was an entire world-view in five songs; it was 'the movement' dramatised, distilled and set to music. The set was what people – the people who cared for that sort of thing – wanted to hear and to believe. The fantasy that songs could change the world was in the Rhode Island air. Still, remember this: at the moment Dylan was being acclaimed as the voice of his generation Jan and Dean's so-so 'Surf City' was the undisputed number one on the *Billboard* chart.

After finishing *The Times They Are a-Changin'* on the last day of October 1963, he would never again be a protest singer. It all stopped, and stopped abruptly. There would be no more songs to which the protest label could be applied easily, and only one – perhaps because it had the word 'freedom' in its title – that might be twisted to fit the case. Electric guitars and pop hits didn't seduce Dylan. Protest ended for him even before the world had begun to absorb his one real protest album. It's a simple, now historical fact: *There were no more of those songs.* He simply ceased to write them. The 'finger-pointing' ceased as though a plug had been pulled. It would not resume until a deity gave Dylan the Word.

Those who charged that he merely used folk music for his own ends would point in their turn to this moment. Folk had taken him to stardom, where he had always wanted to be, and now he had no more use for a movement or its music. On this accounting Dylan was utterly cynical and utterly calculating. If that's your view, his writing can certainly seem to prove as much: the songs of 1964 were to be a world away from the songs of 1963. In 1964 he would discard folk's tropes and conventions almost entirely, reserving them for occasional jokes and allusions. The change was so decisive it can seem as though it must have been born of a decision. So here was another career move.

There were other things going on in his life, however, such of it as remained to him. He had encountered some good, human reasons to look inward for words. Suze Rotolo had transformed his songwriting once by fleeing to Italy. In the autumn of 1963 the looming death of their relationship, and the likely manner of its end, would give plenty of cause for further reflection, and for 'personal' art. Those facts make the tales of commercial calculation superfluous. They certainly help to explain some of the things Dylan would begin to write as the year turned.

He and Suze had 'ostensibly broken up' after Newport. She had moved out of the West 4th Street apartment, but for a while they remained 'in contact by phone at odd and even times'. According to her memoirs, this young woman crushed by accidental fame, his casual cruelty and his selfishness, even came to accept that the 'paranoia and secrecy', evident from the start, 'were essential to his survival later on'.[14] Rotolo wrote that Dylan 'was becoming prey'.

It has been suggested[15] that she attempted suicide at West 4th Street in the aftermath of Newport. Her memoirs, frank enough, make no mention of any such act or intention; other evidence is slight. Instead, not long after moving to live with her sister Carla in a small place on Avenue B, in what would become the East Village, Suze discovered she was pregnant by Dylan. She elected to have an illegal – 'read dangerous' – abortion. He was 'very upset at the idea' but went along with it: 'we', in Rotolo's telling, made the decision. It was a sad and brutally symbolic end – though things dragged on for a while – to a relationship. But if there were suicidal thoughts then she kept them concealed. There might – but only might – have been an allusive hint when she wrote, much later, that the abortion

---

14 *A Freewheelin' Time*, p. 274.

15 Sounes, *Down the Highway*, Ch. 4.

went smoothly, the only complication was my uneasy state of mind. I withdrew more into myself and let people think I was feeling physically weak from the procedure. Instead I was depressed and wanted to sleep reality away.[16]

Then:

One night at Avenue B everything came to a head. Like an overstuffed closet, all the bits and pieces I had shoved away into the dark corners of my brain burst open. I was a mess of whirling, wordless, and no longer containable sounds. There was no going forward for us, that much at long last was settled.

Dylan went out on the road with Baez regardless. You could call that ruthless, no matter how 'upset' he had been at the thought of abortion, no matter that he would continue to telephone Rotolo. You could certainly call it proof that he was devoted, first and last, to the career of Bob Dylan. Baez would claim that he was sometimes cynically dismissive of the protest songs even as they were being acclaimed. She once asked him how he came to write 'Masters of War'. His reply, she said, was that 'he knew it would sell'. Though Baez 'didn't buy it', she did have the wit to notice that Dylan's

active commitment to social change was limited to songwriting. To my knowledge, he never went on a march. He certainly never did any civil disobedience, at least that I knew about. I've always felt that he just didn't want the responsibility.[17]

He wanted exposure; touring with Baez would provide that. She wanted songs; he could supply those. Baez also wanted credibility. Her exquisitely rendered repertoire was all very well, but as she would admit 'We Shall Overcome' was about as radical as it got. Dylan in 1963 was considered incendiary and original; she was tasteful. In consequence, as Baez would recall, some sections of 'her' audience didn't take to the ragamuffin. There was even – a mild introduction to the black art – some booing until she stepped in to put people straight. Dylan would feel patronised by his mentor-love soon enough,

---

16   *A Freewheelin' Time*, p. 281.

17   *And a Voice to Sing With*, Part 2, Ch. 3.

and would fail to return favours when his chance arose. None of it was the basis for a great and enduring passion.

Still: *he just didn't want the responsibility.* Either he was guilty of bad faith, or he understood the nature of the implied responsibility better than Baez ever would. What did she know? What did anyone know who had not been afflicted by the sheer faith of his admirers?

*

At some point in 1963, Dylan came to the attentions of the FBI. This wasn't entirely a big deal. J. Edgar Hoover's voyeuristic bureau paid attention to a lot of people. By the time the decade was done there would hardly be an American of note or independent thought who did not have a file of some description. The FBI literature on the Beatles would become extensive. Its later investigations of John Lennon in his difficult, radical phase could have filled several volumes. Joan Baez, true to her convictions, would be another victim of surveillance and dire, copious official prose. Dylan got noticed, it appears, simply because Phil Ochs got well and truly noticed. They were Village colleagues, friends on and off, and seemingly in the same line of work. So Dylan became collateral damage, oblivious to the fact, in the pursuit of Ochs. It was a case, it seems, of 'add another radical folk singer to the list'.

Dylan's file has yet to be released, but the chances are that he was not treated as public enemy number one. Hoover's FBI merely took the view that cultural figures were more influential than most of the cultural figures realised. Nor is it likely that the bureau took a close professional interest in every detail of Dylan's life. 'Professional' was not always its strong suit: Ochs was frequently written of as 'Oakes' and was still being described as 'potentially dangerous' after his suicide in 1976. On the one hand, he was a real protest singer who continued to fight for his causes until the end. On the other hand, as Ochs knew too well, Dylan was the one with the artistic firepower. Perhaps they suspected him of something. All we know is that, thanks to a fellow folk singer, they took note.

This was the other face of the shining Kennedy era. In that shadow lay segregation, Cold War paranoia and the looming reality of Vietnam. If we say – for it's plainly true – that Dylan stepped away from the fray, we should bear in mind that he was not absenting himself from some tedious right-on debate among right-thinking folk. The issues were big. They would grow bigger before 1963 was done.

Amid all the fears for the safety of the United States it would seem as though, out of the blue, the republic was under assault from within.

*

Dylan began work on *The Times They Are a-Changin'* on 6 August 1963 in Columbia's Studio A with the recording of eight songs. Only 'North Country Blues' would make it to the album. A lesser song, 'Seven Curses', got some consideration, but was excluded, mercifully, from what turned out to be a dour collection. In this regard, at least, *The Times They Are a-Changin'* did not resemble its inventive predecessor. Dylan, overflowing with material, would again record a great many songs, and again leave himself with a great many choices. The first session was not particularly auspicious, however.

Things improved on the following day. 'Ballad of Hollis Brown', 'With God On Our Side', 'Only a Pawn in Their Game' and the sublime 'Boots of Spanish Leather' would each meet with their maker's approval when final decisions had to be made. The third session, five days later, was less useful: nothing would make the album, even if strong claims could be lodged for 'Paths of Victory' and 'Only a Hobo'. Dylan then called a halt, and went off touring with Baez. He was not about to neglect that connection. When he returned to New York, typically, he had a fresh handful of songs ready for recording.

In the last week of October, worthwhile versions of 'The Lonesome Death of Hattie Carroll', 'When the Ship Comes In' and 'Percy's Song' were achieved. The last of these, the longest original thing he had ever done at 7 minutes and 42 seconds, was always liable to lose the fight for album space given the physical limitations of 1963 technology. It is also fair to say that a fine (old) melody did not sustain a track of such length. Dylan might hanker after endless doleful ballads in the manner of ancient 'Barbara Allen'[18]; many in his new audience lacked the taste. To achieve songs of this epic length he would have to master dramatic structure.

---

18 'Barbara Allen', a song as old as most hills, not least those of the Scottish Borders, where the surname is common, would surface finally on Dylan's *Live at the Gaslight 1962*. The album was released in 2005, initially in a distribution deal with Starbucks. A new sort of coffee house for a new age, then. 'A Hard Rain's a-Gonna Fall' with your crème brûlée macchiato.

During the next day the record's title track and 'One Too Many Mornings' were achieved, along with the remarkable 'Lay Down Your Weary Tune'. On 31 October, the final session was expended entirely on that Irish drinking song, the wholly apt 'Restless Farewell'.

The overmatter for *The Times They Are a-Changin'* would have filled another album with songs to spare. Most of the tracks would be bootlegged before long, or dribble out via the snappily titled *The Bootleg Series Volumes 1–3 (Rare & Unreleased) 1961–1991*, a rummage through the vaults conducted by Dylan's manager Jeff Rosen in 1991. Demo versions of nine songs would surface a decade later on *The Bootleg Series Volume 9 – The Witmark Demos: 1962–1964*. Each of these adventures in archaeology would resurrect the question of choices, and renew all the doubts over Dylan's ability to judge his own work. His knack for overlooking or discarding some of his best songs was to become almost a theme of his career. The signs had begun to appear during the making of *Freewheelin'*, but no real harm had been done. *The Times They Are a-Changin'* was a different matter.

The album is easier to admire than to love. Too often it renders Dylan as the protester for all seasons, precisely the type he was supposedly trying to escape. Much of the writing is surprisingly clumsy; many of the sentiments are banal. Of ten tracks only three – 'One Too Many Mornings', 'Boots of Spanish Leather' and 'Restless Farewell' – carry no political freight. Of those ten tracks, half have melodies borrowed, allegedly or demonstrably, from other songs. In one case, with 'Boots of Spanish Leather', Dylan is recycling his own 'Girl From the North Country', itself derived from the old English tune 'Scarborough Fair'. In another instance, that of 'With God On Our Side', the act of creative theft is at first hearing spectacular.

Dominic Behan would rage about it for years afterwards. Even in the months before his early death, aged 60, in 1989 'fuckin' Dylan' could induce a peroration on plagiarism. Dominic could make it sound like an open-and-shut case. What was 'With God On Our Side', right down to its phrasing, if not his own 'The Patriot Game'? The business became strange only if you happened to ask an otherwise endearing man why, if the evidence was plain, he didn't sue.

Somehow the thirst for justice faded then, along with the dying notes, no doubt, of old 'sources' as various – you can take your pick – as 'The Merry Month of May', 'The Nightingale', 'The Shores of Lough Erne' or 'The Grenadier and the Lady'. Dominic had made a great song in 1957 from the contradictions of Irish Republicanism, but the melody had no more belonged to him than it ever belonged to Dylan. The difference, it seemed, was between the methods of *real* folk people and upstart stars growing rich.

All this is evidence, in its way, for the fact that *The Times They Are a-Changin'* was in no sense a great leap forward: Dylan was still depending on tried and tested methods. The album also provided disputable evidence that he was growing tired of the 'protest' label: injustice was his topic, over and over. There is not much light and shade here. He was going through the motions, giving people what they thought they wanted. Listening to the collection now, you can easily believe he was growing tired of it all.

That truth, in turn, might explain something too often forgotten by those who run the title song over monochrome period newsreels and use it to justify the 'voice of a generation' cliché: *The Times They Are a-Changin'* was not a monster hit. Achieving number 20 on the *Billboard* 200 was no disgrace, least of all by the standards of Greenwich Village. But the idea that Dylan swept all before him in the early 1960s is a nonsense. In October of 1964, Nat Hentoff, writing in *The New Yorker*, would report that the first three albums had 'reached a cumulative sales figure of nearly four hundred thousand'. That was good, not great: by 1962, Baez's first three albums had gone gold.

Freewheelin' got to number 22, according to *Billboard*; 1964's *Another Side of Bob Dylan* was very nearly a certified flop, meanwhile, managing only number 43. *The Times They Are a-Changin'*, in that context, was no commercial breakthrough. If anything, it confirmed what people knew about Bob Dylan, if they cared. The belief that a vast American audience was out there, waiting for the message, is not borne out by the music-buying habits of that audience. The early Dylan is better described as a star in Britain, in fact, with each of these early albums showing in the UK's Top 10. Whatever his folk critics thought later of their prodigal son's choices, the fact is that he would only begin to make a real impact when *Bringing It All Back Home*, electric guitars and all, reached six on the *Billboard* chart. Literate, serious, righteous protest music would not be the making of Dylan. That, it seems, was fine by him.

He had yet to break away, however, or breach trust, or betray his admirers, or commit whatever crime it was that ended up on the charge sheet. In one sense, he had yet to show himself for what he was. The role of the honest folk singer fresh from the great American nowhere was one that no longer suited. One good reason was that too many people knew better.

*

On 4 November 1963,[19] 'Bob Dylan' was exposed as a fraud by *Newsweek* magazine. He was outraged, furious and humiliated. He felt he had been set up. In his anger he turned on his family, friends and colleagues. Overnight he grew a carapace of distrust towards journalists and 'media lies'. Yet at this distance in time you wonder: what did he expect?

Most of Dylan's biographers and hardcore fans have echoed Shelton in calling Andrea Svedberg's cover piece 'a hatchet job'. It was nothing of the sort. That it fell some way short of the reverence to which Dylan had become accustomed, chafing at all the praise or not, is certainly true. That Svedberg decided to play rough with a star (and manager) who had chosen to be difficult is also plain. But this was a *Newsweek* cover story – a very big deal, in those days – and Columbia's press department had approached the magazine in search of precisely that coup. Grossman had meanwhile been trying (and failing) to barter his boy's cooperation in exchange for copy approval: why, exactly? Besides, Svedberg wasn't the liar in this quarrel: that was the point. Hers was a legitimate piece of journalism, properly researched and, save in one particular – a large, insinuated particular, it's true – accurate. For Dylan, truth was the problem.

Yet if it hadn't been a *Newsweek* reporter it would have been someone else, sooner or later: he must have known it. His myths, fantasies, contradictions and tall tales were far beyond his control, even by the standards of a business that thrived on creative fiction. It didn't take a genius to check out his background, or to draw an implicit comparison between this denouncer of hypocrites and a few facts gleaned in Hibbing. 'I Am My Words', said the headline: a clever editorial touch. But the piece seemed favourable enough, if routine, to begin with. Svedberg wrote:

---

19 Though printed on the cover, this was the magazine's 'pull date', the date at which it was to be removed from the news-stands. Dylan must therefore have had sight of the story a week before 4 November, probably on or around 29 October, when Shelton was writing his letter of complaint to Svedberg's editor.

He popped up out of nowhere, another unknown, unscrubbed face in Greenwich Village, and now, only two years later, he sits in the pantheon of the folk-music movement. His name is Bob Dylan, he is 22 years old, and his bewildered brown-blond hair trails off into uneven sideburns. He sticks his skinny frame into blue jeans and wrinkled shirts, and he talks hip talk, punctuated with obscenities. His singing voice scratches and shouts so jarringly that his success, at first, seems incredible. Yet his knack for stirring audiences is unmistakable, and it stems, mainly, from the words of the some 200 songs he has written, simple words that pounce upon the obvious – the inequalities, dangers, and deceits of the 1960s – and hammer them home.

Svedberg then observed that for high-school and college students 'Dylan is practically a religion'. Right again. But here it came: in the parlance, the delayed drop:

He has suffered; he has been hung up, man, without bread, without a chick, with twisted wires growing inside him. His audiences share his pain, and seem jealous because they grew up in conventional homes and conventional schools.

The ironic thing is that Bob Dylan, too, grew up in a conventional home, and went to conventional schools. He shrouds his past in contradictions, but he is the elder son of a Hibbing, Minn., appliance dealer named Abe Zimmerman, and, as Bobby Zimmerman, he attended Hibbing High School, then briefly the University of Minnesota.

Interviewed in a New York restaurant, Dylan owned up to Duluth and Hibbing. Fatally, however, 'he denied that Bob Dylan was ever Bobby Zimmerman', and proffered his draft card. Svedberg had taken an elementary precaution against the ploy, stating parenthetically that her subject had 'changed his name legally on Aug. 9, 1962'. He persisted with his fictions. 'I don't know my parents,' he said. 'They don't know me. I've lost contact with them for years.'

A few blocks away, in one of New York's motor inns, Mr and Mrs Abe Zimmerman of Hibbing, Minn., were looking forward to seeing their son sing at Carnegie Hall. Bobby had paid their way east and had sent them tickets, they had told friends in Minnesota.

Svedberg was just warming up. That she had not cared for being messed around by Dylan and Grossman is well attested – presidents changed their schedules for *Newsweek*, after all – but if 'truth' was the game, two could play. In the restaurant, her subject became truculent, probably because he knew where the questions were heading, and ended the interview. It was not a smart move.

> Why Dylan – he picked the name in admiration for Dylan Thomas – should bother to deny his past is a mystery. Perhaps he feels it would spoil the image he works so hard to cultivate – with his dress, with his talk, with the deliberately atrocious grammar and pronunciation in his songs. He says he hates the commercial side of folk music, but he has two agents who hover about him, guarding his words and fattening his contracts. He scorns the press's interest in him, but he wants to know how long a story about him will run and if there will be a photograph. He is a complicated young man, surrounded now by complicated rumors.
>
> There is even a rumor circulating that Dylan did not write 'Blowin' in the Wind', that it was written by a Millburn (N.J.) High student named Lorre Wyatt, who sold it to the singer. Dylan says he did write the song and Wyatt denies authorship, but several Millburn students claim they heard the song from Wyatt before Dylan ever sang it.

The last part was a piece of pernicious nonsense, of course – if Wyatt denied it, why print the legend? – but its use was invoked long afterwards by fans to discredit Svedberg and excuse Dylan. Shelton even wrote to *Newsweek*'s editor to complain of a 'rankly incompetent' piece of hatchet work, and to defend the noble folk tradition of adaptation. (Why this argument was relevant, given that 'Blowin' in the Wind' owed nothing to anyone living, is hard to explain.) The future devoted biographer even copied his pompous letter to various writers, editors and 'music-world leaders'. Politely but firmly, *Newsweek* rejected the complaint.

It is interesting, nevertheless, that Shelton felt the need to defend Dylan's honour. Clearly, he was worried about the article's impact. Did he fear that others might join in the fun with some true stories of their own? If so, he soon changed his mind. Within five years Shelton too would be digging around in Hibbing, excavating the truth and persuading Abe and Beatty to say a few things their son might have preferred them to have left unsaid. Would the biographer have felt able to do so had Svedberg not twisted a few raw nerves and invited her readers to wonder about a singer with a boasted distaste for 'phonies'?

It is a matter of record, in any case, that Dylan was still talking nonsense about his past only weeks before the encounter with Svedberg. Behind the foolish lies there was a compulsive need, and mysteries he did not invent. This appeared, for one example, in the *New York Daily Mirror* in September of 1963:

> His parents and a younger brother are still in Hibbing, Minnesota, where he first tried to leave when he was ten, with his guitar and harmonica. He got 900 miles away before police picked him up and sent him home by train.
>
> 'I got walloped, but not hard enough to make me stay,' Dylan says, 'I took off again at 12 and five times after that, getting caught and walloped each time. But when I was 18 I made it.'
>
> He touched about every state, trying to earn his keep by telling stories of what he saw, but eating more regularly when he trimmed hedges, mowed lawns, or any work he could get. His first New York job earned him $2 for a one-night stand in a village coffee joint. When another folk singer made a record for Columbia he was asked to accompany her on the harmonica. Columbia signed him. He made his first album and was given a Town Hall debut.

The usual stew, then: ingredients that could be identified easily – $2 a night; 'another folk singer made a record' – mixed with some stuff that only the hungry would ever swallow. The point is that, even at this late date, he was *still* keeping alive the fugitive lie of the ten-year-old runaway – 'with his guitar and harmonica', no less – and still pretending he had lived the rambling life and 'touched about every state'.[20] Hence the small mystery in this small controversy. Why would Dylan become quite so furious with Svedberg for eviscerating his deceit over his parents when Hearst's New York tabloid, a title with the second-highest circulation in America, had just located the folks, and his brother, in Hibbing, Minnesota? Plainly, he was deeply

---

20 Dylan was deeply, pathologically reluctant to part with this fiction. Close to a year later, in the edition of 24 October 1964, he was still telling *The New Yorker* that 'I kept running because I wasn't free'. *Newsweek* hadn't cured him: 'When I was 13, I was travelling with a carnival through upper Minnesota and North and South Dakota . . .' Only by 2005, and Scorsese's *No Direction Home*, did he put an obvious fact on the record. He had *seen* carnivals.

wedded to his lies. In some sense, he needed them.

As for Lorre Wyatt, he owned up to everything in due course, a fact that did not prevent the myth of a song's 'disputed' origins lingering for years. He had learned the song from a *Sing Out!* pamphlet before it was recorded by Dylan. Wyatt had then played 'his' 'Blowing in the Wind' with his folk group at their high-school assembly and found himself trapped, so he said, in his own deceit. He nevertheless thereafter enjoyed a small-time career singing and writing songs.

Of all the ironies in this episode – *Newsweek* could have fingered Dylan for any number of borrowings, after all – a couple of entertaining facts survive. One is that Wyatt was reportedly involved subsequently in Pete Seeger's Clearwater environmental project, and sang on the sloop of that name; another is that Seeger recorded one of Lorre Wyatt's very own songs.

'Bob Dylan' was of recent manufacture in 1963, it is true, but *Newsweek*'s 'hatchet job' was the first to raise an enduring issue. Thus: 'Why Dylan . . . should bother to deny his past is a mystery.' You could even add a point or two. First, he must have known that his tales would catch up with him sooner or later. Second, he must have guessed that his obsession with concealment was odd enough in itself to attract attention. Finally, he must have known, if anyone knew, why he was in hiding from himself and from the world, and attempting to hide amid fame, as a public figure. Or was he simply worried that his Village reputation as a musical 'sponge' would become too well known?

In old age he still bends the truth: they call it 'teasing' or 'myth-making'. In old age he knows, better than anyone, that his evasiveness has become almost as big a source of fascination as his music. Yet still he hides within the shell of celebrity. All of it has less to do with Dylan's right to privacy than with the puzzle of his identity. He imagined Bob Dylan. Imagining is what artists do. Then they live with the consequences, if they can.

'Restless Farewell', though it borrowed heavily, even in its lyrics, from the Irish original he had picked up from the Clancy Brothers, was Dylan's non-responsive response to *Newsweek*'s outrageous assault. He thought a song, this song, was as good as a rebuttal.

*

Even *Newsweek* couldn't harm him seriously: that was something else

Dylan should have known. Those high-school and college students were liable, even likely, to write off Svedberg's disclosures as typical of the straight, reactionary world. *Newsweek*, recently acquired by the Washington Post Company, was not a voice to be trusted. Unlike Dylan. Sometimes, despite the goading of press and critics, he would speak free and clear. Sometimes he had a strange way of 'turning his back' on politics.

He was interviewed by Svedberg on 23 and 24 October. On the following night he played Philadelphia's Town Hall. On the 26th, with Abe and Beatty in the audience, he played Carnegie Hall. These concerts were triumphs, and proof that Dylan had begun to reach beyond the usual folk crowd, disconcerting as that was for some. In his biography Shelton unadvisedly mentions 'Dylanmania' to explain the appearance of 'teenyboppers' at these shows. They were evidence of an appeal that was broadening and deepening by the week, despite the hindrance that was 'protest'. *Newsweek*'s efforts changed nothing.

Columbia had recorded the New York performance, apparently intending to combine the result with tapes of Dylan's Town Hall concert from April. The idea, supposedly, was to put out an album for the Christmas market, though how this would have squared with the imminent (January) release of *The Times They Are a-Changin'* is mystifying. By one account the concert record was supposed to go out 'in early summer 1964' but was supplanted by *Another Side of Bob Dylan*. That explanation also seems strange. Why release recordings that would in some cases have been more than a year old, particularly when the artist was developing at Dylan's pace? There were to be many more shows in early 1964 and some – at the Royal Festival Hall in London in May most notably – would be recorded by Columbia.

Solo folk performances were ideal for such ventures, nevertheless, and the fact remains that full-colour sleeve art and a nine-track acetate for *Bob Dylan in Concert* were produced. When the bootleg made its appearance in 1997, it came complete with a longish 'essay' from the singer. Suze also appeared with a bespectacled Dylan in one endearing photograph that would never have been sanctioned in the summer of 1964, or afterwards. In the prose piece – actually a column entitled (imaginatively) 'Blowin' in the Wind' that he had written in November when Shelton was struggling to edit a doomed magazine named *Hootenanny* – Dylan asserted:

One reason why I could never be a cop in this system under all systems is that the persons I'd be bustin' would be commitin' crimes that ain't on any books yet – crimes that ain't on any records yet – that nobody's got any laws for yet . . .

There followed a long tale about sitting in a club audience with a friend while 'two Negroes were well lit up an' singin' an' actin' out dances that the prisoners do on the chain gangs', to the writer's disgust.

Shelton named this pair as 'Ira and Inman', though they performed as Inman and Ira. The biographer had Dylan objecting to their 'slick, pandering, bowing-and-scraping black music for whites'. This was unjust. Leroy Inman and Ira Rogers had released a couple of albums by this time. 'Pop-folk' they may have been, but the records contained songs that had to be misrepresented utterly to justify Dylan's indignation. This was the same Inman and Ira who had caused a sensation by performing Alan and David Arkin's 'The Klan' on the *Today* show in 1961. So who was indulging in caricature? Dylan, who could never be wrong when he was righteous, nevertheless turned his face away from minstrel spectacle

to Jim Foreman [*sic*] who I stood next t on a Mississippi sound truck an watched his face while he told the people why they gotta go vote – I started thinkin' about John Lewis whose speech was cut down in Washington cause some people were afraid t speak on the same platform with somebody who could actually think t say 'We shall march thru the South like Sherman's Army.'

The piece went on to talk about racism's victims, civil-rights organisers and the Freedom Riders. If Dylan was already growing uneasy with 'politics', this declaration allowed no room for ambiguity. It was acute, too, in its understanding of the comfortable liberal conscience. So the writer thought about

headlines that tell stories like they were happenin' in a faraway country an tell 'm in the kinda way t make people sit around analizin' an discussin' an philosophizin' and theorizin' like some kinda college sociology problem was takin' place and nothin' more.

The sub-Huck Finn prose palls after a while. The attendant roll of honour – Miles Davis, Mavis Staples, Paul Robeson, Diana Sands, James Baldwin – feels contrived. A passage on the plight of 'the poor petty robber' who steals for the sake of 'his wife an kids' is meanwhile a routine Guthrie trope, and a then-standard Dylan inquiry: who are the real criminals? But had the album been released, essay or no essay, his chances of escape from a political 'leadership role' might have been slim. He wasn't trying to hide: these were his beliefs, as he understood belief. His self-evident sincerity is also a reminder of why quite so many people were to feel quite so betrayed when Dylan made for the ideological exits. You didn't mess around with this sort of commitment. A pity, though – not for the first time or the last – about the facts.

It has been said that the album was pulled, despite publicity material having been distributed around New York, because the Columbia suits couldn't cope with 'Last Thoughts on Woody Guthrie', the prose poem and eulogy delivered at Town Hall. This is possibly true. On the bootleg version it appears, dauntingly, as the opening track of *In Concert*: 'Last' would be first.

It has also been claimed that the album was abandoned because it was 'out of date' by the year's end. This is certainly true. But the 'lost' record remains a mesmerising sampling of two mesmerising concerts.[21] It answers one accusation: Dylan didn't quit folk music just because of mere opportunism and the main chance. Late in 1963, he had the world at his feet. He could easily have become the biggest thing the genre had ever seen. The trouble was, that wasn't such a big thing, and nor was it readily understood. Dylan was not yet part of the cultural language. The arbiters were still struggling to come to terms with him.

Witness Shelton's *New York Times* review of the Carnegie Hall show. With certain familiar reservations – 'Mr Dylan is far from being a "finished" artist' – it's another laudatory notice. But it misrepresents

---

21 In 2005, Columbia issued a promotional six-track version of *In Concert* entitled *Live at Carnegie Hall 1963* to publicise Scorsese's *No Direction Home*. Two further songs appeared on the film's 'soundtrack' album, another pair having appeared on *The Bootleg Series Volumes 1–3*. The cover art echoed the design planned for the aborted 1963 record, but the choice of tracks – 'Lay Down Your Weary Tune' aside – differed. First you have to wonder if the bootleg version is correct, then ask yourself why 'Hattie Carroll', first performed at Carnegie Hall, is represented in none of these collections.

its subject utterly. What were the unwary to make of this artist when the omniscient *Times* could declare:

> To regard Mr Dylan as merely an entertainer is to slight his importance. Rather, he is a moralist, a pamphleteer, an angry young man with a guitar, a social protest poet, a latter-day James Dean who knows what he is rebelling against, perhaps an American Yevtushenko (the Russian poet).

Dylan (the American poet) could still be upbraided mildly for 'songs [that] were almost speeches delivered to guitar chording'. Worse, 'Some of his lyrics have been left unwrought.' *Unwrought*? In this underwrought review Shelton allowed that these observations were 'trifles'. Instead, his praise at the conclusion of the notice did the real damage. Dylan might have begun to tire of political responsibility. That was his tough luck. The man from the *Times* decreed that he was 'assuming the role of radical spokesman, with music as his vehicle'. The response from the Carnegie Hall audience suggested that he was, like it or not, 'speaking for them, too'.

*

He worked fast in those days. He would never show much patience for the studio, but in his first flowering 'historic' tracks would be knocked off, time and again, in one take or two. Then, like as not – another abiding creative tic – he would discard a song that astonished all who heard it. 'Lay Down Your Weary Tune' was one such.

Perhaps the fact that this was another song with obvious antecedents swayed the singer, though that consideration was rarely an obstacle for Dylan or any of the folk-scene magpies. Perhaps he felt forced to choose between this track and 'Restless Farewell', a song supposedly intended as a rebuke to *Newsweek*'s newshounds. Perhaps, guided by what he wanted to hear in his head, he judged the song a failure. His apparent profligacy has often been guided by motives that seem opaque, to say the least, to his fans. The fact remains that inferior stuff could have been dumped, and no harm done, from *The Times They Are a-Changin'*. 'Lay Down Your Weary Tune' was an early example of a theme that would preoccupy followers of his career: the abandoned masterpiece.

Dylan has recalled that the song was written in California, at Joan

Baez's house 'outside Big Sur' in the Carmel Valley. He has remembered[22] immersing himself in Scottish ballads, and a particular ballad 'on an old 78 record that I was trying to really capture the feeling of, that was haunting me'.

> I couldn't get it out of my head. There were no lyrics or anything. It was just a melody, had bagpipes and a lot of stuff in it. I wanted lyrics that would feel the same way. I don't remember what the original record was, but this was pretty similar to that, the melody anyway.

Bagpipes: right. And a ballad without words. And another of the old things to which he could not, for the life of him, put a name. The album he was making echoed with the ghosts of the Scottish tradition, in any case, and with their perennial themes of life, death and remembrance. But this was a Dylan song, and another single take captured in Columbia's New York studios on 24 October 1963. Just a week later, in Washington DC, the President of the United States said to his wife: 'We're heading into nut country today. But, Jackie, if somebody wants to shoot me from a window with a rifle, nobody can stop it, so why worry about it?'[23]

> Struck by the sounds before the sun
> I knew the night had gone
> The morning breeze like a bugle blew
> Against the drums of dawn
>
> Lay down your weary tune, lay down
> Lay down the song you strum
> And rest yourself 'neath the strength of strings
> No voice can hope to hum

It is recorded that some people around the president were uneasy about a trip to Texas. It was no secret that politics had become viscerally nasty and habitually sectarian. The background noise of right-wing chatter was audible and growing louder. Bobby Kennedy had been advised to keep JFK away from Dallas. While the Secret Service and the FBI worried about the fringe right-wingers who

---

22 Interview with Cameron Crowe, *Biograph* booklet (1985).
23 Dallek, *John F. Kennedy: An Unfinished Life* (2003).

damned the president for being soft on Communism or too interested in black Americans, the guardians overlooked – so runs the narrative – a Castro sympathiser who had spent three years in Russia, and who happened to work in a building on Dealey Plaza. Why did Lee Harvey Oswald do it, if he did it? Amid all the documented facts, the answer to that question is still missing. The central fact is that half an hour after the third and last shot, in the early afternoon of 22 November, the wife of the President of the United States knew she was a widow. In a 'fear-filled world', as Suze Rotolo remembered, it didn't end there.

> Bobby, Carla, and I were together at the Avenue B apartment sitting on the rickety wicker couch, cigarettes in hand, in front of the old black-and-white television set to watch Lee Harvey Oswald, the alleged lone assassin, be arraigned. We watched him get shot right there, live, on national TV. If we'd turned to flick an ash, we would have missed it.
>
> Chaos ensued, both on TV and everyplace else.
>
> Did you see that?!
>
> The three of us froze and went deadly serious. There was no instant replay; these were the days before video cameras. The attack had been captured on film. The news commentators would have to explain what they saw or knew until the film was processed. Bob barely spoke and could not leave the TV. He was fastened to it. Everyone was.[24]

*

The third record, *The Times They Are a-Changin'*, was released mere weeks after Kennedy's burial in Washington's Arlington Cemetery. A coincidence, obviously. To those inclined to believe such things, however, Dylan seemed near-prescient. By another coincidence, he and Kennedy had started out in the same freezing January week in 1961, JFK taking his oath while a kid blew into New York on a blizzard. By the time 'Lay Down Your Weary Tune' was written the kid and the president were gone. Yet if there was truly such a thing as 'capturing the national mood' in the aftermath of the assassination, Dylan caught it, square in the palm of his hand.

Kennedy's murder was a shock as profound for Americans, historians tend to say, as Pearl Harbor. The three shots fired (supposedly) from a

---

24 *A Freewheelin' Time*, p. 261.

sixth-floor window of the Texas School Book Depository on Dealey Plaza, Dallas, had killed a man and seemed to paralyse a country. Darkness had spilled forth from JFK's 'nut country', where the John Birch Society, the racist right, the McCarthyite survivors, the big crooked money and all the rest of the unreconciled were united in the belief that somehow their country's president had no right to the office. The killing also left as a legacy an inextinguishable paranoia. The conspiracy theory, universal doubt, a refusal to trust even the plain truth if its source seemed tainted or merely unwelcome, had begun to reshape the national character. Henceforth, people would think twice before they believed *them*. 'Don't,' as someone would later observe, 'follow leaders.'

Still, in November of 1963 the common questions were simple questions. How could this happen? Why did this happen? What was wrong with America? Amid a group of rough, disconnected verses, Dylan would write:

> stunned by disbelief
> as everybody in the room
> we watched Walter Cronkite
> half asleep tryin his best
> t fasten rumor t'gether
> it was friday mornin
> yesterday a riot started up
> in Harlem
> t'day at least for now it is no more[25]

One loner had destroyed Kennedy and struck at the nation through its overarching institution and symbol. Echoes of Lincoln's death and the Civil War, that blood feud between the two halves of America's being, were audible. Protest? The word hardly seemed adequate. Still: *Come gather 'round people . . .*

Dylan seemed to face the darkness without flinching. The sort of people who could attempt to murder America's democracy, who simply refused to accept that their 'patriotism', God, hatred or fear were subject to the popular will, were the sort of people who would kill Medgar

---

25 From the so-called – that is, never by Dylan – 'Kennedy Poems', themselves a group of bits and pieces from what are known as the Margolis & Moss Manuscripts, a disparate bunch of typescripts reputedly purchased by Graham Nash at the end of the 1980s. Margolis & Moss are rare-book dealers based in Santa Fe, New Mexico.

Evers, or claim the same God on their side for every act. As ever, or so it seemed, Dylan knew what to say. He could express – and they would call it art – how people felt.

He was of his time and in those times. After Kennedy was slaughtered, his music was part of America's mourning. It seemed to say, above all, that something had to change. The problem was that the catalyst for change, at least in the eyes of some folk types, already had certain reservations about his assigned role, and about anyone who accepted such a role. Other things were running through his brain. So they called him a cynical opportunist.

There are those who still believe it. Other evidence says instead that Dylan wouldn't allow himself simply to accept at face value the questions, far less the answers, that were placed before him. The evidence of the songs meanwhile says that art was making a greater demand on his attention than ideology. But if he was growing sceptical about the political simplifications endemic in the folk movement, he was as capable of near-blasphemy amid the national mourning over JFK as he was of writing 'Lay Down Your Weary Tune'. He was drunk when he blasphemed, reportedly, and wouldn't make the same mistake again. But no one could say he was dishonest.

*

In 1962, the National Emergency Civil Liberties Committee marked Bill of Rights Day by giving its Tom Paine Award to the philosopher Bertrand Russell. In December of 1963, in the grand ballroom of the Americana Hotel in New York, amid 1,500 of the liberal great and good, with the writer James Baldwin in attendance, the committee honoured Bob Dylan.

He wasn't stupid: he didn't deserve it. 'A few songs' from a 22-year-old hardly counted as a life of achievement in the struggle for human dignity. Tom Paine himself, who knew how to upset a patron, might have thought otherwise. Evidently Dylan felt patronised and exploited as the 'protest' type with a hotline to youth. He was therefore nervous, angry, unprepared and drunk – to the point of throwing up in the men's room beforehand – and in no state for a foray into public speaking. Any lingering temptation to enlist in someone's cause was cured on the evening of 13 December. Dylan began by accepting the award on behalf of Phillip Abbott Luce and 58 other supporters of the Student Committee for Travel to Cuba who had visited the island in July in defiance of a State Department ban. Then he said that all the old, balding stalwarts of the left 'should be at the beach' because 'it is not an old people's world'. He rambled on, mentioned Woody, said that when it came to race he saw no colours, dismissed politics as 'trivial', talked of *his* black friends and the March on Washington. There was laughter at times, and applause. Perhaps encouraged, Dylan then said something he felt to be true.

> So I accept this reward – not reward [laughter] – award in behalf of Phillip Luce who led the group to Cuba which all people should go down to Cuba. I don't see why anybody can't go to Cuba. I don't see what's going to hurt by going any place. I don't know what's going to hurt anybody's eyes to see anything . . . I'll stand up and to get uncompromisable about it, which I have to be to be honest, I just got to be, as I got to admit that the man who shot President Kennedy, Lee Oswald, I don't know exactly where . . . what he thought he was doing, but I got to admit honestly that I too – I saw some of myself in him. I don't think it would have gone – I don't think it could go that far. But I got to stand up and say I saw things that he felt, in me – not to go that far and shoot.
>
> [Boos and hisses.]
>
> You can boo but booing's got nothing to do with it. It's a – I just a – I've got to tell you, man, it's Bill of Rights is free speech and I just want to admit that I accept this Tom Paine Award in behalf of James Forman of the Students Nonviolent Coordinating Committee and on behalf of the people who went to Cuba.
>
> [Boos and applause.]

Gauche? Certainly. Ill-advised? Probably. Accounts of the event agree that the hisses and boos were more intensely heartfelt than the transcript might suggest. For many who attended, the idea that Lee Harvey Oswald might have possessed a civil right was beyond comprehension, and Dylan's honesty merely a provocation, even a calculated insult. When a long 'message' of apology was extracted from him, he attempted again to explain himself to people who didn't want to understand. At one point he wrote:

> I do not claim t be smart by the standards set up
> I dont even claim to be normal by the standards
> set up
> an I do not claim to know any kind of truth

Dylan was attempting to be conciliatory towards those of whom he fundamentally approved. His remarks had cost the committee several thousand dollars in donations, for one thing. Still, this was no recantation.

> when I spoke of Lee Oswald, I was speakin of the times
> I was not speakin of his deed if it was his deed.
> the deed speaks for itself
> but I am sick
> so sick
> at hearin 'we all share the blame' for every
> church bombing, gun battle, mine disaster,
> poverty explosion, an president killing that
> comes about.
> it is so easy t say 'we' an bow our heads together
> I must say 'I' alone an bow my head alone
> for it is I alone who is livin my life
> I have beloved companions but they do not
> eat nor sleep for me
> an even they must say 'I'
> yes if there's violence in the times then
> there must be violence in me
> I am not a perfect mute.
> I hear the thunder an I cant avoid hearin it
> once this is straight between us, it's then an
> only then that we can say 'we' an really mean
> it . . . an go on from there t do something about
> it

Six months later, Nat Hentoff was composing a profile of Dylan for *The New Yorker*. By then, the singer was certain he was 'part of no Movement. If I was, I wouldn't be able to do anything else but be in "the Movement". I just can't have people sit around and make rules for me . . . I fell into a trap . . . . when I agreed to accept the Tom Paine Award.'

Trap or not, he was done with politics. As he also said in Hentoff's presence: 'I tell you, I'm never going to have anything to do with any political organisation again in my life.' The self-denying ordinance would endure, with modest exceptions, for the rest of his career. Some people had plenty of rules and precious little human understanding.

He wanted no part of them, despite the self-evident fact that his music had expressed his own convictions – political, like it or not – with rare brilliance.

*

What is a protest song? What is its purpose, how does it function and whom, if anyone, does it serve? The term seems to make things obvious: here's a song of complaint bearing the implication that something needs to be done, something can be done and something must be done. About something. *The Times They Are a-Changin'*, with its black-and-white cover photograph of Dylan in a work shirt, for all the world like a Walker Evans Dust Bowl portrait, seemed to summon a radical past even as it pointed to the future.

Yet there is an odd fact attached to the album that sealed the singer's reputation as a protest singer. Anyone familiar with Dylan's work from this period could sketch all the themes. Injustice, civil rights, struggle, truth and lies and politics: that's obvious. But let the tracks play through, attend to the lyrics, and you will not hear much, if anything, that amounts to an actual explicit protest. As for 'messages', these have more to do with doubt and hesitation than with a call to arms.

There are any number of biblical echoes and allusions. There are pieces of indignant reportage attached shakily to disputable facts. There are love songs, bleak songs, songs that draw from tradition or the daily news. There are touches, now and then, of prophetic vision, as in the title track or the majestic 'When the Ship Comes In' (even if that was only written, according to Joan Baez, because the scruffy Dylan had trouble getting into a hotel). But there are precious few lines in any of the songs that do more than assail injustice, deceit and hypocrisy generally. Who admits to being in favour of those? And how many times does it have to be said?

'When the Ship' *might* be akin to the old union anthems dedicated to a new socialist Jerusalem. It *might* be about political demands and the sweeping away of the boss class, 'the foes'. But where do the words demonstrate that this isn't a song about the Second Coming and salvation?

Then the sands will roll
Out a carpet of gold
For your weary toes to be a-touchin'

And the ship's wise men
Will remind you once again
That the whole wide world is watchin'

Political agitators of the nineteenth and early twentieth centuries once used religious language without hesitation, almost unconsciously. Many believed they had God on their side and were happy enough to claim Jesus as an egalitarian. The music of black slaves, equally, was drenched in the Bible's promise of redemption, conflating the salvation offered by faith with liberation from temporal bondage, Moses with Lincoln. Even as Dylan was writing Martin Luther King was speaking of a promised land. Which one? A better America or God's kingdom? Both, of course: exceptionalism, the devout self-regard that said the country was divinely chosen, was an old American conceit. It had begun to drive the nation's politics as never before. It helped to explain why Dylan's only other extended adventure with protest song would coincide with his being 'born again'.

In 1964, even as the appointed voice of his generation, Dylan was never so overt. He knew enough, even at this early point in his career, to cultivate ambiguity. People could take what they needed from such songs. But how was that *protest*?

Context explains a lot. In early 1964 it was still more or less unheard of for popular music even to hint at social comment. In an America just emerging from the red-baiting hysteria, equally, anyone who recalled past American wars with distaste, and called on God – an even-handed or disinterested God, to boot – to stop the next one, was probably a Communist. In a society still unthinkingly racist, speaking out for black Americans was 'controversial'. And Dylan, like all those New York types, didn't seem too enamoured of the patriotic Bomb, or the military-industrial complex that was fostering right-wing politics in the sunshine states. Explicit protest, in that sense, was superfluous. It was perfectly clear what Dylan was about: change.

The songs are hedged around, nevertheless, with qualifications. Sometimes ambiguity was useful; sometimes it satisfied his contrarian instincts. However much he may have approved of a cause, Dylan was a self-identified radical individualist. This would become patently clear with hindsight, but not for the first time or the last people heard what they wanted to hear.

Still you wonder: why was it so terrible to be identified with a cause and with protest? There are dozens of statements by Dylan testifying, variously, to beliefs, allegiances, opinions. He had a good, full mind, a keen eye and a keener ear. Nor did he attend the March on Washington on the last Wednesday in August 1963 out of idle curiosity. What convinced him, even before the Tom Paine debacle, that his acclaimed 'protest' songs achieved nothing, that in fact they offered only the delusion of optimism and political hope? What was it about a mere label that could scare him away from his beloved folk music? Bluntly, why should art and politics have struck him as antithetical, oil and water, mutually destructive?

*

What's the problem, in any case, with political art? Is there even a problem? Dylan knew more than enough about the career of Woody Guthrie to know that his hero had stepped up willingly when the poor and dispossessed were in trouble. He knew perfectly well that the performer he admired more than any other had identified himself explicitly with the radical, anti-fascist left, written for a Communist Party newspaper and vouched for Steinbeck's *Grapes of Wrath* in 'The Ballad of Tom Joad'. Woody had even paraphrased the famous words Dylan had absorbed at high school.

> Then it don' matter. Then I'll be all aroun' in the dark. I'll be ever'where
> – wherever you look. Wherever there's a fight so hungry people can eat,
> I'll be there. Wherever they's a cop beatin' up a guy, I'll be there. If Casey
> knowed, why, I'll be in the way guys yell when they're mad an' – I'll be
> in the way kids laugh when they're hungry an' they know supper's ready.
> An' when our folks eat the stuff they raise an' live in the houses they
> build – why, I'll be there. See?

There had been no hesitation on Guthrie's part, nor any suggestion of the phoney. Woody, above all others, had been authentically human in his politics. When Dylan stepped back from the collective struggle he was denounced instantly as a phoney himself, even as a hypocrite, a parasitical fake who had exploited life-and-death issues for something as tawdry as a mere career.

He also knew, however, that Guthrie had never toed the Communist line, and had avoided joining the party whenever he was pressed to accept the obligation. Woody had remained a man of independent mind, writing his 'Woody Sez' columns for a CPUSA paper, but never selling the paper, as good comrades did, or selling himself.

Dylan's dilemma, if he thought of it as such, was an old one: individual or collective? The unfettered mind or the greater good (as defined on high)? It's no stretch to say that in the end he reacted to politics much as he had reacted to the faith of his fathers (and to his father): he had a problem with authority figures. The problem became most intense when it became obvious that he was not only supposed to hold the correct political beliefs, but express them in the correct musical fashion. To play his part in 'the movement' he had to imprison himself in freedom songs.

The trouble would come to a head, once and for all, at Newport in 1965, but there is more than one way to consider that infamous estrangement. Who was ever capable of holding Dylan to a political programme when fame had made him a bigger deal to the wider world than any folklorist? It was hardly a fair contest. And what if the Newport confrontation, so perfectly realised, was not exactly as it seemed? To mould a hero, you must first provide opponents, whether the adversaries are willing or not. Some people would certainly attempt to tell Dylan what he shouldn't be singing. Can anyone name the individual who ever told him *exactly* what he ought to write and sing? Or would that spoil an old, favourite story?

*

At the end of January 1964, he began to put it about that he was writing more than ever. In fact, he was writing a novel. No, make that a novel *and* a play. Dylan said as much to the *Toronto Telegram* then, within days, to the Canadian magazine *Gargoyle*. So it had to be true. Such was the regard for this prodigy's talents otherwise sensible people took every claim seriously. Just to have Dylan talk about a novel was almost as good, perhaps exactly as good, as a Dylan novel. It was a kind of pre-postmodern thing. He talked about the novel very well, after all.

Almost simultaneously, however, *Broadside* was dutifully publishing 'A Letter From Bob Dylan' suggesting both that his prose needed a little work, and that the process of stepping up to 'real literature' might be more complicated than the poet-novelist-playwright-singer-spokesman had yet anticipated. In part, the letter read (rendered with Dylan's spelling, punctuation and the rest):

my novel is going noplace

absolutely noplace
like it dont even tell a story
it's about a million scenes long
an takes place on a billion scraps
of paper . . . certainly I can't make nothin out of
it.
(oh I forgot.
hallelujah t you for puttin Brecht in your
same last issue. he should be as widely known as
Woody an should be as widely read as Mickey Spalline
an as widely listened to as Eisenhower.)

anyway I'm writin a play out of this here so called
novel (navel would be better I guess)
an I'm up to my belly button in it.
quite involved yes
I've discovered the power of playwriting means
as opposed t song writing means
altho both are equal, I'm wrapped in playwriting
for the minute, my songs tell only about me an how
I feel but in the play all the characters tell how
they feel. I realize that this might be more confusin
for some but in the total reality of things it might
be much better for some too. I think at best you could
say that the characters will tell in an hour
what would take me, alone, two weeks t sing about

Like, *it dont even tell a story*. His songs were going in one, non-narrative direction, slipping the bonds of ballad, yet he expected to summon narrative on demand. He also seemed a little perplexed by a new discovery: some kinds of writing were harder than they looked.

Up to his neck or navel or not, Dylan was on his way out of New York on 3 February, preparing to drive across America with three cronies in tow and a typewriter on his lap. It may be that he got out of town just in time. Some sounds he had been hearing lately were crossing the Atlantic even as he headed out of North Carolina after a visit to the aged and distinctly nonplussed poet Carl Sandburg.

All through Friday, 7 February, the disc jockey Murray the K had been using station 1010 WINS as a loudhailer to send out news of Pan Am flight 101's impending arrival at Idlewild, otherwise the airport newly renamed as John F. Kennedy International. The DJ's hard-pressed local radio rivals, WABC and WMCA, with no news of their own, had simply copied his reports. As a result, 5,000 people, most of them teenage girls, most of them out of their minds with desire and delight, were waiting with 200 baffled journalists when the flight touched down at 1.20 p.m. Film of the event made that night's TV news. A pop record was about to be released in America.

'I Think I'll Call It America'

Passing the visions, passing the night . . .

Walt Whitman

WHEN RAMBLIN' JACK ELLIOTT MET JACK KEROUAC IN THE VILLAGE IN 1953 or thereabouts, the novelist remarked, 'I like the language of bums.' Elliott took out his guitar and played some Woody Guthrie songs. Kerouac responded – or retaliated – by reading the entire manuscript of *On the Road* aloud over three consecutive nights.[1] Some of it, Ramblin' Jack would say many years later, 'seemed like my own experiences'. And some of it wasn't so close.[2] Sometimes things only seem to connect.

Jack Elliott had imitated Woody to the point of impersonation. Lacking the real, functioning thing for the purposes of study, Dylan had then imitated Jack imitating the man they both wanted to be. Like some bohemian sequential movie franchise, 'son of' had bred 'son of son of'. Among the records Dylan had stolen from Jon Pankake back in Minneapolis in 1960 were albums Elliott had made in London in the mid-to-late 1950s, records full of Guthrie songs and Guthrie-sounding songs that helped to cure the young Zimmerman of his *On the Road* fever. Among the records Ramblin' Jack would later make, by no coincidence, was one he called *Kerouac's Last Dream*. When first released there was a photograph on its cover of a lost American highway touching the blue horizon's vanishing point, and it relied heavily, as ever, on Woody Guthrie songs . . .

For all his talk, Dylan had never been on the road in Kerouac's sense, far less in the sense understood by Guthrie. Student dropout jaunts and a professional folk singer's itineraries had allowed only

1 Nicosia, *Memory Babe: A Critical Biography of Jack Kerouac* (1983), Book Two, 'Double Vision'.

2 Interview with *Thirsty Ear* magazine, July 2002.

303

brushes with the mythos of hard travel and self-discovery, never mind the grubby reality. The voice of his generation didn't actually know his country well. As 1964 began he could count one trip to Colorado, the excursion to Mississippi, a few gigs in the Chicago area, and a couple of recent flights to California: beyond the eastern seaboard and the North Country vast tracts of the United States were mysterious to him. Inevitably, he wanted to know more. It was almost his last chance to ramble, and his first real chance to give substance to all those 'Bob Dylan' tales. Almost exactly three years after blowing into New York, he decided to trace a few footsteps.

*

On a cold, dry, late Monday afternoon at the beginning of February 1964, Dylan headed out onto the New Jersey Turnpike and found the endless highway. Moriarty and Paradise and the rest were not in the car, not even in restless spirit, though they were probably invoked by someone. Instead, there was a 'road manager', Victor Maymudes, and a couple of selected accomplices, Paul Clayton and Pete Karman. The three hipsters might have been mistaken for retainers. Each would certainly come to know his place. If they needed to, the trio would also learn that Dylan was no longer the mimetic shadow of all his old heroes, or even the almost-famous Newport protest singer. People said he was a poet in his own right. He was certainly the presence around whom all else now revolved. This new star held lesser bodies in his orbit.

The car the group drove is usually described as a Ford station wagon, probably a Country Squire, of powder blue. In the back, along with the luggage, 'was used clothing that Dylan had collected for the striking miners in Kentucky'.[3] The vehicle would carry the quartet all the way to California, where a concert at the Berkeley Community Theater was scheduled for 22 February. Along the way, on a route that would trace wide circles on the map, Dylan would perform in Atlanta, Georgia, in Tougaloo, Mississippi, and in Denver, Colorado.

Robert Shelton would afterwards do his reliable best to endow this eccentric vacation with the quality of legend. Amid 'detours to see embattled miners in Kentucky, a father-poet, Mardi Gras, and southern civil rights fighters', Dylan 'rolled like thunder across America's landscape, right through Whitman's "Open Road", Guthrie's *Hard*

---

3   Anthony Scaduto, *Dylan* (1972).

Travellin', Kerouac's *On the Road*, Hopper and Fonda's *Easy Rider*, and Kesey's *Acid Test*.[4] Reality was a little less cooperative than all the famous fables.

It was a weird trip nevertheless: one folk messiah, three not-so-wise men, a car, a typewriter, a guitar, booze, the lesser drugs and whatever else each individual could bring to the expedition. Amidst it all Dylan would write himself towards new kinds of song.

*

The country he was about to traverse was still deep in profound, near-physical shock: the usual word is *trauma*. The Kennedy killing and four days of national mourning had sent America into a fit of recrimination and self-interrogation. Those who celebrated the slaughter – and there were some – did so discreetly. The rest wondered: what kind of a nation could do this to its democracy, to its leader, to itself? The JFK myth of sacrifice, a bigger thing than mere reality could sustain, had already begun to form. Dylan had discovered as much, to his cost, during the fiasco of the Tom Paine Award ceremonials.

Kennedy's best recent biographer[5] can fairly state that had his subject 'never become president, it is doubtful that biographers, historians and the mass public would have had a lot of interest in him'. The Dallas killing, that 'death in the American family', had changed everything. In the estimation of the Nielsen ratings agency 93 per cent of the TV sets in the United States had been tuned to the funeral coverage. 'Kennedy Victim of Violent Streak He Sought to Curb in the Nation', a doleful subheading on the front page of the *New York Times* had said. The paper's editorial on 23 November had called the loss to the country and the world 'historic and overpowering'.

In 1964 no one wanted the truth about Kennedy's behaviour during the red scare or the civil-rights struggle. No one wanted to hear about the calculating private man. Above all, his compulsive sexual excesses were a well-kept secret, in the public sphere at least. In a society that separated church and state, murdered John Kennedy had become sacred. The sin was on his country. It was making the country as strange as any car full of beatnik types loaded with grass, speed, ideas, wine and song.

Old and new were overlapping in peculiar ways. Regarded

---

4   *No Direction Home*, Ch. 7.

5   Dallek, *Kennedy: An Unfinished Life* (2003), Epilogue.

superficially, America could still seem like the big, bold, energised country of cliché and saturated colours, the one fixated with modernity and trips to the moon, a country that discarded its past as easily as it demolished old buildings. Appearances were deceitful. The America of progress and hustle possessed a stubbornly conservative heart, always nearer to God – well over 40 per cent of citizens were attending church each week[6] – than to the latest urban Gomorrah. Thanks to Lyndon Johnson, the war in Vietnam was escalating early in 1964; protests against the war were not. The people Richard Nixon would one day claim for his silent majority were perplexed instead by fads and frenzies among the young. Those people were worried, too, by foreign ideas, and disturbed by foreign threats. They feared the erosion of essential American values. They didn't like long hair much, either. They were beginning to stir.

Senator Goldwater of Arizona would speak for those Americans in 1964. That summer he would say: 'Our people have followed false prophets. We must, and we shall, return to proven ways – not because they are old, but because they are true.' The Republican candidate, praised by Nixon as 'Mr Conservative', would also put a paraphrase of Cicero to patriotic use: 'I would remind you that extremism in the defense of liberty is no vice. And let me remind you also that moderation in the pursuit of justice is no virtue.'[7]

A former actor named Ronald Reagan would step up to endorse Goldwater, and assert that the issue facing the electorate was simple. It turned on a single proposition: 'Whether we believe in our capacity for self-government or whether we abandon the American revolution and confess that a little intellectual elite in a far-distant capitol can plan our lives for us better than we can plan them ourselves.' The senator from Arizona would fail catastrophically in his presidential endeavour, but that wasn't really the point. Almost undetected abroad, and still overlooked at home, the shift from self-assured Kennedy liberalism to a new conservatism was already under way.

In many parts of America, equally, the past was still going on.

---

6   According to William G. Mayer's *The Changing American Mind: How and Why American Public Opinion Changed Between 1960 and 1988* (1992), church attendance had risen to 47 per cent in the mid-1950s, commenced 'a period of modest decline' around 1964 and fallen to 40 per cent by 1971.

7   Nomination acceptance speech at the Republican Party National Convention, San Francisco, July 1964.

Poverty, poverty insulted by all the talk of universal prosperity, had not disappeared just because it had been long ignored. Kentucky, as ever, was among the worst-afflicted states.[8] Appalachian music would one day become central to the 'Americana' with which Dylan would be identified as a prime mover, but Appalachian reality in 1964 was less sweetly pastoral than utterly grim.

Suddenly people were beginning to remember the poor. Less than a month before Dylan's expeditionary party found their way through the Holland Tunnel, President Johnson had declared 'unconditional war on poverty in America' in his State of the Union address. The statistics, like Johnson's opponents, said there was no need. Officially, poverty rates were falling: by 1964 'only' one American in every five lacked the means necessary to secure minimal health. In the places where the poor tried to live statistics didn't mean much. LBJ intended to fight his war on a broad front, and to reach the people and places that seemed to have fallen off the map. It was good politics, too: here was one of the fallen leader's causes.

On 8 January in Washington, Johnson had devoted expanses of rhetoric to those living 'on the outskirts of hope'. He had called poverty 'a national problem', and said that each arm of government in America, national and local,

> must pursue poverty, pursue it wherever it exists – in city slums and small towns, in sharecropper shacks or in migrant worker camps, on Indian Reservations, among whites as well as Negroes, among the young as well as the aged, in the boom towns and in the depressed areas . . . Our aim is not only to relieve the symptom of poverty, but to cure it and, above all, to prevent it. No single piece of legislation, however, is going to suffice.
>
> We will launch a special effort in the chronically distressed areas of Appalachia . . .

In 1962, a historian and Kentucky legislator named Harry Caudill, himself raised in poverty in the coalfields, had published *Night Comes to the Cumberlands*, a book that laid the blame for the region's long history of woe squarely on the mine-owners and their investors in the

---

8   By the time of the Obama presidency, 29 of the 100 poorest counties in the United States, as measured by median incomes, were in Kentucky. According to the 2010 census, the measure of 'persons below poverty level, percent, 2009' as applied to the state stood at 18.4 per cent. By all accounts, the situation has since deteriorated.

North-east. In the autumn of 1963, inspired by Caudill's revelations, a *New York Times* reporter named Homer Bigart – better known, appropriately perhaps, as a war correspondent – had filed a piece that began, 'Hard times – the worst since the great depression – have come again to the coal fields of Southeast Kentucky and the southwest tip of Virginia.'

Digging machines were replacing men and the coal owners were laying off workers. Operators had begun to claim that they could not afford the wages agreed in the union contract. Worst of all, for mining families, the smaller companies were failing to pay the royalty – 40 cents for each ton hewn – that was supposed to provide free medical care after the pits had removed limbs and the coal dust had destroyed lungs. The United Mine Workers union, deprived of income, was closing its own hospitals, and facing the rage of its desperate members. There was no other work to be had, but a lot of agitation, some of it violent. This had been going on for over a year by the time Dylan arrived in the region. In Kentucky's Harlan County alone 13,056 people were classified as destitute in a population of around 51,000.

Caudill's book and Bigart's dispatches first attracted the attention of the Kennedy White House (a White House looking for a cause that didn't necessarily involve blacks). Soon the old story of rural poverty was news again. The January 1964 issue of *Life* was devoted to Appalachia's travails. People – and not just folk singers – began to inundate the region with donations of food and clothing. Dylan might have been responding to a deep, instinctive sympathy for a people in crisis. He might have believed, thanks to all the old Guthrie songs and his North Country memories, that he understood what was at stake. But he was also reacting to headlines: such were the perils of 'topicality'.

America's outpouring of concern was well meant, but often foolish, and it did nothing to address causes. The town of Harlan, for one, found itself with an entire railcar packed with ten tons of cabbages that soon began to rot and stink. No one knows what became of one celebrity's bundles of unwanted urban apparel. As the *New York Review of Books* had remarked in its notice of Caudill's volume:

> For years these hills have been scrutinized by social scientists, their folk art has been collected and catalogued, their unfortunate people have been organized and reorganized by the mining companies, by the UMW, and by various government agencies. Communists, novelists,

photographers, cartoonists, and song-pluggers have, for decades, been bringing word of these mountains to the rest of the country. But to no avail.

So here was Dylan, his new album with its riveting blues about the abused mining towns of the Iron Range just three weeks in the stores, with LBJ's speech still a topic of national discussion, heading off to Kentucky with that car full of groovy companions and used New York garb 'collected for the striking miners'. Jack Kerouac had never thought of that. It was a Woody kind of thing to do. But, not for the first time or the last, the voice of a generation was naive, and imagining himself into a role.

If mean-spirited, you could even say he was boarding a bandwagon. There had already been benefits for the miners at the Village Gate in New York, with Phil Ochs their driving force. A few weeks after Dylan's mercy mission, in fact, a whole platoon of big-city folk-types would descend on Appalachia at the invitation of the Highlander Research Center to witness conditions in the mining areas. Tom Paxton, one of the group's leading lights, would describe the trip in November's issue of *Sing Out!* (an edition Dylan would remember for other reasons). Paxton would write:

> Over the Easter weekend, my wife Midge and I, along with Phil Ochs, Carolyn Hester, Alix Dobkin, Eric Anderson [sic], Danny Kalb, and some others, got down to Hazard, Kentucky, to meet some of the miners who have been on strike and starving for over a year. If a man wants to scab, he can put in a 12-hour-day in an unsafe mine ('dog holes', they call them) for anywhere from three to eight dollars a day. Things are rigged so if he won't scab, it's seen that he's unable to get food stamps for the government rations. This 'high sheriff' runs the county the way he likes. As the song says, he's part-owner of a mine himself, so the miners have learned not to expect too much from him – except trouble.

The song mentioned by Paxton was his own 'The High Sheriff of Hazard'. He at least had bothered to understand some of the issues at stake for miners and their families, and attempted – in proper protest style – to put them into words. Ochs and Andersen would do the same. Dylan had no such interest. The songs in question had some of the honest virtues and all the flaws of the musical polemic. Thus Paxton:

It seems to be so since this old world began
That some folks are willing to scheme and to plan,
To gouge out a fortune from the poor working man . . .⁹

Thus Ochs:

Well, minin' is a hazard in Hazard, Kentucky,
And if you ain't minin' there,
Well, my friends, you're awful lucky,
'Cause if you don't get silicosis or pay that's just atrocious
You'll be screamin' for a union that will care.

'Ain't minin' there' applied equally to Ochs and his comrades. They could write touchingly, as in Andersen's 'The Blind Fiddler' ('I lost my eyes in the Harlan pits in the year of 56'), or ferociously, but they could never resist idealising the proletariat. They did so, at least in part, because of Dylan, but also because of Dylan's 'last hero', Woody Guthrie, and songs like 'The Dying Miner'. It meant they had to overlook a few things. The violence in Kentucky – shootings, beatings, bombings and arson – was not one-sided. Some of the workers were at war with their own union, and with their own kind. Ochs would write no fewer than three songs in solidarity with a people who did not *necessarily* share all his urban-intellectual views on politics or, come to that, religion. One of those songs would be called 'No Christmas in Kentucky'. To the tune of 'Wabash Cannonball', it would assert that 'if you knew what Christmas was, I think that you would find / That Christ is spending Christmas in the cold Kentucky mine'. Dylan wrote nothing about the miners. In 1964, he would never have written *that*.

Bathetically, there was no hero's welcome in the town of Hazard, and Dylan did not stick around for long. People were busy. Though it has sometimes been claimed that he offered to stage a benefit concert for the miners, no one has produced evidence that he made the slightest preparations for such an event, or that he warned harried union organisers of any such intention. It seems the locals were friendly enough, but most, it seems, didn't know much about him, if they had

---

9   'The High Sheriff of Hazard' from the album *Ramblin' Boy* (1964). The Ochs song 'Hazard, Kentucky' was released finally on *The Broadside Tapes 1: 1962–64* (1989). Andersen's 'The Blind Fiddler' appeared on the album *'Bout Changes and Things* (1966).

heard of him at all. No doubt he bore a distinct resemblance to a well-meaning tourist. Anthony Scaduto would allege that Dylan resented a failure to pay him proper attention, but the first of the biographers had only Pete Karman's word for that.

Of slightly more interest is a remark Dylan would make in January of 1966, during a long interview/performance on a Bob Fass phone-in on WBAI-FM in New York. One caller wanted to know what the mention of Hazard, Kentucky, would 'mean' to the star. After an evasive exchange, Dylan said: 'You shouldn't just know about Hazard, man. Hazard's just a . . . Hazard's just a propaganda.'

In February 1964 thanks were made, the clothes were distributed and his little group went on their way, apparently none the wiser. A couple of nights later they were shooting pool and enjoying what Shelton termed 'a nudie movie'. No protests there. But that, too, was 'the real America'.

*

Their next stop was at the home of the blameless old poet who had also never heard of Bob Dylan, and probably had no desire to hear anything about or from Bob Dylan. Carl Sandburg was then a tiny 86-year-old who lived quietly and wrote Pulitzer Prize-winning books about Abraham Lincoln while his wife raised champion dairy goats. The aged populist had himself taken a deep interest in folk song in his younger days. In fact, Sandburg too had been a guitar player and singer, once upon a time, performing the likes of 'Casey Jones' and 'Steamboat Bill' along with his poetry when Woody Guthrie was still a child and the Carter Family had only just begun to record.[10]

Never a folklorist in the pure, academic sense – and probably just as well – Sandburg had collected hundreds of songs during his annual lecture and reading tours, a haul published in 1927 as *American Songbag*, his 'ragbag of strips, stripes, and streaks of color from nearly all ends of the earth'. It would become a famous text. The poet had been a 'musical expeditionary' long before the rest, putting around 100 (so he reckoned) of the 280 songs in his volume into print for the first time, and later recording a good few of them. Unlike John Lomax, Sandburg had enjoyed no institutional support in his labours, nor gone into 'the field' with a musicologist's preconceptions. Instead, he had understood and appreciated folk music simply because of the people

---

10 Not just any guitarist: Sandburg had once been a pupil of Andrés Segovia.

who produced it. Sandburg was an inadvertent purist. He was also – as Dylan might have heard – something of an American icon.

He had once been a shoeshine boy, and a bricklayer, and a farm labourer, and a coal heaver, and a soldier, and a journalist with socialist inclinations. He had even been an actual hobo. In old age he was staunch still for civil rights, and still uneasy about the lusts of American capitalism. His poems were too easy for some tastes, even simplistic, and certainly 'too political'. But Carl Sandburg had earned the right to be called the real thing. So why was he being bothered by a strange young man?

Quite what Dylan wanted from the poet at Connemara Farms other than recognition, esteemed writer to esteemed writer, is hard to name. Once again he had given no warning of his arrival, but he had not simply stumbled across Carl Sandburg. Instead it had been a case, as Pete Karman would recall, of 'Dylan studying the map . . . "Hendersonville, North Carolina," he said. "You gotta take this highway" – shoving the map in front of Clayton – "and right outside Hendersonville is where he has his place, Flat Rock. That's where he lives."'[11]

The group found the poet's home eventually. By Karman's account – the only account there would ever be – Dylan announced his arrival as he reached the antebellum porch, telling Mrs Sandburg, 'I am a poet. My name is Robert Dylan, and I would like to see Mr Sandburg.' It doesn't sound like him, but who knows? Perhaps he was adopting an unaccustomed manner for an august occasion. Lilian Sandburg was probably used to young disciples of the poet's art turning up whenever they pleased: her husband was said to receive between 200 and 400 letters a week. When it became Dylan's turn to have fans thieving his time and attention he would be less tolerant than an old couple confronted out of the blue with four itinerant freaks.

What *did* he want? Or rather, what did he expect Sandburg to say? It is as though the pilgrimages to Woody had inculcated a fantasy that allowed no arguments: 'I am a poet.' If that's what he said, Dylan had, for the moment at least, lost his ambivalence towards the claim.

Throughout his career he would embrace and reject the poet's role. A year after the visit to Flat Rock he would tell the *LA Free Press*: 'I can't define that word poetry, I wouldn't even attempt it.' On the other hand – with Dylan there is always another hand – he wasn't shy in

---

11 Scaduto, *Dylan*.

this period about having his verses and his prose experiments printed on his album jackets and elsewhere. The *Times They Are a-Changin'* sleeve boasted 11 brand-new 'Outlined Epitaphs'; the next album of the year would advertise its ragged-right lines as 'Some Other Kinds of Songs'; Dylan texts would adorn the packaging on three out of four hit albums thereafter. In 1964, he would have a book publishing contract, too, if not a book. A lot of people *said* he was a poet. And he read a lot of verse.

At the time of *Freewheelin'* Dylan had said the only distinction between songs and poems depended on what could be sung and what could not: simple as that. The real, practical difference might have been that he put great care, generally, into the words for which he found music; the other sort of writing tended to be hammered to the page in bouts of Beat-like 'spontaneity'. It was an odd misapprehension on the part of a natural craftsman. The songs, most of them, came quickly, but then underwent careful revision, on the page or in performance. The poems and prose came fast and formless, as though Dylan thought structure would take care of itself, conjured by the force of his personality alone. Sometimes he got lucky, but not often.

He made a poor choice of literary role models, too: many did, in that period. Can anyone truly pull off a Whitman line apart from Walt Whitman? Frank O'Hara or John Ashbery, both coming into their own as American poets in those years, could just about manage it, if only for fun. Lawrence Ferlinghetti's *Starting From San Francisco* (1961) had done it explicitly. Not Dylan, even when he attempted to disguise the effort by chopping lines arbitrarily. So did all of Suze's interesting foreign-language poets survive translation well enough to be of any real use? Did the 'poetics' of Ginsberg or Kerouac's *Mexico City Blues* (1959) make the kind of sense that could be absorbed instantly, like an old folk melody? Not as such. There was the deeper problem, in any case, of competing musics, of the structures of verse, even of free verse, colliding unstoppably with the structures of melody. On the evidence of what he was publishing by 1964, however, it was not a problem that Dylan was able to confront. That didn't mean the problem would go away.

The sleeve of the record he would release in August would cram them in regardless, these 'other kinds of songs', the type size reduced to a tiny minimum to accommodate 'Poems by Bob Dylan'. Unlike the actual songs, there were many more misses among them than hits. Only the blindly devoted could have overlooked the fact that this writer

313

would have remained deep in obscurity had he ever depended on text alone. It was not, or not yet, his métier.

> i talk t people everyday
> involved in some scene
> good an evil are but words
> invented by those
> that are trapped in scenes

At Connemara Farms the bard handed Sandburg a copy of *Times* – Clayton gave an album of his own – and its 11 pieces of verse. What the old man made of the texts or of the songs is not recorded. He was polite, he chatted, but evidently minds did not meet. Sandburg had undergone this sort of trial by flattery many times before; Dylan would endure it too, for decades. In truth, he had endured it often enough by the time he got to Flat Rock. The fact made his clumsy overtures all the more tactless. Suze Rotolo had been a witness:

> After *The Freewheelin' Bob Dylan* had been out awhile, at parties I noticed that people would approach him with reverence and tell him involved stories about their lives and then wait for him to speak. They wanted him to suggest solutions for them, to enlighten them in some way . . . It made him uneasy.[12]

Plainly, Dylan thought a grand old man was better equipped to handle that sort of thing. Or, more likely, it didn't cross his mind that he – *a poet* – could resemble an importunate fan. Sandburg seems to have concluded otherwise. Pete Karman would tell Shelton that there was 'an immediate, unspoken communication' between Dylan and his hapless host, but 'unspoken' was how it stayed.

This counts as ironic. Dylan was becoming a poet, a better one in certain songs than Sandburg with his elliptical, homely and melancholy fragments, his romanticised reports of human nobility, his big heart on his patriotic sleeve and his formal inadequacies. Dylan was probably drawn to the aged writer because Sandburg had made the business of poetry seem human, unpretentious, a vernacular art. In reality most of the venerable poet's verse was crafted rhetoric, natural-sounding artifice: Dylan could do that. Crudely put, Sandburg possessed only a

---

12   *A Freewheelin' Time*, p. 274.

couple of literary tricks; Dylan had already mastered a dozen. There were songs on the album he left at Flat Rock that did the job better than the grand old man had ever managed.

Dylan supposedly wanted 'to see manuscripts and books', to be granted intimacy and access. You can only believe he wanted something resembling the recognition he believed he had received from Woody Guthrie. Instead, there was 20 minutes of small talk before Sandburg made his excuses. Karman, as quoted by Shelton, contradicted himself, but probably said it all:

> We had a definite feeling of disappointment, mainly because Sandburg had never heard of Bobby. As I recall, during the rest of the trip Sandburg was never mentioned again. Dylan sank into one of his quiet funks.

*

He got over it soon enough. He had three boon companions, after all, and a jolly three too. Mostly. Unlike an octogenarian poet, they all thought Dylan was the key to something. What they thought about the purpose of the trip is less clear. A whim? The young star's attempt to break away from oppressive fame, however briefly, and connect again with the real world? On the one hand, there seemed to be no itinerary to speak of for this journey; on the other hand, says one version of the tale, their drugs were posted ahead to towns along the way to await collection. Spontaneity had its limits.

In one breath this is a wild, instinctive voyage into the American heartland, with destinations, encounters, the booking of hotel rooms and much else besides left to chance. Then Dylan has promises to keep, shows to give, places he has to be. Whatever the claims made subsequently for this 'legendary' trip, it's hard to escape the feeling that he was living out the old, fantastic idea of himself as a rootless soul, and acting on the same impulse that had caused him to invent all the stories about running away from home and travelling with the carnival. Given his devotion in later life to the endless road, the Dylan glimpsed in 1964 is, almost in his entirety, an act of the imagination: *I am a poet*. He was living in his own movie, or in one of his own songs.

Victor Maymudes, stuck behind the wheel while Dylan scribbled, typed or dozed, was the only member of the praetorian trio who was getting paid for the peregrination; the other two were along for the ride, esteemed freeloaders on the production-company tab. Suze would remember Maymudes as 'silent and creepy'; others have called him 'worldly and engaging', 'a philosopher', 'Dylan's right-hand man', 'a bodyguard', 'a mentor' and a counter-culture pioneer. A few years older than the others, he was supposed to have produced Odetta's first concerts. He was certainly involved in setting up Unicorn, the first Los Angeles coffee house featuring live music and poetry, on Sunset Boulevard in 1955. He had travelled to New York with Jack Elliott and found himself meeting Dylan's requirements: tour manager, driver, factotum, chess opponent, hired hand, whatever. He would serve those diverse and ill-defined functions for two long spells over thirty-five years, the second ending in what court reporters like to call acrimony.

Paul Clayton had laboured long amid mixed blessings. Known as 'the most recorded young folk artist in America', he had made a lot of worthy records and precious little money by the time he encountered Dylan. A gay man trapped in 1964, 'Pablo' Clayton was bewitched, in awe and perhaps in love. Dylan was, to begin with, impressed by a real folklorist who seemed to know any song that anyone could name. One posthumous record-company advertisement would describe Clayton as 'the missing link' between Woody Guthrie and Dylan. By 1964, he was a glutton for music and amphetamines, a forgiving victim of the star's 'creative' borrowings, the melody to 'Don't Think Twice' – robbed wholesale from Clayton's already 'adapted' 'Who's Goin' to Buy You Ribbons When I'm Gone' – not least, and already a sad case.

By his own account, Pete Karman had started in newspapers as a copy boy, a dogsbody in the hot-metal days when typewritten stories and galley proofs had to find their way between reporters, editors and printers. By 1964 he was a *New York Daily Mirror* journalist whose claim to fame was that he had written the city's first review of Dylan. He was also a friend of Suze Rotolo who advertised the fact that he was unimpressed by the songwriting sensation of the hour, though happy enough to hang out in his vicinity. Karman, in the usual accounts of the expedition, heard all and saw all. Or rather, he was the only one of the four later to give an account of what he saw and what he heard. He has been quoted to the (faintly preposterous) effect that he was along for the ride as Rotolo's nominated 'chaperone', as though Suze didn't know by 1964 that Dylan had elastic notions of fidelity. It has also been suggested that the reporter was supposed to inhibit contact between Dylan and Baez. The criteria for guardianship, as for the best-buddy role, were far from clear. Why bring along 'a long-time friend of the Rotolos' when the relationship with Suze was in its last days? Why bring along someone who didn't think much of the music? Short answer: we don't know.

*

After North Carolina, the jolly band headed south, making for New Orleans. Despite the presence of a 'tour manager', the trip wasn't a tour, but Dylan still had a handful of dates to fulfil. One concert was near Atlanta, at Emory University's Glenn Auditorium, on 7 February. Gratifyingly, fame had on this occasion preceded the evening's attraction. That night, the students 'knew nearly every song by its opening phrase'. Afterwards there was a party, encounters with civil-rights activists, and – duly noted by Karman – Dylan's liaison with a willing girl he happened to meet. None of the four was in a position to pass judgement. The mystical road trip was, as often as not, a bad boys' party. Its contacts with the authentic heart of America were not always edifying. They drank a lot, did plenty of drugs, took in the reality of segregation and other strange sights, and rambled on.

The striking thing is not that Dylan began to write this or that song on this or that disputed date as America fell beneath the wheels of the Ford; the striking thing is that he managed to write anything at all. Over the ensuing couple of years the gift would come in handy. What separated this writer from most other producers of masterpieces was the ability to come up with his finest work in the least promising of circumstances. In Karman's account of the road trip the prevailing theme is of mild craziness, substance abuse and hangovers. Somehow, when he needed to, Dylan could shut out the chaos.

*

Two days after he gave his concert at Emory University, 73 million Americans were tuning in to CBS for *The Ed Sullivan Show*. No one was walking out this time. Had Sullivan or the undead from 'program practices' decided that the night's headliners were in some way unsuitable entertainment for the nation's youth, the suits would probably have been torn into small pieces and fed to New York's pigeons. America's teenagers, chiefly its teenage girls, had been raised to a rare pitch of hysteria. In Studio 50 on Broadway at 8 p.m. Eastern Time the veteran host, all big smile and befuddled eyes, was spinning out a typically inept introduction for 'these youngsters from Liverpool,

317

who call themselves the Beatles'. Sullivan said: 'Now tonight, you're gonna twice be entertained by them. Right now, and again in the second half of our show. Ladies and gentlemen, *the Beatles!* Let's bring them on.' Then McCartney counted in. For teen America, the '60s began.

One of the most tantalising images of a paraphrased decade arises from a conjunction. It was, of course, the merest coincidence. Yet while the four Liverpudlians were tearing New York apart, Dylan was working steadily, amid the self-created weirdness of his ramshackle trans-American journey, on a song he would call 'Chimes of Freedom'. In Studio 50 a generation was being exposed to the purest pop yet created. Far to the south, lyrics were coalescing on a pad and a portable typewriter, some clumsy and some inspired, that would not be contained within anyone's idea of popular music. Fundamental choices were being made.

Dylan grasped the meaning of the Beatles soon enough. He understood their art and craft, the way in which they had revived rock and roll yet added several new and unexpected dimensions to the form. They gave an impetus, clearly, to some of his own thoughts about musical 'directions'. No doubt the vast, unprecedented scale of their success also gave him pause. Within weeks, famously, the English quartet would occupy the top five spots on the *Billboard* singles chart. Come March, 'Can't Buy Me Love' would sell only slightly fewer than one million copies on the day of its release in the United States. In that sort of company, Dylan was the complete unknown: hence, perhaps, the modest blue station wagon. He was an East Coast phenomenon, not yet a real star; a favourite of urban 'intellectuals', not the mass audience. He would never once experience the sort of preposterous acclaim enjoyed by the Beatles. But in the space of the same few hours in February 1964, two different kinds of revolution were coming into being.

There was a paradox at work, too. For all their innovations, the Beatles would become the template for pop in its classical form, the cornerstone of a tradition. Dylan, forged in the traditions of folk music, would make something strange and antithetical with songs that were apparently anything but traditional. He was already becoming the alternative to 'alternative culture' and 'Chimes of Freedom', assembled by stages, would be one of his prototypical gestures.

Despite its title, it wasn't really the sort of song his folk fans were looking for. Because of its title – and its sentiments, its ideas, its delivery, its seven-plus minutes length – it was also a wide universe away from anything the vast multitude of Beatles fans would ever embrace. It was, in a particular sense, one of the first true Bob Dylan songs. For the journey it offered, he didn't need a Ford station wagon.

> Far between sundown's finish an' midnight's broken toll
> We ducked inside the doorway, thunder crashing
> As majestic bells of bolts struck shadows in the sounds
> Seeming to be the chimes of freedom flashing

*

The actual trip might simply have been Dylan's idea of a holiday from his several selves. Mardi Gras in New Orleans, thought Shelton, supplied the sort of images that would turn up in *Blonde on Blonde*, but it would probably have been hard to separate the fatigued group who appeared in the city on a Monday night, long hair aside, from any other bunch of inebriated young tourists. Fat Tuesday in the French Quarter, running into the early hours of Ash Wednesday, was not the ideal time for a study trip to the town that gave birth to jazz and 'Tutti Frutti'. The sole advantage for Dylan, so it seems, was that he could still move around the crowded streets without being recognised too often. Drunk, he got into a brief fight over segregation; mixed with sailors and transvestites; talked about authors with high-school teachers; and sprained his ankle.

> we charge thru casa
> blazin jukebox
> gumbo overflowin
> get kicked out of colored bar
> streets jammed
> hypnotic stars explode
> in louisiana murder nite
> everything's wedged
> arm in arm
> stoned galore . . .[13]

In one moment of intoxicated enthusiasm Dylan also told Karman that he intended to write like Rimbaud. Not, be it noted, that he *hoped*

---

13 'Some Other Kinds of Songs', *Another Side of Bob Dylan* (1964).

or *wanted* to write like the master of a language he could neither read nor speak, but that he would. It was that sort of vacation: anything was possible.

What thereafter became commonplace, though, was the kind of dim associative logic that gets passed off as critical analysis. Dylan mentioned Rimbaud while writing 'Chimes': *therefore* . . . In reality, 'therefore' is hard to identify. You could say the same about Dylan and most of his alleged poetic antecedents: as often as not, the evidence of genuine influence is thin. What he got from the Frenchman was an idea about creativity, not a literary method. To say otherwise is akin – and it happens – to invoking William Blake just because the words 'mad mystic' turn up in a song, or because someone is rounding up the usual visionary suspects. The attempt always to justify Dylan by citation, by reference to the quick and the dead he is supposed to echo and resemble, is beside the point. He didn't and does not need it. There were influences and inspirations, as with any writer, but a little perspective is required. A lot of young poets and folk singers had read the perennially fashionable Arthur Rimbaud.

Dylan's hubris in 1964 shouldn't be mocked. He had come a very long way in a short space of time by attempting things that were supposed to be beyond him, by failing (or refusing) to recognise his limitations, and by daring to fail. Besides, it was the expeditionary's task to strike out for new territory. Dope, drink and admirers tended always to agree that this was a good idea. With quantities of each at his disposal, and no one to explain that there was more to writing like Rimbaud than 'a long, involved, and logical derangement of all the senses' ('un long, immense et raisonné *dérèglement* de *tous les sens*'),[14] he would nevertheless achieve his own kind of success. Not as a seer, perhaps, but as a writer who seemed to many people, sometimes too many people, like the next best thing.

Those who embraced Rimbaud's advice on sensory overload in the 1960s generally overlooked the whole story, if they even knew it. The 16-year-old Frenchman, fond enough of his vices for their own sakes, had also announced that the first task for anyone wishing to become a poet and *voyant* was 'to know himself completely', the better to turn 'one's soul into a monster'.

Dylan could manage monstrous; real self-knowledge was as yet

---

14 Letter to Paul Demeny, Charleville, 15 May 1871. From *Rimbaud Complete*, translated and edited by Wyatt Mason (2002).

another matter. As the years passed he and a multitude of admirers would quote another of Rimbaud's lines, as though to explain away the problem of Bob Dylan, truth and identity. *Car Je est un autre*, the poet had said; 'For I is someone else/another.' Metaphysically true, no doubt, but what did it otherwise mean? It could sound like an alibi. Who – or what – marks the boundary between this I and this other? If the paradox makes sense, which Dylan do we trust to make the statement?

He hasn't said. In an interview published in the notes to the 1985 *Biograph* box set he would assert, 'I don't think of myself as Bob Dylan. It's like Rimbaud said, "I is another."' Near the conclusion of *Chronicles: Volume One*, almost 20 years on, he would recall that Suze had introduced him to Rimbaud's poetry. It was no small matter. In the volume supplied by his girlfriend he had come across the Frenchman's famous letter containing that famous phrase. On this occasion it emerged as 'I is someone else'. Dylan responded as to a fundamental truth of existence. His only regret was that no one had shared the insight sooner.

Not only would he claim to have found perfected meaning in words discovered some time in 1963, he would go on to associate the statement with his primary influences in the period: Robert Johnson's interior darkness; Woody Guthrie's propagandising rhetoric; and the structure for song provided by Brecht and Weill's 'Pirate Jenny'. Whatever anyone thinks of *Chronicles* as a witness statement, or of its unreliable narrator as a witness, this is unambiguous: Rimbaud's paradox mattered. It explained something to Dylan. It did not explain Dylan to anyone else.

All of this is complicated by the transparent desire among his admirers for him to *be* a Rimbaud for the age, as though that would settle all arguments over status and artistic seriousness. In the 1960s, assertion became fact. The actual fact is that you can find interesting parallels between the lives of two young men, but little in the way of literary correspondence. The parallels are tantalising for different reasons. Take that 'famous, syntactically improbable pronouncement', *Je est un autre*, and the Dylan who turned away from Hibbing, Judaism and poetry:

> He was speaking of the transforming powers of the imagination, of poetry as a kind of latter-day shamanism, but I hear this phrase echoing on throughout his driven, restless, nomadic life. He is a man on the run. He has turned his back on family and friends, on the comforts of home, on his own brilliant future as a poet. He has broken the ties which bind the rest of us, the ties which most of us are, sooner or later, glad to be

bound by. He has seen enough and known enough: he is out in the wilderness of Africa, 'far from everywhere', hurrying on towards that last, impossible freedom, which is to lose yourself, to become somebody else entirely.[15]

On the last night of October in the year 1964, on the night when children go disguised and pretend to believe there is more to the world than appearances allow, Dylan would give a concert at Manhattan's grand Philharmonic Hall. After a new, dark song of epic length and power he would joke with the audience. In those days, high spirits could still prevail. 'It's Halloween,' he would say. 'I got my Bob Dylan mask on. I'm masquerading!' The crack would be funny on, as they say, several levels. It would serve to show how little he cared about those who called him a fake. It would remind the audience that, contrary to whatever they might be hoping, he was a performer; they didn't know him or own him. But it would be a joke at his own expense, too. He was Bob Dylan; Bob Dylan was a mask; and 'I' was another. Tricky.

He made sense of things, when he could, through songs. One of the songs that had begun to assemble itself in the drunken, doped, hit-and-run visit to New Orleans would still be new to most of the Philharmonic audience in October. In it he would sing that his senses had been stripped, that he was ready to go anywhere, under a spell, beyond memory and fate, and plead to be allowed to forget about tomorrow and today. Anything was possible.

*

At the black college of Tougaloo, for a promise kept, more civil-rights activists were encountered. Dylan performed briefly, but someone – Maymudes, presumably – realised on this Wednesday night that the star had to be in Denver, one thousand miles away, by Saturday. Dylan promptly decided that the group would head through Dallas, Texas.

They went to Dealey Plaza, of course. Like almost everyone in America they doubted that Lee Harvey Oswald had acted alone. In the aftermath of the assassination belief in a vast conspiracy – Soviet, Cuban or right-wing fanatical – had been insistent throughout the country. An attack on America had to be big, not obscenely, pathetically

---

15 From Charles Nicholl's *Somebody Else: Arthur Rimbaud in Africa 1880–91* (1997), p. 12. This fine book begins with two epigraphs. One is 'Je est un autre . . .', the other a quotation from 'It's Alright, Ma (I'm Only Bleeding)'.

random. Few believed the story of the lone nut, murdered in his turn, who had declared himself 'a patsy'. Studying the Book Depository, the sometime protest singer and his fellow instant experts duly decided that anyone who could make the shots for which Oswald was held responsible had to be a supreme marksman.

The larger significance of the event did not need to be discussed: an understanding of the symbolism, if not the motive, had become commonplace, an instant cliché. Besides, Dylan had dispensed, as he would soon assert, with 'finger-pointing'. What was there still to say about bloody murder? Had he required confirmation of his reservations over protest songs and their morality-to-go, the Kennedy killing supplied it. Expressions of horror, outrage or hope probably made people feel better, but that wasn't his job. Not any more.

In due course it would be asserted that the opening lines of 1965's 'Desolation Row' were an oblique reference to the assassination. Nothing in the song supports the idea. Instead, you are reminded that by leaving the literalism of protest behind Dylan acquired a new set of literary tools with which to expand the notion of meaning. In 1964, he wasn't there yet. There would be false starts. The real mistake is to believe that he had a choice in the matter.

He was working, though, on that Liberty Bell of a song, the one he seems to have begun while in Toronto for a TV appearance at the end of January, just before the road trip commenced. It was one he would sing for the first time (probably) in Denver. Perhaps by saying less about 'issues' he could say more.

'Chimes of Freedom' was certainly a new thing, politically and lyrically, for Dylan and for his audience. Amid several lines that failed to ring, it said that liberty took many forms, personal and political, civic and artistic, spiritual and physical, even – whatever the word truly meant – existential. A lot of the writing wasn't as good as it might have been: that 'mad mystic hammering of the wild ripping hail', to name one overburdened line, was almost juvenile. But the writer was still finding his way: such would be the theme of the year 1964. Phrases and lines creaked because he was asking too much of them.

In performance, though, Dylan would sweep that minor difficulty aside. 'Chimes of Fredom' would be among the first of his songs truly to pose what might be termed the problem of poetry. Clearly, what was on the page disagreed formally, in poetry's terms, with what would be recorded. Yet what was recorded justified itself utterly as art, verbal art, words with a metrical structure, in couplets and rhyme. Anyone reading 'Chimes' on the tyrannical page might pause before calling it a poem. Anyone listening would hesitate to call it *just* a song in the manner of 'She Loves You' or anything else written for the mass market in the twentieth century. If it wasn't poetry, what was Dylan doing?

*

He was becoming still another Bob Dylan. The reincarnation cycle had resumed. It is too easy to say that 'disillusionment' alone caused him to turn his back on political songwriting. It is tempting, meanwhile, to mark the coincidence that saw his relationship with Suze Rotolo, 'the political one', approach its terminus at precisely the moment – give or take – that he began to write verses with no explicit political content. But did that explain everything? A truly ruthless Dylan would have stuck with the money-making folk-protest seam and dumped the girl.

It is beyond glib, meanwhile, to claim that the casting aside of those protest songs was proof of cynical opportunism, start to finish. Dylan could certainly talk, as Joan Baez well remembered, as though he was just giving the left-liberal suckers what they wanted. Telling people only what they want to hear is almost the definition of one sort of political rhetoric. Yet it seems more likely that Dylan was, as usual, striking a devilish pose and hoping to shock the sanctimonious Queen of Folk. By 1971, in his interview with Jann Wenner for *Rolling Stone*, he had become more subtly disingenuous:

> I never did renounce a role in politics, because I never played one in politics. It would be comical for me to think I played a role.

All of these attempted explanations overlook two plain facts. One is that Dylan's desertion caused genuine anguish among his friends and admirers. Anger – and it was heading straight for him as 1965 approached – was not far behind. Naive, simplistic, possessive and puerile some of the anger might have been. It might have overlooked a gigantic contradiction – what use are songs of freedom if there is no artistic freedom? – but it arose from a second plain fact. No one could have faked those songs. The best that cynicism can manage is bargain-basement psychology: if the Dylan of protest was a fraud, he had to fool himself first.

It sounds ridiculous. It overlooks the fact that any genuine artist will develop, grow and refuse to be confined by prescriptive acclaim. Sooner or later, he will break the chains. On that accounting, Dylan simply grew up too quickly as a poet and musician for fans who – let's be honest – liked him just the way he was.

But listen to 'When the Ship Comes In'. Try to listen to 'A Hard Rain' as the first audiences heard it, to 'Masters of War', 'The Times They Are a-Changin'', 'Paths of Victory' or 'Only a Pawn in Their Game': scepticism begins to seem perverse. He was sincere, clearly, even – especially – if he was fooling himself. If he then left those songs behind, it is because he left that person behind. He discarded the rhetoric of protest in the same manner that he became 'politicised' to begin with: he became a Bob Dylan for the moment. Then the words, the writing itself, began to disagree with his choice. The insistent writing won, as it always would. Besides: in February of 1964 Dylan heard the Beatles. He was not the only one who was caused to think twice by the experience.

Whatever his originality, this is a man who has existed within a cliché since he first attempted to write a song: his art is his life. It is, profoundly, who he is. Dylan doesn't control the art; the art controls 'Bob Dylan', and remakes him time after time.

If there needs to be an argument about this version and his loss of commitment – or faith – in 1964, one simple test is useful. Which were the songs that had marked him out at this point in his career, the ones that had brought the most attention and real acclaim?

Songs of protest and topicality were the least of his output, numerically and artistically. Only 'The Times They are a-Changin'' still earns its place alongside the too-vague-for-protest 'Blowin' in the Wind', 'Girl From the North Country', 'Don't Think Twice', 'Boots of Spanish Leather' or 'It Ain't Me, Babe'. Of the major songs, the apocalyptic poetry of 'A Hard Rain's a-Gonna Fall' was only ever mistaken for protest because it appeared amid the shadowlands of the Cold War. In another era, it could as easily have been taken for a born-again song about the end of days. Count yourself lucky.

'Chimes of Freedom', like 'A Hard Rain', like 'Lay Down Your Weary Tune', is only political in the sense that existence is political. 'When the Ship Comes In' is as political as you like, but in any sense you like. The explicit stuff – 'With God On Our Side', 'Hattie Carroll', 'Only a Pawn in Their Game', 'Masters of War' – never truly dominated a Dylan album and never came close to matching those 'personal' songs. He knew it, too. What he happened to believe about politics didn't matter. Here was where art was leading.

*

After Dallas, the merry troupe in the dusty blue station wagon crossed the Texas Panhandle. In the twenty-first century, publicising an album, Dylan would proclaim himself a Texan for the benefit of one interviewer. By the sounds of it, that was one of his serious jokes. The fact remains that the 1964 road trip allowed his first sighting of an America that had hitherto existed only in his fantasies and his favourite movies. Soon enough, the iconography of the South-west, and of the Old West, would begin to soak into his music. He already knew plenty of cowboy songs, a compulsory module on the standard folk singers' course of study, but the ancient landscape was utterly new. It entered his imagination.

In Ludlow, Colorado, the group halted briefly at a memorial to coalminers and their families massacred in 1914 during a strike over pay, recognition, safety and the iniquitous company store. One of Woody's better-known ballads had been dedicated, as Dylan well knew, to the victims of this confrontation between corporate power and the common man in which at least 19, babies included, had been killed. Guthrie had written his song 30 years after the events at Ludlow, inspired, yet again, by 'Mother' Ella Reeve Bloor's unreliable autobiography, *We Are Many*. But here was Dylan, fully 50 years after the fact, paying a kind of homage of his own. First Harlan County, then Ludlow, with visits to civil-rights workers and to the site of a president's assassination in between: he had become apolitical in a peculiar manner.

The motley crew only just made it to the Denver show. If this was the first public performance of 'Chimes of Freedom', no reviews of the concert have turned up. It's doubtful, in any case, that many in the typical Dylan audience of the day would have absorbed the implications of the song instantly. On cursory examination, what with the refrain and the context of the Kennedy murder, it probably sounded – as it can still sound – like still another protest number, even if Dylan was extending his concern to 'every hung-up person in the whole wide universe' (no less). What separates the song from its predecessors is a profligate use of imagery and a staging, while skies explode, worthy of the Romantic poets.

In January of 2012 a vast compendium of his work – 76 songs by 80-odd artists – would appear. Its title, *Chimes of Freedom*; its beneficiary, with Dylan's blessing and the cooperation of his office, Amnesty International. 'Bob Dylan's music endures because he so brilliantly captures our heartbreak, our joy, our frailty, our confusion, our courage and our struggles,' said a representative of the charity founded to protect political prisoners. The album's closing track was Dylan's original 1964 recording of a song whose meaning was perfectly well understood by human-rights activists. So who dismissed a 'comical' political role?

A lot has been said about the song's imagery, and about Dylan's fitful brilliance in orchestrating a metaphysical storm from flashing lightning in real skies. In 1964, attentive Americans would have caught other echoes, familiar to them since birth, painfully familiar since the Kennedy killing, the unthinkable event that had almost inspired ('as cathedral bells were gently burnin'") a Dylan poem.[16] In that regard, his universal song was wholly American, its central idea wholly traditional. You might even say clichéd. After all, Philadelphia's cracked Liberty Bell, rung like all the others for the Declaration of Independence, bears an inscription from Leviticus: 'Proclaim LIBERTY throughout all the land unto all the inhabitants thereof.' At the March on Washington, only six months before, Dylan had been among the hordes who had heard Martin Luther King make incantatory poetry for his dream of justice:

> Let freedom ring from the snowcapped Rockies of Colorado!
> Let freedom ring from the curvaceous slopes of California!
> But not only that; let freedom ring from Stone Mountain of Georgia!
> Let freedom ring from Lookout Mountain of Tennessee!
> Let freedom ring from every hill and molehill of Mississippi.
> From every mountainside, let freedom ring.

King in his turn was making explicit use, of course, of that song known to every American, Samuel Francis Smith's 'My Country, 'Tis of Thee' ('America'), the one enjoining the 'sweet land of liberty' to 'let freedom ring'. Bruce Springsteen would introduce his own performance of 'Chimes of Freedom' during a 1988 Amnesty show in Stockholm with those self-same words. Bells had tolled everywhere for John Kennedy. Dylan's transition from protest to supposedly Rimbaldien poetry was far from clear-cut.

Besides, as with Rimbaud's advice on the derangement of the senses – convenient wisdom in the mid-1960s – it is hard to lay hands on a piece of the Frenchman's verse, particularly in translation, and identify

---

16 The fragment in question, scribbled out at the time of the assassination, is only six lines long.

precisely the seeds of Dylan's new-found method. Influence, if influence there was, seems to have been informal. A translator's description of Rimbaud's poems – 'vessels of indeterminacy, ambiguity and frequently strange beauty'[17] – might suggest affinities. But it is a stretch to claim the Dylan who wrote 'Chimes', or any other song, as a Symbolist in the nineteenth-century French manner. If he took much from Rimbaud, he took a sense of the expansiveness of language, a liberation from literalism, the idea that images need not be connected laboriously. As for actual borrowings, there are (at best) hints. For 'Chimes of Freedom', fragments of Rimbaud's 'The Drunken Boat'/'Le Bateau Ivre' are generally nominated:

> I know skies split by lightning, waterspouts
> And undertows, and tides: I know the night,
> And dawn exulting like a crowd of doves.
> I have even seen what man dreams he has.
>
> I have seen the low sun stained with mystic horror,
> Lit with long violet weals like actors
> In some ancient play, waves unrolling
> Their shuddering paddles into the distance.[18]

Skies, lightning, night, dawn, 'mystic horror': obvious, isn't it? Less obvious is the persistent need to explain Dylan through complicated webs of presumed creative relationships, genius to genius, as though an artistic DNA can be identified in scraps of verse. And all because, greatly the worse for wear, he once said he wanted to emulate a dead poet? Sometimes interpreters try too hard.

In any case, his 'new-found method' might just as easily have had a very long gestation. Most accounts insist that Dylan first encountered Rimbaud's poetry in Greenwich Village, with Suze Rotolo making the introductions. Dylan says as much in *Chronicles*. But in an article in praise of *Tarantula* – one reprinted by the official and authorised bobdylan.com, indeed – the poet and novelist Mark Spitzer has this to say:

> Growing up in Minnesota, then going to the U of M . . . I studied the

---

17 Mason, *Rimbaud Complete* (2002), Introduction, p. xxix.
18 Trans. Mason, p. 86.

same books Dylan did. I know this because, back in those days at the university library, you had to sign a slip of paper inside the back cover whenever you checked out a book. And in the books by Arthur Rimbaud, the mythic name of Zimmerman was always there, scrawled in the same ink in which passages were underlined in French as well as English.[19]

'Chimes of Freedom' was certainly something new, but also something flawed. In places it is thrilling, even yet; in other spots it is loosely and horribly overwritten: too many words do no work. Despite Dylan's intentions, meanwhile, the song has continued to be burdened with a *specifically* political meaning. The four-CD tribute from Amnesty in the twenty-first century made that clear. Dylan would perform the piece for the remainder of 1964 and then discard it until a whole new generation of underdog soldiers had been born and raised, 23 years later. Then – did he do requests? – he would sing 'Chimes of Freedom' at Bill Clinton's first inauguration in 1993, when hope for America had reared its battered head once more.

*

A stop at Central City, as though to prove Dylan really had worked there back in 1960, was a little anticlimactic, given that the Gilded Garter had been shut down for the winter. Still, it transpired that the star actually did know his way around: one of his unlikely tales had turned out to be true, more or less. The Denver show dealt with, the troupe made for the Rockies as the radio in the station wagon played 'I Want to Hold Your Hand'. Dylan got it straight away – 'Their chords were outrageous, just outrageous, and their harmonies made it all valid' – instantly grasping what was at stake. In another version he already knew plenty about the Beatles, thanks partly to Suze and other early adopters. In those days the quartet were hard to avoid. What is striking is that his epiphany was delivered by a track whose lyrical content was, let's say, negligible. Those chords, and whatever it was that the Beatles had as performers, were another matter. 'The poet' was a musician, first and above all.

After passing through a snowstorm in the mountains, Dylan touched down in San Francisco, last redoubt of what was still being passed off as Beat writing. Short of born-again revelation, he would suffer no more pernicious influence in his artistic life. The prevailing aesthetic

---

19 'Bob Dylan's Tarantula', first published in *JACK* magazine, 2003.

of a fading 'movement' was sloppy – not always but too often – and invariably pretentious. It seemed to suggest that the making of literature depended on the type of person doing the writing. This was not, ironically enough, necessarily the fault of the original Beats themselves, or of the loosely associated poets of the 'San Francisco Renaissance', but it was a consequence of their work. For a brief while Dylan was drawn to it all – the attitudes, the works, the ramshackle theoretical justifications – like a moth to a blazing metaphor.

In point of fact, nevertheless, the labels used to describe Beat's leading lights (and friends) encompassed intellectually serious writers, whatever their private habits, with authentic lineages within the American tradition. The likes of Ginsberg, Gregory Corso, Gary Snyder, Lawrence Ferlinghetti, Kenneth Rexroth, Robert Creeley and Robert Duncan – 'schools' became confused; those labels were accepted and rejected – made technical choices because they understood technique. The same could not be said of most of their imitators.

In an often-quoted 1960 lecture to mark his National Book Award for *Life Studies*, Robert Lowell had observed two types of American poetry, 'a cooked and a raw', in competition.[20] He was a master chef, most of the time, but he understood, and worried over, the appeal of the allegedly unprocessed art called Beat. 'There is a poetry that can only be studied,' Lowell had said, 'and a poetry that can only be declaimed, a poetry of pedantry and a poetry of scandal.' Many of those who followed the Beats (in both senses) had arrived at the same conclusion, albeit with less eloquence. The received rules, whether of prosody or the seminar room, need not apply. It was also the old problem of *vers libre*: so what makes a bunch of lines poetry? With the liberating attractions of drink, drugs, radical politics, eclectic sex, 'altered consciousness', exotic religions and rampant individualism there was, often enough, no contest. The Beats *seemed* to say that poetry was not, among other things, a rule-bound craft that had to be mastered like carpentry. If you didn't fuss too much over the details of Allen Ginsberg's poetics, it was as easy, metrically, as breathing. A lot of bad writing followed; some of it was Dylan's.

He had met Ginsberg late in the previous December at a party held in the 8th Street Bookshop in Manhattan. The two were supposedly introduced by the importunate *New York Post* music journalist and

---

20 See Ian Hamilton's *Robert Lowell: A Biography* (1982), Ch. 16.

career disciple Al Aronowitz.[21] The poet would later claim that Dylan 'invited me to go on tour with him', though the only 'tour' then on the cards was the road trip. Ginsberg, a born enemy of self-effacement, further reported that 'if I'd known then what I know now, I'd have gone like a flash. He'd probably have put me onstage with him.'[22] Probably. Instead, laurels were distributed. What Ginsberg liked about the young singer, what everyone liked who tried to sneak Dylan into the pantheon, were his images, those 'chains of flashing images'.

According to the journalist Ralph J. Gleason, who seemed to believe he heard it first, the phrase explained everything. 'Dylan thinks of songs – all songs, his own included – as pictures, "chains of flashing images",' Gleason wrote in 1966.[23] (Soon enough the reference to 'all songs' – an important detail, you might have thought – would be forgotten.) The journalist was meanwhile another of those who pioneered comparisons with Rimbaud. He found the parallel 'striking'. After all, 'Rimbaud not only was a child prodigy of poetry, but, like Dylan, ran away from home again and again.' Indeed.

It is now close to impossible to find anything written about the Dylan of the 1960s that does not include the flashing chains. It is a lovely accolade. So what does it mean? What decent poetry does not involve enchained – flashing, if you like – images? Yet this single phrase has been taken to explain everything about Dylan's literary method in 'Chimes of Freedom', 'Mr. Tambourine Man' and most other songs of the period. It is then called in aid when someone wants to invoke the youth from Charleville. The trouble is, it explains nothing at all about the way Dylan broke apart the logic of imagery. It certainly doesn't tell us why, when the connective tissue of verse has been dissolved, his 1960s lyrics are not gibberish.

A poetic remark to explain poetry: does it help? Ginsberg would not have flinched. Grant the older man – by 15 years – this much: he

---

21 Interviewed by *Sing Out!* in 1968, Dylan, unreliable as ever, remembered the bookshop, but guessed that the meeting with Ginsberg 'and his friend Peter Orlovsky' had taken place 'in the fall of '64 or '65'. Aronowitz was also writing for the *Saturday Evening Post*, having produced a *12-part* series on the Beats for that title in 1959.

22 *Deliberate Prose: Selected Essays: 1952–1995* (2001). The poet would also claim, notoriously or comically according to taste, to have been 'afraid I might become his slave or something, a mascot'.

23 'The Children's Crusade', *Ramparts* magazine, March 1966.

recognised the literary merit of the 'protest singer' long before academia caught on. He was star-struck, too, as later events would make comically plain, but the friendship between the two was real. Ginsberg was no Carl Sandburg or Robert Lowell, even if his talent for talking fine-sounding semi-sense never failed him. Here he is discoursing on Dylan, circa 1965:

> His image was undercurrent, underground, unconscious in people . . . something a little more mysterious, poetic, a little more Dada, more where people's hearts and heads actually were rather than where they 'should be' according to some ideological angry theory.[24]

Ginsberg had already decided, in any case, that the writer who had brought him to tears with 'A Hard Rain' bore the mark of the poet. In San Francisco, Lawrence Ferlinghetti was moved to agree. He had met Dylan a few months previously and had made an attempt to secure the young singer's book-in-the-making, whatever it might be, for City Lights, Ferlinghetti's bookshop-imprint, the cult publisher of *Howl* and other primary Beat texts. In the end Dylan (or Grossman) decided against – that year City Lights got Frank O'Hara's *Lunch Poems* instead – but did not reject the attention. He was a poet, and he had the plaudits to prove it. He also had Ferlinghetti as his guest at the Berkeley Community Theater on the 22nd. On Parnassus, poets keep company.

When Dylan sang, he earned the right to be called just such a poet. When he wrote, putting words naked on the page, the description was implausible. The fact was that many of the verses the world called lyrics – in the sense meant by the music industry – functioned better on the page than anything he could yet write for the printing press. The album he would make in a blur on the night of 9 June would show that he had not understood, far less mastered, this problem. One attitude towards writing bled into the other. He still believed he could do anything to which he turned his hand.

*

Suze Rotolo believed it too. Though she could no longer tolerate the man, she did not once question his genius. That was no doubt part of the intractable problem. Fame, the cult of 'Bob Dylan', was destroying their relationship as surely as his near-addiction to infidelity. All that remained was to put this love affair out of its misery. Dylan, deservedly,

---

24 *Deliberate Prose: Selected Essays, 1952–1995* (2001).

lost his self-respect in the process. The final scenes were ugly. They earned a song that was uglier still, cheap, nasty and – you could call this poetry's revenge – an abysmal piece of self-indulgence.

It isn't entirely clear why the relationship had endured into 1964. Dylan was still seeing Baez – Karman, the 'chaperone', was sent home from California, glad to leave, with a certain Bobby Neuwirth filling his seat – and stayed at her Carmel house before heading on to Los Angeles for more concert dates. After a show at the Santa Monica Civic Auditorium he was mobbed by fans, chased by teenage girls, and given to understand the incontrovertible truth: he was locally famous, taken seriously, solicited for his opinions on anything and everything, and deferred to at every turn. He had mastery of a world he had only glimpsed back in Hibbing, barely five or so years before. It did not do him a world of good.

Suze was still stuck in that cheap apartment on the Lower East Side, and yet still expected to be Dylan's New York companion. He was, it appears, oblivious to all the contradictions. After her abortion, things inched towards their conclusion. At some point in March after his return from the West an argument became a fight. Carla Rotolo, her former admiration for Dylan long since dissipated, joined in when shouting turned to screaming. All that remained was for Dylan to have the last word in song.

Two decades later he had the good grace to regret 'Ballad in Plain D', telling Bill Flanagan, 'I look back and say "I must have been a real schmuck to write that." I look back at that particular one and say, of all the songs I've written, maybe I could have left that alone.'[25] In the same year, interviewed by Cameron Crowe, Dylan explained why 'You're a Big Girl Now' from *Blood on the Tracks* was not 'confessional', and insisted that he didn't write such songs. Then he remembered that 'actually I did write one once and it wasn't very good – it was a mistake to record it and I regret it . . . Back there somewhere on my third or fourth album.' Clearly, it was not a memory he treasured. After making 'Boots of Spanish Leather' for Suze he had subjected her to a song that was the equivalent of domestic abuse.

'Ballad In Plain D' was miswritten in Greece, mostly, where Dylan had wound up in a village outside Athens after a concert at the Royal Festival Hall in London in May. At that show he had performed a song better suited to his impending album – to any album – than the bitter,

---

25 *Written in My Soul* (1990).

juvenile thirteen verses and eight-and-some endless minutes of the 'Plain D' ballad. The contrast is striking. Most agree that he made a start on 'Mr. Tambourine Man' during or after the visit to New Orleans. It was more or less complete, in all its dreaming glory, when he astonished the London audience – if the recorded applause is anything to go by – on the third Sunday in May. Yet when he came to make *Another Side of Bob Dylan* he filled almost one-sixth of its running time with the woeful ballad and left out the masterwork.

True, he botched his attempt to record 'Tambourine Man' in the summer of 1964, thanks not least to the weird decision to include an entirely superfluous guest vocalist in the shape of Ramblin' Jack Elliott. Perhaps he concluded that he would give this of all songs the treatment it deserved, or wait for a more propitious moment. Such is the usual assumption. What is baffling still is how the same talent could have been applied to *the writing* of these two songs at almost the same moment and yet with such wildly different results. The Bob Dylan who was writing 'Tambourine Man' also wrote this:

Of the two sisters, I loved the young
With sensitive instincts, she was the creative one
The constant scapegoat, she was easily undone
By the jealousy of others around her

Those 'traditional' inversions – the mark of bad poetry for 200 years – provide neither excuse nor camouflage. It doesn't much matter, either, that Dylan was self-consciously following a traditional ballad model. Truly: so what? Here was a demonstration that an actually personal song involving psychological truths – about himself, above all – was beyond his reach. He had never written anything as thoroughly bad as this before, and would not do so again for years to come. 'Ballad in Plain D' sticks out like an infected thumb from the body of his work in 1964.

It is only explicable if you accept that Dylan could not, at this moment, handle material that touched his life, or facts that drew near to the person he was. He had not, it is slightly surprising to realise, even cracked the formula for revenge. The honesty required was beyond him. None of that explains an absolute failure of syntax, phrasing, prosody and taste. The young genius had limitations and no one dared to mention it. Instead, a kind of justice was done to Suze Rotolo: with this ballad, Dylan humiliated himself.

Few people, even among the most slavish of his fans, have a good word to say for 'Plain D'. Some of its verses have achieved a kind of perverse celebrity just for being breathtakingly inept. If this had truly been the best Dylan could manage, protest song would have remained an honourable calling. Rimbaud would have been affronted by comparisons with this *rimeur*.

> With unseen consciousness, I possessed in my grip
> A magnificent mantelpiece, though its heart being chipped
> Noticing not that I'd already slipped
> To a sin of love's false security

*

After astonishing London, he was reunited briefly with his friend Hugues Aufray in Paris. Thanks to the French singer's introductions, he thereafter enjoyed an interlude with the singer Nico, travelled with her to her native Germany to view the Berlin Wall and made his way finally to Greece. There Dylan wrote for over a week, or rather continued to write, in circumstances more congenial than usual. It would be his last respite, creatively, until the day he parted company with a motorcycle on a country road. At the start of the second week in June he was back in a New York recording studio.

Another Side of Bob Dylan is still accorded a kind of reverence, less for its content than for the supposedly remarkable manner of its creation. A whole album, start to finish, in a single recording session? You could admire the audacity. Given the complications attending the birth of *Freewheelin'*, you could even sympathise with the desire for spontaneity, the wish – an abiding wish for Dylan – to capture the moment *in* the moment. You could also call the act cavalier and careless. *Another Side* could have stood a few second thoughts and revisions.

This was 1964. It was not yet conventional for popular entertainers to spend the time it takes to acquire a college degree on the recording of a few melodies. Dylan completed his album in six hours, it is said, but most of its eleven songs were well prepared in advance, and he had a few more to spare if the need arose. Besides, he used only his voice, guitar, harmonica and a bit of rackety, not-necessarily-in-tune piano. (An electric guitar had been rented after the road trip, but Dylan wasn't yet ready to explore *that* other side.) If he had nothing to add in terms of performance, how much time in the studio did he really need?

A couple of hours spent reconsidering his choice of songs wouldn't have hurt. Not for the first time or the last, material was excluded that should have remained, and vice versa. The decision to throw out the lovely and sly 'Mama, You Been On My Mind' remains inexplicable. The gift of 'I'll Keep It With Mine' to Nico might have been a nice keepsake after their brief, trans-European affair, but the loss of that graceful song made the gesture seem profligate. Dylan's inability to achieve a satisfactory rendering of 'Tambourine Man' can meanwhile be blamed on the drunken speed-reading of half-realised verses that the night's session became. He had performed the piece to perfection in London. In New York, he lost the plot and the point. He was 'just too out of it'. Besides, 'It was all done too fast.'[26]

What Dylan failed to explain was the reason for haste. Which malign power had forced him to complete an entire album in half a dozen hours? Not Albert Grossman, not his touring schedule (he would give only 28 performances in the course of the year). The idea that Dylan and his producer, Tom Wilson, were under an implacable pressure to deliver a new record overnight is hard to fathom.

Wilson would nevertheless tell Nat Hentoff of *The New Yorker*, who was present at the session, that 'this album has to be ready for Columbia's fall sales convention'. That event certainly took place – at the Sahara Hotel in Las Vegas – at the end of July. Dylan's album was then listed by *Billboard* among '29 pop and jazz LPs' due out in August and September from the likes of Barbra Streisand, Miles Davis and the Clancy Brothers. That said, even a company eager for product would surely have sanctioned a couple more sessions. Dylan couldn't have worked on Monday as well as Tuesday? The record industry of the time might have struggled to grasp why a folk-type singer-guitarist could possibly require more than half a dozen hours to make an album. (The Beatles had spent just under ten hours on *Please Please Me*.) Dylan, over-confident or not, must have known better. Besides, he had licence. The only identifiable person in a rush on the evening of 9 June was the artist. As Wilson also told Hentoff: 'Except for special occasions like this, Bob has no set schedule of recording dates. We think he's important enough to record whenever he wants to come to the studio.'[27]

The choice was his. Even with the sales convention looming he could have set to work earlier instead of leaving things, as was clearly the

---

26 Interview with Robert Shelton, March 1966, *No Direction Home*, p. 360.

27 *The New Yorker*, October 1964.

case, until the last possible moment. It counted (again) as hubris. As with his attempts at Beat-like verse and prose, 'spontaneity' became the enemy of creativity.

For years afterwards Dylan would claim that working fast and loose was always his preferred method. Inconveniently, he was a recording artist who disliked the recording process, forever pretending that modern 'product' could be knocked off with the easeful insouciance of an old bluesman singing into a tin-cup microphone in a dusty San Antonio hotel room. He thereby caused himself no end of grief.

Another Side of Bob Dylan is a mixed bag. By one account, its vapid title was supposed to announce the artist's solemn renunciation of protest and politics. The artist himself would disown that title as none of his doing, and yet claim credit – to Nat Hentoff – for the absence of those 'finger-pointin' songs'. He would stand behind the records he had made before, meanwhile, but they belonged to the past. Dylan said: 'From now on, I want to write from inside me, and to do that I'm going to have to get back to writing like I used to when I was ten – having everything come out naturally.' To this day the critical consensus holds that with *Another Side of Bob Dylan* he drew away, decisively and permanently, from monosemous political writing and outright political commitment. Here was when he told them where to stick it.

It depends what you mean by politics. 'Chimes of Freedom' and 'My Back Pages' might not involve explicit 'issues', mercifully, but they are born of a working political consciousness. In any case, how much actual agit prop finger-pointing was there in Dylan's catalogue by the time he made *Another Side*? The tricky fact is that the extent of his 'political role' in the first half of the 1960s has been exaggerated wildly, along with the tally of his overtly political songs. He was never a Seeger or a Phil Ochs.

Before he entered the studio that June evening Dylan had released thirty-six tracks on three albums in his own name. The first of those collections involved no politics of any description bar a couple of lines in 'Song to Woody'; the second had five songs among thirteen, the comedy-satire of 'Talkin' World War III Blues' included, that could be called political, more or less. A reputation as a 'protest singer' rests almost entirely on *The Times They Are a-Changin'*, and on a single year, 1963. If it is true, in any case, that Dylan quit the political game with *Another Side*, certain subsequent songs require explanation. He wasn't done with the rat-race choir. The issue had to do with method, perspective and, above all, language.

In reality, the importance of the second album of 1964 was not that it said farewell to politics and 'movements', but that it marked Dylan's abandonment of folk, or what had come to be known – thanks to him, in no small part – as folk. It was not a moment too soon, but few at the time paid much attention. The cherished Gibson 'Nick Lucas' flat-top acoustic and the harmonica were still in place: such was 'folk', for most listeners. A few Village arbiters would fret that personal songs were displacing those crucial, socially responsible anthems. The important fact is that Dylan's repudiation was musical, and melodic.

A couple of the songs on *Another Side* might have had antecedents within the folk canon, but it no longer mattered. This, had he been ready and prepared to book more than 360 minutes of studio time, could have been the first 'electric' album without the slightest difficulty. The Byrds, preparing to appropriate four songs from *Another Side*, plus 'Mr. Tambourine Man', for the sake of a 'folk-rock' collection (1965's *Mr. Tambourine Man*) and a later single ('My Back Pages'), demonstrated how easily it could have been done. Angelic harmonies were not Dylan's forte; his edge was harder and keener than anything possessed by Roger McGuinn and friends; but his second album of 1964 could have been written for a band.

So what did he create instead with a few bottles of red, friends and hangers-on (and their children) in tow, a half-refurbished literary method and a resolve to avoid pronouncements on current affairs? Unlike the recording, the writing had not been done in haste. The choices were made freely. After a little under six hours in the studio he emerged with five very good songs, a couple of them flirting with greatness; three decent songs; and three stinkers. By the standards of the time, when an album involved a hit cemented into place with filler, there was no shame in that. But such standards were not supposed to apply to Dylan.

Another Side is an oddity, part heartfelt and part slapdash. Supportive listeners like to call it 'transitional'. The reality is that the album does not contain an actually great song – a preposterous demand, no doubt, but Dylan set the bar – yet includes tracks that are authentically awful. The quality varies, then. 'Ballad in Plain D' is beyond redemption; 'Motorpsycho Nitemare' is about as funny as any farmer's daughter joke; and 'I Shall Be Free No. 10' palls faster than a sitcom. Some people are fond of 'All I Really Want to Do' and 'My Back Pages': the fairest word is 'middling'. 'Black Crow Blues' meanwhile has the charm of a demo: real but limited. What remains are five tracks and a question. 'Chimes of Freedom' aside, which of these songs demonstrates that this 'personal' writing has that familiar universal power? The case is hard to make. Hence the reason to regret the absence of 'Tambourine Man'. That song doesn't just make an argument for Dylan's 'new style'; it settles the argument.

So what of the claim that the author was just a little too intoxicated to give the masterpiece its due? What, equally, of the idea that he would not release 'Mr. Tambourine' in a state that was anything less than perfect? If that was the honest intention, he had a funny way of showing it.

On 9 June, Ramblin' Jack Elliott ran into Dylan and Victor Maymudes on the street. 'Son-of son-of' was no longer the sleeve-tugging acolyte, nor was he the waifish hobo. Long discarded – perhaps somewhere in Kentucky – were 'the denim work shirts and laced work boots of *The Times They Are a-Changin'* era'. Dylan had a new haircut, fancy boots and cool clothes. He was on his way to record. Did his former mentor want to tag along?[28]

Elliott had heard Dylan sing 'Tambourine Man' precisely once, either in Woodstock or – accounts differ – at an apartment his former wife was sharing with Albert Grossman's then girlfriend, Sally Buehler. He was a little bemused, therefore, to be called to the studio floor by the artist and told, 'Jack, sing on this.' Nor did Tom Wilson have any idea of what was going on, or why Dylan suddenly felt the need for a backing vocalist. Bob Dylan didn't use backing vocalists. For the producer's preference, amidst a recording session in which time was supposedly of the essence, he didn't use backing vocalists who had no proper grasp of the song's lyrics. Then again, though supposedly in possession of a typed manuscript – one he refused to share with Elliott – Dylan himself seemed to allow a few of the words to slip his tipsy mind. The result was predictable.[29] So 'Mr. Tambourine Man', beyond question the finest song he had yet written, failed to find a place on *Another Side of Bob Dylan*.

Funny things happen when people are drunk. Self-sabotage is sometimes one of those things. The Byrds, who got their first taste of

---

28 These details, and parts of the explanation for the 'Tambourine Man' debacle, are drawn from Hank Reineke's *Ramblin' Jack Elliott: The Never-Ending Highway* (2009), pp. 157–8.

29 These days available to all on *The Bootleg Series Volume 7: No Direction Home: The Soundtrack* (2005).

'Tambourine Man' thanks to the Dylan-Elliott farrago, might have reimagined the song in terms of chiming harmonies. No one else thought of Dylan in those terms. Either he was arrogant enough to believe that the rest of the material allotted to *Another Side* was plenty good enough, or he didn't want the song on the album. Why bother to record it, then, and why implicate Jack Elliott in the mess?

Whatever the pressures attending its creation, *Another Side of Bob Dylan* is proof that Tom Wilson was right: the singer had absolute licence. No one told him what to write and sing, or *how* to write and sing. No one attempted to dictate the direction he should follow. If Dylan thought it sufficient just to turn up and stand before a microphone for a few hours, no one was arguing. In the case of *Another Side of Bob Dylan* the result was one of his lesser works, and very close to a flop. Yet when he next exercised absolute creative autonomy Dylan's judgement would be almost unerring.

*

By the summer of 1964, the United States had 23,000 troops in Vietnam. The Ho Chi Minh trail, winding through Laos, was being bombed by mercenaries in America's pay, using aged American aircraft. Robert McNamara, LBJ's defence secretary, was meanwhile telling the South Vietnamese that 'We'll stay for as long as it takes'. In the White House, the idea had taken root that if Communism could be halted in South East Asia it could be contained around the world. As Dylan raced through the making of an album, plans for the bombing of North Vietnam were being discussed.

He had nothing to say about any of this, not even obliquely. As US Navy warships massed in the Gulf of Tonkin, the writer who had damned the masters of war was silent. The composer of 'With God On Our Side' explored his private truths behind a wall of public reticence. He had picked quite a moment to 'turn his back on politics', but that didn't seem to bother Dylan. Not so many months before he had been filleting newspapers for song ideas. He probably noticed, then, that in the May week before his trip to Europe students had been marching through Times Square in what is generally recognised now as the first major protest against the war. San Francisco, where poetry was made, saw 700 take to the streets. Joan Baez would join the non-violent fray before the year was out. The sorts of people who expected things of Bob Dylan – people who expected too much, who demanded the obvious and predictable, who nonetheless believed in him – had begun to wake up to the things being done in their name.

It is customary to admire Dylan for defending his artistic integrity against all the clamant voices: those who thought they could conscript creativity, who wanted slogans-on-demand, who believed that poets had a duty to enlist in the higher – always higher – cause. The admiration is justified. Had Dylan remained the writer and performer of *The Times They Are a-Changin'*, he would these days be remembered in footnotes, if at all. Equally, as 'Chimes of Freedom' demonstrates, he did not become truly apolitical in 1964. Instead, he acquired a larger idea of politics; more importantly, of the ideas behind politics. That does not excuse him from a simple, inconvenient question, however. What would it have cost him just to have said, once or twice, that as a matter of personal opinion he, too, opposed a pointless war?

He would be asked a version of the question in 1968 by John Cohen and Happy Traum in a *Sing Out!* interview. The proposition for debate was that Dylan could not possibly 'share the same basic values' as a 'certain painter' of his acquaintance who, claimed Dylan, supported the Vietnam incursion. 'People just have their own views,' he said finally. 'Anyway, how do you know I'm not, as you say, for the war?'

Dylan reconciled this rhetorical stratagem with the writing of 'Masters of War' by asserting, blandly: 'There were thousands and thousands of people just wanting that song, so I wrote it up.' Obviously enough, the real answer was his refusal to answer. The evasiveness that had once been playful or mocking had become a ritual defence. Even Vietnam, the most important event to affect his generation, the great calamity that would offer neither victory nor affirmation, would not cause him to loosen his armour. The closest he came to frankness was a form of self-diagnosis: 'I no longer have the capacity to feed this force which is needing all these songs.'

Interviewed by Hentoff for *Playboy* in the autumn of 1965, Dylan had nevertheless been frank enough in his contempt for political activism.[30] He had no quarrel with principles, but he had become allergic to organised emotions, programmatic thinking and the delusion of ideological obedience. Asked if it was 'pointless to dedicate yourself to the cause of peace and racial equality', Dylan said:

---

30 Hentoff, though he kept the fact to himself in the interview, was no stranger to activism. His books of the period were dedicated to the common good. In a long career, he distinguished himself as an advocate for civil rights and free speech. Was Dylan aware that he was talking to the author of *The New Equality* (1964)?

Not pointless to dedicate yourself to peace and racial equality, but rather, it's pointless to dedicate yourself to the *cause*; that's *really* pointless. That's very unknowing.

Pressed again by Hentoff over 'those who have risked imprisonment by burning their draft cards . . . and by refusing – as your friend Joan Baez has done – to pay their income taxes as a protest against the government's expenditure on war and weaponry', Dylan gave an answer that would become notorious. It would also set a test for the liberal-left sorts prepared to defend his artistic autonomy. Given the pointlessness of causes, he advocated doing *nothing at all* about Vietnam.

Burning draft cards isn't going to end the war. It's not even going to save any lives. If someone can feel more honest with himself by burning his draft card, then that's great; but if he's just going to feel more important because he does it, then that's a drag. I really don't know too much about Joan Baez and her income tax problems. The only thing I can tell you about Joan Baez is that she's not Belle Starr.

None of this was off the cuff. Hentoff would later explain that he had conducted the interview twice, the second time by telephone at Dylan's insistence, after *Playboy*'s editors had enraged the subject by putting his words through the editorial wringer. The published piece, the one Dylan 'made up' (as Hentoff claimed), was often brilliantly inventive and gloriously funny. Where politics, war, conscience and commitment were concerned, though, he meant what he said.

Baez's 'Institute for the Study of Nonviolence' was up and running in Carmel by 1965. She was not alone in her tax protest. That year the likes of Lawrence Ferlinghetti, Noam Chomsky and Albert Szent-Györgyi, the Nobel Prize-winning physiologist, had joined the singer and several hundred others in publicising their refusal to fund the war. Shortly afterwards Joan Didion would knife Baez as 'the Madonna of the disaffected', a 'pawn of the protest movement' – therefore not its queen – in an article about the 'peace school'.[31] Dylan didn't need to

---

31 'Where the Kissing Never Stops', first published in the *New York Times Magazine* and collected in Didion's *Slouching Towards Bethlehem* (1968), her acidulous account of the California counter-culture. The Didion manner has since fallen out of fashion somewhat. As Barbara Grizzuti Harrison remarked percipiently as early as 1980, 'Didion uses style as argument.'

be told. In him, there was little distinction between the personal and the political. He could discard both at will.

Something gets overlooked, nevertheless, in the familiar tale of the Dylan who refused to be used by propagandists and promoters of 'the cause'. He preserved his artistic integrity and gave himself respite from impossible demands, no doubt, when he rejected the spokesman's job. In the process, however, he did something remarkable: he surrendered wholesale his right to express a simple opinion, to speak his mind. Refusing to speak for all, he ceased to speak for himself. Just to get the political types off his back, he censored himself.

At this distance in time it seems clear, in any case, that there was more at stake than Dylan's art for its own sake. Chafing at *causes*, at movements and organisations, he was asserting a traditional, if wholly conservative, American individualism. The predilection for outlaws, movie cowboys, renegade poets, runaway teenagers, Brando, Dean and wandering Woody Guthrie had become a private mythology. Its appeal would not diminish as his career progressed. No one was going to tell him how to think, even if their opinions happened to be all but identical to opinions he had held the day before yesterday. The attitude that had first drawn him to folk radicalism could as easily cause him to rebel against compulsory rebellion. Dylan had his fill of radical chic long before Tom Wolfe came up with the phrase.

Besides: *how do you know I'm not, as you say, for the war?* Every account of the great epochal schism between Dylan and the political left holds the suggestion to be unthinkable. It is presumed that he retained his beliefs privately while tiring of the unsought public role. He simply didn't need the sort of hassle he had endured at the Tom Paine award ceremony.

So where's the evidence? Dylan would in due course utter some deeply conservative remarks after finding himself born again in Christ. Was he simply programmed by evangelicals? It hardly matters. The individual forever struggling to emerge from 'Bob Dylan' could turn on a dime and alter out of all recognition almost, it seems, overnight. It was less a matter of disguises – for he did not try to hide these transformations – than of *becoming* someone else. The important evidence says that any one of these Dylans could reject a previous 'Bob Dylan', right down to his dearest beliefs, as though he had never existed. This happened time and again. And what had he actually meant, in any case, by the stuff about understanding Lee Harvey Oswald?

It is also entirely possible that Dylan was better attuned to the national mood than the average dissident. His conversion to evangelical Christianity would occur, after all, amid another country-wide religious revival. The progenitor of *Americana* had a clear enough sense of middle America. It's where he came from. This is not to claim that he was any sort of conservative in the mid-1960s, only that he was alert to what was really going on. In the American heartland, far from the Village, the campuses and the counter-culture, old attitudes, attitudes that had never disappeared, were being reasserted by the middle (working) class, Democrats not least. One modern account of the resurgence of American conservatism after 1964 captures the flavour of things.

> For many activists, the Vietnam war was the greatest evil of the day – and the counter-culture was a natural accompaniment to a life of protest. For many rank-and-file Democrats, however, the anti-war movement was an abomination. What did the average working man have in common with hippies who spent their time taking drugs and squandering their families' trust funds? Or with students who desecrated the American flag? The anti-war protesters, most of whom would have been given student deferments rather than being sent to fight, were even more unpopular than the war itself. Far too many of them seemed not just hostile to this or that American policy, but to America in general.[32]

*

As the *Sing Out!* and *Playboy* interviews made clear, Dylan was always liable to wonder why the opinions of 'the average working man' seemed to count for nothing among Movement types. It was not for him to say what or how people should think. That was the essence of his native individualism. So why would anyone else have the right? And how could they dare to be so certain?

> Anybody can be specific and obvious. That's always been the easy way. The leaders of the world take the easy way. It's not that it's so difficult to be unspecific and less obvious; it's just that there's nothing, absolutely nothing, to be specific and obvious *about*.[33]

---

32 John Micklethwait and Adrian Wooldridge, *The Right Nation: Why America Is Different* (2004), Ch. 3.

33 Interview with Nat Hentoff, *Playboy*, March 1966.

Something else needs to be observed where Dylan, politics, individualism and the 1960s are concerned. He was not alone in his dissent from the old certainties. As it began to emerge the counter-culture would also begin to make a fetish of personal autonomy. By the decade's end, that liberty would be indistinguishable from self-indulgence. Desperate protests against the Vietnam War would continue and intensify, but the business of turning on, tuning in and dropping out would cause a great many of Dylan's generation – this is putting the matter kindly – to look inwards, to approach the doors of perception rather than the gates of the White House. Drugs and third-hand 'philosophies' would play their part, but a belief in the collective yielded to an obsession with the self. Come 1967, Dylan would show his absolute disdain for that development, too, but one charge sticks: he started it. He made personal liberty paramount.

*

The critics were a little perplexed by *Another Side of Bob Dylan*. The public reaction was less ambiguous: deep dyed fans bought the record, many others didn't bother. The album just made it into the Top 50 in America (though it managed number 8 in Britain), and that counted as a setback, even a humiliation.

At Newport that year Dylan received the now-customary hero's welcome but not, perhaps, a wholehearted hero's ovation. He had become a puzzle. For the first time, though not the last, people didn't quite know what to make of him. Those in the Village who thought they had deciphered the deviationist thinking of the prodigal were putting fresh ribbons into their typewriters and dipping their pens. They wanted to set Dylan straight on a few points. More in sorrow than in anger, you understand.

For him, the real joy of the festival was a chance to meet Johnny Cash and seal a friendship. It was an aspect to Dylan that his folk fans didn't often care to notice: *his* idea of a contemporary musical hero was a Nashville star, albeit one in the throes of a severe amphetamine and tranquilliser problem that would see Cash busted – sentence suspended – in October 1965. It's true, equally, that Dylan's new friend was no standard-issue Music Row cornball. Cash's hit albums in 1964 were *I Walk the Line*, a partial reworking of his old Sun material, and *Bitter Tears: Ballads of the American Indian*. Hence his two big singles of the year: Peter La Farge's 'The Ballad of Ira Hayes' and a certain

'It Ain't Me, Babe'. Cash, as the now-official 'bootleg' commemorates, would do a fine, personalised version of 'Don't Think Twice' for the Rhode Island crowd, and praise 'the best songwriter of the age'.[34] No one said a word about an electrically operated guitar polluting the sacred stage. No one seems even to have asked whether a hit-making country and western star was an appropriate choice for the festival. Pete Seeger introduced Cash, and very nicely, too.

The scrupulousness of the folk scene, and hence of the Newport organisers, otherwise allowed for what now seem like odd spectacles. A modern festival would probably not give the biggest name in attendance his first outing at a daytime 'topical song workshop', or have him perform on a rickety marquee's stage with a battered upright piano for a backdrop. Even the Dylan of 1965 would not have countenanced allowing a watchful Seeger to sit a few feet away on the stage itself, as though about to raise a scorecard.

In 1964, it was no big deal. Only a couple of new songs were at stake during the workshop performance, and one of those went down very well indeed: that would be the one he was excluding from his new album. Dylan enjoyed the song he called 'Hey, Mr. Tambourine Man' so much – smiling knowingly at the close, with just the odd 'jingle jangle' forgotten – that he did it twice at Newport. Yet on the Sunday night, after four of the new songs, he allowed himself to be dragged back for an encore, submitting yet again to a 'With God On Our Side' duet with the nerve-piercing trills of Baez in his ear. You can see why people became confused. Dylan's own feelings as he sang must have been complicated too.

At Woodstock in upper New York State, where Grossman kept a house for his star's convenience, there was a new woman in his life. The affair with Baez had run its course, or perhaps – you can take your pick – served its purpose. Oblivious, she was still around in the summer of 1964 and still, to all appearances, his inamorata, close enough at hand that August to observe his working (and drinking) habits. The important truth is that Dylan was hiding in plain view. He had managed to meet the woman he would sincerely want to marry. She was a friend of his manager's partner. Her name was Sara Lownds.

A conundrum, then. If Suze Rotolo is granted credit for raising Dylan's political consciousness, how much recognition is due to Sara

---

34 Johnny Cash, *Bootleg Volume 3: Live Around the World* (2011, Columbia/Legacy).

for the songs he began to write in the second half of 1964, those multifaceted pieces that spoke of a consciousness altered and fragmented, that look inwards, not out at the public world? Clearly, he had embarked on this path with 'Chimes of Freedom' and 'Tambourine Man' (always her favourite) before the relationship commenced. Those songs, in turn, could be said to amplify previously existing lyrical traits: his development was never neat and orderly. Nevertheless, if Dylan is to be subjected to the biographical fallacy that links every event in a life with a moment in art, the appearance of Ms Lownds surely counts for something. *He* certainly regarded her as a woman very like a muse. Equally, the songs written for Sara are a match, if such is your idea of a contest, for the songs written for Suze.

*

There are other explanations. One is that Dylan was also applying himself in those months to book-type writing. He had been wearing out typewriter ribbons on the road trip, at the Baez residence in Carmel and at Woodstock. For his part Grossman had reached, or was in the process of reaching, an understanding with the Macmillan publishing house that promised a better return than Lawrence Ferlinghetti and City Lights could ever provide. General acclaim for Dylan's way with words indicated a potential income stream, and Albert was not known to overlook one of those. Besides, his client was keen: he believed – and why would he not?   that he had a book in him. No one was presumptuous enough to enquire about the nature of the work, or its possible contents. Anything Bob Dylan chose to write would be fine by them.

Its final title was *Tarantula*. To this day, no one knows why, and Dylan isn't saying. Theories with citations are available, of course. Demonstrably true is the fact that the author spun out a web, never silken, and stretched it over 137 pages at first printing. When we juveniles once upon a time handed over our money, we consoled ourselves with the image of Dylan at the web's centre, spinning his weird tales. Disloyal thoughts of a tangled sticky mess were not far behind.

Because most of what appears in *Tarantula* has been called prose – or 'prose poems', or poetic prose, or some other hybrid variant – the Rimbaud of *Illuminations* has again been invoked. You never know. The obstacle to all theory is that Dylan was writing, as ever, in the

American vernacular, in his own self-conscious, orthographically quirky sub-Beat idiom. His language in no sense resembled Rimbaud's language, even in translation. Nor did he share the long-gone French youth's concerns. Nor did he deliver much that was seer-like – this does not count as a pity – with his scattergun assaults on the page. He was beginning, nevertheless, to try to make a book.

A better clue to this disregarded work, important to Dylan for half a year but a dead zone in most of the books about him, lies in the poetry and prose of Kenneth Patchen, the stubborn, semi-crippled writer who collaborated with John Cage and Mingus, and who released three albums of his performance-readings on Folkways between 1959 and 1961. Suze Rotolo was reading *The Love Poems of Kenneth Patchen* (1960) in 1964. Dave Whitaker, the Dinkytown 'Svengali-type' who had loaned Dylan *Bound for Glory* – and all but taught him to read, supposedly – would later claim he had put Patchen on the protégé's reading list back in Minneapolis. It's just as likely, though, that Dylan had come across *The Journal of Albion Moonlight*, Patchen's 1941 pacifist 'dream-vision' of a novel, when it was republished by New Directions in 1961. There are plenty of Bob-like bits to be found.

> People don't want to be healed. They want a nice juicy wound that will show well when they put neon lights around it.

> May 19. I have forgotten my mask, and my face was in it.

The usual thing to say is that Patchen was 'surrealist-influenced'. This is usually said when people have nothing better to say, least of all about this hugely important American poet. It is common, too, to see Patchen's name corralled with the Beats, presumably because he lived for a time in the Village, performed with jazz musicians and still fits few of the usual canonical moulds. That's neither particularly true nor even slightly fair. Patchen himself refused to be associated with a 'synthetic Bohemian spectacle'. (Pressed about common ground with the Beats, he said, 'I breathe the same air as Liberace.')[35] Some of those same Beats, and some of those roped in to Beatdom, Ferlinghetti and Rexroth in particular, were fans or friends. But Patchen was ahead of them all: his first book, *Before the Brave*, was published in 1936, when he was 25. Ginsberg might just

---

35 Larry Smith, *Kenneth Patchen: Rebel Poet in America* (2000), Ch. 14.

have come across it, you suspect, before writing 'Howl'. One poem began:

> Let us have madness openly, O men
> Of my generation. Let us follow
> The footsteps of this slaughtered age . . .

Parallels with Dylan, if nothing more, meanwhile abound. Henry Miller called Patchen 'the living symbol of protest', a 'sort of sincere assassin' and 'a fizzing human bomb'.[36] These things were said in 1946, five years after *The Journal of Albion Moonlight*, and five years after the poet had decided to oppose *the* war, the good war, and (come to that) any war. Mostly bedridden, in constant pain from a severe spinal injury and the incompetent surgery that had almost crippled him, Patchen developed his art unhindered by the usual literary trends. He was prolific, experimental, independent and, for most of his career, obscure. He framed *The Journal* loosely around 'Tom a Bedlam'/'Tom o' Bedlam', the astonishing, anonymous seventeenth-century beggar-ballad rendered in the voice of a crazed wanderer. From Patchen's own poetic voice came things far closer to *Tarantula* than the ritually invoked Rimbaud. As here:

> Seemed enough ambition for anyone with sense.
>
> Scant matter with what. Be it only with the serenity of veils at the funeral of a river, or even with the compassion of first snow upon a blackened wood. (Of course taste did set certain limits: a bit of all too responsible soul-baiting went a long way to Redjellyhead Fair.) . . .

Or here:

> Hey there, you in the macadam suit! Mr U.S. Highway #1 –
>   How's that for a fancy name, eh?
> Or maybe you're only some casual man of leaning like me, huh?
> Spooking up pals out of shadows, making buddies from candy
>   and cigarette wrappers?

The second excerpt, should it matter, is from a poem entitled 'Just

---

36 *Patchen: Man of Anger and Light* (1946).

Outside Tombstone', the first from 'To Be Charmed'. If nothing else, they suggest that those who reject Dylan as a poet know too little about the sort of American poetry that interested him. He doesn't write like Robert Frost: who knew? Despite his ruthless folksiness, that laureate did not in fact encompass his country's entire literary tradition. Dylan admired Ginsberg from the start, but there were others who stirred his urge to imitate and emulate. Unfortunately, they didn't help to rescue *Tarantula*.

Two things redeem the novel's two-finger exercises. First, Dylan's wit. Once you struggle through his sometimes laborious attempts to reproduce common speech, some of the stuff that became *Tarantula* is very funny. Second, hard work was producing results. Certain of his pages are wine-stained, metaphorically. Some stand as 'proof', apparently, of narcotised energy: on this evidence his attention span could have been timed with a stop watch. Nevertheless, according to Baez's testimony he was 'tapping away relentlessly for hours' at his typewriter. Slowly, steadily, his writing was getting better. Dylan was learning things from these prose experiments, things to do with structure, rhythm and the conjunction of images. These discoveries did nothing much for any hopes he might have entertained for a publishable book, but they were altering his songwriting.

In 1965, Dylan told Nat Hentoff that he had worked 'about six months, off and on', for the sake of the prose work he called a novel. There were 'about 500 pages of it', but he had ceased to believe or pretend that he was composing a great literary statement. When it escaped into the world in 1971 – though its copyright date was 1966 – this *Tarantula* was met with bewilderment, derision, mockery, hilarity, irritation, bad jokes, straightforward insults and most of the other critical reactions a first-time author dreads. Dylan, in contrast, was not even slightly surprised.

By 1971, the proverbial slim volume had been 'delayed' for five years precisely because he had lost whatever faith he ever had in the writing. Crude loose-leaf bootleg copies had in any case entered circulation in San Francisco almost at the instant he stopped typing in the summer of 1965. By 1971, Dylan may have ceased to give a damn: his *Self Portrait* album had been trashed comprehensively, often by the same critics who would despise his prose, just the year before. He had recovered some credibility with *New Morning* late in 1970, but the set's title stated his position. He was moving on; the book was already ancient, just back pages; so let them have it. They let him have it instead.

Even today, any good word said about *Tarantula* is held to be perverse. Since the book is obviously unreadable, anyone who claims to enjoy reading it has to be kidding: unlike the book, that stands to reason. The view is not *necessarily* unfair. As writing, the volume escapes definition. In place of a structure it has patterns and insistent rhythms. You can't easily crack its spine and spoon out its meaning, image by image, metaphor by metaphor. Some of its jokes are private or obscure. It does not defer even for a paragraph to the reader's assumptions about narrative or the authorial voice: *Tarantula*'s voices are as cacophonous as a multiple personality disorder. It offers less a stream than an entire floodplain of consciousness. The book's few devoted fans don't help much, tending invariably to believe that a mention of Rimbaud (as ever) or James Joyce will render Dylan's efforts respectable, like a classical tag pasted to a college essay.

Judging by his remarks over the years, one of his problems with *Tarantula* had to do with the business of writing itself. It was impossible to compose a book with the spontaneity and speed with which he could construct an album of songs. Writing was extended labour. Nor was that difficulty solved by the quantity of pages he could produce: 500 of those – or the 'billion' he once mentioned despairingly – did not necessarily amount to a book. Yet it is obvious even to the cynical reader that Dylan wanted to give his pages the pace and attack of his songs, or at least to attempt the 'spontaneous prose' of Jean-Louis Kerouac. Some optimists have therefore suggested that *Tarantula* is best read aloud. But don't try this at home.

The book requires cooperation. Implicit in its style is a kind of special pleading: don't judge this as you would other books; trust it as you would trust a weird Dylan lyric; go with it. The author misunderstood the difference between reading and music, the active and passive, but the unspoken advice is sound. Once you stop asking why the work is odd or ill-constructed or wilfully obscure, *Tarantula* is a lot of fun.

It fits no category. Even the usual invocation of Joyce's *Finnegans Wake* is misleading: Dylan isn't attempting to reinvent the language, or delve into the bowels of culture itself. *Tarantula* is a succession of false starts, a collection of shards, an interlaced series of voices in which spaces and silences – the punctuation is the opposite of casual – count for almost as much as the words. Those, in turn, perform the tricks of assonance and alliteration that Dylan was deploying in song. Then, apropos of nothing obvious, there are the 'letters' from various characters, like comedy walk-on parts, interspersed in the text, acting as still more punctuation, as chorus. When any of this comes off – the exception rather than the rule – the effect is memorable.

> in a sunburned land winter sleeps with a snowy head at the west of the bed/Madonna. Mary of the Temple. Jane Russell. Angelina the Whore. all these women, their tears could make oceans/ in a deserted refrigerator carton, little boys on ash wednesday make ready for war & for genius . . . whereas the weary archaic gypsy – yawning – warbles a belch & tracking the cats – withstanding a ratsized cockroach she hardly appears & looks down upon her sensual arena

Dylan's careful punctuation shapes the elisions and dislocations familiar from his songs of the period. The sleeping figure depicted as a cold landscape 'at the west of the bed' yields at an actual stroke to typecast femininity, Madonna to whore by way of Mary and a movie star – a sly comment, perhaps, on cliché and the status of women. Their tears making oceans then connect to little boys making 'ready for war & for genius' on Ash Wednesday, day of repentance. Finally, in a bleak chamber where roaches dart, there is that brilliant little image of contested sexuality: 'her sensual arena'.

It's not to every taste. It is, equally, an ambitious exercise in technique for a first-time 'novelist': a failure was almost guaranteed. But *Tarantula* is not an unmitigated failure. It's not half as good as Dylan must have hoped, and not half as bad as the book's first reviewers, brutal or gleeful, maintained. Most of those regarded themselves as hip, and perhaps even as literate, but they spoke invariably for rock's dumbass tendency. By 1971, they felt able to tell Dylan to stick to his last.

One legacy of the book, nevertheless, was an idea of character and characterisation. Here they came, the menagerie of strange and symbolic types, the Dylan repertory company of parodies, avatars, archetypes and everyday freaks, each one identified by a trait or, more usually, an action: they enter, they leave. These figures would people song after song in the mid-'60s. They are everywhere, meanwhile, in *Tarantula*.

In the book we meet 'aretha', 'the good samaritan', Judy the Wrench, 'homer the slut', 'the dada weatherman', 'a strange man we're calling Simply That', Unpublished Maria, 'truman peyote', Plague the Kid, 'herold the professor' and, of course, the lumberjacks. In the songs there's 'the ragman', Shakespeare in the alley, Captain Arab, Miss

Lonely, Dr Filth, Mack the Finger, Saint Annie and Sweet Melinda and Sweet Marie. And so ever on. In this manner Dylan could put any words he wanted into any mouth he chose. It allowed him to turn songs into dialogues and miniature dramas. In the book, in the absence of a presiding voice, it works somewhat less well. In *Tarantula* there's

> the senator dressed like an austrian
> sheep. stopping in for coffee & insulting
> the lawyer/ he is on a prune diet &
> secretly wishes he was bing crosby
> but would settle for being a close
> relative of edgar bergen

In a better-known song the stock character reappears:

> Now the senator came down here
> Showing ev'ryone his gun
> Handing out free tickets
> To the wedding of his son

In *Tarantula*, in one of many such passages, the first traces of a psychological landscape, and of the Dylan *mise en scène*, begin to appear:

> you are in the rainstorm now where your cousins seek raw glory near
> the bridge & the lumberjacks tell you of exploring the red sea . . . you
> fill your heart with rum & heave it into the face of hailstone & not
> expect anything new to be born

In due course, such elements would offer up a better idea:

> When you're lost in the rain in Juarez
> and it's Eastertime too
> And your gravity fails
> And negativity don't pull you through . . .

You could go on. By 1971, the critical consensus held that it would have been better if Dylan had not. The opinion remains prevalent, especially among those who appear not to have read the book. Dylan never did harness his gifts to poetry in the usual sense, yet *Tarantula* was anything but a waste of time. It added to his armoury and expanded his range. None of the 'singer-songwriters' had begun even to think in this manner. That the dumbass tendency (and 15-year-olds) failed to spot even that much was hardly his fault. On the other hand, the author hadn't made it easy for anyone, least of all himself.

*

Towards the end of 1963 the *New York Post* journalist Al Aronowitz had begun to attach himself to Dylan like creeping ivy to a cold stone. Often described – often enough by himself – as 'the godfather of rock journalism', Aronowitz in those days compiled a column entitled 'Pop Scene' for the tabloid while turning out lengthier pieces for the *Saturday Evening Post*, the *Village Voice* and others. His career would come to a bad end,[37] but in his pomp he was the epitome of a familiar newspaper type, the star-struck entertainment journalist, the reporter turned courtier. To accuse Aronowitz of sycophancy towards Dylan in 1964 is to underestimate the versatility of the verb 'to fawn'. It was not a tendency the hack bothered to conceal. After the dust had settled he truly believed that 'the '60s wouldn't have been the same without me'. The only point of a newspaper job was to get Al Aronowitz to the heart of the action. Objectivity and impartiality were secondary, and by a distance. 'Modesty,' as the *Washington Post* said after his death, 'was not one of his more notable traits.' Aronowitz's own words on the matter best described his relationship with Dylan.

> Assigned months earlier by the *Saturday Evening Post* to write an article about Bob, I instead had fallen in love with him. To me, no other artist had ever come along with such wit, perception, insight, charm, cleverness and charisma. To me, Bob was going to revolutionize contemporary culture. To me, Bob was doing more to change the English language than anybody since Shakespeare. I decided for certain that, in Dylan, I was witnessing the greatest ever. For me, nobody could beat Bob, nobody past or present.

---

37 Fired from the *Post* for flagrant conflicts of interest when he took to managing musicians, Aronowitz became addicted in the 1970s to freebase cocaine and turned to dealing. Reputedly, Dylan 'banned' the former acolyte from his concerts. Freed finally from his addiction, Aronowitz attempted to rehabilitate himself as a web-based writer. Styling himself 'the Blacklisted Journalist', he published *Bob Dylan and the Beatles* in 2004. He died in New Jersey in 2005.

Then, later, when I was also assigned by the *Saturday Evening Post* to write an article about the Beatles, I fell in love with them, too.[38]

Aronowitz had managed to install himself both in Dylan's life and in his home. He had been present, so he claimed, during the writing of 'Mr. Tambourine Man'. (Chez Aronowitz, in this version, with Marvin Gaye playing in the background.) He was present again on 28 August 1964, when the auguries were propitious, demigods walked among us and Mr Dylan took weed with the Beatles at the Hotel Delmonico on Park Avenue. Twenty-two-year-old Paul McCartney also discovered the meaning of life, then forgot what the meaning meant.[39] You know how it is.

It was an incident of no importance whatever, or 'a legendary meeting' between the central figures of a cultural revolution: a matter of perspective. The reality was that after awkward introductions everyone got on just fine. They had fun and laughed a lot, just as God and weed intended. Clearly, all concerned had decided that their interests did not conflict. Neither party threatened the other. Besides, respect was mutual. The tale about Dylan introducing four naive English lads to the art of spliff has been contradicted,[40] however, while McCartney's glimpse of the meaning of everything remains difficult to corroborate. Dylan and the Beatles became friends, to varying degrees, inasmuch as their worlds allowed. But those were worlds apart.

Aronowitz's memoirs, gleeful even in hindsight, the prose beside itself with remembered excitement and self-satisfaction, fail to mention conversations of any interest after towels were stuffed around the doors of the hotel suite to keep the cops in the corridor off that distinctive scent. The journalist, like many others since, was engaged in permanently adolescent counter-cultural nonsense. If Bob met the

---

38 From 'Let's 'Ave a Larf (1995), first published online at Aronowitz's website The Blacklisted Journalist. An earlier version of the piece had appeared in Q magazine in May 1994.

39 It has something to do with 'seven levels'. Not six, not eight: *seven*.

40 'We first got marijuana from an older drummer with another group in Liverpool. We didn't actually try it until after we'd been to Hamburg. I remember we smoked it in the band room in a gig at Southport and we all learnt to do the Twist that night, which was popular at the time . . . Everybody was saying "This stuff isn't doing anything."' George Harrison in *The Beatles Anthology* documentary series (1995).

Beatles, it had to be a moment of significance and consequence. A year before his death from lung cancer, Aronowitz was still telling Newark's *Star-Ledger* that the meeting 'didn't just change pop music, it changed the times'. In reality, the five young men, Brian Epstein, the Beatles' factotum Mal Evans, and the intrepid reporter were each merrily, in the parlance, off their faces. Forever young.

Aronowitz's last words give a flavour, nevertheless, of pop culture's presumptuousness. 'Changed the times'? Which battle in a Vietnamese jungle was postponed because Bob was due to smoke a joint with the Beatles? Dylan himself had at least begun to understand – to insist – that songs and their singers had no such potency.

*

Sara Lownds is almost as tantalising a figure as the man she married. Some choose to find mystery in her unshakeable insistence on privacy, but such has been her choice down the years. It was a choice born, presumably, of hard experience during her second marriage to a difficult man in the public eye. The result is that Sara is almost wholly absent from the journalistic record. This is no mean feat, under the circumstances.

The stories told about her are almost as contradictory as some of the tales Dylan invented about himself. Was she born Shirley Marlin Noznisky in Delaware in 1939? Dylan's mother said her name was Novoletsky. Was her father, Isaac, shot dead during a hold-up when she was five? You would have to trust Aronowitz for that one. Did her mother, Bessie, die shortly afterwards, having been incapacitated by a stroke? There is an Internet fan page that makes the claim.

Was Sara first married to an older man named Hans Lownds, a photographer who obliged her to lose her given name? But isn't he sometimes identified still as *Lowndes*, formerly Lowenstein? Previous authoritative accounts named the husband as a *Playboy* executive named Lowndes. Or was it Lownes? Neither of those was relevant. There is, though, a photograph of Sara during her early days in New York, dressed for work as a *Playboy* bunny. Strangely, however, no photographs whatever have turned up from her 'well-documented' spell as a model with the Ford agency, or from her work as a stage actor.

Stranger still, examples of pictures taken by Hans, professionally or privately, have eluded the hunters of Bob trivia. So had Sara first met Dylan in the Village in 1962 or thereabouts, as claimed by her first husband's son, or were they only introduced – it makes slightly more sense – when her friend the former waitress Sally Buehler married one Albert Grossman in November of 1964?

So where does that leave the better-than-true story told by Mel Howard, later the 'producer' of Dylan's *Renaldo and Clara*, in which he and his first wife introduced Sara ('a friend of ours') to Bob 'back in the early sixties'?[41] After all, Howard further said that at the time 'Sara was acting in the Broadway production of *Dylan*, a play about the great Welsh poet Dylan Thomas'. Perhaps, just possibly, she was. But not on the opening night at the 1,000-seat Plymouth Theatre in the middle of January 1964, with Alec Guinness playing the lead – and set to win a Tony Award for his efforts – she wasn't. Where and when had she acquired the theatrical experience, in any case, to be keeping that sort of company?

All of this is trivial. The former Mrs Dylan has guarded her privacy and covered her tracks supremely well: a shared trait, perhaps. The couple's son Jakob, almost as reticent as his parents, has merely said of his mother: 'She's a real individual. I don't think she's been affected by the things around her. She was too strong for that stuff, that lifestyle you see a lot of other "wives-of" pursuing.'[42]

The facts are few and apparently simple: that Sara was born a Jew, that Dylan loved her deeply and that he chose to marry her. He chose, that is, to embark on family life without hesitation amid the chaos that rolled around and through him. Because so very little is known about his first wife, however, nothing useful can be said about his reasons or his desire.

Plenty can be said about what came next. A domestic idyll, if such was the plan, would have to be postponed for a long while. Sparks were about to fly. There was an electrical storm coming. Dylan had picked the least propitious moment to think about marriage.

---

41 As reported by Clinton Heylin in *Behind the Shades Revisited*, Ch. 9.

42 Interview with David Fricke, *Rolling Stone* (2000).

Once Upon a Time . . .

Tin Pan Alley is gone. I put an end to it.

Interview with Cameron Crowe (1985)

A black leather jacket; a fop's shirt; an electric guitar; and a blues band. A lot of noise, on stage and off. No one can truly say they didn't see this coming, nor can they claim that anyone other than the protagonist is responsible. The choice is his: that is not, and never will be, disputed. One 45 rpm single has appeared like a comet's tail in March, an album fewer than three weeks later. The second side of the long-player, with its four mordant 'poems' and its reassuring acoustic guitar, might have fooled a few of the folk-pure into believing that all was not lost; certain of the preceding songs argued otherwise, loudly. When another thundering 45, the most audacious yet, begins to assault the *Billboard* chart in these dog days of July notice is served. If Bob Dylan is once again to grace the Newport Folk Festival, he will play his latest hits. What else would he do? For that purpose, he needs a band.

In his later telling, it was that simple. The entire exercise – this 'new direction', this 'betrayal', this 'revolution' – was perfectly logical. Dylan was writing in a wholly new style; therefore he required a new musical setting. He had begun to hear his songs with a band behind them; that was all the reason he needed to resume a failed 'rock and roll' experiment. *Bringing It All Back Home* was not designed to break anyone's heart – though it wouldn't hurt to try – but recorded according to the needs of particular songs. The decision had been coming for a while.

Folk music destroyed itself. Nobody destroyed it. Folk music is still here, if you want to dig it. It's not that it's going in or out. It's all the soft mellow shit, man, that's just being replaced by something that people know there is now. Hey, you must have heard rock & roll long before the Beatles, you must've discarded rock & roll around 1960. I did that in 1957. I couldn't make it as a rock & roll singer then.[1]

Anyone who had paid attention to *Another Side of Bob Dylan* and to a singer shedding the thin skin of protest, folk and topicality would have understood what was going on. Most of the songs on that album had stood in need of a few good players to help the wayward strummer along. There was no gimmickry to *Bringing It All Back Home*, in any event. The choices made were appropriate choices, apposite choices: the words were served. Though it's now possible to contrast and compare the band-accompanied and single-handed versions of 'Subterranean Homesick Blues' – thanks to 1991's *The Bootleg Series Volumes 1–3* – the song is lodged permanently in every mind that knows as 'electric'. Somewhere there is a celestial cue card. The track makes no sense in any form other than the form first offered. The words need the noise, the noise needs the hailstorm of language. That was Dylan's point.

He set out to prove it, too. The year 1965 would see the release of two entire albums. In the space of fourteen months, in fact, Dylan would place three new collections, eight vinyl sides of music, one hundred and seventy minutes of song, before the public. This would stand as an unparalleled achievement in its own right, even in a decade in which pop's indentured labourers were obliged to be prolific. It was also a surge of creativity, of electricity, from which there could be no recanting: after this adventure-in-song, Dylan couldn't go back to being anyone's troubadour. His direction was unspecified – there was no master plan – yet somehow fixed, artistically and personally. Along the way he would enjoy and endure a few other adventures, and come very close to destroying himself, but he would not deviate from the pressing logic of the music and the words.

In this context, the Beatles' incursion into America, the *deus ex machina*, is generally mentioned. The quartet's effect on Dylan was no doubt – every pun intended – electric. Patently, the fabulists had given pop a whole new lease on life, and revealed startling vistas lurking beyond the horizon. They were strip-mining money, too. No one was

---

1   Interview with Paul J. Robbins, *LA Free Press*, March 1965. Aside from claiming that he had given up on rock and roll at 16 – 'joining Little Richard' apparently forgotten – Dylan went on to mention his piano playing and to claim, 'I made some records, too.' Which ones, Bob?

left untouched by the phenomenon. Nevertheless, where influence is concerned certain things need to be remembered.

First, from the Beatles' initial encounter with *Freewheelin'* onwards, the current flowed in one direction, from Dylan to the Liverpudlians. That dismal word, *Dylanesque*, began to be applied to certain of their songs, for certain straightforward reasons. John Lennon in particular, competitive as a rutting stag, was quick to take up the challenge of 'serious' writing. Yet there was no truly reciprocal process, barely a trace of one. There is hardly a line in a Dylan song of the period that can be bent – though a few unconvincing attempts have been made – to fit a shape called *Beatlesque*. There are a handful of knowing private jokes in certain of the lyrics perhaps, but nothing more. You couldn't say the same about Lennon's 'Norwegian Wood': he had been paying very close attention.

Thanks to its circular melodic logic and its (apparent) subject matter, *Blonde on Blonde*'s '4th Time Around' would in due course provoke the usual paranoid anxiety in the Beatle, but the joke – if a joke it was – doesn't begin to explain the song. If anything, Dylan would flaunt the fact that *he* was impervious to peer pressure and influence, so called, and could embezzle a tune to prove it. Lennon did *Dylanesque* and was mocked by his bandmates for his pains; Dylan produced a Bob Dylan song.[2] Like all those supposedly notorious thefts of melodies and arrangements from the Gerde's days and before, '4th Time Around' would demonstrate a stubborn truth. He made things his own.

It is far from obvious, in any case, that Dylan hired an electric guitar and began to recruit a bunch of musicians just because he heard those early Beatles singles. Some of the cartoon histories of music in the 1960s seem to say that switchblade R&B would never have occurred to him without the quartet's intervention. The belief misrepresents the evidence. Dylan was done with the *J'accuse* songs before 1964 began. His melodies were meeting the new pop halfway – at the very least – before the new pop had begun to establish itself. Besides, he differed from the Beatles in one fundamental manner. They were fascinated by the potential of recording technology; Dylan spent his time – and much of his life thereafter – trying to evade its clutches.

---

2   Cf. Ian MacDonald's *Revolution in the Head: The Beatles' Records and the Sixties* (2nd rev. ed., 2005), p. 163. A footnote quotes Alan Price, then of the Animals, remembering that even before 'Norwegian Wood' was recorded the other Beatles were 'taking the mickey' out of Lennon for copying Dylan.

He truly believed in spontaneity and instinct, for better or worse.

What *Another Side* did make plain was that the familiar guitar-harmonica settings would no longer do for some of the things Dylan was writing. The Animals' version of 'House of the Rising Sun', released within weeks of the appearance of his album, had taught him absolutely nothing about the song. The reedy sound of a Vox Continental combo organ aside, the English band had simply lifted the arrangement *he* had lifted from Dave Van Ronk. The sound of Alan Price's organ, the sound for its own sake, was not incidental, however.

Dylan didn't need to be told anything twice. His songwriting had already begun to alter and stretch beyond 'folk' before music's world was turned upside down. He didn't require lessons from the Beatles, or from anyone else. He took advantage of the environment the British groups had created – and much good it did him – but his direction of travel was already clear. Yet if 'Mr. Tambourine Man' and all that followed was *sui generis*, entirely of its own kind, so was his use of hard-wired 'backing'. Hitherto he had shaped words; now he would shape words and noise together. The synonymic consequence was pandemonium.

A second fact is therefore worth bearing in mind. While white American pop surrendered gratefully to the British invasion, Dylan went on making indigenous music. The idea of borrowing R&B or 'rock and roll' *back* from the interlopers never once occurred to him. Later, he would observe mildly that the supposedly epochal *Sgt Pepper* was 'overproduced'. He appreciated the Beatles, liked them (to varying degrees) and respected them as rivals, but imitation on any level would have been ludicrous. Warming up and messing around in a studio in New York in the spring of 1970 with his friend George Harrison, Dylan would take a sardonic crack at McCartney's revered 'Yesterday'. The gesture was intended, you suspect, merely to tease a guest escaping the wreckage of Beatledom just weeks after the band's break-up. (As the song fades Harrison can be heard to mutter, 'Dub some cellos on.') The Dylan who could open his eyes and ears to every influence was almost untouched, artistically, by the British revolution. That became one subtext to his extraordinary output in the middle years of the 1960s: here was *Americana* in the proper sense. Dylan's electric music owed almost nothing, start to finish, to the dominant anglophone trends in pop-type entertainment.

The fact raises an interesting question. He had started out as an imitator, a copyist, a mimic. He had taken what he needed from any source available. To whom, or what, could he now turn for inspiration?

The question of originality was about to receive a definitive answer.

Dylan's accomplishment in the recording studios between the first days of 1965 and March 1966 continues to grow in stature as a singular moment in American culture. If benchmarks matter, it deserves to be reckoned alongside *On the Road*, Coltrane's *A Love Supreme*,[3] John Berryman's *Dream Songs*, Jasper Johns' *Flag* or Aretha Franklin singing 'Respect'. Dylan's songs in those months were never intended as a single body of work: that wasn't how he operated. He didn't know, often or clearly, where the writing was taking him: his statements only hint at what he had glimpsed. Yet they hang together, these Dylan albums, whatever their differences, like three movements in a larger piece of art, like a triptych. The reliable cliché is accurate. It hardly matters who noticed or who didn't, or that Dylan's achievement is still imperfectly understood: everything changed.

In 1962, coincidentally, a book by the Berkeley philosopher Thomas Kuhn had introduced the world to the notion of the paradigm shift, an idea about scientific progress that was thereafter debased as often as it was misapplied. Among many other things, Kuhn had argued that abrupt revolutions scatter 'the entire constellation of beliefs, values, techniques, and so on shared by the members of a given community'.[4] To wit: a Newton or an Einstein (disguised or not) comes along. Kuhn had also mentioned that one paradigm puzzle-solution tends to create still more puzzles.

Dylan didn't know anything about that, and he was not discarding every 'technique', but the songs he was recording might have been made to illustrate the thesis. In 1965 his puzzling revolution was happening, moreover, in the studio, that detested arena. The drama of Newport, for all the fuss and contested legends, for all the 'controversy' over amplification, distortion, offence, personalities, ideology and indignation, was in reality a sideshow. It helped to sell some records, though.

> I just went through that other thing of writing songs and I couldn't write like that anymore. It was just too easy and it wasn't really 'right'. I would

---

3   Recorded in December of 1964 and therefore contemporaneous, just about, with *Bringing It All Back Home*.

4   Postscript to *The Structure of Scientific Revolutions* (2nd ed., 1970). Kuhn didn't come up with the actual phrase 'paradigm shift'. It was simply too good for commentators to miss, and promptly appropriated to explain all sorts of events and human endeavours that were no business of an analytic philosopher of science.

start out, I would know what I wanted to say before I wrote the song and I would say it, you know, and it would never come out exactly the way I thought it would, but it came out, you know, it touched it. But now, I just write a song, like I know that it's going to be all right and I don't really know exactly what it's all about, but I do know the minutes and the layers of what it's all about.[5]

They call that poetry, sometimes, at least in terms of the method described. You could as well call it a demand for job satisfaction: Dylan needed to keep himself interested. He wanted to be surprised by the mysterious act of creation. Such was the growth in his confidence, in any case, that he no longer needed to worry over what a song might be 'about': the work didn't require justification. The results turned out to be *about* a great number of things, but the manner of working, that spontaneous overflow, meant he would no longer be available to write to order when a cause demanded or his generation called. Not that he was interested – this would be *his* political point – in any such activity. He wouldn't be making tomorrow's old news any more.

Increasingly, his writing involved ideas of texture, juxtaposition, voice, metaphor, persona and the startling, kaleidoscopic effect one apparently misrelated image could have on another. Soon enough, some people would begin to say that his verses were 'surreal'. They forgot how the word stands, by definition and derivation, in relation to what most people know as reality.

> The foreign sun, it squints upon
> A bed that is never mine
> As friends and other strangers
> From their fates try to resign
> Leaving men wholly, totally free
> To do anything they wish to do but die
> And there are no trials inside the Gates of Eden

The verse, like the song, isn't asking who killed Davey Moore. 'Gates of Eden' seems to have been one of the earliest of the pieces written for *Bringing It All Back Home* and had its first public performance – a memorable performance, too – at the 1964 Philharmonic Hall Halloween show. It is littered with the existential paradoxes – paupers exchanging

---

5   TV press conference, KQED (San Francisco), December 1965.

possessions, discussions of what's real and what is not in a place where an answer no longer matters, the truth that there is no truth, the worth of meaning in dreams – that were ever after to preoccupy Dylan. If the reference point is the art of William Blake, as is often supposed, there are images sufficient to fit the bill: a 'candle lit into the sun', wailing babies, the Golden Calf, a singing bird and those 'kingdoms of Experience'. The song's paradoxes could be taken, too, as a nod to the Blake who wrote, 'Without Contraries is no progression,' and said, 'There is a place where Contrarieties are equally True.'[6] Circa 1793 Blake produced a series of engravings and aphorisms (for children) depicting the human condition and entitled *The Gates of Paradise*. At around the same time the poet composed the prose and verse of *The Marriage of Heaven and Hell* as precisely the sort of dialectic with which Dylan would juggle. Besides, Allen Ginsberg was a fervent advocate of Blake, his visionary and Romantic crazy-poet precursor. Dylan is unlikely to have escaped a tutorial.

William Blake was also obsessed periodically – if a 50-odd-page poem entitled *Milton* is anything to go by – with the author of *Paradise Lost*. John Milton's concluding Book XII gave the Western world its enduring image of Adam and Eve being hustled like mortgage defaulters from the gates of Eden ('th' Eastern Gate', at least) by the archangel Michael, and cast out for yielding to the temptation of knowledge. But Milton, contrary to rumour, does not treat this Fall as an unalloyed curse. Like Dylan, if euphoniously, he considers it an introduction to reality, ready or not, as though Eden itself is the delusion. There are no guarantees. After paradise, the pair 'wip'd' their tears:

> The World was all before them, where to choose
> Thir place of rest, and Providence thir guide:
> They hand in hand with wandring steps and slow,
> Through *Eden* took their solitarie way.

Alternatively: 'there are no truths outside the Gates of Eden.' Instead, there are gates of horn and gates of ivory. As with 'A Hard Rain's a-Gonna Fall', the song produces an instant response in anyone who has ever thought about Dylan's careening progress as a writer, amid all those periodic jolts and jump-cuts, during the '60s. Where did *that* one come from, in the middle of 1964? Is it also likely that he knew

---

6   In *The Marriage of Heaven and Hell* and *Milton* ('Book the Second') respectively.

of Blake's literary assaults on his 'Milton' character for an alleged perversion of ancient visions in the name of organised religion, or that the lead character in the *Milton* poem treats readers to a final speech on the need for poetic self-annihilation? In 1800, Blake would make a small painting regarding a gilded bovine mentioned in Dylan's song. *Moses Indignant at the Golden Calf* was not meant to express approval of those who hand down laws.

As an example of Dylan's new songwriting 'Gates of Eden' is certainly 'Blakean' enough, then, not least for its attitude towards the fixed polarities of established religion. But that's not all it is. Part of the fascination of the songs Dylan began to write in the second half of 1964 is that they do not yield easily or ever to the source-hunting that has become criticism's default method. So William Blake is hauled in for questioning. So he coughs up a few half-answers. What about all the parts of this song that don't remotely fit with Blake's theomantic psycho-melodramas?

> The savage soldier sticks his head in sand
> And then complains
> Unto the shoeless hunter who's gone deaf
> But still remains
> Upon the beach where hound dogs bay
> At ships with tattooed sails
> Heading for the Gates of Eden

Whatever the verse concerns, the burden is not Blake's universe. Its world is closer to the dream of *Seeräuber-Jenny* and her (mistranslated) Black Freighter, with a dash of *Robinson Crusoe* for good measure. The opposed images – the deaf hunter and the baying hounds; 'tattooed sails' on an Edenic course – are ominous. The skies above that sea are not blue. The verse carries this echo of 'Pirate Jenny', the 'tempered' version of a Bertolt Brecht song of revenge Dylan had heard to staggering effect, thanks to Suze Rotolo, at the Sheridan Square Playhouse in the late spring of 1963, but transforms it. He had never drawn – would never draw – the intended Marxist conclusions from the piece. He had first taken an idea of retribution and turned it into a song of liberation with 'When the Ship Comes In'. In 1965 he would follow another course mapped by Brecht and explore the idea of revenge, revenge for its own implacable sake, to exquisite effect in 'Like a Rolling Stone', 'Positively 4th Street' and other songs besides.

Here, however, Jenny's dream – to make them pay, *'Hoppla!'* – is a fleet looming from the horizon, as though to make everyone pay. What message is borne by the tattoos on those sails? It isn't good news. For Crusoe, it isn't rescue.

It's just possible, equally, that the contradictions and the sense of existential futility in 'Gates of Eden' derive from quiet evenings at the movies with Suze. There is certainly a coincidence worth noticing. Those people in the song struggling to decide what's real and what is not, free to do 'anything they wish to do but die', have their direct counterparts in Luis Buñuel's *The Exterminating Angel*, a picture released in 1962. A song that ends at dawn when a lover 'tells me of her dreams' is lodged within the universe of the master surrealist.

In Buñuel's film, a film as jaundiced in the face of organised religion as any Blake poem, a group of dinner-party guests, deserted by their servants, are somehow trapped within a music room. They are trapped, it seems, by their freedom of choice, by free will. In this dream these sheep are condemned to repeat their failures. The biggest failure of all is sheer, monotonous and hellish repetition. There are pointless deaths, mystifying suicides, morphine, collective desperation. Religion in its usual trappings gives the group no relief and at the picture's end Buñuel makes no attempt to fill the ditch of meaning in this dream. Gunshots do the job instead.

Whether Dylan saw the film or not is almost beside the point: these enquiries were in the air in the early '60s. His 'taste in movies could be quite conventional', as Suze would remember. He had been as baffled as most people, for example, by the elliptical Alain Resnais flick *Last Year at Marienbad* (1961), a movie that turns entirely on the question of 'what's real and what is not'. He would one day nominate François Truffaut's *Shoot the Piano Player* (1960), that film about fluid facts and mistaken identity, as one of his favourite pictures, and spend idle hours in 1972 on the set of *Pat Garrett and Billy the Kid* talking with the writer Rudy Wurlitzer about producing a remake.[7] Storytelling – as if you need to be reminded – was important to Dylan. Storytelling is also the art of what is true and what is not. But the sequence of

---

7   In 2002, predictably, bootleg recordings of Dylan performing in California would appear under the title *Don't Shoot the Piano Player*. Truffaut's film was actually called *Tirez sur le pianiste*: a different proposition. In 1987, Dylan would name Charles Aznavour, the star of the movie, as one of the greatest live performers he had seen. The French-Armenian 'just blew my brains out'.

albums begun with *Bringing It All Back Home* was full of stories as odd as anything being produced by the *nouveau roman* crowd, stories which felt like dreams, allegories, black comedies and surrealist parodies. European art movies played their part in the process more than once: hence, for example, Dylan's mention of Federico Fellini's *La Strada* (1954) as an element within 'Mr. Tambourine Man'.

*

You could call these three collections of songs a trilogy, as some do, though there is no evidence that this was ever Dylan's design, or that he had a design. Language, rather than musical style, instruments or subject matter, made the connections between *Bringing It All Back Home*, *Highway 61 Revisited* and *Blonde on Blonde*. Language, 'the minutes and the layers', the liberation implied by the freely associated words themselves, pulled everything together. You could as well say that the three collections are bound together by Dylan's intuitions, by his sensibility.

A lot of former fans were not ready for that, but some had certainly seen it coming. *Another Side of Bob Dylan* had caused disquiet and several growls of public complaint. That fact gives the lie to one legend. Before anyone decided that 'electricity' was the issue an old guard (some of it not so old) was already talking about sell-outs and betrayals *simply because of the words*. In 'My Back Pages' the words had been plain enough, while 'Chimes of Freedom' had offered the only track on the record that sounded properly, if mystically, if mistily, 'political'.

After the 1964 festival at Newport, Irwin Silber had written an 'open letter' to the artist through the pages of *Sing Out!* while one David Horowitz – as though on behalf of the central committee – had condemned an 'unqualified failure of taste and self-critical awareness' from a performer who had become that abominated thing, a commodity.[8] In *Broadside* 53, in December of 1964, Paul Wolfe had also decided that at Newport the singer had 'degenerated into confusion and innocuousness'. Picking a fight on their behalf between Dylan and hapless Phil Ochs – the latter was furious – Wolfe juxtaposed 'meaning vs. innocuousness, sincerity vs. utter disregard for the tastes

---

8   Horowitz was then a self-defined Marxist, somewhat intolerant and full of conviction. These days he is a self-advertising neo-conservative, entirely intolerant and full of bilious certainty. *C'est la guerre.* 'Islamofascism Awareness Week' was one of his recent contributions (in 2007) to the rich tapestry of American political life.

of the audience, idealistic principle vs. self-conscious egotism'. Wolfe had then trashed 'free verse uninhibited poetry' for good measure.

As Marxist commentary, this was trite stuff, but it represented a strand within the folk revival and the intellectual procedures of the Left that stretched back to the Roosevelt era and to social (sometimes socialist) realism. Dylan wasn't thinking the correct thoughts, or using the correct words, and he was making money: all was explained. The language of abuse would not have been out of place in the councils of the old USSR's Union of Soviet Writers. They might as well have denounced Dylan as a decadent artist and an enemy of the people.

The commodity himself had merely hated the album's typically Columbia title, so he said, accurate though it happened to be.[9] Still, anyone dismayed by Dylan's base commercial motives could have pondered a more important fact: *Another Side of Bob Dylan* had not performed impressively, reaching only 43 on the *Billboard* 200. The sell-out wasn't selling too well.

The standard accounts of the '60s tend to skip the fact that in 1964 Dylan's music wasn't exactly sweeping the nation. Nor was youth flocking en masse to the sound of the poet. He remained a cult figure, if that. People were paying more attention to him than to his records. Dylan had solid artistic reasons for hiring himself a band in 1965 – three albums offer proof of the self-evident sort – but sound business imperatives were also at work. The *Billboard* chart didn't lie. It wasn't just protest that was played out by the time work began on the 'electric' recordings in January. On this evidence, the whole beloved lone acoustic strumming idealist thing was over. So Dylan left that to others, to all those wan, sweet-voiced singer-songwriters he had made possible.

This did not mean, though, that the new electric pop sound offered any guarantees. 'Subterranean Homesick Blues', that glitterball of a song, sparkling with verbal invention and serrated wit, the Beat lyric the Beats forgot to write, had reached only 39 in the US singles chart. True, *Bringing It All Back Home* would make number six, and *Highway 61* would do better still, but Robert Shelton was overstating the case, and more than somewhat, when he wrote that by the eve of Newport '65 Dylan's releases had done 'fabulously well'. It can't be said too often: irrespective of anything disaffected folkies with sheltered lives might have believed, Dylan was a star only in the most limited sense

---

9   It still seems strange that Dylan could be given the freedom to write and record whatever he liked, but no liberty, supposedly, to choose an album title.

on Sunday, 25 July 1965. August 1965 was a different matter.

He had contributed 'notes' of sorts ('Good God, there's a thousand angry plumbers all in chrome suits. They've smashed the gates.') to the festival programme, as though to prove that, if nothing else, tolerance for even the least of his prose was infinite. He called the piece – with a certain disarming honesty – 'Off the Top of My Head'. Shelton had meanwhile written a plea 'for tolerance toward folk-related popular and country music' for the same publication, reminding those who needed to be reminded that others besides the 'middle-class collegiate audience' deserved to be served. The detail is interesting. Clearly, the journalist knew that something was going on, and going wrong. The chasm between Dylan and his former patrons was evident, then, before the racket began.

*

A black leather jacket; a fop's shirt; an electric guitar; and a blues band. A lot of noise, only some of it rational. At Newport, in July of 1965, Dylan's brief electric set was a lit match set to kerosene. Or so the story would go. In fact, as has been mentioned, some of those who would affect outrage had been rehearsing their lines for quite a while before the event. Some of the others in the *ancien régime* would insist only that the sound engineering and/or the PA had been woeful, to the point where few could even hear Dylan sing as the band hammered away.

There was truth in that, but not enough to explain the grand controversy. A lot of revisionism has taken place since. Memories have been lost and recovered, sometimes selectively. Pop history meanwhile prefers the simple, dramatic notion of symbolic conflict, of open combat between artist and audience. We hear precious little of those who just enjoyed the show, and bought the record, and were changed utterly. One way or another, nevertheless, the festival would inaugurate 11 weird months of astonished acclaim interspersed with barracking, insults and incomprehension for Dylan.

For all that, it is still worth wondering why he even bothered with Newport in 1965. Grossman, a stalwart supporter of an event liable to promote his acts, no doubt booked the gig; the engagement must have seemed like an obvious choice. But Dylan's surge of electricity did not remotely resemble Shelton's 'folk-related popular and country music'. At Newport, it certainly bore no resemblance to the bastard form the music press had just decided to call 'folk-rock'. What sort of reception did Dylan honestly expect from people who had paid for the comradely minstrel-poet and his readings from folk's old-time religion? Either his performance was a calculated provocation, or it was a spontaneous choice. Or perhaps it was just an honest mistake.

> Everything is changed now from before. Last spring, I guess I was going to quit singing. I was very drained, and the way things were going, it was a very draggy situation – I mean, when you do 'Everybody Loves You for Your Black Eye', and meanwhile the back of your head is caving in. Anyway, I was playing a lot of songs I didn't want to play. I was singing words I didn't really want to sing. I don't mean words like 'God' and 'mother' and 'President' and 'suicide' and 'meat cleaver'. I mean simple little words like 'if' and 'hope' and 'you'. But 'Like a Rolling Stone' changed it all: I didn't care anymore after that about writing books or poems or whatever. I mean it was something that I myself could dig. It's very tiring having other people tell you how much they dig you if you yourself don't dig you.[10]

*

Words like 'God' and 'mother' and 'President' and 'suicide' and 'meat cleaver' might have served a purpose in the year ahead. In fact, several did. Nevertheless, another of the odd, bathetic synchronicities of 1965 would be the death of T.S. Eliot just nine days before the recording of *Bringing It All Back Home* began, and only months before anyone had the chance to tell the Nobel laureate he had earned an honourable mention in a Bob Dylan song, thus rendering himself 'an influence'.

Erstwhile modernist or not, the old, strange man had embodied an attitude towards literary tradition that would never accommodate an ill-schooled backwoods punk with a guitar. Eliot was high church and high culture, the epitome of the polyphiloprogenitive snob, anti-Semitic and unsympathetic, mostly, to the variety of poetry on which Dylan was drawing in the middle '60s. A solitary line in 'Desolation Row' would shortly earn far too many citations. The fact remains that the technique of juxtaposing images with no obvious connection had once mattered as much to Eliot and his fascist friend Ezra Pound as it would to Dylan in 1965. It is also oddly intriguing – nothing more – to bring to mind some of Eliot's made-for-quoting lines in the context of the 'new sound' of the anathematised singer.

---

10 *Playboy* interview with Nat Hentoff, March 1966.

Thus: 'Genuine poetry can communicate before it is understood.' Thus: 'Only those who will risk going too far can possibly find out how far one can go.' Thus: 'You are the music while the music lasts.' Thus: 'Anxiety is the handmaiden of creativity.' Thus: 'The last thing one discovers in composing a work is what to put first.'

Time hustled on. Just after *Bringing It All Back Home* was complete, on 21 February 1965, three men shot and killed Malcolm X, otherwise El-Hajj Malik El-Shabazz, with a sawn-off shotgun and semi-automatic hand weapons in the Audubon Ballroom in New York's Washington Heights, just north of Harlem. This was to be the year of the Voting Rights Act. This was the year inaugurated by the death of an individual who had told America that the Kennedy killing was a sign of chickens coming home to roost. Malcolm X was murdered by three members of the Nation of Islam, but his death seemed all too convenient in a country fast earning a reputation for its public executions. Whatever the motives behind the assassination, here was a disputatious black man, another black man, being put to death in the land of the free. America's self-image was breaking apart.

> I repeated that my friends
> Were all in jail, with a sigh
> He gave me his card
> He said, 'Call me if they die'

It mattered to a few people. In another reality the big deal in March, when vinyl began to be pressed for *Bringing It All Back Home*, was the release of the movie version of Rodgers and Hammerstein's *The Sound of Music*. Here was actual popular culture, the authentic sound of the '60s. It was, in fact, the people's music. Anyone perturbed by Vietnam or civil rights was offered a nicely white and properly melodic alternative to reality for their suburban stereophonic pleasure. In 1965, *The Sound of Music* soundtrack album would dislodge Bob Dylan's latest and best from the top of the British charts effortlessly, almost on the moment of its release, and then go on to sell a dozen million copies.

What passes for history misrepresents 'the '60s' wilfully. In the process, Dylan's significance is exaggerated and underestimated. In April of 1965, when Grammy Awards were given away at the Beverly Hilton Hotel, Petula Clark would be recognised for 'rock and roll', 'The Girl from Ipanema' exalted as record of the year and Gale Garnett's

'We'll Sing in the Sunshine' honoured as the very best 'folk' recording a decent youngster could buy. Some Beatles would be mentioned that year, almost in passing, but only as a top-notch 'vocal group'. The clichés attached to 'the '60s' manage to forget that the decade was both bloody and bland, sometimes decadent and yet, for most, as decently dull as the Eisenhower years. In order for a counter-culture to pretend to exist there had to be a solid and complacent mass culture. The point being: Dylan was utterly transgressive in both versions of reality.

*

A black leather jacket; a fop's yellow shirt; a 1962 Fender Stratocaster with a three-tone sunburst; and a blues band. A lot of other noise in the summer air. Some of it echoes still, long after everyone ceased to care about the instruments a musician might employ, in folk or in any other form. Newport, at this distance in time, seems like a very foolish little melodrama, but it no doubt seemed stupid enough to some of those who were present, Dylan not least. The 'controversy' certainly did not deter him in the slightest, though the response at first left him badly shaken. For two years the festival and its organisers had adored him; now he was being denounced. Yet he was still the same person (more or less). A young man denied a fair hearing might have thought: so who's betrayed whom?

As the year began he was at work on Bringing It All Back Home's electrifying music. The album – and so much for those who spoke out for 'folk' – was to be his most successful thus far, and by a long chalk. He had sensed a change, made a change and hastened a change. No doubt the phenomenal success of the Beatles and the other landing parties of the British invasion helped to confirm his choice, or at least persuade him that the risk involved was not huge, but the album pushed at several boundaries simultaneously. It was not a moment too soon.

A strange moment, nevertheless. It is sometimes easy to forget that when Dylan set to work pop was still a juvenile form, and still liable to be dismissed – by folk types, jazz types, serious music types and all fans of *proper singing* – as a fad. Most of the things that are now familiar, that are pop clichés, had simply not been attempted. The pioneers were eager to experiment. In fact, these pathfinders were obliged to experiment. Those with any claim on fickle youth's attention were under a relentless pressure – for it was that sort of decade – to innovate.

In an era that seemed to demand a 'new sound' every other week the leading performers, selling plastic to teenagers, were a gaudy de facto avant-garde, like it or not. Ian MacDonald's *Revolution in the Head* explains, for example, that by mid-1965, in a year full of memorable pop singles, even the deified Beatles were feeling the goad of competition when they set about making *Rubber Soul*. 'If the Beatles didn't find a new road soon,' as the author puts it, 'they risked appearing passé (apart from being boring, pop's only recognised sin).'

Yet MacDonald also reminds us of a neat coincidence. At the start of the year, barely a month after Dylan had finished work on the heretical 'electric' *Bringing It All Back Home* in New York, the Liverpudlians had gathered in Abbey Road's Studio Two to tape 'the first all-acoustic Beatles track', 'You've Got to Hide Your Love Away'. Electric guitars were set aside for a Lennon song that would not have it existed had it not been for *Another Side of Bob Dylan*. The composer of that set would have sneered, of course, at the idea of having flutes disgracing one of his songs. On the other hand, he would probably have been delighted to exchange the praise granted to Lennon's 'mature' *Dylanesque* acoustic efforts for some of the stuff that was about to rain on his own head. In 1965, most of Dylan's peers – the Beatles, the Stones, the Yardbirds, the Who – were bent on new departures. Only his efforts were deemed a sectarian offence. That fact alone marked the clear difference between the folk audience (sections of it, at any rate) and pop's hoi polloi. The latter welcomed upheaval and insurrection. Given the politics supposedly at stake for the Left, old and new, this was ironic.

Yet Dylan was not kidding, it seems, about being 'very drained'. Ennui and exhaustion had combined. The musician tired of 'playing a lot of songs I didn't want to play' was tired of his own writing, too, right down to the pronouns. *Bringing It All Back Home* was not the cure – astonishing as it seems, even those songs were 'words I didn't really want to sing' – but the beginnings of a cure. Mr Dylan's remedy altered his songwriting in specific ways.

Genres ceased to matter, for one thing. Or rather, they became his toys. What was a ballad, exactly? What was traditional and authentic, what was new, if anything? Given some of the attacks on Dylan, honest answers might have caused even the renegade to smile. After all, wasn't it Charles Seeger, Pete's revered musicologist father, 78 when his fragile hearing was assailed at Newport '65, who had observed in 1962 that 'conscious and unconscious appropriation, borrowing, adapting, plagiarising, and plain stealing are variously, and always have been, part and parcel of the process of artistic creation . . . The folk song is, by definition and, as far as we can tell, by reality, entirely a product of plagiarism'?[11]

Melodically, 'Maggie's Farm' was based on an old folk tune, 'Down on Penny's Farm', that Dylan had already 'borrowed' in his earliest days in Greenwich Village for 'Hard Times in New York Town', but the *track*, this new thing, was twisted R&B. It was funny, sour, biting and *fast*. Assigned categories were irrelevant. The backing was exactly what the words required. The result was a contradiction, a song that was both derivative and entirely original.

Arguably, Dylan was simply continuing an old folk tradition of adaptation and renewal: why not? That wasn't what Pete Seeger and the folk crowd heard at Newport when Mike Bloomfield's guitar turned the first note of the tune into 'the loudest thing anybody had ever heard'.[12] A song Dylan probably first came across as it was performed by the Bently Boys on Harry Smith's *Anthology of American Folk Music* became satirical R&B – comic lyrics with a snap and snarl – at the expense of the universal farm; of governments, protest movements, unctuous exploiters, oppressors, all bosses and sanctimonious thieves of every stripe. It was also a song that paid homage to Silas McGee, to Greenwood, Mississippi, and to all those working on real farms, amid real oppression, in an America that had forgotten to ask about the origins and uses of power. Still the folk movement's arbiters didn't get it. The rock types would suffer a similar failure of imagination and empathy when they got their hands on *Tarantula*. That despised little book was an essential preparation for the songs of 1965 and 1966. It was Dylan's laboratory.

Those who blamed the sound system for their reactions at Newport did not recant, as far as anyone knows, when left in the company of the *Bringing It All Back Home* album. Dylan could have set Keats to big beat music (if only to settle a bet) and they would still have howled. Years later, Seeger would claim that he had no problem with 'electric'

---

11 The remark was quoted by Pete Seeger in a *Sing Out!* article, 'The Copyright Hassle', published in the winter of 1963–4, and later reappeared in his *The Incompleat Folksinger* (1972). It is attributed to a piece called 'Who Owns Folklore? – A Rejoinder' contributed by the elder Seeger to the journal *Western Folklore* in April 1962.

12 At least according to Joe Boyd, then the festival's production manager, later the distinguished manager and producer of the Incredible String Band, Nick Drake and a host of others labelled (glibly) 'folk-rock' for a British audience.

and had just wanted to hear the blessed words. The explanation wasn't exactly believable. His optimum conditions for proper appreciation of lyric quality undoubtedly involved the extirpation from Newport and the folk universe of the Paul Butterfield Blues Band and their kind.

The first thing to observe about *Bringing It All Back Home* is that it was misunderstood as thoroughly by some of its admirers as it was by the folk diehards. Both parties failed to hear much beyond the remarkable noise. If they did attend to the words, they found only categories and labels: surrealism, mysticism, introversion, abstraction. All concerned then jumped as one to a conclusion: if the album contained no songs of protest, Dylan had given up on political songwriting. As a matter of fact, *Bringing It All Back Home* is one of the most political albums he ever made.

What it lacks is an identification, even implied, with party, group, cause, faction or even – most important of all – a particular point of view. What it denies is faith in social change for its own sake. Almost 40 years later Dylan would declare that he had never wanted to be 'a political moralist'. He had noticed – apparently some others had not – that 'there are many sides to us, and I wanted to follow them all'.[13] Running through at least half these *Back Home* songs is a nagging question about illusions, about the individual's relationship to the political world when he has refused to be conscripted. The record concludes – and forms a conclusion – with 'It's All Over Now, Baby Blue'. Yet the question of illusion is itself, patently, a political statement.

> Leave your stepping stones behind, something calls for you
> Forget the dead you've left, they will not follow you
> The vagabond who's rapping at your door
> Is standing in the clothes that you once wore
> Strike another match, go start anew
> And it's all over now, Baby Blue

'Subterranean Homesick Blues' is where the needle first found the vinyl's grooves in the pre-digital days when an album's running order was inherent to its design. One part of this design is a proper pop song, shorter even than the classic two and a half minutes, by way of introduction. Dylan would later adduce Chuck Berry's 'Too Much Monkey Business' as a blindingly obvious source code. Jack Kerouac's

---

13 Interview with Robert Hillburn, *Los Angeles Times*, April 2004.

brief novel *The Subterraneans* (1958) was an easy citationist hit – content, themes and intention aside – for the song's title. The simple fact, the important one, is that here was what a lot of people had been talking about: poetry and music. Dylan doesn't so much sing as recite – chant, if you prefer – like a carnival barker in a hurry. His *apolitical phase* begins, then, with this:

Johnny's in the basement
Mixing up the medicine
I'm on the pavement
Thinking about the government

Drugs are on the way; politics on his mind: it could be deemed a prototypically '60s state of affairs. That was hardly Dylan's fault: this *was* 1965. But how 'topical' did he have to be? The phone's tapped, listening devices eavesdrop in the bedroom, the district attorney has ordered arrests, guilt and innocence ('Don't matter what you did') no longer signify: 'Keep a clean nose / Watch the plain clothes.' Here, long before homeland security, is a generation under lockdown. One remark about where all this was heading – 'You don't need a weatherman / To know which way the wind blows' – would even inspire an entire, albeit tiny and inept, Leninist revolutionary movement, the Weather Underground. Bombs in public places and socialist vanguards were not, needless to say, what Dylan had in mind. Perhaps he wasn't *surreal* enough. Just before someone decided that Malcolm X had to die for his disobedience, the singer was plain: 'Don't follow leaders.'

In 2003, Christopher Ricks would publish a book intended to establish Dylan's credentials as an investigator in the sphere of morality and, more importantly, as a poet. Some of the arguments would be complex, in the critical close-reading manner, and one simple: Dylan is a genius with rhyme. The professor would not have much to say about 'Subterranean Homesick Blues' – the issues at stake in the song are not theological – but his point, as a technical point involving perfect rhymes, half rhymes and the elusive knack for turning idiomatic speech into verse (and vice versa), is here demonstrated triumphantly.

Maggie comes fleet foot
Face full of black soot
Talkin' that the heat put
Plants in the bed but

The phone's tapped anyway
Maggie says that many say
They must bust in early May
Orders from the DA.

Dylan employs a kind of sliding rhyme scheme in this little song of paranoia and alienation. The frantic torrent of matching, part matching and force-marched sounds (tiptoes/those) is part of the song's meaning, and the meaning is political: things are becoming dangerous. Pause a while and he'll write it all out on cue cards for you . . .

*

A black leather jacket; a designer shirt; a Strat with S/S/S single-coil pick-ups at the bridge, middle and neck; and an improvised band. The Newport group had been thrown together in haste. They played together for only 15 minutes that July, and performed only three songs. It was a strange sort of ad hoc revolution.

Only a couple of months before Dylan had been performing in the UK and allowing not a hint of what he had in mind. His set had included 'Mr. Tambourine Man', 'Gates of Eden', 'It's All Over Now, Baby Blue' and 'It's All Right, Ma', of course. But the 'other stuff'? There was no band behind him. In Sheffield, Leicester, Manchester and London, with 'Subterranean Homesick Blues' already a big UK hit, he was still giving the crowds 'The Times They Are a-Changin'', 'Hattie Carroll', 'With God On Our Side' and even, at the Albert Hall on 9 May, 'Talkin' World War III Blues'. It wasn't just a case of rambling through his back pages: those pages dominated the set. Yet the pages were full of 'words I didn't really want to sing'.

Dylan could do that. It may be, in fact, that he needed to sicken himself finally of those folk-protest topical songs in order to move forward. It may be, too, that he could make career moves with the best of them, and adjust to market conditions. On 1 June he was performing 'The Ballad of Hollis Brown', for him a song from ancient history, at the BBC Television Theatre in London. By the 15th he was back in Columbia's Studio A in New York to begin recording 'Like a Rolling Stone'. The BBC audience heard 'One Too Many Mornings' and 'Hattie Carroll'. In New York, Dylan was leaving *Bringing It All Back Home* behind him before the month was out as he commenced 'It Takes a Lot to Laugh', 'Can You Please Crawl Out Your Window?' and 'Positively 4th Street'. He had begun to accelerate, to blur. The mind-rattling speed at which he was working still seems impossible to credit. Somehow, nevertheless, he could separate the strands of his writing: old and new, necessary and superfluous, dead and alive.

You wonder, though, about what ran through his head, and about the strains he placed on himself. In London, he had once again picked his way dutifully through 'Boots of Spanish Leather'. In New York, barely two months later, he was shaping 'Desolation Row'. It was, surely, like trying to contain two contradictory ideas simultaneously. The effort produced an irony: the old song, the 'folk song', was the confessional, singer-songwriter piece. The new work, the 'self-indulgent' thing far beyond tradition, was wholly impersonal, a voice outside of time. It told you nothing about Bob Dylan. He wasn't there. After investing so much in successive experiments in identity, he was eradicating the self once more.

> You got to get up and you got to sleep, and the time in between there
> you got to do something. That's what I'm dealing with now. I do a lot
> of funny things. I really have no idea. I can't afford to think tonight,
> tomorrow, any time. It's really meaningless to me.[14]

Most striking of all is the absence, yet again, of self-doubt. Perhaps that's what happens when selfhood becomes provisional, when identity is fragile: 'I' can cease to care. By 1965 confidence was also, no doubt, a by-product of general adulation and the attentions of the lickspittles prepared to say 'genius' in response to any idle thought. Dylan had plenty of that. It extinguished any need to edit his writing, to think twice or hesitate. The stuff poured forth, yet seemed to obey a mysterious internal logic. There was an order in the chaos Dylan was busy embracing: the shape sketched in the process resembled a person. Now even the strangest of his lyrics had a kind of sense within them; even obscure images could resonate. He made the lyrics work, it seems, by refusing to force thoughts or images, and by trusting to his own version of automatic writing. Small wonder he grew weary with all the demands for explanations. He was having enough trouble decoding himself.

There was a risk, too, in all of this. Had he attempted to connect every image with its source in his experience and his thinking, had he tried, like a good little poet, to join every dot, spontaneity would have disappeared. He had arrived at the ideal moment of

---

14 *Chicago Daily News*, November 1965.

unselfconsciousness, and he was not about to insult the muse. *I can't afford to think . . .*

*

At the end of 1964 Dylan, Sara and her daughter Maria had taken a small apartment – number 211, as cultural tourists never forget – at a hotel on West 23rd Street, the Chelsea by name. It appears that Hans Lownds had made some threats, entirely idle, of legal action to gain custody of the child; the 4th Street place was too small even for a small family; Dylan therefore chose to play house in the most bohemian of bohemian establishments. If he wasn't hanging out with cronies at the Kettle of Fish bar on Christopher Street, where Kerouac had done some suicidal boozing, he was leading, by Dylan's unreliable standards, a quiet and uneventful life.

The phrase has a twofold meaning: he was quietly busy, as the world would soon discover, yet we know nothing about his aims, methods or intentions. You could say the same about Dylan's entire career. The famous mystique, like the abhorrence of interpretation, is founded on an implacable reticence. Those cronies who saw him demolish some stray interloper in the Kettle of Fish were never taken into his confidence where art and ideas were concerned. In that sense, Dylan had no confidants. He could and can talk eloquently about technique in music or writing in a general sense. Why *he* happened to write this or that song is the sort of secret he doesn't care to spill.

Sara Dylan keeps her own counsel over what she saw and heard. Those others who observed her partner hunched over his typewriter invariably remember the finished work, claim only to have 'been there' when this or that famous song was written. The interior life of the writer is meanwhile a closed book. Dylan is unusual, if not unique, in that regard. There are no letters known describing what impelled 'It's Alright, Ma (I'm Only Bleeding)', a song whose appearance seems to have astonished even its creator, or 'Love Minus Zero/No Limit', or any of the other works. There are no verbatim notes, no useful memories of conversations, no documented clues. Instead, there are bootlegs and venerated scraps of paper fished from wastepaper pails. There are anecdotes and folk tales. Mostly there is guesswork. That suits him: no statement about a song is ever final.

Dylan's need for privacy, then as now, was artistic as well as personal. It invites you to make another guess, this time about the personality driven by such a need. The songs, like the erstwhile juvenile folk singer, might as well have sprung from nowhere. What do we really know? This much: Dylan the guitarist had a piano installed in the Chelsea apartment.

We also know that Bob 'Bobby' Neuwirth had become a semi-permanent presence during this period. A Boston art-school student who had come through the Cambridge folk scene, he had met Dylan at a folk festival in 1961, but did not join the performer's clique – troupe might be a better word – until the conclusion of the 1964 road trip. Neuwirth these days accounts himself a 'singer, songwriter, producer, performer, painter, improviser, collaborator, and instigator'. He is otherwise self-effacing. In the mid-1960s he was described as acolyte-in-chief, confederate, jester, straight man, the imp to Dylan's perverse streak. The charge is, chiefly, that Neuwirth did not discourage, to put it no higher, the star's taste for cruel wit. On the other hand, no one doubts that this Bobby was smart and talented in his own right, a reliable friend, and an individual who did not – and never would – attempt to exploit the friendship.

He was a conspirator, all the same, on the numerous occasions when Dylan chose to shred the personality or the pretensions of some hapless individual, often enough a journalist, who had come to pay court. Robert Shelton and Al Aronowitz were both put through that mill. The latter, predictably, thought these 'mind fucks' and 'psychic aerobics' a price worth paying; the former seems not have disputed the price. Anyone with a taste for this version of fun can catch its flavour in D.A. Pennebaker's film *Don't Look Back*, in part a documentary account of the British tour that Dylan would undertake in 1965, in part a portrait of fame, ego and a talent under pressure. The famous wit has not worn well. At the time, long before pop videos, the sight and sound of the young poet putting the straights in their place was taken as a kind of droll social comment. It now seems merely vicious, the behaviour of a bully. None of Rimbaud's art-event outrages garland this Bob Dylan convincingly. This wasn't *épater le bourgeois*: this was juvenile, and peculiar.

By common consent Dylan is a shy individual who struggles for small talk. In 1965, given a few drinks, some chemical assistance, too much adulation and too many demands on his attention, he would as often manifest another side of Bob Dylan. Yet again a strange psychological process, that interaction between creativity and a brittle, ill-defined ego, would be on display. That this character could also turn a mean streak into art – in the evisceration of a certain Mr Jones above all – remains his strangest triumph. His protest songs had been associated with a movement dedicated to non-violence. In 1965 Dylan would be armed, dangerous and verbally lethal. Newport provided a couple of incentives, of course.

So here they come: Bob Dylan, every one of him.

*

A leather jacket and all it signified; a shirt never designed for a day's work; a guitar that would never frame a folk song; a band with all that a band implied. Mike Bloomfield, raised on the Chicago blues, had played his own electric guitar on the June sessions at Columbia's 7th Avenue studios. In the middle of the month, in the back room of the Café Au Go-Go on Bleecker Street, he had sat down at a beat-up piano and treated Butterfield and the rest of the group to a version of the tune Dylan was recording. 'Like A Rolling Stone' had impressed Bloomfield, the 21-year-old prodigy, more than a little.

The salient fact concerning Newport in 1965, nevertheless, is that certain of folk's true believers had already begun to have plenty of doubts about Dylan. *Another Side of Bob Dylan* had not been an unalloyed 'critical success'. After Newport '64 Irwin Silber had published his unctuous open letter in *Sing Out!* on 'the paraphernalia of fame'. The editor, remember, had found Dylan's reaction to success 'troubling'. No comrade would tell the young hero what to write, how to write, how to sing or for whom – for freedom was the watchword of *Sing Out!* – but still . . . Silber had noticed that Dylan's 'new songs seem to be all inner-directed now, inner-probing, self-conscious – maybe even a little maudlin or a little cruel on occasion. And it's happening on stage, too.' He had no idea what was to happen on the Newport stage in 1965.

In 2002, the aged Silber was still trying to justify his attack on the errant hero. Interviewed by the author Richie Unterberger,[15] the former Communist, 'Maoist' and stalwart of the people's music admitted that some 'super-purists' – but not Silber – could be pretty rigorous: 'There certainly were people who thought that electricity wasn't compatible with folk music. Some even thought the piano wasn't compatible . . .' *Sing Out!*'s former editor, contrary to any impression he might have given, was not of that school. His

---

15 For the book *Turn! Turn! Turn!: The '60s Folk-Rock Revolution* (2002). The second part of the exhaustive study, *Eight Miles High: Folk-Rock's Flight From Haight-Ashbury to Woodstock*, appeared in 2003.

biggest concern was not with the electricity or the category but with what Dylan was saying and doing about moving away from his political songs. In fact, even saying, well, he just used that for a while in order to get a break and all that kind of . . . And that's what distressed me more than anything else.

I mean, here was a guy who'd come along after I'd spent close to 20 years doing this stuff. And he was the most exciting person I'd heard since Woody Guthrie. And he combined a great artistic feel with a political sense that was poetic, that moved people. And now, to find him turning his back on it, at a time when . . . I mean, remember, I wrote that open letter I guess in '64 when the civil rights movement is at its height, the beginnings of the protest against the Vietnam War, and so on. And after the Fifties, politics was really resurging in a big way. And the left . . . was developing a whole new sense of politics. And to have Dylan deliberately, consciously, moving away from it at that time . . . Well, I really felt bad about that.

The old man still did not believe that a political truth could be delivered to the masses without an 'artistic' mouthpiece. Still he clung to the slander, delivered as innuendo, that it had all been a scam, that the writer of 'A Hard Rain's a-Gonna Fall' had 'just used that for a while in order to get a break'. After the Silber love letter Dylan decided, logically enough, that he no longer wished to see his songs published in *Sing Out!* What point remained? In *Chronicles*, many years later, he would remark that while he liked Silber he could not accept – or understand – the argument being made. Dylan compared himself to Miles Davis and compared his situation in the mid-1960s to the controversy over the jazzman's *Bitches Brew* album.

Dylan reasoned that he had simply added new language and attitudes to very old music. It had to do partly with metaphor, partly with the common speech of the age. In 1965, as far as he was concerned, there were new rules and ordinances at work. Neither Silber nor anyone else had ownership of speech or, come to that, reality, and no right to lecture or reprimand anyone. Above all, the Dylan of the great betrayal was not about to be browbeaten. In *Chronicles* he maintains that he never once considered altering his course.

As it happens, Dylan gives a pretty fair description of the methods he had adopted. Even when he, Bloomfield and the band took to the stage at Newport, the music they played was still founded on those old folk changes, meaning the blues. Metaphor antagonised Silber and others, however: they simply didn't understand what was meant by Dylan's new ordinances, for all the lip service they paid to 'their poet'. In hindsight, it's plain enough: what really angered the diehards were words; words lacking the endorsement of their imagined collective will; words and then *noise*; delinquent words, pop noise, and the sense that capitalist mass entertainment was seducing their favourite son. What was worse, he was making no protest over that. They heard the future and covered their ears. For all their verbiage, they were no different from furious parents around the world: *Turn that down!*

Chronicles, a stratagem disguised as an autobiography, was written with every benefit of hindsight. By the time Dylan began to manufacture his memoirs and make still another puzzle of his life he had heard everyone's opinion, time after time. He knew exactly what 'going electric' was supposed to signify among his back pages. Still: *I knew what I was doing, though, and wasn't going to take a step back or retreat for anybody.*

*

One weird year was almost gone. When he wasn't leading the quiet life at the Chelsea, Dylan did the New York rounds as 1964 wound down and 1965 began. Upstairs at the Kettle of Fish he relaxed among retainers – Neuwirth, Aronowitz, David Cohen ('Blue') – and had his fun picking on the non-famous. Among those who had some claim to public attention the former egalitarian hero was less obnoxious. A friendly encounter just before Christmas with the beautiful and needy model Edie Sedgwick would give rise, for example, to a complicated rumour involving an affair. It would later be said, not least in the court of Andy Warhol, that Dylan's marriage to Sara brought about the blonde's suicide. Setting aside Sedgwick's doleful history of mental frailty, her drug use and her tendency to believe anything she needed to believe, this is fantasy. The affair was with Neuwirth, if it matters.

In any case, Sedgwick had yet to join the Warhol circus as 1964 was ending: what would they know? The tales are self-serving, but lacking in first-hand evidence. One night on the snowy town after the model appeared at the Kettle of Fish in a hired limo was about the extent, as Neuwirth would tell it, of Dylan's involvement with a damaged woman . . . Unless you believe that this particular Miss Lonely is the subject of 'Like a Rolling Stone', that is, *and* the inspiration for the title of an album he would name *Blonde on Blonde*, *and* the shattered victim of the song he would call 'Just Like a Woman'. Some people prefer celebrity gossip, even when the facts refuse to cooperate.

What can be said is that Edie Sedgwick, if or when she materialised in the work, represents a type. The women invoked in Dylan's songs of the period tend to be either enigmatic, magical or wounded: the 'Gypsy gal' of Harlem; the supernatural creative force of 'She Belongs to Me' who can 'paint the daytime black'; or the neurotic victim – Sedgwick was a Boston heiress with a grim record of mental breakdowns – who 'dressed so fine', once upon a time.

It counted as an advance, no doubt, on the ancient Madonna/whore cliché. It was certainly more sophisticated than the perfect-pop misogyny that John Lennon would deposit on vinyl at the end of 1965. Whatever counted as revolutionary on 1965's *Rubber Soul* it was not a song that begins, 'Well, I'd rather see you dead, little girl / Than to be [*sic*] with another man.'[16] Dylan occupied a different moral universe. Nevertheless, his habitual treatment of women in these months exposed a deficiency in characterisation, and therefore in human sympathy. His understanding of one half of the species was limited. He embraced or attacked. Betty Friedan had already published *The Feminine Mystique* (1963). In 1965, the civil-rights movement would begin to be confronted with the truth that the rights of women were among the liberties routinely overlooked, even derided, by its male leadership. Dylan was oblivious to all of that, and would long remain so.

Only in one of his new songs, the one he would eventually call 'Love Minus Zero/No Limit', was there a simple acceptance of a person's existence for her own sake. That was probably Sara's doing, in part, but it also had to do with his evolving dialectical method. Thus: 'She knows there's no success like failure / And that failure's no success at all.' A poet's stylistic gimmick could be applied to life itself. It could tell the truth, and be the truth.

*

Work began on recordings that would become *Bringing It All Back Home* on 13 January, a Wednesday. Outside, the temperature in New York was just above freezing, but the usual snow and sleet would hold off for a few more days. Perhaps because he had no idea how to attempt the feat, Dylan chose not to rehearse with the idiot-proof electric band on that first day. In fact, to begin with, there was only John Sebastian playing bass to help inaugurate the heretic's

---

16 Lennon, to be fair, would later regret, disown and damn the song.

revolution. Some hesitation, even a version of stage fright, might have been involved. It is also possible that Dylan had not yet decided how he wanted to treat his new songs. What seems self-evident now was not obvious at the time. The electric/acoustic organisation of the album – a dialectic in its own right – might seem preconceived. It's just as likely, probable in fact, that Dylan didn't know how to handle the words he had written. He had fewer preconceptions than his followers.

When the musicians were summoned to work on the 14th the ringmaster trusted to luck. He would strike up and they would catch up, if they could: simple as that. By modern standards, the method seems almost suicidal. Dylan didn't waste time on endless takes; he did not spend hours worrying over the textures of this new sound; he did not expend energy wondering about the precise noise a drum might make. The bootlegs from a mere three days' work would deliver slim pickings for avid 'collectors' of his discards. Dylan went about his business at lightning speed, with little real waste. He told the musicians, one by one, what he had in mind, if he could, as best he could. If a take didn't take, he moved on to the next thing. It was, as it remains, a hallmark of his art.

Anyone is entitled to prefer the early attempt at 'She Belongs to Me' that turned up on the *No Direction Home* 'soundtrack' to the version chosen for the album. You can pick over marginal differences in every track that has surfaced in variant editions, legal and otherwise, over the years. The fact remains that Dylan spent *a lot* less time making the actual recordings for *Bringing It All Back Home* than his students have since spent wondering about his choices. They see no irony in that. By 15 January, in any case, he was done.

Done with what? Here was only partial 'amplification': Dylan had not, in fact, embraced rock and roll – more accurately R&B – wholeheartedly. Was he done with 'politics', then? If political writing is defined as an analysis of how the world functions, *Bringing It All Back Home* was one of the most political things he would ever attempt. Marx talked of alienation; church fathers of spiritual desolation; the pop sociologists of the early 1960s of the 'plastic age'. This Dylan, at this moment, was exploring an old theme in a new way: *phoney*, forged reality, false consciousness, manufactured consent. In song after song – in every song – he poked at the guts of an idea. What do we mean by authentic experience, and what do we mean (therefore) by illusion, by truth?

Thematically, the album contains polarities. At one pole is 'Mr. Tambourine Man', at the other 'It's Alright, Ma (I'm Only Bleeding)'. This newborn variety of performer, the personal-and-universal singer-songwriter, gives you the choice: darkness at the break of noon, or a jingle jangle morning. Arthur Koestler's totalitarian eclipse amid Sartre's hell ('other people'), or the chance somehow to go beyond 'the twisted reach of crazy sorrow'? Each song in this album invokes a dream state. Each song questions the dream. The fact that this was not understood as 'political' became a comment in its own right on those who chose to doze.

Still, they called it rock and roll. There was bigotry implicit in a dismissive judgement. The folk-left sort who disliked Dylan's turn towards pop might as well have been railing against 'jungle music', against 'primitive'. At its most banal, the argument became – as banal arguments must – Orwellian: acoustic good, electric bad. Unwittingly, though not unconsciously, the maker of a pop record had also made an argument about art, culture, political worth, trash, value and – above all – *who decides*. The fact that arguments over Dylan's status as a poet began in earnest at this time was no coincidence. It had nothing to do with amplifiers. He had chosen pop, sedative junk, the manipulative stuff fed to the witless. He was disputing art's terms and conditions. Or just – you never know – making an album.

It is not flawless. Dylan was a pioneer of the notion that a long-playing pop record could be more than just a ragbag of songs. He was among the first, in fact, to create an audience devoted to the idea of the album as artwork. But he still attended to mid-1960s notions of light and shade, of necessary contrasts in tone, mood and tempo. A big, dark song had to be matched, supposedly, with something bright and quick. The fact that Dylan was not yet the master of his musicians meant that the first side of *Bringing It All Back* home began with a bang and ended with a comedic whimper. He didn't know how to structure this new form, the album. As subsequent efforts would make clear, the form itself was the problem.

Bringing It All Back Home is at its weakest when the R&B becomes routine, as it does in the last three tracks of side one. How do you follow 'Love Minus Zero'? Not with 'Outlaw Blues', a generic lyric – *Dylanesque*, if you prefer – and a band on autopilot. How do you follow that? Not with, in essence, more of the same, not with the lazy 'surrealism' of 'On the Road Again'. 'Bob Dylan's 115th Dream', for all its winning exuberance, doesn't resolve the problem. You avoid such a sequence, above all, if you expect the purchaser to flip the disc and encounter 'Mr. Tambourine Man'.

He never did solve such problems. Dylan is known to have made some of the most important pop albums yet in existence, but still we pick out this song or that. No structure, least of all a piece of 1960s vinyl, can contain them. *Bringing It All Back Home* feels fragmented, a thing of glittering shards, of shrapnel flying in all directions. That might not be a bad thing, of course: grant him that.

*

Even before John Kennedy was in the ground, Lyndon Johnson had taken an oath in the presence of Henry Cabot Lodge Jr, Nixon's running mate in 1960 and America's ambassador to South Vietnam in 1963–4. 'I am not going to lose Vietnam,' LBJ had said. 'I am not going to be the president who saw Southeast Asia go the way China went.' Even as he spoke, it was already too late. As 1965 began the Johnson White House was embarking purposefully on an imperial war that was, to all intents and purposes, already lost. Two things were striking about the fact. First, such was the faith of the president and his staff in American puissance they could not for an instant imagine such an outcome. Second, it did not once occur to Johnson or to his Republican rivals that the American people would ever rebel against hubris, futility and the blood price expected of their husbands, brothers and sons. As 1965 began, the leaders of the most powerful nation in the world believed they had only just begun to fight their way to inevitable victory. America did not lose wars.

Days after Dylan finished work on his new album, 'professors against the war' at the University of Michigan were attracting a 3,000-strong crowd. Less than a month after the release of *Bringing It All Back Home* the singer's old comrades in the Student Nonviolent Coordinating Committee, along with Students for a Democratic Society, led a 25,000-strong march in Washington DC. Again, the politicians were slow to register what was obvious: America's youth, the inevitable victims of their country's war – if they lacked parents with wealth and pull – had begun to dissent from the demand that they 'serve'. Some were starting to burn their draft cards.

The fact remained, however, that long-haired students were not yet taken seriously by politicians, the media or the wider public. American combat troops were flooding into Vietnam; the US ground war had begun in earnest. The baby boomers, heirs to the long prosperity, were facing ugly new realities. Yet a much-quoted Gallup poll in early summer showed approval for the government's handling of the conflict running at 48 per cent, with only 28 per cent of the citizenry in disagreement.

Dylan, fighting his own pointless little war in the pleasant precincts of Rhode Island, was entitled to deny a role as the voice of a generation. But his generation, his peers, were being poured into the jungles and the paddy fields of a country that meant nothing to most of them, and he had nothing to say about it. That was the charge, supported by the facts. Even with a draft card in his pocket, his public silence was absolute. If you overlooked his songs, that is.

Temptation's page flies out the door
You follow, find yourself at war
Watch waterfalls of pity roar
You feel to moan but unlike before
You discover that you'd just be one more
Person crying

*

Early in Steinbeck's *Grapes of Wrath*, the novel that had transfixed the juvenile Dylan, there is an exchange between Ma Joad and Tom. The mother wants to know if imprisonment has brutalised her son as it brutalised a young man she once knew, a boy named Pretty Boy Floyd. 'I got to know, Tommy,' says Ma. 'Did they hurt you so much? Did they make you mad like that?' Tom Joad answers that he has survived officialdom's routine, manipulative cruelty. They didn't make him crazy. He's all right, just about.

Arthur Koestler's *Darkness at Noon*, though first published in 1940, did not begin to receive international attention until the Cold War became a reality. The novel was a disillusioned Communist's denunciation of totalitarianism and Stalinist show trials. In an album full of contrasting images of light and dark, Koestler's amended title became, in Dylan's hands, an establishing idea for a song he placed at his record's political and intellectual centre.

Here he is no longer interested in left or right. In 'It's Alright, Ma (I'm Only Bleeding)' the encroaching darkness 'eclipses both the sun and moon', and threatens free and prosperous 'silver spoon' America as much as it threatens dictatorship's victims. On this account, all of liberty's battles are already lost. You don't have to be driven mad, as Ma Joad feared, in order to struggle as you 'walk upside-down inside handcuffs', but there is no escape. Preachers, advertisers, warmongers, moralising 'lady judges', the sellers of 'flesh-colored Christs that glow in the dark', presidents of the United States: '. . . the masters make the rules / For the wise men and the fools'. Only what is inside the singer's head, in the last redoubt, remains free. But if 'they' got a glimpse of it, they would stick that head in a guillotine.

The song blazes with an aphoristic vehemence, endlessly quotable, from the money-deity that 'doesn't talk, it swears' to ubiquitous propaganda for parties, religions or consumerism: 'all is phony'. This Dylan neither sees nor seeks consolation. Such a thing isn't possible. Yet this is life, 'and life only': anything else is a pretence.

This song alone – though it is not alone – renders the claim that the writer 'turned his back on politics' with *Bringing It All Back Home* bizarre and comical. The claim is still being made. Yet to this day 'It's Alright, Ma', a song whose insistent need to be born still seems to amaze its writer, can remind you of Dylan's old hero, Marlon Brando, in *The Wild One*, a movie the boy Dylan had adored. What was this singer 'protesting' against? *Whaddaya got?*

*

At first sight, *Bringing It All Back Home* can seem like a compromise, as though two portions of two entirely different records have been welded together. It can also leave the first-time listener wondering if he or she has been misinformed. By what criterion is the 'electric half' of this album rock and roll?

It is nothing of the kind in the classical sense, nor in the Beatles' sense, nor in the sense conveyed by the blues-inflected Chuck Berryisms of the Rolling Stones of 1964–5. *Bringing It All Back Home* isn't truly pop, either. In Dylan's *annus mirabilis* that genre was dominated by the four Liverpudlians, Motown, British acts as strange as Herman's Hermits and Freddie and the Dreamers, the Righteous Brothers, Sonny and Cher, and the Byrds. When Dylan played Newport the Stones were nearing the end of their four-week run at number one in America with '(I Can't Get No) Satisfaction'. Later, just after *Highway 61 Revisited* was released, Barry McGuire would give the grateful public all the protest it could use with P.F. Sloan's issues-to-order (and hilariously *Dylanesque*) 'Eve of Destruction'. At the year's end, Simon & Garfunkel's 'Sounds of Silence' would enthrone the haunted singer-songwriter once and for all. None of this had anything to do with the Dylan who entered the studios on 13 January.

Over the years he has put distance between himself and talk of rock and roll, and for good reasons. The term, in its pure sense, has applied only rarely to his music. The band-aided songs on *Bringing It All Back Home* and *Highway 61* take precious little from Presley, Holly or Berry, and nothing to speak of from Dylan's contemporaries. What isn't wholly his own is R&B, blues and the skeletal remains of mutated folk forms. There are few echoes of Little Richard or Gene Vincent on *Blonde on Blonde* or its pair of predecessors, and nothing of what was going on in the charts. It should go without saying that traces of Woody Guthrie are few. 'Influence' as it related to Dylan was becoming a subtle and obscure business. The magpie had flown. Henceforth, people would steal from him.

Some of the songs recorded over three days in the middle of January had been road-tested. 'Tambourine Man' had been in Dylan's repertoire for almost eight months. 'Gates of Eden' and 'It's Alright, Ma (I'm Only Bleeding)' had been added in October, often interspersed with 'If You Gotta Go, Go Now', a song attempted at Columbia's Studio A but rejected for the album. What Dylan lacked, as a matter of documented fact, was any real notion of how a recanting troubadour was supposed to behave in a studio full of musicians. He had never led a band before. The players, equally, had never dealt with a character such as this before. Nor were any of those present granted the leisure to get acquainted. Columbia indulged Dylan, by its lights, but in 1965 three sessions were still regarded as more than adequate for the making of a long-playing record.

He tended to agree. He still liked to work fast, and could work fast still. Dylan would never see the sense in burying himself in a studio for months on end like his Beatle friends or, to the verge of madness, Brian Wilson. The albums he would make in 1965 say he had a point.

This one would be called *Bringing It All Back Home*. Given its contents, sonic and lyrical, that counted as a declaration, however you care to define the 'it' in question. The title asserted either that Dylan had strayed from his natural territory, electric guitar and all, in the Village years, or that he was gathering in the bounty of his experiences. Back then forward: this was how he functioned. Unlike the asinine title inflicted on his previous album, the caption also spoke of a certain maturity. This time the billing didn't need to mention his name. The apprenticeship was over.

The album is often described as a thing of two halves, but plainly that isn't exactly the case. The second side, as conceived for vinyl, was primarily 'acoustic', it's true, but since the actual first half of the proceedings included 'She Belongs to Me' and 'Love Minus Zero/No

Limit' the distinction is not clear-cut. In subsequent concerts Dylan would present the songs to a more pointed, dramatic effect: first solo, then with his demonic band.

It seems obvious, nevertheless, that *Bringing It All Back Home* was meant to present two faces to the world. For one thing, there is no bootleg evidence showing Dylan toying with full-band arrangements for 'Tambourine Man' or 'It's All Over Now, Baby Blue' as he later would, for one example, with *Blonde on Blonde*'s 'Visions of Johanna'. At this point he was applying his thinking about arrangements, accompaniments and the needs of different songs strictly. Some tracks, generally of a satirical or comic intent, needed a dose of the blues or R&B; the poetry – no one ever accused 'Outlaw Blues' of that misdemeanour – required settings of a more subtle kind.

The decision was logical, but the effect was predictable. Those who deplored this gaudy new sound would dismiss the electric tracks as trivial, almost by definition. Little did they know – a fair enough description – that Dylan had struggled mightily in the studio with the one piece of high literary art he was supposed to know best: on the final day of recording 'Mr. Tambourine Man' required six attempts.[17]

After this song the word 'visionary' would cling to Dylan like his shadow. It was not a word he would employ often in his own behalf. What is there to say, after all, about a prevailing condition of mind? *Pace* Rimbaud and his less-attentive admirers, 'visionary' doesn't, for it cannot, mean much. Like all the presumed but irrelevant drug references supposedly contained in the song, the suggestion of an altered poetic state does not explain the poetry. Let the swirling ship pass.

Such assumptions are about as illuminating as the suggestion that Bruce Langhorne, the guitarist on the track, once used to wander around the Village with a big tinkling Turkish drum, or the claim by Dylan himself that the image of Langhorne playing at an early session with this 'gigantic tambourine . . . big as a wagonwheel' just 'stuck in my mind'. Perhaps it did. The anecdote doesn't have much to do with the song, however, and seems not to have convinced Langhorne. Interviewed years later by the author Richie Unterberger, the guitarist

---

17   A taste of the sessions – though not the travails of 'Tambourine Man' – together with several of Dylan's 1965 concerts, parts of the *Highway 61* recordings, the Newport set piece, interviews, press conferences and the like, can be had from a bootleg set entitled *Bob Dylan: 1965 Revisited*. Just the 14 CDs, you understand, and of 'variable' quality, too.

simply said that Dylan 'has a wonderful sense of humor. And I think that he has a wonderful ability to let people just let out enough rope to hang themselves.'[18]

Dylan's own reference to Federico Fellini's *La Strada* (1954) is more interesting. It reminds you, first, that movies had a profound effect on a young man's imagination; second, that the songs themselves are utterly cinematic, scene by scene. Dylan has always been intrigued, sometimes to disastrous effect, by the possibilities of the industrial art of the moving image. His personal efforts in that direction have been mixed, to say the least. But film has cast its flickering shadow over his songs time and again. The medium, by its nature, is the physical expression of all his questions. He edits songs for filmic effect.

Hence *La Strada*. Here's a film about music, performance, wandering players, a strongman and a ragged clown, a lyrical circus piece both magical and cruel that ends with a desolate soul alone on a beach, consumed by 'crazy sorrow'. Here's Gelsomina, the girl bought as an assistant by the performing brute in this tragedy, a waif who learns to play trumpet and drum (in Italian *tamburo*) for her role in a story that dances between reality and dreams. Part of the meaning of *La Strada*, as one scholar describes it, is the warning that 'A world that has imposed artificial structure at the cost of natural connection and has substituted false consciousness for reality reaches the dead end of consciousness'.[19] 'Mr. Tambourine Man' aches to be reconnected. You suspect, meanwhile, that watching this picture was another lesson for Dylan in the creation of emblematic types: many of the songs of the mid-1960s called surreal could as easily be nominated as Felliniesque.

'Mr. Tambourine Man' is not *La Strada*, but the film and the song have one odd and arresting thing in common. When Fellini's picture was released, Italy's cultural Marxists were loud in their attacks on the director for his self-indulgent betrayal of neo-realism. To quote one history, he had 'abandoned the neo-realist goal of depicting society and had, instead, turned towards the "poetry of the solitary man".' Fellini's response? 'Neo-realism was only a beginning.'[20]

*

---

18 In an interview for *Turn! Turn! Turn!: The 1960s Folk-Rock Revolution* (2002).

19 Frank Burke, *Federico Fellini: Variety Lights to La Dolce Vita* (1984).

20 See Hollis Alpert's *Fellini: A Life* (1986) and Peter Bondanella's *The Films of Federico Fellini* (2000).

After completing his album, Dylan concluded another piece of business. The point at which Joan Baez accepted the end of her relationship with the guest star who had taken over her show is a matter of conjecture and, ultimately, of very slight interest. The great affair had been compromised by calculation from the start. She would later say that discovering the existence of Sara Lownds came as a shock – Suze Rotolo knew that feeling – and Dylan, as ever, would say nothing. The real crisis for Baez, as she would also admit, was that she had been eclipsed utterly as a performer: love, solidarity and ego each had a limit. By the end of March and the first days of April, with *Bringing It All Back Home* beginning to appear in the stores, Dylan was finishing up concerts in California and ending that phase of his life in which any 'queen of folk' could reign or rule. Still she chose to join his forthcoming trip to England.

In the golden west, for contrast, he got to hear what a new group composed of folk refugees calling themselves the Byrds had done with 'Mr. Tambourine Man'. Almost all of his hard-won poetry had been stripped out for the sake of a refulgent pop song; Dylan didn't care. People could *dance* to a song of his, perhaps beneath some diamond sky. That March he told the *LA Free Press*:

> Hey, I'd rather listen to Jimmy Reed or Howlin' Wolf, man, or the Beatles, or Françoise Hardy, than I would listen to any protest song singers – although I haven't heard all the protest song singers there are. But the ones I've heard – there's this very emptiness which is like a song written 'Let's hold hands and everything will be grand'. I see no more to it than that. Just because someone mentions the word 'bomb', I'm not going to go 'Aalee!' and start clapping.

This insight was not shared with those who were buying tickets in smoky English cities to hear the gospel according to a visiting 'protest song singer' who had become the last word in profundity. In Sheffield, Liverpool, Leicester, Birmingham, Newcastle, Manchester and London they were looking forward to a folk performer who was becoming a bigger star among the British than he was in the United States. Dylan didn't disabuse them of their obsolete notions. The Newport festival would be treated to his electrical racket; there would be no band involved when he crossed the Atlantic.

There remains something odd about that. Which album was Dylan promoting on this briefest of English tours? If he wasn't pushing *Bringing It All Back Home*, was he touting a back catalogue – the songs he had supposedly left behind – to a British audience that wasn't yet up to speed? Or had he not settled finally on his infamous new style? So was the subsequent Newport outrage a matter of happenstance, an act committed off the cuff, without premeditation? Did the reactions to that event then incite Dylan to reassemble a band at the Forest Hills tennis stadium in New York at the end of August, and to charge headlong into the storm? The point of the questions is this: he 'went electric' with absolute conviction, but with no apparent attempt at planning.

The short English tour is otherwise remembered mostly because a film was made. *Don't Look Back* (apostrophe optional) would frame Dylan against the footlights of his era for decades to come. Whether it also had anything useful to say about the artist is open to question. In Dylan's view a few concert shots and chaotic hotel-room scenes were not even half the story in the spring of 1965. Posterity is content, for all that, with a collection of famous one-liners, partial accounts of performances, scenes of stress and petulance, some teen hysteria, too many hotel rooms (*int. night*) and that bit involving cue cards.

Bob Dylan's hit single in the United Kingdom in March 1965 was 'The Times They Are a-Changin''. The record wasn't number one – it would go no higher than nine – and merely took its place in the jukebox shuffle alongside Unit Four Plus Two, the ineradicable Cliff Richard and still another Beatles triumph ('Ticket to Ride') when he landed in the country in the second week of April. Nevertheless, one of history's little mysteries involves the song's European release at this juncture. In 1965, six UK singles would be published in Dylan's name. Hindsight would call most of them obvious: 'Maggie's Farm', 'Subterranean Homesick Blues', 'Like a Rolling Stone', 'Positively 4th Street', 'Can You Please Crawl Out Your Window?' So who decided that this musical round should commence, for the sake of an artist supposedly risking everything on a new sort of music, with 'The Times They Are a-Changin'', a single from an album – the album before the last album – that was almost 15 months old when D.A. Pennebaker's camera began to whisper?

It probably had something to do with the fact that Dylan's ascent in the UK had been inexorable but oddly fitful: his biggest hit in Britain in this year would be *Freewheelin'*, hauling the other 'acoustic' records in its train. When that album went to number one in March, however, it was as a 're-entry'. *The Times They Are a-Changin'*, hitting number four, enjoyed the same peculiar resurrection, rising on the chart even as *Bringing It All Back Home*, with all its disavowals of the past, was reaching the stores. Even the first *Bob Dylan* album, his juvenile debut, would reach number thirteen in May while the new, incendiary set was going to number one and 'Maggie's Farm' was failing to crack the Top 20 in the UK singles chart. Columbia would confuse matters further by releasing an EP – extended play – set of four tracks drawn wholly from *Freewheelin'* and *The Times*. In July of 1965, 'Blowin' in the Wind', 'Don't Think Twice', 'Corrina, Corrina' and 'When the Ship Comes In', taken together, would reach number three in Britain just as 'Like a Rolling Stone' was being released.

This mattered in 1965, and would matter more in 1966. The problem would come to a head, for the purposes of legend, with Dylan's second visit to Manchester's Free Trade Hall. But one explanation for an audience liable to turn abusive was simple: they didn't necessarily know who Bob Dylan was, or thought he was. They didn't necessarily hang on his every media-mediated word, or respond instinctively to each of his enigmatic musical moods. If in '66 a youthful fan barracked an artist who had 'gone commercial', that fan wasn't necessarily brain-dead. Dylan's difficulties were not simply the result of that famous backlash from the Stalinists of British folk. Columbia, the artist and the artist's manager didn't help.

A disgruntled youth might have bought his EP in July of 1965. He might have assumed, reasonably, that Bob Dylan was the performer (track one) of 'Don't Think Twice', then of 'Blowin' in the Wind' (track two). The fan might have then concluded that this was what the artist *did.* He might have seen the performer in Sheffield or Newcastle when Dylan was setting no one straight about what lay in store. His audiences in 1965–6 were often confused, but not necessarily stupid. In Manchester, on 7 May 1965, Dylan opened with 'The Times They Are a-Changin''. 'With God On Our Side' and 'Hattie Carroll' were later heard alongside 'Tambourine Man' and 'Gates of Eden'. So what happened to the singer proudly ditching those 'finger-pointing' songs, 'going electric' and 'turning his back' on protest? In this timeline, Dylan's blow for artistic liberty can seem like an unintended consequence of a career-management plan going awry.

The documented facts are all in the documentary, or rather in the bootlegs of the documentary. Pennebaker would claim he came into contact with Dylan because Sara Lownds had been working for Time-Life: the facts were slightly more complicated, but less interesting. The film-maker would also suggest that his subject was already artifice, an *enacted* life, before a foot of celluloid could be processed. What *Don't Look Back* does display, to this day, is a certain unease beyond the camera, as though Dylan himself suspects that something phoney is going on, and that he is the prime suspect in the fraud. To put it no higher, he seems always to be reciting well-rehearsed dialogue.

Some still enjoy his 'confrontations' with hapless media types. The most famous scene, involving the abuse of Horace Judson, a reporter from *Time* magazine, invites the viewer into the world of celebrity mythology, a script Dylan rewrote at will. What's this infernal journalist up to with his passive-aggressive enquiries? Fundamentally, in point of fact, he is asking questions he thinks his readers might ask. He doesn't vouch for their seriousness, nor does he see it as his business to ask questions designed to suit the celebrity's interests or moods. Plainly, Judson couldn't care less about Dylan and his music, but that isn't in fact – despite what the singer chooses to believe – a reporter's job. The journalist has already interviewed the Beatles, with some success. At 34, he isn't entirely geriatric, nor is he demonstrably stupid. Judson's real love is science, and he will one day go on to write definitive (apparently) books on molecular biology, and a much-praised study of fraud (in science). In 1965 the reality is that most of a 30-minute interview goes well enough until Dylan decides verbally to assault the man. Anyone who has not seen *Don't Look Back* needn't bother to guess which portion of the chat makes the final edit.

Time would 'go off the news-stands in a week if they printed the real truth', announces Dylan. It's Judson's doing, somehow, that his magazine doesn't show 'a tramp vomiting, man, in the sewer. And next door to the picture, Mr Rockefeller . . .' There's plenty more in that vein, its best (and funniest) moment involving the singer's boast that he can sing as well as Caruso, and 'hold my breath three times as long'. You could probably argue that Dylan was disputing media-manufactured ideas of truth. You could sympathise with his weariness at witless questions, over and over, about his 'message' or, for a change of pace, his sincerity. But you could also say that he, too, was manipulating the encounter by disputing anyone's right to ask him anything of which he didn't approve. The reporter would later maintain that the entire encounter was premeditated, a set-up, and you can see his point.

After the *Newsweek* 'exposé' Dylan had no reason to love glossy international news journals. He represented himself almost as the persecuted victim of compromised and predatory hacks. The hacks could meanwhile spot widening cracks in the PR veneer. But who had told all those elaborate downright lies, time and again, on Dylan's behalf, from the very start of his career? You might want to excuse the fictions as sophisticated postmodern games – though that wasn't Suze Rotolo's impression – but the consequences were predictable. The self-righteous Dylan who lectured Judson on truth did not have a complete mastery of the concept. An ignorant journalist was treating him as a curiosity, a pop-culture mystery? That wasn't exactly unreasonable.

The *Newsweek* debacle had been a calamity waiting to happen simply because of Dylan's habit of passing off idiotic fictions as fact. He was happy enough with journalism, equally, when it suited his book, and when hacks like Shelton and Aronowitz were compliant. An ancient, self-serving celebrity paradox was in play. If *Time* was despicable, incapable of recognising 'the truth', why waste any time and breath on an interview? *Bringing It All Back Home* could presumably have taken its chances with no publicity and Dylan could have steered clear of *cinéma vérité* documentary films. In point of fact, he submitted to almost three days of media interviews before delivering a single performance in England. He spoke to Judson just before his first reckoning with the Albert Hall, on 9 May, when patently his nerves were less than steady. Desiring fame while hiding from fame is tricky, it seems.

But that equally famous film was the truth, wasn't it? Truth as it happened, unmediated, just as any fly on the wall might have seen it, just as the French phrase itself suggested, made in the finest – and the newest – American style? *Cinéma vérité* had come of age in the United States with Robert Drew's *Primary* (1960). A technique appropriate to the Wisconsin electoral contest between John Kennedy and Hubert Humphrey would surely be resonant and right, then, for Dylan, protest spokesman. Pennebaker had worked as editor on Drew's piece of 'direct cinema'. He subscribed to its ideals – no rehearsals, no editorialising, no dissolves, no added footage or sound, and everything in the order in which it happened – and didn't know much about his latest subject. The last fact could have counted as a virtue. You might therefore count *Don't Look Back* a triumph.

Dylan didn't think so. Pennebaker himself would later be frank about the scenes he was told *not* to film. It might have been fun to see Donovan excuse his attempt to rip off the 'Mr. Tambourine Man' melody on the grounds that such – so he presumed – was Dylan's usual method. The star of the show wouldn't allow Pennebaker to record the moment. As to those famous 'confrontations' with the media, the director told *Time* magazine (of all publications) in 2007: 'The poor souls, they were sent out to interview him and they didn't know much about him. He turned it into a circus. He was enjoying himself. But I never felt that he was being particularly mean in those interviews.'

Angry then, denunciatory, blazing with that familiar righteous poetic anger, but also 'enjoying himself' and never 'particularly mean': it doesn't stack up. By the twenty-first century Pennebaker had also remembered that, despite all the abuse he got, Judson 'wrote a very good piece on Dylan' for *Time*. Few viewers of *Don't Look Back* would have guessed as much. Alert viewers of this piece of *cinéma vérité* would have checked the credits, however, and noticed the name of an executive producer. Albert Grossman did not specialise in the unvarnished truth, or in spending too much money on a promo film. In theory, equally, 'direct cinema' does not submit to the sort of control that honest Albert regarded as his purpose in life. The illusion of candour, a brilliantly constructed illusion, is the story in this picture.

Don't Look Back presents a performance, therefore, by yet another Bob Dylan. He is not, for the most part, setting out to charm. Baez, pathetically persistent, is being shown the door, or having it actually shut in her face. Dylan twists the wigs of Donovan, stray fans and importunate journalists: the ritual becomes repetitive. How many times can it be demonstrated that the artist is misunderstood before the explanations require an explanation? There is added footage, breaking all the sacred *cinéma vérité* rules, taken from the Mississippi voter-registration rally held two years before, showing a singer alleged to have ceased his finger-pointing as he performed 'Only a Pawn in Their Game'. Why is that? There is a row, like a scene from a teen party movie, over some broken bathroom glass. There is, of course, the glorious cue-card business with our Shakespeare in the alley beside London's Savoy Hotel as 'Subterranean Homesick Blues' plays, for which much is forgiven. But that too is out of sequence: another unbreakable rule broken for the sake of cinematic truth and the client's needs.

The new Dylan was glamorous and vicious. Apparently he was sometimes angrier than the kid who had been so furious once about people trying to blow up the world. Speed, methamphetamine, will change a person. If Dylan was not involved with that drug, or with something very like it, several scenes in *Don't Look Back* are hard to explain. Stick-thin psychotics who feel supremely good about themselves when they are not enraged, and feel better still about their distended egos at all times, can also be poets. They can feel like vicious and glamorous geniuses when Bobby Neuwirth, a Beatle, a Stone, Marianne Faithfull and a coterie of complete unknowns have assembled to enjoy the star's upscale room-service hospitality and applaud any psychodrama he cares to stage.

Other forces were at work: Grossman too was always near at hand. In those weeks in England Dylan was gloriously witty, supremely impatient, frequently at the end of his rope, yet also, despite his own rhetoric, prepared to connive in career games. Why was he singing 'Hattie Carroll' to trusting English folkniks at London's resplendent Albert Hall on 9 and 10 May 1965 when that stuff was *over*? Why was he impersonating last year's model of himself for a relentless low-budget movie that, oddly, kept footage of his concert performances to a minimum? When Pennebaker spoke to *Time* in 2007 he had something else to say:

> I didn't know that he was going to leave acoustic. I did know that he was getting a little dragged by it. It was definitely a bore for him to have to go on stage every night while the rest of us were sitting around getting high in the green room.

No Beatle was stupid enough to be caught by the Pennebaker camera: producers of egalitarian pop never forgot the hierarchies. Baez, despite being invited to England by Dylan – in her version – did not get to join her erstwhile lover on stage. Instead, Sara Lownds, already displaying an instinct for discretion, arrived for a holiday in Portugal. Baez 'discovered the truth' thereafter. The gossip is ancient now, the facts matters of opinion.

What you see in *Don't Look Back* are events, some grisly enough, that you are allowed to see. It is one version of what a documentary film can be. The genius of Dylan's performance is that he gives Pennebaker exactly what the director believed he wanted, or what Grossman wanted: the lone artist under pressure, struggling with the rising waters of mad celebrity, battling incomprehension, asserting his creative rights – and then using Neuwirth as his proxy to dismiss Baez from his life. Pennebaker did not 'editorialise' over that detail. Dylan sometimes called the film-maker's camera 'the Eye', but forgot to say that this eye was also another, as phoney as the rest. In June, nevertheless, the Byrds' stripped-down yet gloriously enamelled 'Mr. Tambourine Man' was heading towards number one in the United States. Dylan's last 'acoustic' tour was over. The proposition to be tested henceforth was whether a poet could also be a pop star.

*

'Like a Rolling Stone' existed before *Highway 61 Revisited* had even begun to form. It is easy to lose sight of the fact. Approaching half a century after they were created, the connection between song and album seems absolute: you can't imagine one without the other. The fact remains that 'Rolling Stone' was created for its own sake. It was not intended as part of some grand design, as preface, overture, opening salvo or an argument in a bigger work. It just was; it just is.

You could write whole books about the recording of this pop song. In certain universes someone has probably done exactly that. The effort would be beside the point, clearly, and as useful as an argument in real time against the nature of time itself, but stranger things have been attempted in Dylan's name. So he makes a recording that runs for six minutes and a couple of breaths; in return he gets Borgesian libraries that mimic infinity's pulse. The important thing to remember, perhaps, is the single word with which the song begins: *once*.

Tarantula, the despised little book, deserves most of the credit for 'Like a Rolling Stone': too few of Dylan's fans have dealt with that strange truth. After England, by his own account, and possibly at Woodstock (in another version) the halting adventure in literary art led to one of the few unqualified successes in pop music. The song that began with those famous twenty (or ten) 'pages of vomit' was formed from the same artistic processes that had produced all the baffling prose: free-form, 'spontaneous', the words let loose to take their author where they might. The arachnidan volume had acquired its mystifying title, but as Dylan would explain, the transformation of page upon page of writing into a song, into *this* song, made the book – 'or poems or whatever' – redundant. After 'Like a Rolling Stone' the demands of print could be ignored. Plainly, he was relieved about that. What's clear, however, is that the words involved would probably have been dismissed as just another little-read *Tarantula* mess had Dylan not applied the familiar disciplines of music to his text, even if an early result was, of all things, a song in waltz time.

The legend holds that the track we know as 'Like a Rolling Stone' materialised in a rainstorm. A better fact, or a better metaphor for this moment in the short history of pop, is that the recording came into being during one of the worst droughts experienced on the eastern seaboard of the US in decades, possibly in centuries. It had been going on for five years. New York was under tight restrictions. The region's reservoir system was at 25 per cent of capacity while a dirigible bearing the sign 'Save Water' prowled the city's cloudless skies that summer. The rain came, just as that snare-drum shot came, when the world was arid. That was poetry, too.

In Vietnam, predictably, monsoon storms were hampering operations against the Vietcong, a ragtag army whose successes against their well-equipped South Vietnamese opponents were becoming conspicuous, their meaning unmistakable to anyone willing to understand. That week, another botch disguised as an album – a botch that would sit at number one on the *Billboard* 200 while Newport was unfolding – had been released on the American market as *Beatles VI*. John Lennon had also published his second book, *A Spaniard in the Works*, that June, but never dared to use his 'prose experiments' for sleeve notes. When Dylan was setting to work on 'Like a Rolling Stone' the Liverpudlians were busy with a McCartney song entitled 'Yesterday'. That week, B-52s were preparing for their first bombing runs against North Vietnam and another anti-war protest was being staged at the Pentagon. The Voting Rights Act was about to become law, but for poor black Americans, afflicted by escalating crime on the streets, it would solve few problems. That June, in a commencement address at Oberlin College in Ohio, Martin Luther King judged that 'the problem of racial injustice' was far from solved. A black American – 'the Negro' – 'finds himself perishing on a lonely island of poverty in the midst of a vast ocean of material prosperity'. *The Sound of Music* was then on its merry way to grossing $164 million in the US. Contraception for married couples had been legalised. America was meanwhile getting ready to send a spacecraft all the way to Mars, to look at the view.

There is only ever one moment. History, repetitious or not, is constructed around the fact. In a weird manner it has become Dylan's curse; 'Like a Rolling Stone' came out of a clear, dry sky, once and once only. You can easily believe that *the* version could certainly not have happened before, and probably not afterwards. The grim consequence is the persistent, prevailing conviction that Dylan can forever be fixed, pinned like a butterfly, in one instant at the dead centre of a decade gilded by hindsight's lustre.

The sessions themselves were tricky. The musical crew did not cohere.

They laboured on Tuesday, 15 June, and again on the 16th, for the sake of this unfamiliar notion, a Bob Dylan pop single. False starts proliferated. Dylan's inability to convey what he needed to hear to a band second-guessing themselves, the artist and the song at every turn didn't help. It was a mess. Bootlegs of each failed attempt can be hunted out, if that's your taste, and annotated, if it helps. The important fact is on the album: they went for it, and prevailed, yet didn't realise what they had done until hours after the event.

The abiding memory among those present, reportedly, is of sheer luck. Somehow it came together. The singer liked the keyboard's noise; the wave was caught by musicians who had been adrift, baffled and frustrated. Then the words spoke, in one of those slippery paradoxes, for themselves.

The words. The take of 'Like a Rolling Stone' that astonished those who made the take is beyond unusual, as pop songs go. The words drove everything, defined the required sounds and set the dynamic parameters of the recording. Here was when poetry became both necessary and sufficient. This lyrical construct, this verbal machine, became the most important musical instrument in the room. There was nothing the band could play that was not already in the verses. And in the voice.

This record would not make that instrument less detested. Those who regarded Dylan's singing as an abominable joke were not caused to think twice by 'Like a Rolling Stone'. If anything, the track would become the epitome of all they despised about this 'slurred', 'nasal', 'whining', so-called – or did they mean Jewish? – poet. That part of the audience will not be reconciled to art. Everyone else knows better. But in Dylan's voice there was the sound of a man delivering poetry, and achieving one of the old dreams of American literature: common speech, idiomatic speech, in a shower of uncommon images and wholly 'poetic' constructions. There might even be a moral in there, too.

The evidence was not actually required, but the recording achieved on this afternoon showed Dylan to be a remarkable singer. This, like his use of harmonica or his handling of the guitar, is supposed to be impossible. Even his avowed admirers don't often make a case for his vocal stylings. If you knew nothing about him and believed half the praise, you would think that this Dylan is an absurdity. If you knew nothing about him, you would think he was still the supposedly talentless juvenile loser signed inexplicably by John Hammond. It's a paradox: in 1965, and for almost half a century afterwards, people who enjoy, admire, respect or venerate Bob Dylan still hesitate even to claim that his voice – just his voice – is a revolutionary event in Western art.

The small question follows: so how else should 'Like a Rolling Stone' have sounded? It has been covered times beyond counting, yet no singer apart from its author approaches it with absolute confidence. They know it belongs to him. That too is the condition of poetry.

*

In the summer of 1965 Newport's organisation is in the hands of a board whose composition explains a lot about what follows. There's Seeger, Alan Lomax, the singer Theodore Bikel, Peter Yarrow (colleague to Paul and Mary), Ronnie Gilbert (formerly of the Weavers), Ralph Rinzler (a Greenbriar Boy), Mike Seeger (a New Lost City Rambler) and George Wein, founder of the Newport Jazz Festival. The jury is not exactly stacked in favour of Dylan, or wired for 'electricity'.

On Friday, the opening day, Lomax will introduce the Butterfield band's own set with a rude comment or two – the actual words are disputed, but it is something to the effect that white boys with amplified instruments can't possibly be the real thing – and promptly land himself in a brawl with Grossman. Albert, a founder of the original festival, is the manager of most of the big acts present – Dylan, Peter, Paul and Mary, Buffy Sainte-Marie, the Butterfield group if he has his way – and a man to harbour grudges. The folklorist has been irritated by the band's need to set up their tiny amplifiers, all three of them. He has lectured the crowd on the intimate individual truths and simple instrumentation that must, he says, underpin the blues. Finally he makes a snide remark on 'hardware' and 'Big Albert', the Bear, objects. Lomax doesn't like Grossman; the feeling is mutual; fists fly. Soon enough, according to witnesses, two grown men are rolling around backstage in the dust of symbolic struggle. Does Dylan hear about this hilarious brawl? The forgotten joke is that the Paul Butterfield Blues Band go down like a Windy City storm.

Big crowds have been predicted for the festival: in the end, 71,000 will turn up. An event normally staged at Newport's Freebody Park has therefore been moved to Festival Field, off the Connell Highway to the north of the city. The bill is extensive and eclectic. Four concerts (plus numerous workshops and 'panels') featuring Joan Baez, the Reverend Gary Davis, Son House, the New Lost City Ramblers, Mississippi John Hurt, Memphis Slim, Peter, Paul and Mary, Pete Seeger, Ian & Sylvia, AL Lloyd, Mance Lipscomb, the Chambers Brothers,

Gordon Lightfoot, Mimi and Dick Fariña, Donovan, John Koerner, Mark Spoelstra – and one Bob Dylan – can all be yours for around $30. Eclecticism may yet turn out to be the problem, however.

Newport has heard the clang and cry of electric guitars before. Bo Diddley, Chuck Berry and Muddy Waters have awakened the air on Aquidneck Island, Newport County, with their playing. No one has made a fuss. But those great men were guests of the *jazz* festival years before this encounter between folk's guardians and their worst nightmare. In 1965, even invited black musicians are held to be innocent – by the folk event's ruling class – of the perils of electricity. It still leaves a question unanswered: what do Seeger, Lomax and the rest of those who will soon affect outrage actually expect from Dylan?

He performs with elements of the Butterfield band on 25 July; 'Like a Rolling Stone' has been released on the 20th and has entered the charts on the day before the famous Rhode Island appearance. A lot of people have the good sense to wonder what that portends. *Bringing It All Back Home*, debauched side and chaste side, has been in the stores since the end of March. 'Subterranean Homesick Blues' has made the *Billboard* Top 10, though only just, at the beginning of April. 'Maggie's Farm', supposedly the main cause of all the Newport trouble, is neither a secret nor a surprise to anyone with the slightest interest in Dylan by the time the festival begins. Nor does it seem even slightly plausible that people who have been bewitched by his songs of topical political interest can have failed to notice the abundant media attention paid to his 'new sound'.[21] Anyone who says otherwise has to be kidding.

That will become the story – the folk tale, if you like – regardless. In an odd way, it suits all concerned, even, or especially, because there is no agreement over what actually transpires. The 18-year-old Jonathan Taplin, one of the roadies present,[22] will later testify, for example, that Dylan's decision to perform with the Butterfield band is unplanned and entirely spontaneous. The tale makes sense. Paraphrased, the affronted singer says something like, 'Well, fuck them if they think they can keep electricity out of here.' In this version, the

---

21 To be fair, Columbia's own marketing department had been reluctant to support 'Rolling Stone'. They hadn't got where they were (in the company that turned down both Presley and the first Beatles album) by sanctioning six endless minutes of intimidating racket and garbled imagery.

22 Later a noted film producer and academic, responsible for, among other things, production duties on Martin Scorsese's *Mean Streets* and The Band's *The Last Waltz*.

band is assembled on the night before the show, 'on a whim', after Dylan has turned in three acceptably acoustic numbers at a Newport workshop.

David Dann, manager of the official Mike Bloomfield website, will differ only slightly from this account when he comes to tell the Newport story. Dann has Dylan performing a perfunctory 'All I Really Want to Do' at a 'Ballad Tree' workshop in the middle of Saturday afternoon. Then, 'as the wind rises and the leaves on the trees are tossed about behind the singer, an idea blows into Dylan's consciousness'.

> Here at Newport is the very guitarist who helped make his revolutionary new sound possible. Also in the crowd is his organist – for Al Kooper has come to the festival as a spectator. Bob decides he'll affirm his pivotal role in the evolution of the new music by recreating his electric band from the Columbia sessions a month before. He, Michael Bloomfield and Al Kooper will play the music from his forthcoming LP, including his current single, 'Like a Rolling Stone'.[23]

Dann's thesis is that Bloomfield is the central figure in the great electric controversy, that his performances with the Butterfield band have shattered the defences of folk's old guard even before Dylan plugs in. The blues players have given the singer the idea for this grand confrontation. That invites the question raised by many people since such claims were first made. How did Dylan intend to perform his new material before being struck by the idea of using this hot new blues band? Or had it been his intention to do as he had done in Britain and stick to acoustic songs, old or new, without plugging the new single? And what about those famous displays of audience outrage that – as everyone knows – greeted Dylan and his defiant electric pick-up band?

Al Kooper, interviewed in 2010 by the Minneapolis alternative weekly *City Pages*, would maintain that it simply didn't happen.

> That's a lotta bullshit. That's totally not true. People weren't throwing bottles and people weren't booing. What happened was, everybody played like 45 [minutes] to one hour-length sets at Newport. Bob played 15 minutes. And he was the headliner of the whole thing. That's why people were upset. And then he played like three electric songs. Very Bob.

---

23   'Mike Bloomfield at Newport', mikebloomfieldamericanmusic.com (2009).

The keyboard player reckoned that '85 to 90 percent' of the audience were 'into it' and supportive. The band only played for 15 minutes because they had only prepared three songs. If there was barracking, it was because some in the audience felt short-changed, reasonably enough.

> Rehearsing all night we were only able to nail like three songs. So that's what we did. So a lotta people – college kids – they like migrated there to see Dylan, and they stayed through the whole weekend and watched a lotta stuff that they didn't really particularly wanna see. And then when he played 15 minutes, it wasn't good. They weren't happy. The serious folk music people were probably horrified. But I don't think that that made up more than like 15 percent of the audience.

Kooper concluded that 'It was controversial to the board of the festival, but not to the audience.' Some members of that board, Seeger above all, would in time counter that 'electric' had not bothered them in the slightest. Abysmal sound, distorting Dylan's words or wiping them out entirely, had been the real offence, and the source of another piece of legend. Interviewed for Scorsese's 2005 *No Direction Home*, the venerable Seeger chose to give a rational explanation for a hysterical reaction to 'Maggie's Farm'.

> There are reports of me being anti him going electric at the '65 Newport Folk Festival, but that's wrong. I was the MC that night. He was singing 'Maggie's Farm' and you couldn't understand a word because the mic was distorting his voice. I ran to the mixing desk and said, 'Fix the sound, it's terrible!' The guy said 'No, this is what the young people want.' And I did say that if I had an axe I'd cut the cable! But I wanted to hear the words. I didn't mind him going electric.

Depending on the audience, Seeger's version of events could undergo subtle but interesting alterations. In 2009, interviewed by gibson.com, he had this to say:

> I ran over to the guy managing the controls, and said, 'Fix the sound, so we can understand the words.' And he shouted back, 'No! This is the way they want it!' *They wanted it loud enough that all these folkies would 'boo', because this was Bob's chance to show them he's bidding 'Bye Bye Baby Blue' to them* [my italics].

One interpretation of events has become fact (along with the legendary booing). So Dylan, the lost hero, turns up with a bunch of cacophonous punks who have already been at the centre of festival strife and offers a calculated gesture, or so it seems, of defiance and contempt, and Seeger still *doesn't mind him going electric*? This board member was also oblivious meanwhile to all the tensions between factions and musical philosophies that had begun to characterise the festival? Few disagree that the sound was hideous: Scorsese's soundtrack benefits from the best that twenty-first-century technology can offer, and the result, though thrilling on 'Maggie's Farm', is still raw as an abraded fist. Kooper's explanation for any anger shown to a set comprising a mere three songs, concluded without ceremony, is also plausible: the more devoted the fan, the more likely he or she would have been to become profoundly pissed off. It still doesn't feel like the whole story. It is as though all concerned wanted a symbolic moment.

*

There is, for example, a description of Dylan at a party after the show looking 'stunned, shaken, and disappointed'. There is the aftershock felt among concert audiences around the world in 1966, and all that righteous indignation, whatever it was supposed to mean, towards 'commercialism', Stratocaster and Telecaster guitars, and selling out. There is, for symbolism's purposes, Pete Seeger himself, a man who had been chastised often enough by purists for his own failure to honour authenticity. That detail is often overlooked.

According to his biographer David Dunaway,[24] so dismayed was Seeger by Dylan's performance at Newport in 1965 he withdrew from folk music, for a while at least, to think again. He also resigned from the Newport board and gave up the column he had been writing for *Sing Out!* Ordeal by electricity, taken as a personal humiliation, changed his life and career. Environmentalism, his Hudson River campaign sloop *Clearwater* and anti-Vietnam protests became Seeger's preoccupations.

As Greil Marcus would observe: 'Within a year, Dylan's performance would have changed all the rules of folk music – or, rather, what had been understood as folk music would as a cultural force have all but ceased to exist. The train was leaving the station . . .'[25] Folk had been a brief enough boom. It had not preoccupied the great mass of

24 *How Can I Keep from Singing: Pete Seeger* (1981, rev. ed. 2008).
25 *Invisible Republic: Bob Dylan's Basement Tapes* (1997).

Americans much, or for long. Its political pretensions enabled a lot of middle-class white people to feel good about themselves, even as they treated black and rural performers as fascinating species of noble savage. The arbiters of the revival never had managed to work out what was and what was not 'authentic', nor had they managed to explain why success – reaching the people – constituted betrayal. They had not made a case for their own relevance.

Bruce Langhorne, who saw only part of the Newport show – and therefore could not have seen much – believed the reaction was 'mixed. Some people were going, "What the hell's that?!" And some people were going, "Oh wow!" But my overall impression was that more people were offended than were enchanted. That was my overall impression.' Talking to Richie Unterberger, however, Langhorne also suggested that, among musicians, careers were at stake, that

> there were a lot of people who were very heavily invested in the traditional folk music. And with the folk music revival, these were people who had been playing folk music for years and years and years in obscure venues, and suddenly they saw their time had come. And they probably saw electrification and rock'n'rollation as co-option, total co-option.

Eric Von Schmidt, another witness, would tell the early Dylan biographer Anthony Scaduto that the singer simply couldn't be heard above 'a Butterfield boogie'. There was, effectively, 'no Dylan'. The complaints were against the dire sound, and they grew in volume as the band's volume failed to diminish. Possibly so. The recordings available now have been cleaned up beyond any audio standard achievable in a windy field in 1965. Nevertheless, the tale of the lousy PA system is in danger of becoming another myth. Believe it and you might believe that no one ever objected to this new, electric Dylan, or ever complained that he had deserted folk music. Arguments over ideology and what Langhorne called 'co-option' would not have disappeared had the sound been pristine. The struggle throughout the West between art, consumerism, capitalism and the common will would not have been averted if the young hero had just turned the noise down. In pop's terms, he got the kind of reception that would later be afforded to punk rock.

Dylan blew them away regardless. It counted as an assassination or a mercy killing, depending on your point of view. He abolished an audience. His performance also made an eloquent point about words and their uses. Contrary to Seeger's complaints, it was not always essential to be 'understood' at first hearing. Some things took a while, and were the better for it. The noise mattered for its own sake. It too had a meaning. The only pure, honourable alternative, for any poet, was print, and Dylan was no longer heading in that direction.

Phil Ochs had probably put it best when responding to Paul Wolfe's obnoxious *Broadside* article, 'The New Dylan', at the start of the year. 'To cater to an audience's taste is not to respect them,' Ochs had written, 'and if the audience doesn't understand that, they don't deserve respect.'

'Electricity' was a diversionary argument. Johnny Cash, born in Ozarks poverty of real folk but as invincibly commercial as they came, had enjoyed a big success at Newport in '64. As always Cash and his band had been amplified from start to finish, albeit not egregiously so, and attracted not a murmur. Dylan might have been uncompromising, but he was also the victim of hypocrisy, snobbery and elitism. Ignorance, too.

*

Still: only three songs. Dylan appeared with the Paul Butterfield Blues Band (lacking Butterfield himself) after a long night's rehearsal and could come up with just three numbers? He had Mike Bloomfield (guitar); Sam Lay (drums); Jerome Arnold (bass); Al Kooper (organ); Barry Goldberg (piano); and no shortage of experience to hand. Peter Yarrow, making the introductions, said beforehand that 'the person that's going to come up now has a limited amount of time'. After 'Maggie's Farm', 'Like a Rolling Stone' and a work-in-progress he called 'Phantom Engineer' had faded away, Dylan made his abrupt announcement to the band. He said: 'Let's go, man. That's all.' It didn't sound planned. It sounded as though he was abandoning the stage. You can only conclude that whatever he was hearing, it was not unbridled applause.

You can then notice that Yarrow, audibly uneasy in the face of the audience's reaction, attempted to persuade Dylan to return to the stage, and promised the crowd that the star was fetching his *acoustic* guitar, as though that counted as a placatory sacrifice. What followed, after an E harmonica had been provided, was 'Mr. Tambourine Man'. As in England, Dylan was still prepared to eschew his revolution, if such was required. Clearly, he had been hoping for acclaim, not confrontation. But it was in *this* moment that he turned away.

*

For some, the leather jacket – the jacket that would one day wind up in the Smithsonian Institution's National Museum of American History[26] – was enough, far less the fancy shirt, far less the despised guitar, far less a band of reprobates fighting their way – 'Like A Rolling Stone' barely survived the combat – through a set like a burst of small-arms fire. Todd Haynes could not resist the image when he came to make his 2007 movie *I'm Not There*. The jacket itself instantly became 'a sell-out jacket'.[27] Everything about Dylan was a statement, whether he knew it or not. The problem at Newport in 1965 was that those who failed to grasp the import of the statement were determined to insist on their own interpretations. Chiefly, they were saying that *this artist* could no longer deserve serious attention with that demeanour and that sound. Others might have their amplified noises and their wild clothes and still earn the pretence of respect. Dylan, precisely because of the admiration previously bestowed upon him, was not permitted to deviate. This was politics, of course, in a broad and simplistic sense. Everything about him that year signified a deal with the capitalist devil. Quite how he was expected to make records, fill halls or claim enough of the public's attention to function as 'spokesman' for anyone or anything was a contradiction never explored.

*

Playboy: Mistake or not, what made you decide to go the rock and roll route?

Dylan: Carelessness. I lost my one true love. I started drinking. The first thing I know, I'm in a card game. Then I'm in a crap game. I wake up in a pool hall. Then this big Mexican lady drags me off the table, takes me to Philadelphia. She leaves me alone in her house, and it burns down. I wind up in Phoenix. I get a job as a Chinaman. I start working in a dime store, and move in with a 13-year-old girl. Then this big Mexican lady from Philadelphia comes in and burns the house down. I go down to Dallas. I get a job as a 'before' in a Charles Atlas 'before

---

26 Loaned by an 'anonymous collector' for a 2012 exhibition entitled *American Stories*. The garment went on show alongside Dorothy's ruby slippers, Benjamin Franklin's walking stick, Abe Lincoln's pocket watch, Muhammad Ali's boxing gloves and a fragment of Plymouth Rock. *Americana*, then.

27 Interview with Nora Ephron and Susan Edmiston, 'Positively Tie Dream', August 1965, republished in *Dylan on Dylan: The Essential Interviews*, ed. Jonathan Cott (2006). 'What kind of jacket is a sell-out jacket?' asked Dylan.

and after' ad. I move in with a delivery boy who can cook fantastic chilli and hot dogs. Then this 13-year-old girl from Phoenix comes and burns the house down. The delivery boy – he ain't so mild: He gives her the knife, and the next thing I know I'm in Omaha. It's so cold there, by this time I'm robbing my own bicycles and frying my own fish. I stumble onto some luck and get a job as a carburettor out at the hot-rod races every Thursday night. I move in with a high school teacher who also does a little plumbing on the side, who ain't much to look at, but who's built a special kind of refrigerator that can turn newspaper into lettuce. Everything's going good until that delivery boy shows up and tries to knife me. Needless to say, he burned the house down, and I hit the road. The first guy that picked me up asked me if I wanted to be a star. What could I say?

Playboy: And that's how you became a rock and roll singer?

Dylan: No, that's how I got tuberculosis.[28]

*

Newport only mattered because of what followed. Had Dylan returned to Columbia's Studio A in New York four days after the festival and begun to produce more singer-songwriter poetry appropriate to the type of guitar that doesn't pick fights with the words, the Rhode Island incident would have become a footnote. Newport, and the legend being born in the late summer of 1965, had not yet found its context. *Highway 61 Revisited* would be Dylan's first purely 'rock' album (whatever that means), but it would also be the record that brought his efforts as a writer – the efforts of 'Hard Rain', 'Chimes of Freedom', of *Tarantula*, of 'Tambourine Man' and 'It's All Right, Ma' – to fruition. Whether it counts as a better album than its successor, *Blonde on Blonde*, is a game that endures. Tone, verbal and musical, separates the two sets. The first of the pair can seem chillier than the second, with a keener edge, and that can seem like no accident. There are no love songs on *Highway 61*. It remains a pinnacle, nevertheless.

The bare facts say that Dylan got to the peak in short order. Set aside those two days in June in which 'Like a Rolling Stone' was made, and here's another album forged in the course of – depending on how you calculate these things – three to four days/nights in the studio. This time, it seems, Dylan was ready to manage a band, even if the musicians themselves were often less than sure, start to finish, of what was expected.

28 Nat Hentoff, *Playboy*, March 1966.

One producer, Tom Wilson, had been replaced by another, Bob Johnston, after 'Rolling Stone', for reasons no one has cared to explain. It didn't matter: Dylan was in command, and worked as fast as thought and instinct would allow, as often as not seeming to trust to luck.

The studio annals and anecdotes don't begin to explain everything. Dylan and Sara had bought their own rural retreat at Byrdcliffe, near Woodstock, on his return from England. He would not spend a lot of his precious time there in 1965, or during much of 1966, but would later claim that *Highway 61*, that most urban of albums, a statement on modernity and the condition of man 'in the jungle of cities' (as Brecht's title goes), was composed in sylvan solitude. As ever, we know nothing much about the process, beyond the fact that the creation of 'Like a Rolling Stone' had burst a dam, and that Dylan was hearing echoes of the city – its speech, rhythms and anxieties – in Allen Ginsberg's poetry. We could add something elevated and predictable, say that within the space of weeks Dylan 'reinvented popular song', and it would be true. But what actually went on in a brief period of intensely concentrated writing is a matter of conjecture. Somehow the writer became, in the words of one of his later works, 'a voice without restraint'.

One conjecture is that in the process Dylan learned why a song wouldn't necessarily collapse if the usual props were kicked away. How did he get from his 'twenty pages of vomit' to the four long verses of 'Like a Rolling Stone', after all? 'Editing' would be the usual word, but this was not editing in the usual fashion. What truly happens in this song, and in the other songs of *Highway 61*, is a stripping away of material without regard to narrative. The usual connective matter is discarded; it ceases to signify. Not once does a song or an image explain itself. 'Like a Rolling Stone' tells more of a story (apparently) than most of its companion pieces, but that's the joke implicit in its first line, and in the album's first line: 'Once upon a time . . .' When the set reaches its end, with 'Desolation Row', the idea of coherent narrative, of the traditional song that commences with some version of 'Once upon a time', has been shattered. Dylan had learned that he didn't need the oldest storytelling 'ordinance' of them all in order to make sense. To make his kind of sense, at any rate.

In these nine songs, as in *Tarantula*, characters come and go: six dozen of them, by name or description. In these songs, as in so much of then-recent American poetry, personal pronouns become suspect. It's never entirely clear, track by track, to whom 'I', 'you' or 'me' might refer. Here the writer who made all the self-regarding singer-songwriters possible is casting a lot of doubt over the reliability of authorial voice. The first-person singular makes only intermittent appearances in the ten verses of 'Desolation Row', for example. Is anyone supposed to believe that this is Dylan speaking for himself, even a dream-state self, in the autobiographical manner? Is this imagined 'I' still another, then? Or is this observer merely the narrator in a story whose scenes do not, in the usual sense, connect? There's a fourth, implicit question: who really wants to know, and why would they need to know? Identity, says *Highway 61*, cannot be fixed so easily; words themselves are deceptive. The horde of singer-songwriters appearing to share their *angst* were caught, says this poetic method, in a species of dishonesty.

You could as easily recall, of course, that the real story of this album is only partly to do with words, that its literary interest is in one sense almost beside the point: it's a *pop record*. That description isn't precisely true, but it is always worth remembering the obvious: Dylan is making poetry-in-music. Tunes and musicians are the opposite of irrelevant from the instant 'Like a Rolling Stone' blows open the door. Some species of literary criticism might be necessary, but it is not sufficient where *Highway 61* is concerned. The hard core of musicians who made the recordings – Bloomfield, Kooper, Paul Griffin, Bobby Gregg, Sam Lay, Harvey Goldstein/Brooks – were capable of both lyricism and power. Three of them had been through the Newport storm. The fact didn't necessarily ease their bewilderment at every turn, but they knew enough to realise that Dylan was not looking for the usual by-the-numbers sessions.

Highway 61 was not written in the studio, but it was created there. The band could have played the blues or R&B, old style, for as long as the singer desired. An emphasis on keyboards aside – Bloomfield's contributions were not in fact conspicuous – the set-up was more or less conventional. Instead, after jotting down the chords, Dylan wanted to explore the possibilities of those old, standard forms. The album is least convincing – in 'From a Buick 6', the only outright failure – when it adheres most closely to convention. There are those 'blues changes' aplenty, but what's at stake is a journey in time and space, back and forth. The songs exist in several dimensions, some fantastic, some 'real', some moral, some ancient, some contemporary. Somehow, the players were caused to sense that idea.

Take the album's title. Here's a statement of intent as clear as any he ever made. In Dylan's childhood and youth the highway in question ran all the way from New Orleans to the Canadian border by way of

Duluth, Minnesota. Yet in his yearning juvenile imagination it flowed alongside the Mississippi in the opposite direction, north to south, from an adolescence in the blank middle of nowhere to the home of the blues. As a migratory route, and as a state of mind, the road had long cut its way through numerous of the songs that signified the revelation the young Dylan had called 'the real thing'. After Newport, with this title, he was making his own claim on authenticity. His revolution began with a sense of things revisited.

*

An electric guitar doesn't make a sound. It has no independent life of its own. The lump of wood, plastic, pick-ups and wires depends on an amplifier to kick the electromagnets and paper cones of loudspeakers into life. The musician who adopts an electric guitar is tethered to a transmission system, then to an idea.

The latter is recent: electric guitars became commercially available less than a decade before Dylan was born; the first Fender Stratocaster didn't appear until 1954. Whatever the model, it involves the art of unnatural noise. With an electric guitar you can sculpt the stuff, stretch it and age it and compress it as far as physics and engineering will allow. A conventional hollow-bodied guitar provides no useful guide to any of this. If you choose electricity, you have to think differently. You have to think of a musical instrument as a gesture. For the singer of songs it becomes something more than the folk notion of 'accompaniment'.

In 1965, when Dylan had his spot of trouble at Newport, there was an unspoken assumption in supposedly progressive folk circles: black bluesmen played electric guitars, white musicians did not. It was also taken for granted that an amplified instrument embodied a filthy capitalist industry busy reducing music to 'mindless pop'. In parts of the world, famously in Brazil, the electric guitar could even be taken as a symbol of Yankee imperialism in the mid-'60s. In the American heartland, it was more often a symbol of moral decay. Briefly, it bothered a lot of people.

For Dylan, as for the songs he was writing, this was ideal. The decision to 'go electric' wasn't just a disavowal of a fetishised tradition. Some of the things he was writing in 1965 were unimaginable – could not have been imagined – without amplified sound. He was certainly smart enough, meanwhile, to realise that the folk thing had run its course. Its conventions ordained its conclusions, lyrical, emotional or political. Even at its least 'electric' *Highway 61* takes a scalpel to received opinions concerning the art of song, therefore of art.

ONCE UPON A TIME

Ignore the words, if you can, and 'Desolation Row' could sound like one of those long, ancient ballads in which Dylan had been schooled as a performer. On this basis, it ticks along, like so many others. Charlie McCoy's chiming solo guitar, like something off the streets of old El Paso, might meanwhile give the piece a western tinge, and seem to place the action on the fringes of that great Orson Welles picture *Touch of Evil* (1958), a movie full of grotesques with all the textures of a bad dream. But the most 'folk-sounding' track on *Highway 61* is a folk song only in the oldest, most primal sense – the sense Dylan liked best – and its cinematic expanse rejects all film grammar. It invites you to trust the writer's imagination, to enter the world he has glimpsed through the veneer of presumed reality. Endless interpretations of this song, like every other song on the album, thereafter became almost compulsory. That might be the point: everything is a matter of perception and interpretation. In the middle of the 1960s, in the most powerful country in the world, delivered by a writer who had been born to worry over what was and was not phoney, this was the only statement possible.

One plain historical fact remains paramount: no one else was writing like this in the middle of the 1960s. Few have come close in the decades since. Dylan himself has long maintained that he cannot properly explain how or why he wrote the songs of this period. He only knows that he could not do so again, even if he wanted to. Late in life he can talk, from deep knowledge, about songwriting and technique in the traditional sense, discoursing at will on the importance of Stephen Foster or Chuck Berry to an American art form. Where his own contributions of the mid-'60s are concerned clarity deserts him. This is more than the usual Dylan 'mystique', more than a 'self-mythologising' habit. In 2004, questioned about 'Like a Rolling Stone', he said:

It's like a ghost is writing a song like that. It gives you the song and it goes away, it goes away. You don't know what it means. Except the ghost picked me to write the song.[29]

The idea of the artist as receptacle for the Muse isn't exactly new. Equally, Dylan's unwillingness to attempt to pick apart his songs, line by line, with his life as a footnote, has been consistent. The sense of bafflement – *You don't know what it means* – nevertheless seems sincere. It leaves you wondering: how *does* it feel to sing 'Rolling Stone' year

29 *Los Angeles Times*, April 2004.

after year, decade after decade? You can almost conclude that a song so puzzling to its creator is supposed to be mysterious, not because of the supernatural intervention of Calliope – though for a poet it's a nice thought – but because of the structure of the piece and the process by which it was created.

The Frenchman André Breton (1896–1966) took 'psychic automatism' to be the fundamental method of surrealism in its earliest phase. The prime directive, always, was to avoid the crime of self-censorship. The practical result (in theory) was the voluntary loss of authorial control; the disappearance, in most senses, of the author. The core surrealist belief was that reason had failed. In the first *Manifeste du surréalisme* (1924) Breton had written that through automatism 'we propose to express, either verbally, or in writing, or in any other fashion, the real operation of thought'. Automatism involved 'dictation of thought', as by Dylan's ghost (in the machine). If it helps, Breton also stated:

The most powerful surrealist image is the one that presents the highest degree of arbitrariness, that takes longest to translate into functional language, whether because it contains an enormous quantity of apparent contradiction, or because one of its terms is curiously secret or because it is of a hallucinatory nature, or because it lends very naturally to the abstract the mask of the concrete, or inversely, because it involves the negation of some elementary physical property, or because it unleashes laughter.

Highway 61 doesn't go quite so far, though laughter is certainly unleashed. For one thing, Dylan has here shaped the products of his *Tarantula* automatism into songs. His genius is to avoid wringing the 'hallucinatory nature' out of them. For another thing, Dylan is imposing music – itself a kind of 'dictation of thought' – on words. One way or another, mood and emotional tone, through music, are arrived at by conscious choice. 'Like a Rolling Stone' might have had an early life as a piano waltz, but after *a lot* of false starts it became something else entirely. Many conscious decisions were involved.

The album's preoccupation with revenge, with putting people straight and putting them down, remains startling. Sometimes it amounts to simple assault. 'Positively 4th Street', recorded during the sessions but issued only as a follow-up single to 'Like a Rolling Stone', is almost a blunt instrument, and sounds inescapably like retaliation inflicted on the Newport congregation. This jolly retort from one accused of being 'a master thief' begins as it means to go on: 'You got a lotta nerve / To say you are my friend.' *Highway 61* itself follows the pattern, from 'Rolling Stone' to the public stoning of 'Mr Jones' in 'Ballad of a Thin Man' (for crimes supposedly committed during the English tour). Dylan is nowhere in the business of offering comfort. 'Can You Please Crawl Out Your Window?', also excluded from the album, makes its point with its title alone. Even 'It Takes a Lot to Laugh', ostensibly the gentlest and sexiest of the songs, ends with 'Don't say I never warned you / When your train gets lost.' The persona that had begun to take hold upstairs at the Kettle of Fish had become artistic and actual. As far as the world was henceforth allowed to guess, this individual, lyrical and dangerous, witty and vengeful, accepting no insults, real or imagined, was now Bob Dylan. Once again, art and identity were intertwined.

That doesn't mean the songs were *about* him. 'Just Like Tom Thumb's Blues', for one, is an honourable runner-up in the contest to be named the finest pop song on the album. Here was another example of the knack Dylan and his musicians had acquired since *Bringing It All Back Home*. From somewhere within the sound of keyboards they had found the secret for rendering a track majestic, irrespective of the words. It didn't hurt, of course, that Dylan had meanwhile produced the most concise lyrics of any of those written for *Highway 61*. This song barely attempts to be overtly 'surreal'. Aside from a reference to Edgar Allan Poe's 'The Murders in the Rue Morgue', there are barely sufficient literary allusions to keep a self-respecting critic in business. This is, perhaps as a result, a very clever song, set on the borders of America and of reason, a tale of drugs, failure, prostitution, crooked cops, betrayal, games, more touches of Wellesian evil, with no chance of anyone's redemption, even at Eastertime. There are no resolving choruses, either, not even of Kerouac's Mexican kind.

This listener can't hear the song without thinking of the would-be amateur hoodlum William S. Burroughs on the lam in Mexico City at the end of the 1940s, enslaved to morphine and squalor, shooting and killing his addict wife in 'a game' played out in a room above a bar. You can certainly fit several of Dylan's most-famous lines to the failed legal manouevres conducted on behalf of the writer of *Junkie* – the 'bluff' being that the killing was accidental – before he decided to skip the country. Burroughs, be it noted, was born into wealth.

I started on burgundy
But soon hit the harder stuff
Everybody said they'd stand behind me
When the game got rough
But the joke was on me
There was nobody even there to call my bluff
I'm going back to New York City
I do believe I've had enough

Burroughs was one of the founding Beats, of course. In England, Dylan also seems to have claimed that *Tarantula* owed something to the author's 'cut-up' technique,[30] itself an attempt to achieve the ends advocated by the surrealists. For all that, 'Just Like Tom Thumb's Blues' isn't *about* William Burroughs any more than it is about Bob Dylan. Once again, those personal pronouns dissolve: 'your gravity fails'; 'she takes your voice'; but by the song's end 'I'm going back to New York City'. Border towns, where law ends and craziness begins, recur time and again in the old Hollywood westerns Dylan loved. As cinematic ideas they function much as they function in *Touch of Evil*: civilisations meet, or fade away; restraints are cast off; people lose themselves, as Burroughs tried to lose himself. Sometimes, as this song seems to say, they lose the self and everything else. In Dylan's account, there ceases even to be a difference between 'I' and 'you'. What kind of society produces such an effect?

*

He saw the world anew: sometimes it happens. Those who talk of Dylan and plagiarism therefore tend not to mention *Highway 61 Revisited*. Patently, it is blues-rooted. Patently, you can hunt down the nods to Kerouac or Steinbeck, Robert Johnson or Poe or Burroughs: there are plenty of those. The fact remains that the album is in no obvious sense derivative save where it derives from an imagination left raw and hyper-alert by its attempts to master American reality. The sleeve 'notes' published with the collection might as well be an excerpt from *Tarantula*: that remains a clue as good as any to the making of an utterly original piece of art. Dylan took the now-familiar techniques of literary modernism, the gifts of Ezra Pound and T.S. Eliot – the persistent taste for fragmentation, the relentless allusions, the juxtapositions, the slippery personal pronouns, the characters out of private and actual myth – and

---

30 Clinton Heylin, *Behind the Shades Revisited*, p. 196.

joined them to pop music, then to the vernacular 'American speech' Walt Whitman had sought. Then Dylan sold the result to a mass audience. Would a true poet ever do such a thing?

*

This time, nevertheless, there was no room for doubt: he had achieved a hit album. Not a Beatles-sized hit, but *Highway 61*, released at the end of August, would reach number three in the US and number four in Britain. With 'Like a Rolling Stone' having already achieved number two on the *Billboard* lists, any confusion over what he was about should have been dispersed like a puff of dry dust before concerts were booked for the Forest Hills tennis stadium in Queens, New York, and for the Hollywood Bowl. Dylan, however, was taking no chances.

Reversing the Newport stratagem, he would get his placation in early, or so he thought, by opening with an acoustic set before introducing his band. This format would endure through the long, gruelling months ahead. Some have alleged that it was Grossman's idea. Whoever was responsible – the artist did not rebel – it didn't work in Queens.

Forest Hills on 28 August set a pattern. The bootleg of a concert before a crowd of almost 15,000 reveals the now-familiar Pavlovian reaction. Dylan sang not a single folk-type song that night: such wasn't the problem. He opened with 'She Belongs to Me', gave them 'Gates of Eden', and soon enough the first public performance of 'Desolation Row', the longest and most 'difficult' song he had ever recorded. No one demurred. Indeed, the reception given to the first set was enthusiastic. The dark comedy of 'Desolation Row' even won appreciative laughter. None of it made any difference when Al Kooper, Harvey Brooks and a couple of new guys recruited from a bar band, named Robbie Robertson and Levon Helm, began to play. The murky bootleg says that mostly they played very well, and much good it did them. Harvey Brooks would remember being warned by Dylan in the interval of what lay ahead. That must have been a comfort, of sorts, when 'Tombstone Blues', one of a clutch of songs from the new album, inaugurated the barracking, the fruit-throwing and a couple of attempts to rush the stage. They even knocked Kooper briefly from his chair.

Here was the other side of the coin. Rejecting and rebutting the folk-left was one thing. Having made his bargain with pop and modernity, Dylan had cut off every escape route. His only alternative to forging ahead was humiliation and the repudiation of the music that had refreshed his soul. Perhaps the folkies had been right after all about the corrosive effects of mass culture. A crowd of 15,000, alert enough to catch at least some of the sense of 'Desolation Row', was interested only in punishing the performer for deviance. Art, it seems, was of no interest if it carried an electric charge. Top 40 hits made no difference. They wouldn't listen.

Another illicit tape shows that the Hollywood Bowl concert on 3 September was, interestingly, granted a far better reception than the one Dylan suffered in Queens, but that fact only prevented the California performance from entering legend. The publicity generated by Forest Hills said this artist was at odds with his audience. The publicity would spread like a virus. And so much for *poets*.

*

At the end of the 1840s, scribbling his marginalia in response to something in the *Southern Literary Messenger*, that old Village denizen Edgar Allan Poe had made a different kind of prophetic guess. As an attempt pre-emptively to render redundant most of the nonsense that would be written about Dylan and poetry, it has not been bettered.

There are few cases in which mere popularity should be considered a proper test of merit; but the case of song-writing is, I think, one of the few. In speaking of song-writing, I mean, of course, the composition of brief poems with an eye to their adaptation for music in the vulgar sense. In this ultimate destination of the song proper, lies its essence – its genius. It is the strict reference to music – it is the dependence upon modulated expression – which gives to this branch of letters a character altogether *unique*, and separates it, in great measure and in a manner not sufficiently considered, from ordinary literature; rendering it independent of merely ordinary proprieties; allowing it, and in fact demanding for it, a wide latitude of Law; absolutely insisting upon a certain wild license and *indefinitiveness* – an indefinitiveness recognized by every musician who is not a mere fiddler, as an important point in the philosophy of his science – as the *soul*, indeed, of the sensations derivable from its practice – sensations which bewilder while they enthral – and which would *not* so enthral if they did not so bewilder.

Pain Sure Brings Out
the Best in People . . .

And then folk music came in as some kind of substitute for a while, but
it was only a substitute, don't you understand?

Radio interview with Klas Burling, Sweden, April 1966

IN THE DAMP SPRING OF 1966 BRITAIN IS ADVERTISING ITSELF AS THE
hub of the lucent pop universe. The old, bedraggled, monochrome
country has been reinvented, so they say. Now youth reigns and fashion
rules. Anything novel, stylish, daring or just fun for its own sake is
being embraced. Hedonism is in the fragrant air. Thanks to all those
guitar groups with cute accents pillaging America, Britain leads the
pop-cultural world. Britain is *where it's at*.

The fiction is extravagant. After the long post-war grind there is
some prosperity, in some places, but the phenomenon is so novel
journalists call it affluence. There are a few new planned towns built
to replace a lot of old slums. There is a skeletal network of motorways
connecting a handful of cities, but upwards of 60 per cent of households
do not own a car. Supermarkets are rare and shopping malls almost
unheard of. There are two, count them, TV channels broadcasting for
a few hours each day and a state radio outlet – the only legal indigenous
outlet – with a circumspect attitude towards the music, so called,
enjoyed by anyone breathing and under 25. A very circumspect attitude.

Britain has just got rid of the death penalty, which is something.
The country has also steered clear of the Vietnam debacle (some covert
aid to the US aside) despite LBJ's cajoling. By 1966 Britain's Labour
government has begun to suspect that America cannot win its war in
South East Asia. A vaunted special relationship has become strained.

In March, in a paragraph buried within an article in the London
Evening Standard, John Lennon will remark casually that his band are
'more popular than Jesus now'. The Beatle will also dismiss the Christ's

disciples as 'thick and ordinary'. He won't mention anyone named Judas. Five weeks later, *Time* magazine will grope for the pulse of a small country and nominate London as a 'Swinging City'. Even in the capital's louche precincts, with their 'discothèques' and drinking clubs, this doesn't approach the truth. Beneath stray specks of glitter, London is much as it ever was.

Men in bowler hats still march regimentally to their City offices each morning. The monarchy still expects and receives near-absolute deference. The BBC still sounds like a spoof of a still-vigorous class system. A few 'regional' accents have been allowed to intrude in music, movies and the fashion world: from this, an illusion has been constructed. The promotion of London as the fount of modernity comes as exciting news, for all that, to millions on these islands who still believe, like Lennon and his Beatles, that everything modern in the twentieth century has come from America. Meanwhile, in hundreds of dingy folk clubs across Britain, where intense urbanites gather to sing old peasant songs, there are arguments over what has become of Bob Dylan.

He's a big deal in Britain, though these things are relative. The biggest story Britain will hear in 1966 involves a series of World Cup football matches, not some minority-interest pop concerts. In the circles where songs matter more than sport, nevertheless, Dylan is taken seriously indeed. In Britain, unlike America, he has enjoyed number-one albums in 1965 with *Bringing It All Back Home* and the strangely resilient *Freewheelin'*, hits that already seem now like two faces on a signpost marking a fork in the road.

Britain has suffered no serious red-baiting and felt no need, beyond the north of Ireland, for a civil-rights movement. Unions and the Left have not been weakened; if anything, the reverse is true. The beginnings of mass higher education in the post-war years have seen British universities flooded with stroppy working-class teenagers liable to campaign ferociously against the Bomb, capitalism or, soon enough, 'American imperialism'. If they have not fallen for the skiffle craze towards the end of the '50s, these young people are liable to have found their voices amid the British folk revival. Thanks to Ewan MacColl and others, that movement has defined itself in terms more strictly political – Communist, socialist and beyond – than anything witnessed in the US. By 1965, some of the younger folkies have broken with this 'discipline' and its arcane rules, but a paradox persists.

Britain in the middle of the '60s is a vastly less conservative country than America, more attuned to political dissent, more socially liberal, yet oddly, persistently hidebound. Modern is good; money is tainted. America is envied and admired; 'American' is an object of suspicion. The global phenomenon surrounding the Beatles is a source of bemused national pride and faint derision. The idea that British can still be best cheers up a post-colonial nation; 'commercialism' and hysteria – a million screaming semi-virgins – is deprecated high and low, left and right.

In this world, in a country whose socialist tradition is intact, the idea that Bob Dylan, protesting poet-troubadour, could ever become a pop star isn't just offensive, it's offensively illogical. Many of those whose hard-earned purchases in Woolworths sent *Freewheelin'* to number one struggle with the idea that Dylan should even want to sell records. Give him an electric guitar and he's a traitor, by word and deed.

*

Since Newport, an equivalent resentment has taken root in his own country. These are early days for counter-cultures and alternative attitudes, but Dylan has ignored the fact. Even the killing of John Kennedy, that glimpse into encroaching darkness, has not wrenched every consciousness. The myth of a youth rebellion, '56 to '66, will be applied retrospectively, but in the cities and towns and spreading suburbs of the republic the distinguishing mark of a younger generation is disposable income, not dissent. The freakish are noted – for what else could the adjective mean? – as exceptions to the rule. Despite the Dallas killing emotion and clear thought remain distinct; the times are changing, but not yet changed. Most people, of all ages, are mostly square, and less than hip, and living their lives as though old Ike is still around. In 1966 collective unease – over wars hot and cold, over *the negro question* and divorce rates, over consumerism, crime and culture – is still a vague background noise. There is the appearance, no more, of ferment.

For those still loyal to the folk-music movement the truly important thing is to stand perfectly still. Too often the 'revival' has become a preservation society. Yet thanks to Dylan, a brief fad is ending. There are a great many nice white college kids still trying to sound like suffering black sharecroppers or Virginia mining folk hollerin' in hard times, but they study set texts and master approved melodies. They thieve from the poor and nameless without hesitation. Fidelity to 'the tradition' is a willed act of impersonation among those who, straight-faced, accuse Dylan of plagiarism. Neither Newport nor 'folk-rock' – a term its supposed progenitor despises and rejects – has ended the argument. Everyone, even Pete Seeger, will 'go electric' in the end, but only Dylan will bear the apostate's brand.

Where the singer is concerned, a great many people have taken to behaving like true believers betrayed. Apparently a very young man was somehow supposed to *embody*, to *articulate* and to *represent* a cause, and all decent causes, and *the* cause. All by himself. He was supposed to be a kind of living poetic gesture, absurdly 'the voice of his generation'. No one will ever manage to explain how any human being was supposed to do any of this.

> Sure, you can make all sorts of protest songs and put them on a Folkways record. But who hears them? The people that do hear them are going to be agreeing with you anyway.[1]

He felt himself imprisoned from the moment success came calling. His artistic liberty – far less his room for commercial manoeuvre – was being curtailed as soon as his folk 'anthems' began to be heard. Now, in an America already knee-deep in a south Asian war, as in a complacent Britain, both with their nascent bourgeois *counter*-cultures, they say he has 'sold out'.

You can parse things otherwise. To sell out, you must first have something to sell.

*

Bob Dylan had married his placid Sara without publicity in late November 1965, in a civil ceremony on Long Island. This had been a big step for him; so big he had told almost no one, least of all his parents. Only Grossman and a female friend of the bride had been present. For some time thereafter Dylan would deny that any ceremony had taken place. In those days it was customary, even obligatory, for young pop stars to lie about their marriages. John Lennon had managed to keep his wife Cynthia hidden from the time of their wedding in August of 1962 until almost the end of 1963, but Dylan had not told the truth about himself for a very long time. The latest lie came easily; Sara's thoughts on the matter are not recorded. A public performer who said he didn't care about the opinions of others, who claimed he did what he wanted, the way he wanted, still couldn't shake the illusive

---

1   *LA Free Press*, March 1965.

habits of a lifetime. You can only suspect, equally, that the Bob Dylan who had caused the almighty Newport row was deemed by his wayward inner spirit guide to be an outlaw not made for marriage. A wife didn't suit the latest secretive identity, so she became another secret.

Amid wedded bliss, he got booed, some of the time, but only some of the time. Too many of the tales of 1965 and '66 are told as though the barracking was relentless and universal, as though Dylan ran a gauntlet at every moment along the way as he began to circumnavigate the globe. That never did make sense. When he took to the road in the last week of September 1965, he had a hit album rising in the charts. The people who had bought *Highway 61 Revisited* were unlikely to have been infuriated because he played better than half the tracks, as he generally did, from their latest favourite record. The booing is well attested, but so are the number of sell-out shows. Clearly, righteous exhibitionists, the dog-whistle mob, were outnumbered by those who knew (more or less) what to expect. Not too many would have been especially shocked, either, by bad sound: in the mid-1960s everyone had ratty little speakers, crappy amps and a bad sound. The legend of endless, infernal abuse has a life of its own. At the Hollywood Bowl, after all, the star had felt able to perform an encore. At New York's Carnegie Hall on 1 October, on the first big night of the odyssey, the star was gratified – and reportedly said as much – by the response of the crowd. Still, if you believe half of those who claim to have witnessed the tour, Dylan's performances had a sound that tended to be very bad *and* very loud. To be painfully loud, to forever turn up the dial and ignore the tolerances of the average useless house PA, was his idea. Where punk was concerned, he was a decade early.

He also had a band to remember, and this time not just a scratch team of the best people he could gather from those available at a given moment. Robbie Robertson and Levon Helm had been brought on board the swirling ship for Forest Hills and the Hollywood Bowl. After those shows, Al Kooper had decided not to repeat the weird experience across the length and breadth of the country. Before heading to Austin, Texas, to commence the creation of another of his fables with the first show in an epic tour, Dylan had therefore decided to meet the rest of the group who called themselves the Hawks.

Aside from the songs he gave them and the songwriting he taught them – a big enough aside – The Band's reputation depends rather less on Dylan than many assume. The recorded evidence of their work together was to lie hidden from the larger public, after all, until 1974.

The connection, never a secret, was plain enough when *Music From Big Pink* appeared in 1968, but that was another story. When your first album contains three new Bob Dylan songs, and those three happen to be 'Tears of Rage', 'This Wheel's On Fire' and 'I Shall Be Released', even the casual listener is liable to put five and one together. It remains the case, nevertheless, that The Band made their names thanks to their own gifts. Those were conspicuous.

How good were they in 1965? That's harder to say. The surviving recorded evidence of their pre-existence – effectively a couple of singles – is patchy. Yet they had, as the saying goes, paid their dues with the rockabilly singer Ronnie Hawkins, and on their own behalf, by all accounts working some tough joints along the way. They certainly had more range, in terms of instrumental skills, than was customary in a mid-'60s backing group. Garth Hudson, the prodigal organist, was (as no one forgets to say) classically trained. Robertson would soon enough stand revealed as one of the guitarists of his generation, with an ego to match his talent. Helm, Rick Danko and Richard Manuel were each capable of stopping a show. The sounds at the disposal of this group were almost too many to number, from strings to brass to keyboards. On the other hand, in September of 1965 the Hawks *were* just a bar band, a backing group, hired hands. As events would also demonstrate, they were not yet good enough to carry an album. When Dylan flew up to Toronto for what seems to have been a cursory audition, what did he hear? Or rather, what was he hoping to hear?

The music that would become known as the basement tapes, together with the early albums recorded by The Band on their own accord, would act as a central inspiration for the later idea (such as it is) of *Americana*, of American roots music. That was not the music five men and their new boss began to play in the autumn of 1965. Given that all of the quintet save Mark Lavon Helm were Canadians, the fact is probably apt. Yet it is also patently true that Dylan's live performances during a murderous tour contained no forewarnings of 'Tiny Montgomery', 'You Ain't Goin' Nowhere' or 'Quinn the Eskimo'. The singer was hiring for the psychodrama of 'Ballad of a Thin Man', for the tidal wave of 'Like a Rolling Stone', for the jackhammer of 'Tombstone Blues'. This was entirely American music, but not, even by the broadest categorisation, *Americana*. Nor was it rock and roll in the proper sense, nor authentic R&B, nor even – another idea still hunting a definition – 'rock'. Yet Dylan decided, without much of a second thought, that these Hawks were good enough for him. Rehearsals ensued.

Robertson would later put about the idea that the bar-band veterans schooled the folkie in the secrets of electric pop ensemble music. That doesn't seem likely. The teenage Dylan might not have been the world's greatest rock and roll piano player, but he understood well enough the stuff Ronnie Hawkins had been asking of his boys. There is also the small matter of *Highway 61 Revisited*. Dylan might have had slight experience where playing live with a group was concerned, but his knowledge of the sounds inside his own head was vast. As the album showed, he knew exactly what he wanted to hear. The Hawks had been nowhere close to the kind of music they were about to take around the world. It would be they who would have to work to keep up.

The best you can hope to guess is that Dylan sensed a necessary sympathy in this group of musicians. They were his to command, but better than just a backing group. They got it. They gave him artillery, the heavy kind, when required. Alternatively, they gave him the palette he needed for the piece of performance art he was about to make. His decision to hire the Hawks was intuitive, as usual: they felt right.

Here, nevertheless, is another point at which the tale of this concert tour begins to fray. Dylan never meant for these shows to be turned into the stuff of minor legend. They were never, in that sense, a self-conscious 'piece of art'. Columbia would record some of the concerts – four in England, to be precise – but the next release on this artist's schedule was something else again, and had nothing to do with those tribulations and triumphs. A bootleg of one part of one concert recording would duly become 'legendary'; three decades down the line, a fully rendered account of Dylan and his band on a night in Manchester would qualify as one of the most thrilling live albums released under anyone's name. None of this was part of the artist's intention in 1965 or in 1966. We know that he and his musicians sometimes heard tapes of their performances after the shows – generally while wondering why anyone would barrack such music – but Dylan drew no conclusions. It's a small detail, but important. Most of the time, he isn't impressed by Bob Dylan.

October: New York, New Jersey, Georgia, Massachusetts, Rhode Island, Vermont, Michigan, Massachusetts, Connecticut. November: California, Minnesota, New York, Ohio, Canada, Ohio, New York, Illinois, Washington DC. December: 11 shows in 19 days in the state of California. In the course of 87 days in late 1965 Dylan and his new band performed on 37 occasions. Such a schedule was not regarded as wholly insane in those days – not by people whose sanity was already open to question, at any rate – but for this expeditionary party the continental United States amounted to little more than a warm-up. Between the hours spent in transit in an aged leased jet aircraft Dylan was delivering what were, in effect, two shows at each stop, acoustic and electric. He wasn't singing 'Hang on Sloopy', either: a certain intensity was involved. Meanwhile, he was snatching time in recording studios. *Meanwhile*, he was trying to write. One of the songs we know about he first named 'Freeze Out'. It became 'Visions of Johanna'.

Who copes with such an existence, especially after the year Dylan had already endured and enjoyed? One measure of the chaos and craziness this artist was experiencing (or accepting) can be seen in his personal life. He and Sara married on 22 November, a Monday. On the previous night Dylan had performed in Syracuse, New York; by Friday he would be in wintry Chicago, and no doubt singing 'Love Minus Zero/No Limit' with more than his usual passion. By the customary rough calculation his new wife was by then seven months pregnant; impending fatherhood was therefore no surprise. So why pick such a late, rushed moment to marry? Perhaps because there were so few moments available. Perhaps, too, there was a hint of the sentiment from that old Irish-American folk song he used to perform as a kid, back in the mists of 1961, the one called 'The Girl I Left Behind'. So off to war he went . . .

This version of existence was finite. It would have to end, sooner rather than later, and the chances were that it would end badly. Dylan must have known as much. A 'confession' to Robert Shelton in March of the following year that heroin was part of the struggle – confirmation would have been a better word, judging by surviving photographs – was in one sense a statement of the obvious. Dylan was going to the limit, physically, mentally and creatively. And there, for his instruction and encouragement, was the booing, the nightly ritual, the abuse from those who claimed once to have admired him most.

Those voices, though the loudest, *could not* have been the voices of the majority, but if Dylan ever wanted a taste of crazy, here it was. Who buys tickets just for the chance to be noisily, furiously disappointed? Was the intention truly to bully Dylan back to the path of righteousness and plangent open tunings fit for mature appreciation? Even at this distance in time you still suspect that the anger sprang from an understanding among those jeering that they were a minority. All those records Dylan was selling, and all those people – a little dazed by the noise, perhaps – who did not join the barracking were proof of that. An ideological nonsense, the nonsense on which the folk revival had been founded, was being exposed. No one likes to be wrong. Thanks only to his intuitions, Dylan had taken all the theories about 'cultural commodities', the manipulated masses, passivity and capitalist 'pseudo-individualisation' – all of the international Left's ill-digested Frankfurt School clichés – and ripped them apart. He had meantime destroyed the class assumptions of all the old, infinitely patronising song 'collectors'. Not that his hecklers understood as much, of course.

Dylan, on the other hand, could be almost supernaturally astute. He knew things, by context and implication, that he was not *supposed* to know. In the last month of 1965, for one example, he had the following exchange with a journalist in California.

Reporter: Mr Dylan, how would you define folk music?
Performer: As a constitutional re-play of mass production.

The booing was wearying, for all that. By November's end Levon Helm had suffered enough, and decided to step away from the drum kit, retreating wounded to his native Arkansas. It is to Dylan's credit that he bore Helm no ill will for leaving the party in the lurch. It is to the drummer's credit, meanwhile, that he never ceased to pay tribute to the star's stubborn sense of purpose. According to Helm, Dylan did not once flinch under the pharisaical attack. In fact – and this probably counts as a more significant truth – he seemed truly not to care what anyone thought about his performances or his art. Yet again, the impervious self-belief, the absence of doubt, *the gall*, is startling. Dylan knew he was right; the world would have to catch up. It's entirely possible that heroin and other preparations helped him to achieve this depth of conviction, but the character trait had persisted through each of his identities. Whoever 'Bob Dylan' happened to be, he believed utterly in the art of Dylan.

At November's end, days before the long California leg of the tour was due to commence, he attempted to get his 'Freeze Out' song onto tape. Here was another of those pieces that would give him grief, one of those, like 'Tambourine Man', like 'Rolling Stone', that he knew could not be botched or replaced easily or ever by another improvised masterpiece. In New York on 30 November he brought together musicians old and new, arguably too many of them. He made more than a dozen attempts to get this song right. The bootleg entitled *Seems Like a Freeze Out* – a weird jumble of odd tracks with a treasure, 'She's

Your Lover Now', at its end – would soon disclose a version that was better than pretty good. Dylan wasn't satisfied.

The song was *there*: its essence was present in every complete take, the essentials of the verses, one stray nightingale aside, were intact throughout. Yet neither the singer, his new band nor his old helpers could nail in place this most elusive of his works. Dylan might have esteemed spontaneity. He might have believed in waiting for a song's moment to present itself. Sometimes, equally, he displayed a genius for taking pains. And sometimes, in the worst of times, neither approach did any good. His vexed relationship with the recording studio arose from that fundamental truth. Even for him, no method was ever foolproof. 'Freeze Out' would have to wait.

What became 'Visions of Johanna' has suffered many more interpretations than the number of takes attempted on 30 November. That's understandable: the song is worth some effort. Greil Marcus has mentioned a story about the piece being conceived during the great north-east power blackout of 9 November 1965, when seven states and parts of Canada lost electricity overnight and New York was left in cold darkness.[2] Hence: the night 'plays tricks'; 'We sit here stranded'; 'Lights flicker from the opposite loft'; 'the heat pipes just cough'; and there's nothing, 'really nothing to turn off'. As a proximate cause for images, that's fine, but it does not begin to breach the defences of a song in which some have seen God, some the yearning for inspiration, some a twisted love affair and some the distinction between corporeal temptation ('Louise') and spiritual need ('Johanna'). Marcus has talked of the song in terms of atmosphere and ambience; others have settled for the view that ineluctability is almost the point: *'How can I explain?'* Whatever the case, Dylan dispenses with narrative connections so completely these visions have become, as Shelton put it, 'non-sequential'.

Some movies are like that; this song is like that. 'Visions of Johanna' is 'non-sequential' because its scenes are being played out, as within the time frame of a film, with the illusion of simultaneity. We cut, verse by verse, from scene to scene, from 'this room' to the empty lot, from the entrance of 'little boy lost' to another realm – almost as a script direction – 'Inside the museums'.

In the last verse, Dylan all but shows us the script: 'The peddler now speaks . . .' Then he points his camera: 'We see this empty cage now corrode . . .' Even Madonna, mother of God, is billed as an actor, with

---

2   'Bob Dylan's Dream', *The Guardian*, 21 June 2008.

her 'cape of the stage', in this movie. Because she has not 'showed' for her redemptive role, however, the props are cleared away (mere debris on the back of a fish truck) while the Fiddler steps forward, Prospero or Puck or Rod Serling in *The Twilight Zone*, to offer the resolution: 'He writes ev'rything's been returned which was owed.' By the end, 'these visions of Johanna are . . . all that remain'. Another writer might have said that 'you have but slumbered here, / While these visions did appear'.

The nature of the slumbering has caused some speculation. Louise and her 'handful of rain, temptin' you to defy it' has been taken as a near-straightforward reference to heroin. There is certainly an opiate haze to the song. The sense of atmosphere – or sensation for its own sake – is strong, as Marcus observed. The rain is back at the song's conclusion, a backdrop to the sound of harmonicas – their notes in 'skeleton keys', a pun that will open doors – while a conscience 'explodes' and, finally, only visions remain. You could even, at a stretch, find a drug courier in the 'mule' decked in 'jewels and binoculars'. The 'ghost of 'lectricity', equally, was howling in the bones of Dylan's face in the photographs of this period. And who or what is more useless than a junkie 'Muttering small talk at the wall' while a dealer's customer waits in the hall?

The song doesn't yield so easily. Mercifully, Dylan doesn't want or need to be so literal. Lou Reed had already written and recorded at least one version of his 'Heroin' by the time Dylan set down these visions, but the attempt to capture the nature of a relationship with this particular narcotic was, like addiction, like poetry, wholly personal. 'Visions of Johanna' has more to it than smack, in any case: we never truly discover what those visions contain. Yet when heroin's perceptual distortions and time-dilation effects are once evoked, they seep into any experience of the song. Thus:

Inside the museums, Infinity goes up on trial
Voices echo this is what salvation must be like after a while
But Mona Lisa musta had the highway blues
You can tell by the way she smiles
See the primitive wallflower freeze
When the jelly-faced women all sneeze
Hear the one with the moustache say, 'Jeeze I can't find my knees'
Oh, jewels and binoculars hang from the head of the mule
But these visions of Johanna, they make it all seem so cruel

The image of a smacked-out Mona Lisa ('You can tell by the way she smiles') is appealing. The idea that eternal salvation might resemble a narcotised infinity stuck among museum exhibits, or that existence could embrace 'jelly-faced women' and someone so out of it she (or he) can't stand up, would make any addict's experience 'seem so cruel'. Dylan is not explicit.

Earlier in 1965 he had nominated William S. Burroughs, author of *Naked Lunch*, whom he had read in Minneapolis and met briefly thanks to Ginsberg, as 'a great man'. He had studied his Kerouac, but only small sections of the novelist's *Visions of Cody* had been published by New Directions when 'Visions of Johanna' was being written. Those seem, on any reading, less than pertinent. William Blake certainly preserved 'The Little Boy Lost' (in *Songs of Innocence*) and 'A Little BOY Lost' (in *Songs of Experience*), but the former becomes found and the latter, sacrificed to religious bigotry, has no obvious connection with Dylan's infantile character. The phrase is a label. Guessing games concerning the woman-of-the-title are meanwhile ludicrous: that's not Johanna's function, any more than this is simply 'a drug song'. 'Visions of Johanna' is a kind of crippled romance, too, a parable of relationships, and therefore impossible to decode in terms of she or he. It still has its dizzying narcotic effect, however, and its filmic base, and its roots, above all, in the method Dylan had mastered.

It is the method Ezra Pound had applied when cutting half the lines from T.S. Eliot's *Waste Land* at the start of the 1920s. In that big poem, sections meant to link and 'explain' things were excised, one after the other (one section went from ninety-two lines to ten), to reveal themes and ideas that might otherwise have been hidden. Dylan achieved Pound's editorial insights unaided. Finishing the first draft of his poem, a distressed Eliot wrote to tell Virginia Woolf that 'I wasn't even bothering whether I understood what I was saying'. Dylan had made that kind of remark often enough in 1965. Yet the trouble with the process of stripping away, of concentrating on images for their own sake, was also a difficulty identified by one of Eliot's biographers: 'The poet himself was to be treated as a kind of seer, a position most unsuited to him.'[3] Dylan knew all about that, too.

*

In San Francisco, as December began, he was caught up in a piece of

---

3   Peter Ackroyd, *T.S. Eliot* (1984), Ch. 6.

Beat nonsense as the last survivors of the non-movement gathered at
Lawrence Ferlinghetti's City Lights bookstore to party and stage their
positively final 'last gathering'. On the day after his first show at the
Berkeley Community Theater, Dylan found himself having his
photograph taken by one Larry Keenan – in an alley, with pointed
shoes *sans* bells – alongside Allen Ginsberg, Michael McClure,
Ferlinghetti and Robbie Robertson (who seemed altogether too hip to
be caught among mere poets). Fans were everywhere that day,
reportedly, and they were not looking for autographs from City Lights
authors. Anecdotal history records, in fact, that the Beats were foremost
among the star-struck, only too delighted to yield literature's claims
to a skinny young singer in shades and a polka-dot shirt. Like everyone
else, they couldn't get enough of him. His every whim and half-
statement was their delight.

Thanks to a gift of Dylan's money, Ginsberg at least got a Uher tape
recorder out of the arrangement. America, in turn, duly got a book
entitled *The Fall of America: Poems of These States* (1973) containing all
the poetic anti-war sentiment that progressive America could desire.
Crossing the Midwest, Ginsberg extemporised 'breath unit' upon breath
unit for the benefit of his new toy, mixing bits of newspaper reports,
advertising copy and radio bulletins with observations on the heartland,
curses on Vietnam and thoughts on the condition of language. In
print, he developed the 'stepped triadic' of William Carlos Williams
for poems that asked as many questions about the nature of verse in
relation to the human voice as Dylan ever had. The fundamental
compositional technique, equally, was that of relentless, apparently
unforced juxtaposition. Dylan, inadvertent patron, had given 'the
movement' its radical poet, even if his name happened to be Ginsberg.
With 'Wichita Vortex Sutra', a long piece that would later be folded
into *The Fall of America*, the older man returned the favour with a
passage that would be quoted as often as any part of the work. After
M60 machine guns in La Drang Valley comes

Oh at last again the radio opens
    blue Invitations!
        Angelic Dylan singing across the nation
        'When all your children start to resent you
        Won't you come see me, Queen Jane?'
    His youthful voice making glad
        the brown endless meadows

His tenderness penetrating aether,
    soft prayer on the airwaves,
    Language language, and sweet music too . . .

Who was he now? *Eat the Document*, the almost-film shot in Britain in 1966, would capture fragments of this Dylan in his brief, cometary existence. Short passages of concert footage would reveal the final transformation of the Village kid, full of charm and Chaplin, into the distant individual consumed by the needs of perpetual performance and somehow *fraught*. This was the image that would persist. This face beneath a cloud of hair with its undeceived eyes and unsmiling mouth, cheekbones like napped flint, telling the world everything and giving nothing away, would reappear time and again, first and above all with the cover of the album he had begun to contemplate towards the end of 1965. This Dylan became, in that abused word, 'iconic'.

He looked dangerous; he was certainly a danger to himself. The contests with journalists that were becoming his media trademark were like symbolic representations of what he stood for. Or rather, of what he wouldn't stand for. At the press conference staged to mark his arrival in San Francisco that December a reporter had asked, innocently enough, why Dylan seemed reluctant even to talk about the self-evident fact of his new popularity. The non-answer, four times over, was 'Well, what do you want me to say?' Finally, the soliloquy concluded:

> You want me to jump up and say 'Hallelujah! and crash the cameras or do something weird? Tell me, tell me. I'll go along with you. If I can't go along with you, I'll find somebody to go along with you.

In his semi-private existence reports of simple (if sometimes witty) nastiness were beginning to accumulate. The friends prepared to stick around, musicians aside, were the special, supine kind who would put up with anything. He knew this because he tested the proposition repeatedly. His behaviour might have been one of the tediously predictable effects of celebrity, but it was also curious. Consciously, it seems deliberately, this Dylan was rendering himself friendless. He was *shedding* people, as though creating a new context for another new identity. In the end, there would be only one individual left to destroy.

So it was that hapless Phil Ochs, that old comrade and staunch defender of all things Dylan, found himself being thrown out of the star's limousine that December. As the story goes, his offence was to fail to appreciate the new single, 'Can You Please Crawl Out Your Window?' Or rather, he failed to praise the track as lavishly as, it seems, Dylan had come to expect. Ochs made matters worse by daring to be honest: he just didn't like the record. It wasn't as good, he said, as its predecessors ('Positively 4th Street' and 'Like a Rolling Stone') and probably wouldn't sell. This happened to be true on both counts, as record-buyers would soon confirm. 'Crawl Out Your Window' barely troubled the *Billboard* chart, reaching only number 58. That didn't avert the artist's rage.

Ochs had spoken up eloquently for Dylan during the Newport fuss. He had found *Highway 61* so daring and brilliant it had made him laugh with delight. He had taken his share of bruises in verbal sparring sessions – and sometimes the contests *were* fun – at the Kettle of Fish. Now he was kicked out of the car. Dylan was so furious he called Ochs the worst thing he could think of. 'You're not a folk singer,' he said, 'You're a journalist.' What Dylan probably knew, with his honed instinct for vulnerability, was that a singer he had lauded not so long before – 'he just keeps getting better and better and better' – had once harboured ambitions to enter journalism. Ochs had also stayed true to the topical songs and the causes Dylan had cast aside. The big star was dismissing an honest man's entire existence, an existence that would come to a premature end in 1976 when Ochs committed suicide.

In these moods, Dylan behaved as though he had enemies on every side. The despised journalists had not been incidental to his public profile, but that didn't matter. Some such as Ochs, who had known him since the earliest days in the Village, had been supportive from the start. That, though, seemed to be at the heart of it: they had known him. Reporters, too, were liable to lay hands on some truths here and there, amid their banal questions and 'distortions'. If attack was the best form of defence, this Dylan was capable of total war. He favoured anti-personnel weapons.

Everyone still seemed to want a piece of him, nevertheless. Part of the bond between Dylan, the Beatles and the other glimmering stars of the 1960s was akin to the affinity between combat veterans. Only they had been through it; only they knew what it was like. The problem wasn't just fame. Bizarrely, these young entertainers were supposed to explain things, to explain everything. A certain contempt for the importunate horde might therefore be accounted inevitable. One function of Dylan's verbal 'mind fucks' was to give the civilians a taste of what they didn't, couldn't and would never understand. Besides, inexplicable songs surely warranted inexplicable behaviour. He was Dylan, after all. Everyone knew the name, but he also made sure that no one knew anything important about him. To paraphrase: the only thing they knew for sure about Bob Dylan was that his name wasn't Bob Dylan.

For now and ever afterwards, nevertheless, he owned the name, the look, the voice, supposedly, of the era. Still a lot of people, even esteemed Beat poets, thought they might somehow possess a part of him. The impasse Dylan had attempted to blow apart at Newport endured. As a commentary on need, identity, modernity, art and celebrity, this was unsurpassable, if such is your taste.

You can just about see, nevertheless, why this singer had earned the enmity of those who chose to boo. This 'new Dylan' with his new music was so utterly at odds with the folk singer of recent memory only one conclusion was available: one or other (or both) of these individuals must be, or must have been, a fraud. It wasn't only a judgement on someone's dress sense – though Newport's 'sell-out jacket' had been used in evidence – nor even, for some at least, a judgement on the music *as music*. It had to do with words, with sentiments apparently expressed, and commitments apparently offered. What was it he would say in Manchester, when for history's purposes things would come to a head? He would say, 'I don't believe you.' That was another note within the barracking as Dylan's tour paused for the year's end, for more attempts to commence his third album in a matter of months and for the birth of his first child. *He*, they said, was the liar. The misunderstanding was profound. The noise didn't help.

As it turned out, Dylan's real prophetic gift was his ability to sense a coming disillusionment. His crime was to abandon any hope for politics and political change long before the rest of his generation. There was no going back on that.

*

Touching down in New York, he signed a new and preposterously inequitable publishing deal with Grossman. Albert didn't get the writer's entire soul, just half, his to keep for a decade to come. Dylan also wasted some semi-precious time on Andy Warhol and one of the Factory 'screen tests' the artist used to win people and influence friends. Dylan at least wangled an Elvis silkscreen print for his pains, but in the end traded the thing for one of his manager's spare sofas. Word of the slight got back to a discomfited Warhol, in time. Word, you suspect, was supposed to get back.

More importantly, fresh attempts to create an album were going nowhere. This one would not be conjured out the air. In Columbia's studios towards the end of January 1966 one great song, 'She's Your Lover Now', simply fell apart. The version that would be released on 1991's *The Bootleg Series Volumes 1–3* was halted by a frustrated Dylan before he reached the last verse. A slow, spectral piano-bar account, complete as to lyrics and brilliant in its own way, remains on the illicit list. Attempts were then made at the tune that would become 'Leopard-Skin Pill-Box Hat', but these also foundered. All that Dylan had to show for his efforts after three studio sessions was the miraculous rendering of 'One of Us Must Know (Sooner or Later)' that survives on *Blonde on Blonde*. One year previously *Bringing It All Back Home* had been completed, start to finish, in the time he had now spent producing a single useable track. *Highway 61*, the better record, had not taken much longer to complete than its predecessor. This time around the quicksilver genius was in difficulties.

One conclusion drawn by Dylan from these struggles was never fully tested. After 'She's Your Lover Now' he decided that the Hawks could not meet all his needs in the studio. On the fairest view, you could say they didn't get much of a chance. Nevertheless, Dylan began to fall back on Al Kooper, Paul Griffin and others. He also began to heed the urgings of his producer, Bob Johnston, who argued that a change of scene was needed, and that Nashville, his own home turf, was ideal. Johnston, it so happened, knew the very musicians for the job.

The real problem ran deeper than the quality of accompaniment, however, or the studios available. *Bringing It All Back Home* and *Highway 61* had both been in large part written before Dylan even thought about attempting to record the songs. This time, 'Visions of Johanna' aside, he had no stockpile of material, nor the luxury of a spell in Woodstock in which to work on his verses. Concert commitments were piled up ahead of him: twelve shows in February, then eight in March. Two dozen shows were scheduled for April and May, and these were to take place in Hawaii, in far-distant Australia, in Scandinavia, Ireland, Britain and France. He would barely have time to record, far less to write. Creating an album – one of *his* albums – almost entirely on the run would be

Dylan's biggest test to date. There would be a very slim margin for error.

*

Numerous things have been written about the making of *Blonde on Blonde*; less has been said, a torrent of praise aside, about what was made. There are anecdotes telling of Johnston reconfiguring the studio at Dylan's behest by tearing down the fixed audio baffles designed to prevent one noise from 'bleeding' into another. There are tales of Robbie Robertson and Al Kooper, the only survivors of the New York sessions, crossing the great cultural divide to establish a mutual respect with their Nashville peers. There's the marching band/Salvation Army band story; the assorted (disputed) stories of drugs and personal hygiene; and the droll, remembered interventions of Johnston as finally the pace of recording began to pick up. There's the cameo appearance by a young Kris Kristofferson as the lowly studio janitor who didn't dare speak to the star, but who once saw him sitting alone at a piano. There are all the theories, as usual, concerning the women who may or may not have inspired a song, or *perhaps* inspired – though please doubt it – the album's title. There are tales (not for children) of truly fiendish complexity involving sundry delicate mono mixes, slapdash stereo mixes, various remixes and the eventual fates of said mixes in various editions of the album in different regions of the planet. There are fantastically trivial explanations even for variant renderings of the album's *sleeve*. (My 1970s UK version has that mythical song 'Stuck Inside of Mobile With Thee' – still a great title – listed to the north-west of Claudia Cardinale's head on the gatefold. Is there a prize?) *Blonde on Blonde* has nothing to do with any of this.

Sean Wilentz's book *Bob Dylan in America* (2010) gives a fascinating and exhaustive account of the days and nights in February and March when, finally, things came together as Dylan wrote and revised, wrote and revised – to the evident astonishment of the Nashville crew – to achieve the verses liable to cause 'that thin, that wild mercury sound . . . metallic and bright gold, with whatever that conjures up'.[4] A dozen years after it was all over he would invoke 'my particular sound' in this elemental, synaesthetic fashion. The description was memorable and apt. What it overlooked was the fact that he would never seriously attempt to reproduce the sound he called his own. In 1978, he would confess that he hadn't since 'been able to succeed in getting it all the

---

4   *Playboy* interview with Ron Rosenbaum, March 1978.

time'. By 1978, with the possible exception of a couple of tracks on *Desire* and the opening track of *Street Legal*, there were no examples of him even making the effort. Whatever was found in Nashville had been lost again. That truth points to *Blonde on Blonde*'s molten heart. It was made amid chaos, at a single moment in time. It is 'about' a mind struggling to establish order within that chaos. It has to do with possession and loss and decay. It is an album full of almost-love songs. Above all, it is a collection of songs struggling with the very nature of time.

'Visions of Johanna' seeks to dispute time, movie-style. 'Pledging My Time' is basic-blues explicit, in a form for which time, in the musical sense, is everything. '4th Time Around' is built around a diamond-movement repeating melody. 'Sad Eyed Lady of the Lowlands', a metronome ticking behind its tune, contests time again and again as it rises and falls like a tide. (Tired musicians were baffled by a song that ascended, over and over, to an apparent conclusion, and then *just went on*.) One of the most famous verses in one of the most famous songs, the one that really should have been called 'Stuck Inside of Mobile with Thee', is time-bound:

> And here I sit so patiently
> Waiting to find out what price
> You have to pay to get out of
> Going through all these things twice

Blonde on Blonde has a single feature in common, meanwhile, with 1968's *The Beatles*, otherwise 'the White Album', in the thin ranks of memorable 1960s two-disc pop sets. Artistically, it is that physically impossible thing, three-quarters of a great double album. In many ways, in fact, it is the least coherent of Dylan's triumphant works of 1965–6. Some would simply say that it is unbalanced (or overburdened) by 'Sad Eyed Lady of the Lowlands', but that idea takes the vinyl format too seriously. In its established version, after all, *Blonde on Blonde* comes in at a substantial 72 minutes and 57 seconds. *Time Out of Mind*, Dylan's celebrated 1997 release, clocks up 72 minutes and 50 seconds: time is not always of the essence. If you want to compare one big long song with another big long song, meanwhile, 'Sad Eyed Lady of the Lowlands' got a side of vinyl to itself in 1966, yet lasts 'only' 11:23. In 1997 'Highlands' would consume, for better or worse, 16 minutes and 31 talkative seconds. The important fact is that even if Dylan had been granted the extensible expanses of digital recording in 1966,

Blonde on Blonde would not have been completely unimpeachable.

He should – says one listener – have tried again with 'She's Your Lover Now', the one song that probably was, after all, about lovely, troublesome Edie Sedgwick, her myriad obsessions and delusions, and her affair with Neuwirth. The song speaks, imperiously and wearily, to both, but it is better by far than a mere 'put-down'. 'I'll Keep It With Mine', the one he wrote for Nico that he could never manage to record fairly for himself, should also have been reconsidered. It too contemplates, in exquisite measures, the search for lost time. Dylan wasn't asking anyone's advice about any of this, of course. Still, the absence of this pair of songs points to what is wrong with *Blonde on Blonde*.

Curiously, Dylan's attempts at the blues here feel oddly unsatisfactory and perfunctory, as though he knows he has better things to do, and far better things to write. 'Leopard-Skin Pill-Box Hat' is pallid – a tougher version of an otherwise aimless 'satire' went unused – and 'Obviously 5 Believers' is a makeweight. 'Pledging My Time', the best of this bunch, is on the wrong album. 'Rainy Day Women #12 & 35' is just, in every particular, wrong. If the world didn't need another protest singer, it didn't need another novelty song, least of all a hip and 'knowing' novelty song whose joke died the minute after Nashville's finest had shown what they could improvise to charm a visiting star. These failures, not 'Sad Eyed Lady of the Lowlands', distort and unbalance *Blonde on Blonde*.

The great songs survive. No one can know what it cost Dylan to come up with the words with all those top-dollar musicians hanging around, concerts impending and his own sense of perceived time in question. He did it, for all that. The result, as so often in art, has the appearance of effortlessness, but 'effortless' can take a hideous amount of work. The pieced-together records of the sessions on 14 February show 20 attempts, for example, at '4th Time Around', and 13 takes of 'Leopard-Skin Pill-Box Hat'. Most of these broke down, or were otherwise interrupted, but a lot of attention went into the song of the hat, a slight enough thing on the finished album. On 17 February, similarly, twenty takes were made of 'Stuck Inside of Mobile' in three pre-dawn hours from 4 a.m. onwards.[5] Again, half of these were

---

5   In these matters the researches of Michael Krogsgaard, first published in *The Telegraph* in the winter of 1995, and of Clinton Heylin in *Dylan: Behind Closed Doors – The Recording Sessions (1960–1994)* (1995) are close to definitive. Wilentz, who has heard the session tapes, is illuminating. For documentation – and much else – see also Olof Björner's bjorner.com.

false starts and most of the rest incomplete, but that only underlines the degree of concentration involved in recording a song that is long – 99 lines of verse, as published – lyrically complex and musically tricky. Predictably, the last take was the one chosen for preservation.

Dylan spent no time socialising with his Nashville cats, but gave them plenty of time to socialise among themselves. Session pros, they would remember reporting promptly for work and find themselves lying around dozing or watching TV for hours while he struggled for his verses. These musicians understood a recording session as the efficient dispatch of two-and-a-bit-minute pop tracks, three or more in a working shift. Dylan was looking for five-minute songs, seven-minute songs, an eleven-minute song in an era when an entire album, a *Rubber Soul*, would only rarely edge much beyond a half-hour. As things began to flow – and as the artist's window of opportunity began to close – six whole songs were achieved in a session that began on 9 March and ran into the 10th. Which is to say that, after another spell doing nothing much, the musicians worked from 6 p.m. to 9 p.m., from 9 p.m. to midnight, from midnight to 3 a.m. and then, with a mighty final assault, captured 'I Want You', the last song recorded, between 3 a.m. and seven in the morning. Elvis was known to pull all-nighters, but not day-and-nighters. Yet, of all the tracks on the album, 'I Want You' shimmers with supernatural vitality. Musicians who had been up from morning through to morning – drugs were no prop for these Nashville players – bring every note to dancing life. The singer isn't too bad, either.

Blonde on Blonde probably contains half of the Dylan lines most often remembered. Better yet, it contains the true wild mercury sound, the sound of his voice, a thing of infinite jest, of warmth, wit and layered implicit meaning. On this record, only his harmonica came close. On this record the logic of Ginsberg's breath units and the manner in which Dylan was making poetry began to make perfect metrical sense and came, definitively, to a kind of cock-eyed precision. He would have called it a *mathematical* sense, but that would just have been an instinct for metaphor talking.

Those who say that 'Sad Eyed Lady of the Lowlands' is a mere jumble of images miss a poet attempting, in the ancient manner, to count the ways of love, striving to redefine his own definitions, and to put the mystery of inviolability and passion into words. Those who say that 'I Want You' is a song of frustrated desire must have read the title, and must have then missed the album's idea: 'because time was on his side'. Those who say 'Johanna' is not meant to be understood fail to understand the opportunities for meaning it offers: here is a song whose *sense* of meaning exists outside of time. Those who meanwhile mistake 'Stuck Inside of Mobile with Thee' (as we shall henceforth call it) for the usual parade of characters miss the voice that says, 'And I have sense of time.'

Blonde on Blonde is three-quarters of an astonishing pop record caught up in ideas of chaos, identity and lost time that would have charmed Proust, on a good day. Some pretty fair musicians helped on some pretty fair tunes, too. The game of attempting to track down the sources of Dylan's melodies ended here. Similes attempting to describe how the songs sound do not improve, even slightly, on the singer's invocation of glittering metals susceptible to heat and pressure, flowing and pure. In essence, he had written himself out of trouble. Before long, in any case, the trial of the album's making would seem like an idyll.

*

Amid all this, Dylan and the Hawks were still cutting through the cold skies over America in Grossman's lumbering jet as though Buddy Holly had never fallen to earth. The tour went on. Part of the price paid by the new star for his fancy shirts and his new sound was submission to the standard operating procedures of mid-1960s pop. If there was a record to sell, enough would never be enough.

The Beatles, as Dylan has observed, had one another to lean on; they shared the load. In everything that mattered, he was on his own, writer, producer, director and star in his own apocalyptic vaudeville show. The burden of responsibility earned him no exemptions. Songs of genius were supposed simply to appear, and appear to order. If performances were scheduled, performances were delivered. In the interstices of playing and travelling, in moments when others slept off a hangover or welcomed a firstborn into the world, astonishing recordings were made. Time, like the players' psyches, was bent to accommodate commercial imperatives. Drugs, music's perennial props and catalysts, were almost inevitable on this tour. They were part of the process.

Mickey Jones, a stalwart for Trini Lopez and Johnny Rivers (the latter, for whatever reason, a Dylan favourite), had joined the party by the time they reached Hawaii and Australia at the beginning of April. Sandy Konikoff, another graduate of the Ronnie Hawkins school, had briefly replaced Levon Helm before deciding, like his predecessor in the drummer's chair, that the tour was not a barrel of laughs. Jones had played more than enough rock and roll to fit the bill. He also brought an unpretentious directness to the task that was exactly what was required. It might be accounted blasphemy in some quarters, but the tapes of the 1966 tour don't often indicate that Helm would have done a better job. For that matter, the remaining Hawks would never play in this manner again, and nor would Dylan ask any group of musicians to attempt the feat. Jones went at his kit as though driving a piece of industrial machinery. He did not aspire to be subtle, like Levon, but the time for that had passed.

By some accounts, the booing had begun to die away in North America as the party prepared to cross oceans. Had Dylan remained in the US a while longer, it is possible – no more – that the great and legendary controversy would have blown itself out before Manchester. *Blonde on Blonde* would be released in May (or June, or July; the precise date involves another of this album's finical debates). The refulgent music would duly shut a lot of traps, and make all the debates over 'protest' and 'folk' seem like old news. Pop's audience lacked the patience, in any case, to acquire an attention span. Another round of shows in America might have seen an end to the arguments. As it was, reports of barracking followed the tour across the globe like an advancing weather front.

Dylan was exhausted before he even left his homeland. Whether Grossman noticed or cared is a question that has never been answered, though an answer can probably be guessed. Between the last session for *Bringing It All Back Home* on 15 January 1965 and the final notes of 'I Want You' at the dawn of 10 March 1966, Dylan had completed those three peerless albums, had his trial by fire at Newport, written more and better songs than most artists would manage in a career, struggled to compose a book and given 79 concerts. (In 2011, on another of the tours the press would call never-ending, he would give 89 shows, and create only the vague rumour of recording sessions.) On 11 March 1966, the night after the last of his *Blonde on Blonde* labours, he was performing again in St Louis, Missouri. The next night, it was Lincoln, Nebraska. Dylan was exhausted for some fairly obvious reasons, but Albert, as ever, had plans. The world was waiting.

The concert set list was now more or less established. One bootleg of the show in Sydney on 13 April preserves a performance that concluded with an agreeably intemperate 'Positively 4th Street'; Dylan would offer the same finale – not precisely a gesture of warmth and affection – in the same city on the 16th. Thereafter only one song, the obvious song, would mark the end of each night's labours. Preceding

'Like a Rolling Stone' were the works much as they appear on *The Bootleg Series Volume 4*, and with the same venomous attack. Other bootlegs, the authentic sort, say Dylan did not once ease up. That, too, was a source of strain. Irrespective of audience reactions, of journalists asking the same dumb questions in country after country, of journeys that would be daunting enough in the twenty-first century, never mind in 1966 – Australia to Sweden; a day and a half in a plane? – Dylan showed unswerving commitment to his material.

In effect, once all the components were tuned and ready, he gave two fifty-minute performances each night. On the face of it, that doesn't seem like much in modern terms, not if a Bruce Springsteen iron-man show is your benchmark. What made it arduous for Dylan was that these were two *different* shows. Each night, a mental adjustment was required, a psychological recalibration from 'Johanna', 'Desolation Row' and 'Tambourine Man' to the close combat of 'Tell Me, Momma'. In some sense he had to be two different people each and every time, working – especially in the first half of the show – with songs that required care and attention. He was his own support act.

There was, meanwhile, another consideration to sap his resolve. Whatever the legend might seem to say, London and the Albert Hall on 27 May were never supposed to be the end of it. Grossman's plans involved dozens more American dates, up to and including New York's Shea Stadium. The 1966 tour actually halted, never forget, not in England but with a performance at White Plains, New York, on 16 June. Others were scheduled to follow. Until there was a back-roads mishap with a motorbike, possibly nasty and certainly fortuitous, it must have seemed like a never-ending nightmare.

Even performers who simply went out on the road to sing the songs written for them in 20-minute spots in 1960s revues found such tours tough to handle. Dylan was offering art, however you wish to measure it, alone or with his band. He was giving audiences something that would not be seen or heard again. And he was being barracked, as often as not, for his infinite pains.

Late in 1965, as though in preparation for a year that would see him exceed the recommended dosage for exposure to press conferences, Dylan had given his *Playboy* interview to Nat Hentoff before proceeding to contest the judgements of the magazine's rewrite men. What survived the process – and presumably received Dylan's blessing – was an exchange on the subject of contemporary sanative products. It would be published in March of 1966. Any decent reporter, then or since, would see instantly that Hentoff knew exactly what he was asking, and why. The insinuations are, as these things go, beautifully framed.

Playboy: Paranoia is said to be one of the mental states sometimes induced by such hallucinogenic drugs as peyote and LSD. Considering the risks involved, do you think that experimentation with such drugs should be part of the growing-up experience for a young person?

Dylan: I wouldn't advise anybody to use drugs – certainly not the hard drugs; drugs are medicine. But opium and hash and pot – now, those things aren't drugs; they just bend your mind a little. I think *everybody's* mind should be bent once in a while. Not by LSD, though. LSD is medicine – a different kind of medicine. It makes you aware of the universe, so to speak; you realise how foolish *objects* are. But LSD is not for groovy people; it's for mad, hateful people who want revenge. It's for people who usually have heart attacks. They ought to use it at the Geneva Convention.

Poor Elvis Presley had already talked himself into the belief that any remotely helpful substance capable of being issued on prescription by an ever-helpful MD was 'medicine'. It seems obvious, too, that Dylan had been ingesting some of former assistant professor Timothy Leary's claptrap concerning psilocybin mushrooms and various contemporary tales – as Hentoff's question suggests – of *Lophophora williamsii*, peyote. Allen Ginsberg had been an early enthusiast for Leary's magic mushroom experiments at Harvard. He and the mostly mad shrink had taken it upon themselves to spread the word among receptive progressives that consciousness-altering chemicals had therapeutic uses, and counted as 'medicine'. Dylan had doubtless received the lecture. LSD would not become illegal in America until October of 1966, but the singer's willingness to talk drugs – to appear to 'advocate' drugs, indeed – was rash for a performer about to embark on a world tour. Opium and marijuana had been beyond the law in America since the 1930s; cannabis possession had been illegal in Britain since 1928. Yet here was Dylan speaking, patently from experience, about a range of drugs while Hentoff made a gentle, incisive inquiry concerning the risk of paranoia. The exchange is rendered piquant when the author of 'Can You Please Crawl Out Your Window?' talks of 'mad, hateful people who want revenge'.

He needed his medicine, though, and apparently thought of drugs in those terms. There has been ample speculation over his requirements, the precise ingredients of his favoured sovereign cure for all that ailed him night after night, week upon week, month upon month. Shelton was granted his heroin 'confession', in due course, but kept it to himself. What's worth noting is the difference between the evidence of *The Bootleg Series Volume 4* and actual bootlegs. Aside from that brief, famous exchange with an amateur theologian in Manchester, the official release does not document Dylan's rhetoric between songs. Even the 'Judas' moment makes it plain enough, though, that the singer was functioning under certain physiological and psychic constraints.

Other recordings, hard to transcribe in a way that might convey their tone, prove that on every step of the way in the 1965–6 tour Dylan was on, or under, something. When the end of the road was reached at the Albert Hall in London, when all the 'walkouts' – by those who had paid decent money to walk in – had been suffered, when the Beatles had done their bit to support the genius with the black-and-white 1958 Telecaster, when George Harrison was done shouting at the barracking *idiots*, Dylan attempted – 'I've never done this before' – to introduce his band. Then, as preface to the mightiest 'Rolling Stone' of them all:

> It doesn't mean a thing, y'know what I mean? You don't hafta . . . But they're all *poets*, you understand? If it comes out that way, it comes out that way . . . But all the *poets*, y'know?
> This song here is dedicated to the *Taj Mahal* . . .
> And we're gonna leave after this song. And I want to say goodbye to all of you people. You've been very *warm*, great people. You've been very nice people. I mean, here you are, sittin' in this great huge place . . .
> And believe me, we've enjoyed *every minute of being here* . . .

That wasn't quite the whole truth. The 1966 tour scorched Dylan's soul. It ended him, in this incarnation, once and for all. Manchester wasn't even the half of it. When this carnival train was derailed, he would be forced to become still another person. This is not, or not necessarily, hyperbole. He would have to build a new Bob Dylan from scratch.

First there was another self-inflicted ordeal. For some reason, the star had decided to subject himself to yet another documentary film. This time the magic art was supposed to be under his direction, though D.A. Pennebaker would once again handle the mechanical aspects of the process. Having been less than impressed with *Don't Look Back*, Dylan had – either on a whim or at Grossman's urging – decided to construct the self-portrait known as *Eat the Document*. Filming began when the tour reached Scandinavia and it was, clearly, an obligation he could have done without.

Commissioned for broadcast by the ABC network, this home movie – the fairest description – would be rejected as unfit for its intended purpose. This time, the TV suits were right. *Eat the Document* remains a mess, a curiosity, a treat for voyeurs but bereft of discipline or a central idea. Dylan's apparent belief that he could construct a piece of cinema using the same intuitions he brought to songwriting proved to be horribly mistaken. The actual documentary footage is fine and well, as far as it goes, but the scenes invented or improvised by the star render the thing, at best, a period piece. The one moment of actual drama, the real 'scene' involving an overexcited folk fan with a knife in a Glasgow hotel room (apparently attempting a local version of *Sic semper tyrannis*), was missed. Like *Tarantula*, this movie was another lesson, if needed, that genius was not to be summoned at will.

Nor was stamina. When the tour reached Ireland, Britain and France, audiences were unrelenting. As the bootlegs testify, they booed, jeered, walked out or gave the star of those two number-one albums the slow handclap. More importantly, the disaffected didn't even pretend to give the band a chance: these were not simply complaints over 'a bad PA'. Yet again, however, the tapes make it clear that hostility was far from universal. The suggestion from CP Lee that the dissent was planned and organised, at least in the northern parts of Britain, sounds plausible, according to this recorded evidence. Somehow that only makes the confrontations seem all the stranger.

Heroin or no heroin, it must have seemed like Newport all over again, night upon night. What was it they wanted? How must it have felt to be feted once more by the Beatles and other star-struck peers yet face this raging hostility from paying customers? At times on the bootlegs, especially when he decides simply to mutter hilarious gibberish until the audience shuts the hell up, Dylan's defiance is obvious. That iron self-belief does not desert him. Patently, his conclusion is that if they don't get it, that's their problem. This doesn't quite solve the puzzle.

Dylan's career was not destroyed by the '66 tour. The fact alone is proof that the hecklers represented only one, disaffected part of his audience. He did not, by any stretch, alienate every customer. *Blonde on Blonde*, a difficult concept for a pop audience on any level, would reach number three in Britain and nine in the US before too long. Several singles from the set would do well enough and one, the otherwise dismal 'Rainy Day Women', would deliver a certified hit. Dylan won the war. Clearly, large numbers of those who saw him in Manchester or Edinburgh or London went out dutifully and bought the record at the first opportunity. So what was the war actually about?

This was a period, after all, in which the Beatles could spring practically any surprise on an audience and be guaranteed adoration. The Rolling Stones could desert their blues roots without a second thought, and proceed from strength to strength. The individual with the knife in the Glasgow hotel had supposedly made some sort of noise about a 'traitor to folk music'. Why would that have mattered? Dylan was not doing anything to hinder the folk revival, such as remained.

Clearly, a version of politics was at work, whether Dylan liked it or not. In some manner the singer's decision to don a weird suit and a Telecaster was regarded – bizarre as this now sounds – as an act liable to do political damage. Add his occasional remarks, and occasional they were, on his distaste for affiliations and you can *almost* grasp an argument. If, that is, you accept that the mere sound of an amplified instrument could be an act of cultural vandalism and a symbol of oppression. It would be akin to telling Picasso that he was using filthy capitalist brushes. A movement dedicated to liberty was unforgiving. Nor did it grant much licence to poets or to poetry.

Judas! That was the shout in the darkness. To this day, the insult seems infantile. There were plenty of other singers in the world ready to accept adoration, after all. Yet here was evidence, beyond doubt, of the great virtue and the abiding affliction of the 1960s: music truly matterered.

The argument over art, the individual and political liberty isn't new. What was new in Dylan's case, and in the twentieth century, was the idea that the artist could somehow belong to the audience, become a possession. So the supreme irony here was overlooked by those who heckled this guitar player and called themselves left-wing: they were treating him as a commodity.

*

He had seen enough, in any case. He looked, in every photograph, only slightly better than death. His exhaustion was profound, his mood swings like the arc of a crazed pendulum. As the last shots of Scorsese's *No Direction Home* make clear, after his final show at the Albert Hall he was in no shape for still more concerts. He could barely stand the thought of that ordeal. The tour had been bad enough – could hardly have been worse – but it had come amid sustained bursts of intense creative activity. He had done the near-impossible, but he could do no more. Subsequent events ensured that he was spared the attempt.

He left 'swinging London' to its illusions. His version of modernity, the future that could be glimpsed in his music, was not to every taste. Not for the first or last time, a section of his audience would give up on this contrary star. In more than one sense, Dylan had pushed himself to the edge. He was falling out of step, too, with events in his homeland. What some would call his credibility would depend increasingly on what he had done in his first incarnation, not on what he would do in all the years to follow. *Blonde on Blonde* was all he had left, or so it seemed, to offer. After this, those who bought his records would forever hope for the reappearance of one or other of his former selves. Yet as summer began in 1966, the 'voice of a generation' was already becoming a thing of the past.

Everything ended. His music would never be the same again, and nor would he: that cliché will serve. He would tell people as much for years to come: it was less a case of what he wouldn't do as what he *couldn't* do. For one thing, he could no longer write the words to shape that wild mercury sound. The three albums and the hellish tour had been unique, in the proper sense of being both emotionally and artistically unrepeatable. Anyone who henceforth wanted 'the old Dylan' would be out of luck. He was gone.

Lo and Behold!

I can't even remember it. People have told me they think it's very *Americana* and all that. I don't even know what they're talkin' about.

Interview with *Rolling Stone*, 1984

Later, music and rhyme became games, mere pastimes. The study of this past proves precious to the curious: many get a kick out of reworking these antiquities: let them.

Arthur Rimbaud, letter to Paul Demeny, May 1871

EVENTS IN BOB DYLAN'S LIFE HAVE A NASTY HABIT OF BLEEDING INTO legend. Periods that must have seemed to him like his version of normal – getting up, getting to work, 'drying out', making songs – suffer a metamorphosis in the retelling, generally after hindsight has done its work and significance, always profound, has been discerned. Did he have much on his mind in the summer of 1967? His recovering health aside, not so you could tell.

Certainly he seemed to have no plans for still another of those epochal albums. Some of the songs of that summer were among the finest things that he or anyone else would create, but by the standards of his industry Dylan did nothing serious with them. He never did record the songs 'properly'. The thirty or so tapings made of original work at Woodstock in upper New York State were demos at best – a matter of luck, chance or mood – and he consented to their partial release eight years after the fact, when the bootleggers had taken their fill, only as a favour, so it is said, to his collaborators. Later still, in his own version of hindsight and perverse special pleading, that season's work was deemed the opposite of significant.

I never really liked *The Basement Tapes*. I mean, they were just songs we had done for the publishing company, as I remember. They were used

ONCE UPON A TIME

only for other artists to record those songs. I wouldn't have put 'em out. But, you know, Columbia wanted to put 'em out, so what can you do?[1]

What can you *do*? This from a recording artist with as much autonomy as anyone in his industry, one who had long since ceased to worry much about the cost of studio time, chart placings, popular tastes, critical opinion or the clamorous demands of his very demanding audience. Consider the position from the point of view of those malignant suits at Columbia. By 1967 Dylan had given the label enormous credibility. The *Blonde on Blonde* double set, in format and in execution, had broken new ground in a dozen different ways. He had earned Columbia esteem and a decent amount of money, one way or another – though on unfair terms, Dylan thought – but they had scarcely treated him as indentured labour. He was one of a handful of people in the 1960s who could walk into a recording studio at any time the mood took him, record anything he felt like recording and put it out in any form that took his fancy. Yet still, albeit with work owing, he had gone to ground, armed, or so the average hard-working corporate type might have concluded, with a very convenient medical exemption. All the while he was writing and recording enough material to fill another remarkable double album with ease.

Only 'for other artists to record those songs'? They did, gratefully, in their droves, thanks to a 14-track acetate circulated throughout the industry with Dylan's knowledge and (presumably) consent. But would Columbia have preferred a new Bob Dylan record? A stupid question. As to 'the publishing company', that wouldn't be the enterprise owned and controlled, though disputatiously, by the singer and his manager? Equally, if the work of 1967 was intended as a manoeuvre to keep precious copyrights from the hands of Albert '50–50' Grossman, as has often been claimed, distributing brand-new songs around the music world, on both sides of the Atlantic, amounted to a strange kind of embargo.

Not for the first time or the last, Dylan was manipulating grains of truth in that 1984 interview to shape an unreliable tale. Those were never 'just songs done for the publishing company': he is, generally, too serious a craftsman for that. The works bore his name, and spoke to his reputation. The 14 tracks subsequently offered around may have been a response to certain 'contract issues' in lieu of a new recording

---

1   *Rolling Stone*, June 1984.

deal, but he was under no obvious duress. Yet again he was doing something new, and doing it seriously. He must have known as much. Soon enough most of the people who cared about his work would know it too. A studio album would meanwhile have cost him little effort after the Woodstock sessions, and could have solved a few difficulties into the bargain.

Still, grant him this much: he showed no inclination to 'put 'em out' before 1975. He did not do so even then – more complications – just because of what Columbia wanted. The desire sprang, apparently, from Robbie Robertson and other members of The Band. The label would of course grab 'the legendary *Basement Tapes*' when the chance arose. Who wouldn't? The word of mouth on this one was almost unparalleled. But in 1975, of all his adult years, there was no desperate need for product. Just six months previously, after all, Dylan had given the company a little thing entitled *Blood on the Tracks*.

*

Trivia. Ernest Hemingway said, famously, that 'All modern American literature comes from one book by Mark Twain called *Huckleberry Finn*'. The novel made the language; it spoke to the country and shaped the country. Just as surely, the recovered music of America – music understood consciously as the permanent legacy of the American experience – emerged with Dylan's basement tapes. Dreams and weird beliefs followed. After the fact, old music ceased to be a matter of nostalgia and assumed its proper place as part of the fabric of a lived, and living, culture. Unlike the music of the blues revival, it could not be frozen in time, an exhibited artefact. On the sly, cards stapled to his chest, breathing not a word to anyone, Dylan had achieved what the folk movement had failed to achieve. Call it *Americana*, call it 'roots', call it an understanding that pop music did not have to remain forever in the moment, instantaneous and disposable. There was a hinterland and a history, a memory, demanding to be explored. You could also say that Dylan simply grew up, and then obliged his coevals in the craft of song to do the same. No one – did he? – saw this coming.

It is worth adding, meanwhile, that the attention paid to Dylan's resurrection as an artist in the 1990s and in the twenty-first century was an acknowledgement, mostly unconscious, of what began in 1967. Dylan the historian, the archivist, the curator of American remembrance, first began to emerge down in the basement. He did not become the grand old man of his culture and society without having been the young man who embarked on a musical Lewis and Clark expedition amid the summer of love.

*

All true. The case, made most eloquently by Greil Marcus in his 1997 book *Invisible Republic*,[2] still holds. It has nevertheless been overstated just a little, not least by Marcus. Anyone coming across a more-or-less complete set of the 1967 recordings after *Blonde on Blonde*, and hearing them in the chronological order postulated by Clinton Heylin, is liable to respond – as a critic named Marcus once did when confronted with another Dylan compendium – by asking what *this* shit might possibly be. Let's blaspheme: the basement recordings are not uniformly magnificent.

The idea of a conscious exploration through music of the American interior, historical and psychological, can seem thin indeed when the evidence to hand is of a Dylan failing to find a falsetto voice on 'Try Me Little Girl', or wading through a tedious traditional piece like 'Bonnie Ship the Diamond'. You can't truly fault the singer of 'The Hills of Mexico' who tells Garth Hudson to abort the impromptu recording because it's 'wasting tape'. Even when Dylan and The Band up the pace as the sessions proceed, the listener needs reserves of patience for the comedy stylings (clearly, you had to be there) of 'Bourbon Street', 'The Spanish Song' and several others besides.

The truth of the basement tapes lies somewhere between Dylan's dismissals and the reverence in which the recordings are too often held. The listener has to edit the material, mentally or otherwise, in a way that never occurred to its creators. You have to accept that a great deal of detritus surrounds a hard core of remarkable songs. Above all, as so often with Dylan, it is worth bearing in mind the difference between what he did, what he thought he was doing and what he was thought to have done. This matters.

A bunch of musicians were getting stoned and messing around, not striking out to touch the shadow-essence of America itself. That they did – lo and behold – reach such a destination, and did so simply by dint of seeing what might transpire day to day, tells us something about Dylan's artistic method. '*Americana* and all that'? He demurred; we should hesitate.

---

2   Republished in 2011 as *The Old, Weird America: Bob Dylan's Basement Tapes*.

At issue is a great lost album, but it is a work that survives, just about, amid a great deal of extraneous crap. By reading too much into the basement tapes you can do their creator too little credit. The important fact in the summer of 1967 was the thing he hallows most: his instinct. This was no art project. That makes it all the stranger, and all the more significant. In those months his instinct urged retrospection. Suggest, however, that in the process he founded some sort of movement, his very own unwitting *Pax Americana*, and he will run a country mile.

Still: *something* happened.

*

No sooner had he delivered himself of the febrile masterpiece that was *Blonde on Blonde* than Dylan was throwing himself, so it seemed, into reverse, deep into the mythic and historic past. On the face of it this was an odd thing for Bob Dylan, of all people, to do in 1967, of all years. Back then, a lot of other people wanted to believe that a movement truly was in train. Preposterous hopes were running preposterously high. Altered states of consciousness were expected to alter the world, somehow, and give it a curative jolt of transfiguring love. A lot of people believed this happy talk, and a lot more pretended to believe it. 'Youth' was taking itself very seriously. Any casual remark uttered by a Beatle was near oracular in '67. The straight world was watching and listening, intent and baffled. The year was itself becoming mythical, not to say nonsensical, even as it unfolded. Dylan, all agreed, was supposed to be at the heart of the upheaval. Instead, he had dropped from sight, blending into the scenery, answering no calls, least of all clarion calls. Like the folk movement before it, the counter-culture was somewhat disappointed. Speculation therefore abounded. Simply by stepping back from the microphone, Dylan had become 'a recluse'.

It was news to his neighbours and his family. His wealth meant that the Woodstock resident could hardly be called ordinary – the big Cadillac with the customised sound system and the chauffeur's compartment saw to that – but he was certainly trying his hand at normality in 1967. This part of the standard superstar biography rarely attracts sympathy, but it is pertinent. Anyone whose life is turned inside out at the age of 22, who is glutted with adulation, pawed by sycophants, stuffed with gold and treated – Dylan's special punishment – as though his every stray thought bears the stamp of genius, will struggle. *Normal* becomes a lost habit, a childhood memory. *Normal* is hard to come by. It is the one need that talent, money, a management, a staff, acclaim, an entourage and an army of fans cannot satisfy.

Dylan had been through hell. No one was likely to pity him for it, what with the fame and wealth and talent, but that didn't alter the fact. He had set out to do the thing he most loved in the world, to play his songs for people, and had found himself exhausted, misunderstood and abused. In 1966, siege had been laid to that towering ego. Too often, city by city, he had been rejected. No artist bears that easily. Hence the need for normal, for safe, sure and secure.

It's not much of a guess to say that the need was deeply personal: after the madness, the psychic scalding, Dylan sought 'a tree with roots', something that was not – the word yet again – phoney. As always, it lived in the music, in the emotional reality of music, but not, on this occasion, in the swirling sounds he had heard from the day after tomorrow. *The Basement Tapes* – even that improvised, deceptive, throwaway 'official' title speaks of things uncovered in the depths, things coming from below – reaches back to the homespun pop of childhood, youth and lifetimes long gone. Then it reaches again, deeper into forgotten history. A host of guiding spirits hover over these songs. Huck Finn might even be one of them. Their voices tell stories, dark and comical, surreal and literal, bitter and tragic and sweet: *Americana and all that*. Part of the legend says, nevertheless, that Dylan almost had to die first.

*

He had won himself a respite from the tour, the tour never-ending, that had produced, among other things, the Manchester conflagration and an exhaustion so profound it had left him sick, say several witnesses, to the point of speechlessness. Dylan was in a mess, and in retreat. You catch a sense of his distress in that scene towards the end of Scorsese's *No Direction Home*, when the singer reacts with a kind of psychic dread to the prospect of still more public appearances. Yet amid a brief break his 'personal' manager, Grossman, was busily booking another five dozen tour dates; his book publisher was pressing for the 'finished' version of the *Tarantula* prose poem he could no longer abide; and he had taken charge of the footage that became (after a fashion) *Eat the Document*. To complicate matters further, contract negotiations with Columbia did indeed turn on a pre-existing agreement to provide still more product, an album and/or 14 new songs at the least. In those days, few of those who owned a piece of the talent stopped to wonder what happened when a performer was burned down to a puddle of human wax. Grossman was meanwhile manoeuvring to broker a new deal with a new label, to all appearances oblivious to the beating his boy had taken.

They always say you had to be there, at the heart of it, to know. The Beatles, those rivals and friends from a parallel universe, had hauled themselves finally to San Francisco's Candlestick Park on 29 August 1966. Miserable, playing abysmally, drowning in a weird mixture of fame, hysteria and self-loathing, they no longer felt (if they ever had) 'more popular than Jesus'. Dylan's *Blonde on Blonde* had just appeared, as though to remind the quartet of what a record could be. In Britain, as usual, they had another number-one single ('Eleanor Rigby'). Their own masterwork, *Revolver*, had been in the shops for barely three weeks. But it was over. The insane public ritual of live performance, their private auto-da-fé, was no longer sustainable. In San Francisco, after another wretched, humiliating show, George Harrison told Brian Epstein, the Beatles' manager, that he was quitting the band. Harrison had just turned 23. Dylan, newly 25 at the time, knew the feeling.

Part of the sensation was chemical. Of that there is, if there ever was, not much doubt. Though no one can say precisely which recipes from the recreational pharmacopoeia made themselves Dylan's choice and habit, it is plain that addiction was at some point, as the talk-show types say, an issue. Exactly when and for how long is less clear. A few years later, with his marriage gone, Dylan would offer up a love song, as only he could, recalling having 'taken the cure and . . . just gotten through'. It didn't sound like a metaphor.

In the spring of 2011, in any case, there was a minor hubbub when a revised and expanded edition of Robert Shelton's biography was accompanied by the 'revelation' that heroin had become a problem for Dylan at the end of 1965 (at least), or at the start of 1966. On a private aircraft on its way from Lincoln, Nebraska, to Denver in March of that year he had told the journalist: 'I kicked a heroin habit in New York City. I got very, very strung out for a while, I mean really, very strung out. And I kicked the habit. I had about a $25-a-day habit and I kicked it.'

That love song – 'Sara' from the 1976 album *Desire* – had alluded to New York. After taking the cure, the singer had been 'Stayin' up for days in the Chelsea Hotel / Writin' "Sad Eyed Lady of the Lowlands"

459

for you'. So had he really 'kicked the habit' before unburdening himself to his familiar media confidant? Or had he just substituted one narcotic for another, as addicts will while they boast of vanquishing temptation? After the harder stuff, burgundy – or amphetamines, or cocaine – can seem like a pledge of sobriety.

For many, the Shelton tale only confirmed old news. Those who decrypted Dylan's lyrics had more or less agreed long before that *Blonde on Blonde*, made when the singer was still patently 'very strung out', does not want for drug references. 'Rain' = heroin, with 'Visions of Johanna' as exhibit A. Equally, the Rainman of 'Stuck Inside of Mobile', with his 'two cures' and his invitation to 'jump right in', offered a simple enough code. 'Just Like a Woman' was near explicit: 'Nobody feels any pain / Tonight as I stand inside the rain.'

Interpretative criticism can become addictive. No medical expertise was required – 'And my best friend, my doctor / Won't even say what it is I've got' – to see that the Dylan of 1965–6 was prowling the outer limits of endurance, that speech and body movements were beyond the speed of thought and design tolerances, that he was working at a remarkable pace, and that, one way or another, he didn't look well. In sections of the Manchester concert preserved in *The Bootleg Series Volume 4*, in parts of *Don't Look Back*, in expanses of *Eat the Document*, in several actual bootlegs, it's plain enough: this wasn't the victim of a new-age diet. His body had no fat left to spare, his skin was translucent and his big eyes burned. All you had to do was pick the drug most likely to produce *that* look, or disturb the user's psyche in *that* manner.

Few could have survived the 1966 tour unaided. The emotional assaults, the physical demands, the creative and contractual burdens: these were the superstar's lot, no doubt. But Dylan needed the illusion of energy and the mental armour more than most. It isn't adequate to say, on the basis of a few concert bootlegs, official or otherwise, that he was merely *stoned*, or even – the better description – *out of it*. In those weeks and months he occupied the user's paradox: clarity and dislocation, vitality on demand and reciprocal exhaustion. In such a situation you tailor the drugs to suit, if you can, for as long as you can. Long before he got his shot of love, Dylan paid the price, fully aware – if he allowed the feeling – that it couldn't go on.

The only point that needs to be registered is an objection to the narcotic-visionary fallacy. It is fatuous, and a disservice to the songs, to make the invariable causal connection between Dylan's imagery and drug use, as though everything is thereby explained. The triptych of 1965–6 contained too much clarity for that. The 'rational disordering of all the senses' might have been descriptive of Rimbaud's aesthetic and his world-view. But try it. Follow that injunction to the letter, then try writing your own name, far less three albums of songs in a year and a half.

In Dylan's case, the regimen seems to have had a predictable, inevitable effect. After the world tour, as best we know, the songwriting ceased for at least the remainder of 1966. There is film and audio evidence of half-hearted attempts to write songs with Robbie Robertson while travelling the world in a bubble of ego and rage. Nothing to speak of came of those efforts. Back in America, Dylan enjoyed – the word seems right – the first hiatus in his recording career. One back-roads mishap aside, this appears to have been his choice.

*

There seemed to be a notion abroad, in any case – you could say the writer had only himself to blame – that he could produce masterpieces endlessly, unstoppably and at will. Contrary to anything a man's body and mind might suggest, Dylan was assumed to be inexhaustible. This was *a genius*, after all, one whose fecundity in the business of writing songs had no contemporary rival. Since no one could explain how he did what he did, no one could identify a limit to his energy or inspiration. Dylan was truly a prisoner of his own success, and his gaoler was an enigmatic wizard named Dylan. Small wonder that he was looking for a reason, or an excuse, just to make it all stop.

There was an accident. Or rather, there *was* an accident. For whatever reason, even that simple fact, like so many of the facts of Dylan's life, has been the subject of an indecent amount of rumour, speculation and theorising. People have noted that a spell laid up with an injury suited the hard-pressed singer very well in the summer of 1966. His relations with Grossman, the manager, were close to rupture. All those who were around him at the time agree that he was in desperate need of rest and recuperation. Judging by the work to come, he may have decided he needed something more: contemplation, retreat, a chance to marshal his resources, to think again or just to spend time with his family.

Some have argued that he needed a reason to avoid fulfilling his Columbia contract: hence, supposedly, the indecent burial and strange afterlife of those basement tapes. In 1978, meanwhile, in an interview with *Rolling Stone*, Dylan seemed to say that, as far as *Tarantula* was concerned, the motorbike incident 'just got me out of the whole thing'. It has therefore been concluded that the accident was no accident. That seems to me to be untrue – there are easier ways to hedge your bets, or cleanse body and mind – but the painful event was certainly no outright misfortune.

Back home at his house in Woodstock, Dylan decided – 29 July 1966 – to take an old Triumph motorcycle to a local repair shop. 'It happened one morning after I'd been up for three days,' he later told Shelton. 'I hit an oil slick. The damp weather still affects the wound.'

Which wound? That specific claim has been disputed, just as the extent of the accident has been disputed. On the other hand, 'up for three days' might have been worth a moment's pause. Another biographer[3] has Grossman's wife recalling that Dylan merely 'slipped off the bike' without suffering a visible injury. This biographer reckons it 'a fairly minor fall' exploited thereafter as a dodge. It is recalled, too, that the biker has poor eyesight. Then again, Dylan was observed wearing a neck brace after the incident, and reported to be receiving treatment for cracked vertebrae.

In 1987 he told the playwright Sam Shepard that, unaccountably, he had squinted into the sun, lost his vision, panicked, stamped on the brakes and sent himself skywards. At the time the New York papers instead preferred to believe – no sources were named – that he had come close to his definitive James Dean moment. But even the precise spot of the contested mishap on one of several rough back roads – Zena Road, perhaps? – cannot be established with certainty amid these endless forensic investigations.

It is further suggested that the motorbike had been retrieved from Albert Grossman's garage; that Dylan had only slipped in the manager's driveway and found himself beneath a lump of metal. *But supposedly* no police report was filed, nor an ambulance report, nor a hospital admission document. *Supposedly* the doctor called upon – who didn't live nearby – specialised in substance abuse.

And the whole affair was staged, supposedly, to allow Dylan – myopic, a family man, a public and political figure already older than the average recruit – to dodge the Vietnam draft. And all of it was

---

3   Sounes, *Down the Highway: The Life of Bob Dylan*, Ch. 5, p. 472.

covered up, or made up. And not a single certified on-the-spot witness can be found.

And so what?

Thirty-eight years later, in his truthfully unreliable memoir *Chronicles*, the victim said that there had certainly been a motorcycle accident. He had been injured, but he had recovered. In truth, however, he had decided to make his escape from races and rats. His children had changed his life and begun to absorb his entire attention. By then, nothing beyond his family was of any interest or importance. He had begun to see the world anew.

Elsewhere he has remembered realising, slow on the uptake, that he was 'just workin' for all these leeches'. His brother, David, is meanwhile said to have confirmed to the author Toby Thompson that the legendary smash was really no big deal. Shelton is thought to have held the same opinion. The only important fact is that Dylan withdrew, with a couple of minor exceptions, from public performance, and did his best to retreat from public life. He had reached – no biker joke intended – one of those forks in the road. As the *New York Times* would shortly report, a concert scheduled for the Yale Bowl had been cancelled.

Woodstock would soon become another nightmare as fans, 'moochers', 'dropouts and druggies', 'goons' and 'rogue radicals' descended, some of them breaking into the family house itself, but in mid-1967 Ulster County remained a refuge. You can easily believe that the arrival of a child had changed Dylan's life, his priorities and his interests. Things combined. But the music, too, underwent still another dizzying change. Soon enough an experiment was going on down in that basement. It would have caused his audience's heads to spin – had he bothered to let them know about it.

Add only this: Grossman and his star had not been getting along too well. Regardless of the effects of a hellish tour, Albert had not hesitated to book those dozens of additional dates. Even a faked accident – with Grossman's own wife as the telltale spy? – would have cost a bundle of money, some of it the manager's own. It seems unlikely, therefore, that the grand vizier would have been complicit in a mere scam even as he was booking five dozen halls. The facts are that Dylan abandoned everything and that Albert, by the evidence, made no protest, presumably because he was given no choice.

The withdrawal matters; the reasons do not. Whether there was a wheel on fire, or a careless, sleepless singer mildly injured, Dylan brought a whole career to a shuddering halt. Those who claim the accident as a significant moment get there, unlike the careless biker, in the end. For the first time in five years, perhaps in his life, he was able to pause. For a while it would seem that the pause was a dead halt, that he truly did not want to go on being Bob Dylan.

What's patently true is that he did not mean to go on being *that* Bob Dylan. He had become a burden to himself. To begin anew is one thing: many people make the attempt. The point here is that Dylan's art has everything to do with the way he understands himself at a given moment in time. His writing is his response to a deep problem of identity.

*

The Dylans had acquired Hi Lo Ha, a large Arts and Crafts house set in woodland on Woodstock's Camelot Road, in 1965, when they were expecting Jesse, their first child. It didn't suit the street image of the singer then cutting 'Like a Rolling Stone', and that fact had suited him perfectly well. Thanks to the relentless career that shaped the image, however, Dylan had seen little enough of the place before his accident. Given the chance to settle, he had become, at least by his standards, thoroughly domesticated. In fact, if you believe *Chronicles* he had been fantasising about a nine-to-five life, about tree-lined suburbia, picket fences, roses in the garden. Such was, it seems, his highest aspiration and his deepest hope. Dylan was learning a lesson, however: once gone, privacy is gone for good.

Even a nonentity's life in Hibbing, Minnesota, would probably have seemed nice after his recent experiences. Such confessions would certainly have fascinated the journalists who had attempted to penetrate his armour during the 1966 tour, and would no doubt have appalled any number of 'rogue radicals'. But if Woodstock in the beginning was a good place to find some peace, and a fine place to raise some kids, the yearning it represented also played a part in the music Dylan began to make after the rear wheel locked on his bike. Call it his socially conservative streak – that trait was there from the start – or call it nostalgia. Call it an act of creative purification. Call it an old American urge towards pastoralism. The Woodstock phase in his revolution was to be, in a non-political sense, reactionary. He was digging in, and digging deep.

Clearly, he was dissatisfied with Bob Dylan, and with what that assemblage had become. No one else was complaining. Besides, if he was trapped with this cast of characters, trapped *in* character, that was a consequence of his own choices. Robert Allen Zimmerman was a ghost sustained in the memories of his parents, his brother and a handful of others. He existed nowhere else. That had been Bob Dylan's doing. In 1967, it had become part of his problem.

The trait – restlessness, persistent disquiet, a near-wilful refusal to recognise laurels, far less rest on them – had marked his career. No one else would have objected to *Blonde on Blonde II*, to years spent following the blazed trail. For him, that fact alone rendered such a project impossible. The art was the man, and this young man had concluded that some things would have to change. The future, and his career, could take care of itself.

*

He picked his moment. The summer of 1967 was about to receive a lot of press. Most of the copy would take seriously the idea that deeply important things were happening. Some of the words would be devoted, inevitably, to the absence of Bob Dylan from his proper visionary leadership role – or whatever – in the necessary struggle. Overlooked, always, was the tendency of a children's crusade to confuse every novel idea with a good idea. Hippies – the old label is misleading, but it sticks – chose to believe that the world was being turned upside down. As things turned out, the world had a different opinion. Dylan had no opinion, or no opinion he was prepared to offer.

What was advertised as a new age became a season's fancy. The 'tribes' who gathered in 1967 in San Francisco's Haight-Ashbury, and in cities across America and Europe, turned out to be a distinctly homogeneous bunch in terms of class, age, race, tastes and habits. 'White kids with money' would be another description. They came together, says one generalisation, because of music, drugs, sex, an intellectually vague disaffection and a generous view of the charms of communal living. 'Personal fulfilment' and 'spiritual awakening', those offspring of mumbo and jumbo, began to supplant older, tougher ideas about political work and political change. Any adjustments made to 'consciousness' did not long endure, meanwhile, though the habit of recreational narcotic use persisted. Among musicians the advent of cocaine and heroin would soon bring the summer's dream to a nauseating close. In other respects, the drug most abused was pure, uncut narcissism.

Some of the music would turn out to be pretty good, but certain of the social experiments were disastrous from the start. Acid, LSD, was not the key to the doors of perception; for a few burned souls it became a kind of psychic suicide. The nuclear family into which Dylan had retreated, elsewhere brought into disrepute by superficial readings of R.D. Laing's *Sanity, Madness and the Family* (1964), went on to survive the counter-culture's onslaught mostly because every 'alternative' – the word of the hour – failed to prosper. The harshest judgement on the summer's hopes would be this: a dozen or so years later a good proportion of this 'new generation' voted for Ronald Reagan and Margaret Thatcher; the rest failed utterly in their efforts to prevent a conservative counter-revolution. Disillusionment crept in like a San Francisco fog.

Where Dylan was concerned, nevertheless, they had a point, of sorts, these advocates of alternatives. Hadn't he said that the society in which they had been raised was phoney? Wasn't he the one who had stood against militarism, injustice, preconceptions, the 'nine-to-five existence', bland commercialism, dead art and machine politics? So what had become of the singer who had heard the chimes of freedom? Even those who guessed that Dylan would not have been seen comatose, far less dead, in Haight-Ashbury raised the voice of the New Left to demand his presence.

What happened in 1967? The Beatles produced an album; Monterey held a pop festival; hippies (especially of the weekend variety) became commonplace; Vietnam was subjected to total war; and the cities of America exploded in riots. Some of these events mattered more than others, it's fair to say.

Resistance against the war was a momentous affair: from it flowed a perception of the United States, and of 'US imperialism', that has endured into the twenty-first century. When Martin Luther King denounced his country's descent into colonialism in a speech at New York's Riverside Church on 4 April 1967, he enlarged the argument. King's moral authority was such that protests against the Vietnam adventure could no longer be dismissed as unpatriotic, subversive or as the foibles of spoiled, long-haired youth. The preacher made the issue fundamental to the character of the country:

> Now, it should be incandescently clear that no one who has any concern for the integrity and life of America today can ignore the present war. If America's soul becomes totally poisoned, part of the autopsy must read: Vietnam. It can never be saved so long as it destroys the deepest

hopes of men the world over. So it is that those of us who are yet determined that America will be – are – are led down the path of protest and dissent, working for the health of our land.

The 'race riots' in the cities week upon hot summer week in 1966, '67 and '68 were also symptoms that could not be ignored. Those who tried to portray these events as mere outbreaks of criminality sounded obtuse, at best, and like bland agents of oppression at worst. The trouble was that even those who understood the violence as evidence of a deep malaise had no remedies to hand. LBJ's war on poverty, the Voting Rights Act, the entire Great Society programme: none of these had forestalled, or would forestall, the riots. The House of Representatives was packed with liberals as never before, but it made no difference. The civil-rights movement seemed to have achieved its legislative goals, yet the condition of black America remained dire, its sense of routine, daily injustice palpable. Already there was evidence that young and radical blacks were drifting away from Martin Luther King. Non-violence was a noble aspiration, but no longer, some concluded, a useful strategy. Black people needed power, not prayers.

The times were a-changin', then: the song that was already an editorialist's cliché was not mistaken. So were the Division Street riots in Chicago in June of 1966 – disturbances incited when police shot a young Puerto Rican and a dirt-poor community decided enough was enough – the precise echo of the song's message? That would be a stretch. As Dylan had realised before the rest, the problem for any writer in these times was the very idea of *messages*. What could be written instead? Dylan's solution was to stand apart, to trust his gifts, not the daily news. He had the need, in any case, both physical and mental, to step outside an impossible world.

*

The body of work known as the basement tapes – the mass of recordings made during the summer and autumn of 1967, rather than the officially issued album – can certainly sound like a wholesale rejection of the rat race, above all of the album-tour-album-tour grind. Few of the tracks have the sheen of 'product', even by Dylan's standards. The greatest of the takes, far less the greatest performances, would still strike the most broad-minded studio technician as unacceptably raw, or merely preparatory. Unless he had something utterly subversive in mind, these 'primitive' recordings were not made for release: that part of the tale fits. In 1967, you can be sure, Columbia would have been aghast at the idea. Long before lo-fi, the basement material was no-fi. This doesn't mean that the songs were created artlessly or thoughtlessly, as Dylan has seemed to suggest. It does indicate that he was intent on something antithetical – if only the poor folkies had known – to the usual assumptions of corporate mass entertainment. Ironically, that lack of audio polish is one explanation, though a minor one, for the power of the best of the songs. It does not quite describe what was going on that summer, however, in the Woodstock area.

What do these recordings signify, in the aftermath of 1966? A 'change of direction', obviously, from the headlong charge into a possible lyric future that was *Blonde on Blonde*. Dylan stepped back, and turned away. But that, of itself, was nothing new: it was the pattern of his career. The basement songs stand in relation to the postmodern delirium of 1966 much as Dylan's discovery of folk music had stood in relation to his teenage obsession with rock and roll. Such is his method, if an instinct counts as a method. He returns to his roots time and again, as though caught in a loop between past and present. The irony is inherent: whenever Dylan delves yet again in old music – and only a handful of basement songs sound other than ancient – he seems to wind up pointing to the future. Here was an example, the prime example. In the summer of 1967 no one, not even the survivors of the Village folk crowd, had begun to think properly about *Americana*.

*

On one view, the semi-informal recording sessions that occupied much of Dylan's time in the second half of 1967 were a form of escapism. They constituted, first, a bucolic alternative (soon much imitated) to the industrial processes of the record business. As summer came on, the singer and his musicians – they were still on his payroll, after all – could sing and play up at the big pink house The Band were renting at West Saugerties with the windows open and the warm breeze blowing through. Second, the interludes offered a way to satisfy the industry beast – that album and/or 14 songs owed to Columbia – free of the pressures of the professional studio, the madness of the road, the sticky embrace of the publicity machine or the racket of the critics. No reviews, no fans, no suits, no expectations: such were the emerging ideals of superstardom.

But – and it amounts to a large but – the idea of a Dylan in hiding, obstinately putting aside all thoughts of record-making, is nonsense. If the so-called basement tapes were enough to satisfy Columbia's demands for product, why was he in Nashville before the year's end creating, with speed and deliberation, a record for which the basement sessions provided neither warning nor clue?

John Wesley Harding is another remarkable artefact, but its existence seems never to have depended, in any literal, causal sense, on the basement compositions. *Harding* appeared out of the blue, unheralded, a counter-counter-culture chamber piece. Yet it was fully formed, already written and thoroughly prepared, when Dylan stepped into the studio at the year's end. The Band had no inkling. The record company had no warning. Art aside, Dylan's only available motivation was a new contract guaranteeing a very agreeable royalty rate. A single exposure to the album kills that mundane theory.

It might seem as though a project born of a doped, laid-back, country-kitchen ambience had been laid aside for *Harding*'s ascetic calm. It is more likely that Dylan had compartmentalised his talent, that somehow he had managed to busy himself with two very different groups of songs simultaneously. By any possible chronology, nevertheless, he must have been writing the *Harding* songs – or have begun to write them, at the very least – while still engaged in his basement frolics with The Band. If so, it was quite a trick. It also makes a mockery of the idea that he was on the run from his career and his obligations. Instead, he was running towards something, and leaving the basement tapes behind him in the process, no sooner done than – metaphorically – erased. Why would he do such a thing?

It's not quite true, in any case, that none of the songs done at Big Pink in West Saugerties were remotely suitable for the *Harding* album. 'Too Much of Nothing', 'Tears of Rage', 'Crash on the Levee' or 'You Ain't Goin' Nowhere' have a style, tenor and content that would not have jarred with 'All Along the Watchtower' or 'Wicked Messenger'. Arguably, in fact, there is a third, spectral, never-realised album to be glimpsed on the boundary between the two projects. But Dylan drew that boundary line. When he took himself off to Nashville late in 1967 to record *Harding* it was as though the great basement songs had never existed. As far as the world knew then, that was the case. Who simply discards 'I Shall Be Released'?

No one should rely on bobdylan.com as the last word (or even the first) where the songs are concerned. Yet as a mirror, presumably, to Dylan's attitude towards his work, the site's apparently compendious database devoted to a lifetime's output is fascinating. By this reckoning, he really did not – and does not – hold the basement tapes in high regard. A great song such as 'I'm Not There' does not rate a mention. An equally significant piece such as 'Sign on the Cross' is acknowledged as having existed, but only in a vacuum: no album source is named. Of the rest, officially released and otherwise, only a handful can be said, according to the database listing, to have entered Dylan's concert repertoire. Each of those – 'I Shall Be Released', 'This Wheel's On Fire', 'Crash on the Levee' and the like – is assumed to have come into the world *anywhere but* 'the basement'. 'I Shall Be Released'? If you believe this account, the world knows of the song, it transpires, thanks only to *Bob Dylan's Greatest Hits Volume 2*.

Either he is being stupendously perverse, or he meant exactly what he said: 'I wouldn't have put 'em out.' Someone is mistaken, then. Does Dylan truly misunderstand himself so completely?

*

The literary scholar Alfred Kazin once argued[4] that 'There was a myth about America before it had a name and was a definite place – it was what lay beyond the known world'. It was Kazin's belief that American writing, the literature of successive waves of immigrants, was shaped by responses to the unguessed land itself, to the physical reality and its seemingly endless possibilities, its purity and defilement. This sounds like a fancy way to state the obvious as regards immensity, imagination, and a paradise found and lost, but the idea connects Kerouac flying down the highway to Henry David Thoreau, he who said, 'It takes a man of genius to travel in his own country.' It links Woody Guthrie on his freedom highway to Mark Twain contemplating sunrise on the Mississippi. It links Bob Dylan, still wandering on his never-ending road, to all of them.

Another statement of the obvious: the basement tapes would not have been contemplated, far less recorded, in some studio in LA or New York. If the music of America is in them, so is the land, and the sense of the land. This lost child of immigrants was looking for his country, for F. Scott Fitzgerald's 'dark fields of the republic' rolling on under the night. The search would mark Dylan's work ever after. In *Highway 61* and *Blonde on Blonde* the idea of America – and ideas about America – coursed through an imagination welded to a poetic

---

4   *A Writer's America: Landscape in Literature* (1988).

method. That method, in turn, dislocated and fractured reality. It juxtaposed, shredded and edited remembered experience in a torrent of images, in word-pictures allowed to form in whatever shape a song dictated. In 1967, that method began to fall away. From the basement onwards, Dylan began to look, hear and write in different terms. His America could still seem 'weird', as Greil Marcus has it, but it became solid, historical, actual as the roots of a tree or an ordinary life.

The motorbike accident halted one brief journey and marked the beginning of another, far longer voyage. It became the reason why Dylan is so often associated these days with Walt Whitman. As the shorthand has it, he too hears America singing. From the basement he returned, by some strange roads, to his folk roots, to the things, old and mysterious, he had first heard in folk songs.

*

One sign is that Dylan gave up on *Tarantula*. He had a contract, but no book. It is as though he had forgotten how to understand his own words. It is more likely that he had forgotten how to understand the person who wrote those words. The publishers – not exactly in sympathy with the pop star's masterwork to begin with – believed he was simply checking page proofs and perhaps making a few final changes. Instead, he was looking for a way to disown the work. The phenomenon was persistent: the art and the individual each had an effect on the other. The process was symbiotic: an alteration in one produced its echo in the other. The only mystery is the extent to which true conscious choices were ever involved.

When real decisions were required, particularly by the art of film editing, whimsy and confusion prevailed. Several other people were involved with *Eat the Document*, above all Bob Neuwirth, D.A. Pennebaker and Howard Alk. The last of these had worked on *Don't Look Back* and was supposed to do the actual editing work on the 1966 film. Dylan, however, had control; control and no apparent idea of what he wanted to do with a mass of material, nor the experience needed to turn the material into something he could understand. 'Work' dragged on, by fits and starts, until 1968, by which time Dylan was, self-evidently, out of sympathy with the entire project.

At the end of July 1966, he meanwhile took a motorbike on the road. All of his fitful work came to a stop. The tale of the Woodstock recluse – junkie, crippled, working on his comeback, weirder than ever: pick your rumour – began.

*

If Dylan's life touches legend, no one in his industry complains. Pop, as though to justify its transience, has an overdeveloped taste for the legendary, the purportedly mythic. There is no better publicity. Is Elvis alive? Is McCartney dead? What really killed Jim Morrison? How many near-forgotten just-OK performances these days fail to qualify as 'legendary'? Is there a once-obscure formerly overlooked recording that cannot be accounted a resampled treasure for resale purposes? This lends a little reflected glory, if nothing else, to the person of undoubted wit and taste who can see and hear what others failed to notice first time around. But with pop's youth long gone, these curatorial habits have become a central preoccupation, more's the pity.

It takes nerve, though, to claim that the entire group of recordings known as the basement tapes, some five hours or so in total, is in its entirety a masterwork. It took a certain amount of gall on the part of the artist, his record company and his 'producer'/guitarist, on the other hand, to maintain that the two-disc set released as *The Basement Tapes* in 1975 was an honest reflection of the work done by Dylan and the Crackers, as they sometimes called themselves, in the summer of 1967. The unalloyed truth lies somewhere between the official Columbia release and the near-exhaustive five-CD bootleg (as amended) these days known as *The Genuine Basement Tapes* and/ or *A Tree With Roots*.

The abridged and legal version has been faked up several times over. Even when re-released in elegant packaging in 2009 under the supervision of Dylan's manager Jeff Rosen, the music, though digitally refreshed, retained a spurious 'primitive' false mono. The bootleg, in ironic contrast, mostly offers basic stereo separation. The Columbia version 'compiled' by Robbie Robertson also treats the listener to a succession of guitar, piano and drum overdubs. And were Robertson and The Band entitled to near-equal billing with Dylan on the official artefact? Not, most who care would say, when certain of their contributions – certainly the sublime 'Bessie Smith', possibly 'Katie's Been Gone' and 'Ain't No More Cane' – were not even recorded during the basement sessions. Dylan was absent from fully eight of the twenty-four recordings released in 1975 and 2009, yet a clutch of his original songs, a pair of them very good indeed, are available only on the bootleg even now.

That item, in its most complete form, poses a few problems of its own. There are, roughly speaking, one hundred and a dozen or so extant 'recordings', plus or minus a few jokes and weird bits. But some of these oddment 'songs' are mere fragments, and some are false starts. Some of the jokes are chaotic pieces of nonsense – drink was taken, and a lot of weed – that clearly were never intended to receive further work, far less release. Some listings raise the 'complete' basement total to 137 (or so) by the doubtful expedient that allows inclusion to Band recordings, to a few seconds of melody, or to 'rumoured' songs. Some tracks are meanwhile of a truly abysmal audio quality, despite an impressive twenty-first-century remastering by the bootleg industry. Most of the recordings, good or bad, are cover versions of greater or lesser interest – and Dylan was soon to discover, with *Self Portrait*, that poets are forbidden hokey covers – while the remaining unreleased originals are hardly of uniform quality. But still.

If something remarkable was going on in upper New York State in the summer of 1967, you wouldn't necessarily know it from the official *Basement Tapes*. You would miss, to take the blindingly obvious, 'I Shall Be Released', 'Quinn the Eskimo' and 'I'm Not There'.[5] You would be denied three or four – the usual arguments rage – other notable Dylan songs, not least 'Sign on the Cross' and 'Silent Weekend'. You would have no sense of how any of the work was achieved. Whether you knew it or not, you would be the victim of a kind of fraud, despite the fact – too often overlooked by the devout – that the legal version is a pretty remarkable album in its own right. All that was ever required for a decent account of the basement sessions was an official release omitting those disputable Band tracks for the sake of Dylan's originals. Twenty-four or twenty-five tracks would have done it. Then even *Blonde on Blonde*'s status might have been in question.

That good? Strip away the crud from the basement sessions and there are not many works, in any art, that combine themes of death, betrayal and futility with bawdy high comedy and sardonic wit quite so naturally. Improvised poetry, that dangerous gift, has rarely been

---

5   The last two liberated finally, respectively, in 1991 as part of *The Bootleg Series Volumes 1–3* and in 2007 on the 'soundtrack album' – it is no such thing – of the Todd Haynes film *I'm Not There*.

so accomplished. And no one has worked better in what the poet William Carlos Williams called 'the American grain', meaning the ingrained thought and speech of America, than Dylan in this incarnation. That he chose to do so while the rest of his generation were busy about the child's errand called the summer of love only adds to the piquancy of it all, as though a grown-up had quit the big, foolish party to get some work done in peace and quiet. Add also that the survivor of a locked rear tyre glimpsed a wheel on fire as America sank deeper into the Vietnam apocalypse. Dylan's songs from the second half of 1967 are strangely lit, as though glowing in the darkness. There's a lot, all in all, that can be said about things found down in the basement.

*

There is one thing that should perhaps be said first. Hidden from public view or not, the basement sessions marked the point at which Dylan the unquenchably modern artist became a figure of – and far within – the past. His work in the summer of 1967, and thereafter, became an example of 'learning to go forward by turning back the clock'.[6] Far from reaching to the presumed outer limits of the counter-culture, he laid claim to, and was claimed by, an American past. Instead of searching for the future he went beyond time. This was, of course, the most wilfully avant-garde thing he could have done.

Among other things, it no doubt helps to explain why he was unimpressed by the arrival of the Beatles' *Sgt Pepper's Lonely Hearts Club Band*. When half the world (or so it seemed) was busy being staggered that June by a gaudy audio revolution, Dylan heard only 'production', artifice that he could not – and would not – attempt to match. He saw no point in it. He liked the songs, or so he claimed, but thought *Pepper* 'a very indulgent' and overproduced album. It was as though the Liverpudlians had created a trippy *son et lumière* in day-glo colours while he was down in the cellar with a jug of moonshine knocking together something gnarled and mysterious from lathe, plaster and recovered timbers. But you could just as easily assert that the Beatles had made something that was utterly alien to Dylan. He – and what would the freaks have said? – just didn't get it. He was in another place, another time. His reaction to *Pepper* stood for his reaction

---

6   From Dylan's liner notes, fascinating in themselves, for the 1993 album of old blues and folk songs *World Gone Wrong*.

to all that was going on in the world, in the now. He had no thoughts, publicly, on Vietnam, on cities in flames, on civil rights. A few remarks suggest he wasn't taken with hippy notions. Instead, he was spending a lot of time singing old songs – some of them newly written – and looking at the Bible. For clues.

In those days, nevertheless, rock's royalty were supposed to 'respond' to the innovations of their peers as though to gauntlets tossed. The Rolling Stones, and numberless others, certainly saw *Pepper* in those terms, much as Brian Wilson had set the Beach Boys to work to answer *Rubber Soul* with *Pet Sounds*. Had he been fatuous, and had he cared, Dylan might have seen the reputation of *Blonde on Blonde* as turf to be defended in 1967, of all years. Instead, to all appearances, he goofed around with his musicians. Where the Beatles had toiled hour after meticulous hour[7] to echo the irreality of the acid experience, Dylan just played his guitar. Old songs, new songs, bits of songs, joke songs, stumbling-drunk attempts at songs: Garth Hudson of the Crackers/Band took care of the minimal technical details while the singer presided for a few lazy months over the organic growth of what could easily have become another decisive double set. And then he forgot all about it.

Can he be believed? But then, what other interpretation could there be? It was as though certain Woodstock rooms were turned into a kind of laid-back laboratory for experimental work on the genetic code of American music. Yet when Dylan did set about making a 'real' album towards the end of the year, the result – no less profound – was something else again. The songs on *John Wesley Harding* were news even to the guys in the basement. That fact of itself is a strange and still puzzling clue to what was running through his head.

The *Harding* songs were prefigured, nevertheless, by the work done so casually at Woodstock. Just 26, Dylan altered the terms of engagement for 'rock', shifting his gaze from modern to ancient, changing his tenses. Yet hadn't he been schooled in tradition? Weren't the hoary, shaggy comedies and ragged morality tales of the basement tapes of a piece with all his apprentice folk work in the Village? If that's true then the years of Dylan's greatest public glory are the years that seem anomalous. So were *Bringing It All Back Home*, *Highway 61* and *Blonde*

---

7   According to Ian MacDonald's *Revolution in the Head*, 'A Day in the Life' alone
     required around 34 hours of studio time.

on Blonde the deviations, albeit triumphant, in his career? Not exactly, but the question has a point.

How does an artist relate to tradition? T.S. Eliot, another poet with whose name Dylan has been entangled for no very good reason, made much of this. When you deal in allusion and quotation – or risk the charge of plagiarism – you need to keep an argument handy. Eliot's *Waste Land* is in one part a collage of words, symbols and ideas, much as Dylan has cut and pasted, especially in recent years. It is an artistic method, indisputably, but it can justify, or appear to justify, almost anything, good, bad or indifferent. Cultural reference becomes a kind of self-defence, as though no one would dare pick on the guy who numbers his allies among the quick and the dead. Who would quibble with the basement tapes when Dylan was dabbling – he was, wasn't he? – in the very essence of America? Hence the alarming tendency to treat each whistle and fart on the tapes with reverence. Even when the noise in question is of no account, and was never regarded, by its makers, as being of any account. Even when it's a pig. Some who have written about the basement tapes like the apparent idea of the recordings so much they forget to say that, in fact, the listening experience is not wholly exquisite.

It is unquestionable, nevertheless, that a different sort of poet emerged with these tapes. The icy urban hipster had disappeared. His embrace of chaos was reimagined. His words and music acquired new connections, different root systems. They became, in all definitions of the word, historic. You could say that Dylan was just 'learning to go forward' by stepping back, but the act takes on another layer of meaning when you remember the times. In 1967, only the future was supposed to matter.

The word historic, like 'tradition', like 'folk', is a problem word. Greil Marcus has evoked, with some eloquence, the 'old, weird America' as one entry point to the basement tapes. With less clarity, others have approached The Band's first pair of albums by the same misty route. One reaction is simple: a great deal of actual American history, some of it important, is absent from those artefacts. In Dylan's case, history itself is tangential. Finding his basement songs prefigured by Harry Smith's *Anthology of American Folk Music*, or connected to this old blues or that, is akin to reading Eliot only through the prism of his quotations and allusions, as though those were, of themselves, the point and meaning of the poem. As methodology, it's dubious. Dylan himself has taken in recent years – not plausibly, but insistently – to dismissing the influence of Smith's collection on the development of his work. He doesn't care to conceive of art in those terms, in the traditional, if you like, terms of tradition. These were – a better description – deserter's songs in the midst of war and national turmoil. Or as the weary joke in *Chronicles* goes: 'Spokesman Denies That He's a Spokesman.'

*

It's rough and ready music, albeit delivered by experts. Even in its most recent digitally remastered (official) form, where the pretence of primitivism is less evident, it would make many a studio engineer wince. The earliest of the cuts that remain in bootleg form are meanwhile hideous, technically speaking. For all that Dylan has complained about the cold, dead hand of modern recording technology, the tapes approach the other extreme. Some people mistake that for their point. But then, the tapes were never intended – or so we are asked to assume – as more than an aide-memoire, something for 'the publishing company', recorded while Dylan and The Band had their fun. That might have been true when the sessions began, but it ceased to be true long before their end. Even an artist as perverse as Dylan must have known what he had achieved. The songs were too good to be dismissed.

The bootleggers would prove it before long. At around the time Dylan was releasing *Nashville Skyline*, successor to *Harding*, in the spring of 1969, that 14-track acetate made 'only for other artists to record those songs' was returning to haunt him. The entrepreneurs behind 'Trade Mark of Quality' and its cigar-smoking, shades-wearing, pig's head logo – was Albert Grossman flattered? – were putting together *Great White Wonder*, their cheapo (but never cheap) tribute to genius. The double album was a ragbag. It contained only seven of the basement tracks. Nevertheless, it began the process by which Dylan became – according to the people who measure such things on behalf of the record industry – the most bootlegged artist 'in history'. It also launched the hunt for every last scrap of tape recorded in Woodstock in 1967.

No one really knows what bootlegging has cost Dylan or his record company. Even though he and his manager have been attempting to kill off that industry since the release of *Biograph* in 1985 and the commencement of his own 'official' *Bootleg Series* in 1991, the sums involved must run into many millions. Even now, with so much material on legal sale – but not, conspicuously, the full run of basement recordings – the appetite for concert bootlegs, in particular, is undiminished. There are many hundreds of 'Bob Dylan albums' in circulation, capturing this show or that, on sale – this is barely an exaggeration – the moment the artist has left the stage. Outtakes from his visits to the studio appear and reappear. Tapes of rehearsals, casual sessions with Johnny Cash or George Harrison, things that even Dylan has probably forgotten: it's all grist to a giant mill. Much of it is dire; some of it has caused the singer's admirers to pause, time and again, and wonder *What was he thinking?* when he suppressed this or that recording. Some even contend that some strange conspiracy-within-a-conspiracy is going on.

For present purposes, one point is worth stating: in 1967, Dylan preferred artistic integrity to money, and he has maintained his position ever since. An authorised *Genuine Basement Tapes* would attract the curious in their hordes even now. It would stand very high in his canon. But he made his decision and he sticks to it. He 'never really liked' those songs. And that, supposedly, is that.

*

Can you have serious fun? Some of the basement songs are indeed mere knockabout, but others are fully formed works written and performed in earnest. Some have wondered what Dylan might have made of them in one of the big Columbia studios in Nashville or New York, with expert help to hold everything in balance. Others among us believe that an essence would have been lost. Only in the twenty-first century, acting as his own producer in the guise of chilly Jack Frost, has Dylan come to terms with the studio. (It doesn't mean he's *happy* there, of course.) In years past impatience, unhappiness with a sterile environment, and the pressures that come with absolute control have blighted his judgement too often. In Woodstock, for a while, Dylan was liberated from all of that.

To what purpose? Strip away the legend of those basement tapes and consider their place within his creative progress. Before, there was *Blonde on Blonde*; afterwards there was *John Wesley Harding*. Where does the basement work fit in, if it does fit in? In terms of songwriting, there are clear links and connections. Bear in mind yet again, though, that Dylan himself has treated these 1967 pieces as mere diversions, as being of no account. He has returned, fitfully, to a few of the songs over the years, but refused consistently to value them as they are valued by others. You can say he's dead wrong, but his attitude deserves respect. After all, this trove could have helped him out of a few tight spots in succeeding years. Botched albums could have been rescued, more than once, thanks to things lying ignored in this catalogue. He has never made that compromise. Perhaps he still believes that this lauded collection was a wrong turn, speedily reassessed and discarded. It's impossible to agree.

The Woodstock work, some of it at least, can be depicted as a bridge spanning time and states of mind: many have made that argument, too. You can trace the lyrical path from *Another Side of Bob Dylan* to *Blonde on Blonde* via *Bringing It All Back Home* and *Highway 61*. The writing can be mapped as it develops. What seemed at the time to be giant leaps – an illusion explicable by the choice of instruments and backing musicians – stand now as logical steps. No such sense can be made of the transition between *Blonde on Blonde* and *Harding* unless account is taken of the basement songs. That achieved, things begin to fall into place; they add up; the connections can be made. It's certainly more than can be said about the gulf, the sudden sense of dislocation, between *Harding* and *Nashville Skyline*.

That, though, was 'the amnesia', when Dylan was struck blind and creatively dumb. Or so he said. It becomes the most intriguing episode in this long career. All of a sudden Bob Dylan loses the ability to write, to understand himself, to cope with 'Bob Dylan' and all of the consequences thereof. What's more, he didn't see it coming. And he had – because fate will have its revenge – nothing to say about it. But while there are links between the basement work and *Harding*, and while you can just about trace the links between *Blonde on Blonde* and an album made with just bass, guitar, drums, piano and a touch of pedal steel, the thematic connections can be overstressed. You risk losing sight of what the basement tapes signify in their own right, and on their own terms. The song known variously as 'I'm Not There', 'I'm Not There, I'm Gone' and 'I'm Not There (1956)' is an extraordinary case in point.

As noted, you won't find it on the considerable song database at bobdylan.com, where even songs he didn't actually write are included – by association or mistake? – in his virtual *oeuvre*. You can hear it, presented almost as an afterthought, on the non-soundtrack to the 2007 non-biopic *I'm Not There*. But here's a puzzle for those who like to talk about 'America's greatest living poet': as far as this song goes, no one can agree on the words.

Dylan isn't helping. He discarded the piece, he said once, for the simple reason that it wasn't 'there'. The lyrics are semi-improvised, sometimes ungrammatical, in places incomprehensible. It has often been assumed that he was making this one up as he went along. On the other hand, what seemed to be a partial manuscript turned up in the fanzine *The Telegraph*, having been authenticated – convincingly – by the late John Bauldie and Clinton Heylin.[8] If the singer typed up at least some of the words, how can they be improvised? That might depend on the mood or state Dylan was in when he did the typing. Equally, the verses that do not survive on paper have been heard or misheard by various people, listening hard, in various ways. And each version is perplexing. Compare four different readings from people who have listened to this song *a lot*.

> Now I've cried tonight
> Like I cried the night before
> And I'll feast on her eyes
> But I dream about the door

Or:

> Now I'll cry tonight
> Like I cried the night before
> And I'm released on the heights in
> But I'll dream about the door

Or:

> Now I've cried tonight
> Like I cried the night before
> And I'm leased on the highs
> But I dream about the door

Or:

---

8   See Heylin's *Revolution in the Air – The Songs of Bob Dylan Volume 1: 1957–73* (2009) for a fascinating account of the manuscript and a better-than-most stab at the mesmerising, infuriating song.

Now I've cried tonight
Like I cried the night before,
And I'm knees on the hassle,
But I dream about the door.

Clinton Heylin, in contrast, prefers 'I'm leased on the *height*', but rightly mentions 'the border between *non sequitur* and nonsense'. I hear 'heights', plural, but wouldn't bet my life on it, or begin to attempt to tell anyone what a poet whose words cannot be deciphered is on about, in a song that shimmers with possibilities and uncertainties, possesses few fixed or obvious meanings, and yet leaves you believing you know *exactly* why this song exists, and why it is a great song. Parse that.

It might not matter: what are the chances? People who want to argue over Dylan and literature, for or against, have to contend with this 'Rosetta Stone', as it has been called, and with what it does with categories in the art of writing. The standard literary education that insists on interpretation and explication goes badly wrong when it touches this aspect of Dylan's work. If it's a stretch to accept that a piece of writing can have multiple meanings, how hard is it to grasp that the writer might be toying with the *idea* of meaning?

Dylan has hinted at this possibility often enough. People, he has said, can take whatever meanings from the songs they happen to find. But the offer – for what does he *mean* by it? – makes those same people uneasy. If meaning is fluid, no statement, and least of all an uncertain, improvised piece of song-verse, is worth a damn.

He'd probably call that a victory. Ever since he ceased to point fingers he has questioned certainty and the belief in certainty. His own identity problems might be his starting point, but his mid-'60s jokes about accepting chaos ('Chaos is a friend of mine') solve nothing. If nothing is fixed, where does he stand? Where can he stand? This way of talking about Dylan – and Dylan's way of talking about himself – disappears, sooner or later, into fundamental inanity. By no accident, a person disappears in the process.

*

As far as the world knew, he was doing nothing – 'absolutely nothing', as Robbie Robertson told a reporter – in 1967. After the accident, Allen Ginsberg had brought to Woodstock a box full of books. In effect, there arrived an entire Ginsbergian library of authorised poets for the benefit of the invalid soul (who nevertheless mentioned that he would be up and about in a couple of weeks). Here, reportedly, were works by Thomas Wyatt, Thomas Campion, Emily Dickinson, Arthur Rimbaud, Federico García Lorca, Guillaume Apollinaire, William Blake and Walter 'Walt' Whitman. It was your basic 1960s poet's gift hamper. Set aside the writers with whom, as we know, Dylan was already familiar, and interesting possibilities arise. Wyatt's masterclasses on the art of the sonnet for one, Dickinson on God and brevity for another. We only have Ginsberg's word for any of it. The more interesting detail regarding Dylan's reading habits in 1967 involves a statement by his mother. Beatty would tell Toby Thompson that at around this time her son was devoting many hours to reading the Bible, that 'a huge Bible open on a stand in the middle of his study' was his preoccupation. Scripture, she said after a visit, 'gets the most attention'. It seems the old aptitude of the Hibbing bar mitzvah boy, always a quick learner, had been rediscovered.

The precise date at which Bible study became a habit isn't clear, however. The point at which an individual with an addiction problem felt the need for religious texts – a moment in Manchester would count as too perfect – can only be guessed. Beatty's description does suggest that Dylan was edging towards the deity, if not towards being born again, a lot earlier than most people have realised. Then again, one of the still-unreleased basement recordings makes the process of change perfectly plain.

'Sign on the Cross' begins seriously enough and retreats, by stages, into a Hank Williams preaching spoof. The comedy is a little ill-judged, but the song remains powerful. The writer who had taken religion very ill only a couple of years before in that fun rocker 'Highway 61 Revisited', a cartoon song in which the aims and claims of Old Testament faith are mocked – whistled at, indeed – here thinks again. For this singer this new piece of work, written at this point in his life, is extraordinary. After all, for an artist born a Jew, and raised in Orthodoxy, what would it mean to write and perform a song entitled 'Sign on the Cross', a song whose semi-chorus attests, 'And that old sign on the cross / Still worries me'?

On this point, the New Testament of the Christians doesn't vary much. In Matthew (27:37) the tale is unvarnished. The sign says, 'This is Jesus, King of the Jews.' In Mark, Luke and John we hear of Pilate the Roman's decision to place the description – or mockery, or warning – above the bloodied head of the tortured man in Hebrew, Greek and Latin: 'Jesus of Nazareth the King of the Jews.' What was it about this image that worried Dylan enough to provoke a song?

He had denied his Jewish faith and origins often enough. His relationship with his father had been difficult, meanwhile, until he had decided to pretend, to insist, that his parents had somehow ceased to exist. In reality, his father was Abram, known as Abe, a common enough Jewish name in either form. That playful *Highway 61* song had commenced:

Oh God said to Abraham, 'Kill me a son'
Abe says, 'Man, you must be puttin' me on'
God say, 'No.' Abe say, 'What?'
God say, 'You can do what you want, Abe, but
The next time you see me comin' you better run . . .'

On *Highway 61* it was all a mere comedic conceit, of course, a piece of hip satire. On the other hand, if Abe happens to be the name by which the world knows your father, the joke could carry a certain weight. If you thereafter, born Jewish, write a song that worries over the central symbol of Christianity, and by implication over the ancient blood libel, things have become very complicated indeed. Then there's the third puzzle: a bedevilled pop star associating himself with the King of the Jews? Perhaps 'Highway 61 Revisited' wasn't a joke at all. The mystery of the preaching, born-again Bob Dylan, he of hellfire rhetoric, begins, nevertheless, with 'Sign on the Cross'. While the rest of the world was still talking of his art in terms of alienation and 'existentialism', even of nihilism, he had begun to embrace a rabbi's concerns, but on Christ's terms.

But I was lost on the moon
As I heard that front door slam
And that old sign on the cross
Still worries me

Robert Shelton once pointed out the obvious: there is a lot of nothing in the basement songs. 'Too Much of Nothing'; 'Nothing Was Delivered'; 'nothing is better / nothing is best'; people who 'ain't goin' nowhere': Dylan could not have been more plain as he explored this stretch of Desolation Row. Having run out of road, he wasn't holding out too much hope for his generation. 'The waters of oblivion' held them; the best they could do was say hello, aimlessly, as they drifted and sank. 'This Wheel's On Fire', autobiographical or not, is meanwhile wholly apocalyptic. It exists in a place 'after ev'ry plan had failed'. 'Tears of Rage', one of the greatest of these songs, somehow combining hints of *King Lear* with the sense of an America turning on itself 'on Independence Day', carries the bleakest note of all: 'life is brief'. Shakespeare emerges from his alley with a late tragedy.

The singer has meanwhile lost interest in allusive wit. Most of the time, this Dylan is blunt. He has his linguistic fun, but wordplay for its own sake, one of the delights of *Blonde on Blonde*, has begun to fade. The language is declarative. Even a short, apparently jolly song like 'Odds and Ends' has a cold heart, a matter-of-fact brutality. Each of three bare verses concludes with the same line: 'Lost time is not found again.'

Some of this had something – more than one thing – to do with The Band. The musicians who couldn't achieve the quicksilver changes required for *Blonde on Blonde* are vindicated on the basement recordings. Sometimes the music ambles, sometimes it lopes along. At moments, particularly on the cover versions, there are rumbling echoes of an older world. At other times there is that apparent contradiction, a laid-back intensity. Less than half a year after the last – so it seems – basement recordings were made, with only the 14-song demo to go on, Jann Wenner would write a front-page piece for *Rolling Stone* ('Dylan's Basement Tape Should Be Released') alerting fans to a new, 'distinct sound'. The magazine's founder did not explain – for rock journalism never can – what was involved, or what was implied. Yet in terms of 1960s pop music, of industry standards and professionalism, this was anti-art. In Nashville, Dylan had employed the best in the business to achieve some very tricky things. Here he was employing another kind of expertise, and on a wholly different basis, to explore the kind of music from which Nashville's Music Row (and a lot else besides) had first arisen. Or – for why not take the artist at his word? – he was just making a few tapes with some friends to satisfy the suits.

In either case, The Band were essential. It is impossible to imagine some of these songs without them. That's most obviously true, oddly enough, on the cover versions. The musicians served Dylan's songs well, sometimes exquisitely, but the idea that the making of these basement tapes was a casual affair is another of the singer's fictions. Patently, there was a lot more going on.

In piece after piece Dylan is groping for something, if not for God

– not quite, not yet – then for the theological sense of things that would animate *John Wesley Harding*. That too sprang from the older, other America. In the central basement songs, Dylan experiments, here and there, with (mock) biblical language: the occasional 'unto', the prophecies of 'the meanest flood / That anybody's seen', the advice on forgiving the sick before attempting to heal them. Sometimes he is explicit. Thus: 'In the day of confession / We cannot mock a soul.'

The most obvious product of time spent with that big Bible is 'I Shall Be Released'. The song is generally regarded, reasonably enough, as an anthem for human rights, as another 'political' song. It also exists, in every particular, as a spiritual, and therefore as one profound consequence of America's history. In black slave tradition, after all, such a song involves a liberation that is both religious and secular. The second verse fits that old model almost exactly.

They say ev'ry man needs protection
They say ev'ry man must fall
Yet I swear I see my reflection
Some place so high above this wall
I see my light come shining
From the west unto the east
Any day now, any day now
I shall be released

Elsewhere there is a lot of sheer fun in the basement recordings, a sense of liberation as Dylan and The Band make music for its own sake. The fun is drunken, stoned, carnal; the choices of cover versions endlessly fascinating. They run the gamut, yet it is hard to see that any sort of profound statement – the *Americana* thing – is being attempted. It's more likely that old numbers were chosen without much premeditation. Dylan's intuitions were always his guide.

One of the loveliest of the covers is, for example, Brendan Behan's 'Banks of the Royal Canal/The Auld Triangle'. This one was new to The Band, entirely outside the scope of their experience; Dylan had it from who-knows-where (probably not from Dominic Behan). Nevertheless, on the tape all concerned are in sympathy with a song set long ago and far away in a Dublin prison. How does it connect with a Hank Snow tune, a Johnny Cash song, with a sea shanty, a blues, with the old western number 'Hills of Mexico', with Dylan's own songs? There's nothing obvious. The single plausible idea is that this compendium – this *Self Portrait*, if you like – springs from Dylan's idea of what folk music is, and what its mysteries signify. That, on the other hand, is probably just agreeable speculation. It could be that he and his musicians were only warming up.

The final important thing separating these recordings from *Blonde on Blonde* is that Dylan's voice had changed, becoming at once warmer, more raucous, with more of a country inflection, and somehow – whatever the word conveys – spookier. It could be that the world tour had taken its physical toll. As subsequent decades would show, too many concerts would ravage the vocal cords of a singer who never did acquire Caruso's range. It's just as likely that the strange, familiar phenomenon named Dylan was evident. Here, again, was the metamorphic process that had caused him to sound like an aged bluesman while still a youth and, soon after these basement tapes, would grant him the voice of a 30-year-old teenager. At spots in between he seemed to undergo a transformation as one of his lives ended and another began. It might have been a species of impersonation, of performance, but that's not how it sounds. It sounds like something fundamental to a personality, and to an art.

*

While Dylan was recovering from the motorbike crash, Grossman had kept himself busy. The artist's five-year Columbia contract had expired, save for those few songs still owing, and Albert believed a better deal could be found. There was no reason to doubt it. Negotiations with the MGM label were initiated, but in the end came to nothing. A 'greatest hits' album was put out as a holding operation in March of 1967 and *Don't Look Back* gained a limited release soon after. In the end, inevitably, Dylan got his (greatly improved) royalties deal, but despite all of Grossman's moves and manoeuvres it was again with Columbia. The money was good, but Dylan won something more important: near-complete control over his recorded material.

This was, to say the least, one of the sweeter ironies. At just around the time the contract was signed in July of '67 he was putting 'I Shall Be Released', 'This Wheel's On Fire', 'I'm Not There' and others besides onto Garth Hudson's tape reels while dismissing the idea of handing any of *that* stuff to Columbia. It begins to seem as though he must be taken at his word: he never did want to 'put 'em out'. He could not have been denying Albert his publishing rights, given the 14-track acetate of basement songs that led to numerous lucrative cover versions. Nor could Dylan have been toying with Columbia during those summer months. The contract was settled in July; the *John Wesley Harding* recordings began in October, days (if that) after he emerged from 'the basement'. The single fact is that he wrote and recorded songs of astonishing quality in an astonishing quantity – and rejected them for his own use.

Perhaps Dylan had better things to think about: that July he became a father for the second time, when Sara gave birth to a daughter. Parenthood didn't keep him out of the basement for long, but nor did domestic happiness impinge on his creative decisions. He meant to abandon some of his finest work, come what may. A nagging refrain can be heard once again: *Who does that?*

Gods and Gunfighters

John Wesley Harding was a fearful album – just dealing with fear, [laughing] but dealing with the devil in a fearful way, almost. All I wanted to do was to get the words right. It was courageous to do it because I could have not done it, too.

Interview with *Rolling Stone*, November 1978

BY DYLAN'S OWN ACCOUNT, THE SONG 'JOHN WESLEY HARDING' WAS first conceived as an epic ballad of the old sort, the sort he knew inside out, and from the roots upwards. Its opening line was entirely, or archly, conventional as it introduced that 'friend to the poor'. Then the writer's energy, interest or patience fell away. So he said.

Late in 1969 he would tell *Rolling Stone*:

Well, I called it that because I had that song, 'John Wesley Harding', which started out to be a long ballad. I was gonna write a ballad on . . . like maybe one of those old cowboy . . . you know, a real long ballad. But in the middle of the second verse I got tired. I had a tune, and I didn't want to waste the tune; it was a nice little melody, so I just wrote a quick third verse, and I recorded that.

Whatever the case, the finished song is over almost as soon as it has begun: three verses and out. After it is done the listener knows scarcely more, in terms of mundane biographical information, than he knew at the beginning, and most of what he is told has no basis in reality.

A good thing, too. Whether thanks to dumb luck or to a peerless inner editor, the sketch is the picture entire, complete in its bones. A dozen more verses on the imagined adventures of a reinvented real person, even in the best traditions of cowboy legend, would have added nothing useful. Dylan here is stripping down a myth, subtly but unerringly. He knows better than anyone that folk legends are most effective when they are most mysterious. 'Bob Dylan' was also an elaborate piece of hokum, after all.

Needless to say, and not for the first time or the last in his treatments of real individuals, this John Wesley Harding bears scant relationship to John Wesley *Hardin* (1853–95), a racist murderer from central Texas who killed, so they say, 'well over 20 men' in a single decade, launching his career when he was a mere 15. Like the Earp brothers, Jesse James or Billy the Kid, Wes Hardin was no Robin Hood. On the other hand, the song 'John Wesley Harding' – Why him? 'Fits right in tempo,' the writer said; 'Just what I had at hand.' – is in a line of descent, more or less direct, from the interlocking huddle of medieval ballads celebrating England's woodland outlaw-in-green. All the clichés are present and correct: the poor have a champion, lady at his side, gun 'in every hand', who has never been 'known' – the song mimics the rumours from which legends are born – 'to make a foolish move'. Yet implicit in Dylan's work is a question: why did – why do – people sing songs to honour and remember those who put themselves beyond the law? Why embrace the myth? Who needs heroes?

It has something to do, no doubt, with powerlessness and power. In 1939, to take only one example, Woody Guthrie had written 'The Ballad of Pretty Boy Floyd', a song celebrating a murderous bank robber. The young Dylan had adapted/borrowed one of its better lines – 'Some will rob you with a six-gun, and some with a fountain pen' – and in 1988 would record the song for a Smithsonian Guthrie/Lead Belly tribute album. So was Charles Arthur Floyd, shot dead at 30, just one of the Depression's multitude of victims, driven to a life of crime by hard times and injustice, or merely a parasite? Tens of thousands of Oklahomans turned out for the funeral of this 'friend to the poor', many in the belief that he had been executed by the cops. Pretty Boy had hit the banks that preyed on common folk. Did that place him among the 'social bandits', the 'bringers of justice and social redistributors' identified by the historian Eric Hobsbawm[1] as common in stories and legends around the world? Or was he, as Hardin certainly was, just scum?

The answer depended on what people wanted to believe. Hobsbawm explained that 'banditry as a social phenomenon . . . is about class, wealth and power in peasant societies'. Dylan, ever fascinated by the honesty required to live outside the law, would echo that thought when

---

1   *Bandits*, (1969, rev. ed. 2000).

he came to write about Billy the Kid, George Jackson, 'Hurricane' Carter and Joey Gallo. But the nineteenth-century cowboys singing 'Jesse James', 'Sam Bass' or 'Cole Younger' were not given to Marxist analysis. Often one step ahead of the law themselves, they were showing solidarity among thieves, celebrating their friends and people like them. The songs, bluntly, made excuses. Such was Dylan's hint when he sang,

> 'Twas down in Chaynee County
> A time they talk about
> With his lady by his side
> He took a stand

Whatever 'they' might talk about, no such place as Chaynee County featured in Hardin's history, if it even existed.[2] Any 'lady' by his side was as often as not a prostitute. Any 'stand' he took was invariably for his own benefit. If any situation was 'straightened out' by Wes Hardin an innocent person, usually a poor black person, lay murdered in the aftermath. 'I never killed anyone that didn't need killing,' he boasted once. There's a choice, therefore: either Dylan is just a sucker for a 'social bandit', always prepared to overlook the bloody details, or he knows better. On this occasion, the fact that his song 'about' a real person is pure fiction suggests the latter.

When Dylan went back on the road in 1974 with The Band for his so-called 'Comeback Tour' there was general surprise, reportedly, that he opened his account with 'Hero Blues', a little known mostly-nothing of an early (1962–3) song reportedly intended for *The Times They Are a-Changin'* but withheld until the appearance of 2010's *The Witmark Demos*. The rebuke to an expectant, primed-for-adoration audience in 1974 was veiled, but firm. In his opening shows in Chicago he fiddled a little with the words, but the published version will serve.

---

2   There is a Hardin County in Texas, however, founded by a family member once known as a 'distinguished judge'. The killer was not, on the face of it, a social misfit. His father was a Methodist preacher and lawyer; his grandfather had served in the Congress of the Republic of Texas. The gunfighter's immediate family were most closely connected with Comanche County. The footnote's footnote recalls that the middle name of the Texan Buddy Holly was Hardin.

Well, when I'm dead
No more good times will I crave
When I'm dead
No more good times will I crave
You can stand and shout hero
All over my lonesome grave.

Dylan's horror of being anyone's hero is at the core of his own heroic persona. His tendency to extol heroes, or to render dubious characters as heroic, is another matter. His Billy the Kid is rather closer to handsome Kris Kristofferson in mad Sam Peckinpah's 1973 movie version of a disputed tale than he is to feral, plug-ugly William Bonney. His Joey is a stoical, hounded man of honour, not the psychopathic New York mobster Joseph 'Crazy Joe' Gallo. The Hurricane of Dylan's song bears only a sketchy resemblance to Rubin Carter, the transgressive boxer twice convicted of a triple murder. Mercifully, the singer did get the revolutionary Jackson right – or rather, he got the man right and omitted certain details – but Dylan scores low, generally, whenever he deals with the documented record of anyone's life, even the villains. William Devereux Zantzinger did not kill Hattie Carroll 'with a cane that he twirled 'round his diamond ring finger' at Baltimore's Emerson Hotel in 1963 – and he took his resentment at the libel to his grave – though he probably bullied the poor woman towards a coronary. Dylan may despise journalists, in other words, but his own journalistic failings are numerous. So what is going on in the abbreviated tale of John Wesley Harding?

'When the legend becomes fact, print the legend,' as the hack editor famously observes in John Ford's *The Man Who Shot Liberty Valance* (1962). The smarter gunfighters – never a stiff competition – understood that game long before the West was law-abiding. Dime novelists such as E.Z.C. Judson ('Ned Buntline'), numerous anonymous cowboy balladeers and Hollywood (from the very beginning) had been putting a shine on shit-coloured reality long before Dylan explored American exceptionalism. It is a commonplace now, and it was no secret even when he was assembling the *John Wesley Harding* album in the space of nine hours over three studio days in late 1967, but there was nothing very heroic about the Old West.

Its 'code' was a myth; its gunfighters sociopaths. A great many people were shot in the back. Often enough, like Pat Floyd Garrett, they were assassinated in a cowardly ambush (Garrett while taking a leak). Many died in pathetic squabbles, as often as not because one or other party was drunk. Some were killed for no reason at all – Hardin supposedly murdered a man for snoring – always granting that their assailants could shoot anything with a Colt Civilian .45, a weapon whose cartridges failed continually and whose accuracy was minimal beyond six yards. Larceny, illiteracy, alcoholism, pox, genocide, minimal democracy, wholesale fraud, economic deprivation, sexual abuse and cold-blooded murder are more pertinent historical themes for the old frontier. The yodelling, strumming cowboy meanwhile was an underpaid, overworked, sleep-deprived and bored-witless peasant labourer living on 'sonofabitch stew' in a nasty and dangerous trade. He didn't play guitar, not in the nineteenth century, but sawed on a cheap fiddle. He did sing, though. He can even claim to have contributed, with his comic 'talk songs', to the talking blues of Oklahoma's Woody Guthrie. But a figure of romance, honour and heroism? There are precious few examples.

Something in the American psyche found the facts intolerable. The cowboy and the horse-soldier and the gunfighter were therefore imbued with a simple native decency (and a racial 'purity') that was supposed to serve as a contrast to the corrupt, 'cosmopolitan' and soft ways of the city. The aftermath of the Civil War and the South's experience of vindictive 'Reconstruction' explains much of this (the record of genocide against the country's natives explains most of the rest). In reality, invariably, the famous outlaws had fought for the Confederacy or been raised within it; the lawmen had not. Yet almost from the beginning – which is to say the moment of their passing – sanitised 'heroes' were in demand. When Hollywood took up the challenge, the cause of truth was lost in the dust.

That said, even the mock-chivalric nonsense of the 'Code of the West' was probably a reaction to brutal reality. It provided both an explanation and a justification for homicidal behaviour. In a peculiar way it gave dignity, even honour, to hoodlums. That's what they told themselves, at any rate. As one biographer of Billy the Kid has put it:

> Among the young bravos who flocked to the frontier, the code governed male relationships. 'I'll die before I run,' enjoined the tradition of violent self-defense and self-redress. The code had originated in Texas, flowing northward on the great cattle trails of the post-Civil War decades. Demanding personal courage and pride and reckless disregard for life, it commanded practitioners to avenge all insult and wrong, real or

imagined; never to retreat before an aggressor; and to respond with any degree of violence, even death.[3]

An obvious point of comparison with Dylan's song is the old ballad 'Jesse James', reputedly composed by an 'otherwise unknown' individual named Billy Gashade. It eulogises a former Confederate guerrilla turned killer and thief who supposedly 'stole from the rich and gave to the poor'. Bascom Lamar Lunsford recorded a version in the 1920s, but it was Guthrie, yet again, who turned Jesse into a Robin Hood (and later into Christ's musical twin). James had robbed banks and railroads: therefore, clearly, he was a friend to the downtrodden peasantry. The fact that the James-Younger gang showed no mercy to the occasional interfering peasant was neither here nor there. Hence a central truth about folk song: it can be as 'authentic' as hell, but it needn't be true. The young Dylan certainly performed a ballad – there are multiple versions – that probably first appeared in the aftermath of Jesse's death at the hand of Robert Ford, a fellow gang member, in 1882. Dylan undoubtedly knew the old standard well enough, indeed, to create a lyrical counterpoint in 'Harding'. And he had his own ideas about outlaws.

> Ain't gonna hang no picture
> Ain't gonna hang no picture frame
> Well, I might look like Robert Ford
> But I feel just like a Jesse James[4]

Wes Hardin's world-view was formed amid virulent and unforgiving Texan racism in the wake of the North's victory. No one who knew him thought he was crazy, and thousands of his own folk applauded his murders. He was a cop-killer, nevertheless, and good at it: he took his time aiming with those miserable handguns. Hardin was good, too, at manufacturing the sort of self-serving post facto excuses to which Dylan has always been supremely alert.[5] Yet 'John Wesley

---

3   Robert M. Utley, *Billy the Kid: A Short and Violent Life* (1990). Utley notes that the code as a theme 'is prevalent throughout the historical literature of Texas and New Mexico'.

4   'Outlaw Blues', *Bringing It All Back Home* (1965).

5   *The Life of John Wesley Hardin as Written by Himself* (1896, repr. 1961) is nevertheless these days respected among historians of the American West as a classic of the type, and not badly written, they say.

Harding', at first hearing, serves up nothing more than the usual western myth. Why?

It is probably more interesting to ask why a film director such as Ford, one of Dylan's favourites, felt compelled to turn a brief, chaotic period in the republic's history into the theatre of essential American virtue. The manufacture of John Wayne is the obvious case in point. Here was an impersonator who was taken to represent something authentic – a true fiction, if you like. As though to give a postmodern edge to it all, Wayne himself seemed almost to believe the hoax. Yet he inspired the breast-beating patriotism that has run like a scarlet thread through American conservatism from the House Un-American Activities Committee to Vietnam, Iraq and beyond. At his death the actor, the invention, was mourned sincerely as a 'true American hero'. And he was John Ford's favourite leading man.

So this Wes Hardin 'took his stand'? In his own version, certainly, the killer once faced down Wild Bill Hickok (a contrary account says he escaped through a window in his nightshirt). But Hardin also drank a bit, whored around disgracefully, killed black people without compunction, repented a little in jail, failed as a lawyer, took up with a woman named Beulah Morose, and died in El Paso's Acme bar in August of 1895 with three bullets in the back of his head. None of this is mentioned by Dylan, of course.

Does it matter? If it doesn't, why use the name, plus a superfluous consonant, of a real person? Either a heroic John Ford history is being invoked or a dissection of mythical Old West heroism, concocted and manipulated, is being offered. The myth is central to one of America's many dreams, after all, and Dylan knows it better than most. In an album reeking of God, a record puritanically lean, actually spooked, without a single chorus, composed and recorded at speed in the year in which the Beatles' long-gestating *Sgt Pepper* also appeared, three sketched verses on a character 'never known to hurt an honest man' can amount to one of two possible things: nonsense *Americana*, or a sly, very sly, critique of the legend of the West and a national foundation myth.

The latter sounds like a good reason for brevity. The album's title song was, so Dylan said, a nice melody he didn't want to waste. But it was also 116 words serving both as introduction and as misdirection for what followed. The song is utterly deadpan, too: that should count as a clue. Yet it also works perfectly well, if you want it to, as a little song in praise of one of those ineffable good guys, born saintly and true, who always turn up just ahead of the Lone Ranger to save the homestead and the day.

That can't be the case. Wes Hardin was not one of those, like the Kid, or Hickok, or the James boys, whose lives were reinvented repeatedly and extravagantly by Hollywood in the heyday of the movie western. Dylan isn't playing around with a familiar American folk hero, a gilded household name, in this odd little song. If he knew about Hardin, it was not thanks to any confusion with a major film star. The tale told is not derived from a script doctor's fantasy of the Old West and its 'code'.

Inescapably, this suggests that the title and the hero, 'right in tempo' or not, were derived from reading. But even Hardin's autobiography, though it resorts to bigotry's old excuses, does not lie about central Texas politics and racial crime in the poisonous Reconstruction era. For example, as to his killing, when aged 15, of a former slave named Mage, the 'reformed' gunfighter wrote:

> To be tried at that time for the killing of a negro meant certain death
> at the hands of a court backed by Northern bayonets . . . thus, unwillingly,
> I became a fugitive not from justice, be it known, but from the injustice
> and misrule of the people who had subjugated the South.

Mage's thoughts on justice are not recorded. Even if Dylan was unaware of Hardin's elaborate excuses (the book was reprinted in 1961), he picked the name up somewhere. Was it then possible to become aware of this less-celebrated outlaw and learn nothing whatever of the truth? Reference works on the history of the West tend to cite two studies. Lewis Nordyke's *John Wesley Hardin: Texas Gunman* was published in 1957; C.L. Sonnichesen's *Pass of the North: Four Centuries on the Rio Grande* appeared in 1968. The latter is predated – though tantalisingly, only just – by Dylan's album; the former was still a relatively new book when the singer was recovering from his motorcycle accident, excavating ahistorical America in 'the basement', and composing the parables of *Harding*.

So why name your album after a song that you will claim to find deeply puzzling ('I didn't know what to make of it,' Dylan said in 1985)? Second, if the album in question is supposed to be an exploration of old, deep American realities – or so the critics would in due course claim – why draw attention to a song that is entirely at odds with any possible version of reality? This was 'the one song that I had no idea what it was about, why it was even on the album'. He didn't know why he picked the name – the misspelling was 'a mistake' – or the tale. But he surely knew it wasn't *true*.

In fact, Dylan must have known perfectly well what the song was 'about' – usually a taboo word in his lexicon – and been very clear in his reasons for naming a whole album after an opening track that turns historical fact on its head. What's more, in 1969 *Rolling Stone*'s Jann Wenner was told, first, that no other title for the album was considered, and that serious thought was given to calling the following album – 'the *Nashville Skyline* one' – *John Wesley Harding Volume II*. 'We were gonna do that,' said Dylan. And why? To perpetuate a song about which you had 'no idea'? Even as a joke, that's a little complicated.

The ballad and the album that takes its name carry us to the frontiers of myth-as-reality, to the debatable lands where the American west was 'won' and the country shaped. Dylan was not ignorant about Wes Hardin, I think. We can tell, when the hero in question is Billy the Kid and the album is the soundtrack to a movie that almost tells the truth, that some research has gone into the lyrics. 'John Wesley Harding' tramples on the truth because the writer knows the facts perfectly well. Hence all that gossip in the tale telling only of what was 'known' about the outlaw. Dylan is saying that nothing is known – 'Nothing is revealed,' as another song on the album will say – but plenty is believed. Nor is he echoing John Ford's famous piece of movie dialogue: there was no legend to print where Hardin was concerned, just a plain tale of hatred and murder. He did the crimes, and the time, and made no attempt at denial in a book now 'recognised', as one authority puts it, 'as a classic in western Americana'. And Dylan casts every fact aside.

He is making a larger point then. He is making it, furthermore, with a long song cut short, a song that gives his album its name, that *demonstrates* myth-making, and goes to the heart and core of an American self-image. It is no coincidence that Dylan was composing his album at a time when the movie western was on its last legs, a horse opera flogged once too often. Come 1973 *Pat Garrett and Billy the Kid* would be very close to the last round-up for the genre, a strange and bitter thing, 'realistic' but not truthful, accurate in particular but not in general. Its pair of contrasting central Dylan songs would be the Old West's 'grand finale'. For an alias the guest star, a late addition to the script as written, would select the name Alias. For *John Wesley*

Harding, Dylan had meanwhile chosen to open with an inverted parable, the first of several, for an album of the frontier, wherever it might be.

*

He has never sold a great many records, as these things are measured. The fact tends to surprise people who contemplate all those songs and a 50-year career. Publishing rights have brought him great wealth, of course, but the billion-whatever sales attributed to the Beatles or Presley have never been in his grasp. There have been only six number-one albums in the US, and three of those were achieved in the twenty-first century, when the feat was no longer notable. Nor has critical acclaim always matched public taste. The journalists derided *Self Portrait*, yet it reached number four in 1970; *Blonde on Blonde*, masterpiece or not, got only to number three. Bob Dylan may have sold perhaps 80 million (non-bootleg) albums: it isn't much to show for 50 years. Reputedly, it's why he tours, on and on. These days, that's where the money is.

Those who make the decisions in his industry would argue, no doubt, that he has been his own worst enemy. *John Wesley Harding* would reach number two on the *Billboard* chart, and number one in the UK, but Dylan did nothing to 'support' this tricky album. Jimi Hendrix got the glory – and the composer the royalties, with a storming arrangement for future use thrown in – from 'All Along the Watchtower', released as a single in September of 1968. Ultimately, that was Albert Grossman's doing: he had passed a tape to the guitarist in January. Dylan's own version of the song appeared finally as a single in November, and flopped, predictably enough. He didn't appear to care. He was staying at home, in the real world. And he had no intention whatever of returning to the concert stage.

The odd fact remains, nevertheless, that 'Watchtower', a still-mysterious parable from an album that takes self-effacement as its guiding principle, has become the closest thing Dylan has to a signature tune. If you believe bobdylan.com, where the singer's staff keep score, he has played the song more often in concerts – with everything owed to the Hendrix version – than anything else in his gigantic back catalogue. By the summer of 2012 the number of public renditions exceeded 2,000. The difference between conception and execution must now seem vast.

*

In more than one sense, 1968 was a good year to stay home. There might have been an intense appetite for Dylan's 'leadership', but radicals, hippies, draft-dodgers, dopeheads and Yippies fielding a pig as a presidential candidate didn't pause to explain how the miracle was supposed to be accomplished. 'Genius', it seems, would take care of the details. Even today, the standard potted biographies will note only that a 'disillusioned Dylan' had turned his back on politics. The obvious question is overlooked: what was he supposed to have said, or done, even if the spirit had been willing?

Students were in revolt across the Western world. Vietnam, bad enough as a colonial war, had become symbolic of moral failure and systemic collapse. Anger was the easy part. Was Dylan supposed to come up with some anthem or other gesture appropriate to changing times and make the cosmic difference? Many were playing that game, with risible results. When the Yippies (Youth International Party) faced Mayor Daley's brutish cops to stage their Festival of Life during the '68 Chicago Democratic Convention several singer-songwriters, Phil Ochs included, turned up to play. The infernal A.J. Weberman, 'Dylanologist', 'garbologist' and professional nuisance, was a Yippie from the start, and relentless in his determination to force Dylan to lead the anti-Vietnam struggle. The Weather Underground, 'inspired' by a stray line in 'Subterranean Homesick Blues', would shortly declare war on the United States, and plant a bomb at the Capitol. In March of 1969, meanwhile, John and Yoko would take to a big bed in the Amsterdam Hilton with the world's press on hand and demand peace for all. Reports on that are still coming in . . .

It was a bad year for heroes in 1968, in any case. A cold wind began to howl. In April, Martin Luther King was assassinated at the Lorraine Motel in Memphis, Tennessee, the killing understood instantly as one bloody answer to non-violence, the preacher's stand against the war, and the demand for civil rights. On 5 June, in the kitchen of the Ambassador Hotel in Los Angeles, Robert F. Kennedy was also gunned down, by – or so it seemed to many – no coincidence. 'All Along the Watchtower' could not sound anything other than prophetic that year, but it carried no editorialising comment from its author. Dylan never did 'turn his back on politics'. Political songs would continue to litter his career for decades to come. The change was simply this: he would not tell people what he meant by them, or assist others in their attempts to explain.

*

In print, nine of the twelve songs on *John Wesley Harding* are constructed to the same pattern: three brief stanzas, generally six to eight lines apiece, without choruses or – unless you count a couple of peculiar 'morals' – conclusions. The three-stanza count rises to ten tracks, in fact, if the third verse of 'All Along the Watchtower' isn't broken in two, as it is in editions of Dylan's lyrics, for dramatic effect. There is a formal unity to this collection and it is unlike anything Dylan had attempted previously. Exceptions are made for 'The Ballad of Frankie Lee and Judas Priest' – three-verse ballads being hard to come by; cf. 'Harding' – and for 'I'll Be Your Baby Tonight', a deliberate change of mood at the album's close. The rest abide by a design, and the design has a purpose.

Dylan could as well have been writing sonnets ('little songs'), even if he didn't stick to the traditional 14-line rule. Classically, that type of poem has a problem/resolution structure – a punchline, if you like – with a turn, twist or *volta* at the end. In *John Wesley Harding* the trick is pulled, or subverted, repeatedly. Much of the album is imagistic; most of the songs are elliptical, avoiding endings. This is lyric verse. It is a style – yet again – that he had not attempted previously. Yet again, the use of language itself is altered.

The unmatched example is 'Watchtower'. A dialogue sets the scene. A joker and a thief fret over chaos, truth and an existence that is 'but a joke'. A castle keep, a tower at the borderlands between order and chaos, waiting for the barbarians, is sketched. In atmosphere, in setting, it is redolent of the pre-Christian *King Lear* that Peter Brook would put on film in 1971: the old world is passing. Yet in the song itself nothing actually happens. Instead, these characters wait: *something's coming*.

> Outside in the distance a wildcat did growl
> Two riders were approaching. The wind began to howl

John Wesley Harding is full of presentiments and foreboding. Dylan invests every story – each song save the last is a tale, a monologue, an epistle – with the sense of strange times unfolding. Not a single line makes an obvious reference to a single contemporary event. Within a fortnight of the album's release US divisions would be launching a huge search-and-destroy operation in Vietnam. The racist Lester Maddox would be sworn in as governor of Georgia. Soon enough there would be nuclear tests, military coups in small countries and a 'summer of love', long exhausted, crawling towards terminal disillusionment.

These do not merit so much as the hint of a mention. *Harding* is in no sense 'topical', just pertinent. As with its frequent recourse to a slightly twisted King James Bible language, the album hints at eternal verities. But its 'messages' are as opaque as Zen *koans*.

Again, this is inherent in the structure of the songs and implicit in the cast of characters. These too have changed since *Blonde on Blonde*. They have escaped, one after the other, from religious pseudo-myth and moral fables. Here's Christ-like Wes Harding, the Damsel and 'Tom Paine', the Landlord, the Drifter, 'St Augustine', the Poor Immigrant, the Lonesome Hobo, the Joker and the Thief, Frankie Lee and Judas Priest, and the Wicked Messenger. They can be archetypes. They can stand as Dylan's personalised Tarot pack, or his attempt, this prodigal son, at real parables. Those announced 'morals' may be deliberately platitudinous, but the moral sense behind *John Wesley Harding* is at fever pitch.

From 1963 or thereabouts onwards Dylan has generally been too clever as an artist to allow a single reading of a song, far less a single meaning. That's clearly one reason why he took flight from 'leadership' and protest. How much art can there be in saying that nuclear war is a damnable idea? For his pains, he has seen his songs interpreted to death, but he tends – clever again – to treat that diversion as a hack journalist's tiresome hobby. So *John Wesley Harding* isn't 'about' things. So it tantalises. So the songs refuse resolution, or offer mock resolutions, or finish up with a *deus ex machina* joke:

> Just then a bolt of lightning
> Struck the courthouse out of shape
> And while ev'rybody knelt to pray
> The drifter did escape

The End. The title song concludes, meanwhile, with the empty assurance that Harding 'was never known / to make a foolish move'. 'As I Went Out One Morning' finishes up with 'Tom Paine' apologising for whatever the Damsel *might* have done. 'Frankie Lee' concludes, apparently, with a bland plea for neighbourliness and the counting of blessings (but only after a little boy has muttered that 'Nothing is revealed'). 'I Am a Lonesome Hobo' says it's smart to keep your own counsel. 'The Wicked Messenger' almost pushes the joke too far: 'If ye cannot bring good news, then don't bring any.'

The use of language is fascinating less for Dylan's 'surreal' touches

– those are few – than for its sheer restraint. *Harding* is sparse. Often enough its songs function as monologues, as tales told by the fire. Yet in song after song there is a sense of impending upheaval, of a storm coming or passing. Things end and begin again. The Drifter escapes; Frankie Lee – does the oath 'Judas Priest!' need to be explained? – is transfigured; the wind begins to howl; strange dreams illuminate suffering; visions shatter 'like the glass'. Here's premonition, barely coded: *something's coming.*

A dozen years would elapse before Dylan 'burst / into the arms of Judas Priest' by finding himself born again in the Christian style. Hints litter *Harding*, nevertheless. 'Sign on the Cross', from the basement tapes, is here continued; his mother's tale of a big old Bible open for reference on an antique lectern at the Woodstock house is confirmed. But this is an album notable less for its spot-the-allusion biblical references than for its running argument over faith and meaning.

So the writing is measured, even stately. These lyrics were not fished from any stream of consciousness. There is no 'spontaneous' found poetry in this collection. Every line – and Dylan has said as much – has been crafted to a purpose, with nothing left to spare. Often in the basement recordings we are given the illusion (and sometimes it's no illusion) that Dylan is inventing verses on the spot. *Harding*, in contrast, has been pondered: you can feel the weight of contemplation. Was it really true that the title song became truncated thanks only to Dylan's boredom? I don't think so.

In 1965–6 he had written songs that seemed self-generating, verse after unstoppable verse, songs that halted – or so it seemed – only because he called a halt. Where and why does 'Sad Eyed Lady of the Lowlands' end, precisely? How many verses could 'Desolation Row' or 'Stuck Inside of Mobile' have sustained? What became of the other 19 'pages of vomit' from which 'Like a Rolling Stone' was extracted? In those songs, in those years, Dylan let his writing take him where it might: that was his method. In a banal sense, *Harding* exhibits a belief in less-is-more, in editing. In a real sense it involves a pursuit of the essential, the irreducible. Dylan – who apparently said as much to Allen Ginsberg – wanted these songs to be precise. They are precise in every detail save in their attention to overt meaning.

It's a mode that reappears time and again among poets as they rebel against ornament and excess. It springs from the feeling that sometimes only certain words are right, that dazzling, playful 'surreal' lines are beside the point when life gets serious. It's a matter of concentration, in every sense, a kind of artistic mood swing. Only with *Blood on the Tracks* would Dylan rediscover this kind of deep focus.

In *Harding*'s sleeve 'notes', meanwhile, he continued to have some sardonic fun, not least with those who were about to pore over these long-awaited new songs to count the dozens of biblical allusions and hunt out meanings and messages. Lest some self-congratulatory scholar be warming up for a lecture on the mysteries of the King James version apropos the artist, Dylan got there first. The little tale of three kings, 'a jolly three', in search of Frank, 'the key', counts as somewhat sceptical towards those who always want to know more than the writer is prepared to say. The first king speaks.

'Frank,' he began, 'Mr Dylan has come out with a new record. This record of course features none but his own songs and we understand that you're the key.' 'That's right,' said Frank, 'I am.' 'Well then,' said the king in a bit of excitement, 'could you please open it up for us?' Frank, who all this time had been reclining with his eyes closed, suddenly opened them both up as wide as a tiger. 'And just how far would you like to go in?' he asked and the three kings all looked at each other. 'Not too far but just far enough so's we can say that we've been there,' said the first chief.

*

Dylan went to Nashville in 1967 as winter began with the *Harding* songs written and ready. Kenny Buttrey and Charlie McCoy, drummer and bassist respectively, part of the *Blonde on Blonde* crew, would remember being taken aback. On the previous album they had done their share of hanging around and dozing while Dylan pondered and wrote. Now the star required just three musicians – Pete Drake was brought in on pedal steel for a couple of tracks – and three quick recording sessions. The veterans also noticed that his voice had changed: it was softened, if not subdued. The new songs were put on tape effortlessly. Nothing was left over for the bootleggers, and nothing left to chance.

One cold fact might have affected Dylan's mood and delivery. Just two weeks before the first of the Nashville sessions Woody Guthrie had died, finally. It wasn't exactly a shock. Many people were surprised that Woody had endured for so long, trapped inside his disease. Dylan's immediate response was to call Harold Leventhal, Guthrie's long-term manager – a sad enough role for long enough – to say that he was available, wherever and whenever, if a tribute to his last hero was being planned. With *Harding* wrapped up and released in short order as 1967 drew to a close, he and the still-nameless Band – announced as the Crackers – took to the stage at Carnegie Hall on 20 January. The likes of Ramblin' Jack Elliott, Tom Paxton and Pete Seeger sounded much as ever during a pair of concerts; Dylan and his musicians bore no resemblance to the 1966 troupe. They performed three 'songs for Woody'. Among them was 'Grand Coulee Dam', one of the ballads that had poured from Guthrie when he was roaming the banks of the Columbia River in May of 1941 just as one Bobby Zimmerman was being born.

This gesture of remembrance aside, Dylan had no intention of interrupting his domestic life at Woodstock. It seemed there was no force on earth – and certainly no force named Albert – that could cause him to go back on the road. Only a couple of the usual theories account for what had become a near-total estrangement between the Bear and his erstwhile cub. Either Grossman's eagerness to book still more concert dates after the return from Europe in 1966 had caused Dylan to reassess his manager's character, or the client had at last paused to study his contracts. Neither explanation was liable to fill him with affection. Albert's concern for his well-being – physical, mental or financial – cannot have seemed conspicuous. Lawyers would in due course adopt different language.

*

Press: Do you have a personal message for the kids today?
Dylan: Take it easy and do your job well.
Press conference, Isle of Wight, 27 August 1969

If you believe Dylan, *Nashville Skyline* was almost called *John Wesley Harding II*. Then it was almost called *Love Is All There Is*. Perhaps the idea of entitling an album *Self Portrait* had yet to strike him. To this day, *Nashville Skyline* can sound desperately, deliberately bland, even as a label. But still: *Love Is All There Is*? There have been worse titles, but how many? On the other hand, if that's how the artist truly felt, if the title was an honest description of a state of mind, why reject it after – so he said – very serious consideration? Perhaps it was just too honest, or too corny, even for the new-made contented family man. You might remember how it functions, in any case, this compendious universal devotion: 'it makes the world go 'round.'

Love is all there is, it makes the world go 'round
Love and only love, it can't be denied
No matter what you think about it
You won't be able to do without it
Take a tip from one who's tried

'I Threw It All Away' is actually a lovely thing, by its lights, and certainly one of the best things on the *Nashville Skyline* album, though the consensus says that the competition therein is not intense. At any other time the song's supple melody would have been asked to bear a great deal more of Dylan's lyrical weight. On the other hand, very few songwriters would have cast it aside. As one of those familiar songs offering Advice on What Matters, it contains a single fine image – 'Once I had mountains in the palm of my hand / and rivers that ran through every day' – but the rest seems paltry. Even the rhymes, generally the extra shot in Dylan's locker, are routine-to-trite: 'must have been mad / never knew what I had'; ' think about it / do without it'.

If the world is all that is the case, and if love is all there is, does love's expression have to be so banal? This version of Bob Dylan has gone a long distance out of his way to avoid being mistaken for any of the other Dylans, least of all the groundbreaking, creatively radical crowd of Bobs. This album marks his public embrace – not reciprocated by the folks in the big sparkly hats – of country music, the realm of the less liberal. It amounts to yet another hugely risky move. This is what he releases in the year of the Woodstock Festival? Culling a collection *Nashville Skyline* is one thing. But an album with *Love Is All There Is* for its title, a declaration like something even the high-'60s Beatles might have rejected as puerile, would have sealed it. Put-upon fans would have been liable to say – and quite a few did say – that finally this sell-out had nothing left worth selling.

As it was, those who feared for Bob Dylan's immortal talent (or soul) thanks to *Skyline* were more worried by banality than simplicity, always presuming they could tell the difference. An album so short it could make you wonder about brevity and wit, a set sustained by an old song recycled and an instrumental, a collection composed and recorded in the rhinestone capital of reaction, could only mean one of two things. Either Dylan was running on fumes and memories, or he truly believed he had a shot at a mainstream career. The diehards, forgetting that most of *Blonde on Blonde* was made in Nashville, were left to ponder which might have been worse.

The suggestion that the well was dry, that Dylan was blocked, lacks an explanation. *John Wesley Harding* had been a quiet triumph, written and recorded in almost a single burst with no sign of strain. That had been achieved, meanwhile, in close proximity to the abundant magic of the sessions that led to *The Basement Tapes*. And then everything stopped, just like that? And then he lacked the material, or the ability to create the material, for a single album of respectable length? If so, what happened?

Just over a year had elapsed between the release of *Blonde on Blonde* and the tentative beginnings of the basement sessions. No time at all had passed between the conclusion of the West Saugerties bacchanal and the *Harding* meditations, released officially two days past Christmas in 1967. There was no immense hiatus between that date and the appearance of *Skyline* in the spring of 1969, nor any outward evidence of creative difficulties. It was a longish pause between releases by the standards of the era, and a very long pause when compared with Dylan's output in 1965–6. But if the basement songs and *Harding* are taken as being of a piece, in terms of output and creative energy, the meagre fare of *Skyline* is baffling. As 1967 became 1968 the flood of writing had seemed to be at its height. Yet here he was, suddenly, with a 'country' album and a cowboy hat. But Dylan was all hat, many concluded, and no album.

*

A single biographical fact dominates the period between *Harding* and *Skyline*: Abe Zimmerman was dead. Should we make something of it? Woody Guthrie's passing, when it happened, surprised no one who knew the facts: death had been a long time coming. But of all the possible explanations for the thinness of the material Dylan put out, complete with an excruciating Johnny Cash tribute 'poem', in April of 1969, the passing of Abe is hard to ignore. At Woodstock, with a young family, Dylan had taken a shot at growing up. In June of 1968, just turned 27, the news came from Hibbing that left him with no choice in the matter.

Difficult father; difficult son: sometimes, that's how it goes. Robert Shelton, interviewing Abe shortly before the elder Zimmerman's sudden end, had sensed a man still at odds with himself over his globally famous firstborn. Proud, of course, but with a couple of bones still to pick, perhaps, and evasive when pressed over relations between the child, his parent and his home town.

Dylan could not have *not* known how his father felt, or was liable to feel. Yet what he understood – of himself, his father and how things happen in families – is a question only he could answer. In *Chronicles* he writes that the last chance to explain himself, as he had never been able to explain himself before, was gone. The fact is that he was given no time to think in June of 1968. The blow was sudden. Abe was just 56 when a heart attack (his second) took him. He had 'missed' his son's wedding (because his son had told him nothing about it). News of the motorbike accident had been relayed through the media. Visits back and forth had been rare enough. At 27, it seems, Dylan had not been ready to contemplate the traditional father and son rapprochement. Tot things up: the trauma and exhaustion of '66; the bike crash; Abe's death; his wife's third pregnancy; and all in the space of almost precisely two years. So, ready for your country debut, Mr Dylan?

*

It makes a kind of sense, if all you mean to explain is a man with the wind knocked from his sails. It is tempting, too, to give credence to the seeming significance of calendars. Here was *Nashville Skyline* appearing as the '60s, 'Dylan's decade', approached their end. Here he was with his defiantly retrograde step, anticipating all things retro, as the Beatles were falling apart and the hippy fantasy was descending into squalor. And here was Dylan, seeming to endorse a section of the music industry that saw little amiss with that patriotic business in Vietnam. Here he was – for who could really doubt it? – embracing reaction and evading substance. Not a word of *Nashville Skyline* was even worth the effort of *analysis*. Many took their leave of him.

Thereafter, conclusions were drawn. Either this was a grand, perverse gesture, or he truly had nothing left to say. Judging by the brief duration of an album of meagre songs – from a man who had written a spellbinding chunk of *Blonde on Blonde* on the spot in the selfsame Nashville studios fewer than three years before – the gesture theory could probably be discounted. A generation later Dylan himself would describe himself as disgusted and depressed by the undeclared civil war within American society. Hemmed in, he wanted no part of either side, of any side, in the accumulating conflicts between conservatives and radicals, between the state and the self-declared alternative society. He was unimpressed by modish ideas, dismayed by all the violence, a dissident from all the orthodoxies, old and new. The state of the nation, on this account, made him heartsick. Simply put, he was revolted by what had become of his country. He was a man bent on escape.

At his father's funeral, he wept. It may have been at this moment, for the first time in a long time, that he began to think seriously about his Jewish identity. His interest in Scripture was in any case unabated. His attitude to organised politics was meanwhile unwavering, fixed, and fixed once and for all. Now it was that he gave the interview to *Sing Out!*, in the aftermath of his father's passing, in which he asked why his questioners couldn't imagine him favouring the Vietnam War. In his own reality a third child was born; he took up painting; and wrote a song called 'Lay Lady Lay' for a film entitled *Midnight Cowboy* that was in production in 1968. The picture was based on the novel that had (perhaps) inspired his own tall tales of hustling around Times Square during his very first days in New York: reality has an odd way of confirming Dylan's fictions. Meanwhile, the process of discovering the true extent of Grossman's hold over his affairs – and the extent of his own naivety – continued.

Beyond that, Dylan wasn't doing much at all by way of the art for which he was known. By his own standards, he was barely writing at all. It was one thing to remove ornament and excess from the songs, another to fail to create any kind of song at all. It was as if his talent had disappeared overnight. Something odd was going on.

*

Still, we forget. In the twenty-first century nation states rise and fall in the time it takes recording artists to get a dozen tunes into digital shape. Seasons come and go as teams of studio wizards ponder drum sounds. In the 1960s – in seven years, in point of fact – Dylan wrote and recorded – created – nine albums, and that tally stands before we mention, or measure, the extent of the basement recordings. It could have been a round dozen. By any yardstick, that's a lot.

Others were prolific, of course. In roughly the same period the Beatles produced 12 or 13 albums, according to how you choose to catalogue *Yellow Submarine* and *Let It Be*. Even Lennon and McCartney did not anticipate spending years on a single record, in the modern style. Like Dylan, they started by knocking out whole albums in a couple or three sessions and did not, contrary to legend, spend more than five months on the 'epic' *Pepper*. But the Beatles had one another, if only for the sake of acrimony; Dylan's achievement was his alone. He had no one to fall back on but Bob Dylan, and who could trust that character? What if *Skyline* was just an experiment that went wrong? If he miscalculated or misheard himself, there was no one to set him straight but his disgruntled audience.

It might count, just about, as still another way to explain the sudden falling away that was *Nashville Skyline*. Yet it doesn't ring true. Dylan had removed himself from the grand pop argument before, most obviously in the aftermath of the accident. Country music might have been his honest choice and fancy of the moment. But it is as though, having halted, he had forgotten how to move again, or had lost the will. *Skyline* seems now like a symptom of artistic paralysis. Somehow *John Wesley Harding* and his father's death had drained him. Somehow effortless creativity had disappeared, just like that.

The diagnosis among those who work with words is simple: writer's block. Dylan would in time call it something else: *amnesia*, the loss of creative memory, the loss of artistic identity. In his telling the affliction came out of the blue. A psychologist might say it had been coming for years, fated, inevitable since the moment he had attempted to erase Robert Allen Zimmerman. A best guess, no better than a guess, is that the death of proud Abe Zimmerman, a man who had never once doubted his own identity, had reminded the son of what he had done to himself. It is as though his father's passing posed a question: what had Dylan become? Samuel Clemens had become Mark Twain only once; once was enough for Sam. Bobby Zimmerman had become 'Bob Dylan' serially, time and again. A 'fabricative tendency' is long-lasting, apparently, in cases of what is called mythomania, and the world of entertainment depends on the fact. In 1968, the reality of Abe's death intruded.

*

Ten tracks. One was an old number revived, the product of some amiable and aimless sessions – though the bootleg is fun if the mood strikes – with Johnny Cash. One was a dull-enough pickin' 'rag'. One was 'Lay Lady Lay', a song – most said easily the best of the bunch – that had been commissioned for a movie, not designed to shore up an album. Another track was 'Peggy Day', possibly the poorest song Dylan had sanctioned for release since his earliest apprentice days. Of the rest, only two love songs mattered: 'I Threw It All Away' and 'Tonight I'll Be Staying Here With You'. With 'Lay Lady Lay', that made three from ten. It was Dylan's lowest score as a writer, by such an accounting, since *Bob Dylan*. Even in terms of mere quantity these were – as it were – slim pickings. *John Wesley Harding*, whose songs are mostly brief, comes in at close to 38½ minutes; *Nashville Skyline*, amply padded, struggles to make 27 minutes.

But hold on. A desperate artist (or a cynical one) would simply have taken his pick of the basement material and given it enough of a Nashville gloss to render the Byrds' *Sweetheart of the Rodeo* – released in the previous August, with songs from the basement at its beginning and end – redundant. The world would also have been spared a lot of foolish talk about 'country-rock'. It was one thing for Dylan to say he did not retrace his steps, that he forgot his work the instant it was completed or superseded. That habit was of little use if the landscape was to become littered with half-painted masterpieces. He had plenty of songs. 'Instinct' is a poor excuse, sometimes, for indiscipline.

The further, hopeful theory says that Dylan was again evading his writing responsibilities simply to deprive Grossman of still more unearned wealth. The two were by this point irrevocably estranged, yet thanks to another onerous and absurd contract Dylan had signed without a second thought in 1966, Albert was still entitled to a monumental publishing royalty. As with the notion that the basement songs were buried for 'business' reasons, this neat narrative explains everything except *Nashville Skyline*. It still got made; it still contained original compositions. Dylan was at war with his manager in order to gain control of his art, not deploy it as a poker chip. Equally, the notion does nothing to answer a fundamental question: why country music?

For him, to be fair, it was no novelty. The hip crowd watching *Don't Look Back* might have wondered about the hotel-room scene in which the author of 'Tambourine Man' essayed 'Lost Highway', once a 1949 Hank Williams B-side. Was he being ironic? Only if you overlooked the song's opening line – 'I'm a rolling stone' – and only if you knew nothing about the world in which Dylan grew up. He shared his musical roots with a thousand other singers, but with Presley above all. Rock and roll had always been more than the simple cliché of white meets black, of R&B encountering country encountering blues encountering rockabilly one supernatural day in Memphis. The music was born, if not made, out of economic circumstance, out of patterns of migration, segregation, the spread of radio and recording technology, above all out of poverty. Intercourse had been going on for at least a century.

How did those long-forgotten black cowboys sound when they sang?

Musicologists who write of the cattle-trail crews – on average two men in eight were black – sometimes use the term 'pre-blues'. John A. Lomax, early in the field, first heard 'Git Along Little Dogies' and 'Home on the Range' from a black retired trail cook in 1908. Yet in which genre of modern popular music does the big 'cowboy' hat – one is doffed on the cover of *Nashville Skyline* – loom like a giant trademark? Which genre is deemed to be the music of white middle America? Even that assumption misunderstands the history of country. As Peter Guralnick has observed, matter-of-factly, Jimmie Rodgers and the Carter Family 'unquestionably incorporated both black and white traditions in their music'.[6] You just wouldn't know it from listening to their musical heirs today.

Dylan came to understand country for what it is: one of the folk musics of America, intertwined with others, and part of a continuum. He had grown up with it. Country was in no sense alien to him. In 1969, however, the rock audience had a slightly different perspective. That doesn't explain why he managed to make only half a record.

*

If *Skyline* seems meagre, there might be more than one explanation. You could say, perhaps, that Dylan had only begun to feel his way into the country tradition. He certainly knew the music well enough, but not, I think, the culture that had grown up around it by the end of the '60s. For one thing, it is said that Nashville – John Cash aside – did not go out of its way to make him feel welcome. The rock star – drugs, 'protest', black music, that voice – was not handed an open invitation to reinvent himself. But it has also been pointed out, time and again down the years, that *Skyline* isn't actually country music, not in any real sense, not in any of the genre's old, new or alternative manifestations. The addition of a pedal steel guitar here and there behind a crooning voice does not invest a song with country credentials. Dylan knew that if he knew anything.

You could add, nevertheless, that he had already felt the pull of the pastoral tradition during the basement sessions. Why, for that matter, had he moved his family to Woodstock at all? He had repudiated urban life, found his Walden and his America far from that 'group portrait' of a society 'wrapped up in a blanket of rage'. With a new way of living came a new attitude towards songs, and a

---

6   *Lost Highway* (1999), p. 19.

new idea of what counted. Pastoral and country: a matter of words.

Instinct was one thing; the music itself, as a matter of technical retooling, another. Writing a country song from scratch is not as simple as falling off an old log, even if your skills have not deserted you. *John Wesley Harding* had added a couple of licks and flourishes to Dylan's repertoire, but a properly Nashville album was a different matter, an exercise in musicianship and imagination. It required him to think differently. What was a Bob Dylan record before *Nashville Skyline*? 'Complex' would probably cover it. Though he had recorded the largest part of *Blonde on Blonde* in Nashville, and though he had availed himself of its expert musicians for the job, Dylan was in no position to perform lyrics of that kind, in that town, for this new album. Simplicity – his stated objective – is a complicated business. In that bare context *Skyline* seems now like a tentative step towards disengagement, a first sloughing off.

The album fails both in conception and execution. You can still discern its point, however. It's not nonsensical to argue that Dylan might well have had a *Harding II* in mind: simplicity, heartland music, a stripping away even of the hint of a 'message'. *John Wesley Harding*, though musically unadorned, had been dense with elusive meanings. It was not illogical, then, to make a group of songs to support the argument that only one thing in life truly means anything.

The irony is that Dylan couldn't pull it off. He was more at home with biblical references by the dozen, with surreal characters, odd thematic choices, wordplay and half-buried symbolism. Simple came hard. To this day, he has not fully mastered the trick. Yet when he failed in Nashville he did not reach into his (more or less) secret catalogue of basement songs. He did what he had always done. He put the album out as though to say, 'This is where I am, and what I am.' *Skyline* lacks breadth. It doesn't step into the shadows, or acknowledge the outer darkness fast encroaching in 1969, or even hint at the writer's own creative difficulties. It is indeed a 'sunny', optimistic set, and the picture of a smiling Dylan on its cover is in that sense entirely appropriate: *Here I am.*

*

Let's not indulge our artist too much. He might have had Hank Williams and Jimmie Rodgers in his head when he set out to make *Nashville Skyline*. Fondly preserved voices from his childhood might have persuaded him that the person he had become could find a musical home in that tradition. But the old fans taken aback and dismayed by Dylan's choice of country music had a point. Nashville and all it had wrought possessed a political meaning, like it or not, and a cultural significance. In 1969, country stood on one side of an argument. 'Bob Dylan, country singer' was a contradiction in terms. This was *not* just a rerun of the artistic dispute with the folk radicals of the Village. Dylan was choosing his America: what other conclusion could there be?

If the people of the American South and West despise anything, they despise stereotypes. Randy Newman would speak to that resentment in the 1974 album *Good Old Boys* and in the song 'Rednecks'. Newman would also capture the way in which resentment is manifested as defiant pride. Broad brush strokes leave the culture of the South painted as dumb, racist and reactionary: self-declared rednecks can seem both to embrace and defy the clichés. But then, the history of racism and reaction is not, and never was, some invention of the oppressive North. Country music meanwhile speaks to its people. So what did Dylan's choice – an informed, expert and self-conscious choice – involve?

The dispassionate *Billboard* Hot Country Singles chart is as good a guide to history as most textbooks. Those who wonder about *Nashville Skyline* find their first answers, the obvious ones at least, in its lists. So here's exhibit A, Merle Haggard's 'Okie From Muskogee', sitting at number one on the country chart on 16 November 1969. What more does anyone need to know? This was Nashville's idea of popular song: a rousing tune in support of the troops fighting in Vietnam, in praise of freedom and in baffled contempt for dope-smoking, bead-wearing, draft card-burning hippies.

The first problem is, however, that Haggard was merely – or so he would come to say – satirising the attitudes of all concerned, and most of all satirising the mutual incomprehension among America's constituent communities. A song about 'freedom' had a sly understanding, supposedly, of liberty's nuances. The second problem is, nevertheless, that self-identified middle America, Nixon's silent majority, didn't necessarily hear the song Haggard thought he wrote.

The fact that Haggard would follow this hit with another, 'The Fightin' Side of Me', taking issue with all those 'runnin' down my countrymen' and advising dissenters 'if you don't love it, leave it', suggests that his definition of satire might have been a little fluid, in any case. Bobby Bare, 'adapted' by Dylan for the basement tapes track 'All American Boy', meanwhile had a lesser hit in 1969 with the unambiguous 'God

Bless America Again'. This was standard '60s country fare given a new purpose by Vietnam. This is precisely why the counter-culture found Dylan's latest experiment troubling. It would be a while before sophisticates found ironic uses for 'Okie From Muskogee'. But then, there is no trace of irony in *Nashville Skyline*, either.

Country music depended on family values – and family dysfunction – to a near-fanatical degree. It laid claim to family as it laid claim to God, and gave the deity an American passport. When the California millionaires behind Ronald Reagan began to understand this sort of conservatism – followed soon enough by the millionaires behind George W. Bush, and then by the billionaires who shaped the Tea Party movement – America experienced something akin to a political revolution. But even in 1969 country wasn't perceived as being merely antithetical to 'alternative values': that part of the music industry knew its audience, and knew where its audience stood. The Dylan who sang 'Only a Pawn in Their Game' at the voter-registration rally in Greenwood, Mississippi, in 1963 would have been alert to the facts. A friendship with Johnny Cash didn't change anything.[7]

For all that, the ramshackle recordings the two men made together in February of 1969, hot on the heels of the *Skyline* sessions, are revealing. Cash is clearly the driving force. Dylan even forgets the words – the shame of it – on 'That's All Right, Mama', even with the great Carl Perkins in the band. But when he gets behind a song such as 'I Still Miss Someone' or 'Ring of Fire' one thing is abundantly clear: he believes in himself as a country singer. The '*Nashville Skyline* voice' that would cause such a flutter among critics is no whim. He means it.

Whether he also meant these sessions to result in an album of duets with Cash, as has been alleged, is another matter. Was he so desperate? The country audience might have gone for that sort of thing, but no amount of mutual respect between the two men could bridge the chasm between their singing voices, or disguise the fact that Cash and his band kept things simple to the point of banality. 'Girl From the North Country' on *Skyline* works mostly because Dylan makes it work. The music on the bootleg sounds, with a couple of exceptions, like a bunch of musicians messing around and having fun. Just like Elvis and his

---

7   Predictably enough, Dylan was inducted into the Nashville Songwriters Hall of Fame in 2002. They said he 'brought international prominence to Nashville as a recording center'.

gang at Chips Moman's American Sound in Memphis, but without a Presley. Even as Dylan and Cash were laying waste to 'You Are My Sunshine' on 18 February at Music Row, in point of fact, Elvis was working on 'And the Grass Won't Pay No Mind'. It was a better day's – or rather night's – labour.

Another fact is pertinent: Dylan didn't have to make *Nashville Skyline*. In 1969, Columbia could no longer force product from him. Nor was he under any compulsion from anyone to find another of those 'new directions' on which the basic, repetitive accounts of his career depend. Any intention to continue or expand the music of *John Wesley Harding*, if an intention ever existed, must have been short-lived. As ever, meanwhile, no one was dictating his songs, his vocal style, or his choice of musicians. *Nashville Skyline* might be very slight, if hard to hate, but its creation was deliberate. As for padding, as for a lack of inspiration: Dylan had plenty of songs that had never (officially) seen the light of day. The singer who would shortly embark on a spree of cover versions was not bereft of choices. 'Nothing Was Delivered' would have been apt in any of a dozen different ways.

What we are left with is this: an artist with writer's block, hit harder than he ever believed possible by his father's death, refusing stubbornly to reach into his files and get himself out of a jam. It was perverse, by anyone's standards, or the mark of pride. It was also typical of Dylan.

In the event, the album was accredited a hit – two in the US, number one in the UK – and the critics were respectful. The smarter ones had become wary of speaking too soon where Dylan was concerned. This time, there was no backlash. *Rolling Stone*'s Paul Nelson even wrote that the briefest of sets 'achieves the artistically impossible: a deep, humane, and interesting statement about being happy'. If writer's block was the problem, the word ironic might (or then again might not) spring to mind.

*

In February of 1969 Richard Milhous Nixon had just become President of the United States and Bob Dylan no longer wanted to be Bob Dylan. Or at least, since the invasion and destruction of his Woodstock idyll by his less sane fans, *that* Bob Dylan. He probably understood the black joke. 'Dylan' had been his creation and curse from the start. He could probably have sustained an identity of his own within the shadow of the name, given time, but he could not – or would not; the distinction is almost meaningless – be the Bob Dylan they wanted him to be.

The fact involves a question: what was it that so many people wanted? Had he really made poetry and song matter so much to them, and convinced them so completely that he, just a musician, had special insights and special knowledge? Remarkable, if true. Or was he just another celebrity on the run, discovering that there is no such thing as privacy or an inviolable identity for anyone who presses himself on the public's attention, who chooses – for blind fate wasn't dealing that hand – to get famous just when things were becoming crazy and fame was the only excuse the crazed, believing everything and nothing, would ever need?

Everything about *Nashville Skyline* speaks of a man trying to get out from under. What gives the album its glow is that, in places, he really thinks he has succeeded. What lends a hint of sadness to the music now is that the contemporary listener knows better. 'Bob Dylan' is not a job from which you quit: the contract has no clause covering resignation. It isn't possible, it isn't allowed. That didn't mean he wasn't going to try.

*

If *Nashville Skyline* was made out of need and choice rather than desperation alone, one choice is conspicuous. Shelton made the identification in writing of Dylan's first album: Bob Dylan is a blues singer, a great one. Even in his late period, with the form transformed in his hands – still more insistently mystical, still fixed on mortality – comment returns to this central truth. Both musically and as a species of the American vernacular, the blues is Dylan's mode. And there is not a trace of black America's unique music on *Nashville Skyline*, his whitest – whiter than white – album.

At the time, no one seemed to notice. The critics, dazed, dazzled and confused by Dylan's 'new' voice, certainly didn't notice. Instead, they said he 'crooned'. They said he'd 'found an octave', caught the spirit of Roy Orbison, or even – critics say a lot of things – Elvis. Then they talked about the absence of poetry, the hard-to-miss new-found simplicity, the 'ordinary language' of a (suddenly) ordinary man. Many managed to say that Dylan had even stepped away from the high-plains verities and biblical prophecies of *Harding*. Of the utter absence of his blues heritage there was not a word. Yet if startling gestures were intended with *Skyline*, this was the most startling of all. He had reneged on his crossroads bargain. The album's lack of soul began to make sense.

Just before Dylan's record was released James Earl Ray had pleaded guilty to killing Martin Luther King. Days after *Nashville Skyline* hit the stores black students at Cornell University were locked in a furious confrontation with a college administration they accused of ignoring their needs. In the South, white families were moving house in droves to avoid bussing and the desegregation of schools. The FBI, under J. Edgar Hoover's explicit instruction, had begun to target the Black Panthers.

Dylan's 'Ballad of a Thin Man' had played continuously while the nascent party's founders – Huey P. Newton, Eldridge Cleaver, Bobby Seale and others – were working to put together a newspaper in San Francisco in the summer of 1967. They were fascinated by the song, obsessed with it. One of those photographs that gets called iconic shows a bare-torsoed Newton clutching his copy of *Highway 61 Revisited*. 'Thin Man', another of those supposedly 'post-political' Dylan songs, had spoken to these young black radicals and, they thought, explained the nature of white American society to them.

In South East Asia, where black troops were serving in disproportionate numbers, the carpet-bombing of Cambodia had begun in March of 1969. 'Racial disturbances' were still going on across the US. In Harlem's Mount Morris Park that summer there would be the cultural festival afterwards known as Black Woodstock. The year had begun with Marvin Gaye singing 'I Heard It Through the Grapevine', and had continued with Sly Stone's hit 'Everyday People'. Any historical list is more or less arbitrary, and none of this was necessarily Dylan's business. Still: this was the year in which he chose to make a country album?

No one had told him how his newest record was supposed to sound, or the style it was supposed to adopt. It didn't have to belong to any genre: it was a Bob Dylan album. Given a choice, Columbia would probably not have selected country as an ideal 'new direction' for the hip house laureate, but no choice was offered. Yet again, Dylan was taking sole responsibility for his actions. With *Skyline*, perhaps in an attempt to conceal the fact that suddenly songs were coming hard and slow, if they were coming at all, he chose to begin to explore a new territory.

As Dylan sometimes tells it now, the folk-blues has been the one constant in his life for upwards of 50 years. It's almost true. What is actually true is that his least creative periods as a writer have coincided with his estrangement from the universe beyond time of Charley Patton and Blind Willie McTell. *Nashville Skyline* is a nice album, a restful, 'optimistic' album made by a man exercising his personal freedom in the face of creative difficulties. But it misunderstands the pastoral tradition – a tradition and an idea of natural dignity a mere 2,000 years old – as surely as it forgets what Hank Williams was about. *Skyline* treats country music as a refuge from an artistic problem. Dylan may see equal value in all forms of American music, but inevitably he talks, these days, as though there is a hierarchy. Ultimate seriousness lies in the blues and the ancient wisdom of folk music. In Nashville, those fell silent.

*

The wafting country sound had not, in any case, dispelled that creative problem; quite the opposite. As though in defiance or denial Dylan persisted in trying to work around or through a monumental roadblock. No sooner was *Skyline* a certified hit than he was back in the studios. This time he didn't even pretend to have songs prepared. In April of 1969, in Nashville, he had only two ideas to his name. One was a lame rewrite of a mid-'50s thing called 'Singing the Blues', once a big hit for Guy Mitchell in the US (and for Tommy Steele in the UK), that Dylan would call – even ingenuity eluded him – 'Living the Blues'. The great poet's other notion was an album of cover versions. Bob Johnston would recall the singer turning up with a collection of songbooks to announce the conceptual breakthrough. The producer who had witnessed the upwellings of *Highway 61*, *Blonde on Blonde*, *Harding*, and even – these things turned out to be relative – *Nashville Skyline*, seems not to have believed that it was his to reason why. Yet again, the nuggets and gems of the basement tapes were to be, with a single exception, ignored. That didn't prevent the defiance implicit in Dylan's gesture from becoming almost heroic.

At home in Woodstock, the intrusions of fans, freaks, hippies and worse besides were getting out of hand. The refugee's secret was out. Interlopers were laying siege to his home and, on occasion, even finding their way inside his living quarters. There was to be no relief from being Bob Dylan. As he would write in *Chronicles*, he felt himself ensnared. Furious, he wanted to destroy all the freaks and parasites who still believed he belonged to them. At the end of the year the Dylans would try moving back to New York, specifically to MacDougal Street in the Village, in the hope of eradicating his monstrous persona, but to no avail. A couple of years later they would attempt to live out in the West, in various places, but again fail to escape the paramount fact of his existence. 'Bob Dylan' adhered to his creator. Even an album full of other people's songs wouldn't fix that problem.

In the April of 1969, nevertheless, his second *Self Portrait* session in Nashville saw Dylan attempt a couple of numbers associated with Don and Phil Everly, the old Elvis hit 'A Fool Such As I', and the Davis Sisters' country standard 'I Forgot More Than You'll Ever Know'. On 1 May he turned up – reportedly petrified – on Johnny Cash's TV show, sharing 'Living the Blues' and the *Nashville Skyline* 'Girl From the North Country' duet with America. Two days later he was back in Columbia's Studio A attempting a couple of Cash's old hits and, of all things, 'Blue Moon'. In July, he showed up briefly as a guest at one of The Band's appearances at a festival in Mississippi. This was as aimless, as purposeless, as Dylan had been in a decade.

In August, for all that, he consented to return to England for a performance at a vast festival on the Isle of Wight. His contempt for such events, the one at Yasgur's Farm near Woodstock above all, had become absolute. He wanted no part of the 'bullshit' Woodstock 'nation', nor of any of the counter-cultural masquerades on either side of the Atlantic. He wanted nothing more to do with his manager, either. Nevertheless, an offer from England arranged via Grossman of $50,000, plus substantial expenses, plus a separate fee for The Band, caused Dylan temporarily to suspend these stern judgements. Suddenly he was available. In the nursery nonsense of the times he was supposed to cause 150,000 souls – some estimates exceed 200,000 – to 'sink the Isle of Wight'. That wasn't how it worked out.

Some of the old charisma survived. At a press conference before the big night Dylan maintained that he had come to the island merely to see Tennyson's home. He didn't have any views on drug-taking. He said that a search of the newspaper files would prove he had never made 'too many statements' on big political and international 'issues'. 'I don't want to protest any more,' he protested. 'I never said I'm an angry young man.' He claimed that in the motorbike accident he had 'suffered a broken neck' and 'had to take it easy sometimes'. His behaviour in 1966 had been 'all for publicity'. He conceded that he had become a family man. Just for a change, most of this was mostly true.

Press: What exactly then is your position on politics and music?
Dylan: My job is to play music. I think I've answered enough questions.

Yet again, the bootleg suggests that here and there he put on a pretty fair performance. It in no sense resembled one of the 1966 shows that had already entered legend, however; nor did it reflect the music he was actually making at the time. Few who attended, even those in a position to give the headline act a proper hearing, knew exactly what it was. In part, in fact, the Isle of Wight performance was a kind of Bob Dylan's greatest hits, albeit in a loose and low-key manner: 'She Belongs to Me'; 'Maggie's Farm'; 'Like a Rolling Stone'; 'Lay Lady Lay'; 'Mr. Tambourine Man'; 'I'll Be Your Baby Tonight'. In another part the show was always going to be a tough sell before a crowd of 150,000 plus, a crowd who had, moreover, been kept waiting for over two hours. 'I Dreamed I Saw St. Augustine', 'I Pity the Poor Immigrant' and a lovely account of the Scottish folk standard 'Wild Mountain Thyme' were not exactly ideal for this early attempt at festival rock. Perhaps the most interesting piece played by the bearded figure dressed all in white was the hitherto unknown basement number 'Minstrel Boy', the song that would surface – incongruously, as it turned out – on *Self Portrait*.

Then again, who in the vast crowd knew what the hell *that* saloon-bar lament was supposed to be about? The bootleg, a raw version of recordings allegedly intended for a live album, says that Dylan played for barely 50 minutes. The Isle of Wight 'nation' were distinctly underwhelmed, as were the British media. Few thought they had heard music worth $1,000 a minute. John Lennon, having arrived by helicopter beforehand to make music privately with the visitor and his own fractious band (less McCartney), was merely polite. It was probably as well that Dylan did not attempt 'Blue Moon'.

*

In June of 1970, Greil Marcus commenced his *Rolling Stone* review of *Self Portrait* with four moderately famous words: 'What is this shit?' No one asked a question in return. What did Marcus expect instead? Seriously: what was it he wanted? Which course of creative action was he recommending for the lost leader that summer? Some among us would still like to read an account of that unrealised album, the one that answered every call and met every demand. Or was, at least, better than shit. A lyric sheet would be nice.

Marcus was typical, however. If *Self Portrait* was indeed shit, it earned reviews to match. For the first time since his first album, Dylan had an authentic critical flop on his hands. (The public took a different

520

view. The set made number four in the US. In Britain, it dislodged the Simon & Garfunkel behemoth *Bridge Over Troubled Water* from the top spot, albeit for only a week.) In the press, those who would later laud the musicological instinct that produced all those cover versions up in Woodstock in 1967 did no such favours to this American miscellany. There was a competition, instead, to discover new ways to mourn and abuse its maker. Yet here, nevertheless, whatever anyone says, was the first public example of that vexed and difficult idea, *Americana*.

It's an empty idea, in one sense. Bob Johnston, confronted with that armful of songbooks and the idea for a 'covers' album, is said to have responded (heroically) that if anyone could achieve such a thing it was Dylan. The basis on which the producer could justify the contention has not been identified. In 1970 it was considered shocking – and another betrayal – that the *poet* could be so bereft of ideas as to wish to sing 'Blue Moon' and quirky versions of Everly Brothers tunes. His taste – his loves, affections, memory itself – was a betrayal. It was as though every critic had chosen to forget where all their gods of rock had been born, and where they had grown up, and how they got started as singers and players. They were lucky Dylan didn't take a crack at a Johnnie Ray number.

Reviewers might have been placated had Dylan smuggled a decent album's worth of his own songs into the two vinyl discs of *Self Portrait*. Instead, only eight of twenty-four tracks were his. Two of those were instrumentals; the lyrics of one track contained only a two-line refrain, of four tracks recorded at the Isle of Wight Festival only one involved a song that would have been unfamiliar to the average fan; and then there was (such as it was) 'Living the Blues'. This was the offering after almost a year of work. For the critics, it was equivalent to taking out a closed-for-business ad. True, the fact that the album did contain those eight 'originals' undermines the still-persistent theory that Dylan was again attempting to deny Grossman publishing royalties: the deal had yet to expire. In 1970, a group of tunes so wilfully, woefully slight merely incensed reviewers. Amid it all the rock hacks forgot that Dylan is fascinated by the idea of song.

Self Portrait isn't great. In spots, it isn't even very good. In places, it's awful. If there is anything as elevated as a concept in play the grand design is hard to discern. But the damnation reserved for this collection – disowned as a 'joke' by Dylan himself after the backlash – requires selective memory. First, he had been schooled in borrowed, stolen and 'adapted' music: such songs were his autobiography. Had he compiled the record according to the portraits painted by others, he would doubtless have fitted in a Little Richard tune, something by Guthrie, a blues that actually acknowledged ('It Hurts Me Too' involves no such courtesy) Elmore James, or something so obscure it would have allowed hours of nit-picking pleasure to critics and 'scholars'. But this was a *Self Portrait* of Dylan in his 1969 moment, and in his (mostly) country mode, and in the throes of affection for the virtues of popular song. The choices, like the treatments, are as fascinating as they are confusing. They made one worthwhile point: this, for most ordinary people, was true folk music.

Afterwards, he said he had been trying to rid himself of his unsought messianic 'role'. In that version, the album was a kind of test, as though to say, 'Put up with this shit and you'll see *genius* in anything.' *Self Portrait* was also his 'own bootleg record', as Shelton was informed. Predictably, the remark was given a dose of over-interpretation. Here, supposedly, was a riposte to *Great White Wonder*, the incoherent plain-cover double-disc rip-off that had appeared in the summer of 1969 offering outtakes, stuff from 1961 and Bonnie Beecher's Minneapolis apartment and, of course, a seven-track sampling of the basement tapes.

You needn't believe a word of it. *Great White Wonder* had certainly attracted a lot of attention, and even some West Coast airplay. *Rolling Stone* and others had meanwhile been agitating for the release of the Woodstock recordings. The appearance of *Great White Wonder II* in 1970 – another ragbag compiled from the bootlegs *Stealin'* and *John Birch Society Blues* – would add to the supposed 'pressure' on Dylan. Instead, these records contributed only to his mystique and his irritation. He had no romantic outlaw notions about *these* thieves. But to provide them with some sort of perverse 'answer'? That idea overlooks his pride and his attitude towards criticism. Would he have spent weeks and months in the studios in Nashville and New York for the sake of some counter-culture 'debate'? Hardly. Later bootleggers would give themselves airs with a 'Genuine Bootleg Series' – excellent and fascinating it is, too – as an answer to Dylan's own decision to release selected odds and ends. But these games are beside the point now, as they were in 1970.

Self Portrait suffers mostly because Dylan didn't see the project through, not because he lacked seriousness. Something is thereby overlooked: no artist of his generation, none of the rock aristocracy, had even begun to think about popular song in this way as the 1960s guttered out. The reputation granted to the basement-tape covers – often enough by Greil Marcus, indeed – arrived long after the recordings were made. Would Dylan singing Bob Nolan's 'Cool Water' have been accounted something other than shit in '67, straight after *Blonde on Blonde*? More to the point, would his intention have been understood?

When *Self Portrait* works its cover versions are a match for most of their basement-tape equivalents. Dylan's account of 'Copper Kettle', an invented folk song from the early 1950s that isn't half as authentic as this singer makes it sound, is a glimpse of what the album might have been. The traditional 'Belle Isle' is a marvel of restraint that finds a proper use for the 'Nashville voice'. Gordon Lightfoot's 'Early Mornin' Rain' suffers only – if this counts as a criticism – from being too familiar. 'It Hurts Me Too' should not be dismissed just because of the company it is forced to keep. There are apostates among us, meanwhile, who cannot begrudge a smile at 'Blue Moon' and its homage to Presley, even if Dylan requires an ace fiddle player (Doug Kershaw) to carry the part that young Elvis just *sang*.

The album's real failing, says hindsight, might simply lie in the choices made. The list of outtakes, 20 and more, precious few of which have reached the public, is indisputably impressive, on paper at least. It contains everything from 'Sittin' On the Dock of the Bay' to Eric Andersen's marvellous 'Thirsty Boots' to that old favourite, 'House Carpenter'. Whatever else can be said about the album, the idea that it was some kind of elaborate joke on Dylan's part is impossible to sustain. The collection is horribly ill-designed, even misconceived, but not risible. He was pursuing the 'American songbook' notion, *Americana* in another guise, decades before the idea caught on and made fortunes for lesser lights. In his erratic way, Dylan was asking a question that is both reasonable and important: what is American song? To whom does it speak and why? Perhaps he would have been better off shouting his conclusions through a basement door.

In 1970, *Self Portrait* was a victim both of its times and of that new, strange, slouching beast, 'rock journalism'. Yet a generation later (in 2007) on the website of *Mojo* magazine, you could find it asserted that 'anyone attuned to the old-timey Dylan of *Love and Theft*, *Chronicles* and *Theme Time Radio Hour* will fall upon *Self Portrait* like a new Dylan delight, and one that's a little bit better than – are we allowed to say this? – *Modern Times*'. Indeed.

At the time, even the album's cover design was taken as an obscure provocation. Whatever Dylan's later reputation as a visual artist – and that's a whole other story – the big, primitive, mask-like head of *Self Portrait*, blank-eyed and open-mouthed, crude and apparently slapdash, seemed like a statement in its own right. In reality, it was probably a consequence of the simple fact that Dylan didn't possess much, if any, painterly technique. Years later he would seem to say he had not *intended* to portray himself. In 1970, an apparently obvious conclusion was drawn. The album was called *Self Portrait*; here was a painting of a male head representing an album by a certain male artist. *Ergo*, this was how Dylan saw himself: anonymous, unidentifiable and certainly not 'Bob Dylan'. It could have been anyone. That was assumed to be the idea behind the painting and therefore the idea behind this alienating, self-eradicating collection of songs.

*

One day after the album was released Dylan was awarded, as though for irony's sake, an honorary doctorate in music by Princeton University. The college dropout was granted esteem and a Latin scroll at last, though the accolade came too late for Abe Zimmerman to enjoy. Dylan himself, having just turned 29, doesn't seem to have taken much pleasure from the event on a sweltering June day, with his wife and the singer David Crosby in tow, but at least he got a song from the experience. In 1970, for him, that was no small thing. The noise of cicadas was loud; Dylan decided he heard the ravening sound of locusts. The citation invoked 'the arts of the common people' and 'the authentic expression of the disturbed and concerned conscience of young America'.

Recalling the event in *Chronicles*, Dylan would remember his reaction: a jolt of dismay, a shudder, sheer disbelief that still they were burdening him with their preconceptions and calling the torture an honour. He had been fooled yet again, or so he would write. Instead of talking about his music, they had portrayed him as a self-imprisoned oddball recluse. He kept his face expressionless and his opinions to himself. Inwardly, he seethed.

According to his memoir, Dylan was so angry he felt like gnawing his own flesh that day. He would become accustomed to institutional flattery as the years rolled on, but in 1970 his discomfort was such it invited a simple question. If that was how he felt, what was he doing there? Family man or not – and that too was mentioned by the college president – why was he submitting to the exquisite torture of public praise? In the memoir he says only that, despite everything, he was glad he accepted the degree. It offered credibility, of sorts. It was an acknowledgement by the wider world, misguided or not, and he stood in need of that at a time when his critical standing was in question. *Self Portrait* was hardly calculated to settle things down.

*

In October of 1970, in any case, it seemed for a moment as though Dylan had been stung into granting his critics the kind of answer they thought they wanted. The sudden appearance of an album entitled *New Morning* while *Self Portrait*'s reputation lay bleeding in the gutter looked like a mixture of contrition and defiance. Even the title appeared to say that the artist had put the errors of his recent past behind him. The collection's release a bare four months after the escape of the abominated double-album hotpotch meanwhile gave the impression, understandably enough, that Dylan had rushed into the Columbia studios on East 52nd Street to cover his shame with some half-decent music. That wasn't how it happened.

If *Self Portrait* was an exercise designed to unblock his creative plumbing it had not quite done the trick. *New Morning* simply wasn't good enough to allow anyone to say that a renaissance was afoot, though plenty of reviewers, possibly in desperation, tried to make the claim. Marcus announced grandly that the set was 'an act of vitality'. Various other critics heralded the resurrection (and the life) and the album of the year. Notoriously, Ralph Gleason's *Rolling Stone* notice shouted, 'We've Got Dylan Back Again'. The piece didn't say which Dylan, of course.

In fact, this one could probably best be described as diffident, tentative, less than sure of himself. The Nashville croon was gone, but in truth there was not a lot more to report. The album remains interesting, if slight; pleasant if too rarely compelling. It has its merits, a distinct ambience, four or five (of twelve) better than decent songs, but those are tantalising rather than arresting. Too often they presume that the listener must already know a fair bit about Bob Dylan, who he once was and what he once did. That would be his problem ever after, album upon album. A line of Bob Dylans would stand at his shoulder.

Nashville Skyline had been his last release under Grossman's management. For a while Albert would continue to receive his better than ample dole from Dylan's publishing, though that deal would be modified in due course, but in practical terms the separation became a divorce in April of 1970. There would be plenty of work ahead for the lawyers, and plenty of acrimony between the parties, mostly as a consequence of further contractual haggling in July. In any sense that mattered to him, however, Dylan began the new decade as a free man. As he had contended in song more than once, freedom is a tricky concept.

We don't know how he felt, or if he felt anything at all, about the dissolution of the partnership. In one sense the relationship had been typical of the industry and the period, the usual parable of minnow and shark, of naivety and huckster cynicism. On Grossman's behalf it has been argued, nevertheless, that he took Dylan from dingy Greenwich Village clubs to grand concert halls at lightning speed, that he truly cared about the music, that he was ferocious in defence of his client's interests and that he rarely obstructed the artist's pursuit of his art. Later court arguments would suggest, by contrast, that Albert was merely protective of Albert's considerable interests, that he had a practised eye for a golden goose and that his gall in appointing himself a full and equal partner in the enterprise called 'Bob Dylan' was astounding. The other partner would soon enough allege that Grossman was also guilty of sheer deceit.

Then again, Dylan couldn't say he had not been warned, even as a youngster. Nor could he honestly deny that all his rhetoric on the subject of phonies was made lumbering flesh in a manager whose reputation preceded him like a whiff of acrid cologne, a manager he had chosen. Still, they had been hand in glove for almost five years, and yoked to a relationship for almost three years more. It must have given Dylan plenty to think about. One conclusion drawn, self-evident from his subsequent career, was that he would never again allow himself to be in thrall to any individual. Thereafter, anyone who worked with Dylan in a management capacity would work for him. *John Wesley Harding*'s 'Dear Landlord' is sometimes interpreted as the singer's complaint against having someone 'put a price on my soul', but it doesn't truly fit the bill. *New Morning*, as a title, might better meet the case.

If nothing else the album demonstrated that Dylan had begun to write again, if fitfully, and had begun to do so even as he struggled to make sense of the *Self Portrait* project. Among the list of outtakes for that album are a pair of songs – 'Went to See the Gypsy' and 'Time

Passes Slowly' – that would reappear on *New Morning*. In terms of recordings made, in fact, there was no real gap between the two titles. The overmatter produced, in terms of cover versions, was considerable. Judging by that pile of songs, and by the material Columbia would release in 1973 as the derided *Dylan*, it's not even clear at which point *New Morning* came to be regarded as a separate collection of wholly original songs. Either the singer was still wedded to the idea of performing other people's material, or he still lacked confidence in his ability to sustain a self-written set.

The Princeton experience had given him 'Day of the Locusts', a song that was tagged as having something (or other) to do with Nathanael West's 1939 novel *The Day of the Locust* for no better reason than its title. In fact the track simply (more or less) sketches Dylan's familiar unease with institutions. 'Went to See the Gypsy' is meanwhile purportedly the result of an encounter with Elvis Presley, but no one can say where, or if, such a meeting took place. Clinton Heylin asserts that the two men met backstage in Las Vegas in 'the winter of 1970' – Elvis was certainly in town in the January of the year – but gives no source for the information.[8] The song itself, one of the best of the *New Morning* group, instead refers specifically to a suite in a big hotel and to a 'little Minnesota town'. Dylan himself told *Rolling Stone* in 2009 that he had never met the man: 'I never met Elvis because I didn't want to meet Elvis.' On the other hand, Presley would certainly tape a rowdy, eleven-minute account of 'Don't Think Twice' during a studio jam soon after Dylan's album was released. Again, the details don't have much to do with 'Gypsy', an elliptical song with something to say about performance, faith and illusions.

Elsewhere on the album there were experiments that spoke less of artistic confidence than of sheer indecision. Shelton (and most others) would list Dylan's first prayer, his first jazz song, his 'first Hank Williams-style talking country song' and his first waltz. The inventory is both accurate and trivial: these tracks were the least of the album. The 'jazz' piece, above all, remains a trial. This thing is truly phoney. The cocktail-lounge noise of 'If Dogs Run Free' is all but designed to distract from a lyric that can only have been intended – surely – as a Bob Dylan spoof. It could make anyone think kindly of writer's block.

If dogs run free, why not me

---

8   *Revolution in the Air*, p. 404.

Across the swamp of time?
My mind weaves a symphony
And tapestry of rhyme

'If Dogs Run Free' is an especially egregious example, perhaps, of what went wrong with *New Morning*, but an example all the same. Stuck too often just for words, reputedly his stock in trade, Dylan resorted to gimmicks. When the songs achieved honest simplicity, above all in 'Sign on the Window' and 'Time Passes Slowly', there were once again glimpses, but no more than glimpses, of what might have been. Too often Dylan was still aiming and missing.

For all that, several interesting if unimportant things go on beneath *New Morning*'s calm surface. One involves a group of three songs written at the invitation of the then 78-year-old patrician poet Archibald MacLeish for a dramatised version of the Stephen Vincent Benét short story 'The Devil and Daniel Webster', a piece entitled *Scratch*. Quite why Dylan imagined that 'New Morning', 'Time Passes Slowly' and 'Father of Night' could meet the requirements of such a project is hard to fathom; MacLeish certainly couldn't fathom it. This veteran of first-wave modernism and Paris in the 1920s was well acquainted with the foibles of genius – Hemingway, Fitzgerald, Jean Cocteau, Picasso and the rest – but failed to extract anything usable from Dylan. 'Archie' was planning a drama on the struggle for a man's soul and was offered the jaunty country comforts of 'New Morning'? His chosen songwriter would later claim that a dispute with 'the producer' ended the collaboration. In *Chronicles*, in contrast, he makes it clear he knew, even before a visit to the poet's home, that he had nothing to offer, least of all a single lyric capable of enlarging MacLeish's drama. Dylan was assailed on all sides and deeply confused. He was a man bereft both of optimism and ideas. MacLeish's drama was critically acclaimed without his help and Dylan used the rejected songs anyway. Each was decent enough, in its fashion, and probably helped to get him writing again. Nevertheless, he was still a long way from being out of the dark woods.

Work on the album began in earnest on the first afternoon of May 1970, just days after *Self Portrait* had been consigned to its fate. George Harrison came to town to join what was, in effect, the first session. No album should be judged on tapes illicitly acquired of musicians warming up, but if the guitarist found the last days of the Beatles shambolic, his private thoughts on some of the stuff permitted in

Columbia's New York studios would have been worth hearing. Granted: people were just having fun. It's not always clear that they meant it to be funny, too. A bootleg that begins with what sounds like a bar band the worse for wear murdering '(Ghost) Riders in the Sky' (that one) proceeds to 'Cupid' and 'All I Have to Do Is Dream'. Later, via drive-by shootings of songs by a former Bob Dylan, there's McCartney's 'Yesterday', performed as though the singer bears a grudge, and even 'Da Doo Ron Ron'. Yet somehow Dylan can still, amid what sounds like chaos, manage to amaze. Suddenly, two-thirds of the way through a knock-down contest with twenty songs, as though from nowhere, comes a very fine performance of 'Song to Woody' and a very fair 'Mama, You Been On My Mind'. It's as though there was something he was trying to remember.

An album got made in the end. Released on 21 October, it did well enough, too: number seven in the US and another number one in the UK. It would be three more years, nevertheless, before Dylan enjoyed that sort of success again. At the risk of murdering a metaphor, *New Morning* was a false dawn. He could still make records. He could still command a reverence that verged on the absurd. What he could not do, or could not do easily, was write with the fluency and driven sense of purpose that a few short years before had made him seem like a sanctified freak of nature. It was as though an entire person had disappeared overnight.

Life back in New York wasn't helping. Whatever it was that had possessed Dylan to believe a return to the Village would allow his family peace and anonymity after Woodstock was soon exposed as a delusion. The purchase of a house with a front door opening straight onto the sidewalk at 94 MacDougal Street was a very foolish move. Word got around instantly; out came the freaks. They refused to leave him alone. Nor were his complaints the usual coddled superstar's grumbling: Dylan truly was harassed at every turn, pursued whenever he was spotted. He had been taxed before, often enough, for 'answers', and lectured endlessly on his duties as a leader. This was different. This time the crazies decided he had no say in the matter.

It's fair to say that enough space has been wasted down the years on A.J. Weberman, 'garbology', the art of self-publicity, the 'Dylan Liberation Front', the effrontery and sense of entitlement of reactionary 'radicals', and the mad belief that any and every word or deed of Dylan's is symbolic and worthy of a concordance. It's the stuff of cults, the kind that always end badly, in farce and harm. Most observers still managed to find Weberman the Yippie provocateur hilarious, a portly cartoon burlesque of the counter-culture.

You need only pause for a second and consider things from Dylan's point of view. As 1970 was becoming 1971 he was father to five children. He was trying to rebuild his complicated life and reassess his career. Meanwhile, mobs – by all accounts the word is accurate – were laying siege to his home with loudhailers. 'Dylan's brain belongs to the people, not the pigs!' went one cry. The possibility that the brain in question might belong to its bearer was never addressed. Weberman's crowd in no sense represented Dylan's real admirers, but you can hardly blame the singer if his view of the relationship between pop art and audience was coloured, somewhat. He feared for his family. When the wrong kind of vermin are rooting through your garbage – A.J.'s speciality; nothing to do with Dylan was insignificant – only fury can follow despair.

Last among the least funny jokes is that Weberman to this day enjoys a certain grudging respect among Dylan 'scholars' for his *Dylan to English Dictionary* (2005) and for coining the word – he called it a word – 'Dylanology'. Tapes and transcripts of telephone conversations between the two men in January of 1971 – only Dylan knows what Dylan was thinking – are still pored over by people who would never, of course, dream of going through a writer's garbage. Weberman later became associated with right-wing Zionism, which probably figures. At one point Dylan felt the need to assault this scholarly figure physically, allegedly bouncing his head off a sidewalk, which certainly figures.

In the real world, the artist was still feeling the aftershocks of his father's death. Their most obvious – or at least most public – manifestation came when the Dylans took a holiday in Israel and the singer was photographed at Jerusalem's Western Wall, the Wailing Wall, on his 30th birthday. The media drew their conclusions instantly; this time they were not so far wrong. In *Chronicles* Dylan would snipe at the perfidious press for transforming him into a Zionist, as though the entire exercise had been a piece of deliberate misdirection on his part. That wasn't the case. He had been 'investigating' religion and his heritage since *John Wesley Harding*; he had his memories of Camp Herzl. By the summer of 1971, despite wild rumours about the extent of his commitment, he was serious about his Jewishness. As subsequent adventures in theology would demonstrate, he was not necessarily bound by it, but that's another matter. If nothing else, the pictures of Dylan in his skullcap shed a bright new light on certain of *Harding*'s parables. It became possible to read these frontier outlaw tales in the Talmudic manner, as allegories capable of giving a better sense of the Law. Their composer offered no such explanation. Still, the coincidences – if you can call them that – could not be ignored. The boy who had denied his parents and his faith for the sake of Bob Dylan had turned 30 and returned, in his fashion, as though on the instant, to the fold. He had become still another person. Yet the same old question persisted. What was he supposed to do with this Dylan?

*

At first sight, not much. In the summer of 1971 George Harrison talked him into appearing at two concerts, afternoon and evening, scheduled for Madison Square Garden on 1 August in aid of the people of ravaged Bangladesh. The crowd's welcome for Dylan earned the usual adjectives: ecstatic, delirious, joyous. Part of their delight arose as much from Dylan's appearance and manner as from the music, though the five songs he performed were pleasing. There he was, the figure New Yorkers had thought never to see again: denim jacket, Martin acoustic, harmonica in its rack. His opening song was entirely appropriate for a show meant to raise funds for a country almost destroyed by cyclones and civil war, but that wasn't what the audience heard. They heard Dylan singing 'A Hard Rain's a-Gonna Fall'. For some it was too good to be true, and somehow hard to believe.

He came and went, appeared and disappeared. In the middle of March he had spent a couple of days in the studios – not Columbia's New York studios, however – with the pianist Leon Russell, and emerged, for a miracle, with two whole new songs, written and recorded. That they happened to make much the same statement was no accident. 'Watching the River Flow' commenced as it meant to continue: 'What's the matter with me / I don't have much to say.' While people were 'disagreeing everywhere you look', the singer was happy, or so he said, to sit 'contentedly' and watch the eternal river roll by. Contented or not, he had no choice in the matter. This was no subtle meditation on his withdrawal from a public role: he had few new songs for anyone to argue over. If creativity is a habit, Dylan was all but cured.

The better work, 'When I Paint My Masterpiece', was also the funnier of the two. Here was a hero, of the past and in the present, who had spent far too many hours in combat, 'inside the Coliseum / Dodging lions and wastin' time'. Everything would be different, though, when he painted – for didn't everyone say he surely would? – that masterpiece. Dylan mocked his admirers and his own reputation. For most of the time songs, far less masterworks, eluded him. Any kind of work came hard. Nevertheless, there was a hint, in his delivery and in the song's swagger, that he *just about* wanted to believe the best might still lie ahead.

It wouldn't happen in 1971, however, and nor would it happen in 1972. The pair of new songs assembled that March were part of a pattern: odds and ends, hit-and-run recordings, a desultory life. The two tracks, together with pleasant versions of three basement songs recorded with Happy Traum in September, would pad out that year's album release, November's *Bob Dylan's Greatest Hits Volume II*, and lend a little freshness to a package of otherwise familiar material. Some fans complained at having to pay for a double album just to secure five 'previously unreleased' tracks and the single, 'Watching the River Flow'. The last of these meanwhile counted as a hit only if you stopped counting at number 41 on the US charts.

Tarantula had appeared, finally, to general incomprehension and some outright incredulity, but all talk of Bob Dylan the poet of the age was retrospective. The scholars were arriving on the scene in force only to find the trail going cold. Overpriced bootlegs became a preoccupation – obsession is such a harsh word – for devotees deprived of much else to go on. In the semi-academic terms now being applied, *John Wesley Harding* began to seem like a last flowering among the artist-sanctioned works. Despite sterling efforts in some quarters, nothing Dylan had produced since that album could bear the kind of weight his most eager students wanted to place on his songs. It was becoming plain, too, that no grand renunciation was involved. Dylan wasn't heading, as one critic had suggested, to the creative equivalent of Rimbaud's Abyssinian exile. Instead, he was stranded.

His Columbia contract was about to expire, too, a fact of which he was keenly aware. He might even have been counting on a new deal to apply the kind of spur he needed. As it was, and putting aside the rhetoric of Weberman and other, less intrusive voices, he risked becoming redundant. Just the moment, then, for a protest song. No one was expecting that.

*

It happens that 'George Jackson' is one of the best of the genre, but many of Dylan's admirers hesitate even to mention the work. It seems to make them uncomfortable. One large, recent account of the singer's life contains only a single sentence referring to a 'topical song'. Extolling the flashing chimes of freedom is one thing; celebrating a prison-radicalised Maoist killer and self-styled revolutionary who believed he was at war with America is, it seems, another matter. The Black Panthers meanwhile belong to a history that is fast being erased. In the song Dylan is, in any case, absolutely explicit in his support and sympathy for Jackson. Surely on this occasion he could not be accused of having failed to take sides?

Predictably, typically, he was so accused after the song, issued as a 'double-A' single in band and solo arrangements, appeared in November of 1971. *Rolling Stone* remarked that the song had 'divided speculators [*sic*] into two camps, those who see it as the poet's return to social relevance and those who feel that it's a cheap way for Dylan to get a lot of people off his back'. It was neither. The song was a one-off, written spontaneously and recorded quickly. Jackson's death meanwhile represented a fundamental belief for Dylan, one that had been with him, thanks to Woody Guthrie no doubt, since his earliest days in the Village.

Sometimes I think this whole world
Is one big prison yard
Some of us are prisoners
The rest of us are guards

Did George Jackson deserve the threnody? More than four decades after his death that is held, still, to be 'controversial'. There is no doubt that he was charged with killing a guard at Soledad jail in revenge for the shooting dead, by sharpshooters, of three of his fellow inmates, and was probably facing the gas chamber. There is no doubt that he had been a juvenile criminal – armed robbery, assault, burglary – sentenced at eighteen to the peculiarly American indeterminate sentence of 'one year to life'. There is no doubt that his guards described Jackson as 'antisocial' and the ringleader of what they defined as a prison gang. There's no doubt, too, that the prison authorities at San Quentin, the institution to which he had been transferred, insisted the Jackson they shot stone dead on 21 August 1971 was armed and attempting to escape.

In one of his letters from prison, Jackson had tried to explain what it was like to be 'fair game, hunted, an alien'. He and his supporters said he was a target precisely because 'It's never occurred to me to lie down and be kicked!' and because, thanks to his book, *Soledad Brother*, he was drawing international attention to abysmal (and segregated) conditions within California's penal system. Stephen Bingham, one of Jackson's lawyers and an individual accused of helping to smuggle a pistol to the prisoner despite a series of metal detectors – the attorney was acquitted of all charges – later said his client was 'a marked man', that because 'George was the obvious catalyst for [the] public spotlight, he became Enemy No. 1 to the California Department of Corrections'.[9] Bingham also maintained that the area of San Quentin from which Jackson was supposedly attempting to escape, the 'Adjustment Center', was a prison within a prison, and escape-proof. Jackson had also been strip-searched at least twice, it is further claimed, before he was found – so the authorities said – to be armed. The weapon itself was not afterwards produced.

Dylan didn't tell even half of this contested tale. He didn't mention Jackson's Marxism, or the rhetoric of armed revolution favoured by the prisoner. He didn't say that during Jackson's 'escape attempt' other prisoners broke loose and murdered guards. Dylan picked his side. Yet even the apparently unlikely idea that 'they threw away the key' after locking Jackson up for a mere $70 robbery turned out to be justified. That was the meaning of 'one year to life'. Each time the young Jackson rebelled, the sentence was extended.

Some in the press said Dylan had 'returned to protest' with 'George Jackson'. He had no such intention. All he had done with the song was the one thing demanded of him by 'progressives': he had spoken out. Predictably, the single did only slightly better than 'Watching the River Flow', peaking – if that's the word – at number 33 in the United States. It was nevertheless another reminder, if one was needed, that Dylan would not be categorised, politically or otherwise.

*

In the first months of 1972 he seemed to disappear entirely. This was an absence as complete as any he had or ever would achieve. In his private reality Dylan was living on a ranch he had bought in Tucson, Arizona, absorbing the smells and colours of the desert, soaking up the history of the Old West as though this America was second nature to him. The experience would turn out to be useful. It seems he *might* have been writing a little at the time, though whether he was ready, willing or able to contemplate a new album is far from clear. It would

9   Interview with Joe Allen, socialistworker.org, March 2000.

soon become plain that he had no intention of delivering such a product to Columbia. Master of his own fate at last, Dylan found himself biding his time. He had plenty of that at his disposal.

Richard Nixon would seek re-election in 1972 as a scandal involving some apartment buildings in Washington known as the Watergate began to bubble. In that year America would prepare to withdraw from Vietnam; Israeli athletes would be murdered by terrorists at the Munich Olympics; and a US president would visit Communist China. The headlines would come and go, but Dylan had long since ceased to notice, or to contemplate shaping a front page into a song. Whatever 'George Jackson' had meant to him, the mood had passed. A decade before he would probably have extracted at least a comic talking blues from the figure of Nixon, but that Bob Dylan might as well have never existed. If he even noticed the tenth anniversary of his gauche debut as a recording artist, he didn't let on. In 1972, his own past was alien to him.

Meanwhile, undaunted, his industry was busy manufacturing 'new Dylans'. Anyone liable to pick up a harmonica during the recording of a song they happened to have written unaided got the treatment. John Prine was a notable victim after the appearance of his first album in 1971. Hapless Bruce Springsteen, doubly cursed after being 'discovered' by John Hammond and signed to Columbia in the following year, would have to work long and hard to scrape off the label. The law of supply and demand was in operation. Patently, there was a need for some sort of new Bob Dylan. In 1972, in a moment of conspicuous irony, the writer of that name, still struggling to write, worked instead on his back pages, a volume of his lyrics and old 'liner note' verses that would emerge in time as *Writings and Drawings*.

It would give the critics and the professors something to talk about. Chiefly they would talk about the literary status, if any, of Dylan's verses. People who would struggle to define the word 'poetry' argued back and forth, yet again, and cast their votes for and against: real poet or mere songwriter? The author would call this book *Writings and Drawings*; later editions would settle for 'lyrics'. In 1973, when the volume was published, it would seem that Dylan was taking his song-verses seriously, from the immaculate lines of *John Wesley Harding* to the ridiculous 'If Dogs Run Free'. In fact, the book would open with an actual, quite decent dedicatory poem. That would be followed by four lines in Dylan's hand restating his position, doubly negative, as he sat out a creative drought in the Arizona desert:

If I can't please everybody
I might as well not please nobody at all
(There's but so many people
An I just can't please them all)

A mystique was being constructed around a mundane reality. Dylan was turning apparent self-effacement into an art form, as though consumed by existential weariness, as though only the impossible demand that he 'please everybody' – and when had he ever managed to do that? – was hindering the appearance of those elusive masterpieces. He seemed to say, in this little piece of doggerel as elsewhere, that he was choosing not to write and that somehow this decision was the fault of his audience. It wasn't wholly *untrue*, but he was shaping bricks from rhetorical straw. Something – and bereavement remains the only plausible possibility – had stopped him in his tracks. He could as well have scribbled that in 1972, try as he might, he couldn't please anybody. He hid in a movie instead.

Approached by the screenwriter Rudy Wurlitzer who 'needed a song' for a picture to be entitled *Pat Garrett and Billy the Kid*, Dylan noticed that 'I wasn't doing anything'. He read the script, watched a few of the director's other films, such as *Ride the High Country* and *The Wild Bunch*, and wrote the song 'real quick'. That should have been the end of it. Instead, the screenwriter suggested that Dylan might be suitable for a part in the production. The idea was appealing. Whatever his talents as an actor (minimal), Dylan has never been able to resist the chance to disappear inside a role. Armchair psychologists will draw their own conclusions.

In the wake of *The Wild Bunch*, *Straw Dogs* and *Junior Bonner*, Sam Peckinpah was almost a parody of a big-time Hollywood director. He was also, variously, an alcoholic with a drug problem, a manic depressive prone to violence, a poet of the cinema, a gun nut given to shooting up the joint, a man of honour, a cynical student of American power, a maniac, a romantic, a thug, and an individual revered by those friends and colleagues who could tolerate him for any length of time. He also fought for, and over, his movies, sometimes for the hell of it. Peckinpah affected never to have heard of Bob Dylan.

After lobbying from his two stars, Kris Kristofferson and James Coburn, the director agreed to meet the singer for what turned out to be an audition. Dylan, who must have wanted the tiny part of Alias sincerely, submitted to the indignity, and sang the pair of songs he had to hand. He got the role, whatever it was, and the job of supplying a soundtrack. Kristofferson would later allege, however, that Peckinpah felt he had been put under pressure by the studio, MGM, to hire this pop star. The director certainly didn't go out of his way to turn Dylan's big-screen acting debut into an event of any significance. Anyone else's performance in this bit part would have been forgotten long ago.

Reputedly, most of Dylan's performances ended up on the cutting-room floor as Peckinpah engaged in his usual battles with his studio masters. What was lost? The tricky fact is that even when a director's cut of *Pat Garrett and Billy the Kid* was released in 1988 with 16 minutes restored there was no revelatory Dylan performance to be seen. If Alias has a function in the film, it is as a near-mute witness, the conduit for hearsay and legend. Dylan did his real talking with the soundtrack.

The inevitable bootleg, generally known as *Pecos Blues*, doesn't add much of note to the album as released save for a slight-enough song named 'Goodbye Holly' and two pieces of knockabout, one entitled 'Rock Me Mama (Like a Wagon Wheel)', the other 'Sweet Amarillo' The film, in any of its incarnations, is illuminated instead by the ballad of 'Billy', in its several versions, by Dylan's sun-bleached instrumentals and by that hypnotic death song 'Knockin' On Heaven's Door'. With these, the picture acquired a depth of meaning and a poetry it would otherwise have lacked. Dylan meanwhile acquired his most successful single since 'Rainy Day Women'.

That wasn't the point of his efforts, of course. He and Sara had a miserable time during the Durango shoot, enduring a mixture of tedium and movie-set madness while Peckinpah raged, laboured and fought a running battle with MGM. Cast and crew worked on through Thanksgiving 1973, then through Christmas, then New Year. In January, in Mexico City, Dylan had to begin to pretend he knew how to make film music. This he attempted with a chaotic all-night session that, predictably, produced only one version of 'Billy' fit for use. The real work would be done in Los Angeles in February.

As movie music goes, Dylan's work on *Pat Garrett* seems only to improve with age. It was not received favourably on its release in July of 1973, however. Critics, apparently oblivious to the needs and purposes of this or any film, in effect denounced the release as lazy and self-indulgent. A mere two songs, even those two songs, on the first Dylan album in almost three years counted as a kind of insolence.

After so much praise down the years a touch of open contempt was now evident. The fact that the artist had somehow encapsulated the entire mythos of the Old West in a pair of tunes and some incidental music went almost unnoticed. Both were songs of death, not heroism; both said something about fate and God. 'Knockin' On Heaven's Door' happened to be one of those 'classics' that critics are paid to notice. Instead, the album was treated as more evidence, if required, that Dylan was a busted flush.

*

No one to speak of seems to pay much attention these days to *Planet Waves*. A good song about a good father wishing all that is best for his newborn has become 'anthemic', something for every heart. Nothing else from the collection has lodged in the Dylan canon, and that counts as a shame. 'May you stay forever young': who wouldn't swear by a cliché rendered sincerely? But the work tends to obscure a couple of other songs, and a couple of other questions.

How would it be if Huck Finn lit out 'for the territory' and returned, finally, briefly, after a blur of years? How would things stand if Bob Dylan did the same? And where is that lived and imagined American territory, in any case?

His memoir, *Chronicles*, burns most strongly when he is reaching through the veil of years in the always-doomed effort to touch the lost geography of his childhood and youth. *Planet Waves* was that book's precursor. Dylan has spoken loyally, often enough, of the pure air and killing cold of the North Country. When young, he wanted out, up and gone: landscape and atmosphere were not enough to sustain or hold him. Older, he has returned now and then to a Minnesota farm, so the obsessives report, but he seems – and *Chronicles* agrees – to ache with ambivalence. The past is a remembered country, but the borders are closed.

Yet isn't that most of the point of *Adventures of Huckleberry Finn*, the novel from which America's literature sprang, less as a great whale or a leather-stockinged tracker than as a voice? Without Huck Finn there is no Hemingway, no *On the Road*, no poor Scott Fitzgerald dreaming of the rolling fields of the republic and those bobbing boats, by their tens of millions, drawn ceaselessly into the past. That idea is one of the bedrocks of American literary criticism. Yet where can the voice be heard? In memory, most often. Dylan's Hibbing and Duluth were on the edge of things, but central to the American experience, places filled in his childhood with migrant voices, American voices. And in the *Planet Waves* suite he went back.

It's not a great record, not by his standards. 'Forever Young' is a great *kind* of song, but only great because it does not press or test the audience. It is a song about mortality, not parental sentiment – though let us never knock sentiment – yet the touch of darkness within it tends to be ignored. The song says that things end. The album, equally, can seem like a fit of nostalgia for a lost place and time, but the sense of loss is more than personal. The old America had once belonged to all.

Thus: 'History became a lie! The sideshow took over . . .' So ran Dylan's hand-scrawled sleeve note, later 'suppressed'. The point would be, of course, that 'the sideshow' was also the career he had sought with a feral instinct. You are caused to wonder: what would Bob Dylan's ideal 'Bob Dylan' career have been? Those who complain of vast fame rarely get much sympathy. In the case of this artist, however, a great deal of time has been spent in taking stock. *Planet Waves* is the sort of autobiography that gives little away, but the very fact of its existence makes a statement. In 1973, history was creeping up on Dylan.

Various labels had tried to seduce him; Columbia had not tried hard enough to keep him. We can spare ourselves the corporate politics, or ask why David Geffen's Asylum Records could extract an album from Dylan with no apparent effort when the singer's former associates had been left with only a soundtrack to show for three years of patience. Notoriously, Columbia would retaliate against the ingrate by sticking out a collection of *Self Portrait* and *New Morning* leftovers called, with a certain impertinence, *Dylan*. (It's not half as bad as some maintain, has some nice performances and probably possesses more coherence, as an album, than *Self Portrait*.) The fact that Geffen came up with a one-or-two-record deal that would not tie Dylan down, plus a very generous royalty rate, probably helped. The additional fact that the singer had moved to California might have also been a factor. It's most likely, however, that he was placing himself in exile to demonstrate his worth to Columbia, lest they forget. Hence the convenience of an open-ended commitment to the aptly named Asylum.

Quite why Geffen wanted this performer for his new label is in one sense mysterious. By 1973, Dylan's record sales – in the absence of new records – were not such as to promise a big return. On one brutal reading his career had staggered to a close with the 1960s. Geffen may have been hoping to buy credibility for his revived Asylum label after its merger with Elektra. He may have been – and certainly appears to have been – a sincere fan. He planned the exercise with care. But still: there were plenty of people prepared to say that the man who had been capable of releasing *Self Portrait*, and who had not made an album of consequence in more than three years, was on the wrong side of the hill.

Who were his audience in 1973? The old 'spokesman for a generation' tag still got wheeled out like a premature obituary when Dylan's name came up, but it failed to explain what had become of that generation. The college kids of 1963 were approaching or passing 30. Their younger siblings, if they thought about Dylan at all, had to reconcile *Blonde on Blonde* with *Nashville Skyline* and that *Portrait*. The singer-songwriters who had emerged in the wake of 'Hard Rain' and 'Tambourine Man' had taken the genre, if such it was, in directions Dylan had never indicated. Geffen had to contend with a simple fact: the 1960s, whatever they had meant, were over. His prize signing would have to earn his keep. First the legend would have to prove that he was still a prize.

Proof was not long in coming, but it came in a form disconcerting for artist and impresario alike. *Planet Waves* had been recorded quickly in November of 1973 from such songs as Dylan had been able to put together, in large part because he and The Band were due to commence a 40-date tour of 21 cities in Chicago at the beginning of January. The enormous publicity for 'Tour '74' declared – there was no escape from the claim – that this was, at last, Dylan's 'comeback'. Yet when the long-awaited album appeared it did only moderately well, even when a surge of pre-orders had given the artist his first US number-one album. After the first rush for half a million copies, only a further 100,000 records were sold.

The demand for concert tickets, even at steep prices, meanwhile ran into millions of postal applications. By one estimate there were, in fact, ten million requests to witness the artist's return to the stage. Dylan was a curiosity, it seemed, but his music, the new music so long demanded, the stuff that wasn't country or cover versions or a mere movie soundtrack, was somehow regarded as no big deal. In Britain, so loyal for so long, *Planet Waves* got no higher than number seven.

The record-buyers and the critics had a point. An album Dylan had intended, with a nod to an old song, to call *Ceremonies of the Horsemen* did not exactly draw attention to itself. The opening, self-consciously uptempo number, 'On a Night Like This', was limp and pointless. 'Forever Young', grand as it might have been, was given one version more than was required. Three songs – 'Going, Going, Gone', 'Wedding Song' and 'Dirge' – were bleak and unwelcoming. The songs that lay between were far more interesting than they sounded, but too often they sounded less laid-back than tired. Dylan was back, as every other review managed to say, but he was not the Bob Dylan most recognised.

He had yielded at last to the confessional mode: that much seemed clear at least to the critics. Taken at face value, these were songs about his Minnesota youth ('Never Say Goodbye'), his marriage ('Wedding Song'), one of his children ('Forever Young'), or about his struggles for self-possession ('Going, Going, Gone'). Whether the songs were truly autobiographical is open to argument, however. For this composer, the problem in any such enterprise lay in identifying the person he was able or willing to portray. On this album there is the appearance of revelation, the semblance of intimacy. Many hints are dropped, but hints they remain.

For all that, Dylan had begun, finally, to find reasons to write. It wasn't high art. Nothing on *Planet Waves* would end up in a dictionary of quotations or a seminar room – this is not a criticism, necessarily – and only one of its songs would survive on the tour's set lists from beginning to end. You could call the set a significant minor album. It drew attention to itself because of what it seemed to offer: a Dylan learning to write about himself, past and present.

Such was the ruling from the infallible reviewing fraternity. Few paused to wonder about artistic stratagems and evasions. Apparently – the tricky word – a manner Dylan had avoided throughout his writing career was helping him to save that career. His next studio album would cast a bright light over the question of what was truly at stake in 'autobiography'. First, though, he had to face his public, and face the burden of impossible expectations.

He and The Band had got together a couple of times during the previous autumn to see what remained, musically, of their partnership. That had led to *Planet Waves*. The album and Dylan's deal with Geffen had thereafter made a tour almost inevitable. The singer had not bargained on this tour, on this scale, with this level of public scrutiny. Dylan and his musicians would get the bulk of the millions generated by their performances, but that didn't ease their discomfort. *Planet Waves* didn't justify the private-jet, arena-rock circus that was Tour '74. The audiences exceeded anything the troupe had attracted in 1966 – a fact that did not escape the veterans' notice – and the press were everywhere, jotting down notes. Like it or not, Dylan and The Band were rock stars; Dylan loathed it. As once before, the troupe put their heads down, bullish, and charged. It did the job, but it was the opposite of an artistic triumph.

Anyone who would exchange *Before the Flood*, the resulting live double album, for *Planet Waves* is a dedicated enemy of subtlety. Some bootlegs suggest that there were better shows than those recorded in Los Angeles, at tour's end, but the impression of great songs coarsened, of nuances flattened, of a career rendered into the base metal of nostalgia, persists. Dylan would later call the tour 'the hardest thing I had ever done'. This was, of course, saying something. Rumours as to his private behaviour also began to circulate. There had been good reasons for avoiding a return to the road.

That aside, the millions of dollars and millions of fans solved no problems. City after city might have welcomed the prodigal's return and the crowd might have waved their preposterous cigarette lighters in what passed for homage. All that Dylan had to show for the 1970s, thus far, were two minor albums serving merely to reflect still more glory on his achievements of the 1960s. On this showing, there was no more reason to talk about the art of poetry. He was a prisoner, still, of his past.

Tangled Up in Blue

We allow our past to exist. Our credibility is based on our past. But deep in our soul we have no past. I don't think we have a past, any more than we have a name. You can say we have a past if we have a future. Do we have a future? No. So how can our past exist if the future doesn't exist?

Interview with Rolling Stone, 1978

He once said the songs were inspired by the short stories of Anton Chekhov. In fact, he said, the 'entire album' was 'based on' those Russian tales. Not a soul believed him. As he would recall in his memoirs, the critics decreed that it was autobiographical; he didn't care. In early 1975, in any case, two things were self-evident to most serious observers of serious popular music for the literate AOR audience. First, Dylan had made his best record in half a dozen years. Soon enough, some would vouch that *Blood on the Tracks* was possibly the best record he had ever made, and very possibly one of the best records anyone had ever made. These were defensible statements. That they were important only to those who arrange art by a canonical checklist, a cultural *Billboard* chart, got forgotten, as always. 'The best since . . .' does no honour to this piece of work. Comparisons tend to be invidious for good reasons. Such, nevertheless, was the instant cliché: best since . . . Dylan was *back*, again, never having been too far away.

Second, it was impossible for many listeners to believe that a collection of brooding, intimate songs could be anything other than autobiographical and therefore 'confessional'. Dylan might have invented the singer-songwriter, but by the mid-1970s the paradigm had shifted. By then it involved assumptions and rules for the use of the personal pronoun and the spilling of beans. More than once he has tried to say that a song involving 'I' and 'me' is not *necessarily* an example of true confessions. Then again, he has sometimes let it be

543

known that all the songs are always about him. That, in turn, would depend on what is meant by 'about'. Nevertheless, when *Blood on the Tracks* hit the stores it was generally assumed that any singer performing 'solo' had truth-telling privileges. Once again, the lone acoustic guitar was claiming moral superiority. Solipsism was the unique selling point.

Besides, this suite of songs had a narrative explicable, or just about, in those terms. It spoke – didn't it? – of a marriage gone to the bad. And hadn't there been gossip enough beforehand over the marriage of Bob and Sara Dylan? Years later, one of the couple's children, Jakob, would wrap the matter up for most by asserting that *Blood on the Tracks* was the sound of his parents talking. The idea that an album, or any piece of art, could be two (or more) kinds of thing simultaneously seemed impossible for reviewers to comprehend. So the idea was ignored, by and large. In 1978, in contrast, the singer would tell *Rolling Stone*: 'I've heard it said that Dylan was never as truthful as when he wrote *Blood on the Tracks*, but that wasn't necessarily *truth*, it was just *perceptive*.'

Chekhov wrote often enough, it so happens, about relationships failed and failing. It's not wholly implausible, either, to find echoes of a song like 'Simple Twist of Fate' in certain stories. Chekhov's 'The Lady With the Little Dog' tells of two people, both married to others, who meet in the resort town of Yalta and commence an impossible affair. Gurov, the older of the two, is practised in infidelity. To begin with this jaded, predatory soul doesn't take the trifling amatory business amid the seafront promenades, parks and anonymous hotels seriously. Afterwards, he tells himself he doesn't care. Yet once he is back in Moscow, his old life begins to disgust him, and he seeks her out.

> they felt that fate had intended them to be together, and found it impossible to understand why they were both married to other people; they were like two migratory birds, a male and a female, who had been caught and made to live in separate cages.[1]

People tell me it's a sin
To know and feel too much within
I still believe she was my twin, but I lost the ring
She was born in spring, but I was born too late
Blame it on a simple twist of fate

---

1   From *About Love and Other Stories*, trans. Rosamund Bartlett (2004).

Anyone can play that game, of course. Dylan's remark – joke, if you prefer – contains a serious hint about the craft of storytelling. A study of the Russian master, an attempt to acquire a tone or catch an individual's interior life in a phrase, sounds entirely fitting in the context of *Blood on the Tracks*. Chekhov's melancholia isn't so far distant, either, from the mood of the album's dissociated love songs. Whether actual stories truly served as models is harder to establish. 'Based on' – as Dylan had it in *Chronicles* – is a loose notion. It doesn't really matter. In the songs perspectives are multiplied, time and again. The presentation of character alters in the telling – by whom? – and the retelling. There is a self-evident care, too, in the choice of language, a sparseness, an avoidance of redundancy. It's a matter of technique. The opening song, 'Tangled Up in Blue', makes that much plain. Why wouldn't Dylan, praised so often for his storytelling gift, draw inspiration from a Russian with a genius for concision? The fact is that with this album his writing changed. Yet again.

Contrary to those who insist on true confessions, in any case, *Blood on the Tracks* isn't *about* a single relationship. Dylan and his wife were certainly estranged, and almost finished as a couple, but this is no duologue. Nor, contrary to its reputation, does *Blood on the Tracks* brood from beginning to last. Some of it is dark as hell, but some of it is playful, and some of it, especially at the close, strikes a benign note of resignation and acceptance. In short, there is a lot more going on than a few scenes from a marriage.

In 1975, that was not the consensus. Where singer-songwriters were concerned there was no escape from the biographical fallacy, even if it was tricky to tie Sara to Lily, Rosemary, or even a spousal Jack of Hearts. Where Dylan himself was concerned, praise for the album also came with a nasty little subtext derived from one of his earlier songs: 'Pain sure brings out the best in people, doesn't it?' After the album's success, he would observe in an interview that he couldn't understand people 'enjoying that type of pain'. You can see why this performer, of all performers, would want to keep his distance, and his sense of perspective. Taxed by *Rolling Stone* to explain what *Blood on the Tracks* was 'about', he answered, 'The present.'

As to things tangled and untangled, the first week of April 2012 would bring news from *Variety* magazine that the film rights to the album had been bought, improbably enough, by a Brazilian production company, RT Features. In a press release, chief executive Rodrigo Teixeira would state: 'Our goal is to work with a film-maker who can create a classic drama with characters and an environment that capture the feelings that the album inspires in all fans.' Someone thought they knew what *Blood on the Tracks* might be *about*, then.

Teixeira didn't have a director for his 'classic drama', nor did he mention a writer who might be capable of welding songs such as 'Idiot Wind', 'Lily, Rosemary and the Jack of Hearts' and 'If You See Her, Say Hello' into any sort of coherent narrative. *Variety* meanwhile failed to say whether this English-language venture stood a better than usual Hollywood chance of actually becoming a picture. An attempt to make a movie of 'Brownsville Girl', the actually cinematic 1986 song written by Dylan and the playwright-actor Sam Shepard, had by this point been 'in the works' for two years.

In any case, who had owned the rights in order to sell them? As reports of the RT Features coup went around the world, an outfit named Grey Water Park Productions was mentioned. No one bothered to explain that since 1996 this had been Bob Dylan's production company, with a hand in everything from the film *I'm Not There* to his *Theme Time Radio Hour* to the Scorsese documentary *No Direction Home*.

Perhaps there was something to be said after all for 'enjoying that type of pain'.

*

By celebrity standards the Dylan marriage had endured better than most. Its end was never likely to be easy for either party. They had shared the best part of a decade. There were beloved children involved. The dream they had held in common – the dream of ordinary, of normal – had been precious but impossible. His capacity for fidelity was intermittent, especially during his return to touring in 1974, and Sara Dylan was wounded once too often, according to garrulous 'friends'. In the soap-opera version of events he was also drinking hard. The press were picking up gossip. In the summer of that year the Dylans separated.

Frictions had been evident since the spring. Dylan was no longer eager, far less content, to stay home. Later he would declare that the influence of an older man, a New York artist and teacher named Norman Raeben, had somehow led to problems with Sara. He even uttered the immortal words: his wife didn't 'understand' him after he began to take classes. It's equally possible that she understood him too well, and understood the male definition of life on the road well enough to draw her own conclusions about Tour '74. There were press 'sightings' and claims, after the fact, of affairs. Some were accurate.

In the summer he retreated to a farm he had bought in Minnesota, to the north of Minneapolis, and began to fill up his notebook. His children and a new girlfriend were present; his brother, David, and family were neighbours. Those domestic facts hardly mattered. Equally, anything Dylan has since said about *Blood on the Tracks* – and he has said the usual number of contradictory things – seems extraneous to the interior world of the album.

It's a strange place. There is no trivia in it. Nothing happens that isn't supposed to happen: fate always takes a hand. Every decision is important, personal and moral, even when the situation seems trivial. In this rainy, darkening world existence does indeed feel like a Russian play. In this drama ideas of chance, luck and unintended consequences are as real as Chekhov ever maintained. A track left out of the final reckoning – one of Dylan's larger errors – begins with a bald statement of human truth. 'Up To Me' is a short story in its own right. It commences: 'Everything went from bad to worse. / Money never changed a thing. / Death kept followin', trackin' us down . . .' The characters meet and part, time and again. 'Time is an enemy' and 'life is a pantomime'. Fate takes a hand simply to separate two people – for there is no other explanation who 'both heard voices for a while, now the rest is history . . .'

Blood on the Tracks contains still more evidence, before the bolt from the blue, of a movement towards religious belief. At this point, though, some of the old doubt persists. In 'Up To Me', apparently apropos of nothing else in another of Dylan's episodic narratives, comes

> We heard the Sermon on the Mount and I knew it was too complex
> It didn't amount to anything more than what the broken glass reflects
> When you bite off more than you can chew you pay the penalty
> Somebody's got to tell the tale, I guess it must be up to me

This *seems* to say that Christ's sermon ('too complex') simply describes what a man sees in his broken mirror. Lived reality is more brutal: attempt too much, hope for too much, bite off more than you can chew, and you pay the price. This is the tale that the singer, the only one left of the cast, has to tell. There is no redemption; God had yet to come looking for this Bob Dylan. Instead, he had taken classes with Raeben and learned finally, or so he would say in 1978, to see himself for what he was.

it locked me into the present time more than anything else I ever did. More than any experiences I've ever had, any enlightenment I've ever had. Because I was constantly being intermingled with myself and all the different selves that were in there, until this one left, and that one left, and finally I got down to the one I was familiar with.[2]

On the other hand, there is the contrary evidence of 'Shelter From the Storm', perhaps the album's most singular piece. If you take the claim that *Blood on the Tracks* is wholly autobiographical seriously, here's an early sighting of a Bob Dylan – he would reappear in due course – capable of mistaking himself for a Christ-figure. An album that is supposed to be 'about' a relationship, or relationships, in reality ranges through time and through a series of identities. It would take a dozen films to do the facets of these songs justice. Dylan had to make several attempts at recording his material just to catch its tone, far less its dimensions.

> In a little hilltop village, they gambled for my clothes
> I bargained for salvation an' they gave me a lethal dose
> I offered up my innocence and got repaid with scorn
> 'Come in,' she said, 'I'll give you shelter from the storm.'

*

Where did it spring from, this album? It was not prefigured, not seriously, by *Planet Waves*. The Dylan who wrote these songs was nowhere in evidence on the '74 tour. Prior to this he was stranded, bereft of any sense of direction or inspiration. Suddenly the struggles of the years preceding *Blood on the Tracks* seemed to be swept aside, whether because a cranky painter's advice caused Dylan finally to pay attention, or because strife within his marriage shook him out of his torpor. The former claim provides the more aesthetically pleasing (in every sense) explanation, but the second possibility is more plausible. The techniques of poetry and of the visual arts rarely cross-pollinate. Raeben, if Raeben it was, can only have pointed out an obvious fact about painting as it stands in relation to time. It was left to Dylan to see the possibilities – a stroke of genius, by any standards – and work out how to convey the impression of collapsed or expanding time in the linear medium of song, where there is always a beginning and always an end.

Besides, he had to have something to write *about*. In simple terms,

---

2   Interview with *Rock Express*, April 1978.

he wrote an album of love songs. Specifically, these songs have to do with the way in which perspectives affect attachments. That's painterly, in one sense, but it is also dramatic, literary, even Chekhovian. No painting will tell you what the figures on the canvas are thinking. It will hint, symbolise, even illustrate the possibilities. It cannot, self-evidently, supply the words. If Jakob Dylan was right, some of the words on *Blood on the Tracks* were drawn from, or echoed, married life.

A painting cannot easily show memories or events in flashback, meanwhile, as a 'Tangled Up in Blue' can. Even a narrative painting can't illustrate the scenes and plot lines of a 'Lily, Rosemary and the Jack of Hearts'. Whatever Dylan had to say about Raeben's ability to force a student to focus, the methods applied to *Blood on the Tracks* suggest he wasn't kidding about Chekhov. The techniques at stake are literary. If the dam burst, finally, and his songwriting broke free, it was because he learned to step back from his material. Yet one overriding achievement of the album is the sort of close control that Dylan had exerted only rarely, even in the great days of 1965–6. He had applied it to *Harding*, but those songs were not intimate, certainly not 'personal' in the peculiar, transmuted sense evident in *Blood on the Tracks*.

Raeben, he would say, 'put my mind and my hand and my eye together in a way that allowed me to do consciously what I unconsciously felt'. *Blood on the Tracks*, in this telling, was the product of that insight. Yet there had been no need of a teacher preoccupied with perception and intuition when Dylan was writing 'Mr. Tambourine Man'. That was the other half of the story: the *amnesia*, the blockage.

> Right through the time of *Blonde on Blonde* I was doing it unconsciously. Then one day I was half-stepping, and the lights went out. And since that point, I more or less had amnesia. Now, you can take that statement literally or metaphysically as you need to, but that's what happened to me. It took me a long time to get to do consciously what I used to be able to do unconsciously.[3]

If nothing else, Dylan admits – poetically rather than 'metaphysically' – that something went badly wrong. The paucity of his material at the end of the 1960s and the beginning of the 1970s is more or less acknowledged: he had 'forgotten' how to write songs. Most would

3   *Rolling Stone*, November 1978.

call that writer's block. Nevertheless, Dylan confuses his dates and therefore his story. If the lights went out in the wake of *Blonde on Blonde* – in the wake of the motorbike accident, in other words – where did all those basement songs spring from? How was *John Wesley Harding* created? If those were evidence of the lights dimming he could call off the search for illumination. The only thing that fits, the only blow that fell between *Harding* and *Nashville Skyline*, is the fact of Abe Zimmerman's death. The 'amnesia' ended thanks to a painter's visualisation techniques, or because of a shock to Dylan's marriage: your choice. All anyone knows for sure is that he saw fit to link the two: hence Sara's sudden inability, after all those years, to 'understand' him thanks, supposedly, to his encounters with Raeben.

An audience is brutal. An audience is liable to say, 'Who cares?' What matters to the audience is that with *Blood on the Tracks* Dylan redeemed and renewed himself. Once again, he extended the range of popular music. Once again, it was plausible to talk of his writing in terms of poetry. Whatever old Norman brought to the party, Dylan achieved a technical triumph. The experiment with time and perspective he had first attempted with 'Visions of Johanna' is carried through on *Blood on the Tracks* and, what's more, given a human face. Even if you accept that this is not, or not just, an album of songs about a marriage, the Bob Dylan who sings and tells the stories is undeniably a new character. Previous manifestations – 'all the different selves that were in there' – are banished by a voice that is undeceived, alive to every nuance. For the first time in the 1970s, Dylan managed to produce recordings that stand comparison with his best works of the '60s and yet owe nothing to them.

It took a couple of attempts in studios in New York and Minnesota, with various combinations of musicians, to achieve what he wanted. By all accounts, Dylan's preference for unorthodox guitar tunings didn't help. Some still doubt that he made *exactly* the right choices from the recordings. The bootleg known as *The New York Sessions*, reflecting the album that was almost released until second thoughts were allowed (prompted by Dylan's brother, David, the story goes), is still preferred by many. Most of those tracks are now scattered over the 'official bootlegs', if required. In January of 1975, when such considerations did not apply, *Blood on the Tracks* was recognised instantly for the masterpiece it was, and is. Minnesota's Scott Fitzgerald had coined an adage for the age when he said there are no second acts in American lives. Dylan must have thought so too, for a while. With this album he rediscovered the key to his intuitions.

*

Roughly 70 years had elapsed since the slow, agonising and pathetic death in Marseille of Arthur Rimbaud when Dylan was 'turned on', as someone probably said, to the French poet. A lot has been made of it. Robert Shelton's biography credits the initiation to Dave Van Ronk; Dylan has said that Suze Rotolo made the necessary introductions across the generations. The idea was abroad from an early date, in any case, that poet had spoken to poet. The evidence is less than obvious, but the word poetry was thrown often and indiscriminately at Dylan's name in the mid-1960s: something was bound to stick.

It helped, too, that Rimbaud was talked about more often than he was read, and too often talked about for reasons that had little to do with his work. It was probably inevitable that a connection would be made. The apparent parallels between the Charleville meteor and a shooting star were irresistible to anyone who needed to hear untutored poetry in contemporary song, or believed in protean genius erupting in the backwoods. With Rimbaud in mind even Dylan's drug use could be presented as a striving 'to reach the unknown by the derangement of all the senses'. For his part the 16-year-old Arthur had added a Dylan-like excuse: 'It involves enormous suffering, but one must be strong and be a born poet. It's really not my fault.'

Rimbaud turned up in Paris in September of 1871, a month before his 17th birthday; Dylan reached New York as 1961 arrived when he was just 19. Both had strange and elusive qualities, ambition verging on ruthlessness, a cruel streak interleaved with wit and human sympathy, and scant respect for the truth. Photographs of the young Arthur – hair troublesome, lips tight, eyes hard – have a lot in common with photographs of the proto-Dylan. As to the legendary moment of impact, a passage from Graham Robb's biography of Rimbaud[4] would serve as easily for Greenwich Village as for the capital of France.

> That morning in Paris, several established poets were musing on that great Balzacian theme: the rosy-cheeked prodigy who arrives in the evil metropolis with his sonnets, his illusions and his ludicrously ambitious career plan . . . The 'seer' was practising his magic spells, and the little

---

4   *Rimbaud* (2000), Ch. 9.

village world . . . was about to have its fond illusions shattered beyond repair.

It's almost too perfect. One obvious problem for a theory of creative affinity, however, is that Dylan knew no French. Rimbaud is notoriously tough, meanwhile, to render into useful English without a huge loss in poetry, the stuff, presumably, that is taken to form a background noise in the American's writing. Simply because Van Ronk went on to discover a well-thumbed volume of French Symbolist poetry (in translation) on Dylan's shelves, or because there is a line invoking Rimbaud and his sometime lover Paul Verlaine in a *Blood on the Tracks* song (to a girl), or because the dead poet has been quoted once or twice by the living performer, conclusions have been drawn. Sometimes it is enough for a personage to be mentioned by Dylan for him or her to be added to the list of 'influences'. It doesn't really signify. The singer has also spoken approvingly of Rainer Maria Rilke, apparently in reference to the *Duino Elegies*, but no one has confused him with a gay Teutonic aristo.

Besides, Rimbaud alive published only two bits of verse plus a prose poem (though not just any prose poem). He had given up entirely on poetry before he was 21. Dylan may now and then have romanticised the type – visionary drug-taker, anarchist, gunrunner, martyr, seer – but the Frenchman's later career as a trader in Abyssinia was mostly grim and generally sordid. It ended badly, and left no artistic mark.

He 'started in to dealing with slaves / And something inside of him died'? It fits Rimbaud perfectly, no doubt, but Dylan's 'Tangled Up in Blue', with its doubled perspectives, leans in other directions. 'The first poet of a civilisation not yet born', then, as the French writer René Char alleged of his compatriot? Possibly, though Rimbaud showed little taste for that sort of nonsense. He achieved no public recognition, either, before dying hideously at the age of 37. He was never a media star, nor ever a grand old man. More to the point, he had lost his desire to write – or had repressed the desire – at an age when Dylan could just about manage a pastiche. In that regard the supposed resemblance is invisible. Rimbaud did not play the game, but in quitting poetry without a backward glance he made a grander artistic gesture than any singer-songwriter could contemplate. Dylan has sometimes made a pose of renunciation; Rimbaud did it for real. The young Arthur stepped away from his past more decisively than the young Bob ever did.

Rimbaud was in vogue in the Village nevertheless, thanks largely to Beat propaganda and Enid Starkie's 1947 biography, when Dylan was starting out. The New Directions publishing house had made *Illuminations* available to an American audience during the second war; *The Anchor Anthology of French Poetry*, perhaps the volume Van Ronk spotted, had appeared in 1958; and a complete edition of the forever-young delinquent's verse in translation was to be published in 1962. Rimbaud – vagabond, outlaw, bohemian, juvenile poetic revolutionary – was a name to drop among those who said they read.

Was Dylan one of them? He has said plenty of things to demonstrate that he knows many varieties of poetry. In the early years, when he was hammering a typewriter relentlessly in the approved Kerouacist fashion, he had a hankering to write for the page. Few of the results were encouraging and the experience of composing 'Like a Rolling Stone' showed him, so he would claim, that the literary life was not his destination. Dylan's stripped senses no doubt experienced their share of derangement and rearrangement, but doing recreational drugs is not – and here's news – the key to creativity.

Even the Beat connection is less solid than it has sometimes seemed. Dylan has admitted that he caught only the 'tail-end' of the phenomenon. Arguably, he was privy to less than that. By the time he met Allen Ginsberg in the Village in the last week of 1963 little remained of the Beats beyond a media burlesque. They had suffered the fate that would befall protest singers: journalists would go on applying the label long after it had ceased to make sense.

Set aside Ginsberg's relentless urge to create advertisements for himself, remember that this loose fraternity had its origins when Dylan was still a child, recall that the central pieces of writing had been published – often years after they were composed – well before the young folk singer arrived in New York, and you reach a crude conclusion: Beat was a '50s thing. By the time William Burroughs managed to publish *Naked Lunch* in Paris in 1959 it was over. The fact that the novel did not achieve a legal existence in the United States until 1962 is a historical detail. The only life left in the 'generation' by then was supplied by *Life* magazine.

In the long aftermath Ginsberg would make a lot of claims on behalf of the Beat upheaval; Ginsberg always made a lot of claims. He was the barker for this brief carnival. Writing in 1981,[5] he would allege that most of the significant events in American life in the third quarter

---

5   'A Definition of the Beat Generation', republished in *Deliberate Prose: Selected Essays, 1952–1995* (2001).

of the twentieth century were Beat-inspired, the 'essential effects' of his coterie. You name it, for he did: sexual liberation, drug decriminalisation, rock and roll's emancipation ('as a high art form'), the alleged new spiritualism, most political activism, environmentalism, rage against the machine. What had a small group of chaotic individuals not done?

'Honoured their talents' would be one answer. Dylan was influenced by the Beats: of that there is no doubt. But we also know that he regarded the ability to absorb any influence as a simple matter of opening his eyes and ears. Ginsberg flattered him shamelessly at every turn, and for years. Dylan appreciated the appreciation, even when it was manifested as an ill-concealed sexual infatuation. He was not, however, a Beat writer. He adopted the manner momentarily, for a brief period, took what he needed and made that his own. Even then, he preferred Ginsberg's *Kaddish* to 'Howl' – the choice itself a mark of a repressed Jewish identity – contrary to the usual story.

Dylan read. The Bible, old ballads, newspapers – no one escaped those when the world was about to end – and perhaps, thanks to Suze Rotolo, Bertolt Brecht, another balladeer in 'the jungle of cities'. There is a lot of 'poor BB' in Dylan's early three-cent operas. It amounts to a social realism that is never properly realistic. In those works there is also a lot of what was then fashionable, and much that later proved useful. If he did nothing else Dylan patently read in and around modernism – Pound et al.; Ginsberg by way of William Carlos Williams and Black Mountain – sufficiently well to understand that images need not form an orderly queue on their way to a conclusion. He grasped enumeration and repetition, too.

One typical summary of modernism's arrival in America speaks of poets investigating 'fragmentation, ellipsis, allusion, juxtaposition, ironic and shifting personae, and mythic parallelism'.[6] The description fits the Dylan of the mid-1960s like a mitten. It became the Beat template, after all. But something else needs to be remembered when the discussions of Dylan and poetry, Dylan as a poet, and the 'problem' of reconciling his printed lyrics with the usual idea of a poem resume: he has never been wedded for long to a single style.

Dylanesque can't be stretched to accommodate all the many ways

---

6   'Poetry of the United States: Modernism and After' at the website Blurb Wire. See also Malcolm Bradbury and James McFarlane (eds) *Modernism: A Guide to European Literature 1890–1930* (1991).

he has approached writing. The verses on *Blonde on Blonde* – the admired ones, at any rate – bear no resemblance, in style or intent, to the couplets and quatrains of *John Wesley Harding*. There are worlds of difference between the basement-tape songs and *Blood on the Tracks*. Arguably, Dylan has been several poets. Those 'reinventions' were never just a case of picking a band and a musical genre.

Perhaps critics have an excuse. After all, Dylan remains unmistakably Dylan even when decades have intervened, or when the songs at issue range from extraordinary to the far side of banal. It's not just the voice: that too has altered drastically, unavoidably. Anyone who didn't know would not necessarily guess that the ragged glory of *Together Through Life* belongs to the person who once sang 'Don't Think Twice'. Yet there is, as the lumbering phrase goes, an artistic unity to his writing despite the many changes in style. The born-again Christian is united with the junior sceptic, the voice coming off a basement's concrete wall with the voice powering through the juxtapositions of 'Jokerman'. It's more than just a 'unique gift' for a turn of phrase (though it's certainly that). Many strands of the American experience, and hence of American writing, are stitched together – there are dropped stitches, too – in Dylan's songs.

God under Whom there is one nation? Whitman proceeded from the assumption that if the language of the King James version was good enough for the deity, it was good enough for Walter. Miss Dickinson, soul afire in Amherst, rewrote the hymnal in search of a poetics that would fit. This is facetious and conventional, but also true.

Dylan and the American land itself, in *Harding*, *New Morning* or *Time Out of Mind*? The imagination's response to that great mass was there from the start. It demanded 'pastoral', and more. In 1956 John Berryman, noted despiser and grudging admirer of Dylan, published *Homage to Mistress Bradstreet*, a meditation on the 'Tenth Muse Lately Sprung Up in America', famously 'America's first published poet'. In 1657, *she* wrote:

My winters past, my stormes are gone,
And former clowdes seem now all fled;
But, if they mvst eclipse again,
I'le rvn where I was succoured.
I haue a shelter from the storm . . .

A common phrase. You could trawl American literature and find any number of echoes to fit a Dylan song, much as you can track a multitude of biblical references. A literate man talking about God can't escape those. An American poet in the shadow of Walt Whitman, whose lines are the echoes of the cadences of the King James Bible, can't easily escape those, either. Allusion-hunting is sometimes just a party trick. So Dickinson wrote 'Success is counted sweetest / By those who ne'er succeed'? Surely she meant to say there's no success like failure? Some accounts of Dylan's writing are based on slimmer pickings. Persistent, inevitable, are the multitude of ways in which he deploys an American voice. If it's genius we seek, that's where the genius lies. It is also why the confessional singer-songwriter model doesn't fit a writer who turned himself into a character to give voice to other characters. His art is an infinity effect. As we have seen, he favours that Rimbaud thing, in theory: there is no I. So who said that?

*

Just as *Blood on the Tracks* was being released certain of the Watergate conspirators were being put on trial and America was preparing to abandon Vietnam. If those were portents, they did not seem favourable. The country was beginning to prepare for its bicentennial with some doubts over what there was, exactly, to celebrate. A sense of aftermath hung over culture and public affairs. Amid the exultations over Dylan's album no one bothered to fret just for once over his lack of political engagement. If anything, his 'personal' songs seemed more in keeping with the times. Even 'Idiot Wind', *appearing* to connect the individual with the collective, offered little to chew on. Dylan had won the argument over his refusal to argue about politics. In this, he began to seem prescient. *Blood on the Tracks* had made the case, overwhelmingly, for art. That fact marked a new era if anything did.

*

A biographer[7] once described Walt Whitman's notebooks of the 1850s as 'the fossil remains of an unexampled upheaval, one of the puzzles of American literature: the emerging, with no apparent preliminaries, of a poet'.

In the beginning, people had much the same thoughts about Bob Dylan. Where had he sprung from? How had he become an 'unexampled' artist with none of those 'apparent preliminaries'?

---

7   Paul Zweig, *Walt Whitman: The Making of the Poet* (1984), Ch. 5.

Because he was supremely facile, or utterly dedicated, or just lucky? In Greenwich Village, where the old hands could spot theft and impersonation, it seemed easy at first to nail the youngster. Once the more-or-less original songs began to appear, doses of 20–20 hindsight were needed. The well-versed could still identify the Scottish ballad or the blues tune that had been pillaged. They could not say why these songs, even the flagrant steals, became entirely Dylan's possessions.

Amended opinions required further amendment when it became plain that the writer was no more likely to be bound by his successes than he was by his failures. Year after year, regardless of acclaim or derision, he discarded versions of himself in a blur of creative fire. These acts of self-obliteration baffled many and, famously, angered more than a few. Folk's great hope to rock star in one lightning move: it caused heads to swim.

Dylan could have ridden the folk wave to wealth, fame and seminar-room appreciation for decades. He could have gone the way of soft-focus 'acoustic singer-songwriter' stupor and filled his walls with gold discs in the 1970s and 1980s. Most of those who made the big money were to take their inspiration from his early example, after all. Yet he did nothing of the sort. Wouldn't or couldn't?

Hence the persistent question concerning Dylan and poetry. It ought to be settled by now. He seems to have settled it in his own mind long ago. An ambition to achieve in print something approaching his achievements in song dissolved years ago into sub-Beat jottings and the failure he called *Tarantula*. Decades on, *Chronicles* proved that writing, as writing, was never the problem. Some such as Robert Shelton once convinced themselves, on the other hand, that Dylan could write 'anything'. But the verses he makes these days, given the absence of any evidence to the contrary, are composed exclusively for the purposes of song. So must the oldest art, the poetic art, expand to accommodate Bob Dylan? Or are the dismissals of a near half-century, the ones founded on the belief that real poetry can only be a metrical arrangement capable of being read and recited, still the only criteria? If so, we are judging this arranger of words by the standards of Victorian prosody. Those are tough standards.

The word poet is used freely, nevertheless. The Nobel literature prize is mentioned routinely. Distinguished universities bestow honorary degrees. Then some people become annoyed, while others are baffled: conferences are held. Poems that cannot be read, read *profitably*, from a page? Poems that might cease to function if the voice – phrasing, intonation, intent – is not Dylan's voice? Song-poems that might disintegrate if the musical setting is not precisely – yet indefinably – right? This is to stretch every definition until it snaps, surely?

If nothing else, it seems to demand a privileged notion of what a poem can be. The folklorists have made a big deal of the idea that some kinds of musical art are best understood, and perhaps can only be understood, in the context of performance. Given the claims made for Dylan, those explanations sound like special pleading. If half of what has been said is halfway true, the successive editions of his lyrics should function far better than they do as naked text. No one who has read poetry with any degree of attention makes that claim.

Such strictures are fair enough, but they miss something important. It amounts to this: if Dylan's larger works are not to be called poems, what are we to call them, exactly? If they are songs, mere songs-performed, the advisers on verse and metrical purity had best explain when, and why, songs ceased to be poems.

*

Nobody's perfect. *Blood on the Tracks* might well count as one of the best things Dylan ever did, but parts of it seem less impressive now than once upon a time. When the album was released a lot of fuss was made, for example, over 'Idiot Wind', apparently for no better reason than that the track was lengthy. This was taken as the equivalent of significant. In fact, it's a small song trying to sound big, a bombastic and self-serving (not to say self-pitying) piece dressed up as a state-of-the-nation address. It's not why *Blood on the Tracks* matters.

'Tangled Up in Blue', the opening song, makes the better argument both for what Dylan said he was attempting and – an unusual coincidence – for what he actually did. In performance he has tinkered with it repeatedly over the years, especially where pronouns are concerned, as though to prove that perspective is everything. In this song, time stops and starts. Even while seeming to review episodes in an affair, the narrator remembers that 'the past *was* close behind'. As the song approaches its end, he says

So now I'm goin' back again
I got to get to her somehow
All the people we used to know
They're an illusion to me now

Memory and reality have parted company. With a certain sure brilliance, Dylan is telling us something simple and complicated: this is just one man's story. How did things seem to her? Love alone can't solve that problem. Thus: 'We always did feel the same / We just saw it from a different point of view.' *Blood on the Tracks* pulls off this trick, if trick is the word, time and again.

*

As a working entertainer, Dylan does not always strive for art. Never has. Sometimes, he just puts words to a decent tune. Sometimes he offers less than that, sometimes a great deal more. Sometimes, though, he says that putting together words as best he can for the best melodies he can find is all he has ever done. In this story he has played no part in giving people big ideas about his work. That, he likes to suggest, is their problem.

On the other hand, the problem of Bob Dylan's poetry is poetry's problem. So much was true for over a decade as the 1960s became the 1970s, yet those who construct definitions for the art of verse still evade the difficulty. Dylan doesn't have to answer for poetry's problems; someone should.

Print and literary speech intersect tangentially, momentarily, with music and popular song, but that explains very little about Dylan's power as a shaper of words. Which is to say: it really does depend on what you mean by poetry. With most of the formal rules long gone, the chances of consensus are remote. Some have been puzzled since the appearance of *vers libre* among the Victorians, Walt Whitman and the French Symbolists. Poets, it seems, are always found wanting until the wider audience opens its eyes and its ears.

So is it this: Bob Dylan's poetry is Bob Dylan performing a Bob Dylan song *and nothing else*? Much that is contained in the books of his lyrics wouldn't pass for verse among most readers if the music was erased from their memories. Equally, there are here and there beautifully written sets of words that count among his least successful songs. In that sense, the poetry fails. Why so?

Or rather, what makes a Bob Dylan song poetry? In the usual explanation, that's not so complicated: it's the way he sings. To put it otherwise: the act of singing imposes a metrical scheme that is nowhere inherent or obvious in the words alone. Dylan's enunciation, his habit of slurring and stressing, his propensity to speak rather than sing a word or line, his pauses, his pitch and timbre, even his snarls – these,

559

with and against the flow of the music, its support and implicit comment, create the poetry. Probably.

'Like a Rolling Stone' is as good an example as any. The fixed points of rhyme aside – and even those are tested almost to destruction – there is very little to connect any possible printed version with what goes on in the recordings, and each of those differs. The page cannot reflect the emphases, the stretching of vowels, the silent beats taken or the crowding of words into single lines. Because this is pop music pushed to its limits, Dylan is able to appear to sing, mimic conversational speech and assemble a poem simultaneously. The page is one-dimensional. It does not exist in time as a performed song does. You cannot bend and mould metre within its confines. Dylan meanwhile allows no room whatever for the traditional 'voice in your head' that makes the reading of verse from a page private and unique. Arguably, in fact, few of us are in a position now to *read* Dylan's greatest poems: the tunes are in our heads, impossible to shift.

And so what? You could say, quite correctly, that what takes place in a Dylan performance is what happens with the performance of any song. The point is that his delivery, at its best, suggests calculation. He is working to achieve poetry, or an effect equivalent to poetry. It's less that he 'can't sing' – his range was never great, and what of it? – than that he deploys aspects of his voice deliberately to create the song-poem. Some people write words to fit a tune, or vice versa. Dylan fits everything available – words, melody, his voice, his band, implicit and explicit meaning – around the idea of the poem.

The playwright and actor Sam Shepard, who collaborated with Dylan in the writing of the glorious 'Brownsville Girl', the sole redeeming feature of the otherwise lamentable 1986 album *Knocked Out Loaded*, is hardly a stranger to literary composition. Yet even he was astonished by Dylan's method, his sureness of touch, and by the relationship between writing and performance. As Shepard recalled:

> I think the most surprising thing is his phrasing. I'd say, 'But how the hell are you going to fit this into the melody?' He said, 'Don't worry about it. It'll work.' And inevitably it did. The way he squashes phrasing and stretches it out is quite remarkable.'[8]

Dylan makes poetry: why not? The rhymes are there. You have your

---

8   Reported by Howard Sounes in *Down the Highway*.

images, your allusions, your symbols and your language, most of the time, under pressure. There is emotion recollected in tranquillity, or at least in the emotional space created in the studio on the fifth take at 2 a.m. If the objection is that Dylan's words don't 'work' on the page, where stands all the verse that could never support a tune?

*

> For my own part, I would much rather have
> written the best *song* of a nation than its noblest *epic*.
>
> Edgar Allan Poe, 'Marginalia' (1849)

The poet William Carlos Williams, a New Jersey baby doctor who kept his art in his office drawer, possessed a clear idea of what it meant to be an American writer. Williams, a mentor of sorts to the young Allen Ginsberg, did not grant a choice in the matter. You could 'make it new', as his friend Pound liked to urge, but the thing made, if worth a damn, could only bear the stamp of origins. Which is to say: Dylan occupies a paradox. Wholly original, if that word means anything, yet a typical product, a pure product, of an American circumstance.

Where art is concerned he could, if larcenous, appropriate a statement left in a notebook by Mark Twain in the 1890s when the storyteller was cooped up in Europe. 'Are you an American?' Twain enquired of himself. 'No, I am not *an* American. I am *the* American.' Pound would use similar words when talking about Whitman, the poet who had tended, obligingly, to offer the selfsame definition on his own behalf. Ernest Hemingway would then say something very similar about Twain and the creation of Huck Finn. In America, it appears, the need for founding fathers runs deep. For those who care, the relationship of the artist to the republic matters most of all. He gives it voice.

Dylan was shaped as a writer by blues and folk. They provided vocabulary, forms, imagery, metaphor and most of his early modes of expression. They nevertheless stood outside – or far beyond – the canonical. 'Real' poets could attempt ballads and songs, and often had, but they managed only rarely to strike the balance between the living voice and the inert page. Poetry as Dylan began to write and understand it had a lineage that stretched back beyond moveable type. Yet generally he typed up his verses before giving them a voice: which criterion applies?

The blues and folk, the open-source code, were the heart of his education. In seeming to touch a deeper reality, the old songs had the resonance of poetry. That was surely what the youngster in Minnesota meant when he shouted about 'the real thing'. The music's enduring effect on the country's culture was in precise parallel to American literature's long struggle to find itself, to escape the grip of English tradition, to speak of America with an American voice. In Dylan's hands the blues and its descendants served the same function as the verses of Kenneth Patchen, William Carlos Williams or Allen Ginsberg.

Williams only rarely wrote 'real verse' in the traditional sense. John Berryman's dream songs were never *quite* sonnets. Patchen, Rexroth, Ginsberg, even Lowell: in these writers the pseudo-classicism of the English tradition with its elegies and odes and pulse-beat iambs – to generalise, somewhat – gives way to an obsession with voice. Free verse had raised all the questions asked by Dylan's talent long before he began to write. If you cannot put a metrical lock on a group of words, and cannot easily apply classical terms for meter – few of which describe English in any case – the attempt to outlaw Dylan begins to falter. Modern poetry occupies his paradox: it too fails to fit the rules, as often as not.

For what truly matters, one of the first of Dylan's literary fans left us a clue. You needn't take Allen Ginsberg's theories on poetics entirely seriously to see that in explaining the method he employed in 'Howl' he was describing Dylan *exactly*. Those 'breath units'; that 'elastic line with a fixed base'; the connectives omitted for the sake of juxtaposition; the 'speech-rhythm prosody' reclaimed from Whitman: this is Dylan's poetry. If it's acceptable from Ginsberg, if it justifies much recent American verse, especially of the 'open form' variety, the attempt to exclude this artist from consideration is fatuous. And revealing.

His poetry lives because it breathes. In that, it achieves the condition to which all poetry, the descendant of song, aspires. What became, once upon a time, of the bards who didn't understand music, who couldn't carry a tune? Bob Dylan's breath units breathe life into the idea of poetry.

*

After the album went to the top of the American charts, Dylan and his wife attempted a reconciliation. It didn't work. Both still seemed to believe there was a lot worth saving in the marriage, but a lot more had been lost for good. Dylan would spend his 34th birthday in France, in Savoie, attempting to assuage a desolate loneliness with occasional bad behaviour in the company of the painter David Oppenheim. Casual debauchery did no good. In effect, he was bereaved; on top of the world again as a musician, yet bereaved.

In southern France, he paid a visit to the king of the Gypsies, an old man with 'twelve wives and a hundred children'. Dylan was fascinated. Perhaps he glimpsed a future. Perhaps he realised that *Blood on the Tracks* was not just a memoir or a set of stories. Perhaps it, too, foretold a gypsy future.

Acknowledgements

A number of Bob Dylan's songs, as listed below, have been quoted for purposes of criticism and review:

p. 18 'Like a Rolling Stone' (Copyright © 1965 by Warner Bros. Inc.; renewed 1993 by Special Rider Music); p. 38 'Song to Woody' (Copyright © 1962, 1965 by Duchess Music Corporation; renewed 1990, 1993 by MCA); pp. 64, 65 'North Country Blues' (Copyright © 1963, 1964 by Warner Bros. Inc.; renewed 1991, 1992 by Special Rider Music); p. 70 'Absolutely Sweet Marie' (Copyright © 1966 by Dwarf Music; renewed 1994 by Dwarf Music); p. 85 'The Death of Emmett Till' (Copyright © 1963, 1968 by Warner Bros. Inc.; renewed 1991, 1996 by Special Rider Music); p. 88 'Desolation Row' (Copyright © 1965 by Warner Bros. Inc.; renewed 1993 by Special Rider Music); p. 133 'Ballad of a Thin Man' (Copyright © 1965 by Warner Bros. Inc.; renewed 1993 by Special Rider Music); p. 223 'Let Me Die in My Footsteps' (Copyright © 1963, 1965 by Warner Bros. Inc.; renewed 1991, 1993 by Special Rider Music); p. 245 'Oxford Town' (Copyright © 1963 by Warner Bros. Inc.; renewed 1992 by Special Rider Music); p. 249 'Restless Farewell' (Copyright © 1964, 1966 by Warner Bros. Inc.; renewed 1992, 1994 by Special Rider Music); p. 253 'You've Been Hiding Too Long' (Copyright © 1985 by Special Rider Music); p. 255 'I Shall Be Free No. 10' (Copyright © 1971 by Special Rider Music; renewed 1999 by Special Rider Music); p. 259 'Last Thoughts On Woody Guthrie' (Copyright © 1985 by Special Rider Music); pp. 264, 364, 365, 366, 367 'Gates of Eden' (Copyright © 1965 by Warner Bros. Inc.; renewed 1993 by Special Rider Music); p. 270 'Only a Pawn in Their Game' (Copyright © 1963, 1964 by Warner Bros. Inc.; renewed 1991, 1996 by Special Rider Music); pp. 271–2 'Maggie's Farm' (Copyright © 1965 by Warner Bros. Inc.; renewed 1993 by Special Rider Music); p. 290 'Lay Down Your Weary Tune' (Copyright © 1964, 1965 by Warner Bros. Inc.; renewed 1992, 1993 by Special

ACKNOWLEDGEMENTS

p. 484 'Odds and Ends' (Copyright © 1969 by Dwarf Music; renewed 1997 by Dwarf Music); p. 485 'Crash on the Levee (Down in the Flood)' (Copyright © 1967 by Dwarf Music; renewed 1995 by Dwarf Music); p. 485 'I Shall Be Released' (Copyright ©1967, 1970 by Dwarf Music; renewed 1995 by Dwarf Music); pp. 490, 491, 495, 501 'John Wesley Harding' (Copyright ©1968 by Dwarf Music; renewed 1996 by Dwarf Music); p. 492 'Hero Blues' (Copyright © 1963 by Warner Bros. Inc.; renewed 1991 by Special Rider Music); p. 494 'Outlaw Blues' (Copyright © 1965 by Warner Bros. Inc.; renewed 1993 by Special Rider Music); pp. 497, 501 'The Ballad of Frankie Lee and Judas Priest' (Copyright © 1968 by Dwarf Music; renewed 1996 by Dwarf Music); p. 500 'All Along the Watchtower' (Copyright © 1968 by Dwarf Music; renewed 1996 by Dwarf Music); p. 501 'Drifter's Escape' (Copyright © 1968 by Dwarf Music; renewed 1996 by Dwarf Music); p. 501 'The Wicked Messenger' (Copyright © 1968 by Dwarf Music; renewed 1996 by Dwarf Music); p. 502 'I Pity the Poor Immigrant' (Copyright © 1968 by Dwarf Music; renewed 1996 Dwarf Music); p. 504–5 'I Threw It All Away' (Copyright © 1969 by Big Sky Music; renewed 1997 by Big Sky Music); p. 526 'Dear Landlord' (Copyright © 1968 by Dwarf Music; renewed 1996 by Dwarf Music); p. 527 'Went to See the Gypsy' (Copyright © 1970 by Big Sky Music; renewed 1998 by Big Sky Music); p. 527–8 'If Dogs Run Free' (Copyright © 1970 by Big Sky Music; renewed 1998 by Big Sky Music); p. 531 'Watching the River Flow' (Copyright © 1971 by Big Sky Music; renewed 1999 by Big Sky Music); p. 531 'When I Paint My Masterpiece' (Copyright © 1971 by Big Sky Music; renewed 1999 by Big Sky Music); p. 533, 534 'George Jackson' (Copyright © 1971 by Ram's Horn Music; renewed 1999 by Ram's Horn Music); p. 544 'Simple Twist of Fate' (Copyright © 1974 by Ram's Horn Music; renewed 2002 by Ram's Horn Music); p. 545 'She's Your Lover Now' (Copyright © 1971 by Dwarf Music; renewed 1999 by Dwarf Music); p. 547 'Up to Me' (Copyright © 1974 by Ram's Horn Music; renewed 2002 by Ram's Horn Music); p. 548 'Shelter from the Storm' (Copyright © 1974 by Ram's Horn Music; renewed 2002 by Ram's Horn Music); pp. 552, 558, 559 'Tangled Up in Blue' (Copyright © 1974 by Ram's Horn Music; renewed 2002 by Ram's Horn Music).

Bibliography

Dylan, Bob, *Tarantula* (1971).
   Writings and Drawings (1973).
   Lyrics 1962–2001 (2004).
   Chronicles: Volume One (2004).

Aronowitz, Al, *Bob Dylan and the Beatles* (2004).
Bauldie, John (ed.), *Wanted Man: In Search of Bob Dylan* (1992).
Engel, Dave, *Just Like Bob Zimmerman's Blues: Dylan in Minnesota* (1997).
Flanagan, Bill, *Written in My Soul* (1990).
Gray, Michael, *Song and Dance Man III: The Art of Bob Dylan* (2000).
   The Bob Dylan Encyclopedia (2006).
Hajdu, David, *Positively 4th Street: The Lives and Times of Joan Baez, Bob Dylan, Mimi Baez Fariña and Richard Fariña* (2001, 2nd ed. 2011).
Heylin, Clinton: *Dylan: Behind Closed Doors – The Recording Sessions 1960–1994* (1995).
   Bob Dylan: Behind the Shades Revisited (2003).
   Revolution in the Air – The Songs of Bob Dylan Volume 1: 1957–73 (2009).
   Still on the Road – The Songs of Bob Dylan Volume 2: 1974–2008 (2010).
Lee, CP, *Like the Night* (1998), *Like the Night (Revisited)* (2004, rev. ed.).
Marcus, Greil, *Mystery Train: Images of America in Rock 'n' Roll Music* (1975, rev. ed. 2008).
   Invisible Republic: Bob Dylan's Basement Tapes (1997), republished as *The Old, Weird America: Bob Dylan's Basement Tapes* (2001, 2011).
   Like a Rolling Stone: Bob Dylan at the Crossroads (2005).
   Bob Dylan by Greil Marcus: Writings 1968–2010 (2011).
Marqusee, Mike, *Chimes of Freedom: The Politics of Bob Dylan* (2003), revised and expanded as *Wicked Messenger: Bob Dylan and the 1960s* (2005).
Marshall, Lee, *Bob Dylan: The Never Ending Star* (2007).

Ricks, Christopher, *Dylan's Visions of Sin* (2003).

Rotolo, Suze, *A Freewheelin' Time: A Memoir of Greenwich Village in the Sixties* (2008).

Scaduto, Anthony, *Dylan* (1972).

Sheehy, Colleen J., and Swiss, Thomas (ed.), *Highway 61 Revisited: Bob Dylan's Road from Minnesota to the World* (2009).

Shelton, Robert, *No Direction Home: The Life and Music of Bob Dylan* (1986, rev. ed. 2011).

Sloman, Larry 'Ratso', *On the Road with Bob Dylan* (1978).

Sounes, Howard, *Down the Highway: The Life of Bob Dylan* (2001).

Thompson, Toby, *Positively Main Street: Bob Dylan's Minnesota* (1971, rev. ed. 2008).

Weberman, A.J., *Dylan to English Dictionary* (2005).

Wilentz, Sean, *Bob Dylan in America* (2010).

Ackroyd, Peter, *T.S. Eliot* (1984).

Baez, Joan, *And a Voice to Sing With* (1987).

Berryman, John, *Collected Poems 1937–1971* (1989).
The Dream Songs (1990).

Blake, William, *Poems and Prophecies* (ed. Max Plowman, 1927).

Breton, André, *Manifestoes of Surrealism* (1969).

Burke, Frank, *Federico Fellini: Variety Lights to La Dolce Vita* (1984).

Caudill, Harry, *Night Comes to the Cumberlands* (1962).

Chekhov, Anton, *About Love and Other Stories*, trans. Rosamund Bartlett (2004).

Converse, Philip E., et al., *American Social Attitudes Data Sourcebook 1947–1978* (1980).

Cray, Ed, *Ramblin' Man: The Life and Times of Woody Guthrie* (2004).

Dallek, Robert, *John F. Kennedy: An Unfinished Life 1917–1963* (2003).

Davies, Hunter, *The Beatles* (rev. ed. 1985).

Didion, Joan, *Slouching Towards Bethlehem* (1968).

Dunaway, David, *How Can I Keep from Singing: Pete Seeger* (1981, rev. ed. 2008).

Eliot, T.S., *The Sacred Wood* (1920).

Ferlinghetti, Lawrence, *A Coney Island of the Mind* (1958, reissued 2005).
Starting from San Francisco (1961).

Ginsberg, Allen, *Selected Poems 1947–1995* (1996).
Deliberate Prose: Selected Essays, 1952–1995 (2001).

Gioia, Ted, *Delta Blues: The Life and Times of the Mississippi Masters Who Revolutionised American Music* (2008).

BIBLIOGRAPHY

Green, Martin, *New York 1913* (1988).

Guralnick, Peter, *Lost Highway: Journeys and Arrivals of American Musicians* (1979).

Guthrie, Woody, *Bound for Glory* (1943, 1971).

Hajdu, David, *The Ten-Cent Plague: The Great Comic-Book Scare and How It Changed America* (2008).

Hamilton, Ian, *Robert Lowell: A Biography* (1982).

Heat-Moon, William Least, *Blue Highways: A Journey into America* (1983).

Hobsbawm, Eric, *Bandits* (1969, rev. ed. 2000).

Hoffman, Andrew, *Inventing Mark Twain: The Lives of Samuel Langhorne Clemens* (1997).

Honan, Park (ed.), *The Beats: An Anthology of 'Beat' Writing* (1987).

Hughes, Langston, *The Big Sea: An Autobiography* (1940).

Kazin, Alfred, *A Writer's America: Landscape in Literature* (1988).

Kerouac, Jack, *On the Road* (1957).

   The Subterraneans (1958).

   Mexico City Blues (1959).

   Visions of Cody (1960).

   Desolation Angels (1965).

Klein, Joe, *Woody Guthrie: A Life* (1980).

Kuhn, Thomas, *The Structure of Scientific Revolutions* (2nd ed. 1970).

Lowell, Robert, *Collected Poems* (2003).

Jackson, George, *Soledad Brother: The Prison Letters of George Jackson* (1970).

MacDonald, Ian, *Revolution in the Head: The Beatles' Records and the Sixties* (2nd rev. ed. 2005).

Mariani, Paul L., *Dream Song: The Life of John Berryman* (1990).

Mayer, William G., *The Changing American Mind: How and Why American Public Opinion Changed Between 1960 and 1988* (1992).

Meyers, Jeffrey (ed.), *Robert Lowell: Interviews and Memoirs* (1988).

Micklethwait, John, and Wooldridge, Adrian, *The Right Nation: Why America Is Different* (2004).

Nicholl, Charles, *Somebody Else: Arthur Rimbaud in Africa 1880–91* (1997).

Nicosia, Gerald, *Memory Babe: A Critical Biography of Jack Kerouac* (1983).

O'Neill, William L., *American High: The Years of Confidence 1945–1960* (1986).

Patchen, Kenneth, *The Collected Poems of Kenneth Patchen* (1968).

   The Journal of Albion Moonlight (1941).

Pearson, Barry Lee, and McCulloch, Bill, *Robert Johnson: Lost and Found* (2003).

Poe, Edgar Allan, *Marginalia* (John Carl Miller intrd. 1981).

Prévert, Jacques, *Paroles* (1946).

Prial, Dunstan, *The Producer: John Hammond and the Soul of American Music* (2006).

Reineke, Hank, *Ramblin' Jack Elliott: The Never-Ending Highway* (2009).

Richards, Keith, *Life* (2010).

Robb, Graham, *Rimbaud* (2000).

Rimbaud, Arthur, *Rimbaud Complete* (trans. Wyatt Mason, 2002).

Rosenstone, Robert A., *Romantic Revolutionary: A Biography of John Reed* (1975).

Sandburg, Carl, *The American Songbag* (1927).
Complete Poems (1950).

Sante, Luc, *Low Life* (1991).

Seeger, Pete, *The Incompleat Folksinger* (1972).

Smith, Larry, *Kenneth Patchen: Rebel Poet in America* (2000).

Talese, Gay, *New York: A Serendipiter's Journey* (1961).

Terkel, Studs, *American Dreams: Lost and Found* (1980).

Thompson, Hunter S., *The Proud Highway: Saga of a Desperate Southern Gentleman 1955–1967 (The Fear and Loathing Letters, Volume 1)* (ed. Douglas Brinkley, 1997).

Unterberger, Richie, *Urban Spacemen and Wayfaring Strangers* (2000).
Turn! Turn! Turn!: The '60s Folk-Rock Revolution (2002).
Eight Miles High: Folk-Rock's Flight From Haight-Ashbury to Woodstock (2003).

Utley, Robert M., *Billy the Kid: A Short and Violent Life* (1990).

Völker, Klaus, *Brecht: A Biography* (1976).

Wald, Elijah, *Escaping the Delta: Robert Johnson and the Invention of the Blues* (2004).

Woliver, Robbie, *Hoot! A 25-Year History of the Greenwich Village Music Scene* (1986, reissued 1994).

Zweig, Paul, *Walt Whitman: The Making of the Poet* (1984).

Index

573

INDEX

Silver, Roy 230, 235
Silver Legion of America 52
Simon, Paul 129, 240n
Simon & Garfunkel 129, 240, 390, 520
Sing Out! 178n, 217, 239, 259, 285, 331n, 341, 344, 368, 382
Singers' Club 237
Sloan, P.F. (Philip Gary Schlein) 390
Smart, Christopher 94
Smith, Bessie 27
Smith, Harry, see Anthology of American Folk Music
Smith, Larry 351n
Smith, Samuel Francis 327
Smithsonian Institution 411
Snow, Hank (Clarence Eugene Snow) 84, 92, 485
Snyder, Gary 330
Socialist Party of America (SPA) 76
Son House (Eddie James House Jr) 404
Songs of Experience, see Blake, William
Songs of Innocence, see Blake, William
Sonnichesen, C.L. 496
Sonny & Cher 390
Sorensen, Ted 173
Sound of Music, The 372, 402
Sounes, Howard 56n, 58, 80n, 137, 237, 275n, 462
Southern Literary Messenger, see Poe, Edgar Allan
Spaniard in the Works, A, see Lennon, John
Spanish Civil War 136
Spiegel, Der 107
Spin (magazine) 69
Spitzer, Mark 328–9
Spoelstra, Mark 175, 188, 405
Springsteen, Bruce 260n, 327, 446, 535
Stalin, Joseph 238
Staples, Mavis 288
Star-Ledger, The (Newark, NJ) 356

Starkie, Enid 552
Steele, Tommy 518
Steeleye Span 240
Steinbeck, John 82, 203, 298, 389, 419
Stevenson, Adlai 75
Stevenson, Robert Louis 55
Stewart, James 47
Stone, Ben (BD's maternal grandfather; formerly Benjamin David Solemovitz) 129
Stone, Florence (BD's maternal grandmother) 65
Stone, Sly (Sylvester Stewart) 517
Stookey, Noel Paul, see Peter, Paul and Mary
Strada, La, see Fellini, Federico
Stravinsky, Igor Fyodorovich 219
Streisand, Barbra 171, 219, 336
Structure of Scientific Revolutions, The, see Kuhn, Thomas
Student Committee for Travel to Cuba 293
Student Nonviolent Coordinating Committee (SNCC) 174–5, 269–70, 272, 294, 388
Students for a Democratic Society (SDS) 231–3, 388
Sullivan, James 86
Sun Records 83, 200, 345
Supreme Court of the United States 85, 174–5, 244
Svedberg, Andrea 281–6
Swiss, Thomas, 82n
Szent-Györgyi, Albert 342

taconite process 65, 65n
Talese, Gay 197
Tamla Motown 106
Taplin, Jonathan 405
Teixeira, Rodrigo 545–6
Telegraph, The (fanzine) 442n
Ten Days That Shook the World, see Reed, John
Ten O'Clock Scholar (coffee house) 139–44

INDEX